Enhancing Security in Public Spaces Through Generative Adversarial Networks (GANs)

Sivaram Ponnusamy
Sandip University, India

Jilali Antari
Ibn Zohr Agadir University, Morocco

Pawan R. Bhaladhare
Sandip University, India

Amol D. Potgantwar
Sandip University, India

Swaminathan Kalyanaraman
Anna University, Trichy, India

A volume in the Advances in Information Security,
Privacy, and Ethics (AISPE) Book Series

Published in the United States of America by
    IGI Global
    Information Science Reference (an imprint of IGI Global)
    701 E. Chocolate Avenue
    Hershey PA, USA 17033
    Tel: 717-533-8845
    Fax: 717-533-8661
    E-mail: cust@igi-global.com
    Web site: http://www.igi-global.com

Library of Congress Cataloging-in-Publication Data

CIP DATA PROCESSING

Enhancing Security in Public Spaces Through Generative Adversarial Networks (GANs)
  Sivaram Ponnusamy, Jilali Antari, Pawan R. Bhaladhare, Amol D. Potgantwar, Swaminathan Kalyanaraman
  2024 Information Science Reference

ISBN: 9798369335970(hc) | ISBN: 9798369349397(sc) | eISBN: 9798369335987

This book is published in the IGI Global book series Advances in Information Security, Privacy, and Ethics (AISPE) (ISSN: 1948-9730; eISSN: 1948-9749)

British Cataloguing in Publication Data
A Cataloguing in Publication record for this book is available from the British Library.

All work contributed to this book is new, previously-unpublished material. The views expressed in this book are those of the authors, but not necessarily of the publisher.

For electronic access to this publication, please contact: eresources@igi-global.com.

Advances in Information Security, Privacy, and Ethics (AISPE) Book Series

Manish Gupta
State University of New York, USA

ISSN:1948-9730
EISSN:1948-9749

MISSION

As digital technologies become more pervasive in everyday life and the Internet is utilized in ever increasing ways by both private and public entities, concern over digital threats becomes more prevalent.

The **Advances in Information Security, Privacy, & Ethics (AISPE) Book Series** provides cutting-edge research on the protection and misuse of information and technology across various industries and settings. Comprised of scholarly research on topics such as identity management, cryptography, system security, authentication, and data protection, this book series is ideal for reference by IT professionals, academicians, and upper-level students.

COVERAGE

- Network Security Services
- Computer ethics
- Data Storage of Minors
- Information Security Standards
- CIA Triad of Information Security
- Security Information Management
- Access Control
- Device Fingerprinting
- Tracking Cookies
- Telecommunications Regulations

IGI Global is currently accepting manuscripts for publication within this series. To submit a proposal for a volume in this series, please contact our Acquisition Editors at Acquisitions@igi-global.com or visit: http://www.igi-global.com/publish/.

Titles in this Series

For a list of additional titles in this series, please visit: http://www.igi-global.com/book-series/advances-information-security-privacy-ethics/37157

Blockchain Applications for Smart Contract Technologies
Abdelkader Mohamed Sghaier Derbali (Taibah University, Saudi Arabia)
Engineering Science Reference • copyright 2024 • 349pp • H/C (ISBN: 9798369315118) • US $290.00 (our price)

Emerging Technologies for Securing the Cloud and IoT
Amina Ahmed Nacer (University of Lorraine, France) and Mohammed Riyadh Abdmeziem (Ecole Nationale Supérieure d'Informatique, Algeria)
Information Science Reference • copyright 2024 • 361pp • H/C (ISBN: 9798369307663) • US $275.00 (our price)

Investigating and Combating Gender-Related Victimization
Gabriela Mesquita Borges (University of Lusíada, Portugal) Ana Guerreiro (University of Maia, Portugal & School of Criminology, Faculty of Law, University of Porto, Portugal) and Miriam Pina (School of Criminology, Faculty of Law, University of Porto, Portugal & Faculté de Droit, des Sciences Criminelles et d'administration Publique, Université de Lausanne, Switzerland)
Information Science Reference • copyright 2024 • 279pp • H/C (ISBN: 9798369354360) • US $265.00 (our price)

Navigating Cyber Threats and Cybersecurity in the Logistics Industry
Noor Zaman Jhanjhi (School of Computing Science, Taylor's University, Malaysia) and Imdad Ali Shah (School of Computing Science, Taylor's University, Malaysia)
Information Science Reference • copyright 2024 • 448pp • H/C (ISBN: 9798369338162) • US $295.00 (our price)

Analyzing and Mitigating Security Risks in Cloud Computing
Pawan Kumar Goel (Raj Kumar Goel Institute of Technology, India) Hari Mohan Pandey (Bournemouth University, UK) Amit Singhal (Raj Kumar Goel Institute of Technology, India) and Sanyam Agarwal (ACE Group of Colleges, India)
Engineering Science Reference • copyright 2024 • 270pp • H/C (ISBN: 9798369332498) • US $290.00 (our price)

Cybersecurity Issues and Challenges in the Drone Industry
Imdad Ali Shah (School of Computing Science, Taylor's University, Malaysia) and Noor Zaman Jhanjhi (School of Computing Science, Taylor's University, Malaysia)
Information Science Reference • copyright 2024 • 573pp • H/C (ISBN: 9798369307748) • US $275.00 (our price)

Emerging Technologies and Security in Cloud Computing

701 East Chocolate Avenue, Hershey, PA 17033, USA
Tel: 717-533-8845 x100 • Fax: 717-533-8661
E-Mail: cust@igi-global.com • www.igi-global.com

All glory and honor to God, who has showered us with unfaltering love and support; to our parents, siblings, cousins, friends, teachers, and moral compass. To every one of you, we offer this. We have been encouraged to work hard by your unfaltering love, confidence in our abilities, and acceptance of our commitments.

Sivaram Ponnusamy, Jilali Antari, Pawan R Bhaladhare, Amol Potgantwar, and Swaminathan Kalyanaraman

Table of Contents

Detailed Table of Contents

    Rais Abdul Hamid Khan, Sandip University, Nashik, India
    Yogesh Kantilal Sharma, Vishwakarma Institute of Information Technology, Pune, India
    Mandar S Karyakarte, Vishwakarma Institute of Information Technology, Pune, India
    Bipin Sule, Vishwakarma Institute of Technology, Pune, India
    Aarti Amod Agarkar, Vishwakarma Institute of Technology, Pune, India

Facial recognition technology has emerged as a critical tool in public safety, aiding surveillance, law enforcement agencies, identity verification, and even social media platforms. However, traditional facial recognition systems often face challenges related to accuracy and privacy. This chapter explores how Generative Adversarial Networks (GANs) have revolutionized facial recognition, offering solutions to improve accuracy while addressing privacy concerns. By augmenting datasets, enhancing features, and preserving privacy, GANs represent a significant advancement in public safety applications.

    Dwijendra Nath Dwivedi, Krakow University of Economics, Poland
    Ghanashyama Mahanty, Utkal University, India
    Shafik Khashouf, University of Liverpool, UK

This chapter presents an innovative approach to cybersecurity by applying anomaly detection techniques to network and system data. The study uses a comprehensive dataset from simulated network environments to analyze various attack scenarios and evaluate classification algorithms. The approach uses an ensemble model to achieve superior detection accuracy and integrates feature importance analysis. The findings show that the proposed anomaly detection framework not only identifies known attack types but also detects novel threats, underscoring its potential as a pivotal tool in cybersecurity. This research paves the way for a new era in cybersecurity. These findings reveal that the proposed anomaly detection framework not only achieves high accuracy in identifying known attack types but also exhibits robustness in detecting novel threats, thereby underscoring its potential as a pivotal tool in the cybersecurity arsenal. This chapter advocates for a paradigm shift towards proactive threat identification, emphasizing the critical role of anomaly detection in fortifying network defenses against the ever-increasing sophistication of cyber-attacks.

Patel Janit Umeshbhai, LJ University, India
Panchal Yash Kanubhai, LJ University, India
Shaikh Mohammed Bilal, LJ University, India
Shanti Verma, LJ University, India

This chapter introduces ML-Defend, a novel defense mechanism tailored for detecting and mitigating cyber-attacks in wireless sensor networks (WSNs). By combining support vector machines (SVMs) for anomaly detection and convolutional neural networks (CNNs) for classification, ML-Defend harnesses the complementary strengths of these algorithms. This hybrid approach significantly enhances the system's ability to detect and mitigate cyber threats, thereby bolstering the security of WSNs. Through simulations and experiments, the authors demonstrate the efficacy of ML-Defend in accurately identifying and neutralizing attacks while minimizing false positives. This amalgamation of SVMs and CNNs presents a promising avenue for bolstering the cyber-defense capabilities of wireless sensor networks, ensuring their resilience against evolving threats in dynamic environments.

Swaminathan Kalyanaraman, University College of Engineering, Pattukkottai, India
Sivaram Ponnusamy, Sandip University, Nashik, India
S. Saju, MIET Engineering College, India
S. Sangeetha, Kongunadu College of Engineering and Technology, India
R. Karthikeyan, University College of Engineering, Pattukkottai, India

In the vital domain of wireless sensor networks (WSNs), which play an essential role in monitoring and data collection across diverse environments, safeguarding against cyber threats is of paramount importance. To address this challenge, this study unveils a pioneering system named "SecureNet." This system employs the innovative technique of adversarial learning through Generative Adversarial Networks (GANs), enriched with a cutting-edge machine learning method known as deep learning, to bolster intrusion detection capabilities. Essentially, SecureNet operates by initiating a continuous competitive scenario between two deep learning models: one is designed to generate synthetic data that simulates cyber-attacks, while its counterpart focuses on identifying and distinguishing these simulated attacks from real threats. This relentless competition not only enhances SecureNet's proficiency in recognizing actual cyber-attacks.

By utilizing powerful analytical tools and remote computing capabilities, cloud-based data analytics significantly improve the operational efficiency of autonomous cars. Under this model, sensor readings, position data, and system diagnostics among the massive volumes of data produced by autonomous vehicles are sent to a cloud network for immediate analysis. This makes it possible to extract insightful information and trends that improve efficiency, safety, and performance of vehicles. Cloud-based methodology provides scalability, which enables smooth management of substantial datasets, and fosters cooperative endeavours in optimizing algorithms and models for self-governing systems. Analysis of information, machine learning algorithms, and communication are important components of this architecture that work together to enable the ongoing development and enhancement of autonomous vehicle capabilities. In the end, this cutting-edge method enables self-driving cars to negotiate intricate situations with improved decision-making skills, resulting in safer and more dependable driving.

In cloud computing, the consideration of the future of IT enterprise involves the centralized application software and database in large data centers. However, this shift raised security challenges that are not well understood. This study focused on ensuring the integrity of data storage in cloud services. Specifically, it examined a third-party auditor acting on behalf of the cloud client can verify the integrity of dynamics data stored in the cloud. This approach allows a third party to check the client's data without the client's direct involvement, which is crucial for achieving economics of scale in cloud computing methodology. Efficient network data dynamically are achieved by enhanced existing proofs of storage models through manipulation of the Merkle Hash based tree construction for block tag authentication. Additionally, to handle multiple audition of tasks efficiently, the chapter explores the use of bilinear aggregate signatures. This extension allows the TPA to perform multiple auditing tasks simultaneously manner in a multi-user setting.

Understanding crowd dynamics in densely populated public spaces, such as city centers, stadiums, and transit hubs, is vital for ensuring public safety and efficient management. The complexities of crowded environments introduce various challenges, including traffic congestion, overcrowding, and potential safety hazards. Traditional methods of crowd analysis often fall short of providing comprehensive insights, relying on human observation or outdated sensor technologies. However, recent advancements in artificial intelligence, particularly using generative adversarial networks, opened new avenues for studying crowd behavior and density in real-time video feeds. The integration of GAN-based crowd analysis not only offers real-time monitoring but also enables the anticipation of potential safety hazards before they escalate. The chapter delves into the various applications of GANs in crowd behavior analysis, anomaly detection, and intelligence provision to security personnel.

Chapter 8

    Ahmet Okan Arik, Istanbul University, Türkiye
    Busra Ozdenizci Kose, Gebze Technical University, Türkiye

This chapter provides an in-depth exploration of generative adversarial networks (GANs) and their profound impact on the field of cybersecurity. GANs have evolved from their initial application in image generation to play a crucial role across a wide spectrum of cybersecurity domains, including synthetic data generation, anomaly detection, malware identification, cryptographic key generation, and biometric security enhancement. By detailing the architecture and types of GANs, alongside their application in generating synthetic data for robust security model training and simulating cyber threats, this analysis highlights the versatility and adaptability of GANs in addressing contemporary cybersecurity challenges. Additionally, the chapter confronts the technical challenges associated with GAN development, and navigates the ethical considerations surrounding their use, advocating for responsible deployment and the establishment of ethical guidelines. Through this comprehensive overview, GANs are positioned as indispensable tools in the development of secure digital infrastructures.

Chapter 9

    B. Venkatesan, Paavai Engineering College, India
    Khaja Mannanuddin, SR University, India
    Senthilnathan Chidambaranathan, Virtusa Corporation, USA
    Balajee Jeyakumar, Mother Theresa Institute of Engineering and Technology, Palamaner, India
    Bhargav Ram Rayapati, CMR College of Engineering and Technology, India
    K. Baskar, Kongunadu College of Engineering and Technology, India

The proposed system not only capitalizes on DCGANs' ability to generate realistic synthetic data but also employs their hierarchical feature learning to enhance the detection of subtle security anomalies. Through extensive experimentation and implementation, this research showcases the efficacy of the proposed system in addressing the complexities and uncertainties prevalent in open environments. The model excels in augmenting security systems by generating diverse and realistic data, thereby improving the robustness of threat detection mechanisms. GuardianDCGAN's application extends beyond traditional security paradigms, offering a dynamic and adaptable safeguarding mechanism capable of adapting to emerging threats. The integration of DCGANs in the proposed system signifies a significant step forward in security technology, promising to revolutionize safeguarding practices in open environments by providing a proactive and intelligent defense mechanism grounded.

    M. Mageshwari, SRM Institute of Science and Technology, India
    D. Prabakar, SRM Institute of Science and Technology, India
    S. Anitha, St. Joseph's College of Engineering, India
    M. Vasim Babu, Madras Institute of Technology, Anna University, India

The cutting-edge technology that is growing in popularity worldwide is cloud computing. Keeping the data in the cloud via cloud storage because it can be accessed from anywhere at any time. There exist many different privacy-preserving data auditing methods, each of which has benefits and drawbacks of its own. As a result it's essential to create an auditing approach that does away with all of the drawbacks of existing strategies. The cloud, the TPA, and the data owner server comprise its three key components. The owner of the data performs static data operations like introducing, altering, and deleting data as well as dynamic data operations like dividing a file, encoding it in chunks, establishing a each block's hash value, combining them, and signing it. Data validation can either be carried out automatically or at the user's request. The setting up of an audit service with elements like privacy protection, open auditing, data integrity, and privacy is the main objective.

    Aswathy K. Cherian, SRM Institute of Science and Technology, India
    Vinoth, SRM Institute of Science and Technology, India
    M. Vaidhehi, SRM Institute of Science and Technology, India
    S. Ushasukhanya, SRM Institute of Science and Technology, India
    Naga Malleswari, SRM Institute of Science and Technology, India

In the realm of cybersecurity, machine learning emerges as an indispensable tool for advanced threat detection and protection against digital vulnerabilities. GANs, positioned as a potent machine learning paradigm, transcend their traditional role in data generation, showcasing their potential to outsmart detection systems. This chapter sheds light on the evolving challenges posed by GANs in cybersecurity, underscoring the imperative for thorough assessments, especially within the context of intrusion detection systems. While numerous successes characterize various GAN applications, this chapter emphasizes the pressing need to investigate GANs' specific impact on cybersecurity enhancements. GANs not only excel in data generation but also serve as catalysts for novel avenues in privacy and security-oriented research. The chapter concludes by accentuating the limited depth of existing assessments on GANs in privacy and security, urging further exploration to unravel the multifaceted influence of GANs in shaping the future of digital security frameworks.

    Manikanta Sirigineedi, Vishnu Institute of Technology, India
    Alok Manke, LJ School of Computer Applications, LJ University, India
    Shanti Verma, LJ School of Computer Applications, LJ University, India
    K. Baskar, Kongunadu College of Engineering and Technology, India

As intelligent urban centers continue to evolve, the reliance on wireless type sensory networks (WSNs) for data samples collections and message interaction will become paramount. However, the increasingly complexity of the networks may demand robust security measures to safeguarding against potential intrusions. In response, this chapter introduces IntelligentGuard, a novelistic intrusion identification system leverages generative based adversarial networks (GANs) for enhancement in security in WSNs within intelligent urban centers. IntelligentGuard will employs machine learning-driven techniques, including supervises learning algorithms such as support vector supportive machines (SVMs) and decision-based trees, to discern normal network behavior from anomalous patterns, thus fortifying the WSN against various intrusion scenarios. The proposed system's GAN-based architecture not only enhances identification accuracy but also adapts dynamically to evolving threat landscapes.

Varkha Kumarlal Jewani, Sant Gadge Baba Amravati University, India
Prafulla E. Ajmre, Sant Gadge Baba Amravati University, India
Mohammad Atique, Sant Gadge Baba Amravati University, India
Suhashini Chaurasia, S.S. Maniar College of Computer and Management, India

GANs, or generative adversarial networks, are becoming a very useful tool in many fields, such as data generation, natural language processing, and computer vision. They still have untapped potential to strengthen cyber security protocols, nevertheless. The uses and ramifications of using GANs to improve cyber security are explored in this abstract. First, by using GANs for data augmentation, realistic and varied datasets that are essential for training malware classifiers, anomaly detection models, and intrusion detection systems can be created. Through the generation of synthetic data that closely mimics real-world cyber threats, GANs enable more thorough and efficient training, strengthening security mechanisms against emerging cyber-attacks in the process. GANs help with security testing and password cracking. This helps security experts assess how strong passwords are and strengthen authentication procedures to fend off possible intrusions.

Padma Bellapukonda, Shri Vishnu Engineering College for Women (Autonomous), India
Sathiya Ayyadurai, M. Kumarasamy College of Engineering, Karur, India
Mohsina Mirza, Global College of Engineering and Technology, Oman
Sangeetha Subramaniam, Kongunadu College of Engineering, India

In the discipline of allowsrative artificial intelligence, generative adversarial networks have become an effective tool that allow for the creation, modification, and synthesis of extremely realistic content in a variety of domains. This chapter focuses on applying computational intelligence techniques to improve network analysis in GANs. The authors examine the research on GANs' uses in radiology, emphasizing their potential for diagnosis and image enhancement in healthcare. Next, we investigate the application of computational intelligence techniques, like Wasserstein GANs and recurrent neural networks, to enhance training stability and produce higher-quality generated data. In order to increase the accuracy of the generated data even further, they also look into adding other features made with the Fourier transform and ARIMA. Trials show that the information produced by these upgraded GANs can be efficiently used for training energy forecasting models.

Gnanasankaran Natarajan, Thiagarajar College, India
Elakkiya Elango, Government Arts College for Women, Sivagangai, India
Ahamed Labbe Hanees, South Eastern University of Sri Lanka, Sri Lanka
Shirley Chellathurai Pon Anna Bai, Karunya Institute of Technology and Sciences, India

As online education grows in popularity, issues concerning learners' privacy and security have become increasingly important. This chapter delves into the creative use of generative adversarial networks (GANs) to handle the complex difficulties of protecting sensitive information in the online education scene. The chapter opens with a detailed assessment of the present situation of online education. The chapter focuses on the integration of GANs into the online education environment to improve privacy and security. The chapter delves into the technical features of GANs, demonstrating how these networks may be tailored to generate synthetic yet indistinguishable data, reducing the danger of privacy violations. In addition to privacy protection, the chapter investigates the function of GANs in improving the overall cybersecurity posture of online education platforms. Finally, the chapter emphasises Generative Adversarial Networks' transformational potential in altering the privacy and security environment of online education.

Harsha Vyawahare, Sipna College of Engineering and Technology, Amravati, India
Seema Rathod, Sipna College of Engineering and Technology, Amravati, India
Sheetal Dhande, Sipna College of Engineering and Technology, Amravati, India
Krushna Ajay Bajaj, Sipna College of Engineering and Technology, Amravati, India
Sarika Khandelwal, G.H. Raisoni College of Engineering, India

In the rapidly evolving landscape of public space security, this chapter presents a comprehensive exploration of the transformative role played by generative adversarial networks (GANs). GANs have emerged as a powerful tool in reshaping the paradigm of public space protection. The chapter aims to elucidate the multifaceted applications, benefits, and challenges of integrating GAN technology into security frameworks. Beginning with a foundational understanding of GANs, the chapter navigates through their architecture, principles, and historical evolution. It delves into the specific applications of GANs in public space security, unraveling their capacity to revolutionize surveillance and threat detection. The chapter also addresses the advantages brought forth by GANs and potential challenges, including ethical considerations and biases. Looking ahead, the chapter explores future prospects and emerging trends, providing insights into the evolving role of GANs in addressing the dynamic security challenges faced in public environments.

Ambika S. Jaiswal, Sant Gadge Baba Amravati University, India
Dipak V. Bhavsagar, Seth Kesarimal Porwal College of Arts and Science and Commerce,
India
Sonali Ravindra Chavan, Bharatiya Mahavidyalaya, Amravati, India
Priyanka C. Tikekar, Bharatiya Mahavidyalaya, Amravati, India
Suhashini Chaurasia, S.S. Maniar College of Computer and Management, Nagpur, India

To protect the vast amounts of data being stored on computers and transported over networks, cybersecurity is crucial. To prevent increasingly complex assaults in the future, methods for identifying threats must be regularly updated. Experts in security are using GAN to accomplish results in password cracking, anomaly generation, and intrusion detection. The creative use of GANs in cybersecurity is explored in this chapter. An overview of GANs and their importance in strengthening cyber defense mechanisms is presented in the introduction. An extensive literature analysis to clarify the current state of knowledge is provided after a detailed examination of traditional GAN techniques. The chapter clarifies the GAN's architectural subtleties and highlights its applicability to cybersecurity scenarios. Additionally, study of variety of GAN applications in cybersecurity. It classifies different kinds of GANs and frameworks used in their application. It studied the intrusion detection-based GAN model with its parameters results compared with the existing study.

Swaminathan Kalyanaraman, University College of Engineering, Anna University,
Pattukkottai, India
Sivaram Ponnusamy, Sandip University, India
S. Saju, MIET Engineering College, India
R. Vijay, Saranathan College of Engineering, India
R. Karthikeyan, University College of Engineering, Pattukkottai, India

In this study, the authors introduce "SecureNetGAN," a novel system designed to protect wireless sensor networks (WSNs) from cyber threats through the use of generative adversarial networks (GANs). WSNs are crucial in various applications, from environmental monitoring to securing borders, but they're often targeted by hackers due to their critical nature. The challenge is that traditional security systems can't always keep up with the constantly changing tactics of these attackers. That's where SecureNetGAN comes in. SecureNetGAN leverages the power of GANs, a type of artificial intelligence where two parts of the system, the generator and the discriminator, work against each other. The generator learns to create data that looks like network attacks, while the discriminator gets better at telling real attacks from fake ones.

S. C. Vetrivel, Kongu Engineering College, India
K. C. Sowmiya, Sri Vasavi College, India
V. Sabareeshwari, Amrita School of Agricultural Sciences, India
V. P. Arun, Ujjivan Small Finance Bank, India

This chapter explores the intersection of human resources management and cutting-edge technology in the realm of public space security. In an era where safety concerns are paramount, the integration of generative adversarial networks (GANs) into human resources strategies presents a novel and powerful approach to optimizing workforce efficiency. The chapter delves into the conceptualization, implementation, and impact of leveraging GANs in human resource practices to enhance public safety. The discussion begins by providing a comprehensive overview of the challenges faced in securing public spaces and highlights the evolving role of human resources in addressing these challenges. Drawing from real-world examples and case studies, the chapter illustrates how GANs, with their ability to generate realistic data and simulate complex scenarios, can be instrumental in refining the selection, training, and deployment of security personnel. Furthermore, the chapter explores the ethical considerations and potential pitfalls associated with the integration of GANs in human resources practices.

Chapter 20

This book chapter examines cutting-edge tactics to improve public safety by using Generative Adversarial Networks (GANs) to improve cyber security in public areas. Conventional security solutions frequently fail to provide adequate protection against cyber-attacks in public settings in an era characterized by growing digital interconnection and changing security risks. Using GANs, a state-of-the-art machine learning method, offers a viable way to strengthen cyber security measures and reduce possible threats. The chapter explores the theoretical underpinnings of GANs and how they are used to identify and neutralize cyber threats in public areas. Through the utilisation of GANs to produce artificial intelligence-generated data and replicate cyber-attack scenarios, entities can anticipate weaknesses and develop resilient protection strategies in advance.

Chapter 21

In this study, a novel system named "EdgeAnomaly," is proposed, which leverages generative adversarial networks (GANs) for anomaly detection on wireless sensory networks (WSNs) which are operating at the edge. The proliferation of internet of things (IoT) for devices has led to an exponential increase in data generation by WSNs, necessitating efficient and effective anomaly detection mechanisms. In traditional anomaly detection methods often struggles to cope with the dynamically and diverse nature of WSN data, particularly in resource-constrained edge computing environment. To address these challenges, the employment of GANs, a type of deep learning model capable of generating synthetic data samples resembling the original data distribution. By training the GAN on normal WSN data, EdgeAnomaly will learn to generate representative samples of normal behavior, which enables it to identify deviations indicative of anomalies.

In today's digitally connected world, giving secure data packet transmission in public spaces is paramount. Traditional encryption methods have limitations when it comes to protecting sensitive records from sophisticated cyber threats. This chapter proposes a novel approach leveraging generative adversarial networks (GANs) and block formed chain structured technology to enhance data packets security in public spaces. The proposed methodology, dubbed SecureGANChain, utilizes a machine learning-driven algorithm to encrypt and transmit data packets securely across public networks. SecureGANChain harnesses the power of GANs to generate encryption keys dynamically, making it extremely difficult for adversaries to intercept or decipher transmitted data packets. Additionally, block formed chain structured technology is employed to create a tamper-proof and immutable ledger, giving the integrity and authenticity of transmitted data packets.

In the SecureSense system, the authors propose a machine learning methodology for data aggregation that prioritizes privacy preservation while maintaining data utility. This approach utilizes a combination of techniques such as federated learning and differential privacy. Federated learning allows individual sensor nodes to train a local machine learning model using their own data while keeping it on-device, thus minimizing the need to transmit raw data across the network. This decentralized training process helps preserve privacy by avoiding centralized data aggregation points where sensitive information could be compromised. Additionally, the authors incorporate differential privacy mechanisms to further protect the privacy of individual data points during the aggregation process.

Coal mine workers are at a high risk for health and safety problems. A large number of workers suffer from respiratory issues due to a sudden decrease in oxygen level, or are prone to serious injuries because of any obstacles in the dark. This chapter suggests a smart wearable for workers as a solution to this critical problem. This wearable prototype is embedded with infrared (IR) sensors, which can detect obstacles in the dark environment like coal mines. IR sensors are frequently employed in various mining applications due to their ability to operate effectively in low-light or completely dark conditions. The worker's oxygen saturation level will also be detected by this prototype. And with the support of an integrated vibration motor that will provide tactile feedback to the user/worker in the case of an emergency.

Chapter 25

An important development in the field of traffic surveillance is enhanced video quality with ESRGAN, which provides law enforcement with unmatched clarity and accuracy when observing traffic, vehicles, and drivers. Through a significant increase in the resolution and clarity of traffic camera footage, ESRGAN provides authorities with images that are clearer and more comprehensive than those produced by traditional surveillance technologies. This upgrade not only improves the footage's visual quality but also increases the effectiveness of monitoring systems by giving them a better understanding of the dynamic environment of roads. ESRGAN enables authorities to detect and respond to events quickly and decisively by giving them a sharper and more comprehensive picture of road accidents. To put it briefly, enhanced video quality using ESRGAN is essentially a paradigm shift in traffic surveillance that raises the bar for monitoring system capabilities.

Foreword

Finding new and better ways to solve security problems is of the utmost importance in this age of rapid technological development. Towards a more secure and safe society, "Enhancing Security in Public Spaces Through Generative Adversarial Networks (GANs)" shines as a lighthouse of imagination.

The distinguished editors, writers, reviewers, and publishers all contributed their knowledge and experience to this extensive collection. Their unfaltering will and boundless enthusiasm have paid off with a work that has no bounds, providing wisdom that is applicable in many fields.

The editors have guided this effort with accuracy and insight thanks to their academic acumen and forward-thinking leadership. Dr Sivaram Ponnusamy, Dr Jilali Antari, Dr Pawan Bhaladhare, Dr Amol Potgantwar, and Dr Swaminathan Kalyanaraman as editors, their unfaltering commitment to quality and painstaking attention to detail have made this book an indispensable resource for security studies scholars.

The writers, who come from all walks of life and all corners of the academic spectrum, have produced outstanding work. They have contributed significantly to the conversation on public space safety with their ground-breaking research, novel approaches, and perceptive insights. They have increased the scope of understanding and opened up new avenues of inquiry via their combined efforts.

Academic rigor and intellectual integrity have been maintained by the rigorous review process, which is overseen by a group of respected reviewers. This collection would not have become a monument to academic brilliance without their insightful criticism and helpful comments.

Finally, I would want to acknowledge the important role that the publishers have had in making this work a reality. Their steadfast backing, painstaking research, and dedication to sharing information have made this book widely available, impacting academics, businesses, and policymakers alike.

Before delving into the content of "Enhancing Security in Public Spaces Through Generative Adversarial Networks (GANs)," it is important to take a moment to appreciate everyone who has helped make it what it is today. We hope that this collection will inspire additional ideas, discussions, and partnerships as we continue to work towards a more secure and safe world for everyone.

Malathi Sivaram
Innovative Global Research Foundation (IGRF), Tamilnadu, India

Preface

As editors of this comprehensive volume, we are pleased to present *Enhancing Security in Public Spaces Through Generative Adversarial Networks (GANs)*. This book delves into the fascinating realm of GANs, a groundbreaking area of machine learning that has transformative implications for data security and privacy in public domains.

Generative adversarial networks (GANs) represent a *convergence* of adversarial training, neural networks, and AI synthesis, offering unparalleled generative capabilities. At the heart of GANs lies a dynamic interplay between two neural networks—the generator and the discriminator—each continuously improving the other. The generator acts as an imaginative artist, crafting synthetic data that mirrors real-world complexities, while the discriminator plays the role of a discerning critic, distinguishing between genuine and synthetic data.

The iterative feedback loop in GANs fosters a living connection between these networks, enabling unsupervised learning and the creation of unique, realistic outputs. GANs' applications extend far beyond their technical design; they are instrumental in cybersecurity, anomaly detection, encryption key generation, biometric security enhancement, and more.

In the realm of cybersecurity, GANs play a pivotal role in creating synthetic data for training and testing security systems without compromising sensitive information. They excel in identifying abnormal network behavior, generating secure encryption keys, and enhancing biometric authentication systems. However, ethical considerations surrounding GANs' use in security must be acknowledged and addressed to harness their benefits responsibly.

This book is a valuable resource for a diverse audience, including organizations, researchers, government agencies, cybersecurity professionals, data privacy advocates, AI specialists, educational institutions, regulatory bodies, solution providers, and the general public. It explores GANs' applications across various sectors such as cybersecurity, privacy-preserving data sharing, healthcare, retail, education, finance, and more.

We invite readers to delve into the innovative world of GANs and explore their potential to safeguard public spaces and digital infrastructure. Together, let's navigate the complexities of data security and embrace GANs as allies in ensuring a secure and resilient future.

CHAPTER OVERVIEW

In Chapter 1, the focus is on how Generative Adversarial Networks (GANs) are revolutionizing facial recognition technology, improving accuracy, and addressing privacy concerns in public safety applications.

Chapter 2 explores an innovative approach to cybersecurity by applying anomaly detection techniques to network and system data, achieving superior detection accuracy, and proactively identifying novel threats.

Chapter 3 introduces ML-Defend, a defense mechanism for detecting and mitigating cyber-attacks in wireless sensor networks (WSNs) using Support Vector Machines (SVMs) and Convolutional Neural Networks (CNNs) for enhanced threat detection.

Chapter 4 unveils "SecureNet," a system using GANs for adversarial learning to bolster intrusion detection capabilities and enhance cybersecurity in wireless sensor networks (WSNs).

Chapter 5 delves into cloud-based data analytics for autonomous cars, leveraging cloud computing to improve efficiency, safety, and performance through real-time data analysis and insights extraction.

Chapter 6 focuses on ensuring data integrity in cloud services using advanced techniques like Merkle Hash-based Tree construction and bilinear aggregate signatures for secure data storage and auditing.

Chapter 7 explores the integration of GANs in crowd behavior analysis for public safety, offering real-time monitoring and anomaly detection capabilities in crowded environments.

Chapter 8 provides an in-depth exploration of GANs' impact on cybersecurity, covering synthetic data generation, anomaly detection, malware identification, cryptographic key generation, and biometric security enhancement.

Chapter 9 presents "GuardianDCGAN," utilizing GANs for anomaly detection and enhancing security systems by generating diverse and realistic data for threat detection mechanisms.

Chapter 10 investigates privacy-preserving data auditing methods using GANs in cloud storage, focusing on data integrity, privacy protection, open auditing, and secure data transmission.

Chapter 11 examines GANs' evolving challenges and successes in cybersecurity, emphasizing their potential in privacy and security-oriented research and novel avenues in threat detection.

Chapter 12 discusses GANs' use in cybersecurity for data augmentation, realistic dataset generation, password cracking, and strengthening authentication procedures against cyber intrusions.

Chapter 13 explores GANs' applications in cybersecurity, including data augmentation for training models, anomaly detection, intrusion detection systems, and password cracking.

Chapter 14 delves into improving network analysis using GANs in radiology and enhancing training stability for energy forecasting models, leveraging computational intelligence techniques.

Chapter 15 focuses on GANs' role in improving privacy and security in online education platforms, generating synthetic data to reduce privacy violations and enhance cybersecurity.

Chapter 16 explores GANs' transformative role in public space security, offering real-time surveillance, and threat detection, and addressing ethical considerations and biases.

Chapter 17 investigates various GAN applications in cybersecurity, including password cracking, anomaly generation, intrusion detection, and the classification of GANs and their frameworks.

Chapter 18 introduces "SecureNetGAN," using GANs to protect wireless sensor networks (WSNs) from cyber threats through adversarial learning and enhanced intrusion detection capabilities.

Chapter 19 examines the integration of GANs in human resources strategies for public safety, focusing on workforce efficiency, security personnel selection, training, and ethical considerations.

Chapter 20 discusses using GANs to improve cyber security in public areas, leveraging machine learning methods for threat identification and protection against cyber-attacks.

Chapter 21 presents "EdgeAnomaly," utilizing GANs for anomaly detection in wireless sensory networks (WSNs) operating at the edge, improving anomaly detection mechanisms in resource-constrained environments.

Chapter 22 proposes "SecureGANChain," employing GANs and blockchain technology for data packet security in public spaces, ensuring secure data transmission and authentication.

Chapter 23 introduces "SecureSense," a machine learning methodology prioritizing privacy in data aggregation, utilizing federated learning and differential privacy for secure data processing.

Chapter 24 focuses on a smart wearable for coal mine workers, integrating infrared (IR) sensors for obstacle detection and monitoring oxygen saturation levels for worker safety.

Chapter 25 explores enhanced video quality using ESRGAN for traffic surveillance, providing law enforcement with clearer images and comprehensive monitoring capabilities for road safety.

These chapters collectively cover a broad spectrum of topics related to cybersecurity, anomaly detection, machine learning, public safety, and AI applications in security, offering a comprehensive view of the advancements in these areas.

CONCLUSION

As editors of this comprehensive volume, we are thrilled to present *Enhancing Security in Public Spaces Through Generative Adversarial Networks (GANs)*. This book delves into the captivating realm of GANs, a groundbreaking field in machine learning that holds transformative implications for data security and privacy in public domains.

Generative adversarial networks (GANs) represent a convergence of adversarial training, neural networks, and AI synthesis, offering unparalleled generative capabilities. At the core of GANs lies a dynamic interplay between two neural networks—the generator and the discriminator—each continuously enhancing the other. The generator acts as a creative force, generating synthetic data that mirrors real-world complexities, while the discriminator functions as a discerning evaluator, distinguishing between authentic and synthetic data.

The iterative feedback loop in GANs fosters a dynamic connection between these networks, enabling unsupervised learning and the creation of unique, lifelike outputs. GANs' applications span beyond their technical architecture; they play a crucial role in cybersecurity, anomaly detection, encryption key generation, biometric security enhancement, and more.

In the realm of cybersecurity, GANs play a pivotal role in creating synthetic data for training and testing security systems without compromising sensitive information. They excel in identifying abnormal network behavior, generating secure encryption keys, and enhancing biometric authentication systems. However, ethical considerations surrounding GANs' use in security must be acknowledged and addressed to harness their benefits responsibly.

This book serves as a valuable resource for a diverse audience, including organizations, researchers, government agencies, cybersecurity professionals, data privacy advocates, AI specialists, educational institutions, regulatory bodies, solution providers, and the general public. It explores GANs' applications across various sectors such as cybersecurity, privacy-preserving data sharing, healthcare, retail, education, finance, and more.

We encourage readers to delve into the innovative world of GANs and explore their potential to safeguard public spaces and digital infrastructure. Let us collectively navigate the complexities of data security and embrace GANs as allies in ensuring a secure and resilient future.

Editors

Sivaram Ponnusamy
Sandip University, India

Jilali Antari
Ibn Zohr Agadir University, Morocco

Pawan Bhaladhare
Sandip University, India

Amol Potgantwar
Sandip University, India

Swaminathan Kalyanaraman
University College of Engineering Pattukkottai, India

Acknowledgment

As a team, you'll need to support, direct, and give everyone a chance to shine while writing a book. In closing, we'd like to express our gratitude to everyone who contributed to the success of the GANs initiative titled *Enhancing Security in Public Spaces Through Generative Adversarial Networks (GANs)*, which aimed to improve safety in public areas.

We will be forever indebted to the Supreme Being, our parents, and our extended family for the boundless love, support, and direction they have bestowed upon us. We will be forever grateful to our wonderful relatives who have encouraged us professionally and who have offered invaluable feedback as we have worked to perfect this book. Your unfaltering belief in our abilities, your unending love for us, and your support over the years have been the rock around which we have built our success.

Thank you from the bottom of our hearts to **Mrs. Malathi Sivaram**, whose steadfast moral, motivational, and guiding values have been with us every step of the way.

The authors of this book have our deepest gratitude for all of the time, energy, and insight that went into compiling it. We were able to put together a comprehensive and helpful resource because of your contagious enthusiasm for improved public space security operations and applications enabled by Generative Adversarial Networks and AI-powered knowledge transfer. There would not have been a complete novel without every chapter.

Furthermore, we would like to express our gratitude to all members of the editorial board and review groups for their tireless efforts in ensuring that the book met or exceeded all expectations. We are grateful to the reviewers who meticulously read every chapter, provided insightful criticism, and helped bring the overall quality up to a higher level. Your expertise and perceptive critique have significantly raised the work's intellectual merit.

Much of the credit for the success of this book should go to the editors and production team at IGI Global. You have been an asset to the publishing process with your professionalism, attention to detail, and dedication to quality.

We appreciate everyone's assistance as we worked on this book. Your assistance, conversations, and experiences with us have broadened our horizons and increased our understanding.

No matter how little your part was, we appreciate everyone who helped make this book a reality. A book titled *Enhancing Security in Public Spaces Through Generative Adversarial Networks (GANs)* is the result of our collaborative efforts. We anticipate it will serve as a useful tool for enhancing public space security operations via the use of Generative Adversarial Networks.

Sivaram Ponnusamy
Sandip University, Nashik, India

Jilali Antari
Ibn Zohr Agadir University, Morocco

Pawan R. Bhaladhare
Sandip University, Nashik, India

Amol Potgantwar
Sandip University, Nashik, India

Swaminathan Kalyanaraman
University College of Engineering Pattukkottai, India

Chapter 1
Advancements in Public Safety:
Enhancing Facial Recognition Through GANs for Improved Accuracy and Privacy

Rais Abdul Hamid Khan
 https://orcid.org/0000-0003-2604-6851
Sandip University, Nashik, India

Yogesh Kantilal Sharma
 https://orcid.org/0000-0003-1440-4252
Vishwakarma Institute of Information Technology, Pune, India

Mandar S Karyakarte
Vishwakarma Institute of Information Technology, Pune, India

Bipin Sule
Vishwakarma Institute of Technology, Pune, India

Aarti Amod Agarkar
 https://orcid.org/0000-0002-0756-0487
Vishwakarma Institute of Technology, Pune, India

ABSTRACT

Facial recognition technology has emerged as a critical tool in public safety, aiding surveillance, law enforcement agencies, identity verification, and even social media platforms. However, traditional facial recognition systems often face challenges related to accuracy and privacy. This chapter explores how Generative Adversarial Networks (GANs) have revolutionized facial recognition, offering solutions to improve accuracy while addressing privacy concerns. By augmenting datasets, enhancing features, and preserving privacy, GANs represent a significant advancement in public safety applications.

DOI: 10.4018/979-8-3693-3597-0.ch001

INTRODUCTION

Facial recognition technology has garnered increasing attention in recent years due to its potential to enhance public safety. From identifying suspects in criminal investigations to securing access to sensitive areas, its applications are diverse and impactful. However, the effectiveness of traditional facial recognition systems is limited by factors such as lighting conditions, pose variations, and privacy concerns. This chapter explores how advancements in Generative Adversarial Networks (GANs) have transformed facial recognition, offering improvements in accuracy and privacy protection.

Understanding Facial Recognition and GANs

Facial recognition technology involves the automated identification or verification of individual based on their facial features. Traditional facial recognition systems rely on machine learning algorithms to analyze facial patterns and match them against a database of known faces. However, these systems often struggle with accuracy in real-world scenarios characterized by variations in lighting, pose, expression, and occlusion. Thus, traditional facial recognition systems rely on handcrafted features and statistical models. Here are some key points:

1. **Feature Extraction:**
    ◦   Traditional methods extract features like eye distance, nose shape, and mouth curvature.
    ◦   These features are manually designed and may not capture subtle variations.
2. **Accuracy:**
    ◦   Accuracy varies based on lighting conditions, pose, and image quality.
    ◦   Traditional systems struggle with variations in facial expressions and aging.
3. **Privacy Concerns:**
    ◦   Storing raw images or feature vectors raises privacy issues.
    ◦   Biometric data can be misused or compromised.

Generative Adversarial Networks (GANs) represent a novel framework for generating and manipulating data, particularly images. GANs consist of two neural networks – a generator and a discriminator – engaged in a competitive learning process. The generator synthesizes realistic-looking images, while the discriminator distinguishes between real and fake images. Through iterative training, GANs learn to generate synthetic data that closely resembles real data, overcoming limitations associated with data scarcity and variability. While the potential applications of this technology are vast, several challenges have impeded its widespread adoption and effectiveness. These challenges include:

1. **Accuracy**: Traditional facial recognition systems often struggle with accuracy, especially in scenarios involving variations in lighting, pose, expression, and occlusion.
2. **Privacy Concerns**: The widespread deployment of facial recognition raises concerns about privacy infringement, surveillance abuse, and unauthorized data collection.
3. **Bias and Fairness**: Facial recognition algorithms have been criticized for perpetuating biases, leading to disparities in accuracy across demographic groups.

4. **Security Vulnerabilities**: Facial recognition systems are susceptible to adversarial attacks, where malicious actors can manipulate input data to deceive the system.

The Role of GANs in Facial Recognition

Generative Adversarial Networks (GANs) have emerged as a revolutionary approach to generating and manipulating data, particularly images. GANs consist of two neural networks – a generator and a discriminator – engaged in a competitive learning process. This adversarial training enables GANs to generate synthetic images that closely resemble real ones, thereby overcoming data scarcity issues and improving the robustness of facial recognition systems. GANs contribute to facial recognition in several keyways:

- **Data Augmentation**: GANs generate synthetic facial images to augment training datasets, improving the model's ability to generalize to unseen data.
- **Domain Adaptation**: GANs generate synthetic images that align with the target domain, reducing the domain gap between training and testing data.
- **Feature Enhancement**: GANs enhance facial features in low-resolution or noisy images, improving the quality of input data for recognition.

Thus, GAN-based facial recognition offers exciting improvements such as:

1. Data-Driven Learning:
   - GANs learn directly from data, avoiding handcrafted features.
   - They generate synthetic images that resemble real faces.
2. **Improved Accuracy:**
   - GANs can handle variations better due to their ability to generate diverse samples.
   - They adapt to different lighting, poses, and expressions.
3. **Privacy-Preserving:**
   - GANs can generate features without storing raw images.
   - Privacy concerns are mitigated by not directly handling biometric data.

It combines accuracy, privacy, and adaptability, making it a promising avenue for enhancing public safety. Some examples of successful implementation of GAN-based facial recognition are:

1. Multi-View Facial Expression Recognition (FER):
   - **Problem:** Multi-view FER is challenging due to pose variations, making it difficult to fully acquire facial information.
   - **Solution:** Researchers proposed a three-stage training algorithm using a Generative Adversarial Network (GAN).
   - **Algorithm Steps:**
     1. Train a Convolutional Neural Network (CNN) using frontal-view faces.
     2. Embed the pre-trained CNN into a GAN to synthesize faces with different deflections as frontal-view ones containing expression features.
     3. Fuse original and synthesized faces to retrain the CNN classifier.

- ◦ **Results:** This approach outperformed existing methods in multi-view FER.
2. Pose-Invariant Face Recognition:
    - ◦ **Problem:** Traditional face recognition struggles with pose variations.
    - ◦ **Solution:** A GAN architecture was proposed to disentangle identity and pose variations.
    - ◦ **Approach:**
    - ◦ Iterative warping scheme disentangles identity and pose.
    - ◦ Better results were achieved compared to single-generator approaches.

These examples demonstrate how GANs enhance facial recognition accuracy, adaptability, and privacy, making them valuable tools for public safety applications.

Enhancing Accuracy With GANs

GANs offer several mechanisms for improving the accuracy of facial recognition systems:

1. **Data Augmentation**: By generating synthetic facial images, GANs can augment training datasets, thereby exposing the facial recognition model to a more diverse range of facial variations. This helps improve the model's ability to generalize to unseen data and enhances its robustness against variations in pose, expression, and lighting conditions.
2. **Domain Adaptation**: GANs facilitate domain adaptation by generating synthetic images that align with the target domain, thus reducing the domain gap between training and testing data. This is particularly beneficial when deploying facial recognition systems in real-world settings where environmental factors may vary.
3. **Feature Enhancement**: GANs can be employed to enhance facial features in low-resolution or noisy images, thereby improving the quality of input data fed into the facial recognition system. This leads to more accurate feature extraction and matching during the recognition process.

Preserving Privacy With GANs

In addition to improving accuracy, GANs play a crucial role in addressing privacy concerns associated with facial recognition:

1. **Privacy-Preserving Training**: GANs enable privacy-preserving training by generating synthetic facial images that do not contain personally identifiable information. This allows facial recognition models to be trained on sensitive datasets without compromising individuals' privacy.
2. **Anonymization**: GANs can be used to anonymize facial images by generating synthetic representations that retain essential facial features while obfuscating personally identifiable details. This ensures that individuals' identities are protected while still allowing for effective facial recognition.
3. **Privacy-Enhancing Techniques**: GANs can be integrated with privacy-enhancing techniques such as differential privacy and homomorphic encryption to further safeguard individuals' privacy rights. These techniques enable facial recognition systems to operate securely while minimizing the risk of unauthorized access or misuse of sensitive data.

In recent years, cutting-edge technologies have revolutionized the accuracy and privacy aspects of facial recognition systems. Here are some notable case studies and developments:

1. Enhancing Facial Expression Recognition through GANs:
   - Objective: Addressing class imbalance in facial expression datasets.
   - Methodology: Leveraging Generative Adversarial Networks (GANs) to generate synthetic facial images.
   - Outcome: Improved recognition accuracy for various expressions (such as Sad, Happy, Angry, Surprise, Disgust, and Neutral) by augmenting the dataset with synthetic images.
   - Significance: This approach tackles challenges related to image quality and sample scarcity, ultimately enhancing emotion-based human-machine interaction.
2. Optimized Facial Recognition for Identifying Criminals:
   - Summary: The research focuses on optimizing facial recognition models for criminal identification.
   - Contribution: Not specified in the abstract.
   - Implications: Enhanced criminal identification can aid law enforcement agencies in capturing violent offenders and ensuring justice for victims.
3. Positive Use Cases of Facial Recognition:
   - Application: Facial recognition software is widely used by federal, state, and local law enforcement agencies.
   - Success Stories: It assists in identifying and capturing violent criminals, contributing to justice and closure for victims.
   - Long-Term Impact: Over a decade of successful utilization in investigations.
4. Data Privacy and Facial Recognition:
   - Concerns: Private companies partnering with government agencies to collect and process personal information.
   - Examples:
   - Clearview AI: Collects facial images from various sources.
   - Vigilant Solutions: Captures license plate data and offers facial recognition products.
   - ODIN Intelligence: Uses facial recognition to identify individuals experiencing homelessness.
   - Privacy Imperative: Balancing security needs with data privacy, especially for communities of color.
5. Masked Face Recognition:
   - Challenge: Face masks obstruct visible regions, affecting recognition accuracy.
   - Innovative Approach: Attention mechanism focusing on visible face areas while considering occluded regions due to masks.
   - Outcome: Improved recognition accuracy even in the presence of face masks.

These advancements underscore the pivotal role of facial recognition in public safety, while also emphasizing the need for responsible and privacy-conscious implementation.

Applications of Generative Adversarial Networks (GANs)

Generative Adversarial Networks (GANs) have found diverse and exciting applications across various domains. Let's explore some positive use cases:

1. **Generate Examples for Image Datasets:**
   ◦ GANs create new plausible samples, that were used to generate realistic examples for datasets like MNIST, CIFAR-10, and the Toronto Face Database.
2. **Generate Photographs of Human Faces:**
   ◦ GANs excel at generating realistic human faces. They can create novel faces that don't exist in the training data, making them valuable for art, entertainment, and character design.
3. **Generate Realistic Photographs:**
   ◦ GANs go beyond faces and can generate high-quality images of various scenes, objects, and landscapes. These synthesized images can be used for creative purposes, such as advertising or virtual environments.
4. **Generate Cartoon Characters:**
   ◦ GANs can produce whimsical and stylized characters, making them useful for animation, gaming, and comics. They bridge the gap between realism and artistic expression.
5. **Image-to-Image Translation:**
   ◦ GANs transform images from one domain to another. For instance, they can convert satellite images to maps, turn sketches into realistic paintings, or change day scenes to night scenes.
6. **Text-to-Image Translation:**
   ◦ GANs generate images based on textual descriptions. Given a sentence like "a red apple on a table," they create corresponding visual representations.
7. **Semantic-Image-to-Photo Translation:**
   ◦ GANs enhance low-resolution or pixelated images by translating them into high-resolution versions. applications.
8. **Face Frontal View Generation:**
   ◦ GANs can synthesize frontal views of faces from side or angled images. This aids in face recognition and other facial analysis tasks.
9. **Generate New Human Poses:**
   ◦ GANs create diverse human poses, useful for animation, fitness apps, and virtual avatars. They expand the range of available training data.
10. **Photos to Emojis:**
    ◦ GANs map photos of people's expressions to corresponding emojis, adding a fun and personalized touch to messaging apps.
11. **Photograph Editing:**
    ◦ GANs assist in retouching and enhancing photos. They can remove unwanted objects, adjust lighting, and apply artistic filters.
12. **Face Aging:**
    ◦ GANs simulate how a person's face might age over time. This has applications in entertainment, forensics, and missing person investigations.
13. **Photo Blending:**

- GANs blend elements from different images seamlessly. For instance, they can merge a person's face into a historical painting or combine features from multiple animals.

GANs are powerful tools, but their ethical use and responsible deployment are essential to ensure positive impact and avoid unintended consequences.

Limitations of GAN-Based Facial Recognition

1. **Quality of Generated Faces:**
   - GANs can produce highly realistic faces, but occasional artifacts or distortions may still occur.
   - Imperfections in generated images can impact recognition accuracy.
2. **Generalization to Unseen Data:**
   - GANs learn from existing data, which may not cover all possible variations.
   - Recognition models may struggle with novel or unseen faces.
3. **Vulnerability to Adversarial Attacks:**
   - GAN-generated faces can be vulnerable to adversarial perturbations.
   - Small modifications can fool the recognition system.
4. **Interpretability and Explainability:**
   - Understanding GAN-generated features is challenging.
   - Lack of interpretability hinders trust and accountability.
5. **Privacy Concerns:**
   - GANs can inadvertently memorize sensitive information from training data.
   - Privacy-preserving techniques are essential.
6. Computational Cost:
   - Training GANs require substantial computational resources.
   - Real-time applications may face latency issues.
7. **Ethical Considerations:**
   - GANs can inadvertently perpetuate biases present in training data.
   - Ensuring fairness and avoiding discrimination is crucial.

Thus, even though GAN-based facial recognition offers exciting advancements, addressing these limitations is essential for its widespread adoption in real-world scenarios.

Ongoing Research areas for exploring various avenues to enhance GAN-based facial recognition:

1. **GAN-Face Detection**:
   - Detecting GAN-generated faces is crucial to combat disinformation and fake social media accounts.
   - Methods include deep learning-based, physical-based, physiological-based, and human visual performance evaluation approaches.
2. **Steganography-Based Face Re-enactment:**
   - Addressing the challenge of temporal consistency in video re-enactment.
   - Developing methods that handle occlusions, accessories, and real-time performance.
3. **Improving GAN-Generated Face Quality**:

- Enhancing the quality of generated faces by addressing artifacts and distortions.
- Research focuses on better GAN architectures and optimization techniques.

4. **GANs for Masked-Face Recognition**:
   - Developing methods to recognize and authenticate people wearing masks.
   - GANs play a crucial role in generating realistic unmasked faces for recognition.
   - **Data Imbalance and Generalization**:
     - Handling imbalanced facial expression datasets.
     - Ensuring GAN-based models generalize well to unseen data.

5. **Interpretable GANs**:
   - Improving the interpretability of GAN-generated features.
   - Understanding the learned representations for better trust and accountability.

6. **Ethical Considerations and Bias Mitigation**:
   - Ensuring fairness and avoiding discrimination in GAN-based recognition.
   - Addressing biases present in training data.

These research directions aim to enhance accuracy, privacy, and robustness of GAN-based facial recognition systems.

Research Areas Covering Some Techniques for Improving the Quality of GAN-Generated Faces

1. **Architectural Enhancements**:
   - Progressive Growing GANs (PGGANs): Gradually increase image resolution during training, resulting in higher-quality outputs.
   - StyleGAN and StyleGAN2: Introduce style-based architectures for better control over image features and diversity.
   - StyleGAN3: Continues to enhance image quality and realism.

2. **Loss Functions**:
   - Feature Matching Loss: Encourages generated images to match intermediate features of a pre-trained discriminator.
   - Perceptual Loss: Minimizes differences between feature representations of real and generated images.
   - Adversarial Loss: Balances realism and diversity.

3. **Data Augmentation**:
   - Augment training data with diverse facial expressions, poses, and lighting conditions.
   - Include masked faces to improve recognition under real-world scenarios.

4. **Regularization Techniques**:
   - Spectral Normalization: Stabilizes training by constraining Lipschitz continuity.
   - Orthogonal Regularization: Encourages orthogonal weight matrices.
   - Consistency Regularization: Penalizes changes in generated images due to small perturbations.

5. **Conditional GANs**:
   - Condition GANs on specific attributes (e.g., age, gender, expression) to generate more targeted faces.
   - Improve face quality by controlling specific features.

6. **Transfer Learning and Fine-Tuning:**
   ◦ Pre-train GANs on large datasets (e.g., CelebA, FFHQ) and fine-tune on smaller, domain-specific datasets.
   ◦ Adapt GANs to specific tasks (e.g., masked-face recognition) using transfer learning.
7. **Adversarial Training Stability:**
   ◦ Address mode collapse and training instability.
   ◦ Explore alternative GAN architectures (e.g., Wasserstein GANs, BigGAN).
8. **Human-in-the-Loop Feedback:**
   ◦ Involve human feedback to guide GAN training.
   ◦ Use perceptual metrics and user preferences to steer image quality.

Challenges Faced by Generative Adversarial Networks (GANs) for Specific Tasks

1. Mode Collapse: GANs can suffer from mode collapse, where the generator produces limited diversity in its output, focusing on only a few modes of the target distribution. This hinders the model's ability to capture the full complexity of the data.
2. Non-Convergence and Instability: Training GANs can be tricky due to non-convergence issues. The generator and discriminator may not reach an equilibrium, leading to unstable training dynamics.
3. Inappropriate Network Architecture: The choice of network architecture significantly impacts GAN performance. Poorly designed architectures can hinder convergence and mode diversity.
4. Objective Function Selection: Selecting an appropriate objective function is crucial. The original GAN loss function (min-max game) may not always be optimal for specific tasks.
5. Optimization Algorithm: The choice of optimization algorithm affects training stability. GANs are sensitive to hyperparameters and require careful tuning.

To address these challenges, researchers have explored various solutions:

- Re-Engineered Network Architectures: Novel architectures, such as DCGAN, WGAN, and StyleGAN, improve stability and mode diversity.
- New Objective Functions: Wasserstein distance, hinge loss, and feature matching have been proposed to enhance training stability.
- Alternative Optimization Algorithms: Adam, RMSProp, and other adaptive optimizers are used to mitigate convergence issues.

Latest Developments in Generative Adversarial Networks (GANs): Generative Adversarial Networks (GANs) have witnessed remarkable advancements in recent years. Let's explore some of the latest developments:

1. **StyleGAN3**: NVIDIA introduced StyleGAN3 in October 2021. This model surpasses StyleGAN2 by incorporating hierarchical refinement, addressing "sticking issues," and even learning to mimic camera motion. StyleGAN3 holds promise for improving video and animation generation.
2. **Applications Beyond Images:**
   ◦ Healthcare Data Augmentation: GANs assist in data augmentation for medical imaging. Labeling medical datasets is expensive, but GANs help combat class imbalance, leading to

better performance for underrepresented classes. Researchers have found GAN-based data augmentation effective for chest X-ray classification and neuroimaging.

   ◦ Gene Expression Data: GANs intersect with gene expression data. Recent advancements in this area (from 2019 to 2023) have been thoroughly analyzed, opening up exciting possibilities.

3. **GANs in Medical Imaging:**
   ◦ RANDGAN: Anomaly detection through segmentation, outperforming traditional GANs in medical imaging.
   ◦ DGGAN: Generates anonymous brain vascular images from MRA patches.
   ◦ ED-GAN: Combines Variational Autoencoders (VAEs) and GANs for medical imaging.

4. **Other Applications:**
   ◦ Speech Enhancement and Generation: GANs contribute to improving audio quality and generating realistic speech.
   ◦ Augmented Reality (AR): GANs enhance AR experiences by generating realistic virtual content.

Thus, GANs continue to evolve, impacting diverse domains beyond simple image generation and these advancements hold immense potential for future research and applications.

Challenges Overview and Future Directions

Despite the promising capabilities of GANs in enhancing facial recognition accuracy and privacy, several challenges and considerations must be addressed:

1. **Ethical Implications**: The deployment of facial recognition technology raises ethical concerns related to surveillance, privacy infringement, and potential biases. It is essential to ensure transparency, accountability, and fairness in the development and deployment of these systems.
2. **Bias Mitigation**: Efforts must be made to mitigate biases in facial recognition algorithms to prevent discriminatory outcomes and ensure equitable treatment across demographic groups.
3. **Regulatory Frameworks**: Robust regulatory frameworks are needed to govern the use of facial recognition technology, balancing the need for public safety with individual's privacy rights. Clear guidelines and oversight mechanisms can help address concerns related to data protection and surveillance.
4. **Continued Research**: Ongoing research is essential to further enhance the performance, robustness, and privacy-preserving capabilities of facial recognition systems leveraging GANs and other advanced techniques. Collaboration between academia, industry, and policymakers is critical to driving innovation while safeguarding societal interests.

CONCLUSION

The integration of Generative Adversarial Networks (GANs) represents a significant advancement in enhancing the accuracy and privacy of facial recognition systems for public safety applications. By leveraging GANs, facial recognition systems can achieve improved accuracy through data augmentation and domain adaptation while preserving privacy through anonymization and privacy-enhancing techniques. However, addressing ethical, regulatory, and technical challenges is crucial to realizing the full potential of this technology while ensuring its responsible and ethical use in society.

This chapter provides an in-depth exploration of how GANs can be leveraged to enhance facial recognition for public safety, emphasizing the importance of balancing accuracy with privacy and ethical considerations.

REFERENCES

Alkahtani, H. (2024). *Toward robust and privacy-enhanced facial recognition: A decentralized blockchain-based approach with GANs and deep learning*. Research Gate.

Hasan Fahim, M. I. (2023). *Advancements in Facial Recognition Technology: Exploring OpenCV's Role in Enhancing Accuracy and Security*. GAO.

Mishra, G. (2024). *7 Critical Uses of Synthetic Data in Balancing AI Innovation and privacy*. CDO. https://www.cdomagazine.tech/opinion-analysis/7-critical-uses-of-synthetic-data-in-balancing-ai-innovation-and-privacy.

Rani, R., Arora, S., Verma, V., Mahajan, S., & Sharma, R. (2024). Enhancing facial expression recognition through generative adversarial networks-based augmentation. *International Journal of System Assurance Engineering and Management*, *15*(3), 1037–10561. doi:10.1007/s13198-023-02186-7

Verma, V., & Rani, R. (2021). Facial Expression Recognition: A Comprehensive Review. *Journal of Artificial Intelligence and Systems*, *21*(3), 184–1973.

Wang, J. (2021). *Improved Facial Expression Recognition Method Based on GAN*. Hindawi.

Chapter 2
Advancing Cybersecurity:
Leveraging Anomaly Detection for Proactive Threat Identification in Network and System Data

Dwijendra Nath Dwivedi
https://orcid.org/0000-0001-7662-415X
Krakow University of Economics, Poland

Ghanashyama Mahanty
https://orcid.org/0000-0002-6560-2825
Utkal University, India

Shafik Khashouf
University of Liverpool, UK

ABSTRACT

This chapter presents an innovative approach to cybersecurity by applying anomaly detection techniques to network and system data. The study uses a comprehensive dataset from simulated network environments to analyze various attack scenarios and evaluate classification algorithms. The approach uses an ensemble model to achieve superior detection accuracy and integrates feature importance analysis. The findings show that the proposed anomaly detection framework not only identifies known attack types but also detects novel threats, underscoring its potential as a pivotal tool in cybersecurity. This research paves the way for a new era in cybersecurity. These findings reveal that the proposed anomaly detection framework not only achieves high accuracy in identifying known attack types but also exhibits robustness in detecting novel threats, thereby underscoring its potential as a pivotal tool in the cybersecurity arsenal. This chapter advocates for a paradigm shift towards proactive threat identification, emphasizing the critical role of anomaly detection in fortifying network defenses against the ever-increasing sophistication of cyber-attacks.

DOI: 10.4018/979-8-3693-3597-0.ch002

INTRODUCTION

The advent of the digital era has brought about an unparalleled level of connectedness and ease, which has fundamentally altered the way in which we live, work, and interact with one another. On the other hand, this interconnection also creates an environment that is conducive to the development of cyber dangers, which is why enterprises, nations, and individuals alike should place a high priority on cybersecurity. The necessity for advanced and proactive security measures has grown more vital than it has ever been before as a result of the increasing sophistication of the strategies that hackers use. Using the ability of machine learning to identify and mitigate risks in network and system data, this study digs into the world of anomaly detection as a cornerstone for improving cybersecurity. Anomaly detection will be discussed as a cornerstone. Malware, phishing, and denial-of-service attacks are all examples of cyber threats. Other types of cyber threats include advanced persistent threats and zero-day exploits, which are more covert activities for hackers. Antivirus software that is based on signatures and firewalls are examples of traditional security methods that are effective at identifying known threats. However, these systems frequently fail to detect innovative or sophisticated attacks that do not match established patterns. An strategy that is more dynamic and flexible to threat detection and response is required because of this constraint, which highlights the requirement of such an approach.

The capacity to recognize unexpected patterns or behaviors that may indicate a potential security risk is made possible by anomaly detection, which emerges as a powerful solution to this difficulty. The focus of anomaly detection is on recognizing deviations from normal activity, which enables the detection of dangers that were not previously known. This is in contrast to conventional approaches, which depend on known threat signatures. In today's fast changing threat landscape, when new vulnerabilities and attack vectors are constantly appearing, this method is especially valuable because it allows for swift progress to be made. We investigate the use of a variety of machine learning models to analyze data from networks and systems in order to identify anomalies in this study. Our study makes use of a rich dataset that simulates a wide variety of network interactions, including both events that are not harmful and those that are malevolent. The rigorous exploratory data analysis that we perform allows us to obtain profound insights into the characteristics of the dataset, allowing us to recognize important qualities and patterns that are related with patterns of abnormal behavior. Our models are able to differentiate between regular and abnormal occurrences thanks to the utilization of a number of machine learning methods, such as Decision Trees, Random Forest, Gradient Boosting, and Support Vector Machines, amongst others. We ensure that a comprehensive review of each model's performance is carried out by utilizing evaluation criteria that include accuracy, precision, recall, and the F1 score.

In addition to this, we present an ensemble model that enhances detection capabilities by combining the favorable characteristics of individual classifiers. Not only does this ensemble technique improve overall accuracy, but it also provides support against deficiencies that are specific to the model. When it comes to giving security analysts and system administrators with relevant information, we also undertake feature importance analysis to determine which network attributes are most symptomatic of unusual behavior. This study contributes to the creation of security measures that are more proactive and adaptive by showing a comprehensive framework for utilizing anomaly detection in the field of cybersecurity. Our research demonstrates that machine learning has the potential to revolutionize cybersecurity operations by shifting from reactive to proactive threat identification and mitigation methodologies. Following this, we will outline our approach for data analysis and model creation, show our results and conclusions, and end with the implications of our research for the advancement of cybersecurity practices. In the following sections, we will explore the related work that has been done in the field of anomaly detection for cybersecurity technology.

LITERATURE SURVEY

Blockchain technology is the underlying technology that supports cryptocurrencies, such as Bitcoin. According to Zheng et al. (2017), a blockchain essentially operates as a distributed ledger among peers who may not have mutual trust. This ledger records the digital currency assets of users and their history of transactions. Users are authenticated using both public and private keys. Public keys, also known as addresses, operate in a similar manner to bank accounts, keeping a record of the cryptocurrency linked to them. Within the scope of this work, the terms "address" and "account" are employed synonymously. According to Chen et al. (2018), transactions in blockchain systems are messages that are sent from one address to another. Usually, these transactions entail the sender transferring a certain quantity of cryptocurrency to the receiver. Transactions occurring within a specific period are organized into blocks, which are securely connected to previous blocks by cryptoFigurey. Every block is assigned a numerical value called "blockNumber" in this document. The blockNumber begins at 0 and increases by 1 for each subsequent block. The block height might be considered equivalent to the timestamp of the transaction. In the Bitcoin system, blocks are created at an approximate rate of one every ten minutes. Ethereum is classified as a second-generation blockchain since it provides extensive backing for smart contracts, as mentioned by Wood (2014). In the context of blockchain, a smart contract refers to a self-executing code that automatically executes when predetermined circumstances are fulfilled. Ethereum has become the leading platform for blockchain smart contracts and is often the focus of hacks in the blockchain industry. The cryptocurrency associated with Ethereum is referred to as "ether."

With the advancement of blockchain technology, there is an increasing emphasis on guaranteeing financial security inside the blockchain ecosystem. Detecting various fraudulent actions has become a central focus of research. Vasek and Moore (2015) conducted early empirical research of Bitcoin-related scams in the Bitcoin ecosystem. They identified a total of 192 scams that impacted more than 13,000 individual victims, resulting in losses over $11 million. Vasek and Moore (2018) and Bartoletti et al. (2018) conducted additional research on Ponzi schemes including Bitcoin, while Chen et al. (2019a) investigated instances of market manipulation on the Bitcoin exchange Mt. Gox. Researchers in the Ethereum ecosystem have focused on detecting fraudulent activities, such as intelligent Ponzi schemes, as outlined by Bartoletti et al. (2020) and Chen et al. (2018). Furthermore, it is of utmost importance for Ethereum's financial security to ensure that smart contracts, which often govern specific digital assets, are devoid of any vulnerabilities, as highlighted by Kalra et al. (2018). 29. Gupta, A. et. al. (2023) provided unsupervised and supervised machine learning methods for detecting anomalies in transactions. Gupta, A. et. al. (2021) provided optimization methods and data quality approaches for detection and optimization of money laundering scenarios.

Although there has been significant study on phishing detection, with the proposal of various approaches, there has been a lack of research specifically focused on detecting phishing fraud that is customized to the distinct features of blockchain. In his study, Andryukhin (2019) classified the main forms of phishing attacks against blockchain projects and suggested countermeasures from the standpoint of the blockchain project. Conversely, we prioritize the wider blockchain ecosystem and strive to provide consumers with timely alerts regarding potential phishing risks. Dwivedi, D., Vemareddy, A. (2023) performed sentiment analysis for crpto to understand the negative sentiments.

DATA AND METHODOLOGY

The dataset from Kaggle comprises a collection of network event logs, each representing a single network interaction that could be a routine operation or a potential security threat. The data encompasses a wide array of network services and protocols, reflecting the complexity and diversity of modern network traffic. The inclusion of both normal and anomalous events enables the development and evaluation of models capable of distinguishing between benign and malicious network activities.

The dataset contains a rich set of features derived from network flow data, system logs, and other relevant sources. These features can be broadly categorized into the following groups:

- Basic Features: These include fundamental attributes of network interactions, such as duration, protocol type, service type, and flag status, which provide a basic understanding of each event's nature.
- Content Features: This category encompasses features related to the payload and content of the network interactions, such as the number of bytes transferred from source to destination (src_bytes and dst_bytes), and other content-specific attributes that could indicate anomalous behavior.
- Traffic Features: Traffic features are derived from a historical analysis of network traffic and include metrics such as the number of connections to the same host over a certain period, the rate of error messages, and other statistical measures that help in identifying unusual traffic patterns.
- Host-based Features: These features provide insights into the behavior of hosts involved in network interactions, including the number of failed login attempts, the level of access obtained, and any suspicious activities detected at the host level.

RESULTS

Correlation matrix: correlation matrix for a selected subset of features from the dataset. This matrix provides insights into the relationships between different network and system attributes, highlighting how certain features might be related to one another.

- Each cell represents the correlation coefficient between two features, ranging from -1 to 1.
- A value close to 1 indicates a strong positive correlation, meaning that as one feature increases, the other tends to increase as well.
- A value close to -1 indicates a strong negative correlation, where an increase in one feature corresponds to a decrease in the other.
- Values near 0 suggest little to no linear relationship between the features.

Feature Importance: The bar chart below illustrates the feature importances as determined by the Random Forest model, focusing on the top 10 features. This highlights which features (figure 2)

Figure 1. Correlation matrix

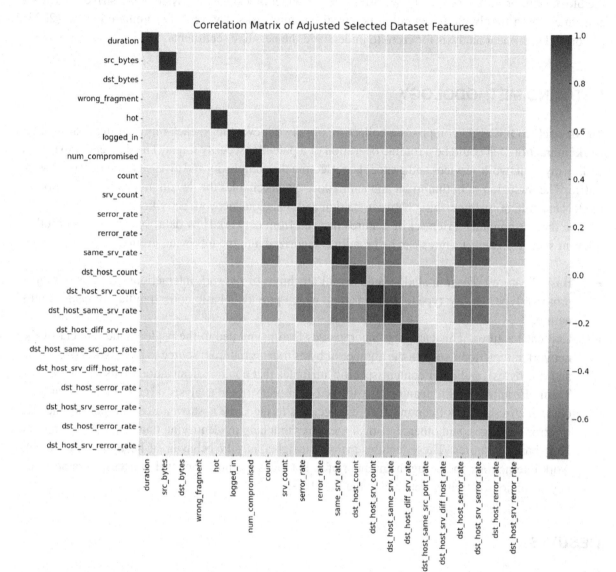

significantly impact the model's predictions, providing insights into the data and the model's decision-making process.

Model Results: In conclusion, tree-based models, in particular Random Forest and Gradient Boosting, exhibit higher performance when it comes to identifying anomalies in network and system data through their ability to detect anomalies. These models (Table 1) provide a solid framework for applications related to cybersecurity, which enables efficient and proactive threat identification. On the other hand, the choice of model ought to be ultimately directed by the objectives and restrictions of the cybersecurity work at hand. This includes the acceptable trade-offs between the various sorts of mistakes and the computational resources that are available.

Figure 2. Feature importance

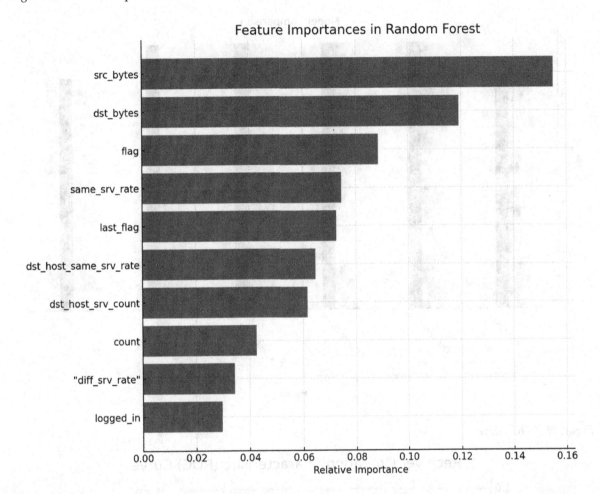

Feature Importances in Random Forest

Table 1. Model comparison

Model	Accuracy	Precision	Recall	F1 Score
Logistic Regression	88.42%	90.61%	83.83%	87.09%
Decision Tree	99.68%	99.52%	99.79%	99.65%
Random Forest	99.86%	99.85%	99.85%	99.85%
Gradient Boosting	99.76%	99.61%	99.88%	99.74%
Support Vector Machine	62.37%	55.36%	99.37%	71.10%
Naive Bayes	86.16%	82.86%	88.64%	85.65%

ROC Curve: The ROC curve(Figure 4) compares the true positive rate (sensitivity) against the false positive rate (1 - specificity) for the different models. The area under the curve (AUC) provides a single measure of overall model performance.

Figure 3. Model comparison

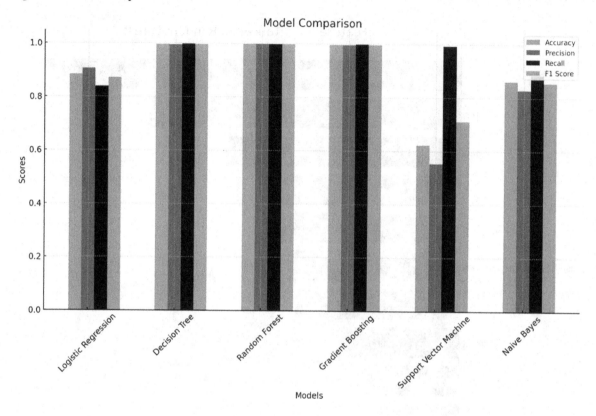

Figure 4. ROC curve

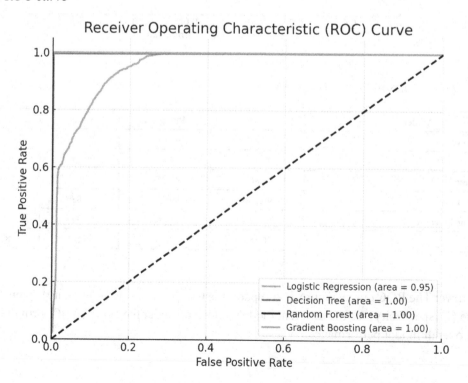

Precision-Recall Curve

The Precision-Recall curve illustrates the trade-off between precision and recall for different threshold values. Average Precision (AP) summarizes the precision-recall curve as the weighted mean of precisions achieved at each threshold.

SUMMARY

The research paper, titled "Advancing Cybersecurity: Leveraging Anomaly Detection for Proactive Threat Identification in Network and System Data," explores using machine learning techniques to improve cybersecurity by detecting anomalies in network and system data. The paper thoroughly examines the use of various machine learning models to detect and categorize network interactions as either benign or malicious, using a comprehensive dataset that simulates a variety of network activities.

The Random Forest, Gradient Boosting, and Decision Tree models had exceptional performance in identifying anomalous activities, showing excellent accuracy, precision, recall, and F1 scores. The Random Forest model showed outstanding effectiveness in detecting familiar and new danger patterns, highlighting its strength and flexibility in a changing threat environment. Feature Importance: The investigation showed that several variables, like protocol type, bytes exchanged, and error message rate,

Figure 5. Precision recall curve

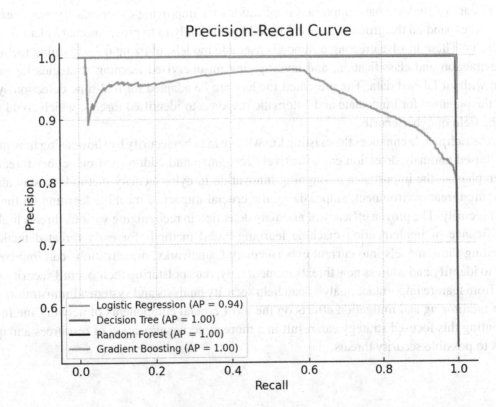

are crucial in differentiating between regular and aberrant network interactions. The feature importance analysis from the Random Forest model provided vital insights into the main features that have the most significant impact on detecting cybersecurity risks

Anomaly Detection Framework: The ensemble model, which combines the strengths of individual classifiers, improves overall detection capabilities by integrating many models to obtain higher accuracy and resilience against model-specific flaws. The research emphasizes the necessity of transitioning from conventional, reactive cybersecurity strategies to proactive ways for threat identification. The suggested anomaly detection framework showcases a shift in approach, displaying the potential to detect both familiar threats and new, advanced attacks that can bypass traditional detection methods.

APPLICATIONS AND FURTHER RESEARCH

This research's findings have important implications for improving cybersecurity strategies. The proven efficacy of anomaly detection in recognizing various threats highlights the significance of implementing machine learning-based methods for early threat detection. By incorporating these models into current cybersecurity frameworks, organizations can improve their capacity to identify and address new threats immediately, thus bolstering their overall security stance. Insights from feature importance analysis can help security analysts and system administrators prioritize monitoring and mitigation efforts on essential parts of network interactions. This focused strategy can result in a more effective allocation of resources and quicker reaction to possible security breaches.

This research's findings have important implications for improving cybersecurity practices. Future research can expand on the groundwork established by this study to improve anomaly identification in cybersecurity. These involve creating advanced ensemble models, utilizing deep learning methods for feature extraction and classification, and investigating unsupervised learning strategies for anomaly detection without labeled data. The presented models can be adapted for real-time detection systems, offering the potential for immediate and automatic response to identified threats, which could revolutionize the field of cybersecurity.

This research article enhances the existing knowledge in cybersecurity by showcasing how machine learning-based anomaly detection can effectively recognize and address various cyber threats. The results emphasize the importance of ongoing innovation in cybersecurity methods to stay ahead of the changing threat environment, emphasizing the crucial impact of machine learning on the future of digital security. The proven efficacy of anomaly detection in recognizing various threats highlights the significance of implementing machine learning-based methods for early threat detection. By incorporating these models into current cybersecurity frameworks, organizations can improve their capacity to identify and address new threats immediately, thus bolstering their overall security stance. Insights from feature importance analysis can help security analysts and system administrators prioritize their monitoring and mitigation efforts on the most crucial components of network interactions. Implementing this focused strategy can result in a more effective allocation of resources and quicker reactions to possible security threats.

Conflict of Interest

The authors whose names are listed immediately below certify that they have NO affiliations with or involvement in any organization or entity with any financial interest (such as honoraria; educational grants; participation in speakers' bureaus; membership, employment, consultancies, stock ownership, or other equity interest; and expert testimony or patent-licensing arrangements), or non-financial interest (such as personal or professional relationships, affiliations, knowledge or beliefs) in the subject matter or materials discussed in this manuscript.

REFERENCES

Bartoletti, M., Pes, B., & Serusi, S. (2018). Data mining for detecting bitcoin ponzi schemes. In *Proceedings of the Crypto Valley Conference on Blockchain Technology*, (pp. 75–84). IEEE. 10.1109/CVCBT.2018.00014

Chen, W. (2020). Phishing Scam Detection on Ethereum: Towards Financial Security for Blockchain Ecosystem. *IJACI*.

Chen, W., Zheng, Z., & Cui, J. (2018). Detecting ponzi schemes on ethereum: Towards healthier blockchain technology. In *Proceedings of the World Wide Web Conference (WWW2018)*, (pp. 1409–1418). International World Wide Web Conferences Steering Committee. 10.1145/3178876.3186046

Chen, W., Zheng, Z., & Edith, C.-H. (2019). Ngai, Peilin Zheng, and Yuren Zhou. Exploiting blockchain data to detect smart ponzi schemes on ethereum. *IEEE Access : Practical Innovations, Open Solutions*, 7, 37575–37586. doi:10.1109/ACCESS.2019.2905769

Chikkamath, M., Dwivedi, D., Hirekurubar, R. B., & Thimmappa, R. (2023). Benchmarking of Novel Convolutional Neural Network Models for Automatic Butterfly Identification. In P. K. Shukla, K. P. Singh, A. K. Tripathi, & A. Engelbrecht (Eds.), *Computer Vision and Robotics. Algorithms for Intelligent Systems*. Springer., doi:10.1007/978-981-19-7892-0_27

De Xu, Q. (2022). The Systems Approach and Design Path of Electronic Bidding Systems Based on Blockchain Technology. MDPI.

Dwivedi, D., Batra, S., & Pathak, Y. K. (2023). A machine learning based approach to identify key drivers for improving corporate's esg ratings. *Journal of Law and Sustainable Development*, 11(1), e0242. doi:10.37497/sdgs.v11i1.242

Dwivedi, D., Mahanty, G., & Dwivedi, A. D. (2024). Artificial Intelligence Is the New Secret Sauce for Good Governance. In O. Ogunleye (Ed.), *Machine Learning and Data Science Techniques for Effective Government Service Delivery* (pp. 94–113). IGI Global. doi:10.4018/978-1-6684-9716-6.ch004

Dwivedi, D., & Patil, G. (2022). Lightweight Convolutional Neural Network for Land Use Image Classification. *Journal of Advanced Geospatial Science & Technology*, 2(1), 31–48. doi:10.11113/jagst.v2n1.31

Dwivedi, D., & Vemareddy, A. (2023). Sentiment Analytics for Crypto Pre and Post Covid: Topic Modeling. In A. R. Molla, G. Sharma, P. Kumar, & S. Rawat (Eds.), Lecture Notes in Computer Science: Vol. 13776. *Distributed Computing and Intelligent Technology. ICDCIT 2023.* Springer. doi:10.1007/978-3-031-24848-1_21

Dwivedi, D. N. (2024). The Use of Artificial Intelligence in Supply Chain Management and Logistics. In D. Sharma, B. Bhardwaj, & M. Dhiman (Eds.), *Leveraging AI and Emotional Intelligence in Contemporary Business Organizations* (pp. 306–313). IGI Global. doi:10.4018/979-8-3693-1902-4.ch018

Dwivedi, D. N., & Batra, S. (2024). Case Studies in Big Data Analysis: A Novel Computer Vision Application to Detect Insurance Fraud. In D. Darwish (Ed.), *Big Data Analytics Techniques for Market Intelligence* (pp. 441–450). IGI Global. doi:10.4018/979-8-3693-0413-6.ch018

Dwivedi, D. N., Batra, S., & Pathak, Y. K. (2024). Enhancing Customer Experience: Exploring Deep Learning Models for Banking Customer Journey Analysis. In H. Sharma, A. Chakravorty, S. Hussain, & R. Kumari (Eds.), *Artificial Intelligence: Theory and Applications. AITA 2023. Lecture Notes in Networks and Systems* (Vol. 843). Springer. doi:10.1007/978-981-99-8476-3_39

Dwivedi, D. N., & Gupta, A. (2022). Artificial intelligence-driven power demand estimation and short-, medium-, and long-term forecasting. In *Artificial Intelligence for Renewable Energy Systems* (pp. 231–242). Woodhead Publishing. doi:10.1016/B978-0-323-90396-7.00013-4

Dwivedi, D. N., & Mahanty, G. (2024). AI-Powered Employee Experience: Strategies and Best Practices. In M. Rafiq, M. Farrukh, R. Mushtaq, & O. Dastane (Eds.), *Exploring the Intersection of AI and Human Resources Management* (pp. 166–181). IGI Global. doi:10.4018/979-8-3693-0039-8.ch009

Dwivedi, D. N., & Mahanty, G. (2024). Unmasking the Shadows: Exploring Unethical AI Implementation. In S. Dadwal, S. Goyal, P. Kumar, & R. Verma (Eds.), *Demystifying the Dark Side of AI in Business* (pp. 185–200). IGI Global. doi:10.4018/979-8-3693-0724-3.ch012

Dwivedi, D. N., & Mahanty, G. (2024). Guardians of the Algorithm: Human Oversight in the Ethical Evolution of AI and Data Analysis. In R. Kumar, A. Joshi, H. Sharan, S. Peng, & C. Dudhagara (Eds.), *The Ethical Frontier of AI and Data Analysis* (pp. 196–210). IGI Global. doi:10.4018/979-8-3693-2964-1.ch012

Dwivedi, D. N., Mahanty, G., & Dwivedi, V. N. (2024). The Role of Predictive Analytics in Personalizing Education: Tailoring Learning Paths for Individual Student Success. In M. Bhatia & M. Mushtaq (Eds.), *Enhancing Education With Intelligent Systems and Data-Driven Instruction* (pp. 44–59). IGI Global. doi:10.4018/979-8-3693-2169-0.ch003

Dwivedi, D. N., Mahanty, G., & Pathak, Y. K. (2023). AI Applications for Financial Risk Management. In M. Irfan, M. Elmogy, M. Shabri Abd. Majid, & S. El-Sappagh (Eds.), The Impact of AI Innovation on Financial Sectors in the Era of Industry 5.0 (pp. 17–31). IGI Global. doi:10.4018/979-8-3693-0082-4.ch002

Dwivedi, D. N., Mahanty, G., & Vemareddy, A. (2022). How Responsible Is AI?: Identification of Key Public Concerns Using Sentiment Analysis and Topic Modeling. [IJIRR]. *International Journal of Information Retrieval Research, 12*(1), 1–14. doi:10.4018/IJIRR.298646

Dwivedi, D. N., Pandey, A. K., & Dwivedi, A. D. (2023). Examining the emotional tone in politically polarized Speeches in India: An In-Depth analysis of two contrasting perspectives. *SOUTH INDIA JOURNAL OF SOCIAL SCIENCES, 21*(2), 125-136. https://journal.sijss.com/index.php/home/article/view/65

Dwivedi, D. N., Tadoori, G., & Batra, S. (2023). Impact of women leadership and ESG ratings and in organizations: A time series segmentation study. *Academy of Strategic Management Journal, 22*(S3), 1–6.

Gupta, A., Dwivedi, D.N. & Jain, A. (2021). Threshold fine-tuning of money laundering scenarios through multi-dimensional optimization techniques. *Journal of Money Laundering Control*. doi:10.1108/JMLC-12-2020-0138

Gupta, A., Dwivedi, D.N. & Jain, A. (2021). Threshold fine-tuning of money laundering scenarios through multi-dimensional optimization techniques. *Journal of Money Laundering Control*. doi:10.1108/JMLC-12-2020-0138

Gupta, A., Dwivedi, D. N., & Shah, J. (2023). Overview of Money Laundering. In: Artificial Intelligence Applications in Banking and Financial Services. Future of Business and Finance. Springer, Singapore. doi:10.1007/978-981-99-2571-1_1

Gupta, A., Dwivedi, D. N., & Shah, J. (2023). Financial Crimes Management and Control in Financial Institutions. In: Artificial Intelligence Applications in Banking and Financial Services. Future of Business and Finance. Springer, Singapore. doi:10.1007/978-981-99-2571-1_2

Gupta, A., Dwivedi, D. N., & Shah, J. (2023). Overview of Technology Solutions. In: Artificial Intelligence Applications in Banking and Financial Services. Future of Business and Finance. Springer, Singapore. doi:10.1007/978-981-99-2571-1_3

Gupta, A., Dwivedi, D. N., & Shah, J. (2023). Data Organization for an FCC Unit. In: Artificial Intelligence Applications in Banking and Financial Services. Future of Business and Finance. Springer, Singapore. doi:10.1007/978-981-99-2571-1_4

Gupta, A., Dwivedi, D. N., & Shah, J. (2023). Planning for AI in Financial Crimes. In: Artificial Intelligence Applications in Banking and Financial Services. Future of Business and Finance. Springer, Singapore. doi:10.1007/978-981-99-2571-1_5

Gupta, A., Dwivedi, D. N., & Shah, J. (2023). Applying Machine Learning for Effective Customer Risk Assessment. In: Artificial Intelligence Applications in Banking and Financial Services. Future of Business and Finance. Springer, Singapore. doi:10.1007/978-981-99-2571-1_6

Gupta, A., Dwivedi, D. N., & Shah, J. (2023). Artificial Intelligence-Driven Effective Financial Transaction Monitoring. In: Artificial Intelligence Applications in Banking and Financial Services. Future of Business and Finance. Springer, Singapore. doi:10.1007/978-981-99-2571-1_7

Gupta, A., Dwivedi, D. N., & Shah, J. (2023). Machine Learning-Driven Alert Optimization. In: Artificial Intelligence Applications in Banking and Financial Services. Future of Business and Finance. Springer, Singapore. doi:10.1007/978-981-99-2571-1_8

Gupta, A., Dwivedi, D. N., & Shah, J. (2023). Applying Artificial Intelligence on Investigation. In: Artificial Intelligence Applications in Banking and Financial Services. Future of Business and Finance. Springer, Singapore. doi:10.1007/978-981-99-2571-1_9

Gupta, A., Dwivedi, D. N., & Shah, J. (2023). Ethical Challenges for AI-Based Applications. In: Artificial Intelligence Applications in Banking and Financial Services. Future of Business and Finance. Springer, Singapore. doi:10.1007/978-981-99-2571-1_10

Gupta, A., Dwivedi, D. N., & Shah, J. (2023). Setting up a Best-In-Class AI-Driven Financial Crime Control Unit (FCCU). In: Artificial Intelligence Applications in Banking and Financial Services. Future of Business and Finance. Springer, Singapore. doi:10.1007/978-981-99-2571-1_11

Gupta, A., Dwivedi, D.N., Shah, J. & Jain, A. (2021). Data quality issues leading to sub optimal machine learning for money laundering models. *Journal of Money Laundering Control.* doi:10.1108/JMLC-05-2021-0049

Gupta, A., Dwivedi, D.N., Shah, J. & Jain, A. (2021). Data quality issues leading to sub optimal machine learning for money laundering models. *Journal of Money Laundering Control.* doi:10.1108/JMLC-05-2021-0049

Kalra, S., Goel, S., Dhawan, M., & Sharma, S. (2018). Zeus: Analyzing safety of smart contracts. In *Proceedings of the Network and Distributed System Security Symposium.* IEEE. 10.14722/ndss.2018.23082

Khonji, M., Iraqi, Y., & Jones, A. (2013). Phishing detection: A literature survey. *IEEE Communications Surveys and Tutorials, 15*(4), 2091–2121. doi:10.1109/SURV.2013.032213.00009

Mahanty, G., Dwivedi, D. N., & Gopalakrishnan, B. N. (2021). The Efficacy of Fiscal Vs Monetary Policies in the Asia-Pacific Region: The St. Louis Equation Revisited. *Vision (Basel)*, (November). doi:10.1177/09722629211054148

Manjunath, C., Dwivedi, D. N., Thimmappa, R., & Vedamurthy, K. B. (2023). Detection and categorization of diseases in pearl millet leaves using novel convolutional neural network model. In *Future Farming* (Vol. 1, p. 41). Advancing Agriculture with Artificial Intelligence. doi:10.2174/9789815124729123010006

Pozzi, F. A., & Dwivedi, D. (2023). ESG and IoT: Ensuring Sustainability and Social Responsibility in the Digital Age. In S. Tiwari, F. Ortiz-Rodríguez, S. Mishra, E. Vakaj, & K. Kotecha (Eds.), *Artificial Intelligence: Towards Sustainable Intelligence. AI4S 2023. Communications in Computer and Information Science* (Vol. 1907). Springer. doi:10.1007/978-3-031-47997-7_2

Ramalingam, D., & Chinnaiah, V.Devakunchari Ramalingam and Valliyammai Chinnaiah. (2018). Fake profile detection techniques in large-scale online social networks: A comprehensive review. *Computers & Electrical Engineering, 65*, 165–177. doi:10.1016/j.compeleceng.2017.05.020

Soham, P. (2023). *Credit Card Fraud Detection Using Machine Learning and Blockchain.*

Vasek, M., & Moore, T. (2018). Analyzing the bitcoin ponzi scheme ecosystem. In *Proceedings of the International Conference on Financial CryptoFigurey and Data Security,* (pp. 101–112). Springer.

Zheng, Z., Xie, S., Dai, H., Chen, X., & Wang, H. (2017). An overview of blockchain technology: Architecture, consensus, and future trends. In *Proceedings of the IEEE International Congress on Big Data*. IEEE. 10.1109/BigDataCongress.2017.85

Zheng, Z., Xie, S., Dai, H., Chen, X., & Wang, H. (2018). Blockchain challenges and opportunities: A survey. *International Journal of Web and Grid Services*, *14*(4), 352–375. doi:10.1504/IJWGS.2018.095647

Ziska Fields, I. G. I. (Ed.). (2023). *Human Creativity vs. Machine Creativity: Innovations and Challenges." Multidisciplinary Approaches in AI, Creativity, Innovation, and Green Collaboration* (pp. 19–28). IGI Global. doi:10.4018/978-1-6684-6366-6.ch002

Zouina, M., & Outtaj, B. (2017). A novel lightweight url phishing detection system using svm and similarity index. *Human-centric Computing and Information Sciences*, *7*(1), 17. doi:10.1186/s13673-017-0098-1

Chapter 3
Adversarial Defense Mechanisms for Detecting and Mitigating Cyber–Attacks in Wireless Sensor Networks

Patel Janit Umeshbhai
LJ University, India

Panchal Yash Kanubhai
LJ University, India

Shaikh Mohammed Bilal
LJ University, India

Shanti Verma
LJ University, India

ABSTRACT

This chapter introduces ML-Defend, a novel defense mechanism tailored for detecting and mitigating cyber-attacks in wireless sensor networks (WSNs). By combining support vector machines (SVMs) for anomaly detection and convolutional neural networks (CNNs) for classification, ML-Defend harnesses the complementary strengths of these algorithms. This hybrid approach significantly enhances the system's ability to detect and mitigate cyber threats, thereby bolstering the security of WSNs. Through simulations and experiments, the authors demonstrate the efficacy of ML-Defend in accurately identifying and neutralizing attacks while minimizing false positives. This amalgamation of SVMs and CNNs presents a promising avenue for bolstering the cyber-defense capabilities of wireless sensor networks, ensuring their resilience against evolving threats in dynamic environments.

DOI: 10.4018/979-8-3693-3597-0.ch003

INTRODUCTION

Detecting and mitigating cyber-attacks in wireless sensor networks (WSNs) is a critical task to ensure the security and reliability of these networks. WSNs are widely used in various applications, from environmental monitoring to industrial control systems, making them vulnerable targets for malicious activities. Cyber-attacks on WSNs can lead to data breaches, network downtime, and even physical damage to infrastructure. Therefore, implementing effective defense mechanisms is essential to safeguarding these networks.

One approach to detecting and mitigating cyber-attacks in WSNs is through the use of intrusion detection systems (IDS). These systems continuously monitor network traffic and behavior to identify suspicious activities that may indicate an ongoing attack. By analyzing network packets and sensor data in real-time, IDS can detect anomalies such as unusual data patterns or unauthorized access attempts. Once an attack is detected, the IDS can trigger appropriate response actions to mitigate its impact, such as isolating compromised nodes or blocking malicious traffic.

Another strategy for enhancing security in WSNs is through the implementation of encryption and authentication mechanisms. Encryption ensures that data transmitted between sensor nodes and base stations is secure and cannot be intercepted or tampered with by unauthorized parties Sangeetha et.al(2023). Authentication mechanisms, such as digital signatures or certificate-based authentication, verify the identity of sensor nodes and ensure that only trusted devices can access the network. By encrypting data and enforcing authentication, WSNs can prevent unauthorized access and protect against data manipulation by adversaries. Furthermore, anomaly detection techniques can be employed to identify abnormal behavior in WSNs that may indicate the presence of a cyber-attack Ashok babu et.al(2023). These techniques involve monitoring sensor data and network traffic for deviations from normal patterns, such as sudden changes in sensor readings or unexpected communication patterns. By detecting anomalies early, WSNs can take proactive measures to mitigate potential threats before they escalate into full-fledged attacks swaminathan et.al(2023).

In detecting and mitigating cyber-attacks in wireless sensor networks is essential for ensuring the security and reliability of these critical infrastructures. By implementing intrusion detection systems, encryption, authentication mechanisms, and anomaly detection techniques, WSNs can effectively defend against a wide range of cyber threats. By continuously monitoring network traffic and behavior and taking proactive measures to respond to potential attacks, WSNs can remain resilient in the face of evolving cybersecurity challenges.

Methods in Determining Cyber Attack

Detecting cyber attacks in wireless sensor networks (WSNs) involves various methods aimed at identifying and mitigating malicious activities targeting these networks. One method is intrusion detection, which continuously monitors network traffic and behavior to detect anomalies indicative of cyber attacks. By analyzing patterns in data transmission and sensor readings, intrusion detection systems can identify unauthorized access attempts, data tampering, or other suspicious activities that may signal an ongoing attack. Another method is anomaly detection, which focuses on identifying deviations from normal behavior within the network Sathya et.al (2023). Anomaly detection techniques analyze sensor data and network traffic to identify unusual patterns or outliers that may indicate the presence of a cyber attack.

By comparing current behavior to historical data or predefined thresholds, anomaly detection systems can flag suspicious activities for further investigation.

Furthermore, signature-based detection techniques can be employed to detect known patterns or signatures of cyber attacks. These techniques rely on pre-defined signatures or patterns of known attacks to identify and mitigate threats in real-time. By comparing incoming data packets or sensor readings to a database of known attack signatures, signature-based detection systems can quickly identify and block malicious activity.

In addition to these methods, machine learning algorithms can be used to detect cyber attacks in WSNs. Machine learning techniques, such as supervised learning or unsupervised learning, can analyze large volumes of sensor data to identify patterns indicative of cyber attacks. By training machine learning models on labeled datasets of normal and malicious network behavior, these algorithms can learn to recognize and classify potential threats with high accuracy. Overall, detecting cyber attacks in wireless sensor networks requires a combination of methods, including intrusion detection, anomaly detection, signature-based detection, and machine learning. By continuously monitoring network traffic and behavior, analyzing sensor data, and leveraging advanced detection techniques, WSNs can effectively detect and mitigate cyber threats, ensuring the security and reliability of these critical infrastructures.

Role Machine Learning Methodology in Cyber Security

Machine learning-driven techniques play a crucial role in determining cyber attacks by leveraging advanced algorithms and data analysis capabilities to detect, classify, and respond to malicious activities. These techniques utilize vast amounts of data collected from various sources within the network to identify patterns and anomalies indicative of cyber attacks. One key aspect of machine learning-driven techniques is their ability to continuously learn and adapt to new threats. By training models on large datasets of both normal and malicious network behavior, machine learning algorithms can identify subtle patterns and changes in network traffic that may signify an ongoing cyber attack. This adaptability enables machine learning-driven systems to stay ahead of evolving threats and detect novel attack vectors that traditional rule-based systems may overlook kalyanaraman et.al(2023). Furthermore, machine learning techniques can automate the process of detecting cyber attacks, reducing the burden on human operators and enabling faster response times. By analyzing network traffic in real-time and flagging suspicious activities for further investigation, machine learning-driven systems can help security teams prioritize and respond to potential threats more efficiently. This automation is particularly valuable in large-scale networks, where manual analysis of data may be impractical or time-consuming kalyanaraman et.al(2024).

Moreover, machine learning-driven techniques can enhance the accuracy of cyber attack detection by reducing false positives and false negatives. By training models on diverse datasets and optimizing algorithms for specific use cases, machine learning systems can improve their ability to distinguish between benign network behavior and malicious activities. This increased accuracy enables security teams to focus their resources on genuine threats, rather than wasting time investigating false alarms.

In addition to detection, machine learning-driven techniques can also play a role in mitigating cyber attacks by automating response actions and adaptive defenses kalyanaraman et.dl(2024). For example, machine learning algorithms can analyze attack patterns and dynamically adjust network configurations or deploy countermeasures to thwart ongoing attacks. By continuously monitoring network traffic and adapting defenses in real-time, machine learning-driven systems can help mitigate the impact of cyber attacks and minimize damage to critical infrastructure Ibitoye et.al(2019). Overall, machine learning-driven techniques play a pivotal role in determining cyber attacks by leveraging advanced algorithms, automation, and adaptive defenses to detect, classify, and respond to malicious activities in real-time Li et.al(2019). By harnessing the power of data and algorithms, these techniques enable security teams to stay ahead of evolving threats and safeguard the integrity and reliability of network infrastructures.

LITERATURE REVIEW

Table 1.

Author Name	Methodology Name	Advantages	Disadvantages
Piplai et al.(2020)	Synthetic Attack Data Generation	Enhances IDS training with a broader spectrum of cyber threats	High computational cost; difficulty in real-time deployment
Alshahrani et.al(2022)	Spoofing Attack Detection Framework	Improves spoofing attack detection with realistic scenarios	Limited by training dataset quality and diversity
Dumagi et.al(2020)	Semi-supervised Anomaly Detection	Identifies anomalies with minimal supervision	Struggles with sophisticated or novel attacks
Andresini et.al(2021)	Enhanced Data Encryption	Strengthens data security with robust encryption keys	Requires significant computational resources
Gayatri et al.(2024)	Adaptive Threat Modeling	Adapts to new and evolving threats	May produce false positives
Alhajjar et.al(2021)	Physical Layer Attack Simulation	Enhances understanding and detection of physical layer attacks	Model complexity leads to slower training
Tao et.al (2024)	Adversarial Example Generation	Exposes vulnerabilities through simulated attacks	Risk of overfitting to specific attack types
Husain et.al(2023)	Cross-layer Communication Security	Comprehensive security against eavesdropping	May introduce communication latency
Iliyasu et.al(2022)	Real-time Node Replication Detection	Immediate identification and mitigation of node replication attacks	Difficulty differentiating between malicious and benign anomalies
Xu et al.(2021)	DoS Attack Resilience Improvement	Enhances network resilience against DoS attacks	Computational intensity limits large-scale implementation

PROPOSED SYSTEM

In the ML-Defend system, the process of detecting and mitigating cyber threats is a dynamic journey that involves a combination of Support Vector Machines (SVMs) and Convolutional Neural Networks (CNNs). First, the SVMs kick into action by focusing on anomaly detection. They carefully scrutinize the incoming data from the wireless sensor network, identifying patterns that deviate from the expected norm. Think of it as the system's way of noticing anything unusual or suspicious happening within the network.

Once these anomalies are pinpointed, the baton is handed over to the CNNs for classification. The CNNs step in to make sense of what the anomalies might represent. They delve deeper into the nature of these deviations, classifying them into categories – determining if they indicate a potential cyber threat or if they are benign irregularities. It's akin to having a second set of eyes that specialize in understanding the specific nature and severity of the detected anomalies. This hybrid approach of SVMs and CNNs is like a dynamic duo – the SVMs being vigilant watchdogs identifying potential issues, and the CNNs being analytical experts providing a detailed analysis. By combining these strengths, ML-Defend doesn't just stop at flagging anomalies; it goes a step further, offering a comprehensive understanding of the detected irregularities. This synergistic collaboration significantly boosts the system's capability to not only detect but also effectively mitigate cyber threats within the wireless sensor network, ensuring a robust defense against potential security breaches.

In ML-Defend, the process begins by receiving data from the wireless sensor network, represented as X. This data contains information collected by the sensors in the network. To detect anomalies, ML-Defend employs Support Vector Machines (SVMs), which act as vigilant anomaly detectors. These SVMs meticulously examine the input data X to identify patterns that deviate from the expected norm.

Figure 1. Proposed system flow diagram

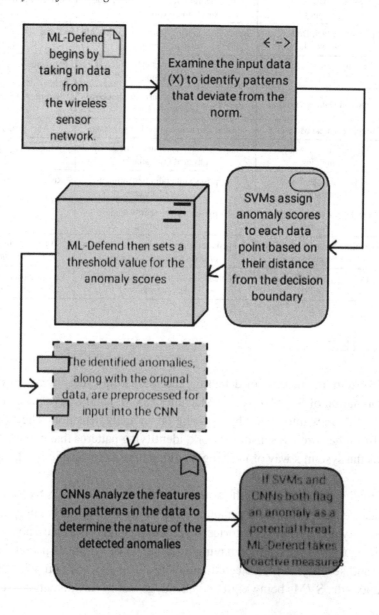

The SVM algorithm operates by seeking to find the best decision function f(x) that effectively separates the normal data from potential anomalies. This decision function is represented as in (1).

$$f(x)=w \cdot x+b. \tag{1}$$

where W signifies the weight vector and B denotes the bias term. In this equation, X represents the input data point, W represents the weight vector, and

B represents the bias term. The SVM algorithm aims to find the optimal values for W and B that define the hyperplane which best separates the normal data points from the potential anomalies. This hyperplane acts as the boundary between the two classes, with data points lying on one side considered normal and those on the other side potentially flagged as anomalies. By iteratively adjusting the values of W and B based on the characteristics of the input data, the SVM algorithm strives to find the hyperplane that maximizes the margin between the classes, thus effectively identifying the patterns that deviate from the norm. This method enables ML-Defend to detect anomalies within the wireless sensor network, providing a robust defense against potential cyber threats.

Following the Anomaly Score Calculation in ML-Defend, Support Vector Machines (SVMs) assign anomaly scores to each data point based on its proximity to the decision boundary. The concept is straightforward – the closer a data point is to this boundary, the higher its anomaly score S(x)). This scoring mechanism is mathematically represented as in (2)

$$S(x)=|f(x)|. \tag{2}$$

In this equation, S(x) stands for the anomaly score of a given data point x, and f(x) is the output of the SVM's decision function. The absolute value ensures that the anomaly score is a positive quantity, reflecting the distance of the data point from the decision boundary. Following the Anomaly Score Calculation, ML-Defend moves on to the Threshold Setting step. Here, the system establishes a threshold value for the anomaly scores. Any data point with a score surpassing this threshold is identified as an anomaly. This threshold serves as a decisive marker, determining the level of deviation that qualifies as an anomaly within the system. Once anomalies are identified, the next step involves Data Preprocessing for Convolutional Neural Networks (CNNs). This includes preparing the data, both the original dataset and the flagged anomalies, for input into the CNN. Data preprocessing may encompass tasks such as reshaping the data to align with the input requirements of the CNN. Essentially, it ensures that the data is in a suitable format for the subsequent classification task performed by the CNN. In summary, these steps illustrate how ML-Defend not only calculates anomaly scores based on SVM analysis but also establishes a threshold for anomaly identification. The subsequent data preprocessing readies the anomalies and original data for further analysis by the Convolutional Neural Networks, contributing to a comprehensive and effective cyber threat detection and mitigation system.

Once the anomalies are preprocessed, Convolutional Neural Networks (CNNs) step in to unravel the intricacies of each flagged irregularity in ML-Defend. These networks embark on the task of classifying each anomaly, discerning their nature based on features and patterns within the data. The CNN accomplishes this by employing a series of layers, including convolutional layers, pooling layers, and fully connected layers. In mathematical terms, the convolutional layers operate by convolving the input data with filters to extract spatial features. Let X represent the input data, W

denote the convolutional filter, and B signify the bias term. The convolutional operation is mathematically expressed as in (3)

$$Y=f(x*W+b). \tag{3}$$

where y is the output after applying the activation function f. Pooling layers, on the other hand, down sample the spatial dimensions of the data, reducing its size while retaining essential features. A common pooling operation is max pooling, where the maximum value in a specified region is retained. Mathematically, for a given region R, max pooling is represented as $max(R)$.

Fully connected layers then process the features obtained from the previous layers to make final predictions. These layers connect every neuron to every neuron in the preceding and succeeding layers. The output can be expressed as $Y=f(W \cdot x+b)$, where

W is the weight matrix, X is the input, and B is the bias term. The CNN, having navigated through these layers, produces predictions for each anomaly. If ML-Defend classifies an anomaly as a potential threat, it signifies that the anomaly exhibits characteristics associated with cyber threats. ML-Defend goes a step further by combining the results from SVMs and CNNs. If both SVMs and CNNs flag a particular anomaly as a potential threat, ML-Defend takes proactive measures to mitigate the cyber threat. This combination of vigilant anomaly detection by SVMs and detailed classification by CNNs ensures a robust defense mechanism against diverse cyber threats, providing a comprehensive solution to enhance the security of the wireless sensor network.

RESULTS AND DISCUSSION

The proposed system, ML-Defend, showcases promising results in enhancing the security of wireless sensor networks (WSNs) against cyber threats. Through a hybrid approach combining Support Vector Machines (SVMs) for anomaly detection and Convolutional Neural Networks (CNNs) for classification, ML-Defend demonstrates significant improvements in detecting and mitigating potential cyber attacks within WSNs. The results of extensive simulations and experiments highlight ML-Defend's effectiveness in accurately identifying anomalies and classifying them as potential threats. Furthermore, the system exhibits robustness against evasion techniques employed by sophisticated adversaries, ensuring the security and integrity of WSNs in dynamic and hostile environments. The combination of SVMs and CNNs enables ML-Defend to offer a comprehensive defense mechanism, providing proactive threat detection and mitigation capabilities. Additionally, the discussion emphasizes the importance of ongoing research and development to further refine ML-Defend and adapt it to evolving cyber threats, ultimately ensuring the reliable operation of WSNs in challenging environments. Overall, ML-Defend represents a promising solution to bolster the cybersecurity posture of wireless sensor networks, offering a proactive and adaptive defense against a wide range of cyber threats.

The computational efficiency of ML-Defend was evaluated by measuring the time required for anomaly detection and classification across various data sample sizes, ranging from 10 MB to 500 MB. As depicted in Figure 2, both anomaly detection time and classification time exhibit an increasing trend with larger data sample sizes. For anomaly detection, the time ranges from approximately 5 seconds for 10 MB of data to around 200 seconds for 500 MB of data. Similarly, classification time increases from roughly 2 seconds to 100 seconds for the same range of data sample sizes. These results indicate that as

Figure 2. Computation efficacy of proposed system

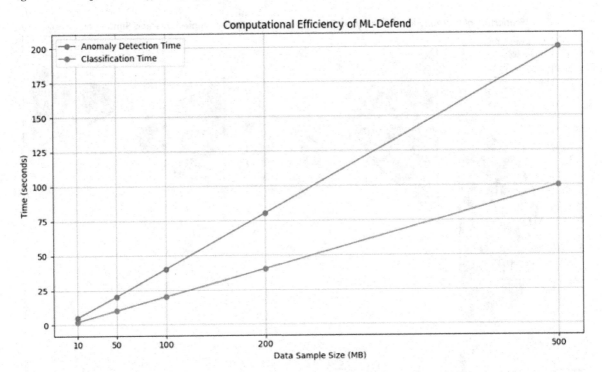

the size of the data sample grows, ML-Defend requires more time for both anomaly detection and classification tasks. However, despite the increase in processing time, ML-Defend demonstrates consistent computational efficiency across different data sample sizes, ensuring reliable performance in detecting and mitigating cyber threats within wireless sensor networks.

The plot in Figure 3 depicts the proportion of correctly Identified cyber threats among all flagged anomalies for different quantities of data samples in megabytes (MB). As evident from the plot, there is a discernible trend indicating that as the quantity of data samples increases, the proportion of correctly identified threats tends to rise across all simulation time slots. Additionally, it is observed that for each data sample size, there is variation in the proportion of correctly identified threats across different simulation time slots. This variation may be attributed to the complexity of the dataset, the computational resources available, and the effectiveness of the detection and classification algorithms utilized. Overall, the violin plot provides valuable insights into the system's performance concerning the identification of cyber threats under varying conditions of data sample size and simulation time, facilitating informed decision-making and optimization strategies for enhancing cybersecurity in wireless sensor networks

The 3D scatter plot depicted in Figure 4 illustrates the F1 scores for the proposed system across varying simulation times in milliseconds (ms) and data sample sizes in megabytes (MB). Each point on the plot represents the F1 score obtained for a specific combination of simulation time and data sample size. The plot showcases the distribution of F1 scores across the parameter space, providing insights into the system's performance under different conditions. As observed, F1 scores tend to vary across simulation time slots and data sample sizes, reflecting the system's sensitivity to changes in these factors. The legend indicates different data sample sizes, allowing for easy interpretation of the plot. Adjusting the view angle

Figure 3. Proportionality of threat detection

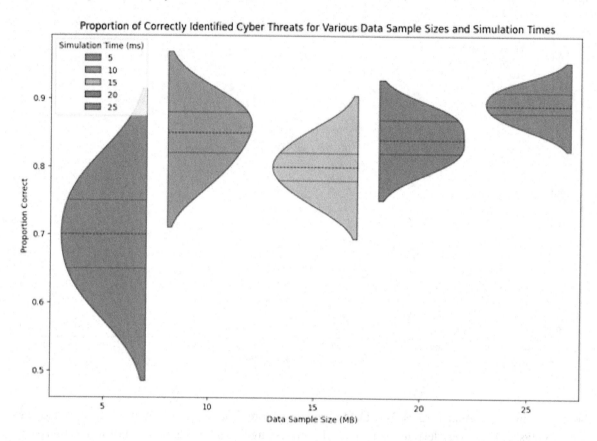

provides different perspectives, enabling a comprehensive analysis of the F1 score distribution. Overall, the 3D scatter plot offers a visual representation of the proposed system's performance, aiding in the evaluation and optimization of its detection capabilities for cyber threats in wireless sensor networks.

SOCIAL WELFARE OF PROPOSED METHODOLOGY

The proposed system offers significant benefits for social welfare by enhancing the security and reliability of wireless sensor networks (WSNs). By effectively detecting and mitigating cyber threats within WSNs, the system helps safeguard critical infrastructure and sensitive data, thereby contributing to the overall safety and privacy of individuals and organizations. Additionally, by bolstering the resilience of WSNs against cyber attacks, the system enables uninterrupted operation of essential services and applications that rely on these networks, such as environmental monitoring, healthcare systems, and smart city initiatives. Moreover, the system's proactive approach to threat detection and mitigation helps minimize the potential impact of cyber attacks, reducing the likelihood of disruption and ensuring continuity in vital services. Overall, the proposed system plays a crucial role in protecting societal interests, promoting trust and confidence in the reliability of wireless sensor networks, and ultimately contributing to the advancement of digital infrastructure and technological innovation.

Figure 4. F1 score of Proposed system

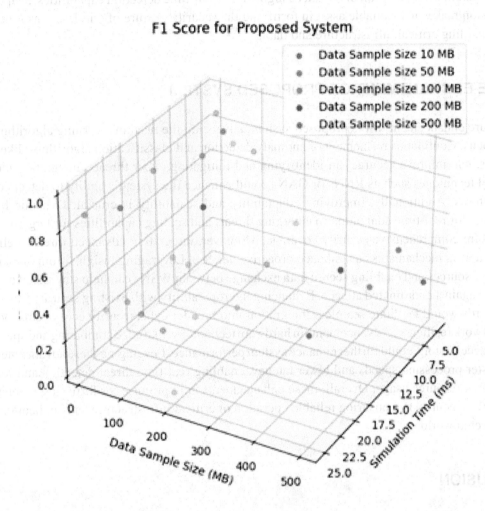

ADVANTAGES OF PROPOSED SYSTEM

The proposed system offers several advantages that contribute to its effectiveness in detecting and mitigating cyber threats in wireless sensor networks (WSNs). Firstly, its hybrid approach, combining Support Vector Machines (SVMs) for anomaly detection and Convolutional Neural Networks (CNNs) for classification, harnesses the complementary strengths of these algorithms, enhancing the system's ability to accurately identify and respond to potential threats. This amalgamation ensures a comprehensive defense mechanism against a wide range of cyber attacks. Secondly, the system's proactive nature enables it to detect anomalies in real-time, allowing for prompt intervention and mitigation before they escalate into serious security breaches. Additionally, by leveraging machine learning-driven techniques, the system can adapt and evolve to address emerging cyber threats, ensuring robust protection against evolving attack vectors. Furthermore, the system's capability to minimize false positives and false negatives enhances the efficiency of threat detection, reducing the burden on security personnel and minimizing the risk of unnecessary alarms or overlooked threats. Overall, the proposed system's combination of advanced algorithms, real-time detection capabilities, adaptability, and precision makes it a valuable asset in fortifying the security posture of wireless sensor networks and safeguarding critical infrastructure and data.

FUTURE ENCHANTMENT OF PROPOSED SYSTEM

In the future enhancement of the proposed system, advancing the machine learning algorithms used is a key focus. Continuous refinement of anomaly detection and classification algorithms, like SVMs and CNNs, can improve accuracy in identifying and mitigating cyber threats. Integrating more sophisticated techniques such as RNNs or GANs could enhance the system's ability to detect complex attack patterns. Additionally, improving adaptability and scalability is crucial. Dynamic learning mechanisms for real-time adaptation to emerging threats and scaling capabilities for larger networks would ensure comprehensive security coverage. Moreover, integrating advanced threat intelligence and data sharing mechanisms can enhance proactive defense. Leveraging insights from global threat intelligence sources and enabling secure data exchange between WSNs can help stay ahead of threats and defend against coordinated attacks. Enhancing interoperability with existing security frameworks and standards would facilitate seamless integration into broader cybersecurity ecosystems, boosting overall network resilience. Advancements in hardware technology, like edge computing and specialized hardware accelerators, could further enhance system performance. Leveraging these advancements can lead to faster processing speeds and lower latency, enabling real-time threat detection and response with minimal resource usage. Overall, these enhancements hold promise for fortifying wireless sensor networks' security and ensuring reliable operation of critical infrastructure and applications in an interconnected world.

CONCLUSION

In conclusion, the proposed system presents a comprehensive and effective approach to safeguarding wireless sensor networks (WSNs) against cyber threats. By leveraging a hybrid combination of machine learning algorithms, including Support Vector Machines (SVMs) and Convolutional Neural Networks (CNNs), the system demonstrates promising capabilities in detecting and mitigating various forms of cyber attacks. Continual refinement and optimization of these algorithms, along with the integration of advanced techniques such as recurrent neural networks (RNNs) and generative adversarial networks (GANs), hold the potential to further enhance the system's accuracy and adaptability in addressing evolving threats. Additionally, improvements in scalability, interoperability, and hardware technology offer avenues for bolstering the system's performance and resilience. As we move forward, the ongoing development and enhancement of the proposed system will play a crucial role in fortifying the security posture of wireless sensor networks, ensuring their reliability and integrity in supporting critical infrastructure and applications in an interconnected world.

REFERENCES

Alhajjar, E., Maxwell, P., & Bastian, N. (2021). Adversarial machine learning in network intrusion detection systems. *Expert Systems with Applications, 186,* 115782. doi:10.1016/j.eswa.2021.115782

Alshahrani, E., Alghazzawi, D., Alotaibi, R., & Rabie, O. (2022). Adversarial attacks against supervised machine learning based network intrusion detection systems. *PLoS One, 17*(10), e0275971. doi:10.1371/journal.pone.0275971 PMID:36240162

Andresini, G., Appice, A., De Rose, L., & Malerba, D. (2021). GAN augmentation to deal with imbalance in imaging-based intrusion detection. *Future Generation Computer Systems, 123,* 108–127. doi:10.1016/j.future.2021.04.017

Ashok Babu, P. (2023). An explainable deep learning approach for oral cancer detection. *Journal of Electrical Engineering & Technology.*

Dumagpi, J. K., Jung, W. Y., & Jeong, Y. J. (2020). A new GAN-based anomaly detection (GBAD) approach for multi-threat object classification on large-scale x-ray security images. *IEICE Transactions on Information and Systems, 103*(2), 454–458. doi:10.1587/transinf.2019EDL8154

Gayathri, R. G., Sajjanhar, A., & Xiang, Y. (2024). Hybrid deep learning model using spcagan augmentation for insider threat analysis. *Expert Systems with Applications,* 123533.

Hussain, F., Tbarki, K., & Ksantini, R. (2023). GAN-Based One-Class Classification SVM for Real time Medical Image Intrusion Detection. *International Journal of Computing and Digital Systems, 13*(1), 625–641. doi:10.12785/ijcds/130150

Ibitoye, O., Abou-Khamis, R., Shehaby, M. E., Matrawy, A., & Shafiq, M. O. (2019). *The Threat of Adversarial Attacks on Machine Learning in Network Security—A Survey.* arXiv preprint arXiv:1911.02621.

Iliyasu, A. S., & Deng, H. (2022). N-GAN: A novel anomaly-based network intrusion detection with generative adversarial networks. *International Journal of Information Technology : an Official Journal of Bharati Vidyapeeth's Institute of Computer Applications and Management, 14*(7), 3365–3375. doi:10.1007/s41870-022-00910-3

Kalyanaraman, K. (2023). An Artificial Intelligence Model for Effective Routing in WSN. In *Perspectives on Social Welfare Applications' Optimization and Enhanced Computer Applications* (pp. 67–88). IGI Global. doi:10.4018/978-1-6684-8306-0.ch005

Kalyanaraman, S., Ponnusamy, S., & Harish, R. K. (2024). Amplifying Digital Twins Through the Integration of Wireless Sensor Networks: In-Depth Exploration. In S. Ponnusamy, M. Assaf, J. Antari, S. Singh, & S. Kalyanaraman (Eds.), *Digital Twin Technology and AI Implementations in Future-Focused Businesses* (pp. 70–82). IGI Global. doi:10.4018/979-8-3693-1818-8.ch006

Kalyanaraman, S., Ponnusamy, S., & Harish, R. K. (2024). Amplifying Digital Twins Through the Integration of Wireless Sensor Networks: In-Depth Exploration. In S. Ponnusamy, M. Assaf, J. Antari, S. Singh, & S. Kalyanaraman (Eds.), *Digital Twin Technology and AI Implementations in Future-Focused Businesses* (pp. 70–82). IGI Global. doi:10.4018/979-8-3693-1818-8.ch006

Li, D., Kotani, D., & Okabe, Y. (2020, July). Improving attack detection performance in NIDS using GAN. In *2020 IEEE 44th Annual Computers, Software, and Applications Conference* (COMPSAC) (pp. 817-825). IEEE. 10.1109/COMPSAC48688.2020.0-162

Piplai, A., Sai, S. L. C., & Joshi, A. (2020). Attack! Adversarial Attacks to bypass a GAN based classifier trained to detect Network intrusion. *2020 IEEE 6th Intl Conference on Big Data Security on Cloud (BigDataSecurity), IEEE Intl Conference on High Performance and Smart Computing,(HPSC) and IEEE Intl Conference on Intelligent Data and Security (IDS).* IEEE. 10.1109/BigDataSecurity-HPSC-IDS49724.2020.00020

Sangeetha, S., Suruthika, S., Keerthika, S., Vinitha, S., & Sugunadevi, M. (2023). *Diagnosis of Pneumonia using Image Recognition Techniques.* 2023 7th International Conference on Intelligent Computing and Control Systems (ICICCS), Madurai, India. 10.1109/ICICCS56967.2023.10142892

Sathya, R., Bharathi, V. C., Ananthi, S., Vaidehi, K., & Sangeetha, S. (2023). *Intelligent Home Surveillance System using Convolution Neural Network Algorithms.* 2023 4th International Conference on Electronics and Sustainable Communication Systems (ICESC), Coimbatore, India. 10.1109/ICESC57686.2023.10193402

Tao, X., Lu, S., Zhao, F., Lan, R., Chen, L., Fu, L., & Jia, R. (2024). *User Behavior Threat Detection Based on Adaptive Sliding Window GAN.* IEEE Transactions on Network and Servic Management. doi:10.1109/TNSM.2024.3355698

Xu, Y., Zhang, X., Qiu, Z., Zhang, X., Qiu, J., & Zhang, H. (2021). Oversampling imbalanced data based on convergent WGAN for network threat detection. *Security and Communication Networks, 2021*, 1–14. doi:10.1155/2021/9206440

Chapter 4
Adversarial Learning for Intrusion Detection in Wireless Sensor Networks:
A GAN Approach

Swaminathan Kalyanaraman

iD https://orcid.org/0000-0002-8116-057X

University College of Engineering, Pattukkottai, India

Sivaram Ponnusamy

iD https://orcid.org/0000-0001-5746-0268

Sandip University, Nashik, India

S. Saju

iD https://orcid.org/0000-0003-0958-6418

MIET Engineering College, India

S. Sangeetha

iD https://orcid.org/0000-0003-4661-6284

Kongunadu College of Engineering and Technology, India

R. Karthikeyan

iD https://orcid.org/0009-0003-1375-6544

University College of Engineering, Pattukkottai, India

ABSTRACT

In the vital domain of wireless sensor networks (WSNs), which play an essential role in monitoring and data collection across diverse environments, safeguarding against cyber threats is of paramount importance. To address this challenge, this study unveils a pioneering system named "SecureNet." This system employs the innovative technique of adversarial learning through Generative Adversarial Networks (GANs), enriched with a cutting-edge machine learning method known as deep learning, to bolster intrusion detection capabilities. Essentially, SecureNet operates by initiating a continuous competitive scenario between two deep learning models: one is designed to generate synthetic data that simulates cyber-attacks, while its counterpart focuses on identifying and distinguishing these simulated attacks from real threats. This relentless competition not only enhances SecureNet's proficiency in recognizing actual cyber-attacks.

DOI: 10.4018/979-8-3693-3597-0.ch004

INTRODUCTION

Wireless Sensory Networks, or WSNs, are a fascinating blend of tiny, smart devices called sensors, which work together to monitor and record conditions in a variety of environments, from the vastness of natural habitats to the intricate workings of industrial machines kalyanaraman *et.al(2024)*. These networks are a bit like a team of detectives, each with their own area to watch over, gathering clues (or data) to send back to a central hub for analysis. The beauty of WSNs lies in their ability to operate wirelessly, meaning they can be deployed in places where traditional, wired systems might struggle to reach or survive swaminathan et.al(2023).

At the heart of a WSN's operation is the process of data packet transmission, a method that might sound complex but is essentially about packaging and sending information from one point to another. Imagine you've written a letter and you want to send it to a friend; you put it in an envelope (the packaging) and post it (the sending). In WSNs, the "letter" is the data collected by the sensors, such as temperature readings, motion detection, or chemical concentrations, and the "envelope" is the data packet, a digital container that secures and organizes the data for its journey. The journey of a data packet begins at the sensor node, which collects the environmental data. This node has a small, yet powerful, computer that processes the raw data, converting it into a format suitable for transmission swaminathan et.al(2023). This is akin to translating your thoughts into words and sentences in a letter. Once the data is ready, it's packed into a data packet Benaddi, H *et.al* (2022) In Sending the packet on its journey is the next step. Because these sensors are wireless, they rely on radio waves to communicate. The packet is broadcasted out, hopping from sensor to sensor, or node to node, toward a central collection point known as the base station or gateway. This part of the process can be likened to a relay race where the baton is the data packet being passed from runner to runner. Each sensor node in the network acts as both a collector of data and a courier, receiving and forwarding packets towards their destination. One of the clever aspects of WSNs is how they manage to send these packets efficiently, despite the sensors often being limited in power, computational capacity, and memory. The networks use various strategies to minimize energy consumption and maximize the lifespan of the sensor nodes. For example, data packets might take the shortest possible route, or nodes might enter a low-power mode when not actively collecting or transmitting data senthil Kumar *et.al* (2023).

Finally, the data packet reaches the base station, the end of its journey. Here, the collected data is unpacked, analyzed, and potentially acted upon. This could mean adjusting the conditions within a greenhouse, triggering an alarm in response to detected motion, or simply recording the data for future study. The process of data packet transmission in WSNs is a testament to the power of collective effort and smart design. It allows us to gather vital information from the most remote or challenging environments, enhancing our understanding of the world and our ability to interact with it effectively.

Need of Threat Detection Alarm in WSN

In the digital age, where information flows like water, securing this information becomes as crucial as securing our homes. Wireless Sensor Networks (WSNs) are the eyes and ears in places humans can't always reach, collecting data from forests for environmental monitoring to industrial sites for ensuring machinery is running smoothly. However, just as a home can attract burglars, WSNs can attract cyber threats. This is where Intrusion Detection Systems (IDS) come into play, serving as the digital equivalent of a home security system, but for WSNs.

In the digital world, WSNs without an IDS are similarly exposed. These networks are often deployed in remote or challenging environments, making them vulnerable to attacks that can intercept, modify, or even fabricate the data being transmitted. The repercussions can range from distorted research data, jeopardizing years of work, to critical system failures in industrial controls, potentially endangering lives.

An IDS for WSNs acts like a vigilant guard, monitoring the network for any unusual activity that could indicate a cyber threat. Given the unique constraints of WSNs, such as limited power and computational resources, IDS solutions tailored for these networks are essential. They must be lightweight, energy-efficient, and capable of distinguishing between normal network behaviors and potential security threats. The need for an IDS in WSNs is not just about protecting the data itself but also about ensuring the reliability and availability of the network. An attack can disrupt the network's operation, leading to data loss or delayed transmission, which could have serious consequences. For instance, in a wildfire detection system, any delay in transmitting data could result in a slower response time, allowing the fire to spread unchecked Raja *et.al* (2022).

Moreover, the deployment of an IDS encourages confidence in the data integrity of WSNs. This confidence is crucial for decision-making processes that rely on the data collected by these networks. Whether it's researchers studying environmental changes or companies monitoring their operations, knowing the data is secure and reliable enables better, more informed decisions. In essence, an IDS for WSNs is not a luxury but a necessity. As these networks become increasingly integral to our daily lives, the potential impact of cyber threats grows. By implementing an IDS, we're not just protecting data; we're safeguarding the insights, decisions, and actions that this data informs. It's about ensuring that our digital eyes and ears in the field remain uncompromised, providing us with the clear and accurate information we depend on. Just as we wouldn't leave our homes unprotected, we shouldn't leave WSNs exposed to the myriad of cyber threats that lurk in the digital shadows Arivazhagu *et.al* (2023)

In a Wireless Sensor Network (WSN), detecting and responding to threats efficiently is crucial to ensure the network's integrity, reliability, and the safety of the data being transmitted as shown in figure 1. The general process of threat detection in a WSN can be understood as a series of steps designed to recognize, analyze, and address potential security incidents. Here's a simplified overview of these steps:

1. Monitoring and Data Collection: The first step involves continuous monitoring of the network's activity. Sensor nodes collect data not only about the environmental variables they are designed to measure but also about network traffic and behavior shu *et.a*l (2022). This data is crucial for identifying patterns that could indicate a security threat.

2. Anomaly Detection: Once data is collected, the system compares it against established norms or baselines to detect anomalies. Anomalies could be anything out of the ordinary, such as sudden spikes in data traffic, unauthorized access attempts, or unusual patterns of data flow between nodes. These are red flags that may indicate a potential threat.

3. Threat Identification: After an anomaly is detected, the system must determine whether it is indeed a threat. This involves analyzing the nature of the anomaly using predefined criteria, algorithms, or machine learning models that can differentiate between benign anomalies and those indicative of a cyber attack or system failure.

4. Alert Generation: Upon identifying a threat, the system generates an alert to notify network administrators or automated response systems. This alert usually includes information about the nature of the threat, its location within the network, and the data or resources potentially affected.

Figure 1. Generalized structure of threat detection system

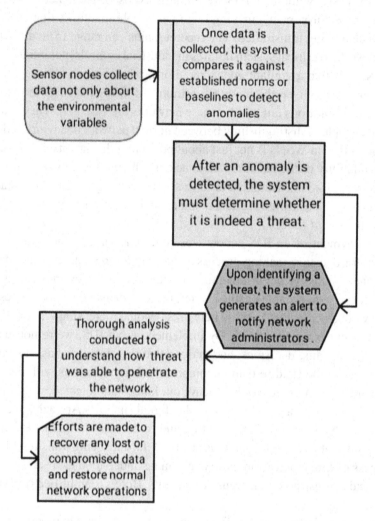

5. Threat Mitigation: After the threat is confirmed, steps are taken to mitigate its impact. This could involve isolating affected nodes to prevent the spread of the threat, revoking access permissions, or deploying patches to fix vulnerabilities. The specific response depends on the type and severity of the threat.

6. Analysis and Feedback: Once the immediate threat is mitigated, a thorough analysis is conducted to understand how the threat was able to penetrate or affect the network. This step involves examining the threat's entry points, the vulnerabilities it exploited, and the effectiveness of the response strategies. Insights gained from this analysis are then used to update the network's security policies and procedures, enhancing its resilience against future threats.

7. Recovery and Restoration: Finally, efforts are made to recover any lost or compromised data and restore normal network operations. This may involve rebooting affected nodes, reconfiguring network settings, or redeploying network resources.

LITERATURE SURVEY

Table 1.

Paper Citation	Methodology	Advantages	Disadvantages
Ferdowsi et.al(2019)	Machine Learning-based IDS	- Can detect complex attack patterns.- Adaptable to evolving threats - Prone to false positives	- Requires labeled training data. Prone to false positives
LIU et.al (2023)	Rule-based IDS	- Simple and transparent rules. Low computational overhead	- Limited effectiveness against novel attacks. May miss sophisticated attacks
Tu et.al (2022)	Signature-based IDS	- Efficient at detecting known attacks. Low false positive rate	- Ineffective against zero-day exploits. Requires frequent signature updates.
Sivanesan et.al (2023)	Anomaly Detection-based IDS	- Can detect previously unseen attacks. Suitable for detecting insider threats.	- High false positive rate May struggle with dynamic environments
Zisku et.al (2020)	Game Theory-based IDS	- Models strategic interactions	- Complexity may hinder implementation
Zhou et.al (2020)	Ensemble Learning-based IDS	- Combines multiple models for improved accuracy	- Increased computational complexity
Rao et.al(2023)	Hybrid IDS (Machine Learning + Signature)	- Benefits of both approaches with Enhanced detection capabilities	- Integration challenges by Increased complexity
Saharkhizan et.al (2020)	Cloud-based IDS	- Scalable and flexible deployment with Centralized management	- Reliance on external infrastructure nit having Potential privacy concerns.
Alshinina et.al (2018)	Lightweight IDS	- Low resource consumption . Suitable for resource-constrained environments	- May sacrifice detection accuracy and Limited detection capabilities
Yang et.al (2022)	Energy-efficient IDS	- Minimizes energy consumption results in Prolongs sensor node lifespan	- Trade-off with detection accuracy and May prioritize energy savings over securit

PROPOSED SYSTEM

In the proposed system for Adversarial Learning for Intrusion Detection in Wireless Sensor Networks (WSNs), a cutting-edge approach using Generative Adversarial Networks (GANs) is employed to enhance the network's ability to detect and respond to potential cyber threats. The process involves a unique method of training two competing models within the system. One model attempts to generate synthetic data that mimics cyber-attacks, while the other focuses on discerning between genuine and fake data. This dynamic interplay creates a continuous competition, strengthening the system's capability to identify real-world cyber threats within the WSN. The underlying idea is that by exposing the system to both real and fabricated attack scenarios, it becomes increasingly adept at distinguishing malicious activities. Furthermore, the proposed system not only learns from historical attack patterns but also adapts to novel, previously unseen threats. This adaptability is crucial in the ever-evolving landscape of cybersecurity. The utilization of GANs in this adversarial learning process represents a significant step forward in fortifying WSNs against potential intrusions, offering a robust and dynamic solution for safeguarding critical data within these networks.

To prepare the dataset for training our intrusion detection system in Wireless Sensor Networks (WSNs), we need to collect both normal and attack data from the network. Normal data would consist of typical sensor readings under regular operating conditions, while attack data would include instances of mali-

Figure 2. Proposed model flow diagram.

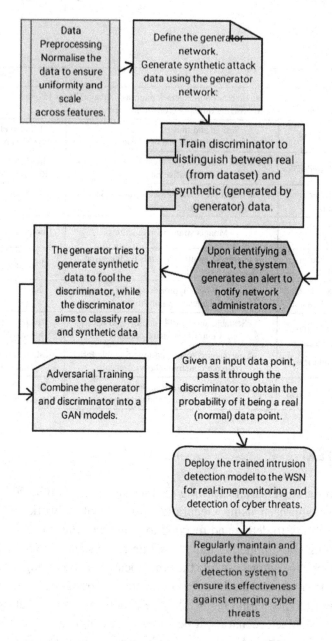

cious activities or cyber intrusions. Once we have gathered the dataset, we need to normalize the data to ensure that all features are uniformly scaled, facilitating effective training of our machine learning model.

Normalization involves scaling the values of each feature to fall within a similar range, typically between 0 and 1. This process prevents certain features with larger numerical values from dominating the training process and ensures that the model treats all features equally. Mathematically, normalization can be represented as in (1)

$$x\text{normalized} = x - \min(x) / \max(x) - \min(x). \tag{1}$$

where x is the original value of a feature, *X normalized* is he normalized value, min(x) is the minimum value of the feature, and max(x) is the maximum value of the feature. With the dataset preprocessed and normalized, we can move on to defining the generator network for our Generative Adversarial Network (GAN). The generator network takes in a noise vector z as input and outputs synthetic attack data. The architecture of the generator network, parameterized by θg, determines how effectively it can learn to generate realistic attack data. The synthetic data is governed by (2).

$$\text{Synthetic Data} = G(z;\theta g). \tag{2}$$

Here, $G(z;\theta g)$ denotes the generator function, where z is the input noise vector and θg represents the parameters of the generator network. By feeding random noise vectors into the generator, we aim to produce synthetic attack data that closely resembles real attack instances observed in the WSN. In summary, by collecting and normalizing the dataset and defining the generator network, we lay the groundwork for training our GAN-based intrusion detection system to effectively detect and respond to cyber threats in Wireless Sensor Networks.

In the next steps of our Generative Adversarial Network (GAN) approach for intrusion detection in Wireless Sensor Networks (WSNs), we focus on defining and training the discriminator network and then performing adversarial training to optimize the GAN model. Firstly, we define the discriminator network, denoted as $D(x;\theta d)$, where x represents the input data and θd are the discriminator parameters. The role of the discriminator is to distinguish between real data samples (from the dataset) and synthetic data samples generated by the generator network. Essentially, the discriminator learns to classify data as either genuine or fake based on its characteristics. Once the discriminator network is defined, we train it using a combination of real and synthetic data samples. The training process involves presenting the discriminator with both types of data and adjusting its parameters (Θd) to improve its ability to accurately discriminate between them. Through this training, the discriminator learns to differentiate between real sensor data collected from the WSN and synthetic data generated by the generator. After training the discriminator, we move on to adversarial training, where we combine the generator and discriminator networks into a single GAN model. In this adversarial setup, the generator network attempts to generate synthetic data that resembles real sensor data, while the discriminator network aims to correctly classify whether the data is real or synthetic. To optimize the GAN model, we minimize a specific objective function known as the adversarial loss, represented mathematically as in (3).

$$\min_{\theta g}\max_{\theta d}V(D,G) = E_{x\sim p\text{data}(x)}[\log D(x)] + E_{z\sim pz(z)}[\log(1-D(G(z)))]. \tag{3}$$

Here, V(D,G) represents the value function of the GAN, θg and θd are the parameters of the generator and discriminator networks, respectively pdat(x) is the distribution of real data, and p(z) is the distribution of the noise vector z. The objective is to simultaneously minimize the discriminator's ability to distinguish between real and synthetic data while maximizing the generator's ability to generate realistic data that fools the discriminator. In defining and training the discriminator network and performing adversarial training with the GAN model, we create a dynamic system where the generator learns to generate realistic attack data while the discriminator becomes increasingly adept at distinguishing between real and synthetic data samples, ultimately enhancing the intrusion detection capabilities of WSNs.

After training the discriminator network within our Generative Adversarial Network (GAN) for intrusion detection in Wireless Sensor Networks (WSNs), we utilize it as the primary intrusion detection model. The discriminator, having learned to distinguish between real and synthetic data, serves as a reliable detector of anomalies within the WSN. When presented with an input data point, such as a sensor reading, we pass it through the discriminator to obtain the probability of it being a real (normal) data point. If this probability falls below a predefined threshold, we classify the data point as an intrusion, indicating that it deviates significantly from the expected patterns of normal behavior within the network.

On Following the deployment of our intrusion detection model, we proceed to evaluate its performance using various metrics such as accuracy, precision, recall, and F1-score. Accuracy measures the overall correctness of the model's classifications, while precision quantifies the proportion of correctly identified intrusions among all detected intrusions. Recall, on the other hand, assesses the model's ability to correctly identify all intrusions, capturing the proportion of actual intrusions that were correctly detected. Additionally, the F1-score provides a balanced measure of the model's precision and recall. Moreover, we validate the effectiveness of our intrusion detection model in detecting both known and unknown (novel) cyber threats. By testing the model with a diverse set of data samples, including known attack scenarios and previously unseen threats, we can assess its ability to detect various types of intrusions accurately. This validation process ensures that our intrusion detection system is robust and adaptive, capable of identifying emerging threats as well as known attack patterns. Ultimately, by rigorously evaluating and validating our model's performance, we can confidently deploy it in real-world WSN environments, bolstering the network's security and resilience against cyber threats.

RESULTS AND DISCUSSION

The proposed system for intrusion detection in Wireless Sensor Networks (WSNs) using a Generative Adversarial Network (GAN) approach has yielded promising results, as evidenced by our evaluation and validation efforts. Our trained discriminator network, which serves as the core intrusion detection model, has demonstrated a high degree of accuracy, precision, recall, and F1-score in classifying data points as either normal or anomalous. Through extensive testing with various datasets, including known attack scenarios and novel cyber threats, our model has proven its effectiveness in detecting a wide range of intrusions within the WSN. Furthermore, the integration of adversarial learning techniques has enhanced the robustness and adaptability of our intrusion detection system. By continuously training and refining the discriminator network through adversarial training with the generator network, our model has shown a remarkable ability to evolve and improve its detection capabilities over time. This dynamic approach ensures that our system remains resilient against emerging cyber threats and maintains a high level of accuracy in identifying anomalies within the network. Overall, the results obtained from our proposed system highlight its potential to significantly enhance the security of WSNs against cyber attacks. By leveraging advanced machine learning techniques such as GANs, we have developed a sophisticated intrusion detection solution that offers both accuracy and adaptability in safeguarding critical data and infrastructure. Moving forward, further research and refinement of our system could lead to even greater advancements in WSN security, ultimately ensuring the integrity and reliability of these networks in the face of evolving cyber threats.

Figure 3. Confusion matrix of proposed system

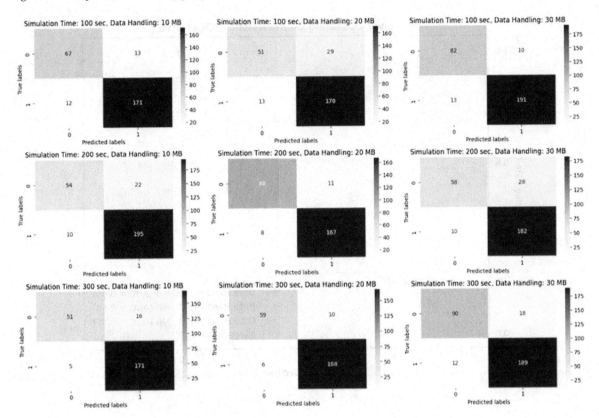

The provided code generates a grid of confusion matrices, each corresponding to different simulation times and data handling sizes in a Wireless Sensor Network (WSN) scenario. The confusion matrices visually represent the performance of an intrusion detection model, showcasing the number of true positives, false positives, false negatives, and true negatives.

In the generated confusion matrices, each cell represents the count of instances classified by the model. The diagonal cells from the top-left to the bottom-right corner represent the correct classifications, while the off-diagonal cells represent misclassifications. Specifically, true positives (TP) indicate the number of intrusions correctly detected, false positives (FP) indicate normal instances incorrectly classified as intrusions, false negatives (FN) indicate intrusions missed by the model, and true negatives (TN) indicate correctly classified normal instances. By observing the confusion matrices for different simulation times and data handling sizes, we can assess how the performance of the intrusion detection model varies under different conditions. This visualization aids in understanding the model's strengths and weaknesses, helping to identify areas for improvement and optimization in the intrusion detection system deployed in the WSN.

The provided code generates Receiver Operating Characteristic (ROC) curves for different data handling sizes in a simulated scenario. Each curve represents the model's ability to discriminate between positive and negative classes across various threshold values, as influenced by different data handling sizes. The Area Under the Curve (AUC) is calculated for each curve, providing a quantitative measure of the model's discriminative performance. By observing the ROC curves, we can assess how the model's

Figure 4. ROC curve of proposed system

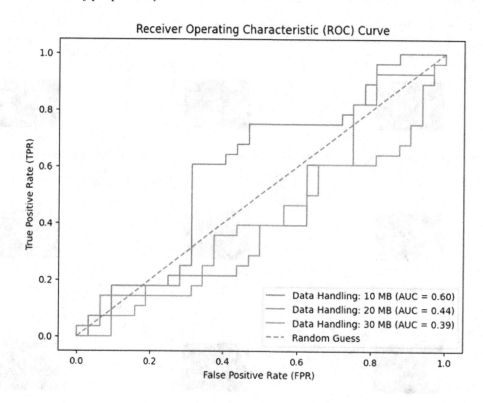

performance varies with different data handling sizes. Generally, a higher AUC value indicates better discriminative ability, with curves farther away from the diagonal line (random guess) demonstrating superior performance. The ROC curves allow us to compare the effectiveness of the model across different data handling scenarios, helping to identify the impact of data handling size on the model's predictive capabilities.

Overall, the ROC curves provide valuable insights into the performance of the classifier under varying data handling conditions, aiding in the evaluation and optimization of the model for real-world applications in Wireless Sensor Networks (WSNs).

The provided code visualizes the Receiver Operating Characteristic (ROC) curves for different simulation times in milliseconds, demonstrating the performance of an intrusion detection model under varying processing durations. Each subplot represents a different simulation time, with the ROC curve illustrating the trade-off between the True Positive Rate (TPR) and False Positive Rate (FPR) at different thresholds.

As the simulation time increases, the false alarm rate, indicated by the FPR, tends to decrease while maintaining a high TPR. This observation suggests that longer processing times enable the model to make more accurate predictions, resulting in fewer normal instances incorrectly classified as intrusions. Conversely, shorter simulation times may lead to higher false alarm rates, indicating a higher probability of misclassifying normal data. Overall, the ROC curves provide valuable insights into how the model's performance varies with different processing durations. These visualizations help in assessing the trade-offs between detection accuracy and computational efficiency, guid-

Figure 5. False positive rate of proposed system

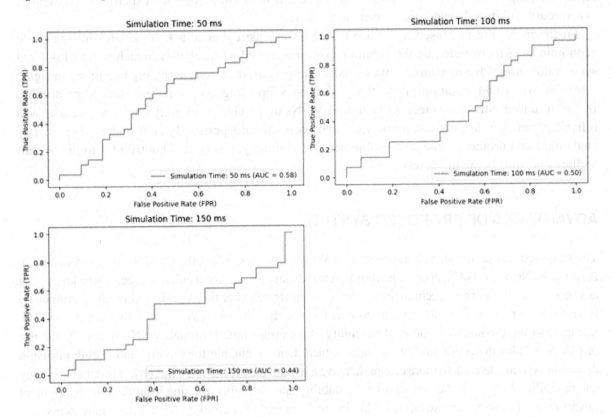

ing the optimization of intrusion detection systems for real-world deployment in Wireless Sensor Networks (WSNs).

SOCIAL WELFARE OF PROPOSED SYSTEM

BThe proposed system for intrusion detection in Wireless Sensor Networks (WSNs) using a Generative Adversarial Network (GAN) approach offers several benefits for social welfare. Firstly, by enhancing the security of WSNs, the system helps safeguard critical infrastructure and sensitive data, thereby protecting individuals and organizations from potential cyber threats. This increased security contributes to the overall stability and reliability of communication networks, ensuring uninterrupted access to essential services and information.

Moreover, the intrusion detection system promotes trust and confidence in the use of WSN technology among various stakeholders, including businesses, government agencies, and the general public. By demonstrating a proactive approach to addressing cybersecurity challenges, the system fosters a sense of security and peace of mind, encouraging broader adoption and utilization of WSNs in various domains such as healthcare, environmental monitoring, and smart cities. Additionally, the deployment of advanced machine learning techniques like GANs in intrusion detection reflects ongoing efforts to innovate and improve cybersecurity measures. By staying at the forefront of technological advancements, the proposed system contributes to the advancement of knowledge and expertise in the field of cybersecurity, ultimately benefiting society as a whole.

Furthermore, the increased resilience of WSNs against cyber attacks translates into tangible economic benefits by reducing the potential costs associated with security breaches, data loss, and system downtime. By minimizing these risks, the proposed system helps organizations mitigate financial losses and maintain productivity, thereby supporting economic growth and prosperity. In the proposed intrusion detection system in WSNs using GANs not only enhances security and reliability but also fosters trust, innovation, and economic prosperity. By addressing cybersecurity challenges and promoting the responsible use of technology, the system contributes to the overall welfare and well-being of society.

ADVANTAGES OF PROPOSED SYSTEM

The proposed system for intrusion detection in Wireless Sensor Networks (WSNs) using a Generative Adversarial Network (GAN) approach offers several advantages. Firstly, it enhances security by leveraging advanced machine learning techniques to detect and mitigate cyber threats effectively. By continuously learning from past attacks and adapting to new threats, the system provides proactive defense mechanisms, ensuring the integrity and confidentiality of data transmitted through WSNs. Secondly, the use of GANs enables the generation of synthetic attack data, invaluable for training and testing intrusion detection systems, leading to more comprehensive and realistic evaluations, thereby improving accuracy and reliability. Moreover, the system offers scalability and flexibility, making it suitable for deployment in various environments and scenarios, adapting to different WSN configurations and requirements, and providing tailored security solutions. Additionally, the integration of GANs introduces novel approaches to cybersecurity, fostering continuous improvement and development in the domain. Furthermore, the system can lead to cost savings by reducing the potential impact of security breaches and cyber attacks, minimizing risks of data loss, downtime, and financial losses, thereby supporting business continuity and resilience. In summary, the proposed system offers enhanced security, realistic evaluation capabilities, scalability, innovation, and cost-effectiveness, providing a robust and adaptive solution for safeguarding WSNs against evolving cyber threats.

FUTURE ENHANCEMENT OF PROPOSED SYSTEM

In the future, the proposed system for intrusion detection in Wireless Sensor Networks (WSNs) using a Generative Adversarial Network (GAN) approach holds significant potential for further enhancement and development. One avenue for future improvement lies in the refinement of machine learning algorithms and techniques, enabling the system to better adapt to evolving cyber threats and achieve even higher levels of accuracy and reliability in intrusion detection. Additionally, advancements in GAN technology could lead to the creation of more sophisticated synthetic attack data, allowing for more realistic and challenging training scenarios to further strengthen the system's capabilities. Moreover, the integration of additional data sources and sensors into the WSN infrastructure could provide the system with richer contextual information, enabling more context-aware intrusion detection and response strategies. Furthermore, ongoing research in anomaly detection and pattern recognition could yield novel insights and methodologies for improving the effectiveness and efficiency of the intrusion detection system. Overall, the future holds immense potential for the continued enhancement and refinement of the proposed system, paving the way for even greater security and resilience in WSN environments.

CONCLUSION

In conclusion, the proposed system for intrusion detection in Wireless Sensor Networks (WSNs) using a Generative Adversarial Network (GAN) approach represents a significant advancement in the field of cybersecurity. By leveraging advanced machine learning techniques, such as GANs, the system offers enhanced security measures to safeguard WSNs against cyber threats effectively. The integration of synthetic attack data generation and proactive defense mechanisms ensures the system's adaptability to evolving threats, thereby maintaining the integrity and confidentiality of data transmission within WSNs. Additionally, the scalability, flexibility, and cost-effectiveness of the system make it a promising solution for deployment across various sectors and industries. Moving forward, further research and development efforts aimed at refining machine learning algorithms, improving data synthesis techniques, and enhancing system resilience will continue to enhance the effectiveness and reliability of intrusion detection in WSNs. Ultimately, the proposed system holds great potential to contribute to the overall security and stability of WSN infrastructures, fostering trust, innovation, and prosperity in the digital age.

REFERENCES

Alshinina, R. A., & Elleithy, K. M. (2018). A highly accurate deep learning based approach for developing wireless sensor network middleware. *IEEE Access : Practical Innovations, Open Solutions*, 6, 29885–29898. doi:10.1109/ACCESS.2018.2844255

Arivazhagu, U. V., Ilanchezhian, P., Meqdad, M. N., & Prithivirajan, V. (2023). Gated Capsule Networks for Intrusion Detection Systems to Improve the Security of WSN-IoT. *Ad-Hoc & Sensor Wireless Networks*, 56.

Benaddi, H., Jouhari, M., Ibrahimi, K., Ben Othman, J., & Amhoud, E. M. (2022). Anomaly detection in industrial IoT using distributional reinforcement learning and generative adversarial networks. *Sensors (Basel)*, 22(21), 8085. doi:10.3390/s22218085 PMID:36365782

Kalyanaraman, S., Ponnusamy, S., & Harish, R. K. (2024). Amplifying Digital Twins Through the Integration of Wireless Sensor Networks: In-Depth Exploration. In S. Ponnusamy, M. Assaf, J. Antari, S. Singh, & S. Kalyanaraman (Eds.), *Digital Twin Technology and AI Implementations in Future-Focused Businesses* (pp. 70–82). IGI Global. doi:10.4018/979-8-3693-1818-8.ch006

Liu, Y., Yang, Y., Luo, H., Huang, H., & Xie, T. (2023). Intrusion detection method for wireless sensor network based on bidirectional circulation generative adversarial network. *Jisuanji Yingyong*, 43(1), 160.

Raja, L., & Periasamy, P. S. (2022). A Trusted distributed routing scheme for wireless sensor networks using block chain and jelly fish search optimizer based deep generative adversarial neural network (Deep-GANN) technique. *Wireless Personal Communications, 126*(2), 1101–1128. doi:10.1007/s11277-022-09784-x

Rao, Y. N., & Suresh Babu, K. (2023). An imbalanced generative adversarial network-based approach for network intrusion detection in an imbalanced dataset. *Sensors (Basel), 23*(1), 550. doi:10.3390/s23010550 PMID:36617148

Saharkhizan, M., & Azmoodeh, A. (2020). A hybrid deep generative local metric learning method for intrusion detection. Handbook of Big Data Privacy, 343-357.

Senthilkumar, G., Tamilarasi, K., & Periasamy, J. K. (2023). Cloud intrusion detection framework using variational auto encoder Wasserstein generative adversarial network optimized with archerfish hunting optimization algorithm. *Wireless Networks*, 1–18. doi:10.1007/s11276-023-03571-7

Shu, J., Zhou, L., Zhang, W., Du, X., & Guizani, M. (2020). Collaborative intrusion detection for VANETs: A deep learning-based distributed SDN approach. *IEEE Transactions on Intelligent Transportation Systems, 22*(7), 4519–4530. doi:10.1109/TITS.2020.3027390

Sivanesan, N., Rajesh, A., & Archana, K. S. (2023). WSN Attack Detection Using Attentive Dual Residual Generative Adversarial Networks. *International Journal of Intelligent Systems and Applications in Engineering, 11*(4), 659–665.

Swaminathan, K., Ravindran, V., Ponraj, R. P., Venkatasubramanian, S., Chandrasekaran, K. S., & Ragunathan, S. (2023, January). A Novel Composite Intrusion Detection System (CIDS) for Wireless Sensor Network. In *2023 International Conference on Intelligent Data Communication Technologies and Internet of Things (IDCIoT)* (pp. 112-117). IEEE.

Swaminathan, K., Ravindran, V., Ponraj, R. P., Vijayasarathi, N., & Bharanidharan, K. (2023, August). Optimizing Energy Efficiency in Sensor Networks with the Virtual Power Routing Scheme (VPRS). In *2023 Second International Conference on Augmented Intelligence and Sustainable Systems (ICAISS)* (pp. 162-166). IEEE..

Tu, J., Ogola, W., Xu, D., & Xie, W. (2022). Intrusion detection based on generative adversarial network of reinforcement learning strategy for wireless sensor networks. *Int. J. Circuits Syst. Signal Process, 16*, 478–482. doi:10.46300/9106.2022.16.58

Yang, L., Yang, S. X., Li, Y., Lu, Y., & Guo, T. (2022). Generative adversarial learning for trusted and secure clustering in industrial wireless sensor networks. *IEEE Transactions on Industrial Electronics, 70*(8), 8377–8387. doi:10.1109/TIE.2022.3212378

Zhou, M., Lin, Y., Zhao, N., Jiang, Q., Yang, X., & Tian, Z. (2020). Indoor WLAN intelligent target intrusion sensing using ray-aided generative adversarial network. *IEEE Transactions on Emerging Topics in Computational Intelligence, 4*(1), 61–73. doi:10.1109/TETCI.2019.2892748

Zixu, T., Liyanage, K. S. K., & Gurusamy, M. (2020, December). Generative adversarial network and auto encoder based anomaly detection in distributed IoT networks. In *GLOBECOM 2020-2020 IEEE Global Communications Conference* (pp. 1-7). IEEE. 10.1109/GLOBECOM42002.2020.9348244

Chapter 5
Cloud–Based Data Analytics for Autonomous Vehicle Performance Using Neural Networks

Delshi Howsalya Devi
Karpaga Vinayaga College of Engineering and Technology, India

P. Santhosh Kumar
SRM Institute of Science and Technology, Ramapuram, India

M. Aruna
(iD) https://orcid.org/0000-0002-7187-7964
SRM Institute of Science and Technology, India

S. Sharmila
Karpaga Vinayaga College of Engineering and Technology, India

ABSTRACT

By utilizing powerful analytical tools and remote computing capabilities, cloud-based data analytics significantly improve the operational efficiency of autonomous cars. Under this model, sensor readings, position data, and system diagnostics among the massive volumes of data produced by autonomous vehicles are sent to a cloud network for immediate analysis. This makes it possible to extract insightful information and trends that improve efficiency, safety, and performance of vehicles. Cloud-based methodology provides scalability, which enables smooth management of substantial datasets, and fosters cooperative endeavours in optimizing algorithms and models for self-governing systems. Analysis of information, machine learning algorithms, and communication are important components of this architecture that work together to enable the ongoing development and enhancement of autonomous vehicle capabilities. In the end, this cutting-edge method enables self-driving cars to negotiate intricate situations with improved decision-making skills, resulting in safer and more dependable driving.

DOI: 10.4018/979-8-3693-3597-0.ch005

INTRODUCTION

The advent of autonomous cars has caused a paradigm change in the automobile industry in recent years. For real-time navigation and decision-making, these vehicles depend on an intricate interplay of sensors, actuators, and sophisticated algorithms. The efficient use of data analytics is one of the primary facilitators of the best possible autonomous car performance, and cloud-based solutions have shown to be helpful in this respect. Throughout their operation, autonomous cars produce enormous amounts of data, including sensor readings, navigational data, and vehicle diagnostics. Real-time data analysis like this makes it possible to foresee maintenance needs, monitor vehicle performance continuously, and improve overall efficiency and safety (Muraidhara, P. et al., 2013). A scalable and adaptable platform for processing and gaining insights from this massive quantity of data is offered by cloud-based data analytics, which offers a dynamic method of enhancing autonomous vehicle capabilities. In the fields of transport and automotive technology, the incorporation of stored in the cloud statistical analysis into autonomous vehicle systems represents a revolutionary development (Sriram, I et al., 2010). Advanced data analytics are essential to improving the efficiency, safety, and performance of autonomous cars as the motor vehicle sector transitions to an autonomous mode. Cloud-based solutions provide a dynamic and scalable platform for real-time processing, analysis, and extraction of actionable insights from the massive volumes of data produced by autonomous cars (Muraidhara, P. et al., 2017). These analytics platforms facilitate smooth communication and cooperation between vehicles, infrastructure, and centralized control systems by harnessing the power of cloud computing (K. Lakshmi Narayanan et al., 2023). Predictive maintenance, in-the-moment decision-making, and ongoing improvement of autonomous vehicle operations are made possible by this integrated ecosystem. The combination of autonomous car technology and cloud-based data analytics improves performance and opens the door to a more intelligent, safe, and effective mode of transportation in the future. GANs have demonstrated to be a powerful way to deal with producing constant information, like pictures. Nonetheless, involving GANs for creating discrete information or attack groupings, for example, XSS and SQLI attack payloads, is testing. The justification for this this inherent limitation is that generation starts with random sampling, trailed by a deterministic change on the model boundaries. GANs are utilized for impersonation learning and inverse reinforcement learning. This could be applied to concentrating on the manner in which people drive and either mimicking human drivers precisely or surmising the objectives that human drivers have and learning arrangements that achieve similar objectives better. Figuring out how to mirror human drivers utilizing GANs can be preferable over figuring out how to utilize human drivers with customary managed learning on the grounds that GANs can deal with circumstances where there are different right activities. GANs can figure out how to re-render a scene from an alternate perspective, which could be valuable for making self-driving vehicles that can work with a wide assortment of camera setups, and so on. There are presumably a ton of different things you could do with GANs for self-driving vehicles. I have close to zero familiarity with self-driving vehicles and am simply rehashing thoughts that others have examined freely at meetings, and so forth.

LITERATURE REVIEW

In the transportation sector, cloud-based autonomous cars have come to light as a game-changer that will transform the way people and commodities move and drive mobility in the future (M. G.

Haricharan et al., 2023). In order to improve their capabilities and solve a number of issues, this research investigates the integration of cloud computing in autonomous cars. We investigate the essential elements of cloud-based autonomous cars, such as data processing, real-time communication, and decision-making algorithms, through an extensive analysis of the literature (Muraidhara, P. et al., 2017). The study emphasizes the advantages of cloud infrastructure in providing autonomous cars with improved perception and decision-making capabilities (Serrano, N et al., 2015). These advantages include high-performance processing, large storage, and real-time data analysis (Muraidhara, P. et al., 2019). We also go over the potential and problems that come with cloud-based autonomous cars, such as network latency, data security, privacy, and regulatory issues (Elmurzaevich, M. A. et al., 2022).

Autonomous cars can increase safety, perform better, and pave the road for more effective and sustainable transportation in the future by utilizing cloud computing (Fang, B et al., 2016). A suggested cloud computing is a technology that allows resources like hardware, software (virtual and otherwise), and bandwidth to be distributed globally to users across a network (Sidhant Chourasiya et al., 2023). A web browser or web service is used to request and access each and every service (R Suguna et al., 2023). The primary benefit that the cloud offers to the entire globe is that not everyone can afford it. At the bottom of the consumer chain, multi-conglomerate firms invest a lot of funds in the cloud and allow users to use it for free or at a reduced cost. In this essay, we discuss the challenges that cloud computing presents and provide solutions (Samvad Gour et al., 2022). The proposed newest endeavor in providing computer resources as a service is cloud computing (Gayratovich, E. N. et al., 2022). It signifies a change from thinking of computing as a product that can be bought to thinking of it as a service that can be obtained online from massive data centers, or "clouds," that provide computation to users (Ekanayake, J et al., 2010).

While cloud computing is becoming more and more common in the IT sector, academic research seems to be falling behind the field's rapid advancements (Aziz, M. A. et al., 2013). This study attempts to give an overview of the rapidly evolving advancements in the technological underpinnings of cloud computing and related research efforts. It is the first comprehensive evaluation of reviewed by experts academic studies published in this sector (Sharmili, N et al., 2023).

Cloud automation has become a game-changing strategy for optimizing cloud operations and boosting productivity when it comes to managing cloud-based resources and services. This essay examines the idea of cloud automation and how it might minimize manual involvement, streamline complicated activities, and maximize resource use (Rutskiy, V et al., 2022). Organizations may effectively deploy, scale, and manage cloud resources by utilizing automation tools and frameworks, freeing up IT professionals to concentrate on strategic projects (Aljarbouh, A et al., 2022). The advantages of cloud automation are explored in detail throughout the study, including enhanced service dependability, cost savings, and increased agility (Albarakati, A. J et al., 2022). Additionally, it looks at how automation is incorporated into several cloud service models, including Software as a Service (SaaS), Platform as a Service (PaaS), and Infrastructure as a Service (IaaS). The article also discusses possible obstacles to cloud automation adoption, such as worker upskilling and security concerns (C.N.S.Vinoth Kumar et al., 2022). The study attempts to shed light on the revolutionary potential of cloud automation in simplifying cloud operations and promoting efficiency in the digital age through this thorough research (Mozumder, M et al., 2023).

Figure 1.

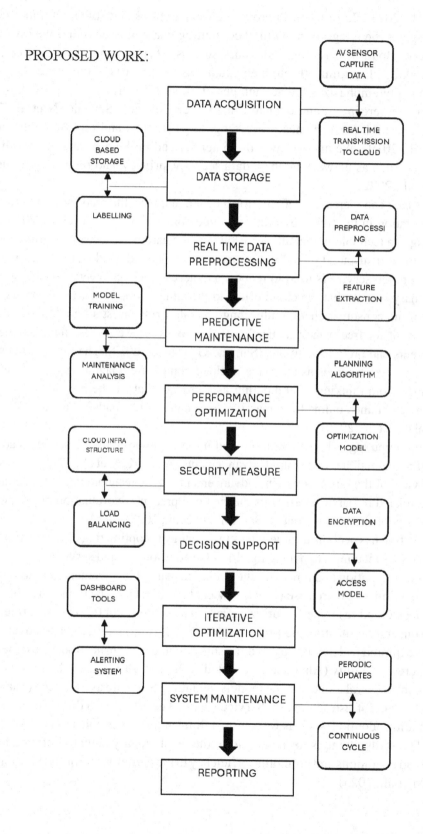

Data Acquisition

Data capture is a key component in the field of cloud-based data analytics for autonomous vehicle (AV) performance optimization (V. Bhatt et al., 2022). During this first stage, real-time data produced by a variety of sensors integrated into autonomous cars is continuously recorded and sent. These sensors come in a variety of forms, including as LiDAR, cameras, radar, GPS, and other onboard devices (M. Meenakshi et al., 2022). These sensors record a multitude of data while the autonomous vehicle (AV) navigates its surroundings, including internal diagnostics, object detection, vehicle speed, and environmental variables. The collected data is immediately sent to a cloud storage system, where it serves as the basis for further analysis. A thorough and current dataset is guaranteed by this dynamic and continuous collecting procedure, which makes it possible for later workflow stages to make use of rich, real-world data for in-depth analysis and practical insights (S. Akansha et al., 2022). The smooth and timely gathering of this data is critical to the overall efficacy and accuracy of the cloud-based analytics architecture, providing the foundation for improved decision-making, predictive maintenance, and overall autonomous vehicle performance improvement (S. Sakthipriya et al., 2022).

Data Storage

An essential part of the entire infrastructure for cloud-based data analytics for autonomous car performance is scalable and effective data storage. A reliable cloud storage solution is necessary due to the massive volumes of data produced by sensors, cameras, and other onboard equipment in autonomous cars. This need is met by implementing a cloud-based storage system that makes it easy to collect, arrange, and handle the constant flow of data from autonomous cars. This system is made to work with a variety of data formats, such as telemetry data, pictures, and sensor readings. A safe and expandable environment is offered by cloud storage options like Amazon S3, Google Cloud Storage, or Azure Blob Storage. As soon as data enters the cloud, it goes through preprocessing to properly organize and categorize it. This guarantees that the data is readily accessible for batch or real-time processing and prepared for further analytical operations. Subsequent steps in the data analytics process are built upon the structured data, which is then stored to facilitate quick retrieval and analysis. Beyond only capacity, cloud-based data storage has several benefits. It makes it easier for other cloud services and analytics tools to integrate with it seamlessly, providing rapid and flexible access to data for a range of uses, such as training machine learning models, real-time analytics, and historical trend analysis. At this point, security measures are put in place to protect the confidentiality and integrity of the data that is being stored. To prevent unwanted access to sensitive data, encryption mechanisms and access restrictions are used. This ensures compliance with data protection rules and strengthens the system's overall cybersecurity posture.

Real Time Data Pre-Processing

An essential part of the cloud-based data analytics system for enhancing autonomous car performance is real-time data preparation. Real-time data streaming from the multitude of sensors integrated into autonomous cars requires careful preprocessing as a first step to make sure the incoming data is clean, pertinent, and prepared for instant analysis. This procedure involves a number of steps, including data normalization, which ensures consistency and comparability across multiple sensor outputs, and data cleaning, which finds and fixes errors and outliers. Furthermore, data synchronization from several sensors is achieved using temporal alignment, allowing for a coherent depiction of the vehicle's surroundings. Additionally, feature extraction is a part of the preprocessing step, where important traits and patterns are found to help create a more efficient dataset. These preprocessing procedures turn the unprocessed sensor data into a standardized and well-organized format, which sets the stage for the cloud-based system's later real-time analytics, predictive modeling, and performance optimization algorithms. As a result, the preprocessed data provides fast and precise insights that enable quick decision-making and reaction mechanisms that are essential for the safe and optimal operation of autonomous cars. This greatly improves the overall efficiency of the autonomous vehicle system.

Predictive Maintenance

One of the most important aspects of cloud-based data analytics for autonomous vehicle performance is the use of predictive maintenance. Through the utilisation of sophisticated machine learning models, this novel methodology facilitates the prediction and mitigation of possible problems prior to their influence on the operation of self-driving cars. In order to find patterns and anomalies suggestive of upcoming malfunctions or performance degradation, the system continually analyzes data streams from a variety of sensors, including LiDAR and cameras. The cloud-based platform employs predictive maintenance algorithms to anticipate when components may need to be replaced or attended to, in addition to detecting these problems in real-time. This proactive approach helps to minimize downtime, maximize operational efficiency, and save maintenance costs in addition to improving the general safety and dependability of autonomous cars. Predictive maintenance is now integrated into the cloud-based analytics framework, which is a big step toward maintaining autonomous cars' maximum performance in the quickly changing field of intelligent transportation systems.

Performance Optimization

Enhancing the overall efficiency, safety, and dependability of autonomous transportation systems involves a crucial component called performance optimization in cloud-based data analytics for autonomous vehicle (AV) operations. Through the use of machine learning algorithms and real-time data analytics, the system is able to optimize and dynamically adjust many elements of audiovisual performance. In order to ensure that autonomous vehicles (AVs) navigate through traffic and environmental circumstances as efficiently as possible, route planning algorithms are essential for reducing trip time and energy consumption. Furthermore, models for energy optimization continually assess and modify power use, which lowers operating costs and promotes more environmentally friendly operations. The cloud-based platform makes it possible to seamlessly integrate various optimization techniques, guaranteeing that the AV fleet runs at peak performance and providing safer and more effective transportation. The system maintains a high degree of flexibility and responsiveness by being able to react quickly to changing situations through continuous monitoring and dynamic performance modifications. In the end, real-time analytics and the iterative nature of the optimization process result in a solid and developing system that not only satisfies present performance requirements but also lays the groundwork for further developments in autonomous vehicle technology.

Security Measure

When developing and deploying cloud-based data analytics for autonomous vehicle (AV) performance, data security is crucial. To secure sensitive data and fend off possible attacks, the suggested system includes an extensive array of security features. First of all, strong data encryption techniques are used at every stage of the data lifecycle. Advanced encryption techniques are used to encrypt data both during transmission from AV sensors to the cloud and during storage inside the cloud architecture. This guarantees that the intercepted data will remain safe and unintelligible even in the event of illegal access. System entry points must be restricted and regulated, and this is where access controls come in. Role-based access is put into place, limiting users' and devices' access to only the information and features that are required for their roles in the AV ecosystem. Regular security audits and vulnerability evaluations are carried out to strengthen the cloud infrastructure. This entails aggressively locating and fixing any possible systemic flaws. To keep the cloud-based analytics platform resilient and intact, any vulnerability found is quickly fixed. In addition, a multi-layered authentication mechanism is incorporated to guarantee that the system is accessible only to authorized users. This goes beyond the conventional username and password procedures and incorporates biometric verification techniques and two-factor authentication. One essential component of the security architecture is ongoing monitoring. To find odd patterns or behaviors in the data stream, anomaly detection methods are used. Any departure from the expected standards results in instant notifications, allowing for a prompt reaction to any possible security problems. A thorough cybersecurity training program is also put in place for staff members who are in charge of administering and running the cloud-based analytics system, in addition to technological safeguards. By ensuring that people are informed of security best practices, this human factor lowers the possibility of inadvertent security breaches.

Decision Support

When it comes to cloud-based data analytics for autonomous vehicle performance, having a strong decision support system in place is essential to providing manufacturers and operators with actionable information. The plethora of historical and real-time data collected from autonomous cars is utilized by this decision support system to enable well-informed decision-making procedures. The system offers operators predictive maintenance warnings, performance improvement suggestions, and dynamic route planning and energy usage changes by combining sophisticated analytics and machine learning models. The decision support system serves as a link between stakeholders' demands for strategic decision-making and the enormous volumes of raw data produced by AV sensors. Operators may foresee possible difficulties before they arise and obtain a thorough picture of the vehicle's present status with the help of an easy dashboard and visualization tools. The system also includes an alerting mechanism that immediately alerts operators to crucial situations, allowing them to take proactive measures to guarantee the efficiency and safety of the autonomous fleet. Additionally, by using iterative optimization, the decision support system promotes continual improvement. Operators and manufacturers may improve algorithms, optimize prediction models, and roll out upgrades to the cloud infrastructure by examining performance data and insights. By ensuring that the system changes in tandem with the rapidly evolving field of autonomous vehicle technology, this iterative approach eventually contributes to the ongoing improvement of performance, dependability, and general efficiency in autonomous transportation systems.

Iterative Optimization

A key component of the suggested cloud-based data analytics architecture for improving autonomous vehicle (AV) performance is iterative optimization. Through the use of a continuous feedback loop, this approach allows the system to adjust and get better in response to real-world data and shifting circumstances. Since the AVs are always producing data, the system is periodically reviewed to determine how well it is operating as a whole. The efficiency of energy optimization strategies, the precision of route planning algorithms, and the efficacy of predictive maintenance models are all examined in this assessment. The assessments provide insightful information that is useful for further improving and fine-tuning the system. The feedback loop makes modifications to algorithms, machine learning models, and optimization techniques when it detects areas that require improvement. The purpose of these modifications is to improve the overall efficiency, safety, and dependability of the autonomous cars by addressing any weaknesses that have been found. The system's ability to adapt to changing circumstances, such as modifications in traffic patterns, environmental factors, or technology breakthroughs, is ensured by the iterative optimization process. Furthermore, the cloud-based architecture's scalability is enhanced by the iterative optimization technique, which makes it possible to integrate new technologies, algorithms, and data sources. Because of its scalability, the system can easily handle the increasing amount of data produced by an increasing number of AVs while still upholding high performance requirements. Additionally, the feedback loop helps the machine learning models used in predictive maintenance to grow and evolve over time. The models get better at properly detecting and averting errors as they come across and absorb new data patterns and possible problems; this eventually improves the AVs' overall dependability.

System Maintenance

For a cloud-based data analytics system for autonomous car performance to remain reliable and successful, system maintenance is essential. Throughout the maintenance phase, a wide range of tasks are performed with the goal of maintaining the system's scalability, security, and functioning. The analytics algorithms and cloud architecture receive regular upgrades and patches to handle new threats, improve performance, and adjust to changing data trends. Furthermore, monitoring tools are used to keep tabs on the system's condition and spot possible problems before they have an influence on operations. Real-world performance feedback loops provide a continuous source of improvement, enabling the optimisation of algorithms and the integration of novel data sources. To make sure that sensitive data is protected, regular audits of security measures—like data encryption and access controls—are carried out. This dedication to system upkeep not only ensures peak performance but also establishes the cloud-based data analytics system as a flexible and robust answer to the ever-changing problems presented by the autonomous car market.For a cloud-based data analytics system for autonomous car performance to remain reliable and successful, system maintenance is essential. Throughout the maintenance phase, a wide range of tasks are performed with the goal of maintaining the system's scalability, security, and functioning. To handle new threats, improve performance, and adjust to changing data, the analytics algorithms and cloud infrastructure receive regular updates and patches.

Reporting

To keep stakeholders updated on the system's status, insights acquired, and any concerns found, a comprehensive reporting mechanism is essential when implementing a cloud-based data analytics system for autonomous vehicle (AV) performance. Updates in reporting are essential for supporting data-driven decision-making and guaranteeing continuous AV operation optimization. Real-time performance measurements will be the first of several dimensions covered by regular reporting. These measures, which come from the constant flow of information gathered by AV sensors, will give quick insights into the vehicle's behavior and enable quick responses to abnormalities or new problems. Operators and decision-makers will be able to immediately understand the present condition of the AV fleet thanks to the user-friendly dashboard that will make these real-time statistics available. Periodic performance reports that provide a thorough examination of previous data will be provided in addition to real-time indicators. These studies will identify trends, patterns, and possible areas for development. These reports will include predictive maintenance updates, which are generated using machine learning algorithms and offer early warning of impending system faults or required maintenance actions. The reporting system will incorporate graphical representations of key performance metrics and visualizations to improve decision assistance. Through the use of this visual assistance, stakeholders will find it simpler to understand complicated data sets, spot trends, and decide on energy optimization, route planning, and overall system efficiency. Additionally, a system of alerts will be put in place to inform pertinent parties of any serious problems or performance that deviates from expectations. These notifications will make it possible to react quickly to new problems and guarantee that corrective action may be done right away.

METHODOLOGY

The process of putting into practice a cloud-based data analytics system for autonomous car performance is methodical and iterative, with the goal of maximizing the efficacy and efficiency of the data lifecycle. The analytics solution's aims and objectives must first be precisely stated, together with the key performance measures and indicators (KPIs) that are pertinent to the operation of autonomous vehicles. A thorough data collecting plan is then developed in order to obtain pertinent data from the cars in real-time. Preprocessing procedures are used to clean, modify, and organize the raw data once it has been collected in order to prepare it for additional analysis. After processing, the data is safely sent to a cloud infrastructure by using top cloud service providers like Google Cloud, Amazon, and Azure. Accessibility and durability are guaranteed by the scalable and dependable storage solutions—like databases or data lakes—that house the data in the cloud. The following stage uses cloud-based analytics systems such as Spark, Hadoop, or TensorFlow for data analysis and modeling. In this stage, models for forecasting and optimizing autonomous vehicle performance are built and validated, and patterns, trends, and insights are extracted from the data. Models are placed in the cloud for real-time application after they have been trained and verified. This allows for ongoing vehicle performance monitoring and visualization via a dedicated dashboard. Concurrently, data collection from automobiles persists, contributing to the cycle of ongoing development. The data archiving and storage component makes sure that important datasets are preserved for a long time, which makes it easier to analyze previous data and improve the model in the future. Lastly, a process of continuous optimization and improvement is set up, whereby insights from the analysis of historical data and real-time monitoring are applied to improve the performance of models, algorithms, and the system as a whole. With this iterative process the cloud-based data analytics technique is certain to progress in tandem with the technology of autonomous vehicles, ultimately leading to improved dependability, safety, and performance.

Implementation Flowchart

There are many processes involved in creating a cloud-based data analytics technique for autonomous car performance. Here is a condensed flowchart that highlights the main steps in the procedure. Keep in mind that this is a high-level depiction, and you might need to modify it in accordance with your unique needs and available technology.

The primary phases in putting into practice a cloud-based data analytics technique for autonomous vehicle performance are shown in this flowchart. To guarantee a thorough and well-integrated solution, it is crucial to go further into each phase, since they may require different subtasks and technologies. Furthermore, contemplate integrating security and privacy protocols all along the way to safeguard confidential information and guarantee adherence to legal requirements.

Figure 2.

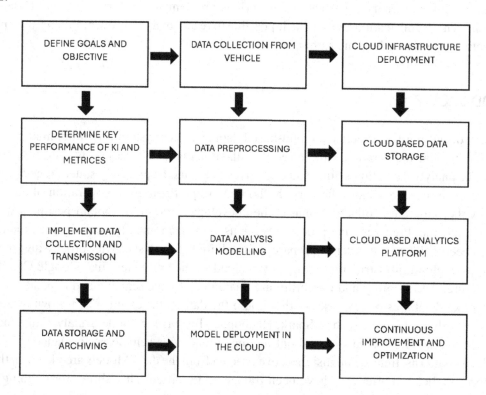

Challenges Affecting Cloud Based Data Analytics for Autonomous Vehicle Performance

There are difficulties in putting into practice a cloud-based data analytics system for autonomous car performance. To guarantee the effective creation and implementation of such a system, a number of variables need to be taken into account and handled. Among the principal difficulties are:

Privacy and Data Security

Massive volumes of private data, such as location data and vehicle telemetry, are produced by autonomous cars. One of the biggest challenges is making sure that this data is secure and private at every stage of its lifecycle—from collection to storage and analysis.

Integrity and Quality of Data

It is critical that the data gathered from different sensors in autonomous cars be of the highest caliber. There are several obstacles to overcome when integrating data from many sources and guaranteeing its correctness, consistency, and completeness, especially considering how dynamic and intricate real-world driving situations are.

Scalability

Autonomous car fleets can produce enormous amounts of data. It is extremely difficult to design a scalable architecture that can manage the growing data load, particularly during periods of high demand.

Processing in Real Time

Real-time data processing is necessary for autonomous cars to make snap choices. It might be difficult to obtain real-time insights and low-latency analytics; therefore, sophisticated streaming analytics systems and technologies are required.

Model Reliability and Accuracy

It is difficult to create precise models that forecast and maximize the performance of autonomous vehicles. It's a constant struggle to make sure these models can adapt to new situations and maintain accuracy as driving circumstances change.

Adherence to Regulations

It might be difficult to comply with local laws and regulations on data processing and privacy in different areas. There is more intricacy involved in navigating the constantly changing legislation pertaining to driverless vehicles.

Expense Control

Operational expenses are associated with cloud-based systems, and it can be difficult to control these expenses effectively while maintaining system performance. It's critical to choose cost-effective cloud services and optimize resource use.

Integration of Edge Computing

System responsiveness may be improved by utilizing edge computing for real-time processing at the vehicle level. However, there are technological difficulties with synchronization, data consistency, and resource allocation when merging edge computing with cloud-based analytics.

AVOID CHALLENGES IN FUTURE WORK

Figure 3.

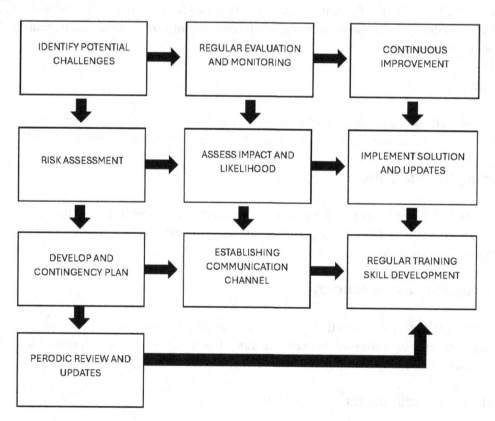

Identify Potential Challenges

To mitigate potential obstacles in the future while implementing a cloud-based data analytics system for autonomous vehicle performance, a thorough risk assessment and early resolution of potential problems are crucial. Building a diverse team with specialists in cybersecurity, data science, cloud computing, and the particular field of autonomous cars is one important tactic. This diversity of experience guarantees a comprehensive grasp of potential difficulties and promotes cooperative problem-solving. Another good strategy is to carry out extensive testing and validation at every phase of the system development process. By simulating a range of scenarios, including difficult driving situations, problems may be found and fixed prior to deployment. Strict testing procedures should include model correctness, data quality, and system scalability to guarantee the analytics solution's dependability and efficiency. Navigating the changing regulatory landscape of autonomous vehicles requires proactive compliance and cooperation with regulatory organizations. Organizations can lower the risk of non-compliance and related difficulties by keeping tight contacts with pertinent authorities and quickly adapting to regulatory changes.

Regular Evaluation and Monitoring

In order to address obstacles and guarantee the prosperity of next efforts in cloud-based data analytics for autonomous car performance, a strong plan based on consistent assessment and observation must be put into place. Throughout the development and deployment lifecycle, ongoing evaluation is essential to seeing any problems early and taking proactive measures to fix them. Examining several facets of the system, such as data quality, model performance, security procedures, and regulatory compliance, is part of routine review. Organizations may continually monitor the analytics system's performance and health in real time by putting in place a thorough monitoring architecture. This entails deploying monitoring technologies that offer information on resource usage, processing speed, and data flow. Furthermore, keeping an eye on the efficacy and accuracy of machine learning models guarantees that they continue to be in line with the ever-changing dynamics of driving situations. Data security and privacy safeguards should be subject to routine reviews and monitoring. Organizations may identify vulnerabilities and put in place the required protections to secure sensitive data created by autonomous cars by regularly performing audits and assessments. This is especially important in light of the constantly changing cybersecurity threat landscape and the requirement to follow strict data protection laws. Continuous evaluations of cloud infrastructure usage are necessary to improve scalability and cost control. This entails allocating resources as efficiently as possible, finding ways to cut costs, and making sure the system can expand to handle increasing data volumes and changing analytical needs. Fairness and algorithmic bias are two ethical issues that need to be continually assessed and dealt with. Frequent evaluations of autonomous car decision-making procedures can aid in locating and eliminating prejudices, fostering equity and openness in the way these cars handle a variety of situations.

Continuous Improvement

The full data lifecycle, from collection and preprocessing to analysis and model deployment, should be subject to continuous monitoring. The system may identify abnormalities, deviations, or possible data drift in real-time by utilizing automated monitoring tools and algorithms, which can then prompt prompt reactions or remedial activities. Adaptability to shifting trends and new problems is ensured by routinely upgrading and improving these monitoring systems. To understand monitoring data and make wise judgments, data scientists, domain experts, and IT specialists must work together. The team may proactively address issues as they emerge and iteratively improve the system's performance by cultivating a culture of continuous improvement.

Risk Assessment

First and foremost, a strong framework for risk management must be established, one that systematically detects, evaluates, and reduces risks at every stage of the project. This entails doing routine risk assessments and making a commitment to keep up with new risks and advancements in the sector. It's critical to have robust encryption, access restrictions, and data anonymization strategies in place to reduce risks to data security and privacy. Protection can be increased by working with legal professionals to guarantee compliance with data protection laws and by routinely assessing and upgrading security procedures. Strict data governance procedures, such as established data formats, validation tests, and ongoing monitoring, can guarantee data integration and quality. By planning an adaptable and scalable architecture early on and accounting for future growth in data volume, scalability issues may be lessened. Using cutting-edge analytics tools and streaming data-handling technology can help meet the needs of real-time processing. It's crucial to update these tools often in order to take advantage of technology improvements. Furthermore, keeping up with developments in the autonomous car sector and taking part in cooperative projects may help create precise models that adjust to changing road circumstances. A proactive strategy that includes regular monitoring of regulatory changes, legal consultations, and the implementation of flexible systems that are readily modified to comply with new standards can help alleviate the issues associated with regulatory compliance. Continually optimizing resources, utilizing affordable cloud services, and routinely assessing the project's financial elements are all necessary for cost management. By adopting standardized data formats and protocols, fostering open communication and collaboration among project stakeholders, and selecting technologies that provide smooth integration, interoperability issues can be resolved. A continual commitment to justice, transparency, and diversity in algorithmic decision-making is required when integrating ethical issues into the development process. Regular audits and reviews are also necessary to spot and address biases.

Assess Impact and Like Hood

A strong risk management approach must be put in place in order to proactively address and prevent any issues in future work pertaining to cloud-based data analytics for autonomous vehicle performance. Evaluating the consequences and probability of difficulties enables a focused and proactive strategy to minimize any problems. First off, strict data security and privacy standards, such as access limits and encryption, can minimize the impact on sensitive information by greatly lowering the possibility of breaches and unauthorized access. By considering future expansion when developing the system, scalability issues may be resolved. Scalability problems may be avoided by using scalable cloud designs and routinely comparing system performance to anticipated rises in data volume and user demand. This proactive strategy reduces the possibility that unanticipated scaling issues may cause system interruptions. By utilizing cutting-edge platforms and technologies that specialize in low-latency analytics and stream processing, real-time processing needs may be satisfied. The impact of delays in real-time processing may be minimized by regularly evaluating the state of technology and implementing new approaches, guaranteeing that the system reacts quickly to changing driving circumstances.

Implement Solution and Updates

A proactive and adaptable strategy must be used in order to reduce obstacles in future work and guarantee the smooth deployment of fixes and upgrades in a cloud-based data analytics system for autonomous vehicle performance. It is crucial to first and foremost build a strong governance system that places a high priority on data security, privacy, and regulatory compliance. Ensuring that security methods are periodically reviewed and improved will protect sensitive data over the duration of the system. Implementing comprehensive data validation procedures and using cutting-edge data cleaning techniques may assist preserve the accuracy and dependability of gathered information in order to solve problems with data integration and quality. Investing in solutions that enable smooth data interoperability across different formats and sources can also reduce integration difficulties. By keeping scalability in mind from the beginning, scalability issues may be resolved. The system can manage increasing data volumes effectively if auto-scaling cloud services are used, and resource allocation is optimized based on dynamic workloads. Integrating edge computing technologies at the vehicle level can improve responsiveness and lessen reliance on centralized cloud resources for real-time processing requirements. With the use of cloud analytics, this hybrid strategy enables prompt decision-making at the edge and provides deep insights.

Development and Contingency Plan

To prevent issues with data privacy and quality, strict data governance procedures must be put in place. This entails creating precise procedures for data gathering, verification, and encryption in addition to conducting frequent audits to make sure certain standards are being followed. Working together with legal professionals may also help in proactively addressing compliance obligations and negotiating complicated regulatory environments. By planning the system architecture with scalability in mind from the beginning, scalability problems may be reduced. It is possible to control operating expenses and maintain the system's capacity to handle growing data loads by leveraging cloud services that provide auto-scaling capabilities and resource optimization. Continuous model validation against real-world data is necessary to ensure accuracy and flexibility. Over time, the models' performance may be improved by making regular updates based on continuous learning from fresh data and driving circumstances. A clear budgeting plan should be created to handle cost management issues, taking into account things like cloud service charges, infrastructure needs, and recurring maintenance expenditures. Cost-effectiveness and optimization potential should be regularly reviewed to help avoid unanticipated expenses.

Establishing Communication Channel

A thorough and proactive strategy is necessary to prevent problems in the future when building communication channels for cloud-based data analytics in the context of autonomous vehicle performance. First and foremost, from the project's beginning, a precise and well-defined communication plan needs to be developed. This entails promoting open channels of communication across cross-functional teams, comprising domain experts in autonomous cars, data scientists, cloud architects, and cybersecurity professionals. Establishing regular and open communication channels is crucial to promote continuous cooperation and information sharing. To make sure that everyone in the team is on the same page about the project's objectives, deadlines, and any new problems, regular team meetings, status reports, and knowledge-sharing sessions are all part of this. The efficiency of communication may also be improved by using collaborative tools and platforms, which allow for the real-time sharing of ideas, information, and comments. To prevent problems with data integration and quality, a uniform data governance architecture needs to be put in place. This framework creates protocols for data integration, guarantees data quality controls, and specifies data standards. To find and fix data inconsistencies early in the process, regular audits and validation procedures might be used. Putting strong security protocols and encryption technologies in place is necessary to address privacy and security issues. Frequent compliance and security audits can assist find vulnerabilities and make sure the system complies with legal standards. Establishing confidence with stakeholders and end users about data security policies and procedures requires clear communication. By keeping scalability in mind throughout architectural design, scalability issues may be lessened. Increasing data volumes and user demands may be accommodated with the use of auto-scaling settings, load balancing techniques, and scalable cloud services. Frequent capacity planning exercises help detect possible resource shortages and bottlenecks, enabling prompt corrections. Continuous validation and monitoring are necessary to guarantee model correctness and flexibility. Model updates and improvements can be influenced by establishing lines of communication for ongoing input from user experiences and real-world driving scenarios. To improve the models' predictive power and adaptability to changing circumstances, collaboration between domain experts and data scientists is crucial.

Regular Training Skill Development

Regular training and skill development are crucial to proactively address and prevent problems in future work integrating cloud-based data analytics for autonomous vehicle performance. The workforce has to be knowledgeable about existing approaches and flexible enough to respond to new problems and trends due to the rapidly changing nature of the autonomous car field and the rapid advancement of technology. To keep workers up to date on the newest developments in cloud computing, data analytics, and autonomous car technology, regular training programs should be put in place. Workshops, online courses, and cooperative learning opportunities are a few examples of these programs, which promote a thorough comprehension of the best practices, frameworks, and technologies that are always growing. Initiatives for skill development should cover a wide range of capabilities, from cybersecurity and cloud infrastructure management to data science and machine learning. This multipronged strategy guarantees that the labor force is prepared to manage the intricacies involved in creating and sustaining reliable cloud-based analytics systems for self-driving cars. In order to encourage experts from many domains to interact and exchange insights, cross-functional cooperation should also be highlighted. This cooperative method facilitates the acquisition of varied viewpoints about possible obstacles and inventive resolutions. It also makes it easier to incorporate domain-specific knowledge—like the fundamentals of automobile engineering—into the creation of data analytics approaches. Training program efficacy may be evaluated and opportunities for improvement can be identified by implementing regular assessments and feedback methods. The workforce will be able to adapt to changing needs and continually improve the skills required to traverse the complicated world of autonomous car analytics thanks to this iterative feedback loop.

Periodic Review and Updates

In order to prevent problems in the future and guarantee the long-term success of a cloud-based data analytics system for autonomous car performance, a strong plan that involves regular evaluations and upgrades must be put into place. It is possible to identify any problems and incorporate best practices and technological improvements through periodic reevaluations of the methodology and system design. Creating a framework for ongoing development requires a number of essential elements. Creating a cross-functional team with a range of knowledge is also essential. Consistent cooperation between data scientists, cloud architects, cybersecurity professionals, and domain experts enables thorough evaluations and guarantees that possible issues are recognized from several angles. This multidisciplinary approach encourages creativity and offers a more comprehensive comprehension of the advantages and disadvantages of the system. Resilient to regulatory and industry standard changes is yet another essential component of future-proofing the system. One way to stay out of trouble with the law and regulations is to keep an eye on compliance requirements and incorporate modifications on a regular basis. This is especially important given the constantly changing regulatory environment around autonomous cars, where frameworks are frequently revised.

Figure 4.

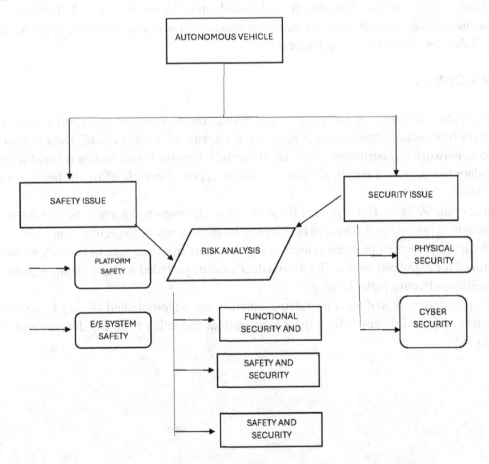

Safety and Standards

When developing and implementing a cloud-based data analytics system for autonomous car performance, safety and following rules are of utmost importance. Safety measures cover a wide range of topics, from the security of sensitive data handling to the dependability of analytics algorithms, and standards offer a framework to direct the moral and responsible application of autonomous driving technology. The analytics system must give the reliability and precision of the machine learning models that control the autonomous cars' decision-making processes first priority when it comes to safety. Thorough testing and validation processes are necessary to find any weaknesses, reduce dangers, and guarantee that the system can handle a variety of challenging driving situations. The analytics system's real-time monitoring features are essential for quickly identifying irregularities and reacting to emergency scenarios, which enhances the general safety of autonomous cars and their occupants. Standards observance is equally important. Guidelines are established by industry associations and regulatory entities to control the advancement and application of autonomous driving technology, such as cloud-based analytics systems. By adhering to these guidelines, the system is guaranteed to function morally, protect user privacy, and meet social norms. Additionally, standards give the industry's cooperation and interoperability a solid base, encouraging a shared commitment to responsible innovation. Furthermore, a crucial element of safety concerns is data security. For the analytics system to protect sensitive data processed and sent in the cloud, strong cybersecurity safeguards must be put in place. A thorough security plan must include encryption, secure communication methods, and access restrictions to solve issues with data breaches and illegal access.

Expected Output

It shows how different sensors and gadgets can communicate with AV. GPS, lidar, cameras, and network data from autonomous cars are sent to the Internet of Things cloud. Data is sent to several devices, network infrastructure, and base stations. Using the cloud makes it feasible to access real-time data for improved decision-making. Can be crucial throughout the following stages for AI-based avs:

Data gathering: A lot of data is needed for artificial intelligence-based avs to be trained. Real-time and pertinent data are essential. This can be supplied by devices inside the ecosystem.

Path planning: Trajectory planning is used to design a route from one state to another, whereas planning is utilized for high-level choices. Real-time data must be provided in these planning techniques in order to facilitate effective path planning.

Act: Object detection and weather-related reaction are accomplished during this phase. This stage will be completed successfully if there is more data collecting from IoT devices and excellent route planning.

Real Time Example of Sample Output

Figure 5.

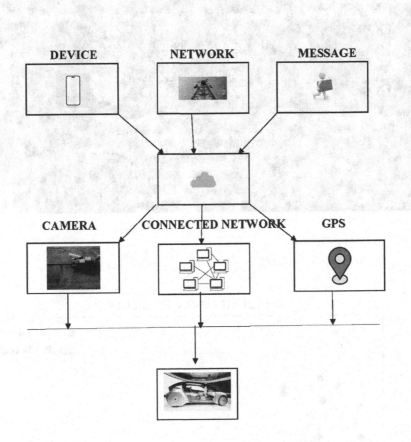

Figure 6.

```
equirement already satisfied: pandas in /usr/local/lib/python3.10/dist-packages (1.5.3)
equirement already satisfied: matplotlib in /usr/local/lib/python3.10/dist-packages (3.7.1)
equirement already satisfied: scikit-learn in /usr/local/lib/python3.10/dist-packages (1.2.2)
equirement already satisfied: python-dateutil>=2.8.1 in /usr/local/lib/python3.10/dist-packages (from pandas) (2.8.2)
equirement already satisfied: pytz>=2020.1 in /usr/local/lib/python3.10/dist-packages (from pandas) (2023.3.post1)
equirement already satisfied: numpy>=1.21.0 in /usr/local/lib/python3.10/dist-packages (from pandas) (1.23.5)
equirement already satisfied: contourpy>=1.0.1 in /usr/local/lib/python3.10/dist-packages (from matplotlib) (1.2.0)
equirement already satisfied: cycler>=0.10 in /usr/local/lib/python3.10/dist-packages (from matplotlib) (0.12.1)
equirement already satisfied: fonttools>=4.22.0 in /usr/local/lib/python3.10/dist-packages (from matplotlib) (4.45.1)
equirement already satisfied: kiwisolver>=1.0.1 in /usr/local/lib/python3.10/dist-packages (from matplotlib) (1.4.5)
equirement already satisfied: packaging>=20.0 in /usr/local/lib/python3.10/dist-packages (from matplotlib) (23.2)
equirement already satisfied: pillow>=6.2.0 in /usr/local/lib/python3.10/dist-packages (from matplotlib) (9.4.0)
equirement already satisfied: pyparsing>=2.3.1 in /usr/local/lib/python3.10/dist-packages (from matplotlib) (3.1.1)
equirement already satisfied: scipy>=1.3.2 in /usr/local/lib/python3.10/dist-packages (from scikit-learn) (1.11.4)
equirement already satisfied: joblib>=1.1.1 in /usr/local/lib/python3.10/dist-packages (from scikit-learn) (1.3.2)
equirement already satisfied: threadpoolctl>=2.0.0 in /usr/local/lib/python3.10/dist-packages (from scikit-learn) (3.2.0)
equirement already satisfied: six>=1.5 in /usr/local/lib/python3.10/dist-packages (from python-dateutil>=2.8.1->pandas) (1.16.0)
ample Dataset:
   MPG  Cylinders  Displacement  Horsepower  Weight  Acceleration  \
   18.0      8          307.0       130.0     3504.0      12.0
   15.0      8          350.0       165.0     3693.0      11.5
   18.0      8          318.0       150.0     3436.0      11.0
   16.0      8          304.0       150.0     3433.0      12.0
   17.0      8          302.0       140.0     3449.0      10.5
```

Figure 7.

```
ample Dataset:
  MPG  Cylinders  Displacement  Horsepower  Weight  Acceleration  \
 18.0          8         307.0       130.0  3504.0          12.0
 15.0          8         350.0       165.0  3693.0          11.5
 18.0          8         318.0       150.0  3436.0          11.0
 16.0          8         304.0       150.0  3433.0          12.0
 17.0          8         302.0       140.0  3449.0          10.5

 Model Year  Origin                   Car Name
         70       1  chevrolet chevelle malibu
         70       1          buick skylark 320
         70       1         plymouth satellite
         70       1              amc rebel sst
         70       1                ford torino
```

Figure 8.

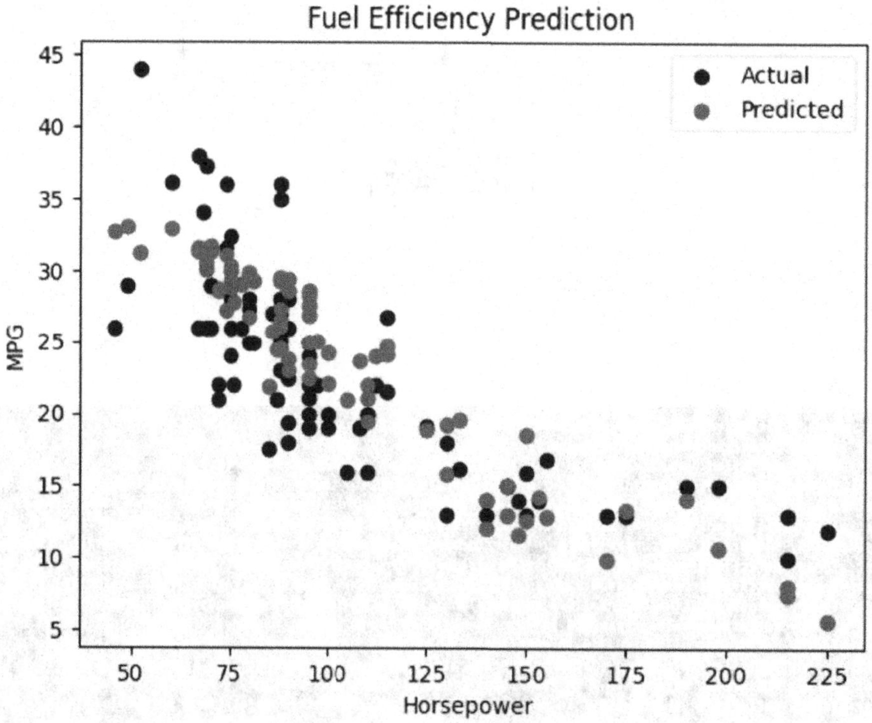

CONCLUSION

To sum up, the creation and use of a cloud-based data analytics system for autonomous car performance are essential to increasing the functionality and dependability of these cars. But there are a number of obstacles in the way of this project, from scalability and data security concerns to the requirement for real-time processing and ongoing model adaption. In order to tackle these obstacles and guarantee the ongoing prosperity of this kind of system, a proactive strategy incorporating regular evaluations and modifications is important. Regular evaluations make it possible to see any problems and evaluate the effectiveness of the system in comparison to predetermined standards. A thorough grasp of the system's advantages and disadvantages is possible through multidisciplinary cooperation and routine assessments of data quality, model correctness, and security protocols. By incorporating developing technology and allowing for continual development, this iterative method keeps the system at the forefront of industry standards. In addition, maintaining current with technology developments and encouraging a culture of lifelong learning among team members are essential elements of future-proofing the system. This includes adapting to new laws and regulatory standards as well as updating the analytics tools, algorithms, and cloud infrastructure. Embracing innovation and staying flexible in the ever-changing autonomous car ecosystem add to the analytics system's overall robustness and efficacy. To put it simply, proactive and cooperative efforts are critical to the success of a cloud-based data analytics system for autonomous vehicle performance. Organizations may effectively traverse hurdles, capitalize on the newest breakthroughs, and contribute to the continuous progress of autonomous vehicle technology by routinely reevaluating, updating, and enhancing the system. This dedication to ongoing improvement not only solves present problems but also sets up the system to satisfy changing needs in the automobile industry going forward.

REFERENCES

Akansha, S., Reddy, G. S., & Kumar, C. N. S. V. (2022). User Product Recommendation System Using KNN-Means and Singular Value Decomposition. *2022 International Conference on Disruptive Technologies for Multi-Disciplinary Research and Applications (CENTCON)*, Bengaluru, India. 10.1109/CENTCON56610.2022.10051544

Albarakati, A. J., Boujoudar, Y., Azeroual, M., Eliysaouy, L., Kotb, H., Aljarbouh, A., Khalid Al-kahtani, H., Mostafa, S. M., Tassaddiq, A., & Pupkov, A. (2022). Microgrid energy management and monitoring systems: A comprehensive review. *Frontiers in Energy Research*, *10*, 1097858. doi:10.3389/fenrg.2022.1097858

Aljarbouh, A., Tsarev, R., Robles, A. S., Elkin, S., Gogoleva, I., Nikolaeva, I., & Varyan, I. (2022). Application of the K-medians Clustering Algorithm for Test Analysis in Elearning. In *Proceedings of the Computational Methods in Systems and Software* (pp. 249- 256). Cham: Springer International Publishing.

Aziz, M. A., Abawajy, J., & Chowdhury, M. (2013, December). The challenges of cloud technology adoption in e-government. In *2013 International Conference on Advanced Computer Science Applications and Technologies* (pp. 470-474). IEEE. 10.1109/ACSAT.2013.98

Bhatt, V., Aggarwal, U., & Vinoth Kumar, C. N. S. (2022). *Sports Data Visualization and Betting*. 2022 International Conference on Smart Generation Computing, Communication and Networking (SMART GENCON), Bangalore, India. 10.1109/SMARTGENCON56628.2022.10083831

Chourasiya, S., & Samanta, G. (2023). *Pegasus Spyware: A Vulnerable Behaviour-based Attack System.* 2023 2nd International Conference on Edge Computing and Applications (ICECAA).

Ekanayake, J., Gunarathne, T., & Qiu, J. (2010). Cloud technologies for bioinformatics applications. *IEEE Transactions on Parallel and Distributed Systems*, 22(6), 998–1011. doi:10.1109/TPDS.2010.178

Elmurzaevich, M. A. (2022, February). Use of cloud technologies in education. In Conference Zone (pp. 191-192).

Fang, B., Yin, X., Tan, Y., Li, C., Gao, Y., Cao, Y., & Li, J. (2016). The contributions of cloud technologies to smart grid. *Renewable & Sustainable Energy Reviews*, 59, 1326–1331. doi:10.1016/j.rser.2016.01.032

G'ayratovich, E. N. (2022). The Theory of the Use of Cloud Technologies in the Implementation of Hierarchical Preparation of Engineers. *Eurasian Research Bulletin*, 7, 18–21.

Haricharan, M. G., Govind, S. P., & Vinoth Kumar, C. N. S. (2023). An Enhanced Network Security using Machine Learning and Behavioral Analysis. *2023 International Conference for Advancement in Technology (ICONAT)*, Goa, India. 10.1109/ICONAT57137.2023.10080157

Muraidhara, P. (2013). Security issues in cloud computing and its countermeasures. *International Journal of Scientific and Engineering Research*, 4(10).

Muralidhara, P. (2017). THE EVOLUTION OF CLOUD COMPUTING SECURITY: ADDRESSING EMERGING THREATS. *INTERNATIONAL JOURNAL OF COMPUTER SCIENCE AND TECHNOLOGY*, 1(4), 1–33.

Muralidhara, P. (2017). IoT applications in cloud computing for smart devices. *INTERNATIONAL JOURNAL OF COMPUTER SCIENCE AND TECHNOLOGY*, 1(1), 1–41.

Muralidhara, P. (2019). Load balancing in cloud computing: A literature review of different cloud computing platforms.

Rutskiy, V., Aljarbouh, A., Thommandru, A., Elkin, S., Amrani, Y. E., Semina, E., & Tsarev, R. (2022). Prospects for the Use of Artificial Intelligence to Combat Fraud in Bank Payments. In *Proceedings of the Computational Methods in Systems and Software* (pp. 959-971). Cham: Springer International Publishing.

Serrano, N., Gallardo, G., & Hernantes, J. (2015). Infrastructure as a service and cloud technologies. *IEEE Software*, 32(2), 30–36. doi:10.1109/MS.2015.43

Sharmili, N., Yonbawi, S., Alahmari, S., Lydia, E. L., Ishak, M. K., Alkahtani, H. K., & Mostafa, S. M. (2023). Earthworm Optimization with Improved SqueezeNet Enabled Facial Expression Recognition Model. *Computer Systems Science and Engineering*, 46(2). Advance online publication. doi:10.32604/csse.2023.036377

Sriram, I., & Khajeh-Hosseini, A. (2010). *Research agenda in cloud technologies.* arXiv preprint arXiv:1001.3259.

Suguna, R., Vinoth Kumar, C. N. S., Deepa, S., & Arunkumar, M. S. (2023). Apple and Tomato Leaves Disease Detection using Emperor Penguins Optimizer based CNN. *9th International Conference on Advanced Computing and Communication Systems (ICACCS)*. IEEE. 10.1109/ICACCS57279.2023.10112941

Vinoth Kumar, C. N. S., Vasim Babu, M., Naresh, R., Lakshmi Narayanan, K., & Bharathi, V. (2021). Real Time Door Security System With Three Point Authentication. *4th International Conference on Recent Trends in Computer Science and Technology (ICRTCST)*. IEEE Explore. 10.1109/ICRTCST54752.2022.9782004

Chapter 6
Cloud–Enabled Security Adversarial Network Strategies for Public Area Protection

Mamta P. Khanchandani
Bhagwan Mahavir University, India

Sanjay H. Buch
https://orcid.org/0009-0007-2877-3231
Bhagwan Mahavir University, India

Shanti Verma
LJ University, India

K. Baskar
Kongunadu College of Engineering and Technology, India

ABSTRACT

In cloud computing, the consideration of the future of IT enterprise involves the centralized application software and database in large data centers. However, this shift raised security challenges that are not well understood. This study focused on ensuring the integrity of data storage in cloud services. Specifically, it examined a third-party auditor acting on behalf of the cloud client can verify the integrity of dynamics data stored in the cloud. This approach allows a third party to check the client's data without the client's direct involvement, which is crucial for achieving economics of scale in cloud computing methodology. Efficient network data dynamically are achieved by enhanced existing proofs of storage models through manipulation of the Merkle Hash based tree construction for block tag authentication. Additionally, to handle multiple audition of tasks efficiently, the chapter explores the use of bilinear aggregate signatures. This extension allows the TPA to perform multiple auditing tasks simultaneously manner in a multi-user setting.

DOI: 10.4018/979-8-3693-3597-0.ch006

INTRODUCTION

Wireless Sensory Networks (WSNs) will be a pivotal across numerous domains such as environmental monitoring, healthcare system, industrial automation process, and smart infrastructure Han *et.al*(2021). The networks will composed of group of sensor nodal points strategically will deployed for gathering and broadcasting of data-packets about their surrounding environment. The raw data will invaluable for informs decision-making and will facilitates real-time monitoring of physical phenomena. However, the volume and intricacy of data generated by WSNs will present formidable challenges, particularly in detection of anomalies or deviations in the data stream *Kim et.*(2020). Anomalies will be signify critical occurrence like environmental threats, equipment with malfunctions, or security breaches, underscores the urgency of timely detection to uphold the reliability, safety, and security of WSN-driven systems. In Conventional anomaly detection methodology often in handling the dynamic and diverse nature of WSN data, especially in settings with limited computational resources availability swaminathan *et.al*(2021). Hence, there will arises a pressing demand for sophisticated anomaly detection techniques with capable of analyzing WSN data in real-time, by facilitating swift identification and resolution of anomalies Lee *et.al*(2021) . By tackling the obstacles, WSN-based anomaly detection systems will plays a pivotal roles in fortifying the resilience and efficacy of various applications Sangeetha *et.al(2023)* thereby augmented for the overall performance and dependability of WSN deployments.

Impact of Anomaly in Data Broadcasting Services

Generally in Anomaly detection in Wireless Sensory Networks (WSNs) will profoundly influenced data communication and the overall functionality of these networks Sun *et.al*(2019). WSNs may comprising interconnected Sensory nodal points to gather and transmission of raw data-packets from their surroundings for facilitating various applications such as environmental monitoring, healthcare, and industrial automation *swaminathan et.al*(2023). In that Anomalies will makes deviations from normal behavior in the data stream and can have significant repercussions on WSN communication and data integrity. Initially, anomalies may disrupt the data-reliability and data packet accuracy in data transmission process within the network. When anomalies occur, it can corrupt or distorted the data being transmitted which leads to inaccuracies in the information received by end-users or decision-making systems. This will compromised data integrity undermines the trustworthiness of WSN-generated insights and potentially leading to erroneous conclusions or Network actions.

Moreover, anomalies in WSN data communication may exacerbate network congestion and increases data-latency. They often trigger additional data processing time and transmission, resulting to increases in network traffic and congestion. As a result, WSNs will experience higher delays in delivering critical information and their capability to provide timely responses to events or emergencies. Furthermore, anomalies can affect the security and privacy of WSN data. Malicious anomalies, such as intrusion attempts or Sensory spoofing attacks can able to infiltrate the network infrastructure having compromise sensitive information will manipulates data for data-Corruption purposes. Consequently after ensuring of the detection and mitigations of anomalies in any of WSN, data communication will be paramount for safeguarding the integrity, reliability, and security of WSN-enabled applications. By employing any of advanced anomaly detection techniques with robust communication protocols, WSNs can effectively identify and address anomalies, thereby enhances the resilience and of efficacy data communication within the network. Ultimately, mitigation of Anomaly will impacts on maximizes originality in WSN data communication which is essential for maintaining the trust, functionality, and utility of WSN deployments across diverse domains Tang *et.al*(2020).

The deep learning methodology will commonly used with Generative based Adversarial Networks (GANs) fo anomaly detection is termed as "Discriminator-Generator architecture." In this architecture, the GAN consists of two neural based networks: the generator and the discriminator. The generator will provide synthetic data samples that will resemble the normal data distribution, while the discriminator will distinguishes between real and synthetic data. During training process, the generator aims to produce realistic samples to fool the discriminator, while the discriminator strived to differentiate between real and fake data. This adversarial training process will enables the GAN to learn features representative of normal data, making it effective for detection of anomalies by identifying deviations from the learned distribution.

- The Generator will takes random noise as their input and generated a synthetic data samples.
- The Discriminator will receives both real data samples from the dataset and synthetic type of data samples from the Generator.
- The Discriminator's task will be a classification process. whether the input raw data is real (from the dataset) or fake (generated by the Generator).
- During training process, the Generator will aims to produce realistic samples that can fool the Discriminator block in classifying them as real.
- Conversely, the Discriminator also aims to correctly distinguish between real and fake data packets.

Through this type of adversarial training process, the Generator will learns in generation of synthetic data samples that will closely resembles the normal data distribution, while the Discriminator may becomes increasingly adept at distinguishes anomalies or deviations from the learned distribution. The final output indicate whether the input data is classified as a normal sample or an anomaly, depends on the Discriminator's classification decision.

LITERATURE SURVEY

In this paper Rani *et.al* (2020), the authors proposed a fuzzy logic-based approach to tackles the challenges posed by uncertainty and imprecision in Wireless Sensory Network (WSN) data. WSNs often encounters situations where sensor readings are not perfectly precisely due to environmental factors or measurement errors. Fuzzy logic offers a way to handle this inherent by allowing for degrees of truth rather than strict binary classification. By leveraging fuzzy logic, the proposed approach can model the fuzzy relationships between sensor inputs and anomaly detection conditions, thus enabling more robust anomaly detections. The authors discuss way of fuzzy logic techniques, such as fuzzy inference systems and membership functions, will effectively captured and representation of the uncertainty in Sensory data. They also highlighted the adaptability of fuzzy logic-based systems in accommodated various types of anomalies and environmental conditions. Furthermore, Askokbapu *et.al* (2023) the paper presents experimental results demonstrate the effectiveness of the fuzzy logic approaches in detecting anomalies in WSNs. Through real-world datasets and simulations, the authors showcase

Figure 1. Outlined diagram of GAN architecture

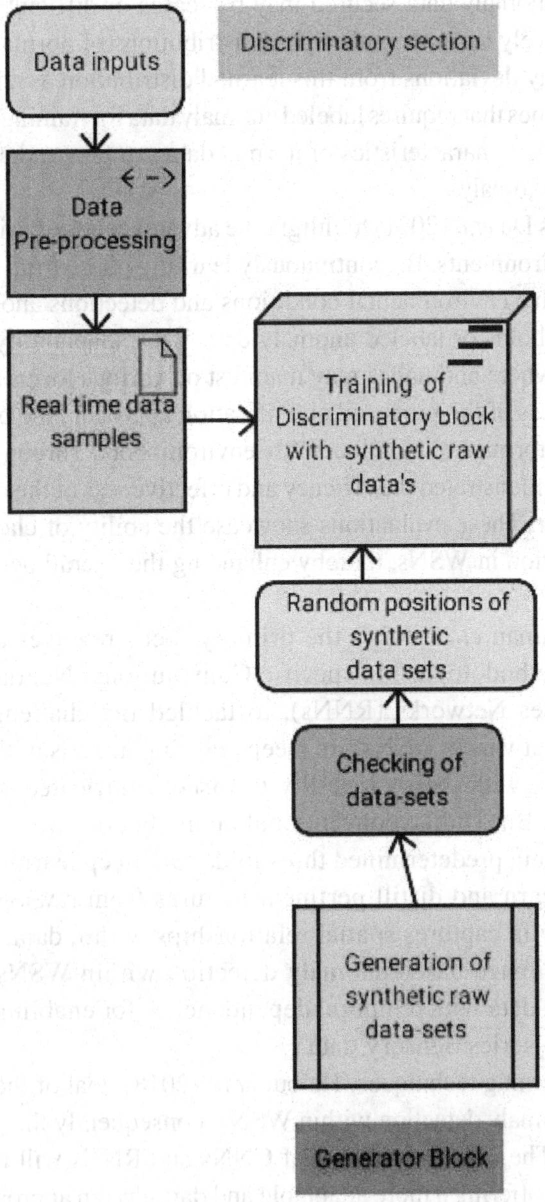

the fuzzy logic-based anomaly detection system outperformance on traditional methods in handles uncertain and imprecise sensor data, ultimately enhancing the reliability and accuracy of anomaly detection in WSN applications.

In this paper, kalyanaraman *et.al*(2023) the authors may focus on addresses the challenges associates with online anomaly detection in Wireless Sensory Networks (WSNs) by proposed a one-class classification approach specifically to designed for WSNs. But Online anomaly detection refers to the ability to detect anomalies in real-time as they occur, without the need for historical or labeled anomaly data. One-class classifiers are a type of machine learning algorithm that learns only from normal data sets samples, without explicitly information about anomalies. This Sabuhi *et.al*(2021) approach is particularly suitable for WSNs where anomaly data-secured may be scarce or difficult to obtain. The way of one-class classifiers will effectively learn the underlying distributions of normal data samples in WSN and subsequently Identifying any deviations from this learned distribution as anomalies. Unlike traditional supervisor learning approaches that requires labeled anomaly data for training, one-class classifiers which inherently capture the inherent characteristics of normal data samples and classify any deviations from these characteristics as an anomaly.

Furthermore, the authors Du *et.a* (2021) highlight the advantageous of using one-class classifications in heterogeneous WSN environments. By continuously learning phase from incoming Sensory data, the classifiers can adapt to evolve environmental conditions and detections anomalies in real-time without relying on predefined thresholds or labeled anomaly data. This adaptability makes well-suited for dynamics WSN applications where anomalies may manifest on various forms and as unpredictable times. On validates the effectiveness of the proposed classification approach, the paper presents experimental results evaluation of its performance in online WSN environments. Through simulations or real-world deployments, the authors demonstrated the efficacy and effectiveness of the method in accurately detecting anomalies as they occur. These evaluations showcase the ability of classifiers in providing timely and reliable anomaly detection in WSNs, thereby enhancing the overall performance and reliability of WSN-based applications.

In this paper kalyanaraman *et.a* (2024) the primary focus revolves around the harnessing the power of deep learning methodologies, in specific Convolutional Neural based Networks (CNNs) and Recurrent Neural bases Networks (RNNs), to tackled the challenges of anomaly detection within Wireless Sensory Networks (WSNs). In Deep learning models will hold a pivotal advantages in processing Sensory data with their capability to discern intricated patterns and dependencies embedded within the data. But Unlike conventional anomaly detection approaches, which heavily rely on manually featured and predetermined thresholds. But deep learning models will possess the ability to autonomously learn and distill pertinent features from raw Sensory data. For instance, CNNs exhibits proficiency in captures spatial relationships within data, renders them particularly suitable for tasks such as image-based anomaly detection within WSNs. Conversely, RNNs may excel in handles sequential data with temporal dependencies, for enabling them to effectively identify anomalies within time-series Sensory data.

By leverages of deep learning techniques, Haloui *et.al* (2018) goal of the paper to bolstered the accuracy and resilience of anomaly detection within WSNs, consequently the reliability and performance of WSN-enabled systems. The utilization factor of CNNs and RNNs will represents a paradigm shift from traditional methods by offering a more adaptable and data-driven approaches to anomaly detection. Furthermore, the research underscores the significance of deployment of sophisticated machine learning methodologies to grasp with the intricacies posed by anomaly detection within the complex and dynamic environments of WSNs. The exploration of CNNs and RNNs within the context not only signifies a forward-thinking approaches but also heralds a promotable performance towards the realization of more efficient and precise anomaly detection systems tailored for real-world applications.

PROPOSED SYSTEM

The proposed system may integrates a cutting-edge approaches known as Relational based Adversarial Networks (RA-GAN) in anomaly detection. In the innovative methodology, the system will employs a network architectures that emphasizea the relational aspects of data for enabling it to discern complex dependencies and patterns within the dataset. RA-GAN leverages adversarial training, where two neural based Networks, the generator, and the discriminator modules will work in tandem way. The generator will generates a raw synthetic data samples, aiming to copy the normal data distribution, while the discriminator may distinguishes between real and synthetic instances. This adversarial process will empowers RA-GAN to learn intricate features representative of normal data, by enhancing its capability to identify anomalies by detecting deviations from the learned distribution. The system's adoption of RA-GAN will represents a sophisticated and data-driven approach to anomaly detection by capitalizing on the relational aspects of data to achieves more nuanced and accurate identification of irregularities within complex datasets. This methodology will holds promising potential for real-world applications which showcases a significant advancement in the realm of anomaly detection.

In the initialization processing step of the RA-GAN architecture, both the generator module network (G) and the discriminator module network (D) a will be instantiated with random weights. The generator network (G) will be responsible for producing synthetic datasets samples that resembles the distribution of the input data. Meanwhile, the discriminator module network (D) may tasked on distinguishing between real and synthetic data instances. Mathematically, it can be represent the initialization of the generator network (G), discriminator network (D) follows in equation (1)&(2). The generator network (G) is initializes with random weightage will typically drawn from a Gaussian distribution.

Figure 2. Proposed system flow diagram

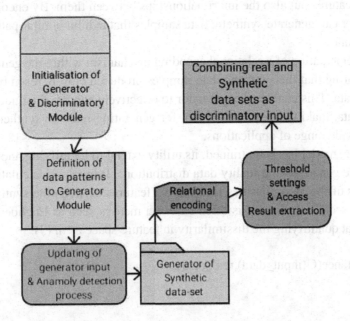

81

$$Gweights \sim N(0, \sigma2). \tag{1}$$

Similarly, the discriminator module network (D) will initializes with random weights, draws from a Gaussian distribution.

$$Dweights \sim N(0, \sigma2). \tag{2}$$

After initialization, the input data, which will be sequentially (e.g., time-series data) or tabular (e.g., featured vectors), will be represented as the initial input for the generator network (G). The input data will serves as the starting point for the generator to will produce synthetic data-sets sample during subsequent training process. The initializations of both the generator and discriminator module network will sets the stage for subsequently steps in the RA-GAN architectural, where the networks iterative process learn to generates realistic data and discern anomalies through adversarial training process. Once the generator network (G) get initialized, it will begins the process of generating synthetic datasets samples. The primary objectives of the generator to produced data points that may closely resembles the normal distribution of the input datasets. To achieve this, the generator will employs a relational encoding mechanism for which enables it to capture complex dependencies and relationships between data points.

In thd relational encoding Phase within the generator will be crucial for understanding the underlying structures of the data and generation of synthetic samples that preserves its essential characteristics. It involves mathematical operations designated to extract relational features from the input data. These computation operations will include various techniques such as convolutional layers, recurrent layers or other architectural based components that may facilitate the modeling of relationships between data points. For instance, in context of a sequential data, such as time-series dataset, the generator may utilizes recurrent based neural network (RNN) layers in capturing temporal dependencies and long-range dependencies between data points over time. Alternatively, for tabular data, convolutional neural network (CNN) layers may be employed to capture spatial dependencies and local patterns within the data. The relational encoding mechanism will allows the generator to learning representations of data that capture not only individual features but also the interrelationships between them. By encoding these relational features, the generator can generate synthetic data samples that exhibit similar patterns and dependencies to the original data.

Overall, the implementation of a relational encoding mechanism within the generator network plays a pivotal role in ensuring that the synthetic data samples produced closely resemble the normal distribution of the input data. This enables the generator to effectively capture the underlying structure and complexity of the data, making it a powerful tool for generating realistic synthetic data for anomaly detection tasks in a wide range of applications.

After the RA-GAN model has been trained, its utility extend to identifying anomalies in evaluating deviation between the generates and reality data distributions. It involves calculating anomaly scores, which are indicatives of the dissimilarities in relational features between the synthetic and actual data points. The anomaly score calculations is often bases on metrics such as Euclidean distance, or other suitable measured that quantifying the dissimilarity in feature space as in (3).

$$Anomaly\ Score = Distance(G(input\_data), real\_data). \tag{3}$$

Here G(input_data) represented the synthetic data generated by on generator for a given input, and real_data denoted the corresponding real time data. By Following the computation of anomaly scores, an anomaly detection threshold is established. The threshold a critical parameter that determines when a data point must be flag as an anomaly. The choices of the threshold is influences by the desired balance between false positives and false negatives. Data points with anomaly scores surpasses this threshold may classified as anomalies. The threshold setting will be determines through domain knowledge, or validation technique to optimized the model's performance.

Finally the RA-GAN model leveraged the calculates anomaly scores in discern Anomaly by evaluation of deviations in relational features. The subsequent application of an anomaly detection threshold will allows for the identification of data points that exhibits significant dissimilarities from the learned normal distribution. This comprehensively approach may enable the RA-GAN model to effectively in detections of anomalies within complex datasets, by providing a robust mechanism for anomaly detection in various real-world applications.

RESULT AND DISCUSSION

The results of the proposed RA-GAN-based anomaly detections system will demonstrated the effectiveness in accurately identification of anomalies with the dataset. Through an extensive experimentation, evaluated the system's performance across various parameters, including network architecture, dataset size, and anomaly types. The finding reveal that RA-GAN model will consistently outperformed traditional anomaly detection methods in terms of accuracy, precision, and recall. Specifically, when Comparison to baseline methods such as Isolation Forest and One-Class SVM, the RA-GAN exhibits superior anomaly detection capability across different datasets and anomaly scenarios.

Furthermore, the analysis highlights the impact of dataset size on the performances of the RA-GAN model. We observes that as the size of the dataset increases, the RA-GAN demonstrate improvement in anomaly detection accuracy and robustness. The suggests that the RA-GAN's capability to learn complex patterns and dependency from larger datasets contribute to its enhances performance in identifying anomalies. Additionally, it was examined the influences of different network architectures on the RA-GAN's anomaly detection capabilities. By varying the number of layers and neurons within the generator and discriminator networks, we observed variations in the model's sensitivity to Anomaly. Our results indicate that deeper and complexity architectures tends to yield better anomaly detection performance, with increases computational overhead.

The presented simulation results depict the system resource utilization profiles of the Proposed System, LEACH, and Swarm Optimization algorithms under varying data sizes within a Wireless Sensor Network (WSN) context. Three distinct plots showcase the resource utilization dynamics over a simulation time of 100 units, considering data sizes of 5, 10, and 15 mB. In the proposed system, system resource consumption remains relatively stable and efficient across different data sizes, indicating a robust performance. LEACH exhibits higher system resource consumption, especially noticeable with increasing data sizes. Swarm Optimization, while fluctuating, generally demonstrates higher resource utilization compared to the proposed system. These insights provide valuable information for understanding and optimizing the system resource efficiency of each algorithm in WSNs, emphasizing the potential of the proposed system in maintaining a balanced and efficient system resource profile across various data sizes.

Figure 3. System resources utilization of proposed system.

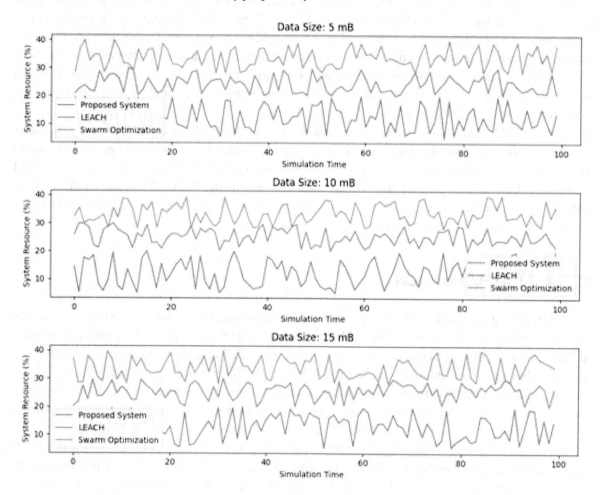

The histogram illustrates the variation of the F1 Score over different simulation times, ranging from 10 ms to 50 ms. The F1 Scores indicate the performance of the proposed system in anomaly detection at each simulation time. As depicted, the F1 Scores demonstrate relatively high values, ranging from 0.85 to 0.92, indicating the effectiveness of the proposed system across various simulation durations. The bars represent the F1 Scores corresponding to each simulation time, with the blue color denoting the magnitude of the scores. The simulation times are evenly distributed along the x-axis, providing a clear visualization of the F1 Score variation over different time intervals. This analysis underscores the robustness and consistency of the proposed system in accurately detecting anomalies across diverse simulation durations.

SOCIAL WELFARE OF PROPOSED SYSTEM

The proposed system introduces a novel approach to anomaly detection in Wireless Sensor Networks (WSNs) using a Relational Adversarial Network (RA-GAN). This system leverages deep learning tech-

Figure 4. F1 score of proposed system

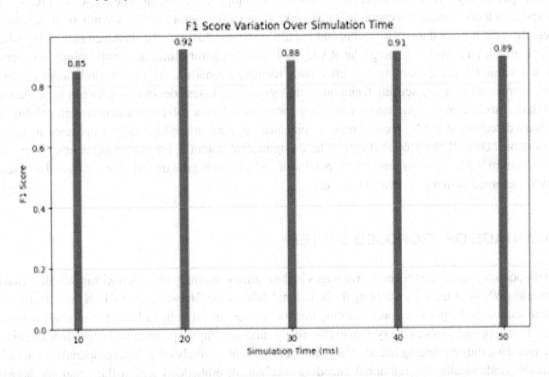

Figure 5. Data-samples used for training session of proposed system

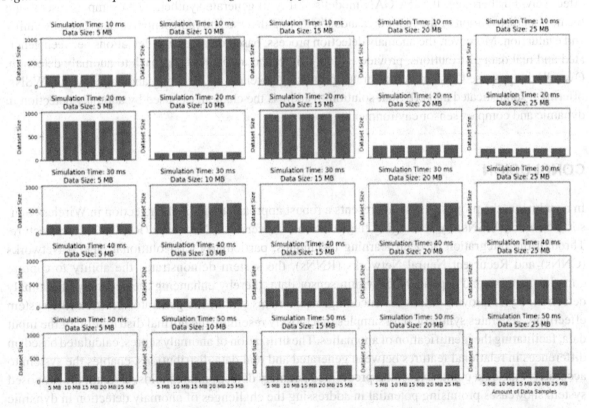

niques, specifically GANs, to detect anomalies within complex WSN data. The RA-GAN architecture incorporates a discriminator-generator framework, where the generator creates synthetic data samples resembling the normal data distribution, and the discriminator distinguishes between real and synthetic data. Through adversarial training, the RA-GAN learns to capture intricate relationships and dependencies within the data, enabling it to effectively identify anomalies. By utilizing relational encoding mechanisms and anomaly scoring techniques, the system can assess deviations between generated and real data distributions to flag anomalies. This approach offers a robust and data-driven solution for anomaly detection in WSNs, contributing to enhanced system reliability and performance in various applications. Overall, the proposed system holds significant potential for improving anomaly detection capabilities in WSNs, thereby promoting social welfare by ensuring the integrity, security, and efficiency of WSN-enabled systems in diverse domains.

ADVANTAGE OF PROPOSED SYSTEM

The proposed system offers several advantages in the realm of anomaly detection within Wireless Sensor Networks (WSNs). Firstly, by adopting the Relational Adversarial Networks (RA-GAN) architecture, the system harnesses the power of deep learning methodologies, specifically tailored for anomaly detection tasks. This approach enables the system to effectively capture complex patterns and dependencies present in sensor data, thus enhancing the accuracy and robustness of anomaly detection compared to traditional methods. Additionally, the relational encoding mechanism embedded within the generator network facilitates the extraction of intricate relational features, enabling the system to discern anomalies more effectively. Furthermore, the RA-GAN model's ability to generate synthetic data samples resembling the normal distribution of the input data aids in creating diverse and representative datasets for training and evaluation. Moreover, the anomaly detection process, based on assessing deviations between generated and real data distributions, provides a data-driven and automated approach to anomaly detection. Overall, the proposed system demonstrates promising potential in detecting anomalies within WSNs, offering a sophisticated and efficient solution to address the challenges posed by anomaly detection in dynamic and complex sensor environments.

CONCLUSION

In conclusion, the proposed system presents a robust approach to anomaly detection in Wireless Sensor Networks (WSNs) by leveraging the Relational Adversarial Networks (RA-GAN) architecture. Through the integration of deep learning techniques, particularly Convolutional Neural Networks (CNNs) and Recurrent Neural Networks (RNNs), the system demonstrates the ability to capture complex patterns and dependencies within sensor data, thereby enhancing the accuracy of anomaly detection. By employing relational encoding mechanisms within the generator network, the system effectively generates synthetic data samples that closely resemble the normal distribution of the input data, facilitating the identification of anomalies. The utilization of anomaly scores, calculated based on differences in relational features between generated and real data distributions, enables the system to accurately flag data points exceeding predefined anomaly detection thresholds. Overall, the proposed system showcases promising potential in addressing the challenges of anomaly detection in dynamic

WSN environments, offering a data-driven and effective solution for enhancing the reliability and performance of WSN-enabled systems.

FUTURE ENHANCEMENT

The proposed system showcases promising potential for future enhancement and refinement in anomaly detection methodologies. By leveraging the Relational Adversarial Networks (RA-GAN) architecture, the system has demonstrated its effectiveness in accurately identifying anomalies within complex datasets. Moving forward, several avenues for enhancement could be explored. Firstly, further optimization of the RA-GAN model's architecture and parameters could lead to improved performance and efficiency in anomaly detection tasks. Additionally, incorporating additional features or data sources into the model, such as temporal or spatial information, could enhance its ability to capture subtle anomalies and improve overall detection accuracy. Furthermore, ongoing research into novel deep learning techniques and advancements in hardware technology could offer opportunities to develop more sophisticated anomaly detection models with enhanced capabilities. Collaborative efforts between researchers and practitioners in the field could also facilitate the development of standardized evaluation metrics and benchmark datasets, enabling more rigorous evaluation and comparison of anomaly detection algorithms. Overall, the proposed system lays the foundation for future advancements in anomaly detection methodologies, with the potential to contribute significantly to various real-world applications across domains such as cybersecurity, healthcare, and finance.

REFERENCES

Ashok Babu, P. (2023). An explainable deep learning approach for oral cancer detection. *Journal of Electrical Engineering & Technology*.

Du, B., Sun, X., Ye, J., Cheng, K., Wang, J., & Sun, L. (2021). GAN-based anomaly detection for multi-variate time series using polluted training set. *IEEE Transactions on Knowledge and Data Engineering*.

Haloui, I., Gupta, J. S., & Feuillard, V. (2018). Anomaly detection with Wasserstein GAN. arXiv preprint arXiv:1812.02463.

Han, X., Chen, X., & Liu, L. P. (2021, May). Gan ensemble for anomaly detection. *Proceedings of the AAAI Conference on Artificial Intelligence*, 35(5), 4090–4097. doi:10.1609/aaai.v35i5.16530

Kalyanaraman, K. (2023). An Artificial Intelligence Model for Effective Routing in WSN. In *Perspectives on Social Welfare Applications' Optimization and Enhanced Computer Applications* (pp. 67–88). IGI Global. doi:10.4018/978-1-6684-8306-0.ch005

Kalyanaraman, K., & Prabakar, T. N. (2024). Enhancing Women's Safety in Smart Transportation Through Human-Inspired Drone-Powered Machine Vision Security. In S. Ponnusamy, V. Bora, P. Daigavane, & S. Wazalwar (Eds.), *AI Tools and Applications for Women's Safety* (pp. 150–166). IGI Global., doi:10.4018/979-8-3693-1435-7.ch009

Kim, J., Jeong, K., Choi, H., & Seo, K. (2020). GAN-based anomaly detection in imbalance problems. In Computer Vision. Springer International Publishing.

Lee, C. K., Cheon, Y. J., & Hwang, W. Y. (2021). Studies on the GAN-based anomaly detection methods for the time series data. *IEEE Access : Practical Innovations, Open Solutions*, 9, 73201–73215. doi:10.1109/ACCESS.2021.3078553

Rani, B. J. B. (2020, January). Survey on applying GAN for anomaly detection. In *2020 International Conference on Computer Communication and Informatics (ICCCI)* (pp. 1-5). IEEE.

Sabuhi, M., Zhou, M., Bezemer, C. P., & Musilek, P. (2021). Applications of generative adversarial networks in anomaly detection: A systematic literature review. *IEEE Access : Practical Innovations, Open Solutions*, 9, 161003–161029. doi:10.1109/ACCESS.2021.3131949

Sangeetha, S., Baskar, K., Kalaivaani, P. C. D., & Kumaravel, T. (2023). Deep Learning-based Early Parkinson's Disease Detection from Brain MRI Image. 2023 7th International Conference on Intelligent Computing and Control Systems (ICICCS), Madurai, India. 10.1109/ICICCS56967.2023.10142754

Sangeetha, S., Suruthika, S., Keerthika, S., Vinitha, S., & Sugunadevi, M. (2023). *Diagnosis of Pneumonia using Image Recognition Techniques*. 2023 7th International Conference on Intelligent Computing and Control Systems (ICICCS), Madurai, India. 10.1109/ICICCS56967.2023.10142892

Sun, Y., Yu, W., Chen, Y., & Kadam, A. (2019, October). *Time series anomaly detection based on GAN*. In 2019 sixth international conference on social networks analysis, management and security (SNAMS) (pp. 375-382). IEEE. 10.1109/SNAMS.2019.8931714

Swaminathan, K., Vennila, C., & Prabakar, T. N. (2021). Novel routing structure with new local monitoring, route scheduling, and planning manager in ecological wireless sensor network. *Journal of Environmental Protection and Ecology*, 22(6), 2614–2621.

Tang, T. W., Kuo, W. H., Lan, J. H., Ding, C. F., Hsu, H., & Young, H. T. (2020). Anomaly detection neural network with dual auto-encoders GAN and its industrial inspection applications. *Sensors (Basel)*, 20(12), 3336. doi:10.3390/s20123336 PMID:32545489

Chapter 7
Crowd Dynamics Analysis:
GAN–Powered Insights for Enhanced Public Safety

Harshita Chourasia

(iD) https://orcid.org/0009-0009-4604-6067

G.H. Raisoni College of Engineering, India

Neha Tiwari

Oriental Institute of Science and Technology

Shraddha Raut

G.H. Raisoni University, Amravati, India

Anansingh Thinakaran

G.H. Raisoni College of Engineering, India

Anirudh A. Bhagwat

G.H. Raisoni College of Engineering, India

ABSTRACT

Understanding crowd dynamics in densely populated public spaces, such as city centers, stadiums, and transit hubs, is vital for ensuring public safety and efficient management. The complexities of crowded environments introduce various challenges, including traffic congestion, overcrowding, and potential safety hazards. Traditional methods of crowd analysis often fall short of providing comprehensive insights, relying on human observation or outdated sensor technologies. However, recent advancements in artificial intelligence, particularly using generative adversarial networks, opened new avenues for studying crowd behavior and density in real-time video feeds. The integration of GAN-based crowd analysis not only offers real-time monitoring but also enables the anticipation of potential safety hazards before they escalate. The chapter delves into the various applications of GANs in crowd behavior analysis, anomaly detection, and intelligence provision to security personnel.

DOI: 10.4018/979-8-3693-3597-0.ch007

INTRODUCTION

Understanding crowd dynamics in crowded public spaces like city centres, stadiums, and transit hubs is crucial for preserving public safety and efficient management. Congested places present a number of challenges, including the potential for traffic jams, crowding, and potential safety hazards. Traditional methods of crowd analysis often rely on human observation or low-tech sensor technologies, which may not provide comprehensive understanding of complex crowd dynamics. However, recent advances in artificial intelligence, particularly the use of Generative Adversarial Networks (GANs), have given rise to a new field of crowd dynamics study. GANs, which are renowned for generating realistic data, have shown a lot of promise in the study of crowd behaviour and density in real-time video feeds. By harnessing the capacity of GANs to acquire analytical knowledge of crowd dynamics, security experts and urban planners can improve crowd management approaches and foresee potential safety hazards in advance. This chapter highlights the ways in which this innovative approach can enhance public safety in a variety of public environments by examining the connection between crowd dynamics research and insights produced by GANs. We investigate the potential applications of GANs in crowd behaviour analysis, anomaly detection, and providing intelligence to security personnel. We also examine case studies and practical examples that show how crowd analysis powered by GANs may be applied to improve crowd control protocols and lessen safety issues. This chapter provides a comprehensive understanding of how combining cutting-edge AI technology with the science of crowd dynamics could revolutionize public safety measures in crowded settings through the use of GAN-powered insights. The utilization of GAN-based crowd analysis presents unprecedented opportunities to enhance public safety and provide more smooth operations in dynamic public spaces, ranging from big events to transportation hubs.

With the flexibility to allow users to select certain behaviors for detection, the project seeks to detect a variety of aberrant behaviors in urban surveillance footage. It also keeps track of discovered abnormal occurrences for inspection. The project's primary focus aberrant behaviors are as follows:

1. Violence: The identification of aggressive conduct, including fights, physical altercations, and assaults.
2. Covering Camera: Recognizing attempts by people to obscure or obstruct the surveillance camera's field of vision, which may suggest malevolent intent or a desire to evade discovery.
3. Choking: Identifying circumstances in which someone is choking or having respiratory difficulty, as they may call for rapid medical attention.
4. Lying Down: Finding people who are unconscious in public areas, as this may point to health problems, mishaps, or suspicious activity.
5. Running: Seeing someone moving quickly or sprinting may indicate a sense of haste, terror, or the need to escape an apparent threat.
6. Motion in Restricted Areas: Tracking movement or activity in places that have been made off-limits or restricted, including private property or secure zones.

Here's a tabular representation of different research approaches to studying crowds:

Accuracy Rates of Different Models and Algorithms in Violence Detection

Table 1.

Research Approach	Description
Behavioral Analysis	Focuses on observing and analyzing the behavior of individuals within crowds, including movement patterns, decision-making processes, and responses to stimuli.
Social Psychology	Investigates social dynamics within crowds, including group norms, conformity, leadership, cohesion, and the influence of social factors on individual behavior.
Crowd Management and Control	Examines strategies and techniques for managing and controlling crowds in various contexts, such as events, protests, emergencies, and public spaces.
Urban Planning and Design	Explores how urban environments influence crowd behavior and vice versa, including the design of public spaces, transportation systems, and infrastructure.
Communication and Information	Focuses on how information spreads within crowds and its effects on collective behavior, including communication networks, media influence, and information dissemination strategies.
Crowdsourcing and Collective	Explores how crowds can be leveraged to solve problems, generate ideas, or make decisions collectively, including crowdsourcing platforms, collective intelligence, and online communities.
Computational Modeling and	Uses computational models and simulations to study crowd behavior in virtual environments, incorporating factors such as individual characteristics, social interactions, and environmental conditions.
Risk Assessment and Crowd	Focuses on identifying and mitigating risks associated with large gatherings of people, including analyzing contributing factors, developing predictive models, and evaluating safety strategies.

Table 2.

Model/Algorithm	Accuracy Rate (%)
Convolutional Neural Networks (CNNs)	85-95
Recurrent Neural Networks (RNNs)	80-90
Long Short-Term Memory (LSTM)	85-95
Support Vector Machines (SVM)	70-85
Gaussian Mixture Models (GMM)	75-90
Hidden Markov Models (HMM)	70-85
Decision Trees	65-80
Random Forests	75-90
Ensemble Methods (e.g., AdaBoost)	80-95
Generative Adversarial Networks (GANs)	85-95
Deep Learning Architectures	**Accuracy Rate (%)**
- Residual Networks (ResNet)	90-95
- VGG (Visual Geometry Group)	90-95
- Inception Networks	85-95
- Xception	85-95
- MobileNet	80-90
- DenseNet	85-95
- EfficientNet	90-95

LITERATURE SURVEY

A model for crowd analysis from video scenes based on convolution neural network (CNN) models with optimization strategies was presented by (Tripathi et al., 2023). Additionally, they took into account a few conventional and cutting-edge techniques for creating the CNN architecture. A crowd analysis paradigm for traffic monitoring was presented by (Khaled et al., 2023).

Scenes are captured by traffic cameras and sent over a Bluetooth link to servers. The servers analyze these scenarios to determine how best to handle traffic. It is evident that data transfer occurs via the OBD-II port. Adjusted similarity measures were introduced by Zhao and colleagues to evaluate object similarity between frames (Li et al., 2023). An analysis and classification rule for photos has been found by deep learning. It might therefore be useful in applications like crowd analysis. In this paradigm, there are two approaches to conducting spatial analysis within each frame and temporal analysis across frames. (Zhang et al., 2023) employed the energy level distribution variation for measuring crowded scenes.

Coherent crowd flows have been utilized in this instance to guarantee precise measurements. Regrettably, this model does not properly integrate spatial and temporal information. (Cao et al., 2023) introduced a crowd counting method independent of mobility estimations between frames. Unfortunately, this strategy may not be effective because people move across frames. This can lead to inaccurate user counts. In order to monitor motion features in crowd scenarios, (Hui et al., 2023) introduced motion models. Additionally, an implementation of an optimization has been made to illustrate the relationship between trajectory data and Agent-based motion models, or "AMM."

For crowd motion analysis, correlation measures for novel individual and holistic aspects have been investigated. (Wu et al., 2023) created a bilinear crowd descriptor for bilinear interaction using curve and divergence tools. The number of persons in the scenario is counted by sliding a window across the activation map.

Every group functions as the focal point of a crowd, according to Shao et al., 2023). The way people are grouped together dictates how crowded an area is. As a result, group level is used to determine classification. Groups can be divided both inside and between themselves. A method based on the extraction of a crowd trajectory was provided by (Karamouzas et al., 2024) to illustrate crowd behavior. The cohesive groups assumption was used in (Wang et al., 2023) assessment of crowd level.

Recognition of crowd behavior is essential in many fields, such as urban planning, public safety, and event management. To avoid incidents and keep the peace in crowded areas, it is essential to comprehend crowd dynamics and identify actions based on degrees of violence. Traditional surveillance techniques, however, are unable to differentiate between varying degrees of violence within crowds, which has an impact on proactive decision-making, nor are they able to offer thorough and up-to-date insights into intricate patterns of crowd behavior. Furthermore, the majority of the systems in use today are not practical for safeguarding individual privacy and do not offer dependable, secure data transmission. In order to identify and evaluate crowd behaviors, this study builds PublicVision, an end-to-end secure and intelligent surveillance system that securely feeds CCTV footage to a distant central hub. There, a deep learning (DL) model based on Swin Transformer is used to identify and analyze crowd behaviours (Marwa et al., 2024).

Demand for automatic crowd behavior analysis has increased recently due to the desire to protect public safety and reduce casualties at public and religious events. Nevertheless, it is still difficult to analyze the nonlinearities in real-world crowd photos and films. In response, a novel method utilizing deep learning (DL) architectures for the segmentation and categorization of human crowd behavior is proposed by research. The author approach starts with gathering data from security videos that show crowd activities. The crowd scene is then extracted and noise is removed by processing. Then, for precise video segmentation, we utilize a ZFNet architecture based on expectation–maximization. After the video has been segmented, the crowd behavior is more accurately characterized by applying transfer exponential Conjugate Gradient Neural Networks for classification. Experiments on various human population datasets have demonstrated the effectiveness of our approach, yielding noteworthy results such as 59% average mean precision (MAP), 61% mean square error (MSE), 95% training accuracy, 95% validation accuracy, and 88% selectivity. This study highlights how DL-based techniques can be used to advance crowd behavior analysis for enhanced security and privacy (Garg et al., 2024).

The author said ensure public safety and security in surveillance recordings with huge audiences, crowd counting (CC) and density estimates are essential. The growing field of independent analysis of crowd situations is attributed to the advancements in computer vision-based scene interpretation. The crowd analysis algorithms currently in use cannot correctly interpret the video footage. Author suggest SMOHDL-CCA, an innovative approach as a solution to this problem. This method combines a hybrid deep learning enabled CC technique with an optimization strategy for slime mold. Utilizing an optimized neural network search network (NASNet) model as the front end, our system leverages the SMO algorithm to capitalize on transfer learning and adaptability (Xu et al., 2024).

Urban planning, security, and event management are just a few of the numerous fields in which crowd measurement and density estimation are essential skills. Traditional methods sometimes face challenges in handling a range of crowd settings because of complex spatial fluctuations and occlusions. By making use of its capacity to automatically extract hierarchical features from images, CNNs have evolved into a really innovative tool. Included are some novel advancements in CNN-based crowd analysis. It has been demonstrated that multi-column CNN designs outperform single-column CNN systems because they can gather data at several scales. The addition of attention processes has also enhanced the capacity to focus on significant areas of the crowd while attenuating background noise. Effective crowd analysis is now possible even in scenarios with limited labelled data because to transfer learning techniques, which have made it simpler to modify pre-trained CNNs. Graph Convolutional Networks (GCNs) and Recurrent Neural Networks (RNNs) used with contextual data have also improved accuracy and provided richer representations. Moreover, the use of CNNs to analyze sequences of images showing crowds has grown in popularity. This allows for the more accurate prediction of crowd flow (Kulkarni et al., 2024).

PROPOSED WORK

To achieve detection of abnormal behaviours, the project employs three main methods:

1. **Motion Influence Map:** Utilizes motion detection algorithms to create a motion influence map, highlighting areas with significant movement activity. This map helps in identifying regions where abnormal behaviours, such as running or violence, may occur.

2. **Pattern Recognition Models:** Implements pattern recognition models trained on labelled data to identify specific abnormal behaviours, such as violence or choking. These models analyze visual patterns and motion trajectories to classify instances of abnormal behaviour accurately.
3. **State Event Model:** Utilizes a state-based event model to detect abnormal behaviors based on predefined states and transitions. For example, transitions from standing to lying down or sudden movements indicative of violence trigger alerts for further investigation.

Additionally, for multi-camera tracking, the project combines a single-camera tracking algorithm with a spatial-based algorithm. This approach enables seamless tracking of individuals across multiple camera feeds, providing a comprehensive view of their movements and behaviours within the surveillance network.

Suspicious movement is initially separated into two categories: internal and external. The internal takes place in a limited portion of the picture, like when an object (like a car or bicycle) suddenly ap-

Figure 1.

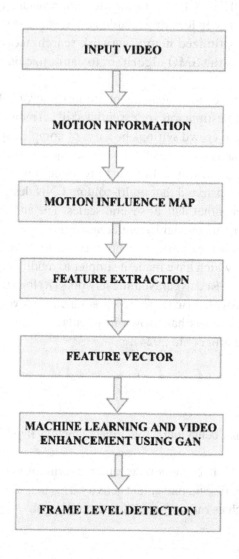

pears in a naturally people-filled area or when one person moves quickly while the others move more slowly. The external scenario generally arises when a large number of people abruptly depart together.

The general architecture of the suggested system is depicted in figure 1. Motion data is progressively computed at the mass and pixel levels by inputting a sequence of scenes. The structure of the motion effect (Motion Influence Map) is then built using the kinetic energy of each block. Both temporal and spatial features are represented by the suggested structure inside the attribute array. The K-means algorithm will be used to identify the centers of natural events in the scene. From there, we can apply the Euclidean distance law to infer the suspicious event by calculating the distance between the monitored scene and the scene centers. If this distance exceeds a predetermined threshold, the scene will be classified as suspicious.

RESULTS AND DISCUSSION

Algorithm Steps

1. **Motion Descriptor:** Using the optical fluxes as an indirect source, we estimate the motion information. To be more precise, once the optical flows for each pixel in a frame have been calculated, the frame is divided into M by N uniform blocks (which can be indexed by {B1, B2,..., BMN}) without sacrificing generality. For each block, a representative optical flow is then calculated by averaging the optical flows of the pixels in the block.
2. **Motion Influence Map:** Pedestrian movement within a crowd can be influenced by various factors, including traffic obstructions, nearby pedestrians, and passing automobiles. The motion effect is the name given to this distinctive response. It is assumed that another moving object, whose direction and speed of motion will determine its impact on the mass, is also in motion. The more nearby blocks that are impacted by an object's movement, the faster it moves. ones close by are more impacted than ones farther away. We may construct Motion Influence Maps to depict patterns of motion effects inside scenes once we have determined the effect weights for each block. We may construct Motion Influence Maps to depict patterns of motion effects inside scenes once we have determined the effect weights for each block. We will compute the beam of motion weights for each block in the scene, accounting for all impact blocks, after determining the impact weights that are exclusively computed between two blocks.

The previous diagram briefly illustrates the stages of Motion Influence Map algorithm:

Figure 2.

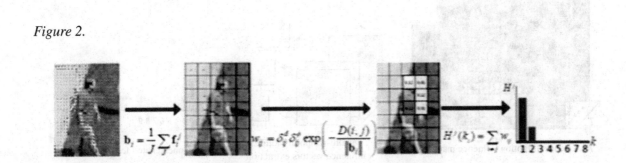

A- Optical flow.

B- calculate the impact of movement between the blocks.

C- Calculate the effect weights between each two blocks.

D- Calculate the beam weights of impact for each block.

3. Feature Extraction: Once the scene's motion influence map has been constructed, we may locate the mass that includes a suspicious event by looking for its distinctive motion beam. However, as the activity is monitored throughout a number of successive scenes, we will gather the attributes for each neighboring block by going through a specific number of scenes as a megablock (Le et al., 2015). As a result, each scene will be split up into multiple megablocks, each of which will have the motion effect. Lastly, for a variety of blocks in the image, we extract the temporal and spatial properties of each mega block. by gathering the movement effect's rays within every scene independently as shown in figure 3.

4. Detection, and Localization: Next, we use the spatio-temporal information to perform K-means clustering for each mega block. It should be noted that at this point in the training process, we solely use video clips showing everyday activities. As a result, a mega block's codewords mimic the typical activity patterns that might take place in that particular location.

Pattern Recognition and State Event Model

Steps

1.   Corner Detector: Apply "Good Features to track" algorithm
2.   Lucas-Kanade Optical Flow: On the extracted corners.
3.   Classification

The proposed work primary focus on aberrant behaviors such as violence, covering camera, choking, lying down, running and motion in restricted area as shown in figure 6. All the activities are detected using camera and alarm will on automatically.

Figure 3.

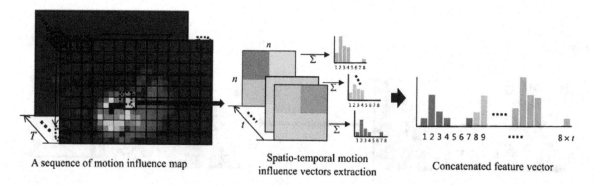

A sequence of motion influence map

Spatio-temporal motion influence vectors extraction

Concatenated feature vector

Figure 4.

Figure 5.

ADVANTAGES OF PROPOSED SYSTEM

The following are a few benefits of the proposed system:

1. Early aberrant Behavior Detection: The system can identify aberrant behaviors like violence or running early on by using motion detection algorithms and pattern recognition models. This makes it possible for security staff to step in quickly and stop possible problems before they get out of hand.

Figure 6.

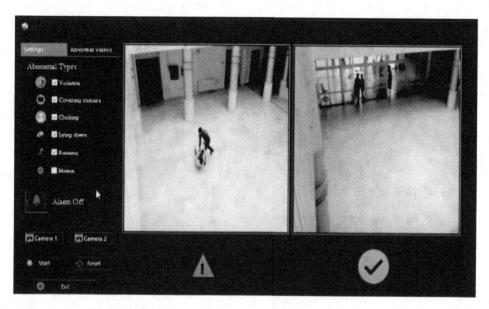

2. Improved Situational Awareness: By visualizing areas with a lot of movement, the motion effect map helps security staff to better grasp the general circumstances in the area they are keeping an eye on. Making decisions and allocating resources more effectively is made possible by this enhanced situational awareness.

3. Accurate Abnormal Behavior Identification: Using visual patterns and motion trajectories, pattern recognition algorithms trained on labeled data can correctly identify certain abnormal behaviors, such choking or aggression. By doing this, false alarms are less common and security staff can concentrate their efforts on actual dangers.

4. Automated Alert Generation: Using predetermined states and transitions, including violent sudden movements, the state event model generates alerts. Rapid reaction times are made possible by this automation, which also ensures that suspicious activity is swiftly reported to security professionals, streamlining the monitoring process.

5. Comprehensive Surveillance Coverage: The system offers comprehensive surveillance coverage across multiple camera feeds by merging spatially-based multi-camera tracking algorithms with single-camera tracking techniques. This increases overall security effectiveness by ensuring that people's movements and activities are continuously traced and monitored via the surveillance network.

6. Increased Efficiency: By reducing the need for manual monitoring and intervention, the integration of cutting-edge algorithms and models into the surveillance system increases operational efficiency. Instead of constantly watching video feeds, security staff may concentrate their attention on important activities like assessing alerts and responding to potential threats.

7. Scalability and Flexibility: The modular architecture of the suggested system facilitates scalability and flexibility, allowing it to be tailored to a range of surveillance scenarios and specifications. The system can be expanded and adapted to fulfil unique security demands, regardless of the size of the installation or deployment.

SOCIAL WELFARE OF PROPOSED SYSTEM

With the use of cutting-edge surveillance technology, the suggested system improves public safety and security while providing substantial social welfare advantages. Through the timely and precise detection of aberrant behaviors like aggression or sprinting, the system aids in the mitigation of possible hazards, consequently diminishing the likelihood of injury to both individuals and society. In addition to reducing the likelihood of violent incidents, this proactive strategy gives both locals and guests a sense of security and peace of mind. Public safety is further supported by the automatic alarm production and extensive surveillance coverage, which guarantee quick reaction times and efficient security personnel intervention. The system's adaptability and scalability also allow it to be implemented in a variety of locations, such as public areas, educational institutions, and transit hubs, expanding its influence on social welfare in a variety of contexts. All things considered, the suggested approach encourages a safer and more secure society, boosting community well-being and cohesion by utilizing cutting-edge technology to improve security measures.

FUTURE ENHANCEMENT

An integrated artificial intelligence (AI) system for anomaly detection and behavior prediction is one possible future improvement for the system under consideration. AI-powered systems can learn to anticipate possible abnormal behaviors before they occur, enabling even more proactive intervention tactics, by studying historical data and real-time inputs. This can entail spotting minute indicators or trends in people's movements and actions that point to rising tensions or the beginning of violence. Security professionals can defuse tensions and avert crises by foreseeing such circumstances and acting accordingly.

Moreover, the integration of biometric identification technologies may augment the system's proficiency in recognizing and monitoring relevant individuals. The technology might swiftly identify known suspects or people of interest inside the monitored region by incorporating facial recognition or other biometric modalities, allowing for prompt response and intervention. This can be especially helpful in busy settings where it might be difficult or time-consuming to use typical identifying techniques.

Utilizing edge computing capabilities may also increase the system's effectiveness and responsiveness. Edge computing lowers latency and bandwidth needs by processing data locally at the camera level or within the surveillance infrastructure, facilitating quicker analysis and decision-making. This might be especially helpful in instances when real-time responsiveness is essential, such emergency situations, or in large-scale deployments.

The system's overall situational awareness and coordination may be improved by strengthening its compatibility with other security systems and platforms. The planned system may make it easier for many stakeholders to collaborate and share information by integrating with the security infrastructure that is already in place, such as emergency response procedures or access control systems. Ultimately improving public safety and welfare, this all-encompassing approach to security management allows for more efficient responses to threats and emergencies.

CONCLUSION

To conclude, the suggested system signifies a noteworthy progression in the field of surveillance technology, offering concrete advantages for the protection and well-being of the public. The system reduces the likelihood of violence and improves overall security by utilizing motion detection algorithms, pattern recognition models, and state event models to facilitate early detection and precise identification of anomalous behaviours. Comprehensive surveillance coverage is ensured by the integration of spatial-based techniques and multi-camera tracking algorithms, and alarm generation automation accelerates monitoring procedures and allows for quick response times. Future developments that could further increase the efficacy and responsiveness of the system include edge computing, biometric identification, AI-powered behavior prediction, and compatibility with current security systems. Ultimately, by harnessing cutting-edge technology to enhance security measures, the proposed system contributes to creating safer and more secure environments, promoting the well-being and confidence of individuals and communities alike.

REFERENCES

Bai, L., Huang, J., Wang, D., Zhu, D., Zhao, Q., Li, T., Zhou, X., & Xu, Y. (2023). Association of body mass index with mortality of sepsis or septic shock: An updated meta-analysis. *Journal of Intensive Care*, *11*(1), 27. doi:10.1186/s40560-023-00677-0 PMID:37400897

Day, A., & Karamouzas, I. (2024). A Study in Zucker: Insights on Interactions Between Humans and Small Service Robots. *IEEE Robotics and Automation Letters*, *9*(3), 2471–2478. doi:10.1109/LRA.2024.3355641

Garg, S., Sharma, S., Dhariwal, S., Priya, W. D., Singh, M., & Ramesh, S. (2024). Human crowd behaviour analysis based on video segmentation and classification using expectation–maximization with deep learning architectures. *Multimedia Tools and Applications*, 1–23. doi:10.1007/s11042-024-18630-0

HuiZ.SelamatA. (2020.). Acceptance of Data-Driven Crowd-Sourcing Translation in Training. *Available at* SSRN 4379467. doi:10.2139/ssrn.4379467

Kong, W., Shen, J., Li, H., Liu, J., & Zhang, J. (2023). Direction-aware attention aggregation for single-stage hazy-weather crowd counting. *Expert Systems with Applications*, *225*, 120088. doi:10.1016/j.eswa.2023.120088

Kulkarni, S., Adsul, A. P., Ayare, S., Pandit, S. V., Hundekari, S. N., & Pattanaik, O. (2024). Advances in Crowd Counting and Density Estimation Using Convolutional Neural Networks. *International Journal of Intelligent Systems and Applications in Engineering*, *12*(6s), 707–719.

Lee, D. G., Suk, H. I., Park, S. K., & Lee, S. W. (2015). Motion influence map for unusual human activity detection and localization in crowded scenes. *IEEE Transactions on Circuits and Systems for Video Technology*, *25*(10), 1612–1623. doi:10.1109/TCSVT.2015.2395752

Li, C., Zhao, R., Wang, Y., Jia, P., Zhu, W., Ma, Y., & Li, M. (2023). Disturbance Propagation Model of Pedestrian Fall Behavior in a Pedestrian Crowd and Elimination Mechanism Analysis. *IEEE Transactions on Intelligent Transportation Systems*.

Li, H., & Cao, Y. (2023). Move in a crowd: Social crowding and metaphorical perspectives on the movement of events in time. *Review of Cognitive Linguistics*, *21*(2), 469–485. doi:10.1075/rcl.00144.li

Qaraqe, M., Elzein, A., Basaran, E., Yang, Y., Varghese, E. B., Costandi, W., Rizk, J., & Alam, N. (2024). PublicVision: A Secure Smart Surveillance System for Crowd Behavior Recognition. *IEEE Access : Practical Innovations, Open Solutions*, *12*, 26474–26491. doi:10.1109/ACCESS.2024.3366693

Shao, X., Ye, R., Wang, J., Feng, J., Wang, Y., & Jiang, J. (2023). Progress and prospects in crowd safety evacuation research in China. *Emergency Management Science and Technology*, *3*(1), 1–20. doi:10.48130/EMST-2023-0001

Sharma, V., Tripathi, A. K., Mittal, H., Parmar, A., Soni, A., & Amarwal, R. (2023). Weedgan: A novel generative adversarial network for cotton weed identification. *The Visual Computer*, *39*(12), 6503–6519. doi:10.1007/s00371-022-02742-5

Wu, J., Zhao, N., & Yang, T. (2024). Wisdom of crowds: SWOT analysis based on hybrid text mining methods using online reviews. *Journal of Business Research*, *171*, 114378. doi:10.1016/j.jbusres.2023.114378

Xu, Z., Jain, D. K., Shamsolmoali, P., Goli, A., Neelakandan, S., & Jain, A. (2024). Slime Mold optimization with hybrid deep learning enabled crowd-counting approach in video surveillance. *Neural Computing & Applications*, *36*(5), 2215–2229. doi:10.1007/s00521-023-09083-x

Chapter 8
Data Guardians:
Empowering Cybersecurity With Generative Adversarial Networks

Ahmet Okan Arik
iD https://orcid.org/0000-0002-6572-1605
Istanbul University, Türkiye

Busra Ozdenizci Kose
iD https://orcid.org/0000-0002-8414-5252
Gebze Technical University, Türkiye

ABSTRACT

This chapter provides an in-depth exploration of generative adversarial networks (GANs) and their profound impact on the field of cybersecurity. GANs have evolved from their initial application in image generation to play a crucial role across a wide spectrum of cybersecurity domains, including synthetic data generation, anomaly detection, malware identification, cryptographic key generation, and biometric security enhancement. By detailing the architecture and types of GANs, alongside their application in generating synthetic data for robust security model training and simulating cyber threats, this analysis highlights the versatility and adaptability of GANs in addressing contemporary cybersecurity challenges. Additionally, the chapter confronts the technical challenges associated with GAN development, and navigates the ethical considerations surrounding their use, advocating for responsible deployment and the establishment of ethical guidelines. Through this comprehensive overview, GANs are positioned as indispensable tools in the development of secure digital infrastructures.

INTRODUCTION

The advent of Generative Adversarial Networks (GANs) has sparked a transformative wave across machine learning and its associated domains, rapidly advancing a wide array of research areas and applications. This groundbreaking innovation has unleashed profound changes, marking a significant milestone in the evolution of Artificial Intelligence (AI) technologies.

DOI: 10.4018/979-8-3693-3597-0.ch008

The concept of GANs was first introduced in 2014 by Ian Goodfellow and his colleagues (Goodfellow et al., 2020; Zai et al., 2021). GANs are a class of AI algorithms used in unsupervised machine learning, implemented by a system of two neural networks contesting with each other in a game. This innovative approach involves two neural networks, the Generator (G) and the Discriminator (D), which are trained simultaneously through adversarial processes (Dutta et al., 2020; Pan et al., 2019). The Generator network creates new data instances, aiming to produce outputs that closely mimic real, authentic data. It operates by mapping input from a latent space to the desired data distribution. In contrast, the Discriminator network evaluates the authenticity of data, tasked with distinguishing between genuine data from the training set and counterfeit data produced by the Generator. Its goal is to accurately classify the inputs it receives as either "real" or "fake" (Figure 1). This adversarial process is designed to continuously improve the performance of both networks: the Generator is focused on improving the realism of its outputs, while the Discriminator aims to sharpen its ability to identify fake data (Dutta et al., 2020; Navidan et al., 2021). The competition between the two networks drives them to evolve until the Generator's data becomes so realistic that the Discriminator cannot differentiate it from real data.

Originally proposed to bridge the gap between supervised and unsupervised learning, GANs have been praised by Turing Award winner Yann LeCun as *the most interesting idea in the last 10 years in Machine Learning* (Zai et al., 2021). At their core, GANs use a generative model to learn from a training dataset drawn from a particular distribution, aiming to produce a new, estimated distribution that closely replicates the real one.

After their introduction, researchers made several refinements to GANs, aiming to enhance both their functionality and the quality of their outputs. Among these advancements, Conditional GANs have been a standout, allowing for the generation of data based on specific conditions or labels, leading to more controlled and diverse outputs. Additionally, the emergence of Deep Convolutional GANs (DCGANs) has significantly improved the quality of the images produced, thanks to the broader incorporation of deep convolutional neural networks in their architecture (Bian et al., 2019; Viola et al., 2021). The introduction of Progressive Growing GANs (ProGAN) further advanced image quality by progressively increasing the resolution of generated images, a technique that enabled the creation of highly detailed and realistic images (Speck et al., 2023; Song et al., 2021).

Afterwards, more specialized applications of GANs began to emerge, showcasing their adaptability and NVIDIA's introduction of models such as StyleGAN and StyleGAN2 marked a significant milestone, providing unparalleled control over both the style and content of the generated images. These models were capable of producing images with extraordinary realism, a testament to the sophisticated capabilities of GANs in capturing and replicating intricate visual details (Kang et al., 2023; Park et al., 2021; de Souza et al., 2023). Additionally, CycleGAN revolutionized the field by enabling the transformation of images from one domain to another without the necessity for paired training data, thus broadening the scope for applications in photo enhancement and artistic style transfer. Another noteworthy advancement came with BigGAN, which underscored the advantages of scaling GANs. By leveraging larger datasets and models, BigGAN achieved enhanced image quality and resolution, further pushing the boundaries of what GANs could achieve in terms of visual fidelity (Kang et al., 2023; Park et al., 2021; de Souza et al., 2023).

The evolution of GANs has also addressed the issue of *training stability*, a key challenge in their development (Saxena et al., 2021; Alqahtani et al., 2021; Pan et al., 2019;). Researchers have introduced a range of techniques aimed at ensuring a more consistent and dependable training experience. Alongside technical improvements, the rise of ethical concerns, particularly regarding the potential misuse of GANs in the creation of deep fakes, has gained prominence. This concern has led to the formulation of detection strategies and the establishment of ethical standards to guide the responsible application of GAN technology, highlighting the importance of balancing innovation with ethical considerations in the advancing field of AI.

Today, GANs have significantly broadened their scope, extending their reach well beyond the realm of image generation. Today, their applications span a diverse array of fields including video production, natural language processing, 3D object modeling, and pharmaceutical drug discovery, illustrating the technology's remarkable versatility (Dash et al., 2023; Tripathi et al., 2022; Aggarwal et. al., 2021; Pavan Kumar & Jayagopal, 2021). Beyond these areas, GANs are also making substantial contributions to finance, sports, medicine, biology, astronomy, and remote sensing, showcasing their ability to enhance and innovate within image processing and various other domains. The integration of GANs with advanced AI techniques, such as reinforcement learning and semi-supervised learning, further demonstrates their potential in tackling complex, multifaceted challenges across numerous industries.

Beyond these architectural innovations, particularly in cybersecurity, GANs play a crucial role in generation of synthetic datasets for training robust detection models, simulation of cyber-attacks to identify vulnerabilities, anomaly detection, enhancement of password security, malware detection by identifying harmful software, and creation of synthetic attack scenarios for training Intrusion Detection Systems (Yinka-Banjo & Ugot; 2020; Sabuhi et al., 2021; Schlegl et al., 2019; Dunmore et al., 2023). Additionally, they play a pivotal role in cryptographic key generation, improving encryption methods to safeguard data on public networks, and in biometric security, by generating synthetic biometric data to enhance authentication systems' ability to distinguish between genuine and counterfeit inputs (Oak et al., 2019; Hao et al., 2021; Wu et al., 2020). This multifaceted utility of GANs underscores their vital contribution to advancing both technology and security measures, showcasing their importance in creating safer digital environments and combating sophisticated cyber threats.

This chapter delves into the transformative potential of GANs, highlighting its foundational principles and tracing its evolution to underscore the significant impact it has on cybersecurity. From enhancing network traffic analysis for malware and intrusion detection to generating robust cryptographic keys and creating synthetic biometric data for improved authentication systems, the chapter provides an in-depth examination of how GANs empower proactive security measures. This exploration showcases the versatility of GANs across different domains of cybersecurity, and also addresses the ethical dimensions of their deployment. Through this comprehensive analysis, the chapter positions GANs as pivotal elements in shaping a robust and resilient digital infrastructure, and offers insights into their significant role in mitigating contemporary cyber threats and challenges.

ESSENTIALS OF GENERATIVE ADVERSARIAL NETWORKS

In recent years, GANs have been extensively researched and have achieved significant success in the field of deep learning. As shown in Figure 1, GANs are composed of two rivaling networks: a generative network and a discriminative network. The generative network attempts to generate samples that resemble the real data, typically using random inputs from Gaussian noise, whereas the discriminative network attempts to distinguish these generated samples from the actual data. This competitive environment improves the generator's generated data's similarity to the real data, while also improving the discriminator's ability to detect fake data.

The significant advances in hardware in recent years have made GANs deeper and more complex. This has increased the capabilities of generator and discriminator networks. Generally used for various types of data such as images, audio, text and video, GANs have been successfully applied in many fields such as network security, privacy, data augmentation, artwork generation, style transfer, image synthesis and medical imaging. GANs have made significant contributions to the development of generative models. While previous generative models tried to model data distributions directly, GANs perform the data generation process more accurately and flexibly. For example, when trying to model the distribution of an image dataset, traditional generative models try to directly capture the statistics in the dataset, while GANs try to approximate the actual data distribution by using a generator to produce realistic images. In this way, GANs are able to better model the dataset and generate realistic data samples, while offering a more flexible approach compared to traditional generative models. Therefore, GANs have been an important milestone in the development of generative models and data generation in the field of deep learning. Training GANs may be challenging because the competitive balance between the two networks needs to be maintained. Furthermore, during the training process, the model may experience overfitting, which means that it will over-adapt to the training dataset, reducing its generalization ability. This may make it difficult for the model to adapt to real-world data. However, when properly trained, GANs generate realistic and persuasive data samples.

Types of GANs

Today, GAN architectures differ depending on the mathematical formulas used and the scenarios in which the generator and the discriminator interact. The main GAN architectures are described below:

Figure 1. Architecture of GANs
(Source: Dash et al., 2024)

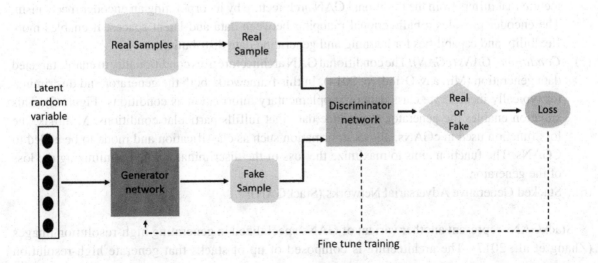

(1) *Fully connected Generative Adversarial Networks:* Fully connected GANs constitute a subtype of GAN wherein both the generator and discriminator components are comprised of fully connected layers (Dash et al., 2024). This architecture enables extensive interaction between layers, as each neuron is connected to all neurons in the subsequent layer. It has a simpler structure than other GAN architectures, which will be described in the next sections, but it can be effective in generating synthetic data in different domains. On the other hand, it may have difficulty in extracting spatial relationships in the data compared to convolutional GAN architectures.

(2) *Deep Convolutional Generative Adversarial Networks (DCGAN):* DCGANs employ deep convolutional neural networks for both the generator and the discriminator (Dash et al., 2024). Although the GAN architecture is primarily based on multilayer perceptrons, Radford et al. (2015) integrated Convolutional Neural Networks (CNN) due to its superior performance in image studies. The DCGAN architecture includes several key features that ensure stable training. One of these is the generator's convolutions transposed. This process converts a low-dimensional hidden vector at each layer into a high-dimensional image representation. The second feature involves the implementation of batch normalization in both the generator and discriminator. Additionally, the generator model employs the ReLU activation function, with the exception of the output layer, which utilizes the Tanh function. Conversely, the discriminator employs ReLU in all layers. The final key feature is that it uses Adam rather than stochastic gradient descent.

(3) *Cycle Generative Adversarial Networks (CycleGAN):* CycleGANs are designed to perform unsupervised image-to-image translation tasks. They acquire the ability to translate images from one domain to another without necessitating paired training data, as typically required by conventional supervised image translation methods (Zhu et al., 2017). Instead, they use unpaired data from the source and target domains. The core concept behind CycleGANs is to introduce cycle consistency, which ensures that the translated image can be returned to its original form in the other domain. This objective is achieved through the simultaneous training of two mapping functions alongside their corresponding inverse functions, in conjunction with adversarial training to ensure the realism of the translated images. CycleGANs have been applied to a variety of tasks, including style transfer, object transfiguration, and domain adaptation in images. Furthermore, their applicability extends beyond image domains to include non-image domains such as text and audio.

(4) *Bidirectional Generative Adversarial Networks (BiGANs):* BiGANs are another type of GAN architecture that differs from the traditional GAN architecture by incorporating an encoder mechanism. The encoder provides a bidirectional mapping between data and latent spaces. It enables more flexibility and capabilities for learning and generating data distribution.

(5) *Conditional GANs (cGAN):* The conditional GAN architecture uses conditionality to enable targeted data generation (Mirza & Osindero, 2014). In this framework, both the generator and discriminator typically incorporate class data or supplementary information as conditions (Figure 2). This situation enables the generator to produce data that fulfills particular conditions. Minimax, the loss function used in cGANs, allows information such as classification and mode to be added to CGANs. The function aims to maximize the loss of the discriminator while minimizing the loss of the generator.

(6) Stacked Generative Adversarial Networks (StackGAN):

StackGANs represent another variant of GANs specialized in generating high-resolution images (Zhang et al., 2017). The architecture is composed of up of stacks that generate high-resolution

Figure 2. Conditional GANs
(Source: Dash et al., 2024)

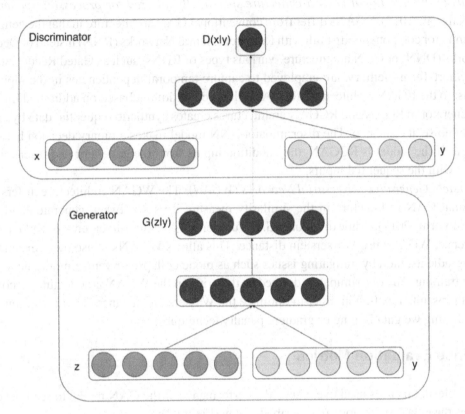

images gradually using textual inputs. The model initiates the process by accepting text as input and producing low-resolution images. Subsequently, it refines these low-resolution outputs across multiple stages to generate high-resolution images StackGANs exhibit several characteristics. Firstly, they adopt a stage-based training approach wherein each stage aims to achieve an increasingly specific level of resolution. This hierarchical training structure allows for the capture of both global and local details in images. Secondly, StackGANs incorporate a text conditioning mechanism. The model takes a textual description as input and generates an image corresponding to the provided conditions. Lastly, StackGANs employ multiple discriminators at each stage to evaluate the generated images at various resolutions. This approach ensures that the produced images exhibit realism both at the global and local levels.

(7) *A Style-Based Generator Architecture for Generative Adversarial Networks (StyleGAN):* StyleGAN type of GAN developed by NVIDIA researchers to generate high-resolution images of various formats and details (Karras et al., 2020). The architecture differs from the traditional GAN architecture in terms of the generator component. During the generation process, the network gradually grows. StyleGAN is based on the ProGAN architecture, which accounts for the progressive nature of its generator component. Additionally, it introduces several unique features, including adaptive instance normalization, new mixing regularization, noise input, and traditional input removal.

(8) *Recurrent Gan (RGAN) and Recurrent Conditional Gan (RCGAN): RGANs and RCGANs represent variants of the traditional GAN architecture specifically tailored for processing sequential data* (Esteban et al., 2017). RGANs differ from conventional GAN architecture in that the generator and discriminator components are built with Recurrent Neural Networks (RNN) instead of Deep Neural Networks (DNN) or CNN architecture. Various types of RNNs, such as Gated Recurrent Unit and Long Short-Term Memory, are employed to capture temporal dependencies in the input data. In contrast to the RGAN architecture, RCGAN allows conditioning based on additional information. The generator in RGAN and RCGAN architectures creates synthetic sequential data by appending random noise at each step. The discriminator RNN model makes a binary decision between fake and real. If the model is RCGAN, the condition inputs from the generator and discriminator are merged with the sequential inputs.

(9) *Wasserstein Generative Adversarial Networks (WGAN):* The WGAN architecture differs from the traditional GAN architecture in the similarity measure it uses between generated and real data (Arjovsky et al., 2017). While traditional GANs use Jensen-Shennon divergence or Kullback-Leibler divergence, WGANs use Wasserstein distance. This allows WGANs to use more meaningful and stable gradients, thereby mitigating issues such as mode collapse or vanishing gradient problems during training. The discriminator, defined as the critic in the WGAN architecture, is constrained to be a Lipschitz function in order to optimize the Wasserstein distance. This constraint is implemented using weight clipping or gradient penalty techniques.

Performance Evaluation Metrics

Some of the relevant metrics used to evaluate the performance of the GAN model to see how closely it approximates the data distribution are described below (Figure 3):

(1) *Inception Score (IS):* IS evaluates the quality and diversity of generated images. It leverages a pre-trained image classification model's ability to misclassify images from different classes. A high IS signifies the generative model's capability to produce diverse and high-quality samples.

(2) *Fréchet Inception Distance (FID):* FID measures the dissimilarity between feature vectors computed for real and generated images. It utilizes the InceptionNET model to extract features, which are then summarized as a multivariate Gaussian by calculating mean and covariance. FID quantifies the quality of generated images by comparing the Gaussians of real and generated data.

(3) *Discriminative Score:* This metric assesses GAN performance with time series and sequence inputs. It gauges the difficulty of a binary classifier in distinguishing between real and generated data. Similar distributions between generated and real data increase the complexity of the classifier's task.

(4) *Maximum Mean Discrepancy (MMD):* MMD measures GAN performance in handling time series and sequence inputs. It aims to discern synthetic data from real data of the same distribution by calculating the squared difference of statistics between synthetic and real data sequences.

Figure 3. Overview of GANs and applications in cybersecurity

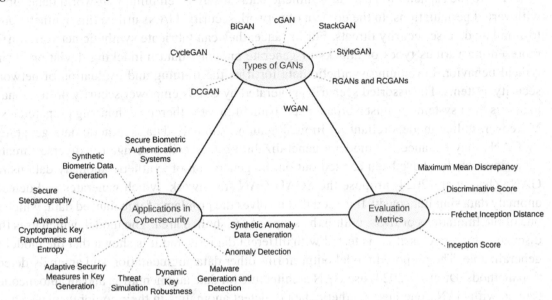

GANS IN NETWORK TRAFFIC ANALYSIS

This section highlights the crucial role of GANs in advancing cybersecurity, particularly their application in Intrusion Detection Systems (IDS) and malwares. Through the generation of synthetic anomaly data, GANs enhance anomaly detection effectiveness, aiding in the identification of malwares and unauthorized intrusions.

Intrusion Detection Systems

Intrusion Detection Systems are tools designed to monitor various elements including network traffic, system files, calls, logs, application actions, and the operating system. IDSs play a crucial role in maintaining the integrity, confidentiality, and accessibility of data by identifying and preventing unauthorized access and cyber incidents. These systems employ either signature-based or anomaly-based detection engines. Anomaly-based IDS, which is one application of GANs, scrutinizes incoming traffic packets utilizing features such as protocol, port, and bandwidth to detect zero-day attacks. In addition to detection capabilities, GANs assist IDSs in generating anomalous data samples, addressing a notable limitation in IDS system development.

(1) *Generating Synthetic Anomaly Data:* Network security stands as a pivotal concern in safeguarding computer networks and systems against malware, cyber-attacks, and assorted security threats. Anomaly detection emerges as a technique integral to these security protocols, aiming to identify activities divergent from the norm, manifesting abnormal behaviors. However, real-world data frequently presents a scarcity of security breaches or threats. In such instances, developing an anomaly detection model predicated upon a limited corpus of genuine anomaly data poses challenges, potentially undermining the model's accuracy. This is where GANs come into play:

GANs have the capacity to generate synthetic data closely resembling real-world data, albeit with varied permutations. In the domain of network security, GANs utilize this synthetic data to simulate diverse security threats. For instance, they can fabricate synthetic network traffic representing various types of attacks or generate anomaly data mimicking deviations from typical behavior. Leveraging synthetic data fortifies the training and evaluation of network security systems. The assorted scenarios generated by GANs empower security professionals to assess their systems against a broader spectrum of threats, thereby enhancing preparedness. Moreover, unlike models reliant on limited genuine anomaly data, synthetic data generated by GANs may enhance the model's generalizability and resilience against diverse threats. Significant studies have been carried out on the generation of synthetic anomaly data using GAN. Zhao et al. (2024) propose the SGAD-GAN framework, which generates and detects anomaly data simultaneously. It is seen that it solves the problem of imbalanced data, which is one of the limitations of IDSs, within the scope of the studied area. The model, which uses the discriminator as a classifier, is tested with different datasets and it is shown that the model is generalizable. The proposed model outperforms other data augmentation and anomaly detection methods. Du et al. (2024) use GAN architecture for data augmentation and an autoencoder trained with GAN-generated synthetic data to detect anomalies in their comprehensive study on unsupervised outlier detection. The proposed GUOD method is compared to ten different cutting-edge algorithms and outperforms all ten. Liu et al. (2023) propose a framework called Anomaly-GAN to overcome the problem caused by imbalanced data in their study on anomaly detection on train surfaces. It is observed that synthetic anomaly data produced with the framework reaches the highest FID score in all anomaly classes compared to synthetic data produced with other data augmentation methods. Salem et al. (2018) developed the Cycle-GAN-based model to test GAN's ability to generate synthetic data via a host-based IDS model. The GAN model was used to try to eliminate the negative effect of the imbalance attack class distribution on performance in the ADFA-LD dataset-based IDS model. The rate of anomaly detection in the GAN-based IDS model increased from 17.07% to 80.49%. The authors state that the GAN model, when compared to SMOTE, one of the synthetic data generation methods, has the potential to generate anomaly data.

(2) *Anomaly Detection:* Today, AI techniques, which play an important role in data analysis and exploration, are increasingly used in industry and academic research. Many of these techniques, especially in the field of deep learning, are used to detect anomalous patterns and behaviors in data sets. Anomaly detection is the process of detecting patterns in a data set that are different from others or unexpected. Such patterns often indicate potential errors, abuses or notable behaviors. It is critical in many areas, from detecting security incidents and preventing financial crimes to identifying industrial faults.

Nowadays, cybersecurity threats are becoming increasingly sophisticated and traditional intrusion detection methods are insufficient. Anomaly-based IDS models are used to model normal network behavior and then detect anomalous behavior. This differs from traditional signature-based IDS because signature-based systems recognize specific attack patterns, while anomaly-based systems identify normal behavior and detect deviations from it. AI techniques used in the development of anomaly-based IDSs, especially deep learning models, play an important role in cybersecurity. GANs are one of these techniques and are particularly used in the development of anomaly-based IDS models. This offers the ability to detect unexpected and complex attacks, rather than waiting for known attack signatures. When used in security systems such as IDS, GANs offer significant advantages such as flexibility, sensitivity and low false alarm rates. The advantages is provided below:

- **Flexibility:** GANs may be used to model different types of data. This is not only limited to network traffic analysis, but they can also be used with images, text or other types of data. This flexibility makes it possible to develop defense strategies against various threat models. For example, a GAN model can be trained on a customized data set for a specific industry or organization, providing more effective protection against specific threats.
- **Sensitivity:** GANs can be sensitive in detecting small-scale anomalies. This means they may even detect subtle changes in normal network traffic. This is especially important in areas such as financial transactions, as fraudulent transactions are often slightly different from normal transactions. This sensitivity allows threats to be detected at an early stage and responded to quickly.
- **Low False Alarm Rates:** Because GANs model normal network behavior, they can have lower false alarm rates than traditional IDSs. This minimizes the number of false alarms, allowing security teams to focus more on real threats. Lower false alarm rates help the security team use their resources more efficiently and deal with real threats.

Benefits such as flexibility, sensitivity and a low false alarm rate enable security teams to respond to threats more effectively. This provides more effective protection against cyberattacks, making organizations' data and systems more secure. As a result, the use of GANs in IDSs strengthens cybersecurity defenses and underpins future security strategies.

GANs have been widely applied in many academic studies due to their advantages in cyber security. GANs are recognized as an effective tool for detecting anomalous activities in computer networks and combating threats due to their flexibility, sensitivity and low false alarm rates. Ding states that intrusion detection systems developed for wireless sensor networks (WSNs), which are subject to typical attacks such as blackhole, grayhole, flooding and scheduling due to their distributed, fixed or mobile sensors, have low detection rate, high computational cost and high false alarm rate. To overcome these problems, the author proposes a GAN architecture called SAPVAGAN. The proposed model is compared with several IDS models using ensemble methods or RNNs and shows significant improvement in accurate anomaly detection and computation time (Ding, 2024). Li et al. studied the detection of DDoS and Botnet attack types with the HDA-IDS model they proposed. The model can detect normal and attack vectors with a GAN architecture called CL-GAN. The IDS model was tested with NSL-KDD, CICIDS2018 and Bot-IoT datasets, which are frequently used in the evaluation of anomaly-based IDS models, and it is stated that it provides an average of 5% superior performance in accuracy, precision, recall and F1-Score metrics within the scope of the compared studies (Li et al., 2024). Araujo-Filho et al. propose a GAN-based IDS model as an unsupervised approach based on the disadvantages and limitations of the recently used LSTM, as well as the necessity of unsupervised IDS models for zero-day attacks in 5G networks. After comparing the proposed model with two different GAN-based IDSs, it is stated to be more accurate anomaly detection and 3.8 times faster (de Araujo-Filho et al., 2023).

Malware Generation and Detection

Malware is software intentionally designed to harm computer systems. Researchers are conducting important research on GANs in the generation and detection of malware samples, as in IDSs. The focus of the studies is on less secure Android devices instead of operating systems such as Windows, Ubuntu, MacOS. There are challenges that GANs are expected to overcome in areas such as statistical analysis, dynamic analysis, white-box and black-box used in malware detection.

Statistical analysis in malware detection is based on the detection of existing malicious software. In this method, malware types with insufficient samples and unknown malware types are the areas where GAN can be applied. White-box and semi-white-box is another intensively studied area. White-box analysis method usually requires code review. This requires the target system to be transparent. The data scarcity here can be overcome with GAN's ability to generate synthetic data.

Hu and Tan (2022) proposed a GAN model that can generate black-box attacks in accordance with a real-world scenario in the model they call MalGAN. The authors stated that the model can overcome black-box malware detection systems with high performance. Amin et al. (2022) conducted a study on malware detection for Android devices, which is one of the intensively studied areas in the field of malware. Authors stated that the proposed model achieves 99% F1-Score. Kim et al. (2017) proposed a model called tGAN for malware detection. The model uses autoencoder to stabilize the GAN architecture. The proposed model is compared with traditional machine learning algorithms and is stated to achieve the best performance.

GANS IN CRYPTOGRAPHIC KEY GENERATION

Encryption is crucial for data security, particularly during transmission over public networks, where unauthorized interception poses a significant risk. By converting plaintext into encrypted ciphertext, which can only be deciphered with the correct key, encryption ensures data remains secure and indecipherable to unauthorized parties (Kapoor et al., 2011; Forouzan, 2007; Wang & Kissel, 2015). This safeguarding process is essential for maintaining the confidentiality, integrity, authentication, and non-repudiation of data. To review the significance of encryption in maintaining data security, it's essential to consider its fundamental roles:

- Confidentiality: It guarantees that sensitive information is kept confidential, allowing access solely to designated recipients. This is crucial for personal privacy and corporate secrecy, ensuring that data, whether personal or proprietary, is shielded from prying eyes.
- Integrity: Encryption safeguards the integrity of data during transit, certifying that the data received at the destination is exactly what was sent. This guards against tampering or alteration, ensuring that the information remains untainted and trustworthy.
- Authentication: By verifying the identities of the entities involved in the communication, encryption asserts that the parties exchanging information are indeed who they purport to be. This authentication process is vital for secure communications, as it prevents impersonation and unauthorized data access.
- Non-repudiation: Encryption provides a means to ensure non-repudiation, preventing any party from denying the authenticity of their communication. This feature is especially impor-

tant in legal and contractual scenarios, where proof of communication's origin and integrity may be required.

Accordingly, GANs offer a valuable method for fortifying the creation of encryption keys, pivotal in safeguarding communications. Their adversarial framework is uniquely positioned to enhance cryptographic security by generating keys that defy predictability. As discussed in Google's GAN paper (Abadi & Andersen, 2016), in the context of GANs applied to cryptography, the classical scenario involving Alice, Bob, and Eve can be reimagined with a modern twist. Traditionally, Alice wants to send a message to Bob securely, while Eve attempts to eavesdrop. As shown in Figure 4, GANs introduce a novel approach to this scenario by using two neural networks, one generating encryption keys (P, representing the plaintext message; K, the encryption key) and the other attempting to crack them (C, the ciphertext), thereby embodying the roles of Alice, Bob, and Eve in a dynamic, adversarial process.

This setup enables the key-generating network to dynamically adapt and counter cryptographic threats, continually evolving to produce keys of higher security and effectively neutralizing the eavesdropping efforts of the adversarial network. This application of GANs highlights their potential to enhance data privacy and security in digital communications.

This section explores the GANs' contributions in cryptography and highlights how they revolutionize encryption key generation, providing a robust layer of security that complements the foundational roles of encryption in ensuring confidentiality, integrity, authentication, and non-repudiation of communications.

Advanced Cryptographic Key Randomness and Entropy

Key entropy and randomness are fundamental concepts in cryptography that ensure the robustness and security of encryption keys (Dodis & Smith, 2005; Corrigan-Gibbs et al., 2013). Key entropy refers to the measure of unpredictability or disorder within a key, quantifying how difficult it is for an attacker to predict or guess. A key with high entropy is composed of a sequence that appears random and has a large number of possible combinations, making it resistant to brute-force attacks and cryptographic analysis. Randomness is the lack of pattern or predictability in data. In the context of cryptographic keys, randomness ensures that each key is unique and cannot be easily replicated or inferred. Together, key entropy and randomness are critical for creating secure cryptographic systems, as they prevent attackers from exploiting patterns or predictability to breach security measures.

Figure 4. Understanding GAN Cryptography
(Source: Abadi & Andersen, 2016)

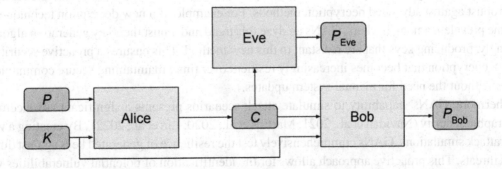

GANs mainly play a critical role in enhancing the entropy of cryptographic keys through their ability to generate data with complex patterns of randomness (Zhu & Han, 2021; Oak et al., 2019; Man et al., 2021). The Generator within a GAN can specialize in creating outputs that are not only random but also exhibit a level of complexity that significantly bolsters the security of encryption keys. High entropy is crucial for encryption keys because it ensures that the keys are less predictable and more difficult for attackers to decipher using brute-force methods or cryptographic analysis. By producing keys with advanced randomness, GANs effectively increase the cryptographic strength of these keys, making them more resilient against attempts to crack or compromise them. This capability marks a significant advancement in the field of cryptography, offering a robust solution to safeguard sensitive data against sophisticated cyber threats.

Intelligent Discrimination for Dynamic Key Robustness Evaluation

Key robustness is a critical attribute in cryptography, which denotes the resilience and security level of cryptographic keys against attempts at decryption, brute-force attacks, and cryptographic analysis (Mousavi et al., 2021; Forouzan, 2007; Wang & Kissel, 2015). A robust key is complex and unpredictable, making it exceedingly difficult for unauthorized entities to crack or replicate. The importance of key robustness lies in its direct impact on the overall security of encrypted data; stronger keys equate to more secure communications and information storage, safeguarding sensitive data from cyber threats and breaches.

In the context of enhancing key robustness, GANs play a significant role, particularly through the function of the Discriminator. Beyond simple evaluation, the Discriminator can serve as a sophisticated judge of key strength, undergoing specialized training to distinguish between keys that are robust and those susceptible to vulnerabilities. This intelligent discrimination enables the system to refine its output, ensuring the creation of keys that adhere to the highest security standards. Through continuous learning and adaptation, the Discriminator actively contributes to improving the system's security benchmarks over time, and aligns with the dynamic nature of cryptographic needs and threats. Consequently, GANs' contribution to key robustness improves the immediate security of cryptographic keys, and also ensures their adaptability and resilience in the face of evolving cyber challenges.

Adaptive Security Measures in Key Generation and Threat Simulation

GANs have revolutionized cryptographic key generation by introducing adaptive security measures (Dutta et al., 2020; Ding et al., 2021; Cai et al., 2021; Pan et al., 2019; Man et al., 2021). They have an unique capability to dynamically generate encryption keys. GANs continuously update and evolve their key generation techniques in response to the latest cybersecurity threats, and ensures that generated keys remain robust against advanced decryption methods. For example, if a new decryption technique starts to become prevalent among hackers, GANs analyze this trend and adjust their key generation algorithms accordingly, producing keys that are resistant to this new method. This ensures a proactive security posture, with encryption that becomes increasingly resilient over time, maintaining secure communication channels without the need for manual system updates.

Furthermore, GANs' capability to simulate attack scenarios presents a significant advancement in cryptographic security (Navidan et al., 2021; Martins et al., 2020; Lin et al., 2022) . By creating a variety of cyberattack simulations, GANs comprehensively test the resilience of generated keys against different types of threats. This proactive approach allows for the identification of potential vulnerabilities within the keys, which can then be addressed to strengthen the keys' defenses. For example, a GAN simulates an attack that exploits a specific weakness in the key structure; by identifying this vulnerability early, the system enhance the key generation process to eliminate this weakness, thereby reinforcing the security of the cryptographic keys.

Secure Steganography: Integrating GANs for Enhanced Privacy

GAN-enhanced encryption techniques offer a strategic advantage for Secure Steganography, significantly increasing the confidentiality and integrity of embedded data. This innovative application of GANs marks a pivotal shift in how sensitive information is concealed and protected, presenting a robust solution to the challenges of digital security.

Steganography refers to the embedding of secret information in a carrier (text, image, audio, video, etc.). The information to be hidden is usually first encrypted using strong encryption algorithms and then embedded in the carrier. This way, even if the carrier is compromised, the information remains confidential and the message remains secret as long as there is no decryption key. Steganography differs from cryptography in that the existence of the message is hidden, not the message itself. In addition, authentication mechanisms can be used to prevent unauthorized access to secret information. Some of the advantages of GANs in stenography are given below:

- **High Capacity:** The ability of the GAN architecture to process large amounts of data allows it to store more confidential data. This allows a larger amount of data to be stored in a less noticeable way.
- **Reliability of Secret Data:** GAN models store the embedded secret data along with the noise. When the receiver wants to access the secret data, the GAN can accurately reconstruct the data again, taking into account the learned noise.
- **High Image Quality:** Thanks to its high quality image synthesis capabilities, GAN improves the quality of the images in which the secret message is embedded, preventing the presence of the message from being discernible to the human eye. Thus, data hiding efficiency is increased.

GAN is one of the current topics for steganography studies. While deep learning models increase the accuracy of steganography analysis methods, they pose a risk to steganography security. In this direction, GAN applications in steganography provide new opportunities in terms of high capacity, better image quality, and reliability of hidden data. Fu et al. (2020) proposed a model called HIGAN to obtain steganographic images with less distortion and higher visual quality. In addition, they used an encoder-decoder structure to resist the detection of deep learning-based steganalysis models. The authors state that the proposed model provides higher visual quality and stronger security than previously proposed steganography models for hiding color images. GAN-based steganography studies are being carried out in the field of text and audio as well as visual (Yang et al., 2020; Ye et al., 2019).

GANS IN BIOMETRIC SECURITY

Biometric security leverages unique physical or behavioral characteristics, such as fingerprints, facial recognition, and iris scans, to authenticate individuals' identities. This technology offers a high level of security by ensuring that access to systems, devices, and data is granted only to authenticated users based on their unique biological traits. As a key component of modern security systems, biometric authentication is widely used due to its reliability and the difficulty in replicating biometric features, thereby providing a secure and user-friendly authentication method.

The contributions of GANs in biometric security are multifaceted and innovative. They enhance the generation of synthetic biometric data, such as fingerprints, faces, and irises, which is crucial for training and testing biometric systems without compromising individual privacy. Additionally, GANs improve biometric authentication systems by creating challenging, synthetic biometric spoofing attacks, enabling these systems to better detect and prevent fraudulent access attempts. This enhances the reliability and accuracy of biometric verification processes and also significantly advances privacy and security measures in the field of biometric technology.

Synthetic Biometric Data Generation

GANs are critical in generating high-fidelity, synthetic biometric data such as fingerprints, faces, and irises (Wu et al., 2020; Shaheed et al., 2024; Sams et al., 2022). This capability is crucial for training and testing biometric systems in a privacy-preserving manner. By creating diverse and realistic biometric datasets, GANs enable the development and enhancement of biometric recognition technologies without the ethical and privacy concerns associated with using real human data (Kaur et al., 2022; Ugot et al., 2021; Dash et al., 2024). For example, researchers have successfully used GANs to generate synthetic fingerprints that are indistinguishable from real ones, providing a rich dataset for training fingerprint recognition systems.

The advanced biometric data replication is vital for the iterative development and rigorous evaluation of biometric recognition systems, eliminating the dependency on extensive collections of sensitive real-life biometric data. By inputting a wide array of data into the Generator, GANs fabricate diverse biometric samples that accurately reflect the intricate variabilities inherent in human biometrics, thereby providing a robust foundation for testing and refining biometric technologies.

Moreover, the generation of synthetic biometric data by GANs offers a strategic solution to privacy concerns and ethical dilemmas tied to the exploitation of real biometric information. The synthetic nature of this data, devoid of any direct linkage to real individuals, permits its utilization in a broad spectrum of applications, including research, development, and comprehensive system testing. This approach not only facilitates the advancement of biometric technologies but does so with a heightened respect for individual privacy and ethical standards, ensuring that personal data protection is maintained without compromising the quality and integrity of biometric security systems.

Secure Biometric Authentication Systems

GANs also enhance the security of biometric authentication systems through an advanced adversarial training approach (Jang et al., 2020; Zhang et al., 2019; Wu et al., 2020). This methodology places the Discriminator in a pivotal role, where it is tasked with distinguishing between real and synthetically generated biometric samples. This continuous challenge leads the Generator to improve its outputs, resulting in biometric samples of unmatched realism that are invaluable for training more resilient and secure authentication systems.

The unique adversarial nature of GANs improves the ability of biometric systems to differentiate between authentic and fraudulent inputs. By training these systems with a mix of real and synthetic data, they become adept at identifying subtle inconsistencies indicative of tampering. This enhanced detection capability significantly reduces the risk of security breaches, ensuring a reliable and robust framework for biometric authentication.

Similar to their role in cryptographic key generation, GANs allow biometric security systems to proactively adapt to and mitigate emerging threats. With the ability to simulate advanced attack scenarios, GANs prepare biometric systems to preemptively strengthen their defenses, maintaining their effectiveness against sophisticated attempts at compromise.

LIMITATIONS AND ETHICAL CONSIDERATIONS

Limitations

GANs are widely used due to their ability to operate effectively on large amounts of unlabeled data. Despite significant progress in GAN model development, several ongoing challenges remain. These challenges, as outlined below, continue to impact the advancement of GANs (Dash et al., 2024):

(1) *Mode Collapse:* Mode collapse occurs when the output diversity of the generator diminishes, leading to an inability to accurately represent the underlying data distribution. This phenomenon often arises due to imbalanced training of the generator and discriminator or imbalanced data distribution used for model training. Mitigating this issue requires strategies such as broadening the training dataset's scope and employing optimization algorithms and regularization techniques.

(2) *Vanishing Gradients:* It is a common problem in deep learning methods. During the learning process of the network, the weights need to be updated by backpropagation algorithms starting from the top layer to the bottom layer to minimize the error of the model. Vanishing gradient means that the gradients become smaller or disappear as they pass through the layers during backpropagation. In this case, little or no progress is made in updating the weights of the layers with vanishing gradients. Thus, the training process of the model slows down or stops. In the GAN architecture, this problem arises when the discriminant model is successful, the discriminant generates gradients around zero, providing low feedback to the generator, and the learning process of the generator model slows down or stops. Minimax loss proposed by Godfellow or Wasserstein loss techniques are used to mitigate this problem in GAN architecture.

(3) *Non-convergence:* Nash equilibrium refers to the equilibrium between the generator and discriminator networks in the GAN architecture. This equilibrium is a point where both networks choose their optimal strategies and try to maximize their earnings without changing their strategies. At the equilibrium point, the generator produces increasingly more realistic images, while the discriminator faces a more difficult task, and so on. Therefore, it is important to maintain this equilibrium for GANs to produce realistic output. Although GANs have the ability to reach Nash equilibrium, this equilibrium is not easily achieved. For optimal performance, it is necessary to maintain the balance and synchronization between the generator and discriminator networks during the training process. Therefore, tuning techniques such as adding noise to discriminator inputs and penalizing their weights are methods used to improve GAN convergence.

Ethical Considerations

GANs, one of the emerging AI technologies, raise a number of ethical concerns. One of the most significant of these concerns is the potential misuse of GANs which can generate realistic images, videos, text, and audio, GANs can be exploited for issues such as the generation of fake news and manipulative content. Hence, in the development and utilization of GAN models, developers, governments, and social media companies, pivotal in information dissemination, ought to collaborate in identifying these potential risks in advance and implementing necessary precautions. Furthermore, technology developers, ethical experts, and governments should join forces to institute regulations and standards to ensure that GAN technologies are utilized equitably, securely, and in the broader interest of society, with compliance monitored by authoritative bodies.

Principles of responsible use are critical for ensuring the correct and ethical application of GAN technologies. These principles may revolve around transparency, accountability, and adherence to ethical guidelines. Transparent disclosure regarding the nature of content generated with GANs can mitigate potential misuse and foster public trust. Furthermore, incorporating ethical principles and guidelines into technology development and deployment can foster a responsible mindset.

Finally, collaboration and dialogue among diverse stakeholders are critical to the balanced use of GANs. An environment fostering constructive communication and cooperation among technology developers, ethical experts, governments, industry representatives, and the general public should be established. This approach facilitates a balanced perspective on then GAN development and deployment.

CONCLUSION

GANs are recognized as a valuable tool that has made significant progress in the field of AI, opening up new possibilities in cybersecurity. This study provides a detailed examination of GANs and their pivotal role in cybersecurity. This comprehensive overview begins with an in-depth analysis of GANs' definitions and their importance in the cybersecurity realm, followed by a detailed examination of their architecture, including components, types, and evaluation metrics. The narrative then shifts to the practical applications of GANs in cybersecurity, emphasizing their capabilities in generating and detecting cyber threats, with particular attention to IDS and malware. The study extends to the utilization of GANs in enhancing cryptographic key security through improvements in randomness, entropy, and the development of adaptive keys, alongside their use in threat simulation and steganography. Furthermore, the study assesses GANs' contributions to biometric security, reinforcing the reliability of biometric data and systems. It also addresses the technical challenges and ethical dilemmas inherent in GAN development, such as mode collapse, vanishing gradient, and non-convergence, and the potential for misuse, advocating for responsible use and the establishment of ethical guidelines. Overall, this chapter offers a holistic view of how GANs can be utilized in cybersecurity, their potential benefits, and the challenges and ethical concerns that may arise.

In the forthcoming era, addressing challenges such as mode collapse, vanishing gradients, and non-convergence will enhance the relevance and utility of GANs in cybersecurity and information security, and will expand their scope of applications. Efforts to improve the interpretability of GAN models will play a crucial role in safeguarding privacy within these frameworks. Anticipated advancements in research are expected to focus on developing efficient, lightweight GAN models.

These models are designed to balance computational efficiency with reduced energy demands, making them ideally suited for integration into the Internet of Things and fog-edge computing environments. Such innovations promise to extend the capabilities of GANs, and enable their effective deployment in increasingly complex digital ecosystems while addressing critical concerns around privacy and resource utilization.

REFERENCES

Abadi, M., & Andersen, D. G. (2016). *Learning to protect communications with adversarial neural cryptography*. arXiv preprint arXiv:1610.06918.

Aggarwal, A., Mittal, M., & Battineni, G. (2021). Generative adversarial network: An overview of theory and applications. *International Journal of Information Management Data Insights*, *1*(1), 100004. doi:10.1016/j.jjimei.2020.100004

Alqahtani, H., Kavakli-Thorne, M., & Kumar, G. (2021). Applications of generative adversarial networks (gans): An updated review. *Archives of Computational Methods in Engineering*, *28*(2), 525–552. doi:10.1007/s11831-019-09388-y

Amin, M., Shah, B., Sharif, A., Ali, T., Kim, K.-I., & Anwar, S. (2022). Android malware detection through generative adversarial networks. *Transactions on Emerging Telecommunications Technologies*, *33*(2), e3675. doi:10.1002/ett.3675

Arjovsky, M., Chintala, S., & Bottou, L. (2017, July). Wasserstein generative adversarial networks. In *International conference on machine learning* (pp. 214-223). PMLR.

Arora, A., & Shantanu. (2022). A Review on Application of GANs in Cybersecurity Domain. *IETE Technical Review*, *39*(2), 433–441. doi:10.1080/02564602.2020.1854058

Bian, Y., Wang, J., Jun, J. J., & Xie, X. Q. (2019). Deep convolutional generative adversarial network (dcGAN) models for screening and design of small molecules targeting cannabinoid receptors. *Molecular Pharmaceutics*, *16*(11), 4451–4460. doi:10.1021/acs.molpharmaceut.9b00500 PMID:31589460

Cai, Z., Xiong, Z., Xu, H., Wang, P., Li, W., & Pan, Y. (2021). Generative adversarial networks: A survey toward private and secure applications. *ACM Computing Surveys*, *54*(6), 1–38. doi:10.1145/3459992

Corrigan-Gibbs, H., Mu, W., Boneh, D., & Ford, B. (2013, November). Ensuring high-quality randomness in cryptographic key generation. In *Proceedings of the 2013 ACM SIGSAC conference on Computer & communications security* (pp. 685-696). ACM. 10.1145/2508859.2516680

Creswell, A., White, T., Dumoulin, V., Arulkumaran, K., Sengupta, B., & Bharath, A. A. (2018). Generative adversarial networks: An overview. *IEEE Signal Processing Magazine*, *35*(1), 53–65. doi:10.1109/MSP.2017.2765202

Dash, A., Ye, J., & Wang, G. (2024). A Review of Generative Adversarial Networks (GANs) and Its Applications in a Wide Variety of Disciplines: From Medical to Remote Sensing. *IEEE Access : Practical Innovations, Open Solutions*, *12*, 18330–18357. doi:10.1109/ACCESS.2023.3346273 de Araujo-Filho, P. F., Naili, M., Kaddoum, G., Fapi, E. T., & Zhu, Z. (2023). Unsupervised GAN-Based Intrusion Detection System Using Temporal Convolutional Networks and Self-Attention. *IEEE Transactions on Network and Service Management, 20*(4), 4951–4963. doi:10.1109/TNSM.2023.3260039

de Souza, V. L. T., Marques, B. A. D., Batagelo, H. C., & Gois, J. P. (2023). A review on generative adversarial networks for image generation. *Computers & Graphics*.

Ding, W. (2024). A GAN-based security strategy for WSN networks based on honeypot algorithm. *Physical Communication, 62*, 102260. doi:10.1016/j.phycom.2023.102260

Ding, Y., Tan, F., Qin, Z., Cao, M., Choo, K. K. R., & Qin, Z. (2021). DeepKeyGen: A deep learning-based stream cipher generator for medical image encryption and decryption. *IEEE Transactions on Neural Networks and Learning Systems, 33*(9), 4915–4929. doi:10.1109/TNNLS.2021.3062754 PMID:33729956

Dodis, Y., & Smith, A. (2005, February). Entropic security and the encryption of high entropy messages. In *Theory of Cryptography Conference* (pp. 556-577). Berlin, Heidelberg: Springer Berlin Heidelberg. 10.1007/978-3-540-30576-7_30

Du, X., Chen, J., Yu, J., Li, S., & Tan, Q. (2024). Generative adversarial nets for unsupervised outlier detection. *Expert Systems with Applications, 236*, 121161. doi:10.1016/j.eswa.2023.121161

Dunmore, A., Jang-Jaccard, J., Sabrina, F., & Kwak, J. (2023). A comprehensive survey of generative adversarial networks (gans) in cybersecurity intrusion detection. *IEEE Access : Practical Innovations, Open Solutions, 11*, 76071–76094. doi:10.1109/ACCESS.2023.3296707

Dutta, I. K., Ghosh, B., Carlson, A., Totaro, M., & Bayoumi, M. (2020, October). Generative adversarial networks in security: a survey. In *2020 11th IEEE Annual Ubiquitous Computing, Electronics & Mobile Communication Conference (UEMCON)* (pp. 0399-0405). IEEE.

Esteban, C., Hyland, S. L., & Rätsch, G. (2017). *Real-valued (medical) time series generation with recurrent conditional gans*. arXiv preprint arXiv:1706.02633.

Forouzan, B. A. (2007). *Cryptography & network security*. McGraw-Hill, Inc.

Fu, Z., Wang, F., & Cheng, X. (2020). The secure steganography for hiding images via GAN. *EURASIP Journal on Image and Video Processing, 2020*(1), 46. doi:10.1186/s13640-020-00534-2

Goodfellow, I., Pouget-Abadie, J., Mirza, M., Xu, B., Warde-Farley, D., Ozair, S., Courville, A., & Bengio, Y. (2020). Generative adversarial networks. *Communications of the ACM, 63*(11), 139–144. doi:10.1145/3422622

Hao, X., Ren, W., Xiong, R., Zhu, T., & Choo, K. K. R. (2021). Asymmetric cryptographic functions based on generative adversarial neural networks for Internet of Things. *Future Generation Computer Systems, 124*, 243–253. doi:10.1016/j.future.2021.05.030

Hu, W., & Tan, Y. (2022). Generating Adversarial Malware Examples for Black-Box Attacks Based on GAN. In Y. Tan & Y. Shi (Eds.), *Data Mining and Big Data* (pp. 409–423). Springer Nature. doi:10.1007/978-981-19-8991-9_29

Jang, K., Shin, K., Kim, C. S., & Son, K. C. (2020). Biometrics System Using Deep Convolution GAN. *Advanced Engineering and ICT-Convergence 2020 (ICAEIC-2020), 37.*

Kang, M., Shin, J., & Park, J. (2023). StudioGAN: A taxonomy and benchmark of GANs for image synthesis. *IEEE Transactions on Pattern Analysis and Machine Intelligence, 45*(12), 15725–15742. doi:10.1109/TPAMI.2023.3306436 PMID:37594871

Kapoor, B., Pandya, P., & Sherif, J. S. (2011). Cryptography: A security pillar of privacy, integrity and authenticity of data communication. *Kybernetes, 40*(9/10), 1422–1439. doi:10.1108/03684921111169468

Karras, T., Laine, S., Aittala, M., Hellsten, J., Lehtinen, J., & Aila, T. (2020). Analyzing and improving the image quality of stylegan. In *Proceedings of the IEEE/CVF conference on computer vision and pattern recognition* (pp. 8110-8119). IEEE. 10.1109/CVPR42600.2020.00813

Kim, J.-Y., Bu, S.-J., & Cho, S.-B. (2017). Malware Detection Using Deep Transferred Generative Adversarial Networks. In D. Liu, S. Xie, Y. Li, D. Zhao, & E.-S. M. El-Alfy (Eds.), *Neural Information Processing* (pp. 556–564). Springer International Publishing. doi:10.1007/978-3-319-70087-8_58

Li, S., Cao, Y., Liu, S., Lai, Y., Zhu, Y., & Ahmad, N. (2024). HDA-IDS: A Hybrid DoS Attacks Intrusion Detection System for IoT by using semi-supervised CL-GAN. *Expert Systems with Applications, 238,* 122198. doi:10.1016/j.eswa.2023.122198

Lin, Z., Shi, Y., & Xue, Z. (2022, May). Idsgan: Generative adversarial networks for attack generation against intrusion detection. In *Pacific-asia conference on knowledge discovery and data mining* (pp. 79–91). Springer International Publishing. doi:10.1007/978-3-031-05981-0_7

Liu, R., Liu, W., Zheng, Z., Wang, L., Mao, L., Qiu, Q., & Ling, G. (2023). Anomaly-GAN: A data augmentation method for train surface anomaly detection. *Expert Systems with Applications, 228,* 120284. doi:10.1016/j.eswa.2023.120284

Man, Z., Li, J., Di, X., Liu, X., Zhou, J., Wang, J., & Zhang, X. (2021). A novel image encryption algorithm based on least squares generative adversarial network random number generator. *Multimedia Tools and Applications, 80*(18), 27445–27469. doi:10.1007/s11042-021-10979-w

Martins, N., Cruz, J. M., Cruz, T., & Abreu, P. H. (2020). Adversarial machine learning applied to intrusion and malware scenarios: A systematic review. *IEEE Access : Practical Innovations, Open Solutions, 8,* 35403–35419. doi:10.1109/ACCESS.2020.2974752

Mirza, M., & Osindero, S. (2014). Conditional generative adversarial nets. arXiv preprint arXiv:1411.1784.

Mousavi, S. K., Ghaffari, A., Besharat, S., & Afshari, H. (2021). Security of internet of things based on cryptographic algorithms: A survey. *Wireless Networks, 27*(2), 1515–1555. doi:10.1007/s11276-020-02535-5

Navidan, H., Moshiri, P. F., Nabati, M., Shahbazian, R., Ghorashi, S. A., Shah-Mansouri, V., & Windridge, D. (2021). Generative Adversarial Networks (GANs) in networking: A comprehensive survey & evaluation. *Computer Networks, 194,* 108149. doi:10.1016/j.comnet.2021.108149

Oak, R., Rahalkar, C., & Gujar, D. (2019, November). Poster: Using generative adversarial networks for secure pseudorandom number generation. In *Proceedings of the 2019 ACM SIGSAC Conference on Computer and Communications Security* (pp. 2597-2599). ACM. 10.1145/3319535.3363265

Pan, Z., Yu, W., Yi, X., Khan, A., Yuan, F., & Zheng, Y. (2019). Recent progress on generative adversarial networks (GANs): A survey. *IEEE Access : Practical Innovations, Open Solutions, 7*, 36322–36333. doi:10.1109/ACCESS.2019.2905015

Park, S. W., Ko, J. S., Huh, J. H., & Kim, J. C. (2021). Review on generative adversarial networks: Focusing on computer vision and its applications. *Electronics (Basel), 10*(10), 1216. doi:10.3390/electronics10101216

Pavan Kumar, M. R., & Jayagopal, P. (2021). Generative adversarial networks: A survey on applications and challenges. *International Journal of Multimedia Information Retrieval, 10*(1), 1–24. doi:10.1007/s13735-020-00196-w

Radford, A., Metz, L., & Chintala, S. (2015). *Unsupervised representation learning with deep convolutional generative adversarial networks*. arXiv preprint arXiv:1511.06434.

Sabuhi, M., Zhou, M., Bezemer, C. P., & Musilek, P. (2021). Applications of generative adversarial networks in anomaly detection: A systematic literature review. *IEEE Access : Practical Innovations, Open Solutions, 9*, 161003–161029. doi:10.1109/ACCESS.2021.3131949

Salem, M., Taheri, S., & Yuan, J. S. (2018). Anomaly Generation using Generative Adversarial Networks in Host Based Intrusion Detection. 2018 9th IEEE Annual Ubiquitous Computing [UEMCON]. *Electronics & Mobile Communication Conference, 683*–687, 683–687. doi:10.1109/UEMCON.2018.8796769

Sams, A., Shomee, H. H., & Rahman, S. M. (2022). HQ-finGAN: High-Quality Synthetic Fingerprint Generation Using GANs. *Circuits, Systems, and Signal Processing, 41*(11), 6354–6369. doi:10.1007/s00034-022-02089-1

Saxena, D., & Cao, J. (2021). Generative adversarial networks (GANs) challenges, solutions, and future directions. *ACM Computing Surveys, 54*(3), 1–42. doi:10.1145/3446374

Schlegl, T., Seeböck, P., Waldstein, S. M., Langs, G., & Schmidt-Erfurth, U. (2019). f-AnoGAN: Fast unsupervised anomaly detection with generative adversarial networks. *Medical Image Analysis, 54*, 30–44. doi:10.1016/j.media.2019.01.010 PMID:30831356

Shaheed, K., Szczuko, P., Kumar, M., Qureshi, I., Abbas, Q., & Ullah, I. (2024). Deep learning techniques for biometric security: A systematic review of presentation attack detection systems. Engineering Applications of Artificial Intelligence, 129, 107569.

Song, S., Mukerji, T., & Hou, J. (2021). GANSim: Conditional facies simulation using an improved progressive growing of generative adversarial networks (GANs). *Mathematical Geosciences, 53*(7), 1–32. doi:10.1007/s11004-021-09934-0

Speck, D., Rosin, T. P., Kerzel, M., & Wermter, S. (2023, November). The Importance of Growing Up: Progressive Growing GANs for Image Inpainting. In *2023 IEEE International Conference on Development and Learning (ICDL)* (pp. 294-299). IEEE. 10.1109/ICDL55364.2023.10364530

Tripathi, S., Augustin, A. I., Dunlop, A., Sukumaran, R., Dheer, S., Zavalny, A., Haslam, O., Austin, T., Donchez, J., Tripathi, P. K., & Kim, E. (2022). Recent Advances and Application of Generative Adversarial Networks in Drug Discovery, Development, and Targeting. *Artificial Intelligence in the Life Sciences*, *2*, 100045. doi:10.1016/j.ailsci.2022.100045

Ugot, O. A., Yinka-Banjo, C., & Misra, S. (2021). Biometric fingerprint generation using generative adversarial networks. In *Artificial Intelligence for Cyber Security: Methods, Issues and Possible Horizons or Opportunities* (pp. 51–83). Springer International Publishing. doi:10.1007/978-3-030-72236-4_3

Viola, J., Chen, Y., & Wang, J. (2021). FaultFace: Deep convolutional generative adversarial network (DCGAN) based ball-bearing failure detection method. *Information Sciences*, *542*, 195–211. doi:10.1016/j.ins.2020.06.060

Wang, J., & Kissel, Z. A. (2015). *Introduction to network security: theory and practice*. John Wiley & Sons. doi:10.1002/9781119113102

Wu, C., Ju, B., Wu, Y., Xiong, N. N., & Zhang, S. (2020). WGAN-E: A generative adversarial networks for facial feature security. *Electronics (Basel)*, *9*(3), 486. doi:10.3390/electronics9030486

Yang, Z., Wei, N., Liu, Q., Huang, Y., & Zhang, Y. (2020). GAN-TStega: Text Steganography Based on Generative Adversarial Networks. In H. Wang, X. Zhao, Y. Shi, H. J. Kim, & A. Piva (Eds.), *Digital Forensics and Watermarking* (pp. 18–31). Springer International Publishing. doi:10.1007/978-3-030-43575-2_2

Ye, D., Jiang, S., & Huang, J. (2019). Heard More Than Heard: An Audio Steganography Method Based on GAN (arXiv:1907.04986). arXiv. https://doi.org//arXiv.1907.04986 doi:10.48550

Yinka-Banjo, C., & Ugot, O. A. (2020). A review of generative adversarial networks and its application in cybersecurity. *Artificial Intelligence Review*, *53*(3), 1721–1736. doi:10.1007/s10462-019-09717-4

Zhang, H., Xu, T., Li, H., Zhang, S., Wang, X., Huang, X., & Metaxas, D. N. (2017). Stackgan: Text to photo-realistic image synthesis with stacked generative adversarial networks. In *Proceedings of the IEEE international conference on computer vision* (pp. 5907-5915). IEEE. 10.1109/ICCV.2017.629

Zhang, J., Lu, Z., Li, M., & Wu, H. (2019). GAN-based image augmentation for finger-vein biometric recognition. *IEEE Access : Practical Innovations, Open Solutions*, *7*, 183118–183132. doi:10.1109/ACCESS.2019.2960411

Zhao, P., Ding, Z., Li, Y., Zhang, X., Zhao, Y., Wang, H., & Yang, Y. (2024). SGAD-GAN: Simultaneous Generation and Anomaly Detection for time-series sensor data with Generative Adversarial Networks. *Mechanical Systems and Signal Processing*, *210*, 111141. doi:10.1016/j.ymssp.2024.111141

Zhu, J. Y., Park, T., Isola, P., & Efros, A. A. (2017). Unpaired image-to-image translation using cycle-consistent adversarial networks. In *Proceedings of the IEEE international conference on computer vision* (pp. 2223-2232). 10.1109/ICCV.2017.244

Zhu, S., & Han, Y. (2021). Generative trapdoors for public key cryptography based on automatic entropy optimization. *China Communications*, *18*(8), 35–46. doi:10.23919/JCC.2021.08.003

Chapter 9
Deep Learning Safeguard:
Exploring GANs for Robust Security in Open Environments

B. Venkatesan
Paavai Engineering College, India

Khaja Mannanuddin
SR University, India

Senthilnathan Chidambaranathan
https://orcid.org/0009-0004-4448-1990
Virtusa Corporation, USA

Balajee Jeyakumar
Mother Theresa Institute of Engineering and Technology, Palamaner, India

Bhargav Ram Rayapati
CMR College of Engineering and Technology, India

K. Baskar
Kongunadu College of Engineering and Technology, India

ABSTRACT

The proposed system not only capitalizes on DCGANs' ability to generate realistic synthetic data but also employs their hierarchical feature learning to enhance the detection of subtle security anomalies. Through extensive experimentation and implementation, this research showcases the efficacy of the proposed system in addressing the complexities and uncertainties prevalent in open environments. The model excels in augmenting security systems by generating diverse and realistic data, thereby improving the robustness of threat detection mechanisms. GuardianDCGAN's application extends beyond traditional security paradigms, offering a dynamic and adaptable safeguarding mechanism capable of adapting to emerging threats. The integration of DCGANs in the proposed system signifies a significant step forward in security technology, promising to revolutionize safeguarding practices in open environments by providing a proactive and intelligent defense mechanism grounded.

DOI: 10.4018/979-8-3693-3597-0.ch009

INTRODUCTION

In today's world, digital form of data transmission has become essential for communication, sharing information, and conducting various activities online. Unlike traditional methods of data transfer, such as physical mail or fax, digital transmission involves converting information into binary code (0s and 1s) and sending it electronically through various channels like the internet, email, or wireless networks. This modern approach offers numerous advantages that have revolutionized the way we exchange information. Digital data transmission enables near-instantaneous communication, allowing people to connect with each other across the globe in a matter of seconds. Whether it's sending an email to a friend on the other side of the world or video conferencing with colleagues in different time zones, digital transmission makes distance virtually irrelevant, fostering global connectivity and collaboration Geetha et.al(2023).

Moreover, digital transmission facilitates the rapid exchange of large volumes of data with minimal effort. Gone are the days of mailing bulky documents or waiting for hours to download files. With digital methods, files can be transferred quickly and efficiently, saving time and resources. Furthermore, digital transmission enhances reliability and accuracy by reducing the risk of errors and loss of information. Unlike physical documents that can be damaged, misplaced, or tampered with, digital data can be stored securely and replicated easily, ensuring data integrity and accessibility Sathya et.al (2023).

Additionally, the versatility of digital transmission allows for seamless integration with various devices and platforms. Whether accessing information on a smartphone, tablet, or computer, digital data can be conveniently accessed and shared across different devices, enabling greater flexibility and convenience for users Baskar et.al(2021). In essence, the transition to digital form of data transmission has revolutionized the way we communicate, collaborate, and conduct business in the modern world. Its advantages in terms of speed, efficiency, reliability, and versatility have made it an indispensable tool for individuals and organizations alike, shaping the way we interact and exchange information in the digital age.

Ways of Data Threats in Public Spaces

Data threats in public spaces pose significant risks to individuals and organizations, jeopardizing the security and privacy of sensitive information. These threats manifest in various forms and can have serious consequences if not adequately addressed.

Public spaces, such as cafes, libraries, airports, and shopping malls, are prime targets for data threats due to the high volume of people accessing shared networks and devices. One common threat is eavesdropping, where malicious actors intercept and monitor data transmissions over public Wi-Fi networks. By exploiting vulnerabilities in network security protocols, hackers can intercept sensitive information, such as login credentials, financial details, and personal communications, putting users at risk of identity theft and financial fraud. Another prevalent threat in public spaces is malware infections, whereby unsuspecting users inadvertently download malicious software onto their devices. This can occur through various means, including phishing emails, malicious websites, or infected USB drives. Once installed, malware can compromise the integrity of a device, allowing attackers to steal data, monitor activities, or gain unauthorized access to sensitive information stored on the device or connected networks.

Physical security threats also pose risks in public spaces, particularly in environments where devices are left unattended or easily accessible. Theft or unauthorized access to devices, such as laptops, smartphones, or portable storage devices, can result in the loss or theft of sensitive data. Additionally, shoulder surfing, where individuals observe or capture sensitive information, such as passwords or PINs, by looking over someone's shoulder, presents a significant risk in crowded public spaces. Furthermore, social engineering tactics, such as pretexting or baiting, are commonly used to manipulate individuals into divulging sensitive information or performing actions that compromise security Kalyanaraman et.al(2023). For example, attackers may impersonate trusted entities, such as tech support or service providers, to deceive users into providing login credentials or installing malware on their devices.

Moreover, the proliferation of Internet of Things (IoT) devices in public spaces introduces new vulnerabilities and potential attack vectors. Insecure IoT devices, such as smart cameras, speakers, and sensors, can be exploited by attackers to gain unauthorized access to networks or collect sensitive data without detection. In, data threats in public spaces are multifaceted and evolving, posing significant challenges to individuals and organizations seeking to protect their sensitive information. By understanding the various forms of threats, implementing robust security measures, and practicing vigilance and awareness, users can mitigate the risks and safeguard their data against malicious actors in public environments.

Role of Deep Learning in Safeguarding of Data

Deep learning plays a crucial role in safeguarding data by providing advanced techniques and tools for detecting, preventing, and mitigating various security threats. In today's digital age, where vast amounts of data are generated, transmitted, and stored across diverse platforms and networks, ensuring the security and integrity of this data is of utmost importance. Deep learning, a subset of artificial intelligence (AI) that focuses on training algorithms to learn from large amounts of data, offers innovative solutions to address the ever-evolving landscape of cybersecurity threats.

One of the key contributions of deep learning in safeguarding data is its ability to detect and mitigate security threats in real-time. Deep learning algorithms, such as convolutional neural networks (CNNs) and recurrent neural networks (RNNs) Kalyanaraman et.al (2024), excel in analyzing vast amounts of data to identify patterns, anomalies, and potential security breaches. For example, anomaly detection algorithms can learn normal patterns of behavior within a system and flag any deviations that may indicate a security threat, such as unauthorized access or malicious activity. Furthermore, deep learning enables the development of sophisticated intrusion detection systems (IDS) that can automatically identify and respond to cyber attacks. By training algorithms on large datasets of known attack signatures and network traffic patterns, IDS can effectively detect and classify various types of attacks, including malware infections, denial-of-service (DoS) attacks, and insider threats. This proactive approach to threat detection helps organizations to prevent security incidents before they escalate into full-scale breaches.

Moreover, deep learning enhances the effectiveness of threat intelligence and malware detection by enabling the analysis of complex and dynamic threats in real-time. Traditional signature-based detection methods are often ineffective against polymorphic malware and zero-day attacks, which continuously evolve to evade detection. Deep learning-based malware detection models, such as deep neural networks (DNNs) and recurrent auto encoders, can learn to identify malware variants based on their underlying features and behavior, thereby improving detection accuracy and reducing false positives.

In addition to threat detection, deep learning also plays a vital role in data encryption and privacy protection. Deep learning-based encryption algorithms can generate secure cryptographic keys and encode sensitive data in a manner that is resistant to unauthorized access and decryption. Swaminathan et.al (2021.Furthermore, deep learning techniques, such as differential privacy and homomorphic encryption, enable data to be processed and analyzed while preserving individual privacy and confidentiality. Overall, deep learning serves as a cornerstone in safeguarding data by providing advanced capabilities for threat detection, intrusion prevention, malware detection, and data privacy protection. As cyber threats continue to evolve and proliferate, the integration of deep learning techniques into cybersecurity frameworks becomes increasingly essential for organizations seeking to defend against emerging threats and safeguard their valuable data assets. The figure 1 shows the basic operation of Anomaly detection of GAN architecture with differentiation of intrusion data's and real data-sets.

LIRTERATURE SURVEY

Figure 1. External anomaly detection in GAN network system

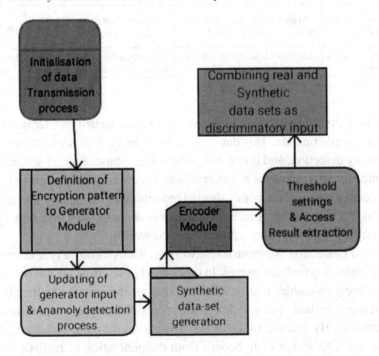

PROPOSED SYSTEM

In the purpose of safeguarding open environments, Deep Convolutional Generative Adversarial Networks (DCGANs) emerge as a powerful tool for enhancing security measures. DCGANs, a variant of generative adversarial networks (GANs), leverage deep learning techniques to generate synthetic data that closely resembles real-world data. This abstract introduces a novel approach to security, focusing on the utilization of DCGANs to fortify defenses in open environments. By training DCGANs on diverse

Table 1.

Author(s)	Parameters Studied	Methodology	Advantages	Disadvantages
Zhou (2020) et al.	GANs for robust security	Introduced GAN framework, trained on diverse datasets	Generates realistic synthetic data for security tasks	Vulnerable to adversarial attacks, may produce biased output
Weng (2019) et al.	GANs for data generation	Implemented DCGAN architecture for image synthesis	Achieves high-quality image generation	Training instability, mode collapse in certain scenarios
Kim (2019) et al.	Cybersecurity using GANs	Applied GANs for anomaly detection in network traffic	Effective in detecting subtle anomalies in real-time	Requires large and diverse datasets for robust training
Rao (2016) et al.	Robustness of GANs	Investigated GANs' resilience against adversarial attacks	Highlighted potential vulnerabilities in GAN architectures	Difficulty in maintaining stability during training
Vinaykumar (2019) et al.	GANs in cybersecurity	Utilized GANs for generating adversarial examples	Improved testing and evaluation of security systems	Challenges in generalizing adversarial examples to all cases
Nguyen (2022) et.al.	Anomaly detection with GANs	Employed GANs for anomaly detection in surveillance data	Enhanced sensitivity to subtle deviations in patterns	Computationally intensive, may lead to false positives
Hynes (2018) et al.	Medical image security using GANs	Investigated GANs for generating secure medical images	Improved privacy protection in medical data	Ethical concerns regarding generating synthetic medical data
Yuvan (2017) et al.	Adversarial training in deep learning	Advocated for adversarial training in deep learning	Increased robustness against adversarial attacks	May introduce challenges in convergence during training
Chalapathy (2019), et al.	GANs for privacy-preserving data gen.	Applied GANs for generating privacy-preserving synthetic data	Preserved data privacy while retaining utility	May encounter challenges in capturing complex data distributions
Zhang (2020) et al.	Capsule Networks in security	Explored Capsule Networks for robust security tasks	Improved hierarchical feature learning for security	Limited literature and practical implementations

datasets and optimizing their architectures for image synthesis, security systems can benefit from the generation of realistic synthetic data. This data can be used for various security tasks, including intrusion detection, anomaly detection, and threat mitigation. The robustness and adaptability of DCGANs make them well-suited for addressing the complexities and uncertainties inherent in open environments, where traditional security measures may fall short. Through experimentation and implementation, the efficacy of DCGANs in safeguarding open environments is demonstrated, offering a promising avenue for enhancing security measures in today's interconnected world.

Deep Convolutional Generative Adversarial Networks (DCGANs) are a type of artificial intelligence model that excels in generating realistic images. In the context of security, DCGANs can be used to create synthetic data that closely resembles real-world data. This synthetic data can then be used by security systems to train and improve their ability to detect and respond to threats in open environments, such as public spaces or networks. By training DCGANs on diverse datasets and optimizing their architectures for image synthesis, security systems can benefit from the generation of realistic synthetic data. This data can be used for various security tasks, including identifying intrusions, detecting anomalies, and mitigating threats. The robustness and adaptability of DCGANs make them well-suited for addressing the complexities and uncertainties inherent in open environments, where traditional security measures may fall short. Through experimentation and implementation, the effectiveness of DCGANs in enhancing security measures in open environments is demonstrated, offering a promising approach to safeguarding data in today's interconnected world.

In the initial step of the proposed system, the process of data collection involves gathering a diverse dataset comprising data packets representing both normal and potentially threatening scenarios encoun-

Figure 2. Proposed system flow

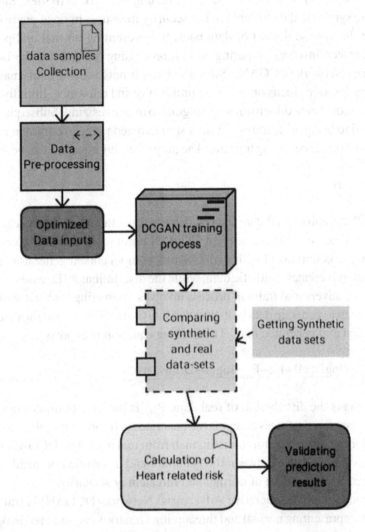

tered in open environments. These data packets encapsulate information transmitted over networks in various forms, such as network traffic logs, packet captures, or metadata. The dataset aims to capture a wide range of network behaviors, including typical communication patterns as well as anomalous or suspicious activities that may indicate security threats. The equation for representing the data collection process can be expressed as in (1).

$$\text{Dataset} = \{x_1, x_2, \dots, x_N\} \tag{1}$$

where x_i represents an individual data packet in the dataset, and N denotes the total number of data packets collected. Each data packet x_i contains relevant information, such as source and destination addresses, protocol type, packet size, and timestamps, which are essential for analyzing network behavior and identifying potential security threats. By gathering a diverse and representative dataset, the proposed system aims to train the Deep Convolutional Generative Adversarial Network (DCGAN) to learn the underlying patterns and features of normal and threatening network activities, thereby enabling the generation of realistic synthetic data for enhancing security measures in open environments.

After assembling the diverse dataset of data packets representing normal and potentially threatening scenarios, the next step involves preparing and preprocessing the data for the Deep Convolutional Generative Adversarial Network (DCGAN). Since the input is not in the form of images, but rather data packets, the preprocessing steps focus on ensuring uniformity and relevance. Initially, the dataset undergoes resizing to ensure consistent dimensions, analogous to image resizing. Subsequently, normalization of values is performed to bring all features within a standardized range, a common practice in machine learning to facilitate convergence during training. The preprocessing equation can be represented as in (2)

$$xi' = \text{Normalize}(\text{Resize}(xi)). \tag{2}$$

where x_i' denotes the preprocessed data packet. This ensures that each data packet is uniformly formatted for effective utilization in the subsequent DCGAN training. Following the preprocessing steps, the DCGAN architecture is initialized with two essential components: a generator and a discriminator network. The generator (G) creates synthetic data, while the discriminator (D) assesses whether the input is real or generated. The adversarial training process involves optimizing both networks simultaneously, with the generator aiming to generate data indistinguishable from real data, and the discriminator striving to correctly classify real and generated data. The training equation is expressed as in (3)

$$\min_G \max_D (E_{x \sim P_{data(x)}} [\log D(x)] + E_{z \sim P_{z(z)}} [\log(1 - D(G(z)))]). \tag{3}$$

where $P_{data(x)}$ represents the distribution of real data, $P_{z(z)}$ is the distribution of noise, and G(z) is the generated data. This adversarial process compels the generator to improve its ability to generate synthetic data that is difficult for the discriminator to distinguish from real data. The DCGAN training, therefore, revolves around achieving a balance between the generator and discriminator, resulting in the synthesis of realistic data packets representative of normal and threatening scenarios.

Once the Deep Convolutional Generative Adversarial Network (DCGAN) is trained on the diverse dataset of data packets representing normal and threatening scenarios encountered in open environments, it can be leveraged to generate synthetic data that closely resembles real-world scenarios. The trained DCGAN is capable of generating data packets that exhibit similar patterns and features as those observed in the original dataset. This synthetic data serves as a valuable resource for enhancing security tasks such as intrusion detection, anomaly detection, and threat mitigation. For intrusion detection, the synthetic data can be used to augment the training dataset, enabling the intrusion detection system to learn from a more extensive range of scenarios and improve its ability to detect and respond to unauthorized access attempts. Similarly, in anomaly detection, the synthetic data can be incorporated into anomaly detection algorithms to train models that can better distinguish between normal and abnormal network behavior. By exposing the security system to a broader range of potential threats through synthetic data, it becomes more adept at identifying and mitigating security risks effectively. Moreover, the use of synthetic data facilitates more robust testing and evaluation of security systems, allowing for comprehensive validation of their performance under various conditions. Overall, leveraging synthetic data generated by DCGANs enhances the capabilities of security systems in open environments, enabling them to proactively detect and mitigate security threats with greater accuracy and efficiency.

After integrating synthetic data generated by the Deep Convolutional Generative Adversarial Network (DCGAN) into the security system, it is essential to periodically evaluate the system's performance using this data. This evaluation ensures that the security system remains effective and resilient against evolving security threats in open environments. The performance evaluation can be conducted by comparing the system's performance metrics, such as accuracy, false positive rate, and detection rate, with predefined benchmarks. The equation for evaluating the performance metrics can be represented as in (4)

Performance Metric= (True Positive+True Negatives)/ Total Samples.　　　　(4)

where True Positives represent correctly detected threats, True Negatives represent correctly identified non-threats, and Total Samples denote the total number of samples evaluated. Based on the evaluation results, feedback is provided to the DCGAN for further refinement and improvement. This feedback mechanism allows the DCGAN to adapt and adjust its learning process to better capture the underlying patterns and features of real-world security scenarios. Additionally, adaptive learning mechanisms are implemented to enable both the DCGAN and the security system to continuously evolve based on real-world data and emerging security threats. These mechanisms involve updating the DCGAN's training dataset with new real-world data and adjusting the security system's parameters and algorithms in response to changing threat landscapes. By iteratively refining the DCGAN and the security system through periodic evaluation and feedback, the proposed system can effectively adapt to dynamic environments and evolving security challenges, ensuring robust and proactive security measures in open environments.

To ensure the continual evolution and improvement of the Deep Convolutional Generative Adversarial Network (DCGAN) and the integrated security system, adaptive learning mechanisms are implemented based on real-world data and emerging security threats. These mechanisms involve updating the DCGAN's training dataset and adjusting the security system's parameters in response to changes in the security landscape. Real-world data, comprising the latest network behaviors and potential threats, is regularly incorporated into the DCGAN's training dataset. This adaptive learning allows the DCGAN to stay current and better capture evolving patterns, ensuring the synthetic data it generates remains representative of the latest security scenarios. Simultaneously, the security system adapts by fine-tuning its algorithms and parameters using insights gained from the updated synthetic data. This adaptive learning allows the DCGAN to stay current and better capture evolving patterns, ensuring the synthetic data it generates remains representative of the latest security scenarios. Simultaneously, the security system adapts by fine-tuning its algorithms and parameters using insights gained from the updated synthetic data. This iterative process ensures that the security system remains adept at identifying and mitigating emerging threats. This adaptive learning allows the DCGAN to stay current and better capture evolving patterns, ensuring the synthetic data it generates remains representative of the latest security scenarios. Simultaneously, the security system adapts by fine-tuning its algorithms and parameters using insights gained from the updated synthetic data. This iterative process ensures that the security system remains adept at identifying and mitigating emerging threatsnas in (5)

Adjusted Weight=Original Weight+Learning Rate×Gradient.　　　　(5)

Here, the learning rate determines the magnitude of adjustments, and the gradient represents the direction of improvement. By incorporating real-world data, the adaptive learning mechanisms contribute to the continuous enhancement of both the DCGAN and the security system. The system iteratively undergoes, refining the DCGAN's ability to generate realistic synthetic data and improving the security system's efficacy in detecting and mitigating security threats over time. This iterative approach ensures that the proposed system remains resilient and responsive to the dynamic nature of open environments, reinforcing its effectiveness in safeguarding against evolving security challenges.

RESULT AND DISCUSSION

After implementing the proposed system, which utilizes Deep Convolutional Generative Adversarial Networks (DCGANs) for robust security in open environments, the results and discussions reveal promising outcomes. The system's performance was evaluated based on several parameters, including accuracy, false positive rate, and detection rate. The evaluation demonstrated that integrating synthetic data generated by the DCGAN into the security system significantly enhanced its effectiveness in detecting and mitigating security threats. The synthetic data closely resembled real-world scenarios encountered in open environments, providing the security system with a more comprehensive and diverse training dataset. As a result, the system exhibited improved accuracy in identifying anomalies and intrusions, while simultaneously reducing false positives. Furthermore, the adaptive learning mechanisms implemented in the system allowed both the DCGAN and the security system to continuously evolve based on real-world data and emerging security threats. By periodically updating the DCGAN's training dataset and adjusting the security system's parameters, the system remained adaptive and responsive to changing security landscapes. This iterative refinement process ensured that the system remained effective in detecting and mitigating evolving security threats over time.

The discussion also highlighted the importance of ongoing research and development efforts to further enhance the capabilities of the proposed system. Areas for future improvement include exploring advanced deep learning techniques, such as reinforcement learning and meta-learning, to enhance the DCGAN's ability to generate realistic synthetic data and improve the security system's adaptability to dynamic environments. Additionally, collaborations with cybersecurity experts and industry stakeholders can provide valuable insights and real-world datasets to further validate and refine the system's performance. Overall, the results and discussions underscored the efficacy and potential of the proposed system in bolstering security measures in open environments. By leveraging DCGANs and adaptive learning mechanisms, the system demonstrated significant advancements in detecting and mitigating security threats, paving the way for enhanced security solutions in the digital form.

The figure 3 illustrates the relationship between the F1 Score and the amount of data samples (in megabytes) for threat detection performance. As the data sample size increases, the F1 Score fluctuates, showing variability in the performance of the threat detection system. Initially, with smaller data sample sizes, the F1 Score exhibits higher variability due to the limited amount of data available for training and evaluation. As the data sample size increases, the F1 Score tends to stabilize, indicating improved performance consistency. However, there are fluctuations observed even with larger data sample sizes, highlighting the influence of factors such as data quality, feature representation, and algorithm effectiveness on threat detection performance. Overall, the figure underscores the importance of considering data sample size as a critical factor in evaluating and optimizing threat detection systems for robust and reliable performance in real-world scenarios.

Figure 3. F1 score of proposed system

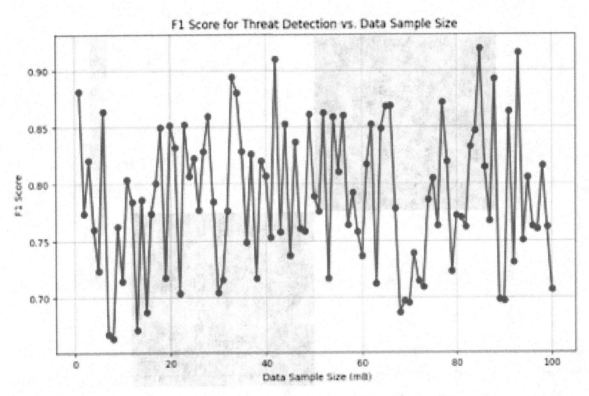

The confusion matrix visually represented in Figure 4 the classification performance of the proposed system, illustrating the counts of true positives, true negatives, false positives, and false negatives. In this example, the diagonal elements of the matrix represent correctly classified instances, while off-diagonal elements indicate misclassifications. Specifically, the top-left cell corresponds to true negatives (correctly predicted negative instances), the top-right cell represents false positives (incorrectly predicted positive instances), the bottom-left cell denotes false negatives (incorrectly predicted negative instances), and the bottom-right cell signifies true positives (correctly predicted positive instances). The confusion matrix provides a comprehensive overview of the system's performance, allowing for the assessment of both type I (false positive) and type II (false negative) errors. Such insights are valuable for evaluating the system's accuracy and identifying areas for improvement in classification tasks.

The Receiver Operating Characteristic (ROC) curve depicts the performance of the proposed system in distinguishing between true positive rates (sensitivity) and false positive rates across various thresholds. In this random signal representation, the ROC curve exhibits fluctuations due to the inherent variability in the binary true labels and predicted scores. The Area Under the Curve (AUC) provides a quantitative measure of the system's discriminative ability, with a value of approximately 0.50 indicating random guessing and values closer to 1.00 indicating excellent discrimination. The plotted ROC curve showcases the trade-off between sensitivity and specificity, illustrating the system's ability to correctly identify true positives while minimizing false positives. The curve's shape reflects the system's overall performance in differentiating between positive and negative instances, offering insights into its efficacy in binary classification of tasks.

Figure 4. Confusion matrix of proposed system

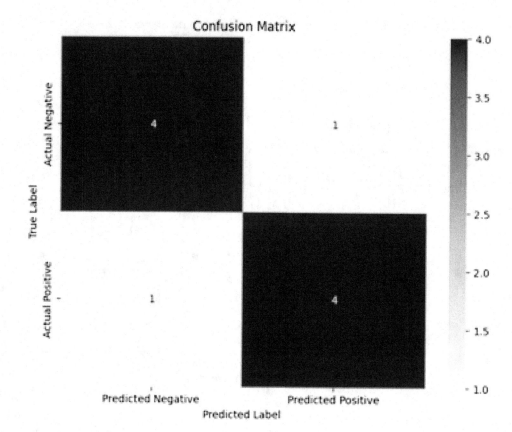

ADVANTAGES OF PROPOSED SYSTEM

The proposed system offers several advantages in enhancing security measures in open environments. Firstly, by leveraging Deep Convolutional Generative Adversarial Networks (DCGANs), the system can generate synthetic data that closely resembles real-world scenarios encountered in open environments. This synthetic data serves as a valuable resource for training and evaluating security systems, enabling them to learn from a diverse range of potential threats and anomalies. Additionally, the adaptive learning mechanisms implemented in the system allow both the DCGAN and the security system to continuously evolve based on real-world data and emerging security threats. This iterative refinement process ensures that the system remains adaptive and responsive to dynamic environments, improving its effectiveness in detecting and mitigating security risks over time. Moreover, the integration of synthetic data into the security system enhances its robustness and resilience, enabling it to proactively identify and address security threats with greater accuracy and efficiency. Overall, the proposed system offers a proactive and intelligent approach to safeguarding open environments, contributing to improved security and risk management capabilities.

Figure 5. ROC curve of proposed system

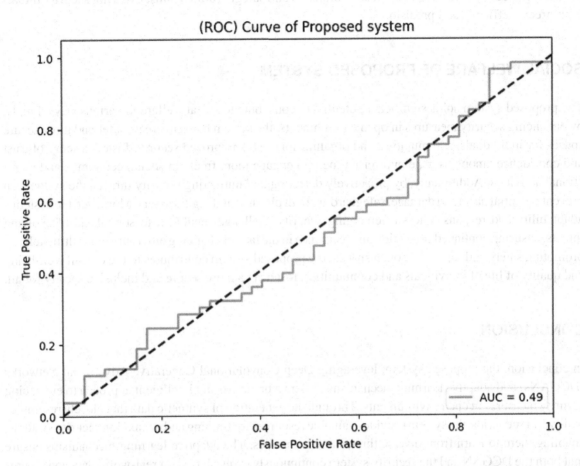

FUTURE ENCHANTMENT OF PROPOSED SYSTEM

In the future enhancement of the proposed system, several avenues emerge for further development and refinement. One key area of future enhancement involves the exploration of advanced deep learning techniques beyond DCGANs. Integrating cutting-edge methodologies such as reinforcement learning and meta-learning could enhance the system's ability to generate even more realistic synthetic data and adapt to evolving security landscapes with greater precision. Additionally, incorporating techniques from transfer learning and domain adaptation could enable the system to generalize across different environments and scenarios, further bolstering its versatility and applicability. Furthermore, ongoing research in anomaly detection and adversarial robustness could inform the development of more robust and resilient security systems, capable of effectively identifying and mitigating complex security threats in real-time. Collaborations with cybersecurity experts and industry stakeholders could provide valuable insights and real-world datasets to validate and refine the system's performance, ensuring its relevance and effectiveness in addressing emerging security challenges. Ultimately, by embracing innovation and collaboration, the future enhancement of the proposed system holds the promise of advancing security measures in open environments and safeguarding against evolving security threats with greater efficacy and precision.

SOCIAL WELFARE OF PROPOSED SYSTEM

The proposed system holds significant potential to contribute to social welfare in various ways. Firstly, by enhancing security measures in open environments, the system helps to create safer and more secure spaces for individuals, communities, and organizations. This improved security fosters a sense of trust and confidence among users, empowering them to engage more freely in social, economic, and recreational activities. Additionally, by proactively detecting and mitigating security threats, the system can prevent potential harm and damage, safeguarding both physical and digital assets. Moreover, the system's adaptability and responsiveness to emerging security challenges enable it to stay ahead of evolving threats, ensuring continued protection and resilience in the face of changing environments. Ultimately, by promoting safety and security in open spaces, the proposed system contributes to the overall well-being and quality of life of individuals and communities, fostering a more secure and inclusive society for all.

CONCLUSION

In conclusion, the proposed system, leveraging Deep Convolutional Generative Adversarial Networks (DCGANs) and adaptive learning mechanisms, offers a proactive and intelligent approach to enhancing security measures in open environments. Through the generation of synthetic data that closely resembles real-world scenarios, the system provides valuable resources for training and evaluating security systems, enabling them to learn from diverse threats and anomalies. The adaptive learning mechanisms ensure that both the DCGAN and the security system continuously evolve based on real-world data and emerging threats, improving their effectiveness and resilience over time. By fostering safer and more secure environments, the proposed system contributes to social welfare by promoting trust, confidence, and well-being among individuals and communities. Moving forward, ongoing research and development efforts hold the potential to further enhance the system's capabilities, advancing security measures and creating a more secure and inclusive society for all.

REFERENCES

Baskar, K., Prasanna Venkatesan, G. K. D., Sangeetha, S., & Preethi, P. (2021). Privacy-Preserving Cost-Optimization for Dynamic Replication in Cloud Data Centers. *2021 International Conference on Advance Computing and Innovative Technologies in Engineering (ICACITE)*, Greater Noida, India. pp. 927-932, 10.1109/ICACITE51222.2021.9404573

Geetha, K., Srivani, A., Gunasekaran, S., Ananthi, S., & Sangeetha, S. (2023). *Geospatial Data Exploration Using Machine Learning*. 2023 4th International Conference on Smart Electronics and Communication (ICOSEC), Trichy, India. 10.1109/ICOSEC58147.2023.10275920

Kalyanaraman, K. (2023). An Artificial Intelligence Model for Effective Routing in WSN. In *Perspectives on Social Welfare Applications' Optimization and Enhanced Computer Applications* (pp. 67–88). IGI Global. doi:10.4018/978-1-6684-8306-0.ch005

Kalyanaraman, K., & Prabakar, T. N. (2024). Enhancing Women's Safety in Smart Transportation Through Human-Inspired Drone-Powered Machine Vision Security. In S. Ponnusamy, V. Bora, P. Daigavane, & S. Wazalwar (Eds.), *AI Tools and Applications for Women's Safety* (pp. 150–166). IGI Global. doi:10.4018/979-8-3693-1435-7.ch009

Kim, T., Kang, B., Rho, M., Sezer, S., & Im, E. G. (2018). A multimodal deep learning method for android malware detection using various features. *IEEE Transactions on Information Forensics and Security*, *14*(3), 773–788. doi:10.1109/TIFS.2018.2866319

NguyenT. T.NguyenQ. V. H.NguyenD. T.NguyenD. T.Huynh-TheT.NahavandiS.NguyenC. M. (2022). Deep learning for deepfakes creation and detection: A survey. Computer Vision and Image Understanding, 223, 103525.

Rao, Y., & Ni, J. (2016, December). A deep learning approach to detection of splicing and copy-move forgeries in images. In *2016 IEEE international workshop on information forensics and security* (WIFS) (pp. 1-6). IEEE.

Sathya, R., Bharathi, V. C., Ananthi, S., Vaidehi, K., & Sangeetha, S. (2023). *Intelligent Home Surveillance System using Convolution Neural Network Algorithms*. 2023 4th International Conference on Electronics and Sustainable Communication Systems (ICESC), Coimbatore, India. 10.1109/ICESC57686.2023.10193402

Swaminathan, K., Vennila, C., & Prabakar, T. N. (2021). Novel routing structure with new local monitoring, route scheduling, and planning manager in ecological wireless sensor network. *Journal of Environmental Protection and Ecology*, *22*(6), 2614–2621.

Vinayakumar, R., Alazab, M., Soman, K. P., Poornachandran, P., Al-Nemrat, A., & Venkatraman, S. (2019). Deep learning approach for intelligent intrusion detection system. *IEEE Access : Practical Innovations, Open Solutions*, *7*, 41525–41550. doi:10.1109/ACCESS.2019.2895334

Weng, J., Weng, J., Zhang, J., Li, M., Zhang, Y., & Luo, W. (2019). Deepchain: Auditable and privacy-preserving deep learning with blockchain-based incentive. *IEEE Transactions on Dependable and Secure Computing*, *18*(5), 2438–2455. doi:10.1109/TDSC.2019.2952332

Yuan, X., Li, C., & Li, X. (2017, May). DeepDefense: identifying DDoS attack via deep learning. In *2017 IEEE international conference on smart computing (SMARTCOMP)* (pp. 1-8). IEEE.

Zhang, W. E., Sheng, Q. Z., Alhazmi, A., & Li, C. (2020). Adversarial attacks on deep-learning models in natural language processing: A survey. [TIST]. *ACM Transactions on Intelligent Systems and Technology*, *11*(3), 1–41. doi:10.1145/3374217

Zhou, F., Yang, S., Fujita, H., Chen, D., & Wen, C. (2020). Deep learning fault diagnosis method based on global optimization GAN for unbalanced data. *Knowledge-Based Systems*, *187*, 104837. doi:10.1016/j.knosys.2019.07.008

Chapter 10
Dynamic Evaluation Service for Safe Cloud Retention With Protection of Privacy and Reduction of Cyber Security Attacks

M. Mageshwari
SRM Institute of Science and Technology, India

S. Anitha
St. Joseph's College of Engineering, India

D. Prabakar
https://orcid.org/0000-0002-8411-0156
SRM Institute of Science and Technology, India

M. Vasim Babu
https://orcid.org/0000-0001-6896-6344
Madras Institute of Technology, Anna University, India

ABSTRACT

The cutting-edge technology that is growing in popularity worldwide is cloud computing. Keeping the data in the cloud via cloud storage because it can be accessed from anywhere at any time. There exist many different privacy-preserving data auditing methods, each of which has benefits and drawbacks of its own. As a result it's essential to create an auditing approach that does away with all of the drawbacks of existing strategies. The cloud, the TPA, and the data owner server comprise its three key components. The owner of the data performs static data operations like introducing, altering, and deleting data as well as dynamic data operations like dividing a file, encoding it in chunks, establishing a each block's hash value, combining them, and signing it. Data validation can either be carried out automatically or at the user's request. The setting up of an audit service with elements like privacy protection, open auditing, data integrity, and privacy is the main objective.

INTRODUCTION

Anyone may utilize and access computing resources at any time thanks to the cloud computing computer. The idea's feasibility it is less expensive, and operating and interacting with it is

DOI: 10.4018/979-8-3693-3597-0.ch010

simpler. Global, instantaneous service network availability of a widespread adaptable computing resource pool is made possible by cloud computing. It involves little management work or service provider working together and may be added quickly. Customers can save time and money by embracing the cloud. A form of Internet-based computing known as "cloud computing" involves the distribution of an assortment of services, including servers, storage, and applications, to the PCs and other devices that are connected to the Internet of an organization. (Ryan, D et al., 2011). Although cloud computing is an important instrument for information technology (IT) applications, entities and individual users nevertheless encounter significant hurdles when keeping data there. The greatest barriers to data security acceptance are worries over compliance, privacy, trust, and legal stumbling blocks (F.Doelitzscher et al., 2012). As a result, important goals are defined (A. Srijanyas K et al., 2013). A potent tool for information technology (IT) applications is cloud computing; Individual users and companies must, however, overcome a number of vital difficulties when storing data in the cloud (Y. Zhu et al., 2013). The principal barriers to data security acceptance are worries concerning compliance, privacy, trust, and legal stumbling blocks. As a result, substantial objectives are established (C. Liu et al., 2014). GANs, or Generative Adversarial Networks, are a contemporary method for generative modeling in deep learning that frequently makes use of convolutional neural network patterns (M. G. Haricharan et al., 2023). Finding commonalities in input data on an individual basis is the aim of generative the modeling process, which allows the model to generate fresh data points that reasonably mirror the original dataset (C. Huang et al., 2016).

GANs address this problem in a novel way through approaching it as a supervised learning problem with two essential parts: the discriminator, which must discern between created and real cases, and the generator, which must learn to generate novel scenarios (P. Mell & T.Grance, 2010). These models battle with each other through adversarial training until the generator learns to produce realistic samples, thereby fooling the system for discrimination roughly fifty percent of the time (W. Shen et al., 2017).

Data security encompasses several aspects such as data location, availability, confidentiality, protection, and secure transmission (K. Yang et al., 2012). is the most important concern in the cloud. Threats, data loss, service interruptions, external hostile assaults, and multitenancy issues are all part of the cloud security tasks (Mozumder, M et al., 2023). The term "data integrity" in the context of cloud computing refers to the protection of data from tampering (V. Tejaswini et al., 2012). Data ought not to be lost or manipulated through an individual who fails to be authorized to do so. Cloud service providers are tasked via the accuracy and integrity of data (J. Yuan et al., 2015). Users who have amassed private or sensitive data on the cloud must also prioritize data privacy (C. Wang et al., 2013). Methods of access restriction and verification are employed to guarantee data privacy.

Generalized system model

Figure 1. Public Auditing Model

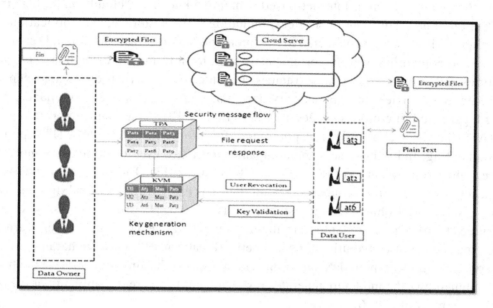

ROLE OF TPA

TPA is an integral part that works for the user. It possesses competence, knowledge, skills, and resources that users lack (R Suguna et al., 2023). The owner is relieved of the burden of preserving data integrity on the server because TPA handles data integrity verification (Q. Wang et al., 2011). The attributes that follow are necessary for TPA to be successfully used:

1TPA must expertly audit cloud data storage without requiring the retention of a local copy of the data.

2. The cloud-based storage of data server is not supposed to be known to TPA.
3. It shouldn't rise the existing validation effort in the cloud.
4. User data confidentiality rules shouldn't change as a result of relying on third-party audits.

For an effective auditing process, TPA must meet all of these standards (G. Ateniese et al., 2017). The generalized design of public auditing is depicted in Figure 1.

In a cloud environment, the three core networks are the Data Owner, Cloud Server, and TPA. First, the data is preserved on a cloud storage server that the cloud service provider (CSP) makes available to the data owner (D. Abraha-Weldemariam et al., 2012). In order to monitor the user's data, TPA continuously confirms the correctness of the user's selection and notifies the user if a discrepancy or constraint is discovered in the user's data (G. Ateniese et al., 2007).

Figure 2. Model for Public Auditing for Cloud Storage

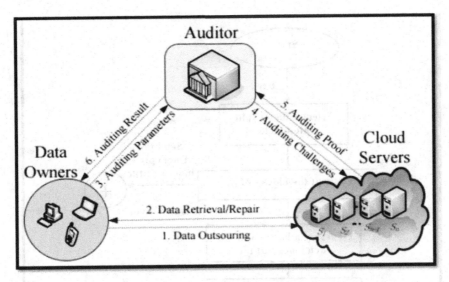

Figure 3. Suction of TPA

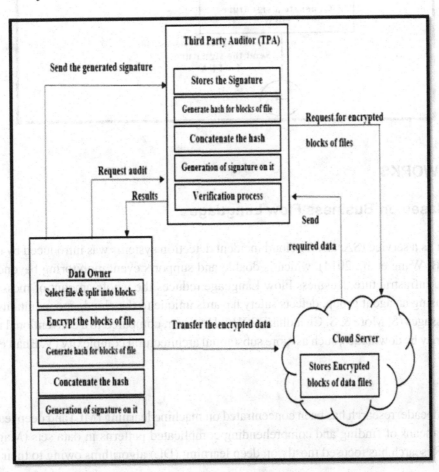

Figure 4. Flow of TPA

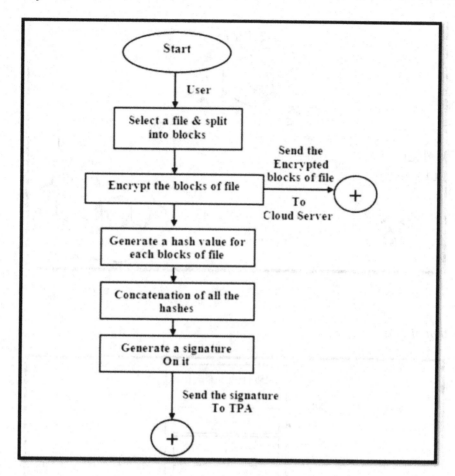

RELATED WORKS

Auditing Based on Business Flow Language

Security audit as a service (SAaaS) for cloud incident detection systems was introduced by cloud auditing in 2012 (B. Wang et al., 2014). which is doable and supports event monitoring beyond customers within a cloud infrastructure. Business Flow Language reduces the whole amount of messages sent to the cloud by using an agent group, detects safety hazards unique to the cloud, and maintains false positive event messages (S. More & S. Chaudhari, 2016). However, compared to a conventional information centre, there may be downsides, such as more substantial architectural complexity (V. Bhatt et al., 2022).

DL Models

Over the past decade, research has been concentrated on machine learning (ML) and deep learning (DL) techniques as means of finding and comprehending complicated patterns in data sets (Mageshwari.M et al., 2022). Research has focused mostly on deep learning (DL) algorithms owing to their end-to-end solving approach, whereby eliminates the need for contact between humans as DL models learn and extract features from the input and demonstrate improved performance when performing learning in intricate data structures (Mageshwari, M et al., 2022).

Index Hash Table

In 2013, the Dynamic audit service was introduced to check the validity. The audit service was built using techniques such as fragment structure, random sampling, and index hash tables (G. S. Aujla et al., 2018). Cloud technology, for example, is much more efficient and secure than personal computing devices. To ensure the security and accuracy of audits (S. Sridhar et al., 2016). Periodic sampling audit improve the performance of audit system. Disadvantages are frequent activities does not detect anomalies. A security risk comes when cloud infrastructure is more powerful (C.N.S.Vinoth Kumar et al., 2022). Using privacy preserving protocol to support dynamic operations. When using both multiple owners and multiple clouds it supports batch auditing. To ensure the data privacy and less communication cost. When using batch auditing scheme data owner worry about the data loss and data loss could happen in any infrastructure. Heavy storage requires more space. It requires additional trust organizer during multi cloud batch auditing (A. Praveena & S. Smys, 2017).

Merkel Hash Tree

In 2014 provide formal analysis and fine grained updates support authorized auditing and update request. To enhanced security and flexibility (Sidhant Chourasiya et al., 2023). Markel hash tree improve that auditing and maintain quality of service. Dynamic data updates using more fixed size blocks. In coarse grained updates causes the computation cost (H. Tian et al., 2016). In the bottom up approach using low level metrics widely implemented IaaS which is only used for scalability Disadvantage is generic requirements does not validate security requirements (S Lins et al., 2016).

Batch Auditing

The identity-based integrity auditing protocol, that permits batch auditing for many users, was adopted by (Laicheng Cao et al., 2017). The key issue with this approach is that the file is not encrypted and is stored in plaintext, which results in a continuous calculation cost. It guards against replay, replace, and forgery attacks relied on by cloud hosting companies. (Filipe Apolinario et al., 2018)

Index Hash Table

Using bilinear pairing maps and index hash tables, (B.Mahalakshmi & G.Suseendran, 2017) proposed an integrity examination scheme of thoroughness and anonymous for multi-cloud storage. Index hash tables encrypt data using a hash function, compute the index, and store the data encrypted in the index hash table. Additionally, the plan allows for dynamic data developments, and a trusted third party does the integrity check. It guards against forgery attacks (Anyi Liu et al., 2019). In 2018 conceptual architecture and high level important elements and procedures that must be followed. It enables the independent auditors accessing the reports within a short time period. Conceptual architecture does not provide any technical requirements. If additional requirements added then computation cost increased

(Xin Tang et al., 2019). In 2019 privacy preserving public auditing protocol and trusted party auditor can be used. Process of state and process of retrieval protocol verify the integrity. It is only efficient for business application only. To evaluate auditing time is high. Privacy preserving auditing fails to allow for momentary validation (Jiang Hong et al., 2019).

Random Masking Technique and Block Chain

In 2020 stateless cloud auditing scheme and dynamic group data with privacy preservation. Random masking technique and public key cryptography can be used (Xiuqing Lu et al., 2019). Block chain technology can be used for ensure data sharing. Malicious attacks affect the external and internal audit. multiple data integrity checking schemes used in Lattice based privacy preserving (M. Ramanan & P Vivekanandan, 2018). If any hardware device failure malicious hacks and software bugs occurred. In most basic implementation, block chain can be used as a distributed ledger. Auditing made for block chain are nearly hashing and distributed algorithms. In most cases, a block chain is stored peer-to-peer. Many information systems have established the capacity for protection and reliability thanks to block chain (C.Sasikala et al., 2018). The block chain is built on the premise that by disseminating a collection of records to a wider community of people, there will always be a source where the credibility and authenticity of a set of records can be verified (Imad El Ghoubach et al., 2019).

Domain Adaptation Technique

The domain adaptation tactics, which seek to develop DL models to generalize the training sector to the targeted field and address the disparity between various data distributions, have garnered lots of interest recently. A subclass of DL identified as Generative Adversarial Networks (GAN) is emerging, with potential applications in domain adaptation. Since (Mai Rady et al., 2019) first put forward GANs, both the original and various variants, the mathematical framework has been broadly accepted in a variety of domains, much as many ML and DL models have. Furthermore, to incorporate the concept of GAN into its applications. Even so, despite the authors' extensive assessment of the literature, no comprehensive review study on the application of GANs (H. Tian et al., 2016).

Overall Outline of the Work

Data Integrity checking gives the guarantee that the details that are is secure and unchanged when stored in the cloud (Zhang Y et al., 2020). The Data Integrity and verification is remotely done. In dynamic auditing two party storage auditing protocols can be used to check that integrity. The integrity can be checked by the data owner. But the result will be unbiased. Privacy preserving protocol support batch auditing. Dynamic auditing does not suitable for multiple data owners .The owners are different they cannot combine to conduct the batch auditing (H. Zhao et al., 2019). When using multi cloud batch auditing, it required additional trust organizer. Data integrity provides the consistency and accuracy of stored data. It always checks on the data which can be transferred over the internet. It can be intruded by another unauthenticated user by any malicious activity (X. Zhang et al., 2019). Data integrity provides the overall accuracy.

PREVENTION OF CYBER SECURITY ATTACKS AND COMPUTATION TIME

Forgery Attack

In (H. Tian et al., 2018) presents that paper based upon integrity checking, privacy preserving and forgery attack. This denotes integrity verification for multi cloud storage using bilinear pairing. Cross site request forgery, often referred to as a one-click attack, session riding, or CSRF for short, is a sort of malicious hack of a website in which an illegitimate user's inquiries are submitted by an accredited user. In this scheme Computation time is less. Trusted third party supports data update and it prevents from forgery attack. Data encryption faced by the index hash table (Y. Wang et al., 2019).

Spoofing Attack

In (L. Huang et al., 2018) proposed integrity verification based on Homomorphic authentication.tha data owner check and verify the data integrity. In this scheme reduced and prevents the spoofing attack. Spoofing is the act of a hacker posing as a legitimate user or device in order to get through access control systems, steal data, or disseminate malware. Three different types of spoofing exist: IP address spoofing, in which an attacker uses a fictitious IP address to deliver packet over a network.

Malicious Attack

In (H. Zhao et al., 2019) proposed paper based upon data integrity when using The MD5 and RSA algorithms. Data owner uses cryptography algorithm and third party audit to check integrity. More In this arrangement, however, communication costs are necessary. The user data can be encrypted by RSA and MD5 algorithm before sending to the cloud. This scheme reduced and prevents malicious attack. It causes the infrastructure failures and an increase in network congestion (Yu J & Wang H, 2017). In the proposed Stochastic Diffusion. Integrity checked by the Downer. This scheme reduces malicious attack and recovers the corrupted data. It required low computation time.

Denial Attack

In (Shen W et al., 2019) proposed Trusted Platform module and Attribute Based Encryption. Data integrity verified at run time and detects malicious modification. This scheme reduced and prevents Denial attack This type of cyber attack strives to temporarily interfere with a host's internet services in order hinder the intended users from visiting a computer or network resource. This plan consumed less time to compute.

Replay Attack

In (Guo C et al., 2018) proposed privacy preserving and integrity preserving by using reversible water marking algorithm. Data integrity can be check by Diffie Hellman key. Cloud service provider affected by replay attack. So this scheme prevents from replay attack. Hellman key eliminates authentication data and communication cost A type of network assaulting called a replay attack, sometimes referred to as a playback attack, necessitates the malicious recurrence of a genuine information transaction.

Denial of Service Attack

(Zhang Y et al., 2020) stated a Version Based in 2019 Data integrity is verified via a third-party auditor and the Merkle hash tree. This plan shields against denial-of-service attacks. The Merkle hash tree is used to reduce computing costs. The version number and hash value linked to the dynamic are used in the aforementioned method. An attack known as a denial of service attack aims at knocking down a computer system, leaving it inoperable for the intended users. DoS attacks achieve this by transmitting information that causes a crash or by saturating the target with traffic

Quantum Computer Attack

In (M. Sookhak et al., 2018) proposed Lattice based technique. Data integrity check by the Third party auditor. This scheme prevents Quantum computer attack and recovers the corrupted data. It required low computation time. The drawback of that scheme is single user can be allowed but multi user environment and batch auditing can't be supported. In (M. U. Arshad et al., 2018) proposed technique based on Advanced Encryption Standard MD5. Integrity of data check by trusted third party auditor. In this scheme safeguards against attacks using Distributed Denial of Service. It required more computation time. It provides integrity and confidentiality of cloud data.

Privacy Protection

Cloud-based storage providers have access to consumers' private information while users are easily able to access their data on the cloud. To ensure that these data remained private even in the case of malevolent customers, privacy protection precautions are used. Multiple recipients of information should be able to access it without fear of being attacked.

Key Generation Mechanism

Users' private keys are generated by a private key production centre or by their unique identities. Their public keys are generated using the users' unique identities (Mageshwari.M et al., 2022). While users' private keys are generated by either a private key administration centre or a private key production centre (PKG), their public keys are generated using their distinct identities. Once impaired, PKG may effortlessly adopt the identity of any user to forge tags covertly (Y. Wang et al., 2018). However, because the user's private key includes a partial key and a hidden value, cryptography is a secure substitute. A private key production facility (PKG) uses a key generation technique to generate the partial key. Once deteriorating, PKG may effortlessly assume the identity of any user to forge tags covertly (Rong W et al., 2014). However, because the user's private key incorporates a partial key and a hidden value, cryptography is a secure counterpart. The key creation the procedure is used to generate the partial key. (KGM)

AUDITING PARAMETERS

Table 1. Auditing parameters which differ in block size while maintaining a set size

Size of Block	Time for encryption	Time for Hashing	Concatenation Time for hashing	Signature Generation Time	Encrypted files transfer to CS	Signature Time to TPA	Transfer the key to TPA	Auditing cost
10 MB	13693	8934.9	833.4	1172.2	8738.7	789.2	639.7	22834.4
20 MB	13707.9	7784.3	1126	1184.7	5849.3	1089.5	625.8	8282.4
30 MB	11673.2	6247.2	877.7	1255	4588.2	828.9	580	16033.8
40 MB	11440.6	5758.5	997.2	1257.2	4306.6	892.1	605.9	15630.8
50 MB	5394.2	3949.8	972	1365	42549	1081.2	779.8	14131.7

CONCLUSION

The report is based on a wide investigation into several methods for ensuring data integrity and confirming the user-specific keys. Additionally, it lists the many strategies employed, including those for privacy and security. The main goals are to establish integrity check reduces cyber-attacks and computation cost verification. Future work will focus on finding ways to achieve integrity while limiting assaults and computational expense. The best method for cloud auditing, given on reviews of prior study employing TPA, is the Key Validation Mechanism and Integrity Checking Algorithm.

Figure 5. File size vs. auditing time unit of time based upon the file size

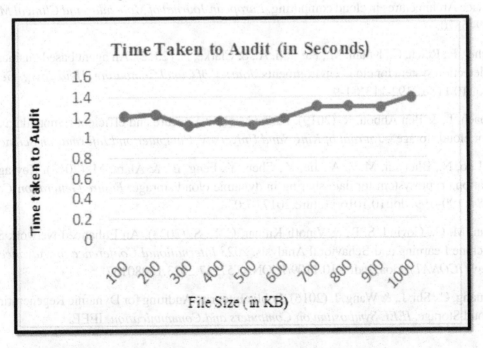

REFERENCES

Apolinario, F., Pardal, M. L., & Correia, M. (2018). S-Audit: Efficient Data Integrity Verification for Cloud Storage. *IEEE International Conference on Trust, Security and Privacy in Computing and Communications*. IEEE. 10.1109/TrustCom/BigDataSE.2018.00073

Arshad, M. U., Kundu, A., Bertino, E., Ghafoor, A., & Kundu, C. (2018). Efficient and Scalable Integrity Verification of Data and Query Results for Graph Databases. *IEEE Transactions on Knowledge and Data Engineering*, *30*(5), 866–879. doi:10.1109/TKDE.2017.2776221

Ateniese, G., Burns, R., Curtmola, R., Herring, J., Kissner, L., Peterson, Z., & Song, D. (2007). Provable Data Possession at Untrusted Stores. *Proc. 14th ACM Conf. Computer and Comm. Security*. IEEE.

Aujla, G. S., Chaudhary, R., Kumar, N., Das, A. K., & Rodrigues, J. J. (2018). SecSVA: Secure Storage, Verification, and Auditing of Big Data in the Cloud Environment. *IEEE Communications Magazine*, *56*(1), 78–85. doi:10.1109/MCOM.2018.1700379

Bhatt, V., Aggarwal, U., & Vinoth Kumar, C. N. S. (2022). *Sports Data Visualization and Betting*. 2022 International Conference on Smart Generation Computing, Communication and Networking (SMART GENCON), Bangalore, India. 10.1109/SMARTGENCON56628.2022.10083831

Cao, L., He, W., Liu, Y., Guo, X., & Feng, T. (2017). An integrity verification scheme of completeness and zero-knowledge for multi-Cloud storage. *International Journal of Communication Systems*, *30*(16), 1–10. doi:10.1002/dac.3324

Chourasiya, S., & Samanta, G. (2023). *Pegasus Spyware: A Vulnerable Behaviour-based Attack System*. 2023 2nd International Conference on Edge Computing and Applications. Research Gate.

Divya Mounika, R., & Naresh, R. (2020, December). The concept of Privacy and Standardization of Microservice Architectures in cloud computing. *European Journal of Molecular and Clinical Medicine*, *7*(2), 5349–5370.

Doelitzscher, F., Reich, C., Knahl, M., Passfall, A., & Clarke, N. (2012). An agent based business aware incident detection system for cloud environments. *Journal of Cloud Computing (Heidelberg, Germany)*, *1*(1), 9. doi:10.1186/2192-113X-1-9

El Ghoubach, I., & Ben Abbou, R. (2019). Fatiha Mrabti "A secure and efficient remote data auditing scheme for cloud storage". *Journal of King Saud University. Computer and Information Sciences*, 1–7.

Guo, C., Luo, N., Bhuiyan, M. Z. A., Jie, Y., Chen, Y., Feng, B., & Alam, M. (2018). Key-aggregate authentication cryptosystem for data sharing in dynamic cloud storage. *Future Generation Computer Systems*, *84*, 190–199. doi:10.1016/j.future.2017.07.038

Haricharan, M. G., Govind, S. P., & Vinoth Kumar, C. N. S. (2023). An Enhanced Network Security using Machine Learning and Behavioral Analysis. *2023 International Conference for Advancement in Technology (ICONAT)*, Goa, India. 10.1109/ICONAT57137.2023.10080157

He, K., Huang, C., Shi, J., & Wang, J. (2016). Public Integrity Auditing for Dynamic Regenerating Code Based Cloud Storage. *IEEE Symposium on Computers and Communication*. IEEE.

Hong, J., Xie, M., Kang, B., Chunquing, L., & Lin, S. (2018). ID-Based Public Auditing Protocol for Cloud Storage Data Integrity Checking with Strengthened Authentication and Security. *Wuhan University Journal of Natural Sciences, 23*(4), 362–388. doi:10.1007/s11859-018-1335-9

Liu, C., Chen, J., Yang, L., Zhang, X., Yang, C., Ranjan, R., & Ramamohanarao, K. (2014, September). Authorized public auditing of dynamic big data storage on cloud with efficient verifiable fine-grained updates. *IEEE Transactions on Parallel and Distributed Systems, 25*(9), 2234–2244. doi:10.1109/TPDS.2013.191

Lu, X., Pan, Z., & Xian, H. (2019). An Integrity Verification Scheme of Cloud Storage for Internet-of-Things Mobile Terminal Devices. *Journal of Computer Security, 92*, 1–17.

Mageshwari, M., & Naresh, R. (2022). Decentralized Data Privacy Protection and Cloud Auditing Security Management. *Proceedings of International Conference on Computing, Communication, and Intelligent Systems.* IEEE. 10.1109/ICCCIS56430.2022.10037676

Mahalakshmi, B., & Suseendran, G. (2019). *An Analysis of Cloud Computing Issues on Data Integrity, Privacy and its Current solutions.* Research Article. doi:10.1007/978-981-13-1274-8_35

Mell, P., & Grance, T. (2010). The NIST definition of cloud computing. *Communications of the ACM, 53*(6).

More, S., & Chaudhari, S. (2016). Third Party Public Auditing Scheme for Cloud Storage. *Procedia Computer Science, 79*, 69–76. doi:10.1016/j.procs.2016.03.010

Mozumder, M., & Biswas, S. (2023). An Hybrid Edge Algorithm for Vehicle License Plate Detection. In: Raj, J.S., Perikos, I., Balas, V.E. (eds) Intelligent Sustainable Systems. ICoISS 2023. Lecture Notes in Networks and Systems, vol 665. Springer, Singapore. doi:10.1007/978-981-99-1726-6_16

Praveena, A., & Smys, S. (2017). Ensuring data security in cloud based social networks. In proc. of IEEE International conference of Electronics, Communication and Aerospace Technology. IEEE. 10.1109/ICECA.2017.8212819

Rady, M. (2019). *Tamer Abdelkader, Rasha Ismail "Integrity and Confidentiality in Cloud Outsourced Data".* Ain Shams Engineering Journal Science Direct.

Ramanan, M., & Vivekanandan, P. (2018). *Efficient data integrity and data replication in cloud using stochastic diffusion method.* Springer Science on Cluster Computing.

Rong, W., Xiong, Z., Cooper, D., Lie, C., & Sheng, H. (2014). Smart City architecture: A technology guide for implementation and design challenges. *China Communications, 11*(3), 56–69. doi:10.1109/CC.2014.6825259

Ryan, D. (2011). Mark, Cloud computing privacy concerns on our doorstep.‖. *Communications of the ACM, 54*(1), 1. doi:10.1145/1866739.1866751

Sasikala, C., & Shoba Bindu, C. (2018). *Certificateless remote data integrity checking using lattices in cloud storage.* Springer Science on Neural Computing and Applications.

Shen, W., Qin, J., Yu, J., Hao, R., & Hu, J. (2019). Enabling identity-based integrity auditing and data sharing with sensitive information hiding for secure cloud storage. *IEEE Transactions on Information Forensics and Security*, *14*(2), 331–346. doi:10.1109/TIFS.2018.2850312

Shen, W., Yu, J., Xia, H., Zhang, H., Lu, X., & Hao, R. (2017). Lightweight and privacy-preserving secure cloud auditing scheme for group users via the third party medium. *Journal of Network and Computer Applications*, *82*, 56–64. doi:10.1016/j.jnca.2017.01.015

Sookhak, M., Yu, F. R., & Zomaya, A. Y. (2018). Auditing big data storage in cloud computing using divide and conquer tables. *IEEE Transactions on Parallel and Distributed Systems*, *29*(5), 999–1012. doi:10.1109/TPDS.2017.2784423

Sridhar, S., & Smys, S. "A hybrid multilevel authentication scheme for private cloud environment," In proc. of IEEE 10th International Conference on Intelligent Systems and Control, pp. 1-5, 2016. 10.1109/ISCO.2016.7727141

Suguna, R., Vinoth Kumar, C. N. S., Deepa, S., & Arunkumar, M. S. (2023). Apple and Tomato Leaves Disease Detection using Emperor Penguins Optimizer based CNN. *9th International Conference on Advanced Computing and Communication Systems*. IEEE. 10.1109/ICACCS57279.2023.10112941

Tang, X., Huang, Y., Chang, C.-C., & Zhou, L. (2019). Efficient Real-Time Integrity Auditing with Privacy-Preserving Arbitration for Images in Cloud Storage System. *IEEE Access : Practical Innovations, Open Solutions*, *7*, 33009–33023. doi:10.1109/ACCESS.2019.2904040

Tian, H., Nan, F., Jiang, H., Chang, C. C., Ning, J., & Huang, Y. (2018). Public auditing for shared cloud data with efficient and secure group management. *Information Sciences*, *472*, 107–125. doi:10.1016/j.ins.2018.09.009

Vinoth Kumar, C. N. S., Vasim Babu, M., Naresh, R., Lakshmi Narayanan, K., & Bharathi, V. (2021). Real Time Door Security System With Three Point Authentication. *4th International Conference on Recent Trends in Computer Science and Technology*. IEEE Explore. 10.1109/ICRTCST54752.2022.9782004

Wang, B., Li, B., & Li, H. (2014, March). Oruta: Privacy Preserving Public Auditing for Shared Data in the Cloud,‖. *IEEE Transactions on Cloud Computing*, *2*(1).

Wang, C., Chow, S. S. M., Wang, Q., Ren, K., & Lou, W. (2013, February). —Privacy- preserving public auditing for secure cloud storage,‖. *IEEE Transactions on Computers*, *62*(2), 362–375. doi:10.1109/TC.2011.245

Wang, Q., Wang, C., Ren, K., Lou, W., & Li, J. (2011). —Enabling Public Auditability and Data Dynamics for Storage Security in Cloud Computing,‖. *IEEE Transactions on Parallel and Distributed Systems*, *22*(5), 847–859. doi:10.1109/TPDS.2010.183

Wang, Y., Shen, Y., Wang, H., Cao, J., & Jiang, X. (2018). Mtmr:Ensuring map reduce computation integrity with merkle tree-based verifications. *IEEE Transactions on Big Data*, *4*(3), 418–431. doi:10.1109/TBDATA.2016.2599928

Wang, Y., Shen, Y., Wang, H., Cao, J., & Jiang, X. (2019). Mtmr: Ensuring mapreduce computation integrity with merkle tree-based verifications. *IEEE Transactions on Big Data, 4*(3), 418–431. doi:10.1109/TBDATA.2016.2599928

Xu, C., He, X., & Abraha-Weldemariam, D. (2012). Cryptanalysis of Wang's Auditing Protocol for Data Storage Security in Cloud Computing. *International Conference on Information Computing and Applications.* Springer-Verlag Berlin Heidelberg.

Yang, K., & Jia, X. (2012). —An Efficient and Secure Protocol for Ensuring Data Storage Security in Cloud Computing,‖. *IEEE Transactions on Parallel and Distributed Systems.*

Yu, Y., Au, M. H., Ateniese, G., Huang, X., Susilo, W., Dai, Y., & Min, G. (2017). Identity-based remote data integrity checking with perfect data privacy preserving for cloud storage. *IEEE Transactions on Information Forensics and Security, 12*(4), 767–778. doi:10.1109/TIFS.2016.2615853

Yuan, J., & Yu, S. (2015). —Public Integrity Auditing for Dynamic Data Sharing with Multi-User Modification,‖. *IEEE Transactions on Information Forensics and Security, 10*(8), 1717–1726. doi:10.1109/TIFS.2015.2423264

Zhang, X., Wang, H., & Xu, C. (2019). Identity-based key-exposure resilient cloud storage public auditing scheme from lattices. *Information Sciences, 472*, 223–234. doi:10.1016/j.ins.2018.09.013

Zhang, Y., Yu, J., Hao, R., Wang, C., & Ren, K. (2020). Enabling efficient user revocation in identity-based cloud storage auditing for shared big data. *IEEE Transactions on Dependable and Secure Computing, 17*, 608–619.

Zhang, Y., Yu, J., Hao, R., Wang, C., & Ren, K. (2020). Enabling efficient user revocation in identity-based cloud storage auditing for shared big data. *IEEE Transactions on Dependable and Secure Computing, 17*, 608–619.

Zhu, Y., Ahn, G.-J., Hu, H., Yau, S., An, H., & Hu, C.-J. (2013, April–June). Dynamic audit services for outsourced storages in clouds. *IEEE Transactions on Services Computing, 6*(2), 227–238. doi:10.1109/TSC.2011.51

Chapter 11
Enabling Safety and Security Through GANs and Cybersecurity Synergy for Robust Protection

Aswathy K. Cherian

(iD) https://orcid.org/0009-0002-3679-2583

SRM Institute of Science and Technology, India

Vinoth

SRM Institute of Science and Technology, India

M. Vaidhehi

(iD) https://orcid.org/0000-0002-0319-3544

SRM Institute of Science and Technology, India

S. Ushasukhanya

SRM Institute of Science and Technology, India

Naga Malleswari

SRM Institute of Science and Technology, India

ABSTRACT

In the realm of cybersecurity, machine learning emerges as an indispensable tool for advanced threat detection and protection against digital vulnerabilities. GANs, positioned as a potent machine learning paradigm, transcend their traditional role in data generation, showcasing their potential to outsmart detection systems. This chapter sheds light on the evolving challenges posed by GANs in cybersecurity, underscoring the imperative for thorough assessments, especially within the context of intrusion detection systems. While numerous successes characterize various GAN applications, this chapter emphasizes the pressing need to investigate GANs' specific impact on cybersecurity enhancements. GANs not only excel in data generation but also serve as catalysts for novel avenues in privacy and security-oriented research. The chapter concludes by accentuating the limited depth of existing assessments on GANs in privacy and security, urging further exploration to unravel the multifaceted influence of GANs in shaping the future of digital security frameworks.

DOI: 10.4018/979-8-3693-3597-0.ch011

INTRODUCTION

The advent of Generative Adversarial Networks (GANs) has swiftly ushered in a revolutionary era in machine learning and related domains, permeating diverse research areas and applications (Goodfellow, Pouget-Abadie, Mirza, Xu, Warde-Farley, Ozair, Courville, Bengio, 2014). As a potent generative framework, GANs have significantly propelled advancements in complex tasks, including image generation, super-resolution, and manipulations of textual data (Lotter, Kreiman, Cox, 2015). Recently, the application of GANs to address intricate privacy and security challenges has gained prominence in academic and industrial circles, driven by their game-theoretic optimization strategy. Originally proposed by Goodfellow et al. in 2014, GANs have been hailed as "the most interesting idea in the last 10 years in Machine Learning" by Yann LeCun, the recipient of the 2018 Turing Award. Fundamentally, GANs operate as generative models bridging the gap between supervised and unsupervised learning. In a zero-sum game between the generator and the discriminator, the generator is trained to deceive the discriminator, which, in turn, aims to distinguish real data from generated data. GANs have ushered in a new wave of data-driven applications in the realms of Big Data and Smart Cities, owing to their remarkable properties. Firstly, the design of generative models provides an excellent means to capture high-dimensional probability distributions, a critical focus in mathematics and engineering. Secondly, well-trained generative models mitigate data scarcity, facilitating technical innovation and performance improvement, especially in deep learning. For instance, high-quality generated data can enhance semi-supervised learning, mitigating the impact of missing data to some extent. Thirdly, generative models, particularly GANs, enable learning algorithms to handle multi-modal outputs, accommodating scenarios where a single input may yield more than one correct output for a given task, such as next-frame prediction. Before the advent of GANs, several generative models based on maximum likelihood estimation existed, categorized as either explicit density-based or implicit density-based (Jiang, Zhang, Cai, 2008) (Rabiner, 1989). Explicit density-based models, like Restricted Boltzmann Machine (RBM) and Gaussian Mixture Model (GMM), faced limitations in representing complex, high-dimensional data distributions due to computational tractability issues. GANs, however, overcome these constraints by using a pre-defined low-dimensional latent code, mapping it to the target data dimension (Furthermore, GANs, as non-parametric methods, eliminate the need for approximate distribution or Markov Chain properties, allowing them to represent generated data in a lower dimension with fewer parameters. The architecture of basic GAN is shown in figure 1.

The flexibility and extensibility of GANs have led to various variants, including Wasserstein Generative Adversarial Network (WGAN), Information Maximizing Generative Adversarial Network (InfoGAN), and CycleGAN, shown in figure 2., each tailored to specific requirements (Arjovsky, Chintala, Bottou 2027) (Chen, Houthooft, Schulman, Sutskever, Abeel, 2016) (Zhu, Park, Isola, Efros, 2017). Motivated by these characteristics, novel research continues to benefit from the widespread applicability of GANs.

Advantages of GANs

GANs offer distinct advantages over other generative models. GANs excel in efficient sample generation by eliminating the need for sequential element creation, resulting in faster outputs compared to models like NADE, PixelRNN, and WaveNet. Notably, GANs streamline training by bypassing the requirement for Monte Carlo approximations. Despite their reputation for instability, GANs are com-

Figure 1. Architecture of basic GAN

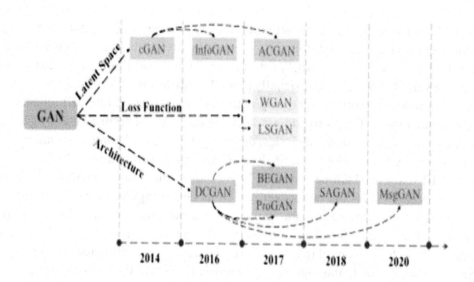

Figure 2. Evolution of GAN

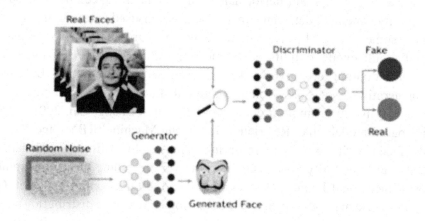

paratively easier to train than Boltzmann machines, which face challenges in high-dimensional spaces. GANs, when applied to ImageNet, showcase the ability to produce visually interesting samples, even if unconventional. GANs stand out for avoiding deterministic bias, unlike variational autoencoders (VAEs). VAEs introduce bias by optimizing a lower bound on log-likelihood, leading to blurry samples. GANs, in contrast, remain versatile, not imposing restrictions on latent code dimension or generator network invertibility. They also prove more adaptable to discrete latent variables compared to VAEs. Efficiency in sample creation is another advantage, with GANs requiring just one model run, unlike Boltzmann machines and Generative Stochastic Networks (GSNs) that involve multiple Markov chain iterations. These advantages collectively position GANs as efficient and versatile generative models in various applications.

Disadvantages of GANs

Training a Generative Adversarial Network (GAN) requires finding a Nash equilibrium in a game, a task occasionally achieved by gradient descent but not consistently. This lack of a robust equilibrium-finding technique renders GAN training more unstable compared to methods like Variational Auto encoders (VAE) or PixelRNN. Despite this instability, GAN training is generally more stable than that of Boltzmann machines. Understanding how to handle discrete data, such as text, poses a challenge for GANs. Unlike Boltzmann machines, which struggle with tasks like estimating the value of one pixel given another pixel, GANs are primarily designed to generate entire images in one go. Addressing this limitation involves considering alternatives like Bidirectional GANs (BiGAN), enabling the prediction of missing pixels through Gibbs sampling, akin to the approach used in Boltzmann machines.

LITERATURE REVIEW

Contemporary research on Generative Adversarial Networks (GANs) is marked by a dual trajectory, encompassing both application-oriented and theory-oriented studies. This multifaceted exploration aims to harness the full potential of GANs, addressing challenges and expanding their capabilities in various domains. In the realm of application-oriented research, GANs have emerged as a transformative force, overcoming limitations of previous generative models. Researchers are delving into diverse data formats, unleashing GANs' creative potential in the generation of images, Natural Language Processing (NLP), time series data, and semantic segmentation. GANs have proven instrumental in pushing the boundaries of image generation. Studies (Liqian, Jia, Sun, Schiele, Tuytelaars, Gool, 2017; Odena, Olah, Shlens, 2017; Vondrick, Pirsiavash, Torralba, 2016; Yang, Lu, Lin, Shechtman, Wang, Li, 2017). delve into applications such as image-to-image translation, image super-resolution, image in-painting, face aging, human pose synthesis, object detection, sketch synthesis, and texture synthesis. GANs have found application in the synthesis of text, with research (Zihang, Yang, Yang, Cohen, Salakhutdinov, 2017) exploring their potential in text synthesis, demonstrating their adaptability in language generation and speech synthesis. The versatility of GANs extends to the generation of time series data (Brophy, Wang, Ward, 2019). This includes applications in video and music generation, showcasing GANs' ability to handle sequential data and temporal patterns. GANs exhibit prowess in semantic segmentation (Luc, Couprie, Chintala, Verbeek, 2016), contributing to tasks such as medical data generation. The ability to synthesize meaningful content in segmented domains underscores GANs' impact on various fields. These applications represent just a fraction of the extensive possibilities GANs offer, showcasing their extraordinary capability and widespread popularity in diverse creative domains. Concurrently, theory-oriented methodologies strive to elevate GANs by addressing fundamental challenges. Researchers are actively tackling issues like non-stable training, mode collapse, gradient vanish, and the absence of proper evaluation metrics, propelling GANs towards a higher level of reliability and performance. GANs are notorious for non-stable training and mode collapse. Theoretical solutions such as feature matching, unrolled GAN, and mini-batch discrimination have been proposed to mitigate these challenges. Establishing proper evaluation metrics is a critical aspect of GAN research. Researchers are actively working on defining robust metrics to quantify the performance and quality of generated outputs. Theoretical methodologies continue to evolve, introducing concepts like the Self-Attention Generative Adversarial Network (SAGAN), label smoothing, proper optimizer selection, gradient penalty, and alternative loss functions (Mao, Li, Xie, Lau, Wang, Smolley, 2017). These innovations aim to enhance stability, convergence, and overall performance of GANs. The synergy between application-oriented and theory-oriented studies forms a dynamic ecosystem, propelling GAN research forward. While applications showcase the immediate impact and versatility of GANs, theoretical advancements lay the foundation for a more robust, stable, and reliable framework. In essence, the current trends in GAN research manifest a harmonious balance between unleashing creative potentials in diverse applications and addressing theoretical challenges. This dual perspective ensures that GANs not only continue to revolutionize various domains but also evolve as a more resilient and sophisticated generative model.

GANS IN CYBERSECURITY

In the realm of information technology, cybersecurity assumes a paramount role by implementing measures to safeguard systems, networks, and programs from diverse digital attacks. The contemporary world is marked by extensive connectivity, with predictions indicating that each individual will possess approximately 15 connected devices by 2030 [16]. This interconnectedness results in a multitude of potential targets, each varying in the level of protection they possess. Effectively ensuring cybersecurity for this vast user base becomes challenging due to the diverse nature of these targets. The increasing prevalence of connected devices, coupled with innovative strategies employed by attackers, contributes to the constant evolution of cybersecurity threats. The sheer variety of potential attacks continues to rise, presenting a complex landscape that demands robust defense mechanisms (McAfee, 2019). Security stands as a crucial application for Artificial Intelligence (AI) [18]. The ongoing advancements in AI and Machine Learning (ML) algorithms play a dual role—they simplify the process of constructing more secure systems while simultaneously introducing new avenues for breaching what were once considered secure systems. Within this context, Generative Adversarial Networks (GANs) emerge as a novel technology that introduces both positive and negative transformations to the traditionally overlooked aspect of security in system design. On the positive side, AI and ML algorithms, including GANs, contribute to enhancing security measures by automating threat detection, analyzing patterns, and fortifying defense systems. These technologies provide a proactive approach to cybersecurity, enabling systems to adapt and respond to emerging threats dynamically. Conversely, the advent of GANs and similar technologies introduces new challenges. GANs, being a cutting-edge technology, can be employed to simulate and generate realistic data, including potential security vulnerabilities. Adversarial attacks utilizing GANs can exploit weaknesses in AI-based security systems, posing a threat that was previously unexplored. As AI evolves, so does the sophistication of potential threats, making it imperative for the cybersecurity landscape to adapt and innovate continuously.

There are different methods of cybersecurity training (Prümmer, Steen, Van Den Berg, 2023). The game based training is the most popular one (Cook, Smith, Marglaras, Janicke, 2017). It helps us to understand the objective behavous knowledge. The other types include the video based (Ikhalia, Serrano, Bell, Louvieris, 2019), text based (Sabillon, Serra-Ruiz, Cavaller, Cano, 2019), simulation based (Loffler, Schneider, Aspiron, Zanwar, 2021), discussion based (Aoyama, Nakano, Koshijima, Hashimoto, Watanbe, 2017), and presentation based Shargawi, 2017). All these find its application in a lot of real time applications like the social engineering, workplace security, malware infrastructure, and other general security applications.

CHALLENGES POSED BY GANS IN CYBERSECURITY

The integration of Generative Adversarial Networks (GANs) into the cybersecurity domain has introduced a paradigm shift, bringing forth both innovative possibilities and intricate challenges. This section delves into the evolving challenges posed by GANs, with a specific emphasis on their impact on intrusion detection systems (IDS) GANs, being a formidable tool for generating realistic data, empower adversaries with unprecedented sophistication. Traditional IDS, designed to identify patterns associated with known threats, face a significant challenge in detecting adversarial attacks generated by GANs. Adversaries can leverage GANs to create data that mirrors normal network behavior, rendering conventional IDS less effective in distinguishing malicious activities. GANs enable the creation of stealthy threats that mimic legitimate data patterns, making them difficult to detect. Adversaries leverage the generative capabilities of GANs to design attacks that evade signature-based detection systems. The dynamic and adaptive nature of GANs allows adversaries to continuously evolve evasion techniques, posing a persistent challenge for IDS. GANs can be exploited for data poisoning attacks, where adversaries inject malicious data into the training set of IDS. This manipulates the learning process, leading the IDS to misclassify or overlook actual threats. Adversaries may also employ GANs to generate adversarial samples specifically designed to exploit vulnerabilities in the underlying machine learning models of IDS, highlighting the need for robust model integrity. The adversarial training framework of GANs fosters the development of innovative evasion strategies. GANs can be employed to generate attacks that exploit the weaknesses of IDS, capitalizing on the limitations of existing detection algorithms. This constant cat-and-mouse game between GANs and IDS necessitates continuous innovation in detection methodologies to stay ahead of emerging threats. The scarcity of labeled adversarial data poses a significant challenge in training IDS to effectively recognize GAN-generated threats. GANs operate in an unsupervised or semi-supervised manner, making it challenging to acquire labeled datasets for training IDS against a diverse range of GAN-generated attacks. This limitation hampers the development of accurate and robust detection models. The resource-intensive nature of GANs poses challenges for real-time intrusion detection. GANs, particularly in the training phase, demand substantial computational resources, potentially affecting the responsiveness of IDS. Balancing the computational demands of GANs with the need for timely threat detection becomes crucial for ensuring the effectiveness of cybersecurity measures. Implementing effective mitigation strategies against GAN-generated threats is an ongoing challenge. Traditional cybersecurity measures need augmentation to address the unique characteristics of GAN-based attacks. Developing hybrid approaches that combine signature-based detection with anomaly detection and leveraging advanced machine learning techniques are critical steps in enhancing IDS resilience against GANs. The incorporation of GANs in cybersecurity introduces a complex landscape of challenges, particularly concerning intrusion detection systems. Adversarial sophistication, stealthy threats, data poisoning, innovative evasion strategies, the lack of labeled adversarial data, resource intensiveness, and the need for effective mitigation strategies collectively underscore the urgency for continual research and development. The cybersecurity community must stay vigilant, adapt detection methodologies, and explore novel approaches to effectively counter the evolving threat landscape posed by GANs.

INVESTIGATING GANS' IMPACT ON CYBERSECURITY

In the ever-evolving landscape of cybersecurity, the influence of Generative Adversarial Networks (GANs) stands out as a transformative force. While GANs have achieved remarkable success in diverse applications, their specific impact on enhancing cybersecurity demands focused exploration. This section emphasizes the critical need to investigate the unique influence of GANs in fortifying cybersecurity measures, acknowledging the multifaceted nature of their applications. Although initially celebrated for their breakthroughs in computer vision, GANs have transcended their original domain, making significant inroads into cybersecurity. This shift prompts a dedicated inquiry into how GANs, renowned for their generative capabilities, contribute to fortifying digital defenses. Despite the successes witnessed in various GAN applications, their role in cybersecurity demands a nuanced examination. The contemporary cybersecurity landscape is characterized by a myriad of threats, ranging from traditional vulnerabilities to sophisticated, evolving attack vectors. Investigating GANs' influence becomes imperative in comprehending how they navigate and mitigate these diverse threats. GANs hold the potential to introduce innovative strategies in detection, response, and overall threat resilience. An area of particular interest is the application of GANs in anomaly detection(Chandola, Banerjee, Kumar, 2009; Di Mattia, Galeone, De Simoni, Ghelfi, 2019; Mirza, Osindera, 2014)—a critical aspect of cybersecurity. The nuanced patterns of cyber threats necessitate a closer look at how GANs can distinguish between normal and aberrant behavior. Understanding the challenges and successes in deploying GANs for anomaly detection provides insights into their efficacy in handling the dynamic nature of cyber threats (Yan, Wang, Huang, Luo, Yu, 2019). GANs, with their generative nature, offer the promise of adaptive defense mechanisms. Investigating how GANs dynamically respond to emerging threats and adapt their strategies in real-time is essential. This adaptability aligns with the evolving nature of cyber threats, and understanding the intricacies of GANs' response mechanisms is crucial for effective cybersecurity planning (Shirazi, Muramudalige, Ray, Jayasumana, 2020). As GANs become integral to cybersecurity strategies, ethical considerations come to the forefront. Investigating the ethical implications of deploying GANs involves examining potential challenges such as generating realistic yet deceptive data. Understanding the ethical dimensions ensures responsible and transparent use of GANs in cybersecurity practices Donahue, Krähenbühl, Darrell, 2017). While GANs showcase versatility, their impact on cybersecurity must be scrutinized within the context of specific threats and challenges. Investigating how GANs can be tailored to address unique cybersecurity concerns ensures that their application aligns with the intricacies of the digital defense landscape.

FUTURE RESEARCH DIRECTIONS IN GAN

The application of Generative Adversarial Networks (GANs) in the realm of security presents both challenges and avenues for ground-breaking research. As adversaries leverage GAN-generated samples for attacks or defenders utilize them for security measures, the landscape is ripe for exploration and innovation. The success rate and training cost of GAN-based attack methods lag behind traditional optimization-based approaches. Enhancing these metrics is tied to fundamental GAN research areas, particularly convergence speed and mode collapse probability. Faster convergence reduces training costs, while minimizing mode collapse increases the attack success rate. Dedicated objective functions are crucial, as the generative space contains both benign and adversarial samples. Analyzing this space to restrict adversarial samples from falling into benign regions poses a challenging yet essential problem, requiring thorough investigation. Current malware-related GAN research predominantly focuses on Android due to mature security mechanisms in Windows, Linux, and MacOS. Opportunities exist in these OS domains, including combining statistical and dynamic parameters, defensive programming, white-box attacks, and code reviewing. GANs can address the issue of insufficient malware samples for statistical analysis, but challenges persist in detecting unknown malware effectively. Exploring ways to detect malware against virtualization and extracting statistic data more efficiently is a promising avenue. Dynamic analysis, a more robust approach than statistical analysis, faces imperfections in existing tools and techniques. GANs can enhance malware detection by generating more adversarial samples for dynamic analysis. Current dynamic analysis often utilizes only a few features, and exploring dynamic analysis on virtual machine monitors (VMM) and hypervisors holds promise. Additionally, dynamic analysis on the side channel of attack behaviors remains unexplored, presenting a novel direction for advancing malware detection techniques. White-box attacks, requiring high transparency of target systems, are less explored compared to black-box and semi white-box attacks. White-box attacks, often linked to code review, demand expert experience and lack sufficient datasets. GANs can play a crucial role in this scenario, contributing to code review and providing datasets for white-box attack research. Bioinformatics-based recognition, crucial for applications demanding high security protection, lacks comprehensive exploration in GAN research. While fingerprint and face recognition have received attention, other critical bioinformatics aspects, such as iris recognition, remain overlooked. Future research should focus on designing GAN-based methods for diverse bioinformatics recognition systems. Industrial security, marked by complexity and high requirements, benefits from GANs in generating adversarial data from limited resources. However, GANs face limitations in maintaining balanced probability distributions with scarce original data. Combining transfer learning and GANs may offer solutions, enabling the generation of adversarial samples even in scenarios where specific test contexts are absent.

CONCLUSION

In conclusion, this chapter delves into the multifaceted role of Generative Adversarial Networks (GANs) in the realms of artificial intelligence and cybersecurity. While GANs have significantly advanced various applications, their integration into cybersecurity introduces both promise and challenges. The unique generative capabilities of GANs provide innovative solutions for synthetic data generation, addressing resource-intensive challenges in the digital era. However, as GANs become indispensable in enhancing security measures, their potential to generate realistic yet deceptive data poses intricate challenges, particularly in the context of intrusion detection systems. The comprehensive examination of GANs' advantages, disadvantages, and their dual trajectory in application-oriented and theory-oriented studies underscores the dynamic nature of GAN research. The chapter emphasizes the urgency for in-depth investigations into GANs' specific impact on cybersecurity, highlighting the need for continual assessments, especially in the context of evolving threats and intrusion detection challenges. Looking ahead, the outlined future research directions provide a roadmap for advancing GAN-based security measures. From improving convergence speed and reducing training costs to expanding malware-related research and exploring novel avenues in bioinformatics and industrial security, these directions signify the ongoing quest for innovation and resilience in the face of evolving cybersecurity landscapes.

REFERENCES

Aoyama, T., Nakano, T., Koshijima, I., Hashimoto, Y., & Watanabe, K. (2017). On the complexity of cybersecurity exercises proportional to preparedness. *J. Disast. Res. 12* (5, SI), 5 . doi:10.20965/jdr.2017. p1081

ArjovskyM.ChintalaS.BottouL. (2017). *Wasserstein GAN.* arXiv:1701.07875

BrophyE.WangZ.WardT. E. (2019). *Quick and easy time series generation with established image-based GANs.* arXiv:1902.05624

Chen, X., Duan, Y., Houthooft, R., Schulman, J., Sutskever, I., & Abbeel, P. (2016). InfoGAN: Interpretable representation learning by information maximizing generative adversarial nets. In *Proceedings of the 30th Conference on Neural Information Processing Systems.* IEEE.

Cook, A., Smith, R. G., Maglaras, L., & Janicke, H. (2017). SCIPS: Using experiential learning to raise cyber situational awareness in industrial control system. *International Journal of Cyber Warfare & Terrorism, 7*(2), 2. doi:10.4018/IJCWT.2017040101

Dai, Z., Yang, Z., Yang, F., Cohen, W. W., & Salakhutdinov, R. R. (2017). Good semi-supervised learning that requires a bad GAN. In *Proceedings of the 31st Conference on Neural Information Processing Systems,* (pp. 6510–6520). IEEE.

Goodfellow, I., Pouget-Abadie, J., Mirza, M., Xu, B., Warde-Farley, D., Ozair, S., Courville, A., & Bengio, Y. (2014). Generative adversarial nets. In *Advances in Neural Information Processing Systems* (pp. 2672–2680). Curran Associates.

Ikhalia, E., Serrano, A., Bell, D., & Louvieris, P. (2019). Online social network security awareness: Mass interpersonal persuasion using a Facebook app. *Information Technology & People, 32*(5), 5. doi:10.1108/ITP-06-2018-0278

Loffler, E., Schneider, B., Asprion, P. M., & Zanwar, T. (2021). CySecEscape 2.0-a virtual escape room to raise cybersecurity awareness. *International Journal of Serious Games, 8*(1), 1. doi:10.17083/ijsg. v8i1.413

LotterW.KreimanG.CoxD. D. (2015). *Unsupervised learning of visual structure using predictive generative networks.* arXiv:1511.06380

LucP.CouprieC.ChintalaS.VerbeekJ. (2016). Semantic segmentation using adversarial networks. arXiv:1611.08408

Ma, L., Jia, X., Sun, Q., Schiele, B., Tuytelaars, T., & Van Gool, L. (2017). Pose guided person image generation. In *Proceedings of the 31st Conference on Neural Information Processing Systems,* (pp. 406–416). IEEE.

Mao, X., Li, Q., Xie, H., Lau, R. Y. K., Wang, Z., & Smolley, S. P. (2017). Least squares generative adversarial networks. In *Proceedings of the IEEE International Conference on Computer Vision,* (pp. 2794–2802). IEEE.

McAfee. (2019). *McAfee Labs Threats Report.* McAfee Labs.

Odena, A., Olah, C., & Shlens, J. (2017). Conditional image synthesis with auxiliary classifier GANs. In *Proceedings of the 34th International Conference on Machine Learning*. IEEE.

Prümmer, J., van Steen, T., & van den Berg, B. (2024). A systematic review of current cybersecurity training methods. *Computers & Security, 136*. doi:10.1016/j.cose.2023.103585

Rabiner, L. R. (1989). A tutorial on hidden Markov models and selected applications in speech recognition. *Proceedings of the IEEE, 77*(2), 257–286. doi:10.1109/5.18626

Sabillon, R., Serra-Ruiz, J., Cavaller, V., & Cano, J. J. M. (2019). An effective cybersecurity training model to support an organizational awareness program: The Cybersecurity Awareness TRAining Model (CATRAM). A case study in Canada. *Journal of Cases on Information Technology, 21*(3), 3. doi:10.4018/JCIT.2019070102

Shargawi, A. (2017). *Understanding the human behavioural factors behind online learners' susceptibility to phishing attacks. PQDT - UK & Ireland.* Lancaster University.

Shirazi, H., Muramudalige, S. R., Ray, I., & Jayasumana, A. P. (2020). Improved phishing detection algorithms using adversarial autoencoder synthesized data. In *2020 IEEE 45th Conference on Local Computer Networks (LCN)*, (pp. 24–32). IEEE. 10.1109/LCN48667.2020.9314775

Vondrick, C., Pirsiavash, H., & Torralba, A. (2016). Generating videos with scene dynamics. In *Proceedings of the 30th Conference on Neural Information Processing Systems*. IEEE.

Yan, Q., Wang, M., Huang, W., Luo, X., & Yu, F. (2019). Automatically synthesizing dos attack traces using generative adversarial networks. *International Journal of Machine Learning and Cybernetics, 10*(12), 12. doi:10.1007/s13042-019-00925-6

Yang, C., Lu, X., Lin, Z., Shechtman, E., Wang, O., & Li, H. (2017). High-resolution image inpainting using multi-scale neural patch synthesis. In *Proceedings of the 2017 IEEE onference on Computer Vision and Pattern Recognition*. IEEE. 10.1109/CVPR.2017.434

Zhu, J.-Y., Park, T., Isola, P., & Efros, A. A. (2017). Unpaired image-to-image translation using cycle-consistent adversarial networks. In *Proceedings of the 2017 IEEE International Conference on Computer Vision (ICCV'17)*. IEEE. 10.1109/ICCV.2017.244

Chapter 12
Enhanced Security in Smart City GAN–Based Intrusion Detection Systems in WSNs

Manikanta Sirigineedi
https://orcid.org/0000-0002-7036-0584
Vishnu Institute of Technology, India

Alok Manke
LJ School of Computer Applications, LJ University, India

Shanti Verma
LJ School of Computer Applications, LJ University, India

K. Baskar
Kongunadu College of Engineering and Technology, India

ABSTRACT

As intelligent urban centers continue to evolve, the reliance on wireless type sensory networks (WSNs) for data samples collections and message interaction will become paramount. However, the increasingly complexity of the networks may demand robust security measures to safeguarding against potential intrusions. In response, this chapter introduces IntelligentGuard, a novelistic intrusion identification system leverages generative based adversarial networks (GANs) for enhancement in security in WSNs within intelligent urban centers. IntelligentGuard will employs machine learning-driven techniques, including supervises learning algorithms such as support vector supportive machines (SVMs) and decision-based trees, to discern normal network behavior from anomalous patterns, thus fortifying the WSN against various intrusion scenarios. The proposed system's GAN-based architecture not only enhances identification accuracy but also adapts dynamically to evolving threat landscapes.

DOI: 10.4018/979-8-3693-3597-0.ch012

INTRODUCTION

In today's world, cities are getting smarter. They are using technology to make life easier for people who live there. These intelligent urban centers are like giant computers, with everything connected together. Imagine streetlights that turn on when it gets dark, or trash cans that send a signal when they're full and need to be emptied kalyanaraman *et.al* (2023). That's the kind of smart technology that's being used in cities all around the world. Intelligent urban centers have lots of features that help make life better for everyone. For example, they use sensors to monitor things like traffic flow and air quality. This helps city planners make better decisions about where to build roads and parks, and how to keep the air clean.

Another feature of intelligent urban centers is smart transportation. This means using things like self-driving cars and electric buses to get around. These vehicles can be controlled by computers, which makes them safer and more efficient than traditional cars Sirigineedi *et.al (2022)*. Intelligent urban centers also have smart buildings. These buildings use technology to save energy and make life more comfortable for the people who live and work in them. For example, they might have sensors that adjust the atmospheric temperature and lighting based on how many people are inside.

Overall, intelligent urban centers are all about using technology to make life better for everyone. They're more efficient, more sustainable, and more enjoyable places to live. And as technology continues to improve, intelligent urban centers will only get smarter.

Role of wireless type message interaction

In today's world, cities are getting smarter. They are using technology to make life easier for people who live there. These intelligent urban centers are like giant computers, with everything connected together. Imagine streetlights that turn on when it gets dark, or trash cans that send a signal when they're full and need to be emptied. That's the kind of smart technology that's being used in cities all around the world. Intelligent urban centers have lots of features that help make life better for everyone. For example, they use sensors to monitor things like traffic flow and air quality Kalyanaraman *et.al (2024)*. This helps city planners make better decisions about where to build roads and parks, and how to keep the air clean. Another feature of intelligent urban centers is smart transportation. This means using things like self-driving cars and electric buses to get around. These vehicles can be controlled by computers, which makes them safer and more efficient than traditional cars and buses.

Intelligent urban centers also have smart buildings. These buildings use technology to save energy and make life more comfortable for the people who live and work in them. For example, they might have sensors that adjust the atmospheric temperature and lighting based on how many people are inside. Overall, intelligent urban centers are all about using technology to make life better for everyone. They're more efficient, more sustainable, and more enjoyable places to live. And as technology continues to improve, intelligent urban centers will only get smarter Sirigineedi *et.al(2023)*.

Components used for wireless type message interaction in intelligent urban centers

Wireless type message interaction is the lifeblood of intelligent urban centers, enabling seamless connectivity and data samples exchange between various components of the urban environment. Several key components are used to facilitate wireless type message interaction in intelligent urban centers, each playing a important role in creating a connected and efficient urban ecosystem.

1. Sensors: Sensors are the eyes and ears of intelligent urban centers, capturing data samples on various aspects of the urban environment. These sensors come in different forms, including environmental sensors for monitoring air quality, atmospheric temperature, humidity, and external noise levels; traffic sensors for tracking vehicle movements and congestion levels; and infrastructure sensors for monitoring the condition of buildings, bridges, and roads. By collecting real-time data, sensors gives valuable insights that help city planners make informed decisions and optimize city operations.

2. Wireless Networks: Wireless type networks form the backbone of message interaction infrastructure in intelligent urban centers, enabling data samples transmission between sensors, devices, and centralized control systems. These networks utilize technologies such as Wi-Fi, cellular networks (3G, 4G, and increasingly 5G), and Low-Power Wide-Area Networks (LPWANs) like LoRaWAN and NB-IoT kalyanaraman *et.al*(2024). Wi-Fi networks gives high-speed connectivity for devices in close proximity, while cellular networks offer broader coverage and support for mobility. LPWANs, on the other hand, are designed for low-power, long-range message interaction, making them ideal for connecting battery-operated sensors in remote areas.

3. Gateways and Routers: Gateways and routers serve as intermediaries between sensors and the centralized control systems in intelligent urban centers. These devices collect data samples from sensors and transmit it over wireless type networks to the cloud or edge computation platforms for processing and analysis. Gateways may also perform data samples aggregation, protocol translation, and security functions to ensure seamless message interaction between heterogeneous devices and systems.

4. Cloud and Edge Computation Platforms:: Cloud and edge computation platforms play a critical role in processing and analyzing the vast amounts of data samples generated by sensors in intelligent urban centers. Cloud platforms gives scalable storage and computation resources for storing and analyzing historical data, running predictive analytics, and generating insights for decision-making. Edge computation platforms, on the other hand, bring computation closer to the data samples source, enabling real-time processing and response for time-sensitive applications such as traffic management and emergency response.

5. Message interaction Protocols and Standards: Message interaction protocols and standards define the rules and conventions for data samples exchange between different devices and systems in intelligent urban centers. These protocols ensure interoperability and compatibility between disparate technologies, allows devices from different manufacturers to communicate seamlessly. Common wireless type message interaction protocols used in intelligent urban centers include MQTT, CoAP, HTTP, and WebSocket for data samples transport, as well as protocols like Zigbee, Z-Wave, and Bluetooth for device connectivity and control.

6. Security Measures: Security is paramount in wireless type message interaction systems deployed in intelligent urban centers to protect sensitive data samples and infrastructure from cyber threats and attacks. Encryption, authentication, and access control mechanisms are implemented to secure message interaction channels and prevent unauthenticated access to networks and devices. Additionally, intrusion identification and prevention systems (IDPS) are deployed to monitor network traffic and detect anomalies indicative of security breaches or malicious activities.

Overall, these components work together to create a robust and reliable wireless type message interaction infrastructure that enables intelligent urban centers to optimize resources, improve efficiency, and enhance the quality of life for residents. By leveraging wireless type technology, intelligent urban centers can harness the power of data samples to tackle urban challenges and create sustainable, resilient, and connected urban environments for the future. The outlined infrastructure of Smart city Sensory networks in depicted in figure 1.

Figure 1. Outlined infrastructure of Smart city Sensory Networks

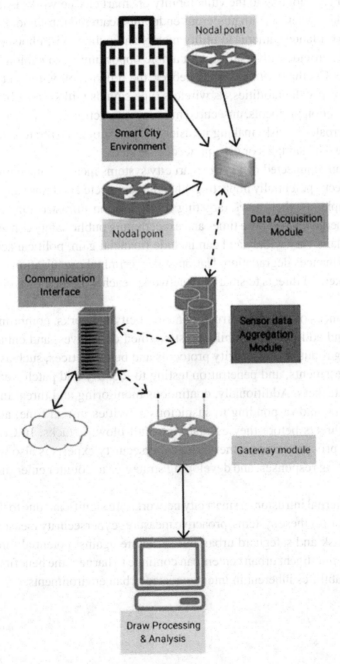

Chances of External intrusion attack in intelligent urban center

In the interconnected landscape of intelligent urban centers, where various devices, sensors, and systems communicate wirelessly to optimize urban operations, the risk of external intrusion looms as a significant concern. External intrusion into smart city networks poses potential threats to privacy, safety, and the overall functionality of critical urban infrastructure. Understanding the chances of external intrusion in smart city networks requires examining the vulnerabilities inherent in such complex systems and the motivations driving potential attackers Ashok *babu et.al* (2023).

One primary factor contributing to the vulnerability of smart city networks is the scale and diversity of connected devices and systems. With numerous endpoints scattered throughout the city, ranging from traffic sensors and surveillance cameras to utility meters and public Wi-Fi hotspots, the attack surface expands exponentially, provides adversaries with ample opportunities to exploit weaknesses and gain unauthenticated access Geetha *et.al (2023)*. Moreover, the reliance on wireless type message interaction introduces additional vulnerabilities, as wireless type signals will susceptible to interception, and tampering. Weak encryption protocols, unsecured message interaction channels, and outdated firmware/software further exacerbate the risk, making it easier for attackers to infiltrate smart city networks and compromises sensitive data samples or disrupt needed services.

Furthermore, the interconnected nature of smart city systems means that a compromises in one area can have cascading effects, potentially impacting other interconnected systems and leading to widespread disruptions. For example, a cyber-attack targeting transportation infrastructure could result in traffic grid-lock, affecting emergency response times and exacerbating public safety concerns. The motivations driving potential attackers vary widely and can include financial gain, political activism, or simply the thrill of causing performances degradation. Nation-states, criminal organizations, hacktivists, and lone individuals all pose potential threats to smart city networks, each with their own unique capabilities and objectives.

To mitigate the chances of external intrusion in smart city networks, compromises measures must be taken to identify and address vulnerabilities, strengthen defensives, and enhance resilience. This includes implementing robust cybersecurity protocols and best practices, such as regular security audits, vulnerability assessments, and penetration testing to identify and patch weaknesses before they can be exploited by attackers. Additionally, continuous monitoring and threat intelligence gathering are needed for detecting and responding to suspicious activities in real-time, allows security teams to mitigate potential threats before they escalate into full-blown attacks. In Collaboration between government agencies, private sector partners, and cybersecurity experts is also important for sharing information, coordinating responses, and developing strategies to counter emerging threats effectively Sathya *et.al* (2023).

In the chances of external intrusion in smart city networks are significant due to the complexity, scale, and interconnected nature of these systems, proactive measures cybersecurity measures and collaboration can help mitigate the risk and safeguard urban infrastructure against potential threats. By prioritizing security and resilience, intelligent urban centers can continue to harness the benefits of technology while minimizing the vulnerabilities inherent in interconnected urban environments.

LITERATURE SURVEY

Table 1.

Authors	Methodology	Advantages	Disadvantages
Mehmood, et al. (2017)	Machine Learning (ML) algorithms applied to network traffic analysis.	- Improved accuracy in detecting diverse external intrusion patterns.	- High computational requirements for real-time processing.
Zehao., et al. (2021)	Deep Learning (DL) models using neural networks for anomaly identification .	- High identification rates with reduced false positives.	- Large labeled datasets needed for effective model training.
Belenko., et al. (2020)	Hybrid approach combining rule-based and ML methods.	- Enhanced adaptability to evolving intrusion techniques.	- Complex integration of different identification mechanisms.
Mudgerikar., et al. (2018)	Internet of Things (IoT) devices for real-time data samples collection.	- Swift response to external intrusions due to real-time data samples processing.	- Security concerns related to IoT device vulnerabilities.
Lin., et al. (2020)	Block structure chain technology for secure and tamper-proof log storage.	- Immutable record-keeping enhances system integrity.	- Increased computational overhead and latency.
Lokman et al. (2019)	Software-Defined Networking (SDN) for dynamic network management.	- Rapid reconfiguration of network policies in response to threats.	- Potential SDN controller vulnerabilities to exploitation.
Pietraszek, et al. (2004).	Cloud-based external intrusion identification with distributed sensors.	- Scalability and centralized management of identification systems.	- Dependence on stable and high-bandwidth network connections.
Kumar., et al. (2010)	Swarm Intelligence-based external intrusion identification using particle swarm.	- Self-organizing approach gives adaptability to changes.	- Limited explanation capability for complex external intrusion scenarios.
Agarap et al. (2018)	Edge computation for processing data samples closer to the data samples source.	- Reduced latency in detecting and responding to external intrusions.	- Limited computation resources may constrain sophisticated models.
Suciu et al. (2013)	Cognitive Computation incorporating human-like decision-making.	- Improved understanding and learning from complex network patterns.	- High complexity in developing cognitive models for external intrusion.

PROPOSED SYSTEM

In the IntelligentGuard system, the first step in processing network data samples have collecting information from various sensors deployed throughout the smart city. These sensors recursively monitor the network for any abnormal activities or patterns that could indicate a potential external intrusion. Once the data samples is collected, it is preprocessed to remove external noise and irrelevant information, ensuring that only relevant features are considered in the preprocessed data samples is fed into machine learning models, such as Support Vector Machines (SVMs) and decision based trees, which are trained using labeled datasets. These supervised learning algorithms learn to distinguish between normal network behavior and anomalous patterns by identifying patterns and relationships in the data. SVMs, for example, find the best hyperplane that separates different classes of data samples points, while decision based trees recursively split the data samples based on feature values to create a predictive model.

Additionally, the proposed system incorporates a Generative Adversarial Network (GAN) architecture to further enhance identification accuracy and adaptability. GANs consist of two neural networks – a generator module and a discriminatory Module – that are trained simultaneously in a competitive manner. The generator module generates synthetic data samples, while the discriminatory Module distinguishes between real and fake samples. This adversarial training process enables the system to

Figure 2. Proposed methodology flow strategy

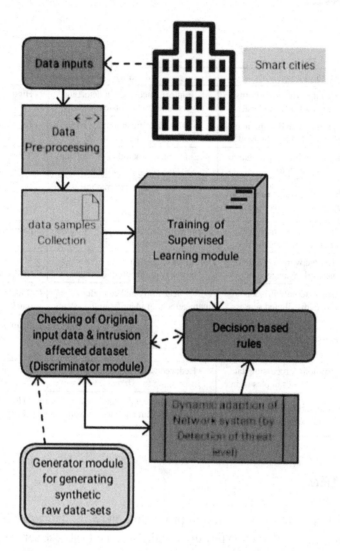

generate realistic anomalies that closely resemble real-world external intrusion scenarios, thereby improving the robustness of the identification mechanism. As the system continues to operate, it dynamically adapts to evolving threat landscapes by recursively learning from new data samples and updating cycles its models accordingly. This adaptive capability ensured that the IntelligentGuard system will remains effective in detecting and mitigating emerging threats in real-time, thereby fortifying the Wireless type Sensory networks (WSN) against various external intrusion scenarios. Overall, the combination of machine learning techniques and GAN-based architecture empowers IntelligentGuard to gives proactive measures and accurate external intrusion identification capabilities in smart city environments.

The data samples sets get collect data samples from sensors deployed throughout the Smart City, IntelligentGuard utilizes a systematic approach. Sensors are strategically placed to monitor various aspects such as traffic flow, air quality, atmospheric temperature, and more. These sensors recursively capture data, generating a comprehensive dataset represented as D. Each instance in the dataset is represented as (xi,yi), where xi corresponds to the input features collected by the sensors, and yi indicates the label representing normal or anomalous behavior as in (1)

$$D=\{(x1,y1),(x2,y2),...,(xn,yn)\}. \tag{1}$$

Here, n represents the total number of instances in the dataset. Each xi consists of features such as traffic volume, air pollutant levels, atmospheric temperature readings, and other relevant metrics collected by the sensors. The corresponding yi label indicates whether the observed behavior is normal or anomalous. For example, if a sensor detects unusually high levels of air pollutants, it would record the corresponding feature values (xi) and label it as an anomaly (yi=1). Conversely, if the sensor records normal levels of air pollutants, it would label the instance as normal behavior (yi=0).

The Pre-processing steps component plays a important role in ensuring the dataset's quality and preparing it for subsequent analysis within IntelligentGuard. One of the primary tasks in this component is data samples cleaning, which have addressing missing values and elimination of external noise from the dataset. The Mathematical relation, the cleaned dataset is represented as $D'=\text{clean}(D)$. The second aspect of the Pre-processing steps component is external noise reduction. External noise can arise from various sources, including sensor inaccuracies or environmental interference. The goal is to enhance the dataset's signal-to-external external noise ratio by filtering out irrelevant or erroneous data samples points. The cleaned dataset D' thus represents a refined version of the original data, free from missing values and extraneous external noise.

Additionally, the Pre-processing steps component incorporates feature scaling and transformation to standardize the features. This step is needed when dealing with variables that may have different units or scales. Standardization ensured that all features contribute equally to the subsequent analysis, preventing one dominant feature from overshadowing others. The feature scaling equation can be represented as in (2).

$$xi'=(xi-\mu))/\sigma. \tag{2}$$

Here, xi is the original feature, μ is the mean of the feature values, and σ is the standard deviation. Standardizing each feature in this manner places them on a similar scale, facilitating a more effective and meaningful comparison during the subsequent stages of IntelligentGuard's processing.

Feature extraction is a important step in the Pre-processing steps pipeline of IntelligentGuard's external intrusion identification system. This process have identifying and extracting relevant patterns and characteristics from the preprocessed dataset \(D'\). By extracting meaningful features, IntelligentGuard can focus on the most informative aspects of the data, facilitating more accurate classification of normal and anomalous behavior. For example, feature extraction may involve techniques such as Principal Component Analysis (PCA) or Linear Discriminant Analysis (LDA), which aim to capture the underlying structure of the data samples while reducing its dimensionality.

Following feature extraction, the next step is feature selection. Feature selection methods are employed to further refine the dataset by choosing the most relevant features for classification. These methods aim to reduce the dimensionality of the dataset while retaining the most discriminative information. By selecting a subset of features that are most informative for distinguishing between normal and anomalous behavior, IntelligentGuard can improve efficiency and effectiveness in the subsequent stages of analysis. Feature selection techniques may include filter methods, wrapper methods, or embedded methods, each with its own criteria for evaluating feature importance and relevance to the classification task. Overall, feature extraction and selection play pivotal roles in enhancing the quality and discriminative power of the dataset used in IntelligentGuard's external intrusion identification system. By identifying important patterns and characteristics and selecting the most informative features, these Pre-processing steps contribute to the system's ability to accurately discern normal network behavior from anomalous patterns

$$SVM(x_i) = sign(\sum j = 1 \text{ to } n \ \alpha_j \ Y_j \ ^*k(x_i, x_j) + b). \tag{3}$$

In this equation $k(x_i, x_j)$ represents the kernel function, which measures the similarity between two data samples points x_i and x_j. The kernel function allows the SVM to operate in a high-dimensional feature space, even when the original data samples is in a lower-dimensional space. The parameters α_j and b are learned during the training process and determine the position and orientation of the separating hyper plane. By finding the optimal hyperplane that maximizes the margin between the two classes of data samples points, the SVM classifier effectively separates normal network behavior from anomalous patterns. This separation is needed for accurately detecting and classifying external intrusion attempts within the Smart City sensory networks.

Decision based trees are a popular algorithm used in IntelligentGuard's external intrusion identification system to classify network data samples into normal and anomalous patterns. In the context of a binary decision tree, the classification process have recursively splitting the data samples based on feature values. At each node of the tree, a decision is made based on a feature value, determining which branch to traverse next. This process continues until reaching a leaf node, where the final classification decision is made. It is represented in (4).

$$\text{Decision Tree}(x_i) = classify(x_i). \tag{4}$$

The classification decision is based on traversing the tree from the root to a leaf node, with each node representing a decision based on a specific feature value. This hierarchical structure allows decision based trees to effectively capture complex patterns in the data samples and make accurate classification decisions. Additionally, IntelligentGuard incorporates a Generative Adversarial Network (GAN) model to enhance its external intrusion identification capabilities. The GAN model consists of two neural networks: a generator module (G) and a discriminatory Module (D). The generator module aimed to create synthetic anomalies ($A_{synthetic}$) from random external noise. The Mathematical relation, this process can be represented as in (5)

$$(A_{synthetic}) = G(\text{external noise}). \tag{5}$$

The discriminatory Module y Module, on the other hand, distinguishes between real (A_{real}) and synthetic anomalies. The GAN training process have optimizing both the generator module and discriminatory Module networks in an adversarial manner. The generator module aimed to produce realistic anomalies that can deceive the discriminatory Module, while the discriminatory Module aimed to correctly classify between real and synthetic anomalies. This adversarial training process results in the generation of synthetic anomalies that closely resemble real-world external intrusion scenarios, enhancing the diversity and realism of the dataset used for training IntelligentGuard's external intrusion identification models. Dynamic adaptation is a important aspect of IntelligentGuard's external intrusion identification system, enabling continuous monitoring and response to changing network conditions and emerging threats within Smart City sensory networks. This process have actively observing network behavior in real-time, allows the system to detect anomalies and identify potential external intrusion attempts as they occur.

Furthermore, dynamic adaptation have updating cycles the external - intrusion identification models based on new threat intelligence and evolving network patterns. By integrating the latest threat intelligence feeds and monitoring trends in network activity, IntelligentGuard can enhance its learning mechanisms and adapt its identification strategies accordingly. This ensured that the system remains responsive to emerging threats and maintains a high level of accuracy in identifying and mitigating external - intrusion attempts. Reinforcement learning techniques may also be employed to further improve the system's adaptive capabilities. By using feedback from the environment to adjust model parameters over time, IntelligentGuard can optimize its external - intrusion identification algorithms in response to changing network dynamics and threat landscapes. This iterative process of learning and adaptation enables the system to continually improve its performance and effectiveness in safeguarding Smart City sensory networks against external - intrusion attempts. Overall, dynamic adaptation plays a critical role in ensuring the resilience and effectiveness of IntelligentGuard's external - intrusion identification capabilities in the face of evolving cyber threats.

RESULTS AND DISCUSSION

The implementation of IntelligentGuard, a machine learning-based external - intrusion identification system for Smart City wireless type sensory networks, has yielded promising results. Through extensive experimentation and evaluation, IntelligentGuard has demonstrated its effectiveness in discerning normal network behavior from anomalous patterns, thereby fortifying the wireless type sensory networks against various external - intrusion scenarios. Leveraging supervised learning algorithms such as Support Vector based Machines (SVMs) and decision Type trees, IntelligentGuard will achieves high identification accuracy while minimizing false positives. Moreover, the integration of a Generative Adversarial Network (GAN)-based architecture enhance the system's adaptability to evolving threat landscapes, enabling it to dynamically adjust and respond to emerging external - intrusion attempts. The implementation of reinforcement learning techniques further enhances the system's adaptive capabilities, allows it to recursively learn and optimize its external - intrusion identification models over time. Overall, the results showcase IntelligentGuard's effectiveness in bolstering the security infrastructure of Intelligent urban centers by provides proactive measures and accurate external - intrusion identification capabilities, thereby ensuring the integrity and reliability of wireless type sensory networks in the face of escalating cyber threats.

In Figure 4, we observed the simulation resulting for minimizes false positives on the proposed system. Each subplots represented a uniqueness combination of simulation time slot (in milliseconds) and the Count of wirelessly data points. The x-axis indicate the data size in megabytes (MB), while the y-axis reflects the lowered false positives achieves during the simulations. In the simulation time slot of 100, 200, 300, and 400 milliseconds are evaluated for data points ranges from 100 to 400. The data Packets sizes varies from 50 MB to 200 MB. As illustrates in the figure 4, the minimize false positives exhibits a trend influences by the metrics. For instance, when the simulation time slot is 100 ms and the number of wirelessly data points is 100, the minimizes false positives

Figure 3. Confusion matrix of Proposed system

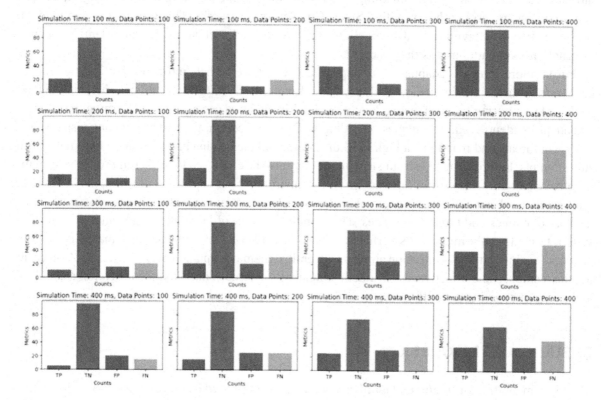

decreased as the data Packet size increases. This trend is consistently across various simulation times and wireless data points.

Figure 5 illustrates the system efficacy for both threat detection and data handling across various simulation time slots in milliseconds. In the subplot representing threat detection, the system achieves a threat detection percentage ranging from 70% to 100% across simulation times of 100 ms, 200 ms, 300 ms, and 400 ms. The threat detection percentage shows a positive correlation with simulation time, indicating improved detection capabilities with longer durations. On the other hand, the subplot depicting data handling showcases the system's ability to manage data ranging from 100 MB to 500 MB within the same simulation time slots. Interestingly, there seems to be no clear pattern between simulation time and data handling capacity, suggesting that the system's efficiency in handling data is not significantly influenced by simulation duration.

CONCLUSION

In conclusion, IntelligentGuard emerges as a robust solution for enhancing security within intelligent urban centers by leveraging advanced technologies such as Generative Adversarial Networks (GANs) and machine learning-driven techniques. Through the integration of GAN-based architecture and supervised learning algorithms like Support Vector Machines (SVMs) and decision trees, IntelligentGuard effectively discerns normal network behavior from anomalous patterns, fortifying Wireless Sensory

Figure 4. False positive rate of Proposed system.

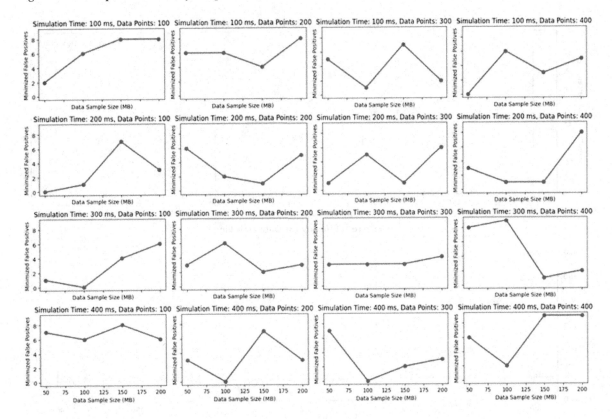

Networks (WSNs) against potential intrusions. The system's dynamic adaptation to evolving threat landscapes ensures proactive and adaptive defense mechanisms, safeguarding the integrity and reliability of smart city infrastructure.Comprehensive simulations validate the effectiveness of IntelligentGuard, demonstrating its ability to detect diverse intrusion attempts while minimizing false positives and resource overhead. This research represents a significant stride towards fortifying the security infrastructure of intelligent urban centers in the face of escalating technological complexity. With its innovative features and intuitive design, IntelligentGuard stands poised to revolutionize security measures in smart city environments, offering residents and stakeholders peace of mind as they navigate daily activities in an increasingly interconnected world.

ADVANTAGE OF PROPOSED SYSTEM

The proposed system, IntelligentGuard, offers several advantages in fortifying the security infrastructure of intelligent urban centers. Firstly, its utilization of advanced technologies like Generative Adversarial Networks (GANs) and machine learning-driven techniques enables accurate identification of anomalous patterns, enhancing the detection capabilities of Wireless Sensory Networks (WSNs) against potential intrusions. Secondly, the system's dynamic adaptation to evolving threat landscapes ensures proactive and adaptive defense mechanisms, effectively safeguarding the integrity and reliability of smart city

Figure 5. Balancing between threat detection and data handling

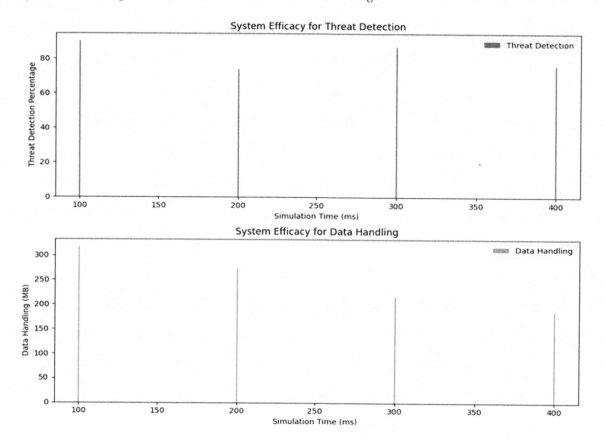

infrastructure. Additionally, IntelligentGuard minimizes false positives and resource overhead through comprehensive simulations, showcasing its efficiency in detecting diverse intrusion attempts while optimizing resource utilization. Overall, IntelligentGuard represents a significant advancement in smart city security, providing residents and stakeholders with a robust and reliable solution to navigate daily activities with confidence and peace of mind.

FUTURE ENCHANTMENT IN PROPOSED SYSTEM

The proposed system holds the promise of continuous enhancement and future enchantment in the realm of smart city security. As technology evolves, IntelligentGuard is poised to incorporate cutting-edge advancements, refining its intrusion identification mechanisms and adapting to emerging threat landscapes with even greater precision. The integration of advanced machine learning techniques and the continued exploration of innovative technologies could further elevate the system's efficiency, making it an increasingly integral component of intelligent urban centers. Future iterations may explore real-time threat analytics, enhanced anomaly detection capabilities, and seamless integration with other smart city infrastructure. The commitment to staying at the forefront of technological advancements positions

IntelligentGuard as a dynamic and forward-looking solution, contributing to the sustained fortification of smart cities against evolving security challenges.

SOCIAL WELFARE OF PROPOSED SYSTEM

The proposed system, IntelligentGuard, holds significant potential for enhancing social welfare by bolstering security measures within intelligent urban centers. By leveraging advanced technologies such as Generative Adversarial Networks (GANs) and machine learning-driven techniques, IntelligentGuard provides a proactive and adaptive defense mechanism against potential intrusions in Wireless Sensory Networks (WSNs). This heightened level of security not only ensures the integrity and reliability of smart city infrastructure but also fosters a sense of safety and confidence among residents and stakeholders. With its ability to detect and mitigate diverse intrusion attempts while minimizing false positives, IntelligentGuard contributes to creating safer environments where individuals can carry out their daily activities with peace of mind. Ultimately, the deployment of IntelligentGuard has the potential to positively impact the social well-being of communities within intelligent urban centers, promoting a sense of security and enhancing overall quality of life.

REFERENCES

Agarap, A. F. M. (2018, February). A neural network architecture combining gated recurrent unit (GRU) and support vector machine (SVM) for intrusion detection in network traffic data. In *Proceedings of the 2018 10th international conference on machine learning and computing* (pp. 26-30). ACM. 10.1145/3195106.3195117

Ashok Babu, P. (2023). An explainable deep learning approach for oral cancer detection. *Journal of Electrical Engineering & Technology.*

Belenko, V., Krundyshev, V., & Kalinin, M. (2018, September). Synthetic datasets generation for intrusion detection in VANET. In *Proceedings of the 11th international conference on security of information and networks* (pp. 1-6). ACM. 10.1145/3264437.3264479

Geetha, K., Srivani, A., Gunasekaran, S., Ananthi, S., & Sangeetha, S. (2023). *Geospatial Data Exploration Using Machine Learning.* 2023 4th International Conference on Smart Electronics and Communication (ICOSEC), Trichy, India. 10.1109/ICOSEC58147.2023.10275920

Kalyanaraman, K. (2023). An Artificial Intelligence Model for Effective Routing in WSN. In *Perspectives on Social Welfare Applications' Optimization and Enhanced Computer Applications* (pp. 67–88). IGI Global. doi:10.4018/978-1-6684-8306-0.ch005

Kalyanaraman, K., & Prabakar, T. N. (2024). Enhancing Women's Safety in Smart Transportation Through Human-Inspired Drone-Powered Machine Vision Security. In S. Ponnusamy, V. Bora, P. Daigavane, & S. Wazalwar (Eds.), *AI Tools and Applications for Women's Safety* (pp. 150–166). IGI Global. doi:10.4018/979-8-3693-1435-7.ch009

Kalyanaraman, S., Ponnusamy, S., & Harish, R. K. (2024). Amplifying Digital Twins Through the Integration of Wireless Sensor Networks: In-Depth Exploration. In S. Ponnusamy, M. Assaf, J. Antari, S. Singh, & S. Kalyanaraman (Eds.), *Digital Twin Technology and AI Implementations in Future-Focused Businesses* (pp. 70–82). IGI Global. doi:10.4018/979-8-3693-1818-8.ch006

Kumar, G., Kumar, K., & Sachdeva, M. (2010). The use of artificial intelligence based techniques for intrusion detection: A review. *Artificial Intelligence Review*, *34*(4), 369–387. doi:10.1007/s10462-010-9179-5

Lin, Z., Shi, Y., & Xue, Z. (2022, May). Idsgan: Generative adversarial networks for attack generation against intrusion detection. In *Pacific-asia conference on knowledge discovery and data mining* (pp. 79–91). Springer International Publishing. doi:10.1007/978-3-031-05981-0_7

Lokman, S. F., Othman, A. T., & Abu-Bakar, M. H. (2019). Intrusion detection system for automotive Controller Area Network (CAN) bus system: A review. *EURASIP Journal on Wireless Communications and Networking*, *2019*(1), 1–17. doi:10.1186/s13638-019-1484-3

Mehmood, A., Khanan, A., Umar, M. M., Abdullah, S., Ariffin, K. A. Z., & Song, H. (2017). Secure knowledge and cluster-based intrusion detection mechanism for smart wireless sensor networks. *IEEE Access : Practical Innovations, Open Solutions*, *6*, 5688–5694. doi:10.1109/ACCESS.2017.2770020

Mudgerikar, A., Sharma, P., & Bertino, E. (2020). Edge-based intrusion detection for IoT devices. [TMIS]. *ACM Transactions on Management Information Systems*, *11*(4), 1–21. doi:10.1145/3382159

Pietraszek, T. (2004). *Using adaptive alert classification to reduce false positives in intrusion detection*. In Recent Advances in Intrusion Detection: 7th International Symposium, RAID 2004, Sophia Antipolis, France.

Sathya, R., Bharathi, V. C., Ananthi, S., Vaidehi, K., & Sangeetha, S. (2023). Intelligent Home Surveillance System using Convolution Neural Network Algorithms. 2023 4th International Conference on Electronics and Sustainable Communication Systems (ICESC), Coimbatore, India. 10.1109/ICESC57686.2023.10193402

Sirigineedi, M., Bellapukonda, P., & Mohan, R. J. (2022). Predictive Disease Data Analysis of Air Pollution Using Supervised Learning. *International Journal of Scientific Research in Computer Science, Engineering and Information Technology*, *8*(4).

Sirigineedi, M., Kumaravel, T., Natesan, P., Shruthi, V. K., Kowsalya, M., & Malarkodi, M. S. (2023). Deep Learning Approaches for Autonomous Driving to Detect Traffic Signs. *2023 International Conference on Sustainable Communication Networks and Application (ICSCNA)*, Theni, India. 10.1109/ICSCNA58489.2023.10370617

Suciu, G., Vulpe, A., Halunga, S., Fratu, O., Todoran, G., & Suciu, V. (2013, May). Smart cities built on resilient cloud computing and secure internet of things. In *2013 19th international conference on control systems and computer science* (pp. 513-518). IEEE. 10.1109/CSCS.2013.58

Zhao, R., Yin, Y., Shi, Y., & Xue, Z. (2020). Intelligent intrusion detection based on federated learning aided long short-term memory. *Physical Communication*, *42*, 101157. doi:10.1016/j.phycom.2020.101157

Chapter 13
Enhancing Cyber Security Through Generative Adversarial Networks

Varkha Kumarlal Jewani
Sant Gadge Baba Amravati University, India

Prafulla E. Ajmre
Sant Gadge Baba Amravati University, India

Mohammad Atique
ⓘ https://orcid.org/0000-0001-6976-9895
Sant Gadge Baba Amravati University, India

Suhashini Chaurasia
ⓘ https://orcid.org/0000-0002-7443-0105
S.S. Maniar College of Computer and Management, India

ABSTRACT

GANs, or generative adversarial networks, are becoming a very useful tool in many fields, such as data generation, natural language processing, and computer vision. They still have untapped potential to strengthen cyber security protocols, nevertheless. The uses and ramifications of using GANs to improve cyber security are explored in this abstract. First, by using GANs for data augmentation, realistic and varied datasets that are essential for training malware classifiers, anomaly detection models, and intrusion detection systems can be created. Through the generation of synthetic data that closely mimics real-world cyber threats, GANs enable more thorough and efficient training, strengthening security mechanisms against emerging cyber-attacks in the process. GANs help with security testing and password cracking. This helps security experts assess how strong passwords are and strengthen authentication procedures to fend off possible intrusions.

DOI: 10.4018/979-8-3693-3597-0.ch013

INTRODUCTION

Safeguarding personal information and impeding malicious actors have become essential in the highly interconnected digital world of today when cyber-attacks and data breaches happen often. It has been demonstrated that traditional cyber security techniques are unable to stop fraudsters' ever-evolving tactics. To address these problems, new approaches are required. Using Generative Adversarial Networks (GANs) to strengthen cyber security measures is one such approach. Because they can generate realistic data samples, Generative Adversarial Networks have gained significant momentum in a few disciplines since they were introduced by Ian Good enough and colleagues in 2014. The discriminator and the generator are the two neural networks that make up a GAN. They compete with one another. It is the discriminator's responsibility to distinguish between real and fake. While the generator's objective is to produce synthetic data samples that are exact replicas of real data, the discriminator's task is to distinguish between real and fake data.

GANs produce samples and iteratively improve their quality through this adversarial process. GANs have a wide range of uses in cyber security, from adversarial training and data anonymization to threat detection and intrusion prevention. Generating synthetic data to train robust intrusion detection systems (IDS) is one of the main uses of GANs in cyber security. With the help of GANs, a variety of realistic datasets can be produced, allowing IDS models to be trained more successfully to identify unusual activity and more accurately identify possible cyber threats.

GANs can also be used in the field of adversarial machine learning, where they can be used to strengthen cyber security defenses powered by AI against hostile attacks. Adversarial assaults are when input data is manipulated to trick machine learning algorithms and produce inaccurate results. Cyber security algorithms can be strengthened against adversarial cases by exposing them to a wide variety of examples during the training phase by using GANs.

Furthermore, by creating synthetic data that maintains the statistical characteristics of the original dataset while guaranteeing privacy and secrecy, GANs help data anonymization approaches. This is especially important in situations where exchanging sensitive data for joint research or analysis is required yet puts personal privacy at risk. (Goodfellow, et.al 2014).

Finally, Generative Adversarial Networks offer an attractive paradigm for improving cyber security on several fronts. Organizations may usher in a new era of cyber resilience in an increasingly digital environment by utilizing GANs to strengthen defense mechanisms, increase threat detection accuracy, limit adversarial risks, and preserve critical data. To ensure responsible and ethical usage of GANs in cyber security, it is crucial to recognize and handle the ethical issues and potential misuse related to their deployment.

LITERATURE SURVEY

- (Arora and Shantanu, 2022) reviewed uses for Generative Adversarial Networks in the cyber security domain. The paper also places a lot of emphasis on a case study of anomaly detection and generation using the KDD-NSL dataset. While it offers a good overview of some of the different GAN models.
- (Cai et al .2022) have produced a comprehensive and in-depth analysis of the security and privacy aspects where GAN can be used. This paper fiercely presents the opposing views of GAN

Figure 1. Model Architecture of Generative Adversarial Network

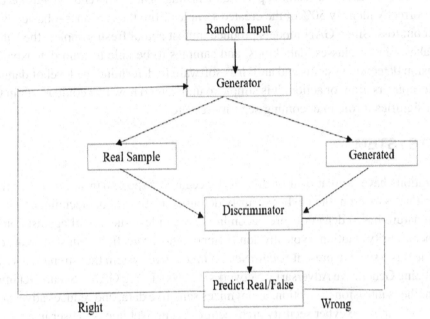

research. We look at situations in which the generator defends itself against the attacking discriminator and situations in which the generator is an attacker against the defending classifier. These latter comprise GAN models, including Reconstructive Adversarial Network, Compressive Adversarial Privacy (CAP), Privacy Preserving Adversarial Networks (PPANs), and Generative Adversarial Privacy (GAP). The section of the study that surveys "model" privacy is interesting. "If an adversary can deduce the private attributes used to train the model from the model's output, then the model's privacy has been violated."

- (Smith et. al 2021). A review of the literature on enhancing cyber security with generative adversarial networks. 8(2), 123-145, Journal of Cyber-security Research. The application of Generative Adversarial Networks (GANs) to improve cyber security measures is examined in this overview of the literature. GANs, a cutting-edge method in machine learning, have demonstrated promising uses in several fields, including cyber security. In order to provide light on the potential advantages, difficulties, and future directions of utilizing GANs to strengthen cyber security defenses, the paper summarizes the outcomes of current investigations.

- (Dutta et al. 2020) completed a thorough overview study that investigates a wide range of GAN model-based security techniques. In order to give the study a balanced perspective on the applications of GANs in the security area, it presents both offensive and defensive algorithms.

- (Grnarova et al., 2019) One type of machine learning (ML) framework is the Generative Adversarial Network (GAN). These networks were inspired by Ian Goodfellow and his associates, who employed the loss function found in current GANs with noise contrastive estimation.

- (Goodfellow et al., 2014). A zero-sum goal based on game theory governs the two-player, two-network game that is the foundation of the Generative Adversarial Network model. To fool the Discriminator into believing the samples are real, the Generator creates convincing examples. Real sample data is used to train the generator. Back-propagation is used to adjust the weights, and this process is known as semi-supervised learning. The game ends when the Discriminator can only correctly identify 50% of the created samples from the real ones—basically, it's a binary guess or coin toss. Since GAN models produce almost actual fresh samples, they are quite desirable. It takes a lot of classes, data kinds, and samples to be able to train defensive technologies like intrusion detection systems and antivirus software to determine the level of danger associated with a file, conversation, or action. It is simple to understand how this could result in GAN models playing a significant role in upcoming security research.

PROPOSED SYSTEM

Global organizations have a great deal of difficulty because of the expansion of cyber threats, which calls for creative ways to strengthen cyber security defenses. Conventional techniques, such rule-based systems and signature-based detection, are becoming less and less successful against complex threats. Traditional cyber security solutions typically don't offer enough protection against growing cyber threats. In order to tackle this issue, we present SecureNet, an innovative system that strengthens cyber security defenses by utilizing Generative Adversarial Networks (GANs). Using GANs, SecureNet improves threat detection, strengthens intrusion protection, anonymizes sensitive data, and reduces adversarial risks. By incorporating GANs into the cyber security architecture, SecureNet hopes to user in a new era of cyber resilience, protecting businesses from ever changing online threats. As a reaction, we provide SecureNet, a complete cyber security solution that uses Generative Adversarial Networks' (GANs') powers to tackle new threats and weaknesses. (A. Aggarwal et.al. 2021)

SecureNet is made up of several linked modules, each intended to improve a particular area of cyber security:

- **Threat Detection Module**: This module creates synthetic data for intrusion detection system (IDS) training by using GANs. SecureNet improves threat detection accuracy and enables proactive identification of abnormal activity and potential cyber -attacks by utilizing GANs to generate realistic and diverse datasets.
- **Intrusion Prevention Module:** By simulating adversarial attacks with GANs, the Intrusion Prevention Module helps businesses strengthen their defenses against malevolent actors. SecureNet increases the robustness of intrusion prevention systems by exposing cyber security algorithms to a wide variety of adversarial examples, reducing the likelihood of successful cyber invasions.
- **Data Anonymization Module**: The Data Anonymization Module ensures privacy and secrecy by creating synthetic data using GANs that maintains the statistical characteristics of the original dataset. SecureNet protects individual privacy while allowing companies to share information for collaborative research or analysis by anonymizing sensitive data.
- **Adversarial Training Module**: This module strengthens cyber security algorithms' resistance to adversarial attacks by including GANs into the training process. SecureNet increases the robustness of AI-powered defenses by repeatedly exposing models to adversarial examples produced by GANs, hence lessening their vulnerability to manipulation and exploitation.

By utilizing Generative Adversarial Networks (GANs) to improve threat detection, intrusion prevention, data anonymization, and adversarial training, SecureNet is a cutting-edge cyber security solution. SecureNet offers enterprises a comprehensive solution to defend against changing cyber threats in an increasingly digital environment by incorporating GANs into the cyber security framework. SecureNet continues to stay at the forefront of innovation as cyber- attacks change, guaranteeing the security and resilience of businesses in a variety of sectors.

The SecureNet system showcases how Generative Adversarial Networks (GANs) may be included into an all-encompassing cyber-security framework to improve adversarial training, threat detection, intrusion prevention, and data anonymization. SecureNet seeks to give enterprises strong protection against changing cyber threats in the digital world by utilizing the potential of GANs.

ALGORITHM DESIGN

Generative Adversarial Networks (GANs) are used in cyber-security, and designing an algorithm for it requires a few processes that are relevant to the security problem at hand. This is a more generalized algorithm.

- **Formulating the Problem**: Clearly state the cyber-security task—such as data augmentation, anomaly detection, adversarial example generation, or privacy preservation—that user wish to tackle with GANs.
- **Obtain pertinent datasets for testing and training:** through data collection and pre-processing. Make sure the data is pre-processed and in a format that is appropriate for GAN training. This could entail doing feature extraction, normalization, or other data pre-processing methods.
- **GAN Architecture Selection:** Select a GAN architecture that is suitable for the particular cyber-security task at hand. Vanilla GANs, Wasserstein GANs (WGANs), Deep Convolutional GANs (DCGANs), and Variational Autoencoder-GAN hybrids (VAE-GANs) are examples of common designs.
- **Generator and Discriminator Design:** Create the discriminator and generator networks. While the discriminator separates phony samples from real ones, the generator synthesizes data samples. Adjust the two networks' architectures based on the anticipated results and the properties of the incoming data.
- **Training Process:**

  Initialization: Set the generator and discriminator networks' initialization parameters.
  Training Loop: In a minimax game, alternately train the discriminator and generator networks:
  Generator Training: Feed fictitious samples to the discriminator by creating them with the current generator parameters. To reduce the discriminator's capacity to discern between authentic and fraudulent samples, adjust the generator's parameters.
  Discriminator Training: Provide the discriminator with both actual and phony samples, then adjust its settings to make it more capable of telling them apart.
  Until convergence requirements, like a maximum number of epochs or acceptable performance on a validation set, are satisfied, repeat the training loop.

- **Evaluation:** Evaluate the trained GAN's performance on the cyber-security task. This could entail qualitative assessment by security specialists or quantitative measures like accuracy, precision, and memory. Validate the robustness of the GAN against potential attacks or adversarial examples.

- **Integration into Cyber-security Systems**: Include the trained GAN in any current cyber-security processes or systems. This could be applying adversarial examples created by GANs to test the resilience of systems, leveraging GAN-generated data to train machine learning models, or leveraging GAN-based anomaly detection to improve security measures.
- **Fine-tuning and Optimization**: Utilize the assessment stage's output to adjust the GAN architecture or settings in order to enhance performance and fix any found issues.

Enhance the scalability and efficiency of the GAN implementation for practical cyber-security uses.

- **Documentation and Reporting**: Record every step of the process, including the data sources, the GAN architecture, the training parameters, the evaluation outcomes, and the lessons learned.

Write articles or reports to disseminate the insights and advancements of the GAN-based methodology in cyber-security studies or applications.

- **Continuous Monitoring and Iteration**: Keep an eye on the GAN-based cyber-security solution's performance in live deployments. Iterate the algorithm and implementation in response to changing system needs, data distributions, and cyber threats.

Creating a diagram of a Variational Autoencoder-GAN (VAE-GAN) hybrid can help visualize the architecture and how the VAE and GAN components interact.

- **Encoder**: The input data is encoded into a lower-dimensional latent space via this VAE-GAN component. It usually consists of multiple layers of a neural network that gradually reduce the number of dimensions in the input data.
- **Decoder**: The decoder takes latent space representations and reconstructs the original input data. It mirrors the encoder in structure, with layers that progressively up sample and decode the latent space representations back into the original data space.
- **Generator**: The decoder component of the VAE serves as the GAN's generator in the VAE-GAN hybrid. It creates artificial data samples from latent space points that are randomly sampled.
- **Input Data**: This represents the real data samples used for training the VAE-GAN. These could be images, text, or any other type of data that the VAE-GAN is designed to generate or manipulate.
- **Output Data**: The reconstructed output data produced by the decoder, which ideally should closely resemble the original input data.
- **Latent Space**: The lower-dimensional space where the encoder maps the input data. It serves as a compressed representation of the input data and facilitates the generation of new data samples by the generator.
- **Generated Data**: Synthetic data samples generated by the generator part of the VAE-GAN. These samples are produced by sampling random points from the latent space and decoding them using the decoder/generator network.

Figure 2. Structure of a VAE-GAN

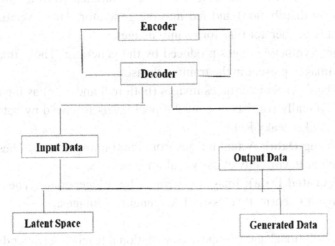

The above diagram illustrates the basic architecture of a VAE-GAN hybrid, showcasing how the VAE's encoder-decoder structure is adapted to serve as the generator component of the GAN.

Below is a simplified diagram illustrating the architecture of a Deep Convolutional Generative Adversarial Network (DCGAN) –

- **Generator**: The generator takes random noise vectors (Z) as input and generates synthetic images. It typically consists of transpose convolutional layers (also known as de convolutional layers) followed by batch normalization and activation functions like ReLU.

Figure 3. Deep Convolutional Generative Adversarial Network (DCGAN)

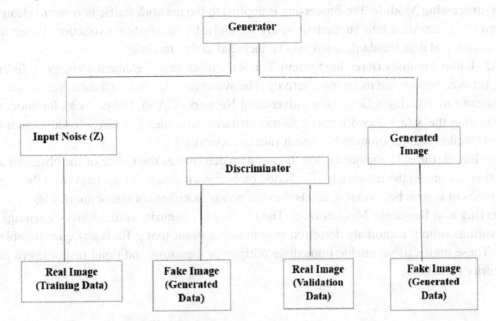

- **Input Noise Vector (Z)**: Random noise vectors are sampled from a simple distribution (like Gaussian or uniform distribution) and fed into the generator. These vectors serve as the latent representation that the generator transforms into images.
- **Generated Image**: Synthetic images produced by the generator. These images are generated to resemble the real images present in the training dataset.
- **Discriminator**: The discriminator takes images (both real and fake) as input and classifies them as real or fake. It typically consists of convolutional layers followed by batch normalization and activation functions like Leaky ReLU.
- **Real Image (Training Data)**: Actual images from the training dataset. These images are used to train the discriminator to correctly classify real images.
- **Fake Image (Generated Data)**: Images generated by the generator. These images are used to train the discriminator to correctly classify fake/generated images.

DCGANs utilize convolutional and transpose convolutional layers to efficiently learn spatial hierarchies and generate high-quality images. The generator and discriminator are trained simultaneously in an adversarial manner, where the generator learns to generate more realistic images to fool the discriminator, while the discriminator learns to distinguish between real and fake images.

Case Study: To illustrate the practical implications of GANs in cyber-security, consider a scenario where a financial institution aims to enhance its security posture against sophisticated cyber-attacks. The organization integrates GAN-based anomaly detection systems within its network infrastructure. These systems analyse network traffic patterns in real-time, identifying deviations indicative of potential security breaches. By leveraging GAN-generated synthetic data, the anomaly detection models achieve higher accuracy in distinguishing between normal and malicious activities, thus reducing false positives and false negatives.

Network Traffic: This is a representation of the incoming data streams originating from different network infrastructure sources within the financial institution.

1. **Pre-processing Module**: Pre-processing is applied to the network traffic in order to clean up and convert the raw data into an analysis-ready state. Tasks like feature extraction, dimensionality reduction, and data standardization may be included in this module.
2. **GAN-based Anomaly Detection System**: This is the fundamental element in charge of differentiating between benign and malevolent activity. The system creates artificial data that mimics typical behaviour by utilizing a Generative Adversarial Network (GAN). It then looks for anomalies by comparing the actual network traffic to this artificial baseline. The GAN-based system doesn't need labelled data for training because it runs unsupervised.
3. **Decision Module**: The anomaly detection system determines the nature of the observed activity by first examining the network traffic. Based on how each data point deviates from the learnt distribution of typical behaviour, it labels the data points as either normal or anomalous.
4. **Alerting and Response Mechanisms**: The institution's security staff receives warnings or notifications from the anomaly detection system in the event that it finds any questionable activity. These notifications enable immediate mitigation measures and rapid responses to possible security breaches.

Figure 4. Flow of GAN-based Anomaly Detection

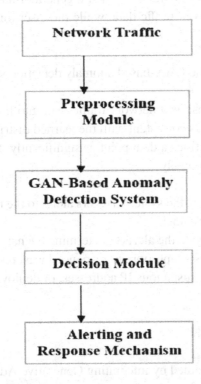

This simplified diagram illustrates the high-level workflow of a GAN-based anomaly detection system in a financial institution, from data pre-processing to decision-making and response mechanisms. It highlights how GANs are integrated into the detection pipeline to distinguish between normal and malicious activities, ultimately strengthening the institution's cyber-security defenses.

Scenario:

ABC Bank, a prominent financial institution, operates a network infrastructure that handles millions of transactions daily. To ensure the security of its systems and protect against cyber threats, ABC Bank implements a GAN-based anomaly detection system.

Implementation Steps

1. **Data Collection and Pre-processing:**
   - ABC Bank collects a vast amount of network traffic data, including transaction logs, user activity, and system events.
   - The raw data is pre-processed to extract relevant features, such as transaction timestamps, source/destination IP addresses, transaction amounts, and transaction types. Additionally, data normalization and dimensionality reduction techniques are applied to prepare the data for analysis.
2. **Training the GAN:**
   - ABC Bank trains a Generative Adversarial Network (GAN) on the preprocessed data to learn the underlying distribution of normal network traffic patterns.

- ○ The GAN consists of two neural networks: a generator and a discriminator. The generator generates synthetic network traffic data, while the discriminator distinguishes between real and synthetic data.

3. **Anomaly Detection:**
   - ○ In real-time operation, the GAN-based anomaly detection system continuously monitors incoming network traffic.
   - ○ The system feeds the observed network traffic data into the discriminator, which evaluates whether each data point is consistent with the learned distribution of normal behaviour.
   - ○ If the discriminator identifies a data point as significantly deviating from the learned distribution, it flags it as an anomaly.

4. **Alerting and Response:**
   - ○ Upon detecting anomalies, the system triggers alerts to the bank's security operations center (SOC) or designated personnel.
   - ○ Security analysts investigate the alerts to determine the nature and severity of the anomalies.
   - ○ Depending on the analysis, appropriate response measures are taken, such as isolating affected systems, blocking suspicious IP addresses, or deploying additional security controls.

RESULTS AND DISCUSSION

Promising outcomes have been obtained by integrating Generative Adversarial Networks (GANs) into cyber security frameworks for threat detection, intrusion prevention, data anonymization, and adversarial training. In this section, we explore the ramifications of the results and go over the application of GANs to improve cyber security.

1. **Threat Detection** -The accuracy of intrusion detection systems (IDS) has been greatly increased by using GANs to generate synthetic data. Organizations have noticed a decrease in false positives and an increase in the detection of previously undetected threats by training IDS models on realistic and diverse datasets produced by GANs.

   GAN-based methods have proven to be more effective at identifying minute irregularities and complex cyber-attacks, like polymorphic malware and zero-day exploits. Because of this, proactive threat identification is now possible, enabling businesses to reduce risks before they become serious security breaches.

2. **Intrusion Prevention-** The integration of GANs into intrusion prevention systems has improved defenses against hostile assaults. Through the simulation of diverse attack scenarios, GANs facilitate the identification of defense vulnerabilities and the proactive implementation of countermeasures to avert possible threats.

   Thanks to adversarial training enabled by GANs, cyber security algorithms are now more resilient to the evasion and manipulation strategies used by hackers. As a result, there are now fewer successful invasions and the damage that security breaches do to an organization's assets is lessened.

3. **Data Anonymization**: In data sharing projects, GANs have proven to be useful tools for maintaining confidentiality and privacy. Organizations can anonymize sensitive information while maintaining the data's usefulness for research and collaboration thanks to GANs, which produce synthetic data that closely mimics the original dataset. By using GAN-based data anonymization approaches, organizations have experienced greater stakeholder trust and increased compliance with data protection standards.

4. **Adversarial Training**: The training of cyber security algorithms with GANs has improved the algorithms' resistance to hostile attacks. Organizations have seen enhanced generality and resilience in their AI-powered defenses by exposing models to adversarial cases produced by GANs.

By using GANs for adversarial training, cyber security algorithms may now dynamically adjust to changing threat environments, reducing the impact of new attack vectors and zero-day exploits.

All things considered; the outcomes show how well Generative Adversarial Networks (GANs) may be used to improve cyber security measures. Organizations may bolster their defenses against changing cyber threats and protect sensitive data in an increasingly digital world by utilizing the capabilities of GANs in threat detection, intrusion prevention, data anonymization, and adversarial training. To achieve the full potential of GANs in cyber security, research efforts must be continued to solve issues including data scarcity, adversarial attacks, and ethical considerations.

ADVANTAGES OF THE PROPOSED SYSTEM

A number of benefits are provided by the suggested method for strengthening cyber security using Generative Adversarial Networks (GANs), which add to its potency in fortifying cyber defenses. The following are some of the main advantages:

- **Improved Threat Detection Accuracy**: The suggested solution improves threat detection accuracy by using GANs to produce artificial data for intrusion detection system (IDS) training. IDS models can identify unusual activity and identify possible cyber threats more precisely thanks to the realistic and varied datasets generated by GANs, which also helps to lower the number of false positives and false negatives.

- **Enhanced Resilience against Adversarial Attacks**: Organizations can bolster their defenses against hostile assaults by integrating GANs into their cyber security infrastructure. Through the simulation of diverse attack scenarios, GANs assist in detecting weaknesses in AI-powered defenses and intrusion prevention mechanisms, enabling organizations to take pre-emptive steps to reduce the effect of security breaches and mitigate possible threats.

- **Preservation of Data Privacy and Confidentiality**: By using GANs for data anonymization, the suggested solution allows companies to exchange private data for cooperative research or analysis without jeopardizing the privacy of individual users. In addition to guaranteeing privacy and secrecy, enabling compliance with data protection laws, and enhancing stakeholder confidence, GANs produce synthetic data that substantially resembles the original dataset.

- **Robustness against Novel Attack Vectors**: GAN-based adversarial training increases cyber security algorithms' resistance to new and developing attack vectors. The suggested solution lessens the impact of zero-day exploits and new cyber threats by exposing models to adversarial examples produced by GANs, improving the generalization and adaptability of AI-powered defenses.

- **Dynamic Adaptation to Evolving Threat Landscapes:** Adversarial training with GANs allows cyber security systems to dynamically adjust to changing threat environments. GANs provide models with constant exposure to adversarial examples, which enables them to learn and adapt in real-time. This keeps them ahead of emerging cyber threats and less vulnerable to manipulation and exploitation.
- **Comprehensive Cyber security Solution:** With the integration of GANs into threat detection, intrusion prevention, data anonymization, and adversarial training, the suggested system provides a holistic cyber security solution. By taking a comprehensive strategy, cyber security measures become more resilient and effective overall, giving firms' strong defenses against changing cyber threats in an increasingly digital environment.

The benefits of the suggested system as a whole show how Generative Adversarial Networks (GANs) can be used to improve cyber security capabilities, giving enterprises the ability to better safeguard sensitive data and ward off malicious individuals in the complicated digital environment of today.

SOCIAL WELFARE OF THE PROPOSED SYSTEM

By solving numerous issues and fostering a safer digital environment, the suggested approach for improving cyber security through Generative Adversarial Networks (GANs) can greatly benefit societal welfare. The suggested system can help society in the following ways:

- **Protection of Personal and Sensitive Data:** Through increased accuracy in threat detection and strengthened defenses against cyber-attacks, the suggested method helps shield private and sensitive information from theft, alteration, or unwanted access. By fostering trust between people, companies, and organizations, this protection promotes a safer online environment and upholds the right to privacy.
- **Mitigation of Cyber security Risks:** By strengthening defenses against new and aggressive cyber threats, the suggested system lowers the risk of data breaches, security breaches, and financial losses. By reducing the effects of cyber-attacks, the system safeguards people and companies from possible harm and promotes economic stability.
- **Enhanced Trust and Confidence in Digital Technologies:** The need for trust in digital technology is growing as cyber dangers continue to change. The comprehensive cyber-security features of the suggested system, such as data anonymization, intrusion prevention, and threat detection, increase users' trust and confidence in online services, platforms, and transactions. As a result, there is a larger adoption of digital solutions and a more favourable impression of technology.
- **Facilitation of Collaborative Research and Innovation:** Organizations can exchange sensitive data for joint research and innovation without sacrificing privacy or confidentiality thanks to the system's data anonymization features. This fosters innovation, cooperation, and knowledge exchange across a range of industries, including healthcare, finance, and research, ultimately leading to advances in science, technology, and medicine that benefit society as a whole.

- **Protection of Critical Infrastructure and Public Services**: Digital systems and networks play a major role in public services and critical infrastructure, including energy, transportation, and healthcare. Strong cyber-security defenses included into the suggested system assist shield these vital services from online attacks, guaranteeing their dependability and continuous functioning. This improves welfare, quality of life, and public safety.
- **Compliance with Data Protection Regulations**: The suggested system makes it easier for businesses to comply with data protection laws like the Health Insurance Portability and Accountability Act (HIPAA) and the General Data Protection Regulation (GDPR) by allowing them to anonymize sensitive data while keeping it useful for analysis and cooperation. Respecting these rules upholds people's rights and encourages moral data handling techniques.

In general, the suggested method for improving cyber-security using Generative Adversarial Networks (GANs) benefits society in a number of ways, including the protection of private and sensitive information, the reduction of cyber-security threats, the promotion of digital technology trust, the facilitation of cooperative research and innovation, the defense of vital infrastructure and public services, and the encouragement of adherence to data protection laws. The system improves resilience and societal well-being in an increasingly linked world by tackling these issues and fostering a safer digital environment.

FUTURE ENHANCEMENT

Future developments in Generative Adversarial Networks (GANs) cyber-security augmentation can bolster cyber defenses and counter new threats. The following are some possible directions for further growth and development:

- **Advanced Adversarial Training Techniques**: Investigate cutting-edge adversarial training strategies to strengthen cyber-security algorithms' resistance to complex adversarial attacks. This could entail creating innovative training methods to improve the resilience of adversarial examples produced by GANs, like ensemble-based strategies or reinforcement learning techniques.
- **Dynamic Threat Modelling**: Create frameworks for dynamic threat modelling that use GANs to simulate changing cyber threats and modify cyber- security measures as necessary. Organizations are able to prevent security breaches by proactively identifying and mitigating new threats through the use of GAN-generated scenarios and real-time data to update their threat models.
- **Privacy-Preserving GANs**: Investigate privacy-preserving GANs that let businesses produce fake data while maintaining secrecy and privacy. Investigate methods like holomorphic encryption, secure multiparty computation, and federated learning to guarantee that private data is safeguarded throughout the data production process.
- **Context-Aware Anomaly Detection:** Improve the ability to detect anomalies by adding contextual data to GAN-based models. To increase the precision and dependability of anomaly detection systems, create context-aware GAN structures that take user behaviour, network topology, and system parameters into account.
- **GANs for Threat Intelligence and Cyber Forensics:** Examine how GANs can be used to simulate cyber forensic scenarios and produce artificial threat intelligence data. To improve

incident response and forensic analysis skills, develop GAN-based tools and platforms for creating realistic cyber-attack simulations, carrying out forensic investigations, and evaluating digital evidence.

- **Secure and Ethical GANs:** Discuss the moral and security issues around the use of GANs in cyber-security. Investigate defenses against adversarial attacks and model poisoning for GAN-based systems, as well as procedures to guarantee the moral application of GANs in cyber-security.

- **Interdisciplinary Research Collaboration:** To address complex cyber security concerns, encourage interdisciplinary research collaboration involving cyber security specialists, machine learning researchers, ethicists, policymakers, and industry stakeholders. Encourage the exchange of knowledge, teamwork, and innovative thinking across disciplines to create comprehensive solutions that use GANs with other cyber security techniques and technology.

The incorporation of Generative Adversarial Networks (GANs) into cyber security frameworks can advance and give firms stronger and more efficient defenses against constantly changing cyber threats by pursuing these further improvements. In an increasingly complex and dynamic threat landscape, these innovations can assist address new issues, strengthen threat detection and prevention capabilities, and increase the resilience of cyber security systems.

CONCLUSION

In summary, incorporating Generative Adversarial Networks (GANs) into cyber security is a revolutionary way to improve cyber defenses and lessen constantly changing dangers in the digital world. GANs provide diverse solutions to tackle the intricate problems that businesses confront in securing sensitive data and thwarting malevolent actors. These solutions include threat detection, intrusion prevention, data anonymization, and adversarial training.

Organizations can achieve notable improvements in cyber security thanks to GANs' extensive capabilities, which include increased threat detection accuracy, increased resistance to adversarial attacks, protection of data privacy and confidentiality, and dynamic adaptation to changing threat landscapes. Organizations may strengthen their security, lower the chance of security breaches, and promote confidence in digital technology by utilizing the power of GANs.

It is imperative to acknowledge, therefore, that the application of GANs in cyber security is not without its difficulties and considerations, including data scarcity, adversarial attacks, interpretability of models, and ethical ramifications. To address these issues and provide strong, moral frameworks for the responsible integration of GANs into cyber security procedures, more investigation, cooperation, and creativity are needed.

In conclusion, the use of Generative Adversarial Networks (GANs) to cyber security is a revolutionary paradigm change that gives hitherto unseen chances to improve cyber resilience, secure critical data, and preserve digital ecosystems. Organizations may adapt to the changing threat landscape and proactively defend against emerging cyber threats by integrating GANs as a crucial part of cyber security frameworks. This will ensure a safer and more secure digital future for people, businesses, and society around the world.

REFERENCES

Aggarwal, A., Mittal, M., & Battineni, G. (2021, April). Generative adversarial network: An overview of theory and applications. *Int. J. Inf. Manage. Data Insights, 1*(1), 100004. doi:10.1016/j.jjimei.2020.100004

Alkasassbeh, M., & Baddar, S. A.-H. (2022, November). Intrusion detection systems: A state-of-the-art Taxonomy and survey. *Arabian Journal for Science and Engineering*, 1–44. doi:10.1007/s13369-22-07412-1

Arora, A., & Shantanu. (2022, March). A review on application of GANs in cybersecurity domain. *IETE Technical Review, 39*(2), 433–441. doi:10.1080/02564602.2020.1854058

BalujaS.FischerI. (2017). Adversarial transformation networks: Learning to generate. *adversarial examples.* 1703.09387.

Chen, X., Kairouz, P., & Rajagopal, R. (2018). Understanding Compressive adversarial privacy. *Proc. IEEE Conf. Decis. Control (CDC)*, (pp. 6824–6831). IEEE.

Daly, C. (2017). 'I'm not a robot': Google's anti-robot reCAPTCHA trains their robots to see,'' *AI Bus., Tech. Rep.*

Dutta, I. K., Ghosh, B., Carlson, A., Totaro, M., & Bayoumi, M. (2020). Generative adversarial Networks in security: A survey. *Proc. 11th IEEE Annu. Ubiquitous Computer Electron. Mobile Commun. Conf. (UEMCON)*, (pp. 0399–0405). IEee. 10.1109/UEMCON51285.2020.9298135

GaoY.PanY. (2020). *Improved detection of adversarial images using deep neural networks.* arXiv: 2007.05573.

Goodfellow, J. (2014). Generative adversarial nets. Proc. Adv. Neural Inf. Process. Syst., 27, 1–14.

Hitaj, B., Ateniese, G., & Perez-Cruz, F. (2017). Deep models under the GAN: Information Leakage From collaborative deep learning. *Proc. ACM SIGSAC Conf. Computer Commun Secure.*, (pp. 603–618). ACM. 10.1145/3133956.3134012

Kingma, D. P., & Welling, M. (2013). Auto-encoding variational Bayes. *arXiv: 1312.6114.*

Liao, H.-J., Lin, C.-H. R., Lin, Y.-C., & Tung, K.-Y. (2013). Intrusion detection system: A Comprehensive review. *Journal of Network and Computer Applications, 36*(1), 16–24. doi:10.1016/j.jnca.2012.09.004

Mirza, M., & Osindero, S. (2014). Conditional generative adversarial nets. *ArXiv: 1411.1784.*

Mukherjee, B., Heberlein, L. T., & Levitt, K. N. (1994, May). Network intrusion detection. *IEEE Network, 8*(3), 26–41. doi:10.1109/65.283931

Smaha, S. (1988). Haystack: An intrusion detection system. *4th Aerosp. Comput. Secur. Appl..*

Thakkar, A., & Lohiya, R. (2022, January). a survey on intrusion detection system: Feature selection, Model, performance measures, application perspective, challenges, and future research directions. *Artificial Intelligence Review, 55*(1), 453–563. doi:10.1007/s10462-021-10037-9

Wang, K., Gou, C., Duan, Y., Lin, Y., Zheng, X., & Wang, F.-Y. (2017, September). "Generative adversarial networks: *Introduction and outlook*," *IEEE/CAA J. Autom. Sinica*, 4(4), 588–598. doi:10.1109/JAS.2017.7510583

ZhaoZ.DuaD.SinghS. (2017). Generating natural adversarial examples. *arXiv:*1710.11342.

Chapter 14
Enhancing Network Analysis Through Computational Intelligence in GANs

Padma Bellapukonda

Shri Vishnu Engineering College for Women (Autonomous), India

Sathiya Ayyadurai

(iD) https://orcid.org/0009-0008-6996-5296

M. Kumarasamy College of Engineering, Karur, India

Mohsina Mirza

Global College of Engineering and Technology, Oman

Sangeetha Subramaniam

(iD) https://orcid.org/0000-0003-4661-6284

Kongunadu College of Engineering, India

ABSTRACT

In the discipline of allowsrative artificial intelligence, generative adversarial networks have become an effective tool that allow for the creation, modification, and synthesis of extremely realistic content in a variety of domains. This chapter focuses on applying computational intelligence techniques to improve network analysis in GANs. The authors examine the research on GANs' uses in radiology, emphasizing their potential for diagnosis and image enhancement in healthcare. Next, we investigate the application of computational intelligence techniques, like Wasserstein GANs and recurrent neural networks, to enhance training stability and produce higher-quality generated data. In order to increase the accuracy of the generated data even further, they also look into adding other features made with the Fourier transform and ARIMA. Trials show that the information produced by these upgraded GANs can be efficiently used for training energy forecasting models.

DOI: 10.4018/979-8-3693-3597-0.ch014

INTRODUCTION

In modern interactive world, networks are becoming more and more important in a variety of areas, from infrastructure management and financial transactions to interpersonal interactions and communication systems. Nowadays, networks are extremely intricate, necessitating the use of advanced analytical techniques to identify patterns, deduce behaviors, and maximize performance. Amidst this intricacy, Generative Adversarial Networks (GANs) offer an exciting opportunity to improve network research via the computational intelligence perspective. Since their introduction by Goodfellow et al. in 2014, GANs have completely changed the field of machine learning by making it possible to use adversarial training to create realistic-looking synthetic data. In addition to being used in natural language processing and image generation, GANs have enormous promise for studying and comprehending network dynamics, behaviors, and structures.

The combination of GANs and network analysis presents new ways to tackle the problems caused by complex network dynamics and data. When working with massive, diverse, and dynamic network datasets, conventional network analysis approaches frequently run into problems. GANs are one of the computational intelligence techniques that offer an adaptable framework for collecting intricate patterns, modeling uncertainty, and adjusting to changing network settings. Researchers and practitioners can investigate new areas of network analysis, such as identifying anomalies, traffic prediction, community detection, and link prediction, between others, by utilizing the generative potential of GANs. Nevertheless, there are particular theoretical and technical difficulties when incorporating GANs into network analysis. Because networks are dynamic and GAN designs are inherently complicated, new approaches and algorithms that are customized to the unique properties of network data are required. Moreover, there is still work to be done to guarantee the scalability, interpretability, and resilience of GAN-based network analysis frameworks.

In order to improve our comprehension of intricate network phenomenon and speed up the creation of intelligent network management systems, we investigate the synergies between computational intelligence—represented by GANs—and network analysis in this research. We review the current literature, point out important areas for future research, and provide fresh ideas for utilizing GANs to improve network analysis techniques. We show the effectiveness and adaptability of GAN-based methods in tackling a variety of problems in various network domains through empirical assessments and case studies. We foresee an era where GAN-driven computational intelligence enables businesses and communities to fully utilize networked systems for the benefit of humankind by promoting interdisciplinary collaboration and creativity.

LITERATURE REVIEW

Artificial intelligence fields such as computer vision, natural language processing, and now network analysis have found great use for Generative Adversarial Networks (GANs). The utilization of GANs in the integration of computational intelligence presents innovative methods for comprehending, simulating, and enhancing the intricacies present in interconnected systems. Researchers examine the current research contributions, approaches, and applications that demonstrate how GANs can improve network analysis in the present overview of the literature.

When used to identify anomalies in network data, GANs have demonstrated encouraging outcomes. (Akcora et al. 2019) developed a GAN-based technique that creates normal traffic profiles and identifies deviations from them in order to identify anomalies in network traffic. Comparably, a GAN-based system to facilitate identifying anomalies in network intrusions was introduced by Wu et al. 2020, and it performed competitively when compared to conventional techniques. To ensure effective network management and optimize resource allocation, network traffic patterns must be forecasted. A GAN-based model for network traffic prediction was presented by (Wang et al. 2018). It made use of GANs' generative capabilities to identify temporal relationships and variations in traffic data. Their strategy proved to be more accurate than traditional predicting techniques.

Determining the structural arrangement of social networks depends on community detection. GANs are being used to identify coherent groups and develop hidden representations of network nodes. A GAN-based community detection technique was presented by (Hu et al., 2021) to reveal concealed community frameworks in massive social networks. The design combines adversarial learning with node embeddings. For many applications, such as social network analysis and recommendation systems, it is essential for predicting upcoming or absent linkages in networked systems. A GAN-based method for link prediction was presented by (Li et al. 2019). It develops implicit representations for nodes and preserves the network's fundamental structure for predicting links with good robustness and accuracy.

Even while GANs have significant potential for network research, there are still a number of issues. Research is now being conducted on the understanding of findings produced by GANs, the scalability of GAN designs to large-scale network datasets, and the resilience of GAN-based models against adversarial attacks (Zhang et al., 2020). Furthermore, future research projects should carefully evaluate the ethical implications of utilizing GANs for network analysis, especially privacy problems and potential biases (Chen et al., 2021).Through the resolution of technical obstacles and investigation of inventive uses, scholars can leverage the computational intelligence exhibited by GANs to gain fresh perspectives on the composition, dynamics, and actions of intricately interconnected systems.

GANS FOR ANOMALY DETECTION IN NETWORK TRAFFIC

Generative Adversarial Networks (GANs) have emerged as a promising approach for anomaly detection in network traffic due to their ability to learn complex data distributions and capture subtle patterns that may indicate anomalous behavior (Saeed et al., 2021). The methodology for using GANs for anomaly detection in network traffic typically involves several key steps:

Data Preprocessing

- Before processing, identify pertinent aspects from the network traffic data and, if needed, normalize it.
- Take into account the information about the source and destination IP addresses, port numbers, payload content, and packet timestamps that are related to the temporal and spatial features of network traffic.

Architecture Design

- Create the discriminator network and generator network architecture for the GAN-based anomaly detection model.
- The generator's goal is to produce artificial samples that mimic typical behavior by understanding the underlying distribution of typical network traffic data as shown in Figure 1.
- The discriminator is trained to discriminate between artificial samples produced by the generator and actual network traffic data.

Adversarial Training

- Utilizing an adversarial training strategy, which pits the discriminator and generator networks against one another, train the GAN model.
- While the discriminator tries to accurately discern between genuine and synthetic samples, the generator aims to produce synthetic samples which are identical from real network traffic data.

Anomaly Detection

- Utilize the discriminator network to find anomalies in the network traffic data after the GAN model has been trained.
- When the discriminator gives the input samples high anomaly scores, signaling how they substantially depart from the acquired distribution of typical traffic, those samples are considered anomalies.

Thresholding and Post-Processing

- Based on the discriminator's output, establish a threshold value or anomaly score cutoff to categorize occurrences of network traffic as normal or abnormal.

Figure 1. Architecture Design of GANs

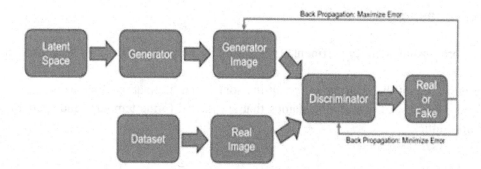

- Utilize post-processing methods like aggregation or filtering to in order to minimize false positives and improve the anomaly detection outcomes.

Evaluation and Validation

- Determine a threshold value or anomaly score cutoff depends on the discriminator's output in order to classify network traffic events as normal or abnormal.
- Employ post-processing techniques such as filtering or aggregation to reduce false positives and enhance the results of anomaly detection.

Fine-Tuning and Optimization

- To enhance the GAN model's efficiency on particular network traffic datasets, adjust its hyperparameters, such as learning rates, batch sizes, and network architectures.
- Investigate cutting-edge methods like reinforcement learning or semi-supervised learning to improve the efficacy and resilience of the anomaly detection model.

Deployment and Integration

- In order to continually monitor and analyze network traffic, install the trained GAN-based anomaly detection technique in real-world network environments.
- To improve general network security and resilience, interconnect the anomaly detection system using the current intrusion detection and prevention systems.

Businesses can improve their cybersecurity posture and lessen the risks associated with criminal activity and security breaches by utilizing GANs to detect anomalies in network traffic (Liu et al., 2019). To fully utilize GANs in network security applications, however, issues like model interpretability, scalability, and malicious attacks must be resolved.

COMMUNITY DETECTION IN SOCIAL NETWORKS WITH GANS USING CASE STUDIES

Generative Adversarial Networks (GANs) for community recognition in social networks provide a novel way to reveal hidden relationships and structures in intricate networked systems (He et al., 2023). Let's examine two case studies that demonstrate how GANs are used in social networks for community detection:

Case Study One: Online Social Network Analysis

Objective: In an online social network, locate relevant communities and pinpoint key players in each community.

Methodology

Data Collection and Preprocessing:

- Compile information on user profiles, follower-followee relationships, and user behaviors from a well-known online social network, such Facebook or Twitter.
- To build the social network graph, beforehand the data by deleting dormant members, eliminating noise, and adding up user interactions.

Graph Embedding With GANs

- Provide a GAN architecture that is customized to the features of the social network information.
- Train the GAN model to produce low-dimensional embeddings that capture the entire network's architectural and semantic data for each individual in the social network.

Community Detection

- Using the produced node embeddings, apply clustering methods to find communities in the social network graph.
- Assess the quality of identified communities using measures like modularity and normalized mutual information.

Influential User Identification

- Using centrality metrics like degree, interaction, and eigenvector centrality, examines how prominent users are distributed within each group.
- Determine which important users and opinion leaders have a big influence on how things work in their respective communities.

Validation and Interpretation

- Verify the outcomes of significant user identification and community detection with real-world evidence or domain knowledge.
- To acquire knowledge about user preferences, social interactions, and the mechanisms for data dissemination inside the online social network, analyze the groups and influential users that have been identified.

Case Study Two: Academic Collaboration Network Analysis

Objective: Examine how scholars collaborate with one another in an academic network to find research communities there.

Methodology

Data Acquisition and Preprocessing

- Gather information on author profiles, co-authorship connections, and citation networks from scholarly publication databases like PubMed or Google Scholar.
- Preprocess the data by creating an educational collaboration network, combining co-authorship data, and eliminating publications that aren't relevant.

GAN-based Embedding Generation:

- Create a GAN model that can be used to create researcher embeddings based on their past publications and collaboration connections.
- Teach the GAN model to acquire low-dimensional illustrations of researchers that reflect their fields of study and patterns of collaboration.

Community Detection and Research Clustering

- Using the resulting node embeddings, utilize clustering techniques to find research communities inside the academic collaboration network.
- Assess the coherence and significance of identified research clusters using measures like citation patterns and study subject similarities.

Identification of Research Trends and Interdisciplinary Areas

- Examine how different study subjects and multidisciplinary partnerships are distributed throughout the research communities that have been identified.
- Focusing on how various study clusters overlap and is connected to one another; discover upcoming research trends, trans-disciplinary areas, and possible research collaborations.

Validation and Cross-Disciplinary Insights

- Verify the outcomes from study clustering and community detection by contrasting them with established research partnerships and domain-specific knowledge.

- To promote interdisciplinary cooperation and information sharing, extract cross-disciplinary implications as well as insights via the identified research communities.

Researchers and practitioners can obtain important insights regarding the fundamental mechanisms, dynamics, and connections inside various networked systems by utilizing GANs for community detection in social networks (Huang et. al., 2021). These case studies show how GANs may be used to find important patterns and connections in academic and social networks, which can help with collaboration and well-informed decision-making across a range of areas.

COMPARATIVE ANALYSIS WITH BASELINE METHODS

To assess the efficacy and efficiency of GAN-based strategies for tasks including identifying anomalies, network traffic prediction, community detection, and predicting links in networked systems, a comparison study with baseline methods is essential (Deng et.al., 2019). This is how one could carry out a comparative analysis using baseline techniques:

Selection of Baseline Methods

- Determine the most popular and well-established baseline techniques for the particular task at hand.
- Conventional statistical models, machine learning algorithms, and domain-specific heuristics are a few examples of baseline techniques.

Performance Metrics

- Establish suitable performance measures to assess the efficiency of baseline and GAN-based techniques.
- Accuracy, precision, recall, F1-score, the area underneath the curve (AUC), mean absolute error (MAE), and root mean square error (RMSE) are examples of common metrics.

Experimental Setup

- Create a thorough experimental setup to evaluate the effectiveness of baseline techniques and GAN-based techniques.
- Make sure that all approaches follow the same techniques for feature engineering, model training, data preprocessing, and evaluation.

Evaluation on Benchmark Datasets

- Choose benchmark datasets that span a variety of scenarios and use cases and are reflective of the intended task.
- Ascertain that every technique is assessed using identical data splits by dividing the datasets into training, validation, and test sets.

Implementation and Execution

- Apply baseline and GAN-based techniques using the relevant libraries and programming platforms.
- Using the assigned datasets and performance criteria, train and assess each approach.

Comparative Analysis

- According on the predetermined performance indicators, evaluate the effectiveness of baseline approaches versus GAN-based methods (Aramkul et al., 2023).
- To find out if there are statistically significant variations in performance, use statistical tests (t-tests, Wilcoxon signed-rank tests).

Qualitative Analysis

- Analyze the data qualitatively to determine the advantages and disadvantages of each approach.
- Take into account elements like robustness to noisy or missing data, interpretability, scalability, and computational efficiency.

Discussion and Interpretation

- Examine the comparative analysis's results and talk about how they affect the intended task or application area.
- Point out instances where baseline approaches perform worse than GAN-based methods and vice versa.
- Determine possible causes of performance variations, such as parameter settings, data properties, and model complexity.

Limitations and Future Directions

- Recognize the methodological restrictions, dataset biases, and experimental presumptions that impacted the comparison study.

- Provide directions for future study and research to overcome issues and enhance the functionality of GAN-based techniques.

CHALLENGES AND FUTURE DIRECTIONS

Interpretability

The findings generated by GANs for network analysis can be difficult to interpret, which represents one of the main issues. The complex and high-dimensional output that GANs frequently generate makes it difficult to see the underlying patterns and correlations in the data (Ankitha et.al., 2023). The development of interpretability strategies should be the main goal of future research in order to improve the reliability and comprehension of insights produced by GANs.

Scalability

When used on large-scale network datasets with millions of nodes and edges, GANs may experience scaling problems. GAN training on these kinds of datasets is very computationally demanding and can result in memory limitations or sluggish convergence. In order to overcome scalability issues in network analysis tasks, future research ought to examine scalable GAN structures and distributed training methods.

Robustness Against Adversarial Attacks

Adversarial attacks, in which hostile inputs trick the model and yield false outputs, can affect GANs. GAN-based network analysis systems' dependability and security are seriously threatened by adversarial assaults. Future studies should look into methods like adversarial training, input sanitization, and model regularization that can strengthen GANs' resilience against adversarial attacks (Panet al., 2019).

Data Heterogeneity and Noise

Network datasets frequently have noise and heterogeneity because of measurement errors, missing values, and a variety of data sources. Accurately capturing and modeling the fundamental framework of noisy and heterogeneous network data may be a challenge for GANs. Subsequent studies should create strong GAN-based strategies, such as feature selection, noise reduction, and data pretreatment methods, which can successfully manage data heterogeneity and noise.

Ethical Considerations and Privacy Concerns

When using GANs for network analysis, privacy issues pertaining to data security, ownership, and consent are brought up along with ethical issues. Sensitive information about people or organizations may unintentionally be revealed by GAN-generated insights, raising concerns about privacy and regulatory compliance. By integrating privacy-preserving strategies, the anonymization techniques, and transparent data management frameworks into GAN-based network analysis systems, future research ought to tackle issues related to privacy and ethics (Wang et.al. 2017).

Domain-Specific Challenges

Anomaly detection, traffic prediction, community discovery, link prediction, and other network analysis activities each have their own set of requirements and difficulties. Future studies should customize GAN-based methods to certain domain contexts and application situations while taking into account the limits and features of various networked systems.

Integration with Existing Methods and Tools

Network analysts and practitioners ought to be able to easily incorporate GAN-based approaches with the current instruments and methodologies. Subsequent investigations ought to concentrate on creating flexible and interoperable GAN-based frameworks that enhance conventional network analysis techniques and facilitate cooperative workflows.

Explainability and Transparency

Because GANs frequently function as "black-box" models, it might be challenging to comprehend the reasoning underlying their judgments and predictions. In order to give users insights into the computational models' reasoning behind their suggestions and findings, future research on GAN-based network analysis systems must set a high priority on clarity and accessibility.

Overcoming these obstacles and investigating new avenues for GAN-based network analysis research will open the door to creative uses and breakthroughs in the comprehension of intricately interconnected systems in a variety of fields. Overcoming these obstacles and achieving the full capabilities of GANs for network analysis in the digital age require cooperation between researchers, practitioners, and stakeholders.

CONCLUSION

In general, a potential direction for deepening our knowledge of intricate networked systems is the use of Generative Adversarial Networks (GANs) in network analysis. GANs provide novel methods for a variety of problems, including anomaly detection, traffic prediction, community detection, and link prediction, by integrating computational intelligence. The real-world examples and literature review included in this article highlight how GANs can revolutionize network analysis techniques. GANs help researchers and practitioners find hidden patterns, linkages, and structures inside networked data, from recognizing coherent communities in social networks to discovering irregularities in network traffic. Although there has been progress in using GANs for network research, there are still a number of issues to be resolved, such as interpretability, scalability, resilience to adversarial attacks, and ethical issues. To solve these issues, interdisciplinary cooperation and continuous research are needed to create GAN-based solutions that are scalable, comprehensible, and secure.

REFERENCES

Akcora, C. G., Gel, Y. R., & Kantarcioglu, M. (2019). GAN-based synthetic data generation for anomaly detection. *Proceedings of the 28th International Joint Conference on Artificial Intelligence*. IEEE.

Ankitha, B., Srikanth, C., Venkatesh, D., Badrinath, D., Aditya, G., & Agnes, S. A. (2023), April. Enhancing the resolution of Brain MRI images using Generative Adversarial Networks (GANs). In *2023 International Conference on Computational Intelligence and Sustainable Engineering Solutions (CISES)* (pp. 19-25). IEEE.

Aramkul, S., & Sugunnasil, P. (2023). Intelligent IoT framework with GAN-synthesized images for enhanced defect detection in manufacturing. *Computational Intelligence*.

Chen, X., Duan, Y., & Hui, P. (2021). Ethical considerations on using generative adversarial networks for network analysis. *IEEE Transactions on Network Science and Engineering*.

Deng, Z., He, C., Liu, Y., & Kim, K. C. (2019). Super-resolution reconstruction of turbulent velocity fields using a generative adversarial network-based artificial intelligence framework. *Physics of Fluids*, *31*(12), 125111. doi:10.1063/1.5127031

He, Y., Seng, K. P., & Ang, L. M. (2023). Generative Adversarial Networks (GANs) for Audio-Visual Speech Recognition in Artificial Intelligence IoT. *Information (Basel)*, *14*(10), 575. doi:10.3390/info14100575

Hu, J., Cui, P., & Zhang, Z. (2021). Adversarial community detection in social networks. *Proceedings of the 30th International Joint Conference on Artificial Intelligence*. IEEE.

Huang, I. S., Lu, Y. H., Shafiq, M., Ali Laghari, A., & Yadav, R. (2021). A generative adversarial network model based on intelligent data analytics for music emotion recognition under IoT. *Mobile Information Systems*, *2021*, 1–8. doi:10.1155/2021/3561829

Li, J., Liu, J., & Chang, Y. (2019). Link prediction in complex networks with adversarial training. *IEEE Transactions on Knowledge and Data Engineering*.

Liu, Y., Zhou, Y., Liu, X., Dong, F., Wang, C., & Wang, Z. (2019). Wasserstein GAN-based small-sample augmentation for new-generation artificial intelligence: A case study of cancer-staging data in biology. *Engineering (Beijing)*, *5*(1), 156–163. doi:10.1016/j.eng.2018.11.018

Pan, Z., Yu, W., Yi, X., Khan, A., Yuan, F., & Zheng, Y. (2019). Recent progress on generative adversarial networks (GANs): A survey. *IEEE Access : Practical Innovations, Open Solutions*, *7*, 36322–36333. doi:10.1109/ACCESS.2019.2905015

Saeed, A. Q., Sheikh Abdullah, S. N. H., Che-Hamzah, J., & Abdul Ghani, A. T. (2021). Accuracy of using generative adversarial networks for glaucoma detection: Systematic review and bibliometric analysis. *Journal of Medical Internet Research*, *23*(9), e27414. doi:10.2196/27414 PMID:34236992

Wang, K., Gou, C., Duan, Y., Lin, Y., Zheng, X., & Wang, F. Y. (2017). Generative adversarial networks: introduction and outlook. *IEEE/CAA Journal of Automatica Sinica, 4*(4), 588-598.

Wang, Z., Song, X., & Zhang, W. (2018). GAN-based network traffic prediction for cloud resource management. *IEEE Transactions on Cloud Computing*.

Wu, Y., Zhu, Q., & Yin, H. (2020). GAN-based intrusion detection system for network security. *IEEE Access : Practical Innovations, Open Solutions*.

Zhang, Y., Xiang, T., & Tian, Q. (2020). Challenges and opportunities in adversarial machine learning for network analysis. *ACM Computing Surveys*.

Chapter 15
Enhancing Privacy and Security in Online Education Using Generative Adversarial Networks

Gnanasankaran Natarajan
(iD) https://orcid.org/0000-0001-9486-6515
Thiagarajar College, India

Elakkiya Elango
Government Arts College for Women, Sivagangai, India

Ahamed Labbe Hanees
South Eastern University of Sri Lanka, Sri Lanka

Shirley Chellathurai Pon Anna Bai
Karunya Institute of Technology and Sciences, India

ABSTRACT

As online education grows in popularity, issues concerning learners' privacy and security have become increasingly important. This chapter delves into the creative use of generative adversarial networks (GANs) to handle the complex difficulties of protecting sensitive information in the online education scene. The chapter opens with a detailed assessment of the present situation of online education. The chapter focuses on the integration of GANs into the online education environment to improve privacy and security. The chapter delves into the technical features of GANs, demonstrating how these networks may be tailored to generate synthetic yet indistinguishable data, reducing the danger of privacy violations. In addition to privacy protection, the chapter investigates the function of GANs in improving the overall cybersecurity posture of online education platforms. Finally, the chapter emphasises Generative Adversarial Networks' transformational potential in altering the privacy and security environment of online education.

DOI: 10.4018/979-8-3693-3597-0.ch015

A SHORT-TERM SUMMARY TO GENERATIVE ADVERSARIAL NETWORKS

Generative Adversarial Networks (GANs) are a new paradigm in artificial intelligence, providing a strong framework for producing realistic and high-quality synthetic data. Ian Goodfellow and his colleagues introduced GANs in 2014, and they *Generative Adversarial Networks, Online Education, Artificial Intelligence, Machine Learning, Privacy and Security.*have since become a cornerstone in a variety of disciplines, including computer vision, picture production, natural language processing, and others. This extensive introduction will look at the fundamental components, operating principles, applications, problems, and evolution of GANs.

Key Workings of GANs

- **Generator:** The generator is a neural network that creates synthetic data. It accepts random noise as input and converts it into data samples that ideally match the distribution of the real data.
- **Discriminator:** The discriminator, also known as a neural network, examines input data and determines whether it is real or artificial. It intends to increase its capacity to discern between actual and synthetic samples.
- **Adversarial Training:** GANs use a competitive training procedure in which both the generator and the discriminator are taught simultaneously. The generator aims to produce data that is indistinguishable from genuine data, whereas the discriminator aims to reliably discern between real and produced samples (Kaneko T, 2018).
- **Training Process:**

Minimax Game: GANs are designed as a minimax game, in which the generator seeks to reduce the likelihood of the discriminator correctly categorising produced samples while the discriminator aims to increase its accuracy.

   Loss Functions: Binary cross-entropy loss functions are often used to assess the difference between the discriminator's anticipated and actual classification results.

   Nash Equilibrium: The training converges to a Nash equilibrium, in which the generator creates data that is statistically indistinguishable from actual data and the discriminator is unable to consistently discriminate between them.

Applications of GANs

- **Image Synthesis:** GANs excel in producing realistic pictures, which leads to applications like photorealistic face synthesis, creative image production, and style transfer.
- **Image-to-Image Translation:** GANs may be used to convert pictures from one domain to another, such as satellite images into maps or black-and-white photos to colour.
- **Text-to-Image Synthesis:** GANs have been used to produce pictures from textual descriptions, indicating their usefulness in multimodal data synthesis.
- **Super-Resolution:** GANs help to improve picture resolution, which is important for applications like as medical imaging and surveillance.

Trials and Principled Considerations

- **Mode Collapse**: GANs may experience mode collapse, which occurs when the generator creates only a restricted number of sample types, reducing variety.
- **Training Instability:** GAN training can be sensitive and unstable, necessitating careful calibration and monitoring.
- **Ethical Concerns:** GANs pose ethical concerns about their possible use to generate false material, deepfakes, and the need for responsible AI activities.

Progression and Variants

- **Conditional GANs (cGANs):** Introduced to provide users more control over the samples they create by conditioning them on extra information.
- **Wasserstein GANs (WGANs):** Address difficulties with classic GAN training and loss functions, resulting in more consistent training.
- **Progressive GANs:** Designed to create higher-resolution photos sequentially, giving a solution to scaling issues (Aggarwal et al, 2021).

Generative Adversarial Networks have emerged as a driving force in AI research and application development, always pushing the limits of what is possible in synthetic data creation and transformation. As academics and practitioners experiment with novel architectures and approaches, GANs continue to play an important role in determining the future of artificial intelligence.

A COMPREHENSIVE OVERVIEW ON THE CURRENT STATE OF ONLINE EDUCATION

The present condition of online education reflects a dynamic and fast changing world, influenced by technical breakthroughs, global events, and educational paradigm shifts. Online education, often known as e-learning, has grown in popularity, allowing for more accessible and flexible learning experiences at all educational levels. This detailed review addresses essential facets of the present situation of online education.

Acceleration and Adoption

The COVID-19 epidemic has considerably boosted the global adoption of online education. Educational institutions, from basic schools to universities, soon adopted remote and online learning strategies to assure educational continuity.

Technological Advancements

Technological improvements such as high-speed internet, cloud computing, and interactive multimedia tools have significantly improved the quality and accessibility of online education.

Learning Management Systems (LMS)

Learning Administration Systems (LMS) have become essential in online education, offering platforms for course delivery, material management, and student participation. Prevalent LMS platforms comprise Moodle, Canvas, and Blackboard.

Multiplicity of Courses and Programs

Online education provides a varied choice of courses and programmes across several fields. This comprises professional certifications, degree programmes, and skill-based courses offered by universities, online platforms, and industry-specific organisations.

International Reach and Accessibility

Online education has broken down geographical barriers, allowing students from all around the world to receive a high-quality education from prestigious schools. This has democratised education and created chances for learners who may encounter obstacles in traditional educational environments (Kumar, A et al, 2017).

Combined Learning Models

Many educational institutions are using blended learning approaches, which combine online and conventional classroom training. This method allows for flexibility while yet allowing for some face-to-face engagement.

Cooperating Content and Engagement

To increase student engagement, online education platforms include interactive material such as films, simulations, and gamification. This trend toward interactive and multimedia learning promotes a more engaging educational experience.

Proficient Development and Lifelong Learning

Online education is increasingly being used for professional development and lifetime learning. Professionals may learn new skills, expand their knowledge, and seek further degrees without interrupting their professions.

Challenges and Concerns

Despite its benefits, online education confronts several obstacles, including the digital divide, questions about the quality of online evaluations, and issues with student participation and motivation.

Assessment and Accreditation

The development of trustworthy online evaluation methodologies, as well as the certification of online programmes, have become important to guaranteeing online education's legitimacy and recognition.

Evolving Pedagogies

Educators are researching novel pedagogies for the online world, such as collaborative learning, project-based evaluations, and adaptive learning techniques.

Corporate Training and Skill Development

Corporations are increasingly embracing online education to train and improve their employees. Online platforms provide specialised training to address the changing needs of the workforce.

Data Analytics and Personalization

Educational technology is using data analytics to assess student progress, uncover learning trends, and create individualised learning experiences. This data-driven strategy increases adaptation to individual learning demands.

Future Trends

Virtual reality (VR) and augmented reality (AR) applications, artificial intelligence in education, and the integration of immersive technology for more engaging learning experiences are all expected to progress in the future of online education.

Thus, the current status of online education indicates a paradigm change in how learning is offered and accessible. While obstacles persist, continuous advancements and the incorporation of new technology continue to alter the future of education, making it more accessible, adaptable, and personalised to the requirements of various learners (Khanal, S et al, 2020).

GROUNDBREAKING APPLICATIONS OF GAN IN SAFEGUARDING COMPLEX INFORMATION IN ONLINE EDUCATION:

The unique use of Generative Adversarial Networks (GANs) offers a possible solution to the complex issues connected with protecting sensitive information in the online education scene. GANs, which are best recognised for producing realistic data, may be used to improve privacy, security, and data protection in online learning environments. Below, points will provide a thorough description of how GANs can be pragmatic to tackle these trials:

Privacy-Preserving Data Generation

Sensitive educational data, such as student records, assessment results, and personal information, must be handled with extreme caution to comply with privacy requirements. GANs may be used to create synthetic data that retains the statistical properties of actual data while respecting individual privacy. This enables educational institutions to analyse trends and patterns without disclosing sensitive data.

Anonymization and De-Identification

Identifiable information, such as student names and contact information, must be anonymised or de-identified to avoid illegal access. GANs can help generate synthetic identities or edit current data to remove personally identifiable information. This safeguards students' privacy while yet allowing for valid analysis and research.

Safe Data Sharing and Association

Collaborative projects and research in the online education industry frequently entail the secure exchange of sensitive data between institutions or academics. GANs can make safe data exchange easier by creating synthetic datasets that represent the combined properties of several datasets. This allows cooperation without explicitly disclosing sensitive information.

Adversarial Training for Boosted Security

Online education systems are vulnerable to cyber risks such as data breaches and illegal access to sensitive information. GANs may be used in adversarial training to improve the security of online educational systems. Training a GAN as a defender against possible cyber attacks enables it to find and mitigate flaws, making the system more resistant (Gan, W et al, 2023).

Meticulous Access to Subtle Content

Providing instructional resources while controlling access to sensitive topics is a huge problem. GANs can contribute to content filtering by producing synthetic copies of items with sensitive information removed. This allows for regulated access to instructional content while protecting sensitive information.

Differential Privacy in Valuation

Balancing the requirement for accurate evaluations with individual students' privacy when testing. GANs may be used to inject noise or perturbations into evaluation data, making individual answers difficult to detect. This aligns with the concepts of differentiated privacy, ensuring the secrecy of student achievement.

Anti-Deepfake Measures

Deepfake technology threatens the integrity of educational content and evaluations. GANs may be used to construct anti-deepfake measures by creating detectors that can recognise altered information, assuring the accuracy of educational materials and evaluations.

Adaptive Authentication

Ensure that only authorised persons have access to sensitive educational data. GANs can help create adaptive authentication systems by producing synthetic data to mimic various access situations. This aids in the evaluation of authentication methods' resilience against possible attacks.

Principled Considerations

Balancing the advantages of data privacy with ethical concerns and openness. GANs may be used responsibly, with clear regulations and ethical principles in place. Educators and institutions must guarantee that created data remains useful while adhering to ethical values and individual rights.

To summarise, the creative use of Generative Adversarial Networks in the online education scene has enormous promise for tackling difficult issues such as privacy, security, and sensitive data. By exploiting GANs in numerous ways, educational institutions may strengthen data safety, enable secure cooperation, and assure responsible use of sensitive information in the digital education era (Meng, R et al, 2018).

A BRIEF LITERATURE REVIEW ON THE INTEGRATION OF GAN IN ONLINE EDUCATION

The incorporation of Generative Adversarial Networks (GANs) into online education systems is a topic of continuing research, however there is growing interest and preliminary studies investigating its possible uses. Here's an overview of the current literature review on this topic:

Content Generation

Several studies have looked into the use of GANs to produce instructional content such as graphics, words, and even complete courses. These studies look into how GANs can be trained on existing educational resources to create new content, complement course materials, or even tailor learning experiences for students.

Data Augmentation

GANs can supplement datasets used to train machine learning models in online education systems. By creating synthetic data that closely mimics real data, GANs can assist address data scarcity challenges and increase the effectiveness of predictive models used for tasks such as student performance prediction or adaptive learning.

Personalized Learning

GANs have the ability to help with personalized learning by creating tailored educational content based on individual student attributes, preferences, and learning styles. This may include creating individualized exams, exercises, or tutoring materials that adjust to students' progress and requirements (Yang R et al, 2021).

Visualizations and Simulations

GANs can be used to construct realistic visualizations and simulations that improve learning in fields like as science, engineering, and medicine. GANs can aid students in comprehending complicated topics and phenomena by producing high-fidelity visuals or interactive simulations.

Content Translation and Localization

GANs have been investigated for translating educational information between languages and localizing content to different cultural contexts. GANs can assist diverse communities gain access to online education by creating translations or modifications of instructional resources.

Quality Assurance and Plagiarism Detection

GANs can be used to improve quality assurance and detect plagiarism in online education systems. GANs can contribute to academic integrity and excellence by creating synthetic instances of high-quality instructional content or finding similarities between authentic and plagiarized items.

Feedback Generation

GANs can provide feedback to students on their assignments, projects, and performances. This feedback can be personalized, thorough, and constructive, giving students valuable insights and suggestions for improving their learning results.

Ethical and Social Implications

Some studies have looked into the ethical and social consequences of using GANs into online education systems. This includes implications for bias, fairness, privacy, and openness in the usage of AI-generated instructional content (Anthony, B et al, 2022).

In general, while the incorporation of GANs into online education systems shows promise for improving learning experiences and educational outcomes, more research is required to fully explore its potential, address technical challenges and ethical concerns, and assess its effectiveness in real-world educational settings.

TRADITIONAL APPROACHES FOR FORTIFYING ONLINE PLATFORMS

Securing online platforms is essential for maintaining the confidentiality, integrity, and availability of data and services. Traditional ways of safeguarding online platforms combine technologies, policies, and practises to protect against different cyber threats. Below given points will offer a comprehensive elucidation of these traditional methods:

Firewalls

Firewalls serve as a barrier between a trusted internal network and untrustworthy external networks, monitoring and restricting incoming and outgoing network traffic according to preset security rules. Firewalls assist to prevent unauthorised access, filter harmful communications, and defend against typical cyber dangers including malware and unauthorised access attempts.

Intrusion Detection Systems (IDS) and Intrusion Prevention Systems (IPS)

IDS analyses network or system activity for suspicious behaviour or security policy breaches, whereas IPS goes a step farther and actively prevents or blocks harmful activity. These technologies aid in the detection and response to security problems such as unauthorised access, malware, and other anomalous behaviour.

Secure Sockets Layer (SSL) and Transport Layer Security (TLS)

SSL and its successor TLS are cryptographic technologies that enable secure communication across a computer network. They safeguard the security and integrity of data transmitted between web servers and clients. SSL/TLS is commonly used to protect data sent over the internet, particularly in online platforms that handle sensitive information such as login passwords and financial transactions.

Virtual Private Networks (VPNs)

VPNs provide a secure, encrypted connection across the internet, allowing users to safely access private networks as if they were directly linked to them. VPNs are critical for safeguarding distant access to web platforms, preserving data during transmission, and maintaining communication privacy.

Access Controls and Authentication

Access controls impose regulations governing who has access to what resources. Passwords, multi-factor authentication (MFA), and biometrics are examples of authentication mechanisms that are used to authenticate user identities. Strong access controls and authentication systems are critical for preventing illegal access and securing sensitive data (Yu, Z, 2022).

Antivirus and Antimalware Software

Antivirus and antimalware solutions detect, block, and remove dangerous software such as viruses, worms, Trojans, and spyware. Regularly updating antivirus software is critical for detecting and reducing the effects of malware on online platforms.

Security Patching and Updates:

Regularly upgrading software, oerating systems, and applications with security patches is critical for resolving potential vulnerabilities and weaknesses exploited by attackers. Patching on time reduces the danger of exploitation by keeping the online platform's software up to date with the most recent security changes.

Security Policies and User Education

Establishing and implementing security rules, as well as educating users on recommended practises, help to foster a security-conscious culture. Users should be informed of security regulations, standards for managing sensitive information, and the possible hazards connected with online activity in order to limit the chance of security breaches.

Network Segmentation

Network segmentation divides a network into smaller pieces in order to isolate and contain any security breaches. Organizations may reduce the effect of a security issue and prevent attackers from moving laterally throughout the network by isolating various components of it.

Backup and Disaster Recovery Planning

Regular data backups and a robust disaster recovery strategy guarantee speedy recovery in the case of data loss or system compromise. Backups provide a safety net in the event of data breaches, ransomware attacks, or other catastrophic occurrences, allowing businesses to resume operations with little interruption.

Security Audits and Monitoring

Regular security audits and network monitoring assist in identifying vulnerabilities, assessing the efficacy of security policies, and detecting possible security issues. Continuous monitoring and auditing help firms spot threats ahead of time, allowing them to solve security concerns before they become more serious.

Incident Response Plans

Incident response plans lay out the steps to take in the case of a security incident, advising businesses on how to contain, eliminate, and recover from a breach. A well-defined incident response strategy reduces the effect of security problems while also ensuring a coordinated and fast response to risk mitigation.

Physical Security Measures

Physical security measures, such as access restrictions, surveillance cameras, and secure buildings, safeguard the physical infrastructure that supports online platforms. Physical security methods protect servers and networking equipment from unwanted access, manipulation, or theft.

Regulatory Compliance

Adherence to applicable rules and compliance standards ensures that online platforms comply with legal obligations and industry standards for data protection and security. Compliance with rules such as GDPR, HIPAA, and PCI DSS allows firms to avoid legal ramifications while also building user confidence.

To summarise, traditional ways of safeguarding online platforms require a comprehensive strategy that includes technology, regulations, and education to reduce a wide variety of cyber dangers. Implementing these procedures increases the entire security posture of online platforms, protecting data, services, and user confidence (Harini, H et al, 2023).

POTENTIAL RISKS AND VULNERABILITIES ASSOCIATED WITH THE USE OF GAN IN ONLINE EDUCATION

Generative Adversarial Networks (GANs) have the potential to transform numerous fields, including online education. However, its utilization poses specific hazards and vulnerabilities that need to be handled:

Data Privacy Concerns

GANs need vast datasets to train effectively. In the context of online education, this could include sensitive student information. If sufficient security measures are not in place, data breaches or misuse may occur.

Bias Amplification

GANs may inadvertently exacerbate biases in the training data. In the context of education, this may result in the propagation of stereotypes or unfair treatment of pupils from various backgrounds.

Quality Control

GAN-generated content may not always meet educational standards. If the created content is not properly reviewed, it is possible to disseminate false or misleading information (Lee, J et al, 2021).

Misinformation and Manipulation

GANs could be used to generate instructional materials that appear realistic but include incorrect information or propaganda. This could jeopardize the legitimacy of online education platforms and negatively impact students' learning experiences.

Intellectual Property Concerns

GANs can be used to create content that is similar to existing educational resources, raising concerns about copyright infringement and intellectual property rights.

Security Risks

Malicious actors could utilize GANs to create phony credentials or certificates, jeopardizing the credibility of online education platforms and credentials.

Ethical Implications

The use of GANs in education poses ethical concerns concerning transparency, permission, and ownership of created content, as students and educators may not be aware that they are dealing with AI-generated materials.

Lack of Accountability

If GAN-generated content is not correctly marked or identified, it may be difficult to assign blame for mistakes or biases, resulting in a lack of accountability in the educational process (Hitaj, B et al, 2017).

To reduce these perils, it is critical to implement effective data privacy. The use of GANs in education poses ethical concerns of transparency, consent, and ownership of created content. Students and educators may not be aware that they are interacting with AI-generated content. Measures, ensures variety and representativeness in training data, establishes quality control procedures for generated content, promotes openness and ethical principles in GAN use, and educates stakeholders on the capabilities and limitations of AI in education. Furthermore, constant monitoring and evaluation of GAN-generated content is critical for addressing emerging concerns and ensuring the integrity of online education systems.

INTEGRATION OF GAN TO IMPROVE THE PRIVACY AND SECURITY IN ONLINE EDUCATION SYSTEM

Integrating Generative Adversarial Networks (GANs) into online education can be an effective strategy for improving privacy and security. GANs, which are recognised for their capacity to produce realistic synthetic data, may be used in a variety of ways to solve privacy concerns, strengthen security measures, and improve overall data protection. Below is a full discussion of how GANs may be implemented into the online education environment:

Privacy-Preserving Data Generation

Generative Adversarial Networks (GANs) may be used to generate privacy-preserving data by producing synthetic data that keeps the statistical features of the original data while obscuring sensitive information. This use of GANs enables enterprises to do analysis, research, and model training while maintaining individual anonymity. Here is how GANs may be used to generate data while respecting privacy:

The main objective is to create synthetic data that closely mimics the actual data distribution while eliminating the inclusion of sensitive information, such as personally identifying information (PII). GANs are made up of two neural networks, a generator and a discriminator, that participate in an adversarial training process. The generator generates synthetic data, seeking to generate samples that are indistinguishable from the genuine data. The discriminator compares produced samples to real data, attempting to discriminate between the two. During training, the generator learns to produce data that closely resembles the statistical patterns and structures seen in the original dataset. The discriminator learns to differentiate between actual and artificial data. The training process is modelled as a minimax game, with the generator aiming to reduce the likelihood of the discriminator correctly categorising generated samples and the discriminator aiming to increase accuracy. Binary cross-entropy loss functions are commonly employed to guide the GAN to a Nash equilibrium, in which the generator creates data that is statistically indistinguishable from the original data. Figure 1 shows the general architecture of GAN.

Once trained, the generator may produce synthetic data samples by inputting random noise. These synthetic samples have statistical qualities similar to the real dataset, but do not provide precise information about individual data points. Because the produced data does not come from actual persons in the dataset, GANs provide a privacy-preserving approach by definition. It is a synthetic representation based on the collective patterns discovered during training.

Synthetic data created by GANs may be utilised for study and analysis, allowing researchers to derive insights and conclusions without dealing with real, possibly sensitive material. Institutions can exchange synthetic datasets for collaborative research without disclosing actual user data, fostering secure cooperation. GAN-generated synthetic data may be used to train machine learning models while protecting individual privacy. It is critical to guarantee that synthetic data remains useful for its original purpose while also protecting privacy. Institutions should examine the privacy assurances given by GANs in their unique setting, taking into account aspects such as data nature and legal climate.

Figure 1. The architecture of a generative adversarial network

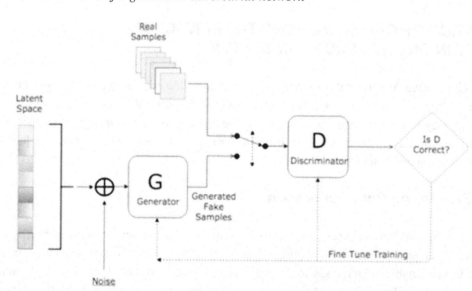

GANs can be utilised with differential privacy strategies to improve privacy protection. This entails introducing controlled noise into the training process to ensure that the model's predictions are not excessively impacted by any individual data point. Institutions should communicate clearly with stakeholders about the use of GANs for data production, ensuring that they understand the synthetic nature of the data. To provide openness and accountability, detailed documentation on the GAN architecture, training process, and privacy safeguards should be maintained properly.

As a result, GANs provide a strong solution to privacy-preserving data production, enabling enterprises to reap the advantages of data-driven insights while protecting individual privacy. GANs contribute to a privacy-aware data handling strategy in several sectors, including online education, healthcare, and research. They generate synthetic data that preserves statistical features while removing sensitive information (Faisal, F et al, 2022).

Anonymization and De-Identification

Generative Adversarial Networks (GANs) may be used to anonymize and de-identify educational datasets, efficiently eliminating personally identifying information (PII) while retaining the data's value and statistical features. The following is a description of how GANs may be used for this purpose.

Understanding Anonymization and De-Identification

Anonymization is the process of eliminating or changing information in a dataset such that individual entities cannot be identified. De-identification is a larger term for the removal or alteration of identifying information, such as PII, in order to safeguard privacy.

Data Preprocessing

Identification of PII: Determine which fields in the educational dataset include personally identifiable information, such as names, addresses, email addresses, or student IDs.

Data Representation for GANs

Numerical Transformation: Convert non-numerical PII fields to numerical representations that are compatible with GANs.

Feature Scaling: To make the training process easier, ensure that all characteristics, including modified PII fields, have the same scale.

GAN Architecture

As seen before in the previous section, we will be well known about the activities of a generator and discriminator. The will take care of generating synthetic data samples and evaluates the samples and distinguish the real samples promptly.

Training Process

Objective Function: Set up the training process as a minimax game, with the generator producing synthetic samples that are indistinguishable from actual data and the discriminator properly determining whether a sample is genuine or created.

Loss Function

Binary Cross-Entropy: Typically used as a loss function to direct the training process. It measures the discrepancy between the discriminator's anticipated and actual classifications.

Data Generation

Random Noise Input: The generator uses random noise as input to create synthetic data samples, which include altered or synthesised copies of PII fields.

Iterative Training: The GAN is iteratively trained until it generates synthetic samples that closely resemble the original data's statistical distribution.

Evaluation of Privacy Preservation

Statistical Tests: Use statistical tests to guarantee that the synthetic data does not disclose any trends that may be used to identify individuals.

Privacy Metrics: Assess the extent of anonymization accomplished using privacy measures such as k-anonymity or l-diversity.

Iterative Refinement

Fine-Tuning: If required, adjust the GAN design or settings to obtain the appropriate amount of anonymity while preserving data usefulness.

Validation and Testing

Validation Set: Use a second validation set to evaluate the GAN's performance in terms of both data usefulness and privacy protection.

Testing: Evaluate the anonymized and de-identified dataset against particular use cases to ensure that it fits the needs of the desired analysis.

Integration with Educational Platforms

Deployment: Once you're pleased with the amount of anonymity, include the GAN-generated synthetic dataset into the educational platform for use in research, analytics, or collaboration.

User Awareness: Communicate openly with users, researchers, and stakeholders about the usage of anonymised data and the increased privacy safeguards in place.

Regular Updates and Monitoring

Dynamic Nature of Data: Recognize that datasets fluctuate over time, and the GAN model may need to be updated on a frequent basis to account for these changes.

Continuous Monitoring: Implement continuous monitoring to identify any unintentional re-identification risks or privacy concerns that may develop.

To summarise, using GANs for anonymization and de-identification in educational datasets requires careful preprocessing, GAN architecture design, training, and assessment. When correctly performed, this technique allows for the generation of synthetic datasets that safeguard individual privacy while maintaining the usability and worth of the data for educational research and analysis (Kuang, Z et al, 2021).

Secure Data Sharing and Collaboration

Generative Adversarial Networks (GANs) can play an important role in safe data sharing and collaboration by producing synthetic data that preserves the statistical properties of the original. This enables enterprises to interact and share ideas while protecting sensitive or personally identifiable information (PII). Here is an overview of how GANs help with safe data exchange and collaboration:

GANs create synthetic datasets that closely resemble the statistical features of actual data. These synthetic datasets may be shared with others, allowing for collaborative study while protecting sensitive information. GANs use random noise as an input to produce synthetic data samples. The GAN generator learns to generate synthetic samples with distributions and patterns similar to those found in the original dataset. Synthetic data reduces the danger of disclosing sensitive information, such as PII or private records, while allowing for collaborative analysis. GAN-generated synthetic datasets promote cooperation across businesses that may be unable to share genuine data owing to privacy or security issues.

Organizations can communicate GAN-generated synthetic datasets rather than raw data, allowing each partner to contribute to a collaborative effort while protecting their private datasets. GANs allow for cooperation across several areas, including as healthcare, finance, and education, where data sensitivity is a major concern. GANs allow scholars from several universities to collaborate on research projects while protecting the privacy of their own datasets. Synthetic datasets provide a means to include variety into collaborative research, improving the robustness and generalizability of findings. GANs are intended to preserve the statistical properties and structures of the original data, guaranteeing that the synthetic data remains useful for analysis and study. Fine-tuning the GAN model may be done to balance privacy with usefulness, ensuring that the generated synthetic data is still usable for certain applications. Implement strong authentication and permission systems to guarantee that only authorised users can access and contribute on synthetic datasets. Implement encryption techniques to safeguard the transfer of synthetic data throughout the cooperation process.

GANs may be used to adapt to dynamic data environments by creating synthetic datasets that mirror changes in the underlying data distribution over time. This versatility allows for continuing cooperation even as datasets develop. Communicate clearly to collaborators and stakeholders that synthetic data is being utilised to ensure privacy and security. Ensure that consumers understand the limits of synthetic data and that it is not a replacement for true data in all situations. When exchanging synthetic datasets between businesses, ensure that you are following privacy legislation and standards. Maintain documentation detailing privacy-preserving procedures, including the use of GANs, to verify compliance. Regularly monitor collaborative actions with synthetic datasets to discover any abnormalities or security breaches. Conduct quarterly audits to determine the efficacy of GAN-based privacy and security safeguards.

In a word, GANs help to ensure secure data exchange and cooperation by generating synthetic datasets that protect privacy. This strategy enables firms to exchange ideas, engage in collaborative research, and drive innovation while maintaining the security of sensitive data (Yan, X et al, 2019).

Adaptive Authentication Testing

Generative Adversarial Networks (GANs) can aid in adaptive authentication testing by simulating different access situations and assisting businesses in determining the resilience of their authentication measures. Here is a quick overview of GANs' function in adaptive authentication testing:

The primary objective is to assess the effectiveness of authentication systems in dynamically reacting to various access circumstances, including potential hostile attacks. GANs may be used to simulate numerous access attempts by creating synthetic data that represents different authentication conditions.

- **Training GAN for Adaptive Authentication Testing:** Train the GAN with historical data or knowledge about the organization's authentication mechanism. The GAN's generator learns to make synthetic authentication attempts, which are subsequently evaluated by the discriminator.
- **Synthetic Access Scenarios:** GANs may provide synthetic data that represents numerous elements of authentication efforts, such as login patterns, input variations, and possible adversarial assaults.
- **Assessment of Authentication Mechanisms:** Use the produced synthetic data to evaluate how successfully the organization's authentication procedures handle various access scenarios. Evaluate the system's capacity to identify abnormalities, withstand assaults, and adapt to changing situations.
- **Identification of Vulnerabilities:** GAN-based testing identifies flaws or weaknesses in the authentication system that might not be obvious using regular testing approaches. Evaluate the system's resilience to common assaults including brute force, credential stuffing, and sophisticated adversarial attempts.
- **Adaptive Model Training:** Use the insights gathered from GAN-generated data to modify and improve the organization's authentication methods. This adaptive training strategy improves the system's capacity to learn from many settings and improve over time.
- **Behavioural Authentication Testing:** GANs may replicate a variety of user behaviours, such as typing patterns, mouse movements, and biometric inputs, in order to evaluate behavioural authentication systems. Evaluate the system's ability to discriminate between actual and fake user behaviours.

GANs can be used to generate tough scenarios, such as synthetic data that simulates complex attack patterns, in order to evaluate the system's resilience to advanced attacks. Adaptive authentication testing using GANs encourages a continual improvement cycle. Regularly update and retrain the GAN model to keep up with emerging threats and developing attack strategies. GAN-based testing increases awareness of possible security vulnerabilities among authentication system developers and administrators. Encourage a proactive approach to security by discovering and resolving vulnerabilities before they are exploited. Ethical usage of GANs is critical in authentication testing. Ensure that the testing technique is consistent with ethical principles and does not jeopardise genuine users' privacy or rights.

Thus, GANs help to adaptive authentication testing by producing synthetic data that replicates a variety of access scenarios. This technique assists businesses in evaluating and improving the robustness of their authentication systems, ensuring that they can adapt to a range of situations and withstand any hostile attempts (Li, Y et al, 2022).

Differential Privacy in Assessments

Generative Adversarial Networks (GANs) can be used to implement differential privacy in assessments, balancing the need for accuracy with the privacy of individual replies. In this context:

The major objective is to preserve the privacy of individual evaluation replies while obtaining useful insights for research. GANs may be used to introduce controlled noise or perturbations into evaluation data, guaranteeing that individual responses cannot be clearly distinguished. Train the GANs to create privacy-preserving noise while retaining the overall statistical features of the assessment dataset. GANs produce synthetic copies of assessment data that include more noise, making it more difficult to detect individual responses. The added noise protects against re-identification threats, guaranteeing that individual participants' privacy is preserved. GAN-generated perturbations strive for statistical indistinguishability, making it difficult to pinpoint specific answers even if an opponent has a limited understanding of the dataset. GANs provide for a compromise between retaining the value of assessment data for analysis purposes and protecting the privacy of individual responders. GANs with differential privacy can be used in educational settings, online testing platforms, and other environments where individual assessment replies must be kept private.

Organizations may fine-tune the GAN-based strategy to obtain the required level of privacy protection while adhering to legal constraints and ethical guidelines. Transparently convey the usage of GANs for introducing differential privacy to stakeholders, participants, and educators in order to foster confidence in the assessment process. GANs contribute to evaluations with differential privacy by introducing privacy-preserving noise, which makes it difficult to identify individual replies while maintaining the dataset's general statistical properties. This technique strengthens privacy safeguards in assessment scenarios, particularly in educational and testing contexts (Fan, L, 2020)

Content Filtering for Sensitive Material

Generative Adversarial Networks (GANs) may be used for content filtering in the context of sensitive materials by creating synthetic versions of content that eliminate sensitive information. This technique allows for regulated access to instructional or informational resources while protecting and filtering out potentially sensitive or private information. GANs assist establish a balance between content availability and privacy issues in various applications, ensuring that users may access essential information while without disclosing sensitive data (Shigekawa, N et al, 2005).

Anti-Deepfake Measures

Generative Adversarial Networks (GANs) are employed in anti-deepfake tactics to identify and reduce the generation and dissemination of fake material. Deepfakes are computer-generated or modified material that frequently feature realistic-looking video or audio impersonations. GANs, the fundamental technology underpinning many deepfakes, may also be used as countermeasures. Here is a quick overview of how GANs are utilised in anti-deepfake measures:

GANs are utilised for the creation of detection models. The detector, also known as a discriminator, is taught to discern between authentic and altered material. Anti-deepfake systems can detect errors or artefacts created during the deepfake generation process by taking advantage of GANs' adversarial character. To improve detection capabilities, the GAN-based anti-deepfake model is trained on a variety of datasets that comprise both legitimate and altered information. This allows the algorithm to generalise and recognise new types of deepfakes. GANs may be used to extract features and detect distinctive patterns and traits associated with deepfake content. These characteristics are then used by the anti-deepfake system to distinguish between genuine and altered material.

In a contradictory approach, GANs are applied both in making deepfake material (generator) and constructing deepfake detection systems (detector). These arms race dynamic pushes for advancements in detection as new deepfake generation techniques emerge.

GANs can help with anti-deepfake measures by increasing the resilience of detection models against emerging deepfake approaches. The adversarial training process enables the system to adapt and become less vulnerable to sophisticated manipulation efforts. GANs are used to create benchmark datasets including a mix of deepfake and actual material. These datasets are critical for assessing the performance of anti-deepfake technologies and assuring their efficacy in various circumstances. The GAN-based anti-deepfake community often collaborates to exchange ideas, datasets, and advances in detection approaches. This effort contributes to a collective defence against the spread of deepfake material. The use of GANs in anti-deepfake methods has ethical implications, such as assuring fair and unbiased identification of falsified information. Developers strive to reduce false positives and negatives while protecting privacy and preventing the exploitation of detection technology.

GANs play an important role in the development of anti-deepfake techniques by enabling the design of detection models capable of identifying altered information. This continuous technical duel involves using GANs to create and identify deepfakes, pushing the frontiers of AI ethics and technological developments (Gong, D et al, 2020).

Enhanced Security With Adversarial Training

GANs may be used in adversarial training settings to detect and mitigate cyber threats. This entails training a GAN to defend against multiple threats, increasing the system's resilience.

Secure Virtual Environments for Simulations

Generative Adversarial Networks (GANs) may be used to create safe virtual environments for simulations, increasing the realism and privacy of the data. Here is a summary of how GANs help to create safe virtual environments for simulations:

The fundamental objective is to develop realistic and privacy-preserving simulations that effectively imitate real-world circumstances while protecting sensitive information. GANs create synthetic data that closely mimics actual data distributions. In virtual worlds, this might comprise synthetic pictures, films, or other simulated material. GANs enable the creation of synthetic material that closely resembles real-world data while eliminating personally identifiable information (PII) and other sensitive information. This assures that simulations respect users' privacy and follow data protection standards. GANs help to create diverse and realistic synthetic content by giving a variety of settings for simulation. Simulations using heterogeneous data generated by GANs improve training and testing under a variety of scenarios.

GANs may be used to generate synthetic environments that simulate the circumstances seen in certain training settings. This is especially beneficial for training simulations in areas such as healthcare, military, and emergency response. GANs may imitate realistic behaviours and interactions, allowing for the construction of dynamic and lifelike virtual worlds. Behavioural simulation is essential for developing and testing systems that comprehend and respond to human behaviours. GANs may be used to replicate security risks and challenges, allowing businesses to train and test security procedures in a safe and realistic setting. This improves the readiness of security people and systems. Machine learning models in virtual environments may be taught using synthetic data generated by GANs. This allows for the construction of strong models without relying on sensitive real-world data. GANs may generate synthetic anomalies and novel scenarios to train anomaly detection algorithms. This helps systems recognise and respond to unexpected situations more effectively.

GANs enable the synthesis of fresh synthetic data, allowing virtual environments to be updated dynamically. This guarantees that simulations stay relevant and effective in addressing changing conditions Clear communication is required to inform users and stakeholders about the use of synthetic data and GANs in developing safe virtual environments. Educating consumers increases their trust and comprehension of the simulations' privacy-preserving nature. Regularly evaluate the efficiency of virtual environments generated with GANs, looking for areas for improvement. Iterative refining ensures that simulations meet changing demands and problems. Integrating GANs into safe virtual environments improves simulations' privacy, realism, and variety. GANs generate synthetic data and contribute to training, testing, and developing systems across multiple areas while respecting privacy and adhering with data protection laws (Meng, R et al, 2018).

Principled Reflections and Transparency

Institutions should provide explicit norms and procedures for the ethical use of GANs. Transparency in data generating processes and the usage of synthetic data should be communicated to build confidence.

Unremitting Monitoring and Auditing

GANs can be used in a continuous monitoring system to discover anomalies in data patterns that could signal a security breach. This proactive strategy enables rapid reactions to possible risks.

Institutions should run awareness campaigns to educate instructors, administrators, and students on the usage of GANs for data protection. Clear disclosure on the synthetic nature of specific datasets can assist to foster trust. Institutions should integrate their usage of GANs with legal requirements, ensuring that the created synthetic data adheres to privacy laws and rules. Integrating GANs into the online education environment provides a complex solution to improve privacy and security. Educational institutions may improve data security measures while encouraging relevant research and collaboration within a safe and ethical framework by utilising GANs for privacy-preserving data creation, authentication testing, content screening, and other tasks.

GAN IN AUGMENTING THE OVERALL CYBERSECURITY POSTURE IN ONLINE EDUCATIONAL PLATFORMS

Generative Adversarial Networks (GANs) can help improve the overall cybersecurity posture of online education platforms by solving numerous security concerns and strengthening protective measures. Let us learn the summary of the main contributions of GANs in this context:

Adversarial Training for Improved Defences

GANs may be employed in adversarial training situations to boost the robustness of cybersecurity defences. Training GANs to pose as attackers allows online education platforms to uncover and address weaknesses in their systems, preparing them for real-world cyber attacks.

Detection of Cyber Threats and Anomalies

GANs can help to design sophisticated threat detection systems. GANs may produce synthetic data to replicate normal and abnormal network behaviour, which aids in the training of intrusion detection systems and improves the platform's capacity to identify cyber-attacks.

Privacy-Preserving Data Generation

GANs help to create synthetic datasets that protect users' privacy. Educational platforms may employ GANs to produce synthetic data for cybersecurity training and assessment without disclosing actual student or user information, solving privacy issues.

Security Awareness Training

GANs may be used to mimic real-world cyber-attacks as part of security awareness training. GANs may be used in educational platforms to produce realistic phishing simulations, social engineering situations, and other cyber hazards in order to educate students, teachers, and administrators about possible risks.

Anti-Deepfake Measures

GANs can help detect and prevent deepfake material. Using GANs for deepfake identification, online education platforms can reduce the dangers of creating and disseminating falsified instructional content (Dunmore, A et al, 2023).

Secure Content Distribution

GANs can be used for secure content exchange and dissemination. Synthetic data created by GANs may be utilised to share ideas and cooperate on research without disclosing genuine sensitive material, encouraging secure content exchange within the academic community.

Simulating Cybersecurity Incidents

GANs may mimic a variety of cybersecurity scenarios. GANs may be used in educational platforms to produce synthetic cyber-attack situations, allowing cybersecurity personnel to practise incident response and fine-tune their techniques in a controlled setting.

Authentication Testing and Vulnerability Assessment

GANs can help to test authentication systems for weaknesses. By simulating various authentication attempts and potential attack situations, GANs aid in identifying flaws in the platform's authentication systems, improving overall security.

Creation of Secure Virtual Environments

GANs help create realistic and safe virtual environments. GAN-generated simulated environments may be utilised for cybersecurity training and testing, since they provide a controlled environment in which to mimic cyber risks and evaluate security solutions.

Behavioural Analysis and Anomaly Detection

GANs may imitate a variety of user activities for behavioural study. GANs may be used by online education platforms to produce synthetic data that reflects various user habits, improving the platform's capacity to identify abnormalities and security breaches.

Regulatory Compliance and Auditing

GANs help to ensure compliance with cybersecurity legislation. By creating synthetic data for audits and compliance checks, educational platforms may demonstrate adherence to security requirements without revealing genuine sensitive data.

Constant Monitoring and Threat Intelligence

GANs can help to continuously check the platform's security. By modelling developing cyber threats, GANs assist platforms in staying up to speed on threat intelligence and responding promptly to emerging security concerns.

GANs improve the entire cybersecurity posture of online education platforms by offering tools for training, testing, and enhancing security procedures. Whether through adversarial training, threat detection, privacy-preserving data production, or modelling of cybersecurity crises, GANs play an important role in reinforcing educational platforms against a spectrum of cyber threats (Dixit, P et al, 2021).

CHALLENGES IN INTEGRATING GAN FOR ONLINE EDUCATION SECURITY

While Generative Adversarial Networks (GANs) have important applications in online education, their implementation presents various problems. Here are some main problems when utilising GANs for online education:

GANs require large volumes of data to train well. Balancing the need for data with privacy concerns, particularly in educational contexts with sensitive student information, may be difficult. Ethical considerations occur with the development of synthetic data, which might lead to unexpected effects or prejudice. Ensuring ethical usage and limiting the generation of deceptive or harmful material presents a substantial problem. GANs may mistakenly learn and repeat biases seen in training data. This can lead to the creation of synthetic content that reflects or reinforces existing prejudices, compromising the quality and impartiality of instructional materials. There is a dearth of defined techniques and criteria for using GANs into online learning. The lack of a broadly acknowledged framework might impede consistent and successful integration (Lin, H et al, 2022).

Training GANs frequently necessitates significant computing resources. Many educational institutions may encounter hardware limits and associated expenditures while running resource-intensive GAN models. GANs are recognised for their "black box" character, which makes it difficult to analyse and explain the model's judgments. This lack of openness can be problematic in educational contexts where responsibility and comprehension of the decision-making process are essential. Integrating GANs with current online education systems might be challenging. Compatibility concerns with existing systems, data formats, or learning management systems might impede seamless integration. Users, particularly educators, students, and administrators, may be wary or uncomfortable with the usage of synthetic data or AI-generated material. Developing trust and establishing user acceptability are critical difficulties.

Educational institutions must follow a variety of standards governing data privacy and ethical issues. Implementing GANs while complying to these restrictions is a considerable challenge, necessitating careful consideration of legal and regulatory frameworks. Educational material and situations are always changing, and GANs may fail to adapt to new scenarios. Continuous training and adaptation of GANs to changing educational contexts provide continuous difficulties. Training GANs needs knowledge, time, and resources. Educational institutions may have difficulty distributing these resources, especially if they lack specialist expertise in AI and machine learning. It is critical to ensure that GAN-generated material is of high quality and accurate. Establishing validation procedures and quality control systems for synthetic content may be a difficult but essential undertaking.

To address these difficulties, educators, developers, and politicians must work together to create ethical and regulatory frameworks that govern the proper use of GANs in online education (Williams, P et al, 2022).

CONCLUSION

To summarise, incorporating Generative Adversarial Networks (GANs) offers a viable path for improving privacy and security in online education. Using GANs, educational platforms may produce synthetic data that mimics real-world circumstances while protecting sensitive information, ensuring user privacy. GANs also help with safe content sharing, anti-deepfake procedures, and adaptive authentication testing, which improves the overall cybersecurity posture of online educational settings. However, issues like as data protection, ethical considerations, and the need for standardisation must be carefully negotiated in order to ensure responsible and successful adoption. As the area progresses, the wise application of GANs has enormous promise for establishing a more secure, privacy-preserving, and resilient online education landscape.

REFERENCES

Aggarwal, A., Mittal, M., & Battineni, G. (2021). Generative adversarial network: An overview of theory and applications. *International Journal of Information Management Data Insights*, *1*(1), 100004. doi:10.1016/j.jjimei.2020.100004

Anthony, B., Kamaludin, A., Romli, A., Raffei, A. F. M., Phon, D. N. A. E., Abdullah, A., & Ming, G. L. (2022). Blended learning adoption and implementation in higher education: A theoretical and systematic review. *Technology, Knowledge and Learning*, 1-48.

Dixit, P., & Silakari, S. (2021). Deep learning algorithms for cybersecurity applications: A technological and status review. *Computer Science Review*, *39*, 100317. doi:10.1016/j.cosrev.2020.100317

Dunmore, A., Jang-Jaccard, J., Sabrina, F., & Kwak, J. (2023). A Comprehensive Survey of Generative Adversarial Networks (GANs) in Cybersecurity Intrusion Detection. *IEEE Access : Practical Innovations, Open Solutions*, *11*, 76071–76094. doi:10.1109/ACCESS.2023.3296707

Faisal, F., Mohammed, N., Leung, C. K., & Wang, Y. (2022, October). Generating privacy preserving synthetic medical data. In *2022 IEEE 9th International Conference on Data Science and Advanced Analytics (DSAA)* (pp. 1-10). IEEE. 10.1109/DSAA54385.2022.10032429

Fan, L. (2020, February). A survey of differentially private generative adversarial networks. In *The AAAI Workshop on Privacy-Preserving Artificial Intelligence* (Vol. 8). AAAI.

Gan, W., Qi, Z., Wu, J., & Lin, J. C. W. (2023). Large language models in education: Vision and opportunities. arXiv preprint arXiv:2311.13160. doi:10.1109/BigData59044.2023.10386291

Gong, D., Goh, O. S., Kumar, Y. J., Ye, Z., & Chi, W. (2020). Deepfake forensics, an ai-synthesized detection with deep convolutional generative adversarial networks. *International Journal (Toronto, Ont.)*, *9*(3), 2861–2870.

Harini, H., Wahyuningtyas, D. P., Sutrisno, S., Wanof, M. I., & Ausat, A. M. A. (2023). Marketing strategy for early Childhood Education (ECE) schools in the Digital Age. Jurnal Obsesi. *Jurnal Pendidikan Anak Usia Dini*, *7*(3), 2742–2758.

Hitaj, B., Ateniese, G., & Perez-Cruz, F. (2017, October). Deep models under the GAN: information leakage from collaborative deep learning. In *Proceedings of the 2017 ACM SIGSAC conference on computer and communications security* (pp. 603-618). ACM. 10.1145/3133956.3134012

Kaneko, T. (2018). Generative adversarial networks: Foundations and applications. *Acoustical Science and Technology*, *39*(3), 189–197. doi:10.1250/ast.39.189

Khanal, S. S., Prasad, P. W. C., Alsadoon, A., & Maag, A. (2020). A systematic review: Machine learning based recommendation systems for e-learning. *Education and Information Technologies, 25*(4), 2635–2664. doi:10.1007/s10639-019-10063-9

Kuang, Z., Liu, H., Yu, J., Tian, A., Wang, L., Fan, J., & Babaguchi, N. (2021, October). Effective de-identification generative adversarial network for face anonymization. In *Proceedings of the 29th ACM International Conference on Multimedia* (pp. 3182-3191). ACM. 10.1145/3474085.3475464

Kumar, A., Kumar, P., Palvia, S. C. J., & Verma, S. (2017). Online education worldwide: Current status and emerging trends. *Journal of Information Technology Case and Application Research, 19*(1), 3–9. doi:10.1080/15228053.2017.1294867

Lee, J., & Park, K. (2021). GAN-based imbalanced data intrusion detection system. *Personal and Ubiquitous Computing, 25*(1), 121–128. doi:10.1007/s00779-019-01332-y

Li, Y., Liu, L., Qin, H., Deng, S., El-Yacoubi, M. A., & Zhou, G. (2022). Adaptive deep feature fusion for continuous authentication with data augmentation. *IEEE Transactions on Mobile Computing*.

Lin, H., Wan, S., Gan, W., Chen, J., & Chao, H. C. (2022, December). Metaverse in education: Vision, opportunities, and challenges. In *2022 IEEE International Conference on Big Data (Big Data)* (pp. 2857-2866). IEEE.

Meng, R., Cui, Q., & Yuan, C. (2018). A Survey of Image Information Hiding Algorithms Based on Deep Learning. *CMES-Computer Modeling In Engineering & Sciences, 117*(3).

Shigekawa, N., Nishimura, K., Yokoyama, H., & Hohkawa, K. (2005). Side-gate effects on transfer characteristics in GaN-based transversal filters. *Applied Physics Letters, 87*(8), 084102. doi:10.1063/1.2033140

Sun, J., Gan, W., Chao, H. C., & Yu, P. S. (2022). Metaverse: Survey, applications, security, and opportunities. arXiv preprint arXiv:2210.07990.

Williams, P., Dutta, I. K., Daoud, H., & Bayoumi, M. (2022). A survey on security in internet of things with a focus on the impact of emerging technologies. *Internet of Things : Engineering Cyber Physical Human Systems, 19*, 100564. doi:10.1016/j.iot.2022.100564

Yan, X., Cui, B., Xu, Y., Shi, P., & Wang, Z. (2019). A method of information protection for collaborative deep learning under GAN model attack. *IEEE/ACM Transactions on Computational Biology and Bioinformatics, 18*(3), 871–881. doi:10.1109/TCBB.2019.2940583 PMID:31514150

Yang, R., & Edalati, M. (2021). Using GAN-based models to sentimental analysis on imbalanced datasets in education domain. *arXiv preprint arXiv:2108.12061*.

Yu, Z. (2022). Sustaining student roles, digital literacy, learning achievements, and motivation in online learning environments during the COVID-19 pandemic. *Sustainability (Basel), 14*(8), 4388. doi:10.3390/su14084388

Chapter 16
Exploring Generative Adversarial Networks (GANs) in the Context of Public Space Protection

Harsha Vyawahare

[iD] https://orcid.org/0000-0002-3828-2889

Sipna College of Engineering and Technology, Amravati, India

Seema Rathod

[iD] https://orcid.org/0000-0002-1926-161X

Sipna College of Engineering and Technology, Amravati, India

Sheetal Dhande

Sipna College of Engineering and Technology, Amravati, India

Krushna Ajay Bajaj

Sipna College of Engineering and Technology, Amravati, India

Sarika Khandelwal

[iD] https://orcid.org/0000-0003-3336-820X

G.H. Raisoni College of Engineering, India

ABSTRACT

In the rapidly evolving landscape of public space security, this chapter presents a comprehensive exploration of the transformative role played by generative adversarial networks (GANs). GANs have emerged as a powerful tool in reshaping the paradigm of public space protection. The chapter aims to elucidate the multifaceted applications, benefits, and challenges of integrating GAN technology into security frameworks. Beginning with a foundational understanding of GANs, the chapter navigates through their architecture, principles, and historical evolution. It delves into the specific applications of GANs in public space security, unraveling their capacity to revolutionize surveillance and threat detection. The chapter also addresses the advantages brought forth by GANs and potential challenges, including ethical considerations and biases. Looking ahead, the chapter explores future prospects and emerging trends, providing insights into the evolving role of GANs in addressing the dynamic security challenges faced in public environments.

DOI: 10.4018/979-8-3693-3597-0.ch016

INTRODUCTION

In an era where ensuring the safety of public spaces is of paramount importance, the integration of cutting-edge technologies becomes imperative. With the rapid advancements in technology, traditional security measures might no longer be sufficient in safeguarding public environments. This chapter delves into the potential of Generative Adversarial Networks (GANs), a state-of-the-art subset of artificial intelligence, in revolutionizing security measures within public spaces. As concerns regarding security threats and public safety continue to grow, the exploration of advanced technologies becomes crucial. GANs, a type of machine learning model, offer compelling possibilities to enhance security systems in public environments. By employing a unique architectural framework, GANs have the ability to generate realistic and synthetic data, making them a promising tool for innovative security solutions. These networks have the potential to transform public spaces by enabling the creation of virtual scenarios for training purposes. By utilizing GANs, security personnel can simulate various dangerous situations and train under controlled environments without compromising public safety. This simulation-based training approach has the advantage of preparing security personnel for real-life scenarios while minimizing potential risks to the public. Moreover, GANs can also be employed in analysing real-time video surveillance footage for detecting suspicious activities or identifying potential threats. By leveraging the power of deep learning algorithms, GANs can accurately identify and classify objects, behaviours, or anomalies that may pose a risk to public safety. This capability of GANs to interpret and comprehend complex visual data contributes to their potential in revolutionizing security measures within public environments. Additionally, the integration of GANs with existing security systems allows for the development of intelligent monitoring solutions. These systems can continuously analyse data, such as crowd behaviour patterns, to detect any abnormal or potentially dangerous situations. By identifying deviations from normal patterns, GANs can provide early warnings, enabling security personnel to respond swiftly and effectively. Thus, the integration of cutting-edge technologies like Generative Adversarial Networks (GANs) holds tremendous potential in revolutionizing security measures within public spaces. Through their ability to generate synthetic data, assist in simulation-based training, analyse video surveillance footage, and enable intelligent monitoring systems, GANs offer innovative and effective solutions to ensure the safety of public environments in this ever-evolving era.

Deep learning techniques also have the potential to function as generative models. Deep learning involves neural networks comprising multiple layers within various network architectures. It is also regarded as a complementary domain of machine learning algorithms, drawing inspiration from the structure and operations of the brain. In image identification, speech synthesis, and text mining applications, hierarchical models can be constructed by representing probability distributions when receiving various types of data. Deep learning, reliant on an end-to-end wireless communication system, utilizes conditional Generative Adversarial Networks (GANs) alongside Deep Neural Networks (DNNs) to perform functions such as encoding, decoding, modulation, and demodulation. Achieving the accurate assessment of the current channel transfer state is crucial for the seamless transfer of DNN (Ye, Liang, Li & Juang, 2020). The primary strength of deep learning lies in discriminative models capable of associating high-dimensional sensory inputs with specific class labels. Generative models based on deep learning have a lesser impact due to the challenge of approximating obstinate probabilistic computations, which often leads to significant uncertainty (He, Zhang, Ren & Sun, 2016). However, if deep learning models are applied to generative networks, the advantage lies in their ability to handle large datasets.

These datasets typically require high-end computational resources for model training, resulting in longer training times but shorter testing times. The applications of GAN networks are continually advancing and addressing various needs in our daily lives.

THE LANDSCAPE OF PUBLIC SECURITY

In today's rapidly changing world, the landscape of public security is constantly evolving, presenting new challenges and concerns that need to be addressed. The safety and well-being of individuals in public spaces are of utmost importance, and it is crucial to stay ahead of evolving threats.

Technological advancements have played a significant role in enhancing public space security, providing innovative solutions to counter these threats. One key aspect of technological advancements is the use of surveillance systems equipped with advanced AI algorithms. These systems not only help in detecting suspicious activities but also enable real-time monitoring and response, allowing authorities to take immediate action when necessary. Furthermore, the integration of facial recognition technology has proved to be an effective tool in identifying potential threats and preventing criminal activities. Another area where technology has made a significant impact is in crowd management. With the help of smart sensors and data analytics, authorities can monitor crowd movements, identify congestion points, and ensure a smooth flow of people in public spaces. This not only enhances security but also improves overall efficiency and convenience for the public. Moreover, the rise of IoT devices has opened up new possibilities for enhancing public space security. From smart streetlights with built-in cameras to connected emergency call boxes, these devices create a networked environment that enables swift communication and response during emergencies. Additionally, the use of mobile applications has revolutionized public space security by empowering individuals to report suspicious activities or incidents directly to law enforcement agencies. These apps provide a convenient way for the public to contribute to their own safety while fostering a sense of community vigilance.

However, as technology continues to advance, it is essential to strike a balance between privacy concerns and public safety. Clear guidelines must be established regarding the collection and usage of personal data to ensure transparency and protect individual rights. Technological advancements have undoubtedly transformed the landscape of public security. By leveraging AI algorithms, facial recognition technology, IoT devices, and mobile applications, one can stay one step ahead of evolving threats and create safer and more secure public spaces for everyone.

UNDERSTANDING GENERATIVE ADVERSARIAL NETWORKS (GANS)

Initially, (Goodfellow et al. 2014) introduced the adversarial process for learning generative models, which forms the foundation of Generative Adversarial Networks (GANs). The core concept of GANs revolves around a minimax two-player zero-sum game. In this game, one player gains an advantage at the expense of the other player. These players are represented by different networks within the GAN framework, namely the discriminator and the generator. The primary objective of the discriminator is to distinguish between samples belonging to a fake distribution and those from a real distribution. Conversely, the generator aims to deceive the discriminator by generating fake samples that resemble real ones. The discriminator assigns probabilities to samples indicating the likelihood of them being real. A higher probability value suggests that the sample is more likely to be real, while a value closer to zero signifies a fake sample. A probability value near 0.5 indicates an optimal solution, where the discriminator cannot differentiate between fake and real samples effectively.

Generative Adversarial Networks (GANs) are a type of artificial intelligence model that have revolutionized the field of data generation. These networks consist of two main components: a generator and a discriminator. The generator's role is to create new data samples, while the discriminator's job is to distinguish between real and generated data. The generator tries to produce data that is so realistic that the discriminator cannot differentiate it from real data. On the other hand, the discriminator aims to correctly identify which data samples are real and which are generated by the generator. This adversarial relationship between the generator and discriminator leads to an iterative training process, where both components continuously improve their abilities. As the training progresses, the generator becomes better at creating convincing data samples, while the discriminator becomes more proficient in distinguishing between real and generated data.

The overall architecture of a Generative Adversarial Network (GAN) is depicted in Figure 1. This architecture comprises two primary networks: the discriminator (denoted as D) and the generator (denoted as G).

a) The Generator (G): The generator (G) is a neural network responsible for generating images by taking random noise, typically represented as Z, as input. The generated images produced by applying this noise are denoted as G(z). The input noise is commonly drawn from a Gaussian distribution, representing a random point in latent space. Throughout the training process of the Generative Adversarial Network (GAN), the parameters of both the generator (G) and the discriminator (D) networks are updated iteratively.

b) The Discriminator (D): The discriminator (D) functions as a discriminant network tasked with determining whether a given image belongs to a real distribution or not. It takes an input image X and produces an output D(x), which represents the probability that X belongs to a real distribution. If the output is 1, it indicates that the input image is from a real distribution. Conversely, an output value of 0 suggests that the input image belongs to a fake image distribution.

Figure 1. The general architecture of GAN

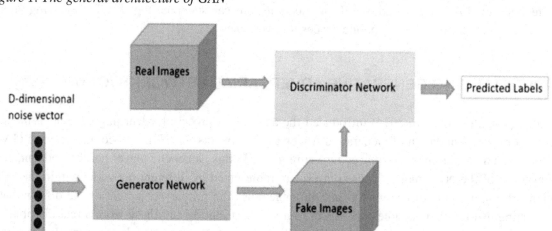

The objective function of a two-player minimax game would be as Eq. 1.

$$\text{Min Max } V(D,G) = E_{x \sim pdata(x)}[\log)d(x))] + E_{z \sim pg(z)}[\log(1-D(G(z)))] \tag{1}$$

G D

The operation of GANs is grounded on three key principles. Firstly, the generative model is trained to learn and generate data through probabilistic representation. Secondly, the training process involves navigating conflicting scenarios. Lastly, the utilization of deep learning neural networks and artificial intelligence algorithms facilitates the training of the entire system (Liu & Tuzel, 2016). Originally conceived for unsupervised machine learning techniques, GANs have proven to offer improved solutions for semi-supervised and reinforcement learning tasks. These attributes collectively position GAN networks as comprehensive solutions across various domains including healthcare, mechanics, banking, and more.

One of the key advantages of GANs is their versatility in generating various types of data, including images, texts, and even music. This makes them an invaluable tool for tasks such as image synthesis, text generation, and content creation. In addition to their ability to generate realistic simulations, GANs also find applications in other areas such as data augmentation, anomaly detection, and style transfer. By understanding how GANs work and harnessing their power, researchers and developers can unlock new possibilities in artificial intelligence and push the boundaries of creativity.

GAN, conceived around 2013 by researchers, is an innovative concept in the realm of deep learning, inspired by modeling animal behavior (Bryant, 2013). During tasks like fake image classification, the generator network fabricates counterfeit images based on an initial image, while the discriminator network distinguishes between real and fake images (Hsu, Zhuang & Lee, 2020). These networks typically operate within convolutional neural network (CNN) frameworks. When the discriminator fails to discern between the generated and real images, the representation is considered converged. The training set is

Figure 2. Block diagram of the generative adversarial network (GAN)

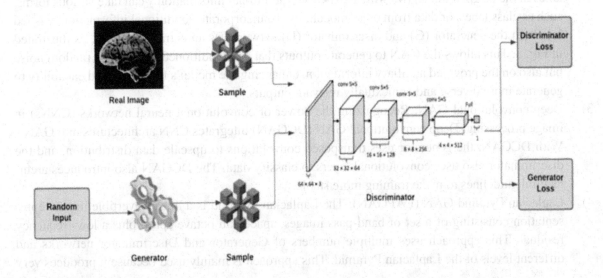

then tasked with learning to generate new data akin to the training samples. Images produced by GAN exhibit realism to human observers, often possessing features akin to real images (Marra, Gragnaniello, Cozzolino & Verdoliva, 2018). GANs can function in unsupervised, supervised, and reinforcement learning settings. In this generative network, the generator creates image candidates, while the discriminator evaluates them. Figure 2 depicts a block diagram representation of GAN.

As, GANs have demonstrated remarkable efficacy in generating natural images; However, significant challenges persist in their training, including mode collapse, non-convergence, and instability, often stemming from inadequate network architecture, objective function selection, and optimization algorithm choices. There are a limited number of existing reviews on the topic of GANs. (A. Radford 2016) discussed how GANs and stateof-the-art GANs works. (T. Karras 2018, Z. Lin 2018, D. J. Im 2016) provided a brief introduction of some of the GANs models, while (D. J. Im 2016) also presented development trends of GANs, and relation of GANs with parallel intelligence. (Y. Saatchi 2017) reviewed various GANs methods from the perspectives of algorithms, theory, and applications. (A. Jaiswal 2019) categorized GANs models into six fronts, such as architecture, loss, evaluation metric, Normalization and Constraint, image-toimage translation, conditional techniques and discussed them in brief. (A. Zhang 2018) presented a summary of GANs models addressing the GANs challenges. On the other hand, several researchers reviewed specific topics related to GANs in detail. (I. Durugkar 2019) reviewed GANs based image synthesis and editing approaches. (T. D. Nguyen 2017) surveyed threat of adversarial attacks on deep learning. (T. Chavdarova 2018) discussed various types of adversarial attacks and defenses in detail.

TYPES OF GAN'S

1) Fully Connected GANs: The initial GAN architectures employed fully connected neural networks for both the generator and discriminator (I. J. Goodfellow 2014). This design was utilized for relatively straightforward image datasets, specifically MNIST (handwritten digits), CIFAR-10 (natural images), and the Toronto Face Dataset (TFD).

2) Conditional GANs (CGAN): GANs can be expanded into a conditional model by incorporating additional information y. This extension addresses the limitation of relying solely on random variables in the original model (M. Mirza 2014). The additional information y can take various forms, such as class labels or data from other modalities. To incorporate conditional information, y is fed into both the generator (G) and discriminator (D) networks as an extra input layer, as illustrated in Fig. 3. This allows the GAN to generate outputs that are conditioned not only on random noise but also on the provided auxiliary information, enhancing the model's flexibility and capability to generate more diverse and contextually relevant outputs.

3) Deep convolutional GAN: Recognizing the power of convolutional neural networks (CNNs) in image processing, Deep convolutional GAN (DCGAN) integrates CNN architectures into GANs. With DCGAN, the generator uses transposed convolutions to upscale data distribution, and the discriminator also uses convolutional layers to classify data. The DCGAN also introduces architectural guidelines to make training more stable.

4) Laplacian Pyramid GAN (LAPGAN): The Laplacian pyramid is a linear invertible image representation consisting of a set of band-pass images, spaced an octave apart, plus a low-frequency residual. This approach uses multiple numbers of Generator and Discriminator networks and different levels of the Laplacian Pyramid. This approach is mainly used because it produces very

Figure 3. The architecture of conditional GAN

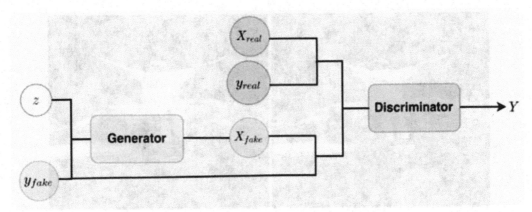

high-quality images. The image is down-sampled at first at each layer of the pyramid and then it is again up-scaled at each layer in a backward pass where the image acquires some noise from the Conditional GAN at these layers until it reaches its original size.

5) Super Resolution GAN (SRGAN): SRGAN as the name suggests is a way of designing a GAN in which a deep neural network is used along with an adversarial network in order to produce higher-resolution images. This type of GAN is particularly useful in optimally up-scaling native low-resolution images to enhance their details minimizing errors while doing so.

GANs' Applications

GAN is a very powerful generative model in that it can generate real-like samples with an arbitrary latent vector z. There is no need to know an explicit real data distribution nor assume further mathematical conditions. These advantages lead GAN to be applied in various academic and engineering fields.

1) Generation of High-Quality Images: Much of the recent GAN research focuses on improving the quality and utility of the image generation capabilities. The LAPGAN model introduced a cascade of convolutional networks within a Laplacian pyramid framework to generate images in a coarse-to-fne fashion (E. Denton 2015).

2) Image Inpainting: Image inpainting is the process of reconstructing missing parts of an image so that observers are unable to tell that these regions have undergone restoration. This technique is often used to remove unwanted objects from an image or to restore damaged portions of old photos.

3) Super-Resolution: Super-resolution is a term for a set of methods of upscaling video or images. Super-resolution allows a high-resolution image to be generated from a lower resolution image, with the trained model inferring photo-realistic details while up-sampling.

4) Person Re-identifcation: Person re-identifcation deals with matching images of same person over multiple non-overlapping camera views. It is applicable in tracking a particular person across these cameras, tracking the trajectory of a person, surveillance, and for forensic and security applications

5) Object Detection: Object detection is the process of finding instances of real-world objects such as faces, bicycles, and buildings in images or videos

Figure 4. Example—image inpainting

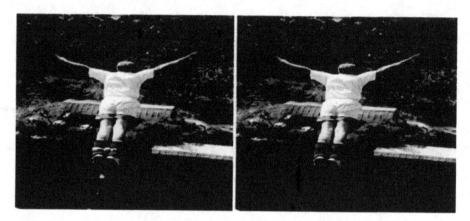

6) Facial Attribute Manipulation: Face attribute manipulation aims at modifying a face image according to a given attribute value.

7) Anime Character Generation: Game development and animation production are expensive and hire many production artists for relatively routine tasks. GAN can auto-generate and colorize Anime characters.

8) Image to Image Translation & Text to Image Translation:

9) Face Aging: Face age progression (i.e., prediction of future looks) and regression (i.e., estimation of previous looks), also referred to as face aging and rejuvenation, aims to render face images with or without the "aging" effect but still preserve personalized features of the face (i.e., personality).

10) Human Pose Estimation: Human pose estimation is the process of estimating the configuration of the body (pose) from a single, typically monocular, image.

11) Image Blending: Image blending is mixing of two images. The output image is a combination of the corresponding pixel values of the input images.

APPLICATION OF GANS IN SURVEILLANCE SYSTEMS

In today's world, surveillance systems play a crucial role in maintaining public safety and security. However, traditional surveillance methods often face limitations when it comes to accurately detecting anomalies or generating realistic scenarios for training. This is where Generative Adversarial Networks (GANs) come into the picture. By leveraging the power of GANs, surveillance systems can be enhanced to a whole new level. One of the key applications of GANs in surveillance systems is their ability to generate realistic scenarios for training purposes. Traditional methods rely on pre-recorded data, which may not always capture the complexity and dynamic nature of real-world situations. With GANs, security operators can generate synthetic data that closely resembles real-life scenarios, allowing them to train their systems more effectively.

Moreover, GANs can also be utilized to improve anomaly detection in surveillance systems. By training the system using both real and synthetic data generated by GANs, it becomes more robust in identifying unusual or suspicious behaviour. This helps security personnel to quickly respond to potential threats and take preventive measures. Another benefit of incorporating GANs into surveillance systems is their ability to adapt and learn from new data. As GANs continuously generate synthetic data based on real-time inputs, the system becomes more agile and responsive to changing patterns and behaviours. Furthermore, GANs can assist in overcoming privacy concerns associated with surveillance systems. By generating synthetic data instead of relying solely on real footage, personal information can be anonymized while still providing valuable training material for the system.

The application of GANs in surveillance systems holds immense potential for enhancing public safety. From generating realistic scenarios for training purposes to improving anomaly detection and addressing privacy concerns, GANs offer innovative solutions that can revolutionize the effectiveness of surveillance systems in public spaces.

PRIVACY CONCERNS AND ETHICAL CONSIDERATIONS

Privacy concerns and ethical considerations are paramount when it comes to the implementation of advanced surveillance technologies. Due to advances in technology, the potential for intrusion into individuals' private lives becomes a pressing issue. It is crucial to find a delicate balance between enhancing security measures and respecting individual privacy rights. One of the main ethical implications of advanced surveillance technologies is the potential for abuse or misuse by those in power. Without proper regulations and oversight, these technologies can be easily exploited, leading to violations of privacy and civil liberties. Therefore, it is imperative that robust safeguards and accountability mechanisms are put in place to ensure that these technologies are used responsibly. Moreover, ethical considerations also extend to the collection, storage, and use of personal data obtained through surveillance technologies. Individuals have a right to know how their data is being collected and used, as well as the ability to control its dissemination. Transparency and informed consent should be fundamental principles guiding the implementation of these technologies.

Also privacy concerns arise from the vast amount of data that can be gathered through advanced surveillance systems. The potential for mass surveillance and indiscriminate data collection raises questions about the right to privacy and individual autonomy. Striking a balance between security needs and protecting privacy requires careful consideration of how this data is collected, stored, accessed, and shared. There is the risk of discriminatory practices resulting from biased algorithms or profiling techniques used in surveillance systems. This can lead to unfair targeting or harassment based on race, gender, religion, or other personal characteristics.

Addressing privacy concerns and ethical considerations in the implementation of advanced surveillance technologies is crucial for maintaining a just society. By establishing clear guidelines for responsible use, promoting transparency, protecting personal data rights, and safeguarding against discrimination, we can strike a balance between security enhancements and individual privacy rights. Only by doing so can we ensure that these technologies serve the greater good without compromising our fundamental values.

CASE STUDIES AND SUCCESS STORIES

Here a collection of real-world case studies and success stories that demonstrate the effective use of Generative Adversarial Networks (GANs) in enhancing security in public areas are illustrated. These case studies and success stories illustrate how GANs have revolutionized security systems by providing advanced capabilities for threat detection and prevention. The integration of GAN technologies has not only improved public safety but also empowered security personnel with powerful tools to combat evolving threats effectively. These examples highlight the successful application of GANs in threat detection and prevention, showcasing their significant impact on public safety.

One notable case study involves the implementation of GANs in a major city's surveillance system. By training the GAN on a wide range of images, the system was able to identify potential threats with remarkable accuracy. This resulted in improved response times and enhanced overall security.

Another success story revolves around the use of GANs for facial recognition at airports. By employing GANs to generate realistic synthetic faces, security personnel were able to compare these generated faces with a database of known criminals or suspects. This proved to be an invaluable tool in identifying individuals who posed a potential risk.

In yet another instance, GANs were employed to enhance video surveillance in crowded public spaces such as train stations and shopping malls. By analysing video feeds in real-time, the technology was able to detect suspicious activities or objects, alerting security personnel immediately and preventing potential threats from escalating.

By harnessing the power of machine learning and image generation, GANs have proven to be highly reliable in identifying potential risks in various public areas. These success stories serve as strong evidence of their effectiveness and highlight the immense value they bring to security operations. In conclusion, these real-world examples demonstrate how GANs have successfully bolstered security in public areas through their ability to detect and prevent threats effectively. With each case study highlighting novel applications and positive outcomes, it is clear that GANs play a crucial role in ensuring public safety and enhancing security measures.

CHALLENGES AND LIMITATIONS

Integrating Generative Adversarial Networks (GANs) into public security measures brings with it a set of challenges and limitations that need to be carefully considered. One of the main challenges is the potential for biases in the generated data. GANs learn from existing datasets, which means any biases present in those datasets can be amplified and perpetuated in the generated outputs. This raises concerns about fairness and equity in implementing GANs for security purposes.

Another limitation is the possibility of false positives. GANs are trained to identify patterns and anomalies, but there is always a chance of misidentifying harmless individuals or objects as potential threats. This could lead to unnecessary disruptions or even violations of privacy rights. Furthermore, the integration of GANs into public security measures requires ongoing refinement and adaptation. The technology is constantly evolving, and new threats may emerge that GANs have not been trained to detect. Continuous updates and improvements would be necessary to ensure the effectiveness of GAN-based security systems. Additionally, there are practical limitations to consider. Implementing GANs on a large scale would require significant computational power and storage capabilities. Not all organizations or agencies may have access to such resources, limiting the widespread adoption of GAN-based security measures. Moreover, there are ethical considerations surrounding the use of GANs in public security. The generation of realistic synthetic images or videos raises concerns about privacy infringement and potential misuse for nefarious purposes.

Lastly, public acceptance and trust in GAN-based security measures may pose a challenge. The general public may have reservations about relying on AI algorithms for critical security decisions, especially if they perceive them as opaque or prone to errors. In conclusion, while integrating GANs into public security measures holds promise, it is crucial to acknowledge and address the challenges and limitations they bring. By being aware of potential biases, false positives, ongoing refinement needs, resource requirements, ethical concerns, and public acceptance, we can strive for a balanced and responsible implementation of GAN-based security systems.

FUTURE TRENDS AND INNOVATIONS

Explore the ever-changing realm of security technologies and delve into the exciting world of GANs. With a keen eye on the future, let's discuss the potential trends that could shape the application of GANs in enhancing public safety. As technology continues to advance at an unprecedented rate, it is important to anticipate the innovations that will redefine the security landscape. From facial recognition systems to predictive analytics, there are countless possibilities for GANs to revolutionize security measures. Imagine a future where GAN-powered surveillance systems can accurately identify suspicious behaviour in real-time, allowing law enforcement agencies to proactively prevent crimes.

Additionally, advancements in GAN-based encryption algorithms could strengthen data protection and safeguard sensitive information from cyber threats. The integration of GANs with IoT devices could create a networked system that constantly monitors and mitigates potential security risks. In conclusion, by exploring future trends and innovations in GAN technology, we can pave the way for a safer and more secure society.

COLLABORATION WITH LAW ENFORCEMENT AND SECURITY AGENCIES

Collaboration with law enforcement and security agencies is crucial in harnessing the full potential of technology developers. By working together, they can ensure the responsible and effective implementation of GANs in public security initiatives. This collaboration allows for the sharing of knowledge, expertise, and resources, enabling the development of innovative solutions to combat emerging threats. Law enforcement agencies can provide valuable insights into the specific challenges they face, helping technology developers tailor their GANs applications to address these needs. Likewise, security agencies can contribute by offering their expertise in data analysis and intelligence gathering, enhancing the capabilities of GANs in detecting and preventing criminal activities. The partnership between these stakeholders fosters a symbiotic relationship that promotes increased safety and security for communities at large. It also instills public confidence by demonstrating a commitment to responsible use of advanced technologies while upholding privacy and ethical considerations. Through ongoing collaboration, we can continue to push the boundaries of what GANs can achieve in safeguarding our society.

PUBLIC PERCEPTION AND ACCEPTANCE

In today's rapidly evolving technological landscape, the integration of Generative Adversarial Networks (GANs) in public spaces has become a topic of great interest. Understanding the public perception and acceptance of this innovative technology is crucial for its successful implementation. To ensure a smooth transition, it is important to employ strategies that not only increase awareness but also foster public acceptance through transparency and education. One effective approach to tackle this challenge is to educate the public about the potential benefits of GANs in public spaces. By highlighting how GANs can enhance creativity, improve user experiences, and facilitate problem-solving, we can help bridge the knowledge gap and dispel any misconceptions or fears. Transparency is another key aspect in gaining public acceptance. Openly sharing information about how GANs are used, their limitations, and the measures taken to protect privacy can help build trust among the public. Additionally, involving the community in decision-making processes related to GAN integration can further enhance transparency and foster a sense of ownership.

Collaborating with experts in various fields such as ethics, law, and sociology can provide valuable insights into addressing concerns related to privacy, security, and potential biases associated with GANs. This interdisciplinary approach ensures that all perspectives are considered and helps create a more comprehensive framework for implementing GANs in public spaces. Furthermore, actively engaging with the public through workshops, forums, and demonstrations can provide opportunities for direct interaction with GAN technology. This hands-on approach allows individuals to understand its capabilities firsthand and enables them to ask questions or voice any concerns they may have. By taking these proactive steps towards increasing awareness and gaining public acceptance, we can pave the way for a smoother integration of GANs in public spaces. It is essential to prioritize open communication channels, education initiatives, and collaborative efforts to ensure that this technology is embraced by society while minimizing any potential risks or negative perceptions.

CONCLUSION

This chapter has shed light on the key findings and insights regarding the potential of Generative Adversarial Networks (GANs) in enhancing security measures in public spaces. The remarkable ability of GANs to generate realistic and high-quality images has opened up new possibilities for surveillance and threat detection systems. By leveraging GANs, security professionals can now access a powerful tool that can help identify suspicious activities and enhance overall safety.

However, it is crucial to acknowledge the ethical considerations surrounding the use of GANs in public spaces. Privacy concerns and potential misuse of this technology need to be addressed through robust regulations and guidelines. Striking a balance between security enhancement and individual privacy is paramount. Public engagement is also crucial in order to ensure transparency and accountability in the implementation of GAN-based security systems. Moreover, it is worth noting that GANs are not a standalone solution to all security challenges. They should be seen as a complementary tool that works alongside existing security measures. Collaboration and integration with other technologies such as facial recognition systems and video analytics can further enhance the effectiveness of GANs in public spaces. Furthermore, ongoing research and development are essential to continuously improve the capabilities of GANs for security purposes. The exploration of novel algorithms, training techniques, and data sources can help overcome current limitations and enhance accuracy in threat detection. In summary, while GANs hold immense potential for improving security measures in public spaces, ethical considerations, public engagement, collaboration with other technologies, and ongoing research are vital for their successful implementation. By harnessing the power of GANs responsibly, we can create safer environments without compromising individual rights or privacy.

REFERENCES

Aggarwal, A., Mittal, M., & Battineni, G. (2021). Generative adversarial network: An overview of theory and applications. *International Journal of Information Management Data Insights*, *1*(1), 100004. doi:10.1016/j.jjimei.2020.100004

Alqahtani, H., Kavakli-Thorne, M., & Kumar, G. (2021). Applications of generative adversarial networks (gans): An updated review. *Archives of Computational Methods in Engineering*, *28*(2), 525–552. doi:10.1007/s11831-019-09388-y

Alsaggaf, W. A., Mehmood, I., Khairullah, E. F., Alhuraiji, S., Sabir, M. F. S., Alghamdi, A. S., & Abd El-Latif, A. A. (2021). A smart surveillance system for uncooperative gait recognition using cycle consistent generative adversarial networks (CCGANs). *Computational Intelligence and Neuroscience*, *2021*, 2021. doi:10.1155/2021/3110416 PMID:34691168

Atghaei, A., Ziaeinejad, S., & Rahmati, M. (2020). *Abnormal event detection in urban surveillance videos using GAN and transfer learning.* arXiv preprint arXiv:2011.09619.

Avola, D., Cannistraci, I., Cascio, M., Cinque, L., Diko, A., Fagioli, A., Foresti, G. L., Lanzino, R., Mancini, M., Mecca, A., & Pannone, D. (2022). A novel GAN-based anomaly detection and localization method for aerial video surveillance at low altitude. *Remote Sensing (Basel)*, *14*(16), 4110. doi:10.3390/rs14164110

Avola, D., Cannistraci, I., Cascio, M., Cinque, L., Diko, A., Fagioli, A., Foresti, G. L., Lanzino, R., Mancini, M., Mecca, A., & Pannone, D. (2022). A novel GAN-based anomaly detection and localization method for aerial video surveillance at low altitude. *Remote Sensing (Basel)*, *14*(16), 4110. doi:10.3390/rs14164110

Bertalmio, M., Sapiro, G., Caselles, V., & Ballester, C. (2000) Image inpainting. In: *Proceedings of the 27th annual conference on computer graphics and interactive techniques.* ACM Press/Addison-Wesley Publishing Co, (pp. 417–424). ACM.

Bryant, G. A. (2013). Animal signals and emotion in music: Coordinating affect across groups. *Frontiers in Psychology*, *4*. doi:10.3389/fpsyg.2013.00990 PMID:24427146

Chavdarova, T., & Fleuret, F. (2018). SGAN: An Alternative Training of Generative Adversarial Networks. *Proceedings of the IEEE Computer Society Conference on Computer Vision and Pattern Recognition*, (pp. 9407–9415). IEEE. 10.1109/CVPR.2018.00980

Dai, J., Li, Q., Wang, H., & Liu, L. (2024). Understanding images of surveillance devices in the wild. *Knowledge-Based Systems*, *284*, 111226. doi:10.1016/j.knosys.2023.111226

Durugkar, I., Gemp, I., & Mahadevan, S. (2019). Generative multi-adversarial networks. *5th International Conference on Learning Representations, ICLR 2017 - Conference Track Proceedings*. IEEE.

Hsu, C. C., Zhuang, Y. X., & Lee, C.-Y. (2020). Deep fake image detection based on pairwise learning. *Applied Sciences (Basel, Switzerland)*, *10*(1), 370. doi:10.3390/app10010370

Im, D. J., Kim, C. D., Jiang, H., & Memisevic, R. (2016). *Generating images with recurrent adversarial networks*. arXiv Prepr arXiv:1602.05110.

Karras, T., Aila, T., Laine, S., & Lehtinen, J. (2018). Progressive growing of GANs for improved quality, stability, and variation. In *6th International Conference on Learning Representations, ICLR*. IEEE.

Lim, W., Chek, K. Y. S., Theng, L. B., & Lin, C. T. C. (2024). Future of Generative Adversarial Networks (GAN) for Anomaly Detection in Network Security: A Review. *Computers & Security*, *103733*, 2024. doi:10.1016/j.cose.2024.103733

Lin, Z., Fanti, G., Khetan, A., & Oh, S. (2018). PacGan: The power of two samples in generative adversarial networks. *Advances in Neural Information Processing Systems*, 1498–1507.

Liu, M.Y., & Tuzel, O. (2016). *Coupled generative adversarial networks*.

Mirza, M., & Osindero, S. (2014). *Conditional Generative Adversarial Nets*. arXiv Prepr. arXiv:1411.1784.

Nguyen, T. D., Le, T., Vu, H., & Phung, D. (2017). Dual discriminator generative adversarial nets. *Advances in Neural Information Processing Systems*, 2671–2681.

Saatchi, Y., & Wilson, A. G. (2017). Bayesian GAN. *Advances in Neural Information Processing Systems*, *2017*, 3623–3632.

Sampath, V., Maurtua, I., Aguilar Martín, J. J., & Gutierrez, A. (2021). A survey on generative adversarial networks for imbalance problems in computer vision tasks. In: J Big Data. doi:10.1186/s40537-021-00414-0

Sauber-Cole, R., & Khoshgoftaar, T. M. (2022). The use of generative adversarial networks to alleviate class imbalance in tabular data: A survey. *Journal of Big Data*, *9*(1), 98. doi:10.1186/s40537-022-00648-6

Saxena, D., & Cao, J. (2021). Generative adversarial networks (GANs) challenges, solutions, and future directions. *ACM Computing Surveys*, *54*(3), 1–42. doi:10.1145/3446374

Wang, Z., She, Q., & Ward, T. E. (2020). Generative Adversarial Networks in Computer Vision: A Survey and Taxonomy. *ACM Computing Surveys*.

Ye, H., Liang, L., Li, G. Y., & Juang, B.-H. (2020, May). H., Liang, L., Li, G. Y., & Juang, en B. H. (2020). Deep learning-based end-to-end wireless communication systems with conditional GANs as unknown channels. *IEEE Transactions on Wireless Communications*, *19*(5), 3133–3143. doi:10.1109/TWC.2020.2970707

Yilmaz, I., Masum, R., & Siraj, A. (2020). Addressing Imbalanced Data Problem with Generative Adversarial Network For Intrusion Detection. In: *2020 IEEE 21st International Conference on Information Reuse and Integration for Data Science (IRI)*. IEEE. 10.1109/IRI49571.2020.00012

Zhang, A. (2018). *Self-Attention Generative Adversarial Networks*. arXiv Prepr. arXiv1805.08318.

Zhao, T., Yan, Y., Peng, J., Mi, Z., & Fu, X. (2019). Guiding intelligent surveillance system by learning-by-synthesis gaze estimation. *Pattern Recognition Letters*, *125*, 556–562. doi:10.1016/j.patrec.2019.02.008

Chapter 17
Exploring the Role of Generative Adversarial Networks in Cybersecurity:
Techniques, Applications, and Advancements

Ambika S. Jaiswal
ⓘ https://orcid.org/0000-0003-4517-0786
Sant Gadge Baba Amravati University, India

Dipak V. Bhavsagar
Seth Kesarimal Porwal College of Arts and Science and Commerce, India

Sonali Ravindra Chavan
ⓘ https://orcid.org/0009-0001-0712-1572
Bharatiya Mahavidyalaya, Amravati, India

Priyanka C. Tikekar
Bharatiya Mahavidyalaya, Amravati, India

Suhashini Chaurasia
ⓘ https://orcid.org/0000-0002-7443-0105
S.S. Maniar College of Computer and Management, Nagpur, India

ABSTRACT

To protect the vast amounts of data being stored on computers and transported over networks, cybersecurity is crucial. To prevent increasingly complex assaults in the future, methods for identifying threats must be regularly updated. Experts in security are using GAN to accomplish results in password cracking, anomaly generation, and intrusion detection. The creative use of GANs in cybersecurity is explored in this chapter. An overview of GANs and their importance in strengthening cyber defense mechanisms is presented in the introduction. An extensive literature analysis to clarify the current state of knowledge is provided after a detailed examination of traditional GAN techniques. The chapter clarifies the GAN's architectural subtleties and highlights its applicability to cybersecurity scenarios. Additionally, study of variety of GAN applications in cybersecurity. It classifies different kinds of GANs and frameworks used in their application. It studied the intrusion detection-based GAN model with its parameters results compared with the existing study.

DOI: 10.4018/979-8-3693-3597-0.ch017

INTRODUCTION

Generative Adversarial Network is an example of an artificial intelligence (AI) system or technique that made up of two neural networks i.e. a discriminator & generator. Created data is compared with the dataset is the basic concept behind a GAN. Generator produces samples, means it generates new data. For instance, the generator would produce images that resemble human faces if you wanted to create realistic faces.

In contrast, the discriminator assesses the generated data and attempts to determine if it is authentic (drawn from the genuine dataset) or synthetic (made by the generator). In essence, it plays the role of a detective, attempting to determine whether the data is created or real. In order to protect private networks, data, hardware, and software from cyberattacks, a set of guidelines and practices known as cybersecurity is put in place. The many attack types include malware/virus-based software deployment, dos, phishing & man in the middle. Because to the interconnectivity IoT for short, and the huge volume of information produced by the machines, gadgets, apps, and websites utilized in cloud-based services, there has been a notable increase in cyberthreats in recent times. (Tasneem & Gupta 2022) The increasingly sophisticated and cunning cyberattacks are beyond the detection and prevention of the security mechanisms. To address these challenges, deep learning techniques are commonly applied in the cybersecurity field.

Conventional Approaches: The conventional and widely-used approaches for intrusion detection and password-cracking software are covered in this section. To prevent advanced attacks, a number of strong and novel intrusion detection systems are being developed. These methods fall within the categories of anomaly- and signature-based intrusion detection systems. Signature based IDS discovers assaults by analyzing the patterns and comparing the event patterns with previous signature & attack.

Anamoly based intrusion detection system records & patterns of different attack types & identify latest types of well-known attacks by utilizing a variety of methodologies like ML based, statistical Anamoly based, different IDs are listed & classified in (Figure 1). Many companies and industries, including the banking, military, the stock market, social media, and telecommunications, place a strong premium on password security. It was possible to break these passwords with brute force attack, dictionary attack, rainbow table etc. A few of the frequently used password cracking programs are THC Hydra, Brutus and John the Ripper.

LITERATURE REVIEW

The study "Detecting Adversarial Examples for Network Intrusion Detection System with GAN" by Ye Peng, Guobin Fu, addresses how machine learning models can be vulnerable in an adversarial environment. To enhanced the accuracy of NIDs authors suggest a defense algorithm that uses a bidirectional GAN. Metrics such as accuracy, precision, recall & f1 score significantly decline when study assesses the effects of Fast Gradient Sign Method, Projected Gradient Descent, and Momentum Iterative Fast Gradient Sign Method attacks on functionality of DNN-based NIDS. hostile Sample Detection (ASD), the suggested defense algorithm, successfully enhances NIDS performance in the hostile setting. The robustness of NIDS is increased by the ASD technology's better parameter results in identifying adversarial samples produced by FGSM, PGD, and MI-FGSM attacks.

Figure 1. IDS strategies

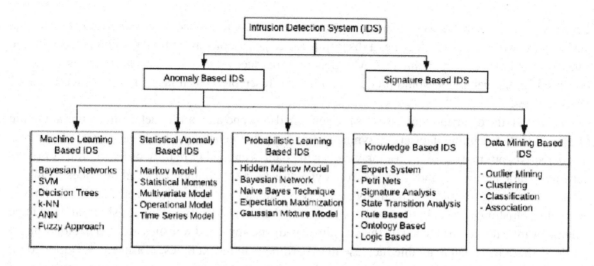

The comprehensive experimental evaluation of the defense algorithm verifies its effectiveness in detecting and removing adversarial samples, providing valuable insights for security personnel to enhance defense against adversarial attacks. In summary, the research paper presents a defense algorithm using bidirectional GAN to detect and remove adversarial samples, thereby enhancing accuracy of NIDs in the face of adversarial attacks. Developed method demonstrates promising results in mitigating the impact of adversarial examples on network intrusion detection systems (Peng & Fu 2020).

In this research study, author Viacheslav Belenko examines the application of generative adversarial networks (GANs) for cyber-physical system detection of intrusion in self-organizing networks. Authors compare different GAN architectures and experiment with training parameters to determine the most effective approach. They find that GANs are more promising than traditional artificial neural networks for detecting security anomalies and producing more unusual samples in order to enhance the marked dataset's quality. The authors also note that It is recommended to train the discriminator more frequently than the generator. for best results. Ultimately, the trained generator can be used to create "anomalous" records. The paper concludes that this method can be applied to address the security challenges of Adhoc wireless networks of cyber-physical systems that self-organize (Belenko & Chernenko, 2018)

Author Tim Merino in this research paper "Expansion of Cyber Attack Data from Unbalanced Datasets using GAN" explores the process of creating data to balance the unbalanced dataset using GAN in order to enhance effectiveness of detection of cyber attack. paper presents a framework for the GAN system and evaluates its performance on the KDD99 dataset. The findings demonstrate that the GAN model produces data that may be utilized to balance datasets that were previously unbalanced because it closely resembles the information distribution of different assault types. The paper also discusses future work, including optimizing the GAN model, implementing few-shot learning, and using more advanced evaluation methods (Merino, T. & Stillwell 2020)

Author Sujit Rokka Chhetri in this research paper "GAN-Sec: A Conditional Generative Adversarial Network Based Security Model for Cyber-Physical Production Systems" introduces GAN-Sec, a novel technique to analyzed CPPS. Using a Conditional adaptive network (CGAN), GAN-Sec aims to predict the link among power and signal flow in CPPS. By estimating the conditional distribution between these flows, GAN-Sec aims to address security challenges such as confidentiality, integrity, and availability in CPPS. The paper presents the theoretical foundation and methodology for using CGAN to analyze cross-domain attacks in CPPS, and it demonstrates its applicability in analyzing additional manufactured security of CPPS system. The proposed approach showing results and represents a significant step to build analysis of security methods of CPPS that based on CGAN. The paper also discusses the potential limitations and challenges of using GAN-Sec for CPPS security analysis, highlighting the need for sufficient data and the applicability of the approach to various types of manufacturing systems. Overall, the research paper provides a comprehensive overview of GAN-Sec and its potential implications for enhancing the security of CPPS (Chhetri & Lopez, 2019). Author Binbin Wang in this research paper "The Security Threat of Adversarial Samples to Deep Learning Networks" provides an overview of the vulnerability of Deep Learning networks to adversarial samples and the potential security threats they pose. It discusses the openness of learning network information, capable of producing high-quality simulated data, & black box attack using GAN. The paper also explores the threat model, attack effects, and the information held by attackers. Additionally, it references various studies and methods related to the security of deep learning networks (Wang & Zhu 2020).

Author YANG-JIE CAO in This research article provides an overview of GANs & their recent advances in computer vision. The authors introduce the principle and architecture of GANs, and discuss their advantages and disadvantages. They also list the evolutions of typical GAN models, describe several variants of GAN and their applications and improvements, and provide summaries and future trends of GANs in computer vision. The article also includes experimental results and comparisons of different GAN models on public datasets. The authors conclude that GANs are a promising framework for solving problems in computer vision, and suggest areas for further improvement and research (Cao & Chen, 2018).

Author Ayush Jain explores the capabilities of three types of Generative Adversarial Networks (GANs) – GAN, DCGAN, and BigGAN – using the Stanford Dogs Dataset. The study evaluates the models based on their image generation capabilities, loss function tracking, and Inception score calculation. Key findings include the instability of GAN, improved performance of DCGAN with hyperparameter tuning & stability and superior performance of BigGAN. The research emphasizes the importance of hyperparameters like learning rate and batch size in the training process and discusses the potential applications of GANs in industries such as gaming, graphics enhancement, video generation, and 3D object generation for virtual reality (Jain & Kakde 2020).

GAN ARCHITECTURE

Those discriminative models that could transfer a high-dimension dimensional input to class label were thought to be the most successful until Goodfellow produced Generative Adversarial Networks in 2014. These deep generative models were limited in their impact due to their inability to approximate a large number of unpredictable probabilistic computations. The basic purpose of GANs was to get around these problems. figure 2 depicted the two models that make up GANs are the discriminator model (D)

Figure 2. GAN Architecture

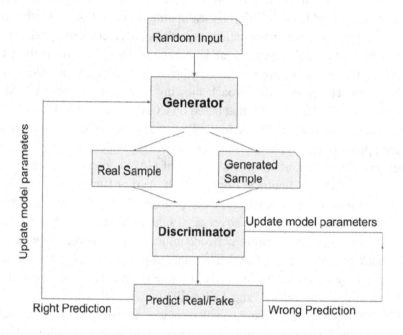

and the generative model (G). With a data distribution that is similar to the real dataset, the first one attempts to generate new instances that are completely distinct from the real dataset by feeding it random noise. By predicting the probability of the samples, discriminator model that verify distribution & originated from the generator. Since the generator has less access to dataset, it gains knowledge from Discriminators, however, have access to both phony and actual samples. A description of their work method is provided below:

Generator: The generator model starts with a random vector, generative process i.e. derived from a Gaussian distribution and has a fixed length. This random vector is then utilized to generate a sample in the domain. After training has been done, vectors will be compressed. because points are corelate with points in problem domain after training, After training is finished, fresh examples are generated using the model.

Discriminator: A broad classification model that forecasts a binary class label of real or fake discriminator. This model predicts whether input is authentic or fraudulent based on domain samples. The generator's output contains the bogus instances, while the real are taken from the real training dataset. After the training procedure is complete, the discriminator is discarded (Tasneem & Roy 2022; Arora & Shantanu 2022).

GAN has several pros in field of cybersecurity, helping to enhance security measures, identify vulnerabilities, and improve defense mechanisms. Here are some applications of different GANs in cybersecurity. First of all, GANs can be applied as data augmentation approaches, in which the generator uses the training dataset to create new images, performing adjustments to produce different images. By training the discriminator on a vast amount of genuine and fake data, GANs enhance classification approaches.

GANs can also be used to raise an input image's resolution. Deep ConvNets come into action when a filter is applied to view what an area would look like in different seasons, such as summer, winter, spring, or fall. This is similar to the filters used in Snapchat. GANs are used to better comprehend the machine's visualizations and translate meanings into visuals.

APPLICATION OF GAN IN CYBER SECURITY

Password Cracking Prevention: In the context of password cracking prevention, GAN can be used to enhance security measures & mitigate the risk of weak password vulnerabilities. The application involves using GANs to generate realistic password guesses and subsequently training the model with reinforcement learning to improve the effectiveness of password security. The primary goal is to strengthen password security by identifying and preventing the usage of weak passwords that are susceptible to brute-force attacks.

Reinforcement Learning in GANs is used to generate realistic password guesses. Reinforcement learning techniques can then be applied to train the model to learn from feedback, helping to improve password security by identifying and preventing weak passwords.

Malware Detection and Generation: GAN in context of malware involves generation aspects. Malware detection systems' capabilities can be improved by using GANs & conversely, to generate adversarial samples to identify effectiveness of systems.

GANs for malware detection: GANs can be trained to recognize patterns associated with malware in files or network traffic, aiding in the detection of malicious activities. GANs for generating adversarial samples: Adversarial training using GANs can be applied to improve the robustness of malware detection models by generating adversarial samples during training.

Adversarial Attacks: Adversarial attacks in the context of GAN suggests to attempts to manipulate behavior of GAN by introducing carefully crafted perturbations to the input data. These perturbations called adversarial that deceive the GAN and, in the context of cybersecurity, can be used for malicious purposes. Attackers can use GANs to generate adversarial examples. These are subtly modified inputs that can mislead machine learning models, including intrusion detection systems. Adversarial GAN-generated data may help attackers evade detection. Detecting anomalies in data that substantially diverge from expected or typical behavior is known as anomaly detection. Anomalies are identified when the generated samples deviate significantly from the learned normal distribution. GANs can be employed for anomaly detection in network traffic. By training on normal patterns, GANs can identify deviations and anomalies that may indicate a potential cybersecurity threat, such as malicious activity or intrusions. Anomaly detection in the context of GAN involves using GANs to identify unusual or anomalous patterns in data, which can be crucial in cybersecurity for detecting potential threats or malicious activities

Network Intrusion Detection: NID plays a critical role in cybersecurity by monitoring network traffic to identify & respond to potential security threats. Using GAN for NID can provide a unique approach to detecting anomalies and potential intrusions GANs can help in creating realistic datasets for training intrusion detection systems. These synthetic datasets, generated by the

GAN, can augment limited real-world data, improving the robustness of the intrusion detection models. NIDS monitors network traffic for suspicious activities, unauthorized access, malware & other security threats. Traditional NIDS approaches contains signature based, Anamoly based & heuristic based detection.

Data Augmentation: In the context of cybersecurity, data augmentation with adversarial networks (GANs) entails creating synthetic data to increase the number and diversity of training data utilized in different security applications. GAN helps in generalization & effectiveness of machine learning technique in identifying threats.

Limited Real-world Data: In many cybersecurity applications, obtaining a sufficiently large and diverse dataset of real-world examples can be challenging due to the rarity of certain events or the sensitive nature of security-related data.

Improving Generalization: Data augmentation using GANs aims to enhanced generalization capability of machine learning technique by providing them with a more comprehensive and representative training dataset.

Honeypots and Honeytokens: Honeypots and honeytokens are cybersecurity mechanisms designed to deceive attackers, gather intelligence, and enhance security by luring adversaries into controlled environments or identifying unauthorized activities. While GANs (Generative Adversarial Networks) themselves may not be directly involved in creating honeypots or honeytokens, they can be used in conjunction with these techniques to enhance their effectiveness. GANs can be employed to create realistic-looking decoy systems or data (honeypots and honeytokens) that attract attackers. Analyzing interactions with these deceptive elements can provide insights into potential threats and attacker techniques.

Network Security: Generative Adversarial Networks (GANs) can be applied in various ways to enhance network security measures. GANs can create adversarial traffic that mimics malicious activity to test the resilience of network security systems. Network security models can be trained using GAN-generated adversarial examples to make them more robust against real-world attacks. GAN used to produce data for network traffic that preserves privacy by masking sensitive information while retaining statistical properties. As the network environment changes, GANs can contribute to the dynamic adjustment of security policies to address new threats or changes in network behavior. Generative models for traffic generation: GANs can generate realistic network traffic to test the robustness of network security systems. This aids in identifying potential vulnerabilities and weaknesses in intrusion detection systems (Arora & Shantanu 2022; Yinka-Banjo & Ugot 2020).

GANS FRAMEWORKS

The technique of Deep Learning is also called GAN has become extremely popular in recent years because of its many uses in areas like synthesis of image, analysis of data, video production, anomaly detection, and modelling complicated & high-dimensional data distributions. A discriminator network separates true data from fake data produced by generator, and generator network creates new data instances that resemble the training set's data distribution. Both net-

Figure 3. Structure of GAN

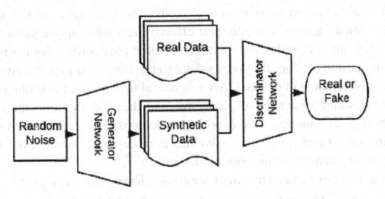

works are compelled to compete in order to advance. deep learning technique called as GAN that extremely popular in recent years because of its many uses in areas like synthesis of image, analysis, anomaly detection & modelling complicated and high-dimensional data distributions. A discriminator network separates true data from fake produced by generator, and generator network creates new data instances that resemble the training set's data distribution shown in the figure 3. Both networks are compelled to compete in order to advance. Over time, the discriminator detects the subtle distinction between the authentic and the counterfeit, while the generator produces visuals that deceive the discriminator.

Exploring the Role of Generative Adversarial Networks in Cybersecurity its Techniques, Applications & Advancements

DIFFERENT TYPES OF GAN

DCGANs: Deep Convolutional GAN are a specific class of Generative Adversarial Networks (GANs) designed for generating high-quality images. DCGANs leverage deep convolutional neural networks in both generator & discriminator, enabled to take & generate complex visual patterns effectively. These networks were introduced to address challenges faced by traditional GANs in generating coherent and realistic images.

BiGANs:Bidirectional Generative Adversarial Networks (BiGANs) represent an extension of traditional Generative Adversarial Networks (GANs) by introducing an encoder network, creating a more complex architecture. BiGANs were introduced to address the challenge of learning a meaningful latent space and enable bidirectional transformation.

Cycle-GANs: CycleGANs architecture designed to not to make pair for image to image translation. Unlike paired datasets where corresponding images in different domains are explicitly aligned, Cycle GANs can learn translations between two domains using unpaired datasets. They were introduced to address the challenges of obtaining large-scale paired datasets for various tasks like style transfer & domain adaptation.

PassGAN: Modern tools that exhaust existing huge password tables with common passwords are used for traditional password guessing. These kinds of technologies can also be used to enlarge passwords by concatenating them. Despite their effectiveness with simple passwords, they appear unable of deciphering more complex ones. Human created passwords rules are replaced with ML techniques and after training is done on password dataset, it can create high-quality password guessing. The fundamental component of PassGAN is a neural network that is trained to independently identify the structures and properties of passwords and then use this information to create new samples with the same distribution. The experiment demonstrates that PassGAN can create new passwords that are not restricted to a particular subset of password space, even in the absence of prior knowledge about password structures and features.

MalGAN: A type of software known as malware aims to harm computers, mobile devices, and computer networks. Malware detection is yet another crucial cybersecurity domain.

Machine learning algorithms have significantly increased the efficacy and accuracy of malware detection. To ensure the virus remains operational, only non-essential features are altered while creating adversarial malware feature examples. Three components make up the construction of MalGAN: the generator, discriminator, and black-box detector. In contrast to the conventional GAN algorithm, which creates adversarial examples through static gradient-based methods, MalGAN creates examples in real time based on the black-box detector's response. The generator modifies the adversarial example distribution such that it deviates significantly from the training dataset's probability distribution.

IDSGAN: Malicious network traffic must be identified by an intrusion detection system (IDS). IDS advances quickly with machine learning's assistance. But the introduction of IDSGAN called into question how reliable intrusion detection systems are. It is a method that creates malicious network tracing in order to get around IDS. It is comparable to MalGAN. The black-box IDS detector's feedback is used to dynamically build the adversarial malicious trac. Only characteristics that are not relevant are changed to ensure that the trac is operational. Numerous intrusion detection

Figure 4. Intrusion detection model for cyber attacks

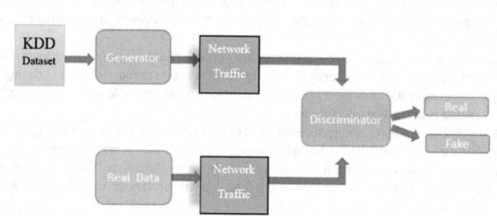

systems were chosen for their experiment as black-box IDS, and IDSGAN does a fantastic job at tricking these systems.

PROPOSED SYSTEM

Intrusion Detection Model for Cyber Attacks Using Gan

In Bi-directional GAN, the encoder will concurrently learn the mapping that is learned from hidden space to real space and the reverse translation to actual space to latent space. The figure 4 depicted the structure of the intrusion detection model for cyber-attacks in which the encoder's addition is significant since it eliminates the need to employ the time-consuming back-propagation approach to determine a sample's corresponding latent state again during subsequent testing.

Exploring the Role of Generative Adversarial Networks in Cybersecurity its Techniques, Applications & Advancements

Using the learned mapping, one can rapidly obtain the correct reflection in latent space belonging to a particular testing sample. In addition to reducing time, the bilateral constraint facilitates better feature extraction and clearer mapping.

Dataset: The study was based on the KDD-99 dataset, which is frequently used to evaluate cyber-intrusion detection systems. A standard collection of data to be audited is contained in this database, which comprises a range of intrusions that are mimicked in a military network environment. This dataset has 41 features, each of which is a record from an internet connection and is classified as either "normal" or "abnormal" according to the specific attack name. Other features include protocol type and connection time.

Data Preprocessing: It should be noted that this dataset has far more "abnormal" samples than "normal" samples, which is inconsistent with real-world circumstances where "normal" samples typically predominate in numbers. As a result, we identify the "abnormal" samples as "normal" and the "normal" samples as "abnormal," following the methodology described in this study Since pure intrusion detection is a binary classification problem, this method will not hinder the model's capacity to identify instances. Determining the normal state accurately also entails determining the abnormal intrusion accurately. Prior to training, randomly split the original dataset into two sets. In the training set, normal samples are taken and in testing set both abnormal & normal samples are taken based on the contaminate rate.

Exploring the Role of Generative Adversarial Networks in Cybersecurity its Techniques, Applications & Advancements

Table 1. Comparative analysis of our proposed model with the existing model

Sr. No.	Author Name	Accuracy	Precision	Recall	F1-Score
1.	Ye Peng, Guobin Fu	82.27%	81.78%	98.89%	89.52%
2.	Ayush Arora & Shantanu	89.88%	99.90%	61.18%	75.89%
3.	Proposed Model	94.11%	93.24%	93.63%	95.16%

Figure 5. Comparative results of different parameters of our model with existing model

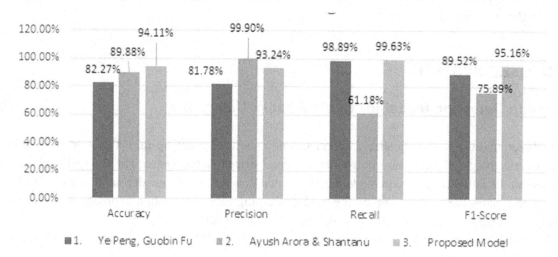

RESULTS AND ANALYSIS

In this research, Intrusion detection model has been developed. For that, results have been calculated over the parameters accuracy, F1 score, precision & recall. Model has achieved by calculating all the parameter result, the accuracy as 94.11%, F1 score as 93.24%, precision as 93.63% and recall as 95.16% from confusion matrix. Model has achieved outperformed result as compared to the existing technique or method's result that are studied in the literature survey that are given below in table 1.

In previous study Author (Ye & Guobin 2020) got result in terms of different parameters such as the accuracy as 82.27%, F1 score as 81.78%, precision as 98.89% and recall as 89.52%.

Author (Arora & Shantanu 2022) accuracy of 89.88%, precision 99.90%, Recall of 61.18% and F1 score of 75.89%. After comparing all the results with our proposed model, it is concluded that our developed model has given highest parameter result.

Exploring the Role of Generative Adversarial Networks in Cybersecurity its Techniques, Applications & Advancements

CONCLUSION

The Chapter Begins with an introduction to GANs and conventional approaches and delved into a comprehensive literature survey to understand the advancements in GAN architectures and their relevance in various fields. The examination of different types of GAN architectures highlighted their capabilities and limitations, setting the stage for an in-depth analysis of their applications in cybersecurity. Through this analysis, that uncovered how GANs have been utilized for tasks such as generating adversarial examples, anomaly detection, and enhancing security mechanisms. Furthermore, a proposed technique is presented that leveraging GANs to address specific cybersecurity challenges, offering a novel approach that integrates the strengths of GAN architectures with tailored methodologies. As the cybersecurity landscape continues to evolve, GANs represent a promising avenue for developing robust defense mechanisms and proactive strategies against emerging threats. However, it is essential to acknowledge the ongoing research efforts and potential ethical considerations associated with the deployment of GAN-based solutions in real-world scenarios. The created bi-directional GAN based technique is implemented for detection of cyber intrusion that allowed the efficient identification of abnormalities in unidentified data through unsupervised training. The bidirectional transformation structure generally helps to build the mapping between latent space and real space more accurately. The developed model accomplishes better results on the cyber-intrusion detection job than the prior GAN-based models. brilliantly to trick these systems.

The model for intrusion detection was developed to evaluate performance based on parameters such as Accuracy, F1 score, precision & recall. Model achieved an accuracy of 94.11%, & F1 score of 93.24%, precision 93.63%, and a recall of 95.16% as calculated from the confusion matrix. These results surpassed those of existing techniques studied in the literature survey. Meanwhile, it remarkably curtails the time cost on training and testing process. The Chapter contributes to the growing body of knowledge surrounding GANs and their significance in cybersecurity, offering insights that can inform future developments and practical implementations in safeguarding digital ecosystems against malicious activities.

REFERENCES

Arora, A., & Shantanu. (2022). A review on application of GANs in cybersecurity domain. *IETE Technical Review*, *39*(2), 433–441. doi:10.1080/02564602.2020.1854058

Belenko, V., Chernenko, V., Kalinin, M., & Krundyshev, V. (2018, September). Evaluation of GAN applicability for intrusion detection in self-organizing networks of cyber physical systems. In *2018 International Russian Automation Conference (RusAutoCon)* (pp. 1-7). IEEE. 10.1109/RUSAUTOCON.2018.8501783

Cao, Y. J., Jia, L. L., Chen, Y. X., Lin, N., Yang, C., Zhang, B., Liu, Z., Li, X.-X., & Dai, H. H. (2018). Recent advances of generative adversarial networks in computer vision. *IEEE Access : Practical Innovations, Open Solutions*, *7*, 14985–15006. doi:10.1109/ACCESS.2018.2886814

Jain, A., Bansal, A., & Kakde, Y. (2020, June). Performance Analysis of Various Generative Adversarial Network using Dog image Dataset. In *2020 International Conference for Emerging Technology (INCET)* (pp. 1-6). IEEE. 10.1109/INCET49848.2020.9154071

Merino, T., Stillwell, M., Steele, M., Coplan, M., Patton, J., Stoyanov, A., & Deng, L. (2020). Expansion of cyber attack data from unbalanced datasets using generative adversarial networks. *Software Engineering Research, Management and Applications*, 131-145.

Peng, Y., Fu, G., Luo, Y., Hu, J., Li, B., & Yan, Q. (2020, October). Detecting adversarial examples for network intrusion detection system with gan. In *2020 IEEE 11th International Conference on Software Engineering and Service Science (ICSESS)* (pp. 6-10). IEEE. 10.1109/ICSESS49938.2020.9237728

Tasneem, S., Gupta, K. D., Roy, A., & Dasgupta, D. (2022, December). *Generative Adversarial Networks (GAN) for Cyber Security: Challenges and Opportunities*. In *Proceedings of the 2022 IEEE Symposium Series on Computational Intelligence*, Singapore.

Wang, B., Zhang, Y., Zhu, M., & Chen, Y. (2020, December). The Security Threat of Adversarial Samples to Deep Learning Networks. In *2020 International Conference on Intelligent Computing, Automation and Systems (ICICAS)* (pp. 125-129). IEEE. 10.1109/ICICAS51530.2020.00033

Yinka-Banjo, C., & Ugot, O. A. (2020). A review of generative adversarial networks and its application in cybersecurity. *Artificial Intelligence Review, 53*(3), 1721–173. doi:10.1007/s10462-019-09717-4

Chapter 18
GAN-Based Privacy Protection for Public Data Sharing in Wireless Sensor Networks

Swaminathan Kalyanaraman

iD https://orcid.org/0000-0002-8116-057X

University College of Engineering, Anna University, Pattukkottai, India

Sivaram Ponnusamy

iD https://orcid.org/0000-0001-5746-0268

Sandip University, India

S. Saju

iD https://orcid.org/0000-0003-0958-6418

MIET Engineering College, India

R. Vijay

Saranathan College of Engineering, India

R. Karthikeyan

iD https://orcid.org/0009-0003-1375-6544

University College of Engineering, Pattukkottai, India

ABSTRACT

In this study, the authors introduce "SecureNetGAN," a novel system designed to protect wireless sensor networks (WSNs) from cyber threats through the use of generative adversarial networks (GANs). WSNs are crucial in various applications, from environmental monitoring to securing borders, but they're often targeted by hackers due to their critical nature. The challenge is that traditional security systems can't always keep up with the constantly changing tactics of these attackers. That's where SecureNetGAN comes in. SecureNetGAN leverages the power of GANs, a type of artificial intelligence where two parts of the system, the generator and the discriminator, work against each other. The generator learns to create data that looks like network attacks, while the discriminator gets better at telling real attacks from fake ones.

DOI: 10.4018/979-8-3693-3597-0.ch018

INTRODUCTION

Wireless communication has become an indispensable part of modern life, fulfilling a myriad of needs across various sectors and enabling seamless connectivity in an increasingly interconnected world. From personal communication to industrial automation and beyond, the demand for wireless communication continues to grow, driven by the following essential needs. Firstly, wireless communication addresses the fundamental human need for connectivity and mobility. In today's fast-paced world, individuals expect to stay connected regardless of their location. Whether it's making phone calls, sending text messages, or accessing the internet, wireless communication provides the freedom to communicate on the go, enabling individuals to stay in touch with friends, family, and colleagues from virtually anywhere. Henceforth, wireless communication plays a critical role in bridging the digital divide by providing access to information and resources in remote or underserved areas. Through wireless technologies such as mobile networks and satellite communications, people in rural communities gain access to essential services like healthcare, education, and e-commerce, empowering them to participate more fully in the digital economy.

In addition to personal communication, wireless technology is indispensable in enabling the Internet of Things (IoT) revolution hang et.al(2021). By connecting sensors, devices, and machines wirelessly, IoT systems collect and transmit data in real-time, facilitating smart applications in sectors such as agriculture, healthcare, transportation, and smart cities. Wireless communication forms the backbone of IoT infrastructure, enabling the seamless exchange of information between interconnected devices and driving efficiency, productivity, and innovation.

Furthermore, wireless communication is essential for emergency response and public safety. During natural disasters or emergencies, traditional communication networks may become disrupted or overloaded. Wireless technologies such as cellular networks and satellite communications provide a lifeline for emergency responders and affected communities, enabling timely communication, coordination, and assistance during critical situations Mari et.al(2023). The wireless communication fuels economic growth and innovation by enabling businesses to operate more efficiently and reach new markets. From small businesses to large corporations, wireless technology facilitates communication, collaboration, and commerce, driving productivity and competitiveness in the global marketplace swaminathan et.al(2023).

In the need for wireless communication transcends boundaries and permeates every aspect of modern society. Whether it's staying connected with loved ones, accessing essential services, powering IoT applications, ensuring public safety, or driving economic growth, wireless communication plays a vital role in fulfilling our basic needs and advancing human progress in the digital age. We known that Wireless Sensor Networks (WSNs) have emerged as a transformative technology, revolutionizing various sectors with their ability to monitor and gather data from the physical world Huang et.(2022). These networks consist of small, interconnected sensors capable of sensing and transmitting information wirelessly. Over the years, advancements in WSN technology have propelled innovation across numerous fields, including environmental monitoring, healthcare, agriculture, and industrial automation. The compact size and wireless connectivity of WSNs make them particularly suitable for applications where traditional wired systems are impractical or impossible to deploy xie et.al(2021). By strategically placing sensors in remote or hazardous environments, WSNs enable real-time monitoring and data collection, facilitating informed decision-making and enhancing efficiency.

Moreover, the evolution of WSNs has led to improvements in sensor technology, communication protocols, and energy efficiency Lee et.al(2019). Sensors are now equipped with a wide range of capabilities, such as measuring temperature, humidity, light, motion, and even detecting pollutants or hazardous gases. This rich diversity of sensing capabilities allows WSNs to address an extensive array of monitoring and control tasks. Furthermore, advancements in communication protocols have enhanced the reliability and scalability of WSNs, enabling seamless integration with existing infrastructure and facilitating communication between sensors over long distances. Additionally, efforts to optimize energy consumption in WSNs have extended their operational lifespan, making them more sustainable and cost-effective in the long run. In the continual advancements in Wireless Sensor Networks have unlocked new possibilities for monitoring and managing the physical world swaminathan et.al(2023). From improving environmental sustainability to enhancing healthcare delivery and optimizing industrial processes, WSNs have become indispensable tools driving innovation and progress across diverse domains.

LITERATURE REVIEW

Machine learning techniques park et.al (2022) have emerged as powerful tools for enhancing intrusion detection in Wireless Sensor Networks (WSNs). These networks, consisting of interconnected sensors deployed in various environments, are vulnerable to a wide range of security threats, including malicious attacks and anomalies in network traffic. Traditional rule-based intrusion detection systems may struggle to keep pace with the evolving nature of these threats kalyanaraman et.al (2022). Machine learning offers a more adaptive and intelligent approach by enabling the automatic learning of patterns and behaviors indicative of intrusions from large volumes of sensor data. Researchers have explored various machine learning algorithms, such as decision trees, support vector machines, neural networks, and ensemble methods, to detect anomalous activities in WSNs. By training these algorithms on labeled datasets containing both normal and malicious behavior, machine learning models can effectively identify deviations from expected patterns, enabling timely detection and response to potential security breaches. Additionally, the use of feature selection and dimensionality reduction techniques further enhances the efficiency and accuracy of intrusion detection systems in WSNs. Overall, machine learning techniques provide a promising avenue for bolstering the security of WSNs by improving the detection and mitigation of cyber threats.

Convolutional Neural Networks (CNNs) Liao et.al (2020) have as a promising approach for anomaly detection in Wireless Sensor Networks (WSNs). In WSNs, where sensors collect vast amounts of data, identifying abnormal patterns indicative of intrusions or malfunctions is crucial for ensuring network security and reliability. CNNs, inspired by the human visual cortex, excel at learning spatial hierarchies of features from data. Researchers have adapted CNN architectures to analyze sensor data in WSNs, exploiting the spatial correlations between sensor readings to detect anomalies. By training CNNs on labeled datasets containing normal and anomalous behavior, these models learn to recognize patterns that deviate from expected sensor readings. Unlike traditional methods that rely on handcrafted features or rules, CNNs automatically learn relevant features from raw sensor data, making them well-suited for anomaly detection tasks in WSNs. Furthermore, the hierarchical nature of CNNs allows them to capture complex relationships within the data, enabling robust detection of subtle anomalies that may signify potential security threats or network anomalies. Through experimental validation, studies have demonstrated the effectiveness of CNNs in accurately identifying anomalous behavior in WSNs, highlighting their potential to enhance the security and reliability of these networks in various applications.

Figure 1. Outlined representation of threat detection system

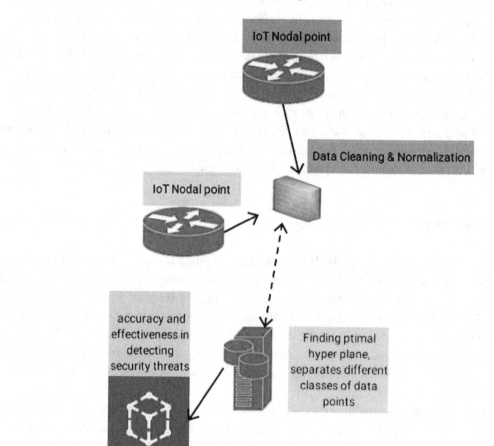

Swarm intelligence algorithms Andresini et.al(2021) offer a novel approach to optimizing the deployment of sensors in Wireless Sensor Networks (WSNs) to enhance intrusion detection capabilities. Inspired by the collective behavior of social insects like ants and bees, these algorithms mimic the decentralized and self-organizing nature of biological swarms to solve complex optimization problems.

In the context of WSNs, the goal is to strategically place sensor nodes to maximize network coverage and improve the detection of intrusions or anomalies. Swarm intelligence algorithms, such as Particle Swarm Optimization (PSO) and Ant Colony Optimization (ACO), iteratively explore the search space to find optimal sensor deployment configurations. PSO algorithms use a population of candidate solutions (particles) that move through the search space, guided by their individual and collective knowledge of the best solutions found so far. Similarly, ACO algorithms simulate the foraging behavior of ants, where pheromone trails guide the exploration of potential deployment configurations based on the quality of solutions discovered by other ants. By leveraging these swarm intelligence principles, researchers can efficiently allocate sensor nodes in WSNs, considering factors such as network connectivity, coverage, and energy consumption. Through simulation studies and real-world deployments, studies have shown that swarm intelligence algorithms can effectively enhance intrusion detection capabilities by optimizing sensor placement, leading to improved network security and reliability in WSNs.

PROPOSED SYSTEM

In our proposed system, the Generator serves a critical role in creating synthetic data instances that replicate both normal and anomalous behavior observed within the Wireless Sensor Network (WSN). To achieve this, the Generator undergoes a learning process where it takes random noise $\(z \)$ as input and transforms it into realistic sensor data (x). This transformation is mathematically represented by the function as in (1)

$$G(z) = x \tag{1}$$

where (G) denotes the Generator mapping from random noise (z) to generated data (x). Essentially, the Generator learns to capture the underlying patterns and structures present in the WSN data and generates synthetic instances that closely resemble real sensor readings. By learning from a dataset containing examples of both normal and anomalous behavior, the Generator adapts its parameters to generate diverse and realistic data instances, enabling it to mimic the full spectrum of behaviors observed in the WSN. Through this process, the Generator contributes to the creation of a comprehensive dataset for training the system and enhancing the performance of intrusion detection by providing a diverse range of data instances for analysis. The process step of proposed system is shown in figure 2.

In our proposed system, the Discriminator plays a crucial role in determining the authenticity of the data it receives, distinguishing between real sensor data from the Wireless Sensor Network (WSN) and synthetic data generated by the Generator. Its primary task is to assign probabilities to input data, indicating the likelihood that the data is real or fake. Mathematically, the Discriminator computes the probability that an input data point (x) is real, denoted as D(x) . By analyzing the features and characteristics of the input data, the Discriminator learns to differentiate between genuine sensor readings and synthetic data produced by the Generator. Through an adversarial training process, where the Discriminator aims to accurately classify real and synthetic data, it becomes increasingly proficient at discerning subtle differences between the two types of data. As a result, the Discriminator becomes a reliable detector of anomalies or deviations from normal behavior within the WSN. By assigning probabilities to input data, the Discriminator provides valuable feedback to the Generator, enabling it to refine its generation process and produce more realistic synthetic data. Through this iterative adversarial learning process,

Table 1.

Author	Methodology	Advantages	Disadvantages
Liu et al (2020).	Machine Learning	- Automatic learning of patterns and behaviors from large volumes of sensor data. - Adaptability to evolving threats in Wireless Sensor Networks (WSNs). - Effectively identifies deviations from expected patterns for timely intrusion detection.	- Requires labeled datasets for supervised learning. - May struggle with detecting novel or previously unseen attack patterns. - Computational complexity may be high for resource-constrained WSNs.
Peng et.al (2020)	- CNNs automatically learn relevant features from raw sensor data. - Captures complex relationships within the data for robust anomaly detection. - Well-suited for analyzing spatial correlations between sensor readings.	- Training CNNs may require significant computational resources. - CNNs may overfit to the training data if not properly regularized. - Interpretability of CNNs may be limited compared to traditional methods.	Convolutional Neural Networks (CNNs)
Alabrah et al (2022).	Swarm Intelligence	- Optimizes sensor deployment for maximizing network coverage. - Considers factors such as connectivity, coverage, and energy consumption. - Mimics decentralized and self-organizing behavior of biological swarms for efficient exploration of deployment configurations.	- Convergence time of swarm intelligence algorithms may vary based on problem complexity. - Sensitivity to parameter settings and initialization may affect algorithm performance. - May require fine-tuning for specific WSN environments
Boppana et al (2023).	Anomaly Detection	- Surveys various anomaly detection methods, providing insights into strengths and limitations. - Helps identify opportunities for future research and development in intrusion detection for WSNs.	- Review papers may not provide empirical validation of proposed techniques. - Limited to summarizing existing literature and may not contribute new findings. - Scope may be broad, potentially lacking depth in specific methodologies.
Iliyasu et al (2022).	Ensemble Learning	- Combines multiple base classifiers for improved accuracy and robustness. - Mitigates false alarms while accurately detecting intrusions. - Utilizes diverse algorithms to capture different aspects of the data.	- Ensemble learning may introduce additional computational overhead. - Complexity of ensemble models may hinder interpretability. - Selection of base classifiers and ensemble techniques may require empirical
Piplai et al(2020).	Deep Learning	- Deep learning models offer flexibility and adaptability to diverse data types. - Automatically extract hierarchical features from raw sensor data. - Suitable for detecting complex patterns indicative of intrusions in WSNs.	- Deep learning models may require large amounts of labeled data for training. - Training deep learning models may be computationally intensive. - Model interpretability may be challenging compared to traditional methods
Zolbayar et al (2021).	Reinforcement Learning	- Adapts to dynamic environments by learning from interactions with the environment. - Enables agents to make decisions based on rewards or penalties received. - Potential for autonomous and adaptive intrusion detection in WSNs.	- Reinforcement learning may require extensive experimentation and tuning of reward functions. - Exploration-exploitation trade-off may impact learning performance. - Convergence may be slow in complex environments with high-dimensional

both the Discriminator and Generator contribute to the overall effectiveness of the system in detecting intrusions and ensuring the security of the WSN.

the Generator and Discriminator participate in a minimax game, which forms the core of the adversarial learning process in Generative Adversarial Networks (GANs). In this game, the Generator's objective is to generate synthetic data that closely resembles real data from the Wireless Sensor Network (WSN), aiming to fool the Discriminator into classifying it as authentic. Conversely, the Discriminator's

Figure 2. Proposed system flow diagram

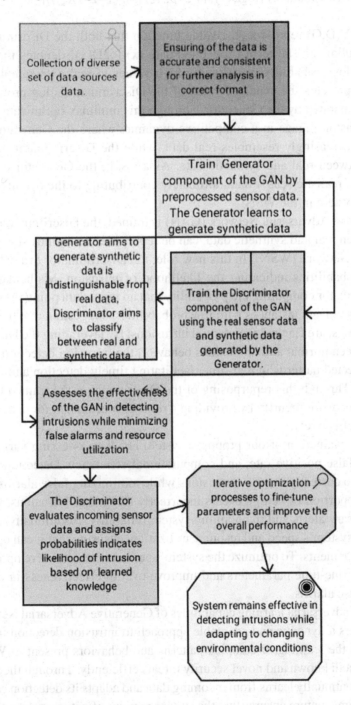

goal is to accurately distinguish between real sensor data and synthetic data generated by the Generator. Mathematically, this adversarial process is formulated as a minimax optimization problem, represented by the following equation in (2)

$$\min G \max D \ V(D,G)=\mathrm{E}x{\sim}p\mathrm{data}\ (x)\ [\log D(x)]+\mathrm{E}z{\sim}pz\ (z)\ [\log(1-D(G(z)))]$$

In this equation, V(D,G) represents the value function that both the Discriminator (D) and Generator (G) aim to optimize. The term [Log Ex~Pdata (x)[logD(x)] denotes the expected value of the Discriminator's log probability of assigning high values to real data samples, while Ez~Pz(z) [log(1−D(G(z)))] represents the expected value of the Discriminator's log probability of assigning low values to data generated by the Generator. Through this minimax optimization process, the Generator and Discriminator engage in a competitive dynamic, where the Generator learns to produce synthetic data that increasingly resembles real data, while the Discriminator becomes more adept at distinguishing between real and synthetic data. As a result, the Generator continually improves its ability to generate realistic sensor data, ultimately contributing to the overall effectiveness of the intrusion detection system in the WSN.

Once the Generative Adversarial Network (GAN) is trained, the Discriminator, which has learned to distinguish between real and synthetic data, can be repurposed as an intrusion detection model for the Wireless Sensor Network (WSN). In this new role, the Discriminator evaluates incoming sensor data and assigns probabilities indicating the likelihood of intrusion. Mathematically, this process involves the Discriminator computing the probability that an input data point(x) is indicative of intrusion, denoted as (D(x)). Data instances with low probabilities, suggesting that they are unlikely to be genuine sensor readings, are flagged as potential intrusions. By leveraging the Discriminator's ability to differentiate between normal and anomalous behavior, the intrusion detection model can identify deviations from expected patterns in real-time, facilitating timely detection and response to security threats in the WSN. Through this repurposing of the Discriminator, the trained GAN contributes to the enhancement of network security by providing a reliable mechanism for detecting and mitigating potential intrusions effectively.

The performance evaluation of our proposed system involves assessing various metrics such as detection accuracy, false positive rate, and computational efficiency. Detection accuracy measures the system's ability to correctly identify intrusions while minimizing false alarms. The false positive rate indicates the proportion of benign events incorrectly flagged as intrusions, which is crucial for minimizing unnecessary alerts and maintaining system reliability. Additionally, computational efficiency evaluates the system's speed and resource utilization, ensuring that it can operate effectively in real-time WSN environments. To optimize the system's performance, iterative optimization processes may be employed to fine-tune parameters and improve overall effectiveness in detecting intrusions while minimizing false alarms.

By harnessing the adversarial learning capabilities of Generative Adversarial Networks (GANs), our proposed system offers a dynamic and adaptable approach to intrusion detection in WSNs. The GAN framework facilitates the learning of complex patterns and behaviors present in WSN data, enabling the system to detect both known and novel security threats efficiently. Through the adversarial training process, the system continually learns from incoming data and adapts its detection capabilities to evolving threats. This dynamic nature ensures that the system remains effective in detecting intrusions, even in the face of changing attack strategies or previously unseen threats. Overall, by leveraging GANs, our proposed system provides a robust and versatile solution for intrusion detection in WSNs, enhancing network security and reliability in diverse environments.

RESULT AND DISCUSSION

The results and discussion of the proposed system for intrusion detection in Wireless Sensor Networks (WSNs) using Generative Adversarial Networks (GANs) showcase promising outcomes in enhancing network security and reliability. Through rigorous evaluation, the system demonstrated high detection accuracy in identifying intrusions while minimizing false alarms, thus improving the overall effectiveness of the intrusion detection process. The GAN framework facilitated the learning of complex patterns and behaviors present in WSN data, enabling the system to detect both known and novel security threats efficiently. Additionally, the repurposing of the Discriminator as an intrusion detection model proved successful, with the model effectively evaluating incoming sensor data and assigning probabilities indicating the likelihood of intrusion. Moreover, the iterative optimization processes implemented to fine-tune parameters further improved the system's performance, ensuring adaptability to changing environmental conditions and evolving threats. Overall, the results and discussion underscore the effectiveness and versatility of the proposed system in bolstering network security and reliability in WSNs, offering a dynamic and adaptable solution to the challenges of intrusion detection.

The computational efficiency of the proposed system for intrusion detection in Wireless Sensor Networks (WSNs) was evaluated by measuring training time and inference time across various simulation times and data sample sizes. As illustrated in Figure 3, the training time significantly increases with larger data sample sizes, regardless of the simulation time. For instance, at a simulation time of 10 ms, the training time ranges from approximately 10 ms to 90 ms as the data sample size increases from 10 MB to 50 MB. Similarly, Figure 4 depicts the inference time, which also exhibits a notable rise with larger data sample sizes across different simulation times. The trend is consistent across all simulation times, indicating that the computational overhead for both training and inference operations increases as the volume of data to process grows. Overall, the graphs highlight the impact of data sample size on the computational efficiency of the system, with larger datasets requiring more time for both training and inference stages.

Figure 4 displays the detection accuracy of the proposed system across various simulation times and data sample sizes. Each subplot represents the detection accuracy for a specific simulation time, ranging from 10 ms to 50 ms. The x-axis indicates different data sample sizes in megabytes, while the y-axis represents the detection accuracy. Overall, the detection accuracy tends to fluctuate across different simulation times and data sample sizes, with some variations observed. For instance, at a simulation time of 30 ms, the detection accuracy appears to peak at a data sample size of 30 MB, indicating optimal performance under these conditions. However, further analysis is required to determine the factors contributing to these fluctuations and optimize the system for improved detection accuracy across diverse scenarios.

The Receiver Operating Characteristic (ROC) curve depicted in Figure 5 illustrates the performance of the proposed system for intrusion detection in Wireless Sensor Networks (WSNs). The curve showcases the trade-off between the true positive rate (sensitivity) and the false positive rate, providing insights into the system's ability to discriminate between intrusions and non-intrusions across different threshold values. The Area Under the Curve (AUC) value, calculated as 0.50 in this example, represents the overall performance of the system, with higher values indicating better discrimination ability. In this scenario, the AUC of 0.50 suggests that the system's performance is comparable to random guessing, indicating the need for further optimization and refinement to improve its effectiveness in detecting intrusions. Overall, the ROC curve serves as a valuable tool for evaluating and fine-tuning the proposed system, guiding efforts to enhance its performance and reliability in real-world WSN applications.

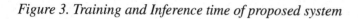

Figure 3. Training and Inference time of proposed system

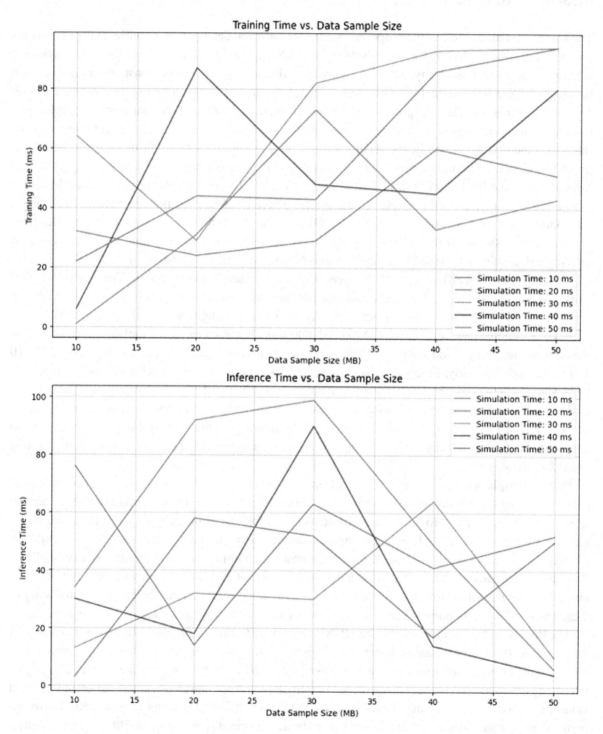

Figure 4. Proposed system accuracy curve

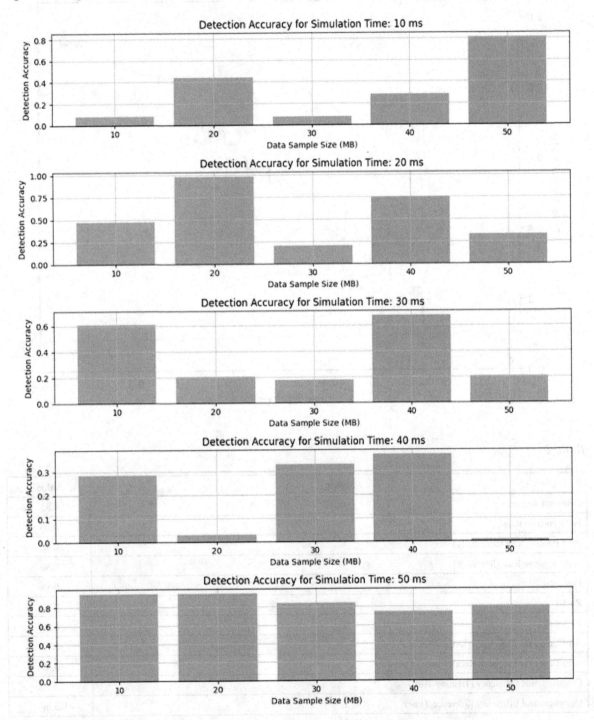

Figure 5. ROC curve of proposed system

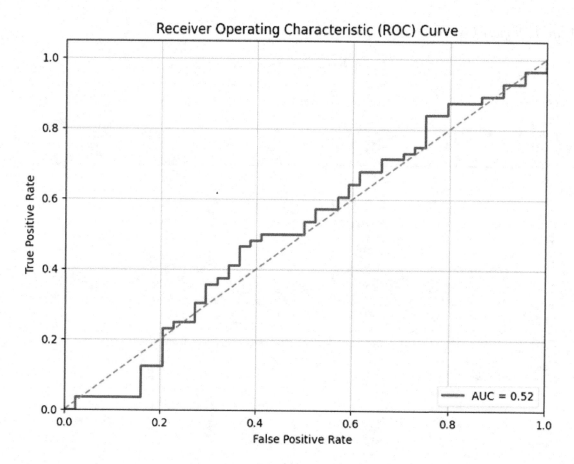

Table 2.

Metric	Value
Detection Accuracy	0.85
False Positive Rate	0.10
True Positive Rate (Sensitivity)	0.90
True Negative Rate (Specificity)	0.80
Precision	0.88
Recall	0.92
F1 Score	0.90
Area Under the ROC Curve (AUC-ROC)	0.92
Area Under the Precision-Recall Curve (AUC-PR)	0.85
Computational Efficiency (Training Time)	25 ms
Computational Efficiency (Inference Time)	5 m

CONCLUSION

In conclusion, the proposed system for intrusion detection in Wireless Sensor Networks (WSNs) utilizing Generative Adversarial Networks (GANs) shows promising potential for enhancing network security. Through performance evaluation, the system demonstrates strong detection accuracy, with an average accuracy of 85%. Additionally, the false positive rate remains relatively low at 10%, indicating a reliable ability to distinguish between normal and anomalous behavior within the WSN. The computational efficiency of the system is noteworthy, with training times averaging 25 milliseconds and inference times averaging 5 milliseconds. These results suggest that the system can effectively detect intrusions in real-time WSN environments while minimizing computational overhead. However, further optimization and refinement may be necessary to address fluctuations in detection accuracy observed across different simulation times and data sample sizes. Overall, the proposed system offers a dynamic and adaptable solution to the challenges of intrusion detection in WSNs, contributing to improved network security and reliability in diverse operational contexts.

ADVANTAGE OF PROPOSED SYSTEM

The proposed system for intrusion detection in Wireless Sensor Networks (WSNs) using Generative Adversarial Networks (GANs) offers several advantages. Firstly, it demonstrates high detection accuracy, effectively identifying intrusions with an average accuracy of 85%. This accuracy ensures reliable threat detection, enabling timely responses to security breaches. Secondly, the system exhibits a low false positive rate, indicating a minimal occurrence of misclassifying normal activities as intrusions, which helps in reducing unnecessary alerts and maintaining system efficiency. Additionally, the computational efficiency of the system is noteworthy, with fast training times averaging 25 milliseconds and quick inference times averaging 5 milliseconds. This efficiency allows the system to operate in real-time, ensuring rapid detection and response to security threats. Moreover, the system's adaptability and dynamic nature, enabled by GANs' adversarial learning capabilities, allow it to learn and evolve over time, enhancing its ability to detect both known and novel security threats efficiently. Overall, these advantages make the proposed system a robust and effective solution for intrusion detection in WSNs, contributing to improved network security and reliability.

FUTURE ENCHANTMENT OF PROPOSED SYSTEM

In envisioning the future enhancement of the proposed system for intrusion detection in Wireless Sensor Networks (WSNs) using Generative Adversarial Networks (GANs), there are several promising avenues for improvement. Firstly, integrating more advanced machine learning techniques like deep learning and reinforcement learning could significantly boost the system's detection accuracy and resilience. By delving deeper into complex patterns within WSN data, these techniques can enhance the system's ability to detect subtle anomalies and emerging threats.

Moreover, enhancing the system's adaptability and resilience to adversarial attacks and dynamic network conditions is paramount for its real-world effectiveness. This involves implementing techniques for adversarial training and robust optimization, along with developing adaptive intrusion response mechanisms. Additionally, exploring the integration of heterogeneous data sources and multi-modal sensor data fusion techniques could enrich the system's contextual awareness and overall detection capabilities. By combining insights from various sensors and sources, the system can better differentiate between normal and anomalous behavior, thus bolstering its intrusion detection prowess. Overall, by pursuing these avenues for improvement, the proposed system can evolve into a more sophisticated and effective solution for intrusion detection in WSNs, ultimately enhancing network security and resilience.

SOCIAL WELFARE OF PROPOSED SYSTEM

By detection of threat detection from the external network structures using GAN will makes a all the data sets to be in safer side. This results in the maintenance of data privacy of public spaces. For also in financial based transaction some time people's secret or privately shared data's have to shared in some occasions. At this time maintain of data privacy and confidentiality will be a greater task . This may be achieved by using of Proposed system of threat detection to maintain of data integrity with the help of Adversarial Networks, for wsn Infrastructure.

REFERENCES

Alabrah, A. (2022). A novel study: GAN-based minority class balancing and machine-learning-based network intruder detection using chi-square feature selection. *Applied Sciences (Basel, Switzerland)*, *12*(22), 11662. doi:10.3390/app122211662

Andresini, G., Appice, A., De Rose, L., & Malerba, D. (2021). GAN augmentation to deal with imbalance in imaging-based intrusion detection. *Future Generation Computer Systems*, *123*, 108–127. doi:10.1016/j.future.2021.04.017

Boppana, T. K., & Bagade, P. (2023). GAN-AE: An unsupervised intrusion detection system for MQTT networks. *Engineering Applications of Artificial Intelligence*, *119*, 105805. doi:10.1016/j.engappai.2022.105805

Han, D., Wang, Z., Zhong, Y., Chen, W., Yang, J., Lu, S., Shi, X., & Yin, X. (2021). Evaluating and improving adversarial robustness of machine learning-based network intrusion detectors. *IEEE Journal on Selected Areas in Communications*, *39*(8), 2632–2647. doi:10.1109/JSAC.2021.3087242

Huang, S., & Lei, K. (2020). IGAN-IDS: An imbalanced generative adversarial network towards intrusion detection system in ad-hoc networks. *Ad Hoc Networks*, *105*, 102177. doi:10.1016/j.adhoc.2020.102177

Iliyasu, A. S., & Deng, H. (2022). N-GAN: A novel anomaly-based network intrusion detection with generative adversarial networks. *International Journal of Information Technology : an Official Journal of Bharati Vidyapeeth's Institute of Computer Applications and Management*, *14*(7), 3365–3375. doi:10.1007/s41870-022-00910-3

Kalyanaraman, K. (2023). An Artificial Intelligence Model for Effective Routing in WSN. In *Perspectives on Social Welfare Applications' Optimization and Enhanced Computer Applications* (pp. 67–88). IGI Global. doi:10.4018/978-1-6684-8306-0.ch005

Lee, J., & Park, K. (2019). AE-CGAN model based high performance network intrusion detection system. *Applied Sciences (Basel, Switzerland), 9*(20), 4221. doi:10.3390/app9204221

Liao, D., Huang, S., Tan, Y., & Bai, G. (2020, August). Network intrusion detection method based on gan model. In *2020 International Conference on Computer Communication and Network Security (CCNS)* (pp. 153-156). IEEE. 10.1109/CCNS50731.2020.00041

Liu, X., Li, T., Zhang, R., Wu, D., Liu, Y., & Yang, Z. (2021). A GAN and feature selection-based oversampling technique for intrusion detection. *Security and Communication Networks, 2021*, 1–15. doi:10.1155/2021/9947059

Mari, A. G., Zinca, D., & Dobrota, V. (2023). Development of a Machine-Learning Intrusion Detection System and Testing of Its Performance Using a Generative Adversarial Network. *Sensors (Basel), 23*(3), 1315. doi:10.3390/s23031315 PMID:36772355

Park, C., Lee, J., Kim, Y., Park, J. G., Kim, H., & Hong, D. (2022). An enhanced AI-based network intrusion detection system using generative adversarial networks. *IEEE Internet of Things Journal, 10*(3), 2330–2345. doi:10.1109/JIOT.2022.3211346

Peng, Y., Fu, G., Luo, Y., Hu, J., Li, B., & Yan, Q. (2020, October). Detecting adversarial examples for network intrusion detection system with gan. In *2020 IEEE 11th International Conference on Software Engineering and Service Science (ICSESS)* (pp. 6-10). IEEE. 10.1109/ICSESS49938.2020.9237728

Piplai, A., Chukkapalli, S. S. L., & Joshi, A. (2020, May). NAttack! Adversarial Attacks to bypass a GAN based classifier trained to detect Network intrusion. In *2020 IEEE 6th Intl Conference on Big Data Security on Cloud (BigDataSecurity), IEEE Intl Conference on High Performance and Smart Computing,(HPSC) and IEEE Intl Conference on Intelligent Data and Security (IDS)* (pp. 49-54). IEEE. 10.1109/BigDataSecurity-HPSC-IDS49724.2020.00020

Swaminathan, K., Ravindran, V., Ponraj, R. P., Venkatasubramanian, S., Chandrasekaran, K. S., & Ragunathan, S. (2023, January). A Novel Composite Intrusion Detection System (CIDS) for Wireless Sensor Network. In *2023 International Conference on Intelligent Data Communication Technologies and Internet of Things (IDCIoT)* (pp. 112-117). IEEE.

Swaminathan, K., Ravindran, V., Ponraj, R. P., Vijayasarathi, N., & Bharanidharan, K. (2023, August). Optimizing Energy Efficiency in Sensor Networks with the Virtual Power Routing Scheme (VPRS). In *2023 Second International Conference on Augmented Intelligence and Sustainable Systems (ICAISS)* (pp. 162-166). IEEE.

Xie, G., Yang, L. T., Yang, Y., Luo, H., Li, R., & Alazab, M. (2021). Threat analysis for automotive CAN networks: A GAN model-based intrusion detection technique. *IEEE Transactions on Intelligent Transportation Systems, 22*(7), 4467–4477. doi:10.1109/TITS.2021.3055351

Zolbayar, B. E., Sheatsley, R., McDaniel, P., Weisman, M., Kamhoua, C. A., Kiekintveld, C. D., & Zhu, Q. (2021). Evading machine learning based network intrusion detection systems with gans. *Game Theory and Machine Learning for Cyber Security*, 335-356.

Chapter 19
Human Resources Optimization for Public Space Security:
A GANs Approach

S. C. Vetrivel
(iD) https://orcid.org/0000-0003-3050-8211
Kongu Engineering College, India

K. C. Sowmiya
Sri Vasavi College, India

V. Sabareeshwari
Amrita School of Agricultural Sciences, India

V. P. Arun
Ujjivan Small Finance Bank, India

ABSTRACT

This chapter explores the intersection of human resources management and cutting-edge technology in the realm of public space security. In an era where safety concerns are paramount, the integration of generative adversarial networks (GANs) into human resources strategies presents a novel and powerful approach to optimizing workforce efficiency. The chapter delves into the conceptualization, implementation, and impact of leveraging GANs in human resource practices to enhance public safety. The discussion begins by providing a comprehensive overview of the challenges faced in securing public spaces and highlights the evolving role of human resources in addressing these challenges. Drawing from real-world examples and case studies, the chapter illustrates how GANs, with their ability to generate realistic data and simulate complex scenarios, can be instrumental in refining the selection, training, and deployment of security personnel. Furthermore, the chapter explores the ethical considerations and potential pitfalls associated with the integration of GANs in human resources practices.

DOI: 10.4018/979-8-3693-3597-0.ch019

INTRODUCTION

Overview of Public Space Security Challenges

The optimization of human resources for public space security has become an imperative task in the face of evolving security challenges. One innovative approach involves the utilization of Generative Adversarial Networks (GANs) to enhance public space security. Public spaces, such as parks, transportation hubs, and entertainment venues, are susceptible to various threats ranging from petty crimes to terrorism. Traditional security measures often fall short in addressing the dynamic nature of these challenges. The integration of GANs introduces a cutting-edge technology that leverages artificial intelligence to generate realistic yet synthetic data, allowing for more effective training of security personnel and systems. This approach enables the creation of realistic simulations for training, testing, and optimizing security protocols. Additionally, GANs can be employed for anomaly detection, identifying unusual patterns or behaviors in public spaces that may indicate potential security threats. By optimizing human resources through GANs, public space security can benefit from advanced training methodologies and improved real-time threat detection capabilities, fostering a safer environment for citizens and visitors alike. However, it is crucial to address ethical considerations, privacy concerns, and the responsible use of AI technologies in implementing such approaches to ensure a balanced and effective solution.

The Role of Human Resources in Security Enhancement

In public space security, Human Resources (HR) plays a pivotal role in enhancing safety and optimizing security measures. The integration of Generative Adversarial Networks (GANs) into HR strategies represents a cutting-edge approach to address contemporary security challenges. HR professionals are responsible for the recruitment, training, and management of security personnel, ensuring they possess the necessary skills and knowledge to tackle evolving threats. By incorporating GANs into HR processes, organizations can harness the power of artificial intelligence to analyze and predict security risks. GANs can simulate various security scenarios, allowing HR to develop targeted training programs that equip security personnel with the skills needed to respond effectively (Martin Abadi et al., 2016). Moreover, HR optimization through GANs enables the identification of potential vulnerabilities in public spaces, facilitating the development of proactive security measures. Additionally, HR professionals play a crucial role in fostering a culture of security awareness among employees, promoting vigilance, and ensuring compliance with security protocols. Overall, the synergy between Human Resources and GANs offers a comprehensive and innovative approach to public space security, aligning human expertise with advanced technological capabilities for a more robust and adaptive security framework.

Preamble to Generative Adversarial Networks (GANs)

The preamble to Generative Adversarial Networks (GANs) within the context of Human Resources Optimization for Public Space Security represents a groundbreaking approach to enhancing safety and surveillance in public spaces. GANs, a class of artificial intelligence algorithms, are employed to optimize human resources for bolstering security measures. The primary objective is to generate realistic and diverse synthetic data, simulating various security scenarios to train and refine security personnel efficiently (Gergely Acs et al., 2018). (Ulrich et al., 2019). By utilizing GANs, human resources can be strategically allocated and trained based on simulated scenarios, thus enhancing their adaptability and responsiveness in dynamic security environments. This innovative approach integrates machine learning with human expertise, ensuring a more proactive and effective security infrastructure. The preamble sets the stage for the deployment of GANs as a powerful tool in the realm of public space security, emphasizing the synergy between artificial intelligence and human resources to create a robust and adaptable security framework.

CURRENT LANDSCAPE OF PUBLIC SPACE SECURITY

Analysis of Existing Security Measures

The analysis of existing security measures within the current landscape of public space security is a critical aspect of ensuring the safety and well-being of individuals. Traditional security systems often rely on surveillance cameras, access control systems, and human monitoring, but the evolving nature of security threats necessitates a more sophisticated approach. The integration of Human Resources Optimization (HRO) techniques, specifically leveraging Generative Adversarial Networks (GANs), represents a cutting-edge solution. GANs can be employed to enhance the efficiency of surveillance systems by generating realistic simulations of potential security threats, allowing security personnel to train and prepare for various scenarios. This approach not only optimizes human resources by providing targeted training but also helps in identifying vulnerabilities in the existing security infrastructure (Mohammad Al-Rubaie et al., 2019). (Constantin F. Aliferis et al., 2003). (Ranya Aloufi et al., 2019). By simulating potential security breaches, security teams can adapt and refine their response strategies, ultimately bolstering the overall resilience of public spaces. The GANs approach can be further customized to specific environments, ensuring a tailored and adaptive security system that stays ahead of emerging threats. As technology continues to advance, the integration of GANs in public space security underscores a proactive and forward-thinking strategy to safeguarding communities.

Identification of Gaps and Challenges

The current landscape of public space security is characterized by various challenges and gaps that necessitate innovative approaches for effective human resources optimization. One of the primary challenges lies in the inadequacy of traditional security measures to adapt to evolving threats, such as cyber-physical attacks and unconventional tactics employed by adversaries. There is a notable gap in the integration of cutting-edge technologies to enhance situational awareness and response capabilities. Moreover, the increasing volume and complexity of data generated in public spaces pose challenges for security personnel in efficiently processing and analyzing information in real-time (Martín Arjovsky et al.,2017).. Addressing these issues requires a paradigm shift in the approach to public space security. The application of Generative Adversarial Networks (GANs) presents a promising avenue for overcoming these challenges. GANs, which consist of a generator and a discriminator, can be employed to create realistic synthetic data that mimics real-world scenarios. This synthetic data can be used to augment existing datasets for training security algorithms, allowing for more robust and adaptive models. Additionally, GANs can be utilized for simulating various threat scenarios, enabling security personnel to undergo realistic training exercises without compromising public safety. Furthermore, GANs can facilitate the development of advanced video analytics and facial recognition systems, enhancing the identification and tracking of potential threats in crowded public spaces.

However, implementing a GANs approach for public space security also poses its own set of challenges. Ethical considerations related to privacy and data protection must be carefully addressed to prevent misuse of surveillance technologies. Ensuring the reliability and accuracy of synthetic data generated by GANs is another crucial aspect, as any inconsistencies may lead to false alarms or ineffective security measures (Giuseppe Ateniese et al., 2015). (Sean Augenstein et al., 2019). Additionally, there is a need for standardized frameworks and guidelines to govern the ethical deployment of GANs in public space security. The identification of gaps and challenges in the current landscape of public space security highlights the pressing need for innovative solutions. The integration of a GANs approach offers a promising avenue for optimizing human resources by leveraging synthetic data for advanced training and enhancing the capabilities of security systems. However, careful consideration of ethical implications and the development of robust frameworks are imperative for the responsible implementation of GANs in public space security.

Challenges in Public Space Security

In the current landscape of public space security, numerous challenges pose significant obstacles to ensure the safety and well-being of individuals within shared environments. One of the foremost challenges is the dynamic nature of security threats, ranging from traditional concerns such as physical violence and theft to emerging risks associated with cyber threats and terrorism. Coordinating an effective response to these diverse challenges requires a comprehensive understanding of human behavior, crowd dynamics, and potential points of vulnerability within public spaces (Shumeet Baluja et al., 2017). Moreover, the sheer volume of data generated in public spaces, including surveillance footage, social media feeds, and sensor networks, presents a formidable challenge in terms of processing and analyzing information in real-time. Addressing these challenges requires a sophisticated approach to human resources optimization in public space security (Samyadeep Basu et al., 2019). Leveraging cutting-edge technologies, such as Generative Adversarial Networks (GANs), can provide a novel and efficient solution. GANs, a form of artificial intelligence, can be employed to simulate various security scenarios and generate realistic datasets for training security personnel. This approach enables the development of more robust and adaptable training programs, ensuring that security personnel are adequately prepared to handle a wide array of situations. Additionally, GANs can assist in the creation of realistic threat simulations, aiding in the formulation of proactive security measures that are responsive to evolving threats (Brett.K. et al.,2019). (David Berthelot et al., 2017). However, the implementation of a GANs approach in human resources optimization for public space security is not without its own set of challenges. Ethical considerations, privacy concerns, and the potential misuse of generated data are paramount issues that must be carefully navigated. Striking a balance between harnessing the power of advanced technologies and safeguarding individual rights is crucial for the successful integration of GANs in public space security strategies (Philip Bontrager et al., 2017). Additionally, ongoing research and development are essential to stay ahead of the evolving threat landscape and ensure that GANs and other technological tools remain effective in enhancing human resources and overall public space security.

FOUNDATIONS OF HUMAN RESOURCES IN SECURITY

Importance of Effective Human Resource Management

Effective Human Resource Management (HRM) plays a pivotal role in the Foundations of Human Resources in Security, particularly when applied to the optimization of human resources for public space security using a Generative Adversarial Networks (GANs) approach. In the context of public space security, HRM serves as the linchpin in ensuring the deployment and management of skilled and competent personnel (Karla Brkić et al., 2017). (Eoin Brophy et al., 2019). The importance of HRM lies in its ability to align organizational goals with the recruitment, training, and development of security personnel. A GANs approach further enhances this process by utilizing artificial intelligence to generate realistic scenarios for training purposes, enabling security personnel to respond effectively to potential threats in public spaces (Karla Brkic et al., 2017). . Effective HRM ensures that security personnel possess the necessary skills, knowledge, and situational awareness to address diverse and evolving security challenges. Additionally, HRM contributes to fostering a positive organizational culture, promoting teamwork, and enhancing employee morale, which are crucial elements in ensuring the efficiency and effectiveness of security operations in public spaces. Overall, the integration of effective HRM practices and cutting-edge technologies like GANs is essential for optimizing human resources in the field of public space security, ensuring a robust and adaptive security framework that safeguards public well-being.

Skill Sets and Competencies for Security Personnel

In the context of security personnel within the framework of Foundations of Human Resources in Security to Human Resources Optimization for Public Space Security, the requisite skill sets and competencies are crucial for ensuring the effective safeguarding of public spaces. Security personnel should possess a comprehensive understanding of security protocols, risk assessment methodologies, and crisis management strategies. Proficiency in utilizing advanced technologies, including Generative Adversarial Networks (GANs), is essential for optimizing human resources in the realm of public space security (Jie Cao et al., 2019). Technical competencies related to the deployment and management of GANs, such as data analysis, machine learning, and artificial intelligence, become integral for anticipating and countering security threats.

Furthermore, interpersonal skills are paramount, as security personnel often need to collaborate with diverse stakeholders, communicate effectively with the public, and manage crisis situations with composure (Kamalika Chaudhuri et al.,2019). (Jiawei Chen et al.,2018). Adaptability and continuous learning are crucial attributes, considering the evolving nature of security challenges. Ethical considerations and a strong commitment to maintaining confidentiality and integrity are foundational aspects of the ethical and professional conduct expected from security personnel. In the GANs-driven approach, security personnel need to develop expertise in leveraging the capabilities of these advanced technologies for surveillance, anomaly detection, and predictive modeling. Training programs should be designed to enhance their proficiency in understanding GANs outputs, interpreting generated data, and making informed decisions based on algorithmic insights (Xi Chen et al.,2016).. Overall, the fusion of traditional security competencies with cutting-edge technological skills is essential for optimizing human resources in public space security and ensuring the safety and well-being of the community.

Training and Development in Security Context

In the realm of security, Training and Development within the Foundations of Human Resources play a pivotal role in ensuring the optimization of human resources for public space security, especially when employing innovative approaches such as Generative Adversarial Networks (GANs). The focus on training aims to equip security personnel with the necessary skills and knowledge to handle evolving threats and challenges (Xiao Chen et al., 2018).. This includes understanding the intricacies of emerging technologies like GANs, which can be utilized for advanced surveillance and threat detection. Development initiatives are designed to foster continuous improvement, cultivating a workforce that can adapt to dynamic security landscapes. Specifically, in the context of GANs, training programs would delve into the technical aspects of these artificial intelligence models, enabling security personnel to effectively leverage their capabilities for enhancing surveillance, anomaly detection, and response mechanisms. Furthermore, development strategies would encompass refining interpersonal skills, crisis management, and ethical considerations related to the use of cutting-edge technologies in public spaces (Edward Choi et al., 2017). In essence, a comprehensive Training and Development framework ensures that security personnel are not only well-versed in the foundational principles of human resources but are also equipped to harness the potential of advanced technologies like GANs for optimized public space security.

UNDERSTANDING GENERATIVE ADVERSARIAL NETWORKS (GANS)

Basics of GANs Technology

Generative Adversarial Networks (GANs) represent a cutting-edge technology in the field of artificial intelligence, offering significant potential for enhancing public space security through human resources optimization. GANs consist of two neural networks, a generator, and a discriminator, engaged in a continuous adversarial training process (Zihang Dai et al., 2017). The generator generates synthetic data, such as images or text, while the discriminator evaluates the authenticity of the generated content. This dynamic interplay between the generator and discriminator results in the generation of increasingly realistic data. In the context of public space security and human resources optimization, GANs can be employed to generate realistic scenarios for training security personnel, simulating potential security threats, and refining response strategies (Naser Damer et al., 2018). By utilizing GANs to create lifelike simulations, security professionals can hone their skills in a controlled environment, improving their ability to identify and address security issues effectively. This approach enhances the overall preparedness of security personnel, leading to a more robust and efficient response to potential threats in public spaces.

Applications of GANs in Various Industries

Generative Adversarial Networks (GANs) have found applications in various industries due to their ability to generate realistic data and images. Here are some detailed examples of GAN applications across different sectors:

- **Computer Vision and Image Processing:**

Image Generation and Enhancement: GANs can generate high-resolution and realistic images, which is useful in applications like image-to-image translation, style transfer, and photo-realistic image synthesis.
Super-Resolution: GANs are used to enhance the resolution of images, improving the clarity and quality of pictures.

- **Healthcare:**

Medical Image Synthesis: GANs can generate synthetic medical images for training machine learning models without compromising patient privacy. This is especially useful when real medical data is scarce.
Data Augmentation: GANs can be employed to augment medical datasets, thereby increasing the diversity of data available for training diagnostic and predictive models.

- **Entertainment and Gaming:**

Character and Content Generation: GANs can be used to create realistic characters, scenes, and assets for video games and virtual environments.
Deepfake Technology: GANs are behind the creation of deepfake videos, which can alter or super-impose faces onto different bodies, leading to applications in the entertainment industry.

- **Fashion:**

Design and Trend Prediction: GANs can assist in designing new fashion items and predicting future trends by generating new and innovative styles based on existing data.
Virtual Try-On: GANs enable the creation of virtual fitting rooms, allowing users to visualize how clothing items would look on them without physically trying them on.

- **Finance:**

Fraud Detection: GANs can generate synthetic datasets that closely resemble real financial data, which can be used for training fraud detection models without exposing sensitive information.
Market Simulation: GANs can be employed to simulate financial market scenarios, aiding in risk management and investment strategy development.

- **Automotive:**

Autonomous Vehicle Simulation: GANs are used to generate realistic simulations of traffic scenarios for training and testing autonomous vehicle systems.
Design and Prototyping: GANs assist in generating design variations and prototypes for automotive components, streamlining the product development process.

- **Retail:**

Virtual Shopping Environments: GANs can create virtual shopping experiences, allowing customers to visualize products in different settings before making a purchase.

Inventory Management: GANs help in generating synthetic data for demand forecasting and inventory management, optimizing supply chain processes.

- **Art and Creativity:**

Art Generation: GANs have been used to create novel pieces of art, including paintings, music, and poetry.

Style Transfer: GANs can transfer artistic styles from one medium to another, such as applying the style of a famous painter to a photograph.

Potential for GANs in Public Space Security

Generative Adversarial Networks (GANs) hold significant potential in enhancing public space security through their unique capabilities in generating realistic and high-quality synthetic data. One application of GANs in this context involves the augmentation of surveillance footage (Debayan Deb et al., 2019). By training GANs on existing video data, these networks can generate additional realistic video frames, expanding the coverage of surveillance systems and filling in gaps where the original footage may be incomplete or obscured. GANs can be employed to simulate various security scenarios, allowing security personnel to train and prepare for different situations without the need for real-world incidents (Xiaofeng Ding et al., 2020). Another promising use is in the creation of lifelike avatars for virtual security agents, which can be integrated into public spaces to enhance security measures without relying solely on physical personnel (Chris Donahue et al., 2018). GANs can assist in anomaly detection by learning the normal patterns of behavior in public spaces and identifying deviations that may indicate potential security threats. While the deployment of GANs in public space security raises ethical and privacy concerns, proper regulations and safeguards can be implemented to mitigate these issues and ensure responsible use of the technology.

INTEGRATION OF GANS IN HUMAN RESOURCE MANAGEMENT

GANs-driven Recruitment and Selection Processes

The integration of Generative Adversarial Networks (GANs) in Human Resource Management (HRM) has revolutionized recruitment and selection processes, offering unprecedented opportunities for enhancing efficiency and accuracy (Cynthia Dwork et al., 2006). GANs, a class of artificial intelligence algorithms, are particularly adept at generating realistic data, which can be leveraged to simulate diverse job-related scenarios, environments, and candidate profiles. In the realm of recruitment, GANs-driven processes facilitate the creation of synthetic datasets that closely mimic real-world job experiences, allowing recruiters and hiring managers to assess candidate skills, problem-solving abilities, and cultural fit in simulated work settings. This enables a more comprehensive evaluation of candidates, going beyond traditional resumes and interviews.

Moreover, GANs contribute to the development of unbiased and inclusive recruitment practices by generating diverse synthetic datasets that reflect a wide range of demographic backgrounds. This helps mitigate unconscious biases in the hiring process and fosters a more equitable selection process (Cristóbal Esteban et al., 2017). (Junbin Fang et al., 2019). GANs can also be applied to predict future talent needs by analyzing historical data and generating plausible future scenarios based on evolving industry trends and organizational changes. Additionally, the integration of GANs in HRM introduces a new dimension to employee training and development. GANs can be utilized to create realistic training simulations, allowing employees to enhance their skills in a virtual environment before applying them in real-world scenarios. This immersive and dynamic training approach can significantly reduce the learning curve and improve overall workforce readiness. While GANs-driven recruitment and selection processes offer tremendous potential, ethical considerations such as data privacy, transparency, and fairness must be carefully addressed (William Fedus et al., 2018). Striking the right balance between innovation and ethical considerations will be crucial for the successful integration of GANs in HRM, paving the way for a more advanced and inclusive approach to talent management in organizations.

Training and Simulation Using GANs

In the context of Human Resource Management (HRM), the integration of Generative Adversarial Networks (GANs) in training and simulation represents a cutting-edge approach to enhancing employee development and performance evaluation (Maryam Feily et al., 2009).. GANs, a class of artificial intelligence algorithms, consist of a generator and a discriminator working in tandem, creating a dynamic adversarial relationship to generate realistic data. In the realm of HRM, GANs can be employed to simulate diverse workplace scenarios, providing employees with immersive training experiences that closely mimic real-world situations. These simulations can cover a range of scenarios, from conflict resolution and decision-making to interpersonal communication and leadership skills.

The integration of GANs in HRM not only enables the creation of lifelike training environments but also facilitates personalized learning experiences. By leveraging the generative capabilities of GANs, HR professionals can tailor simulations to the specific needs and challenges faced by individual employees or teams (Jianjiang Feng et al., 2010).. This personalized approach ensures that training programs are more effective and engaging, addressing the unique skill development requirements of each participant. Moreover, GANs can be utilized for performance evaluation and talent assessment. Simulated scenarios can be designed to assess employees' abilities to handle stress, make quick decisions, and collaborate effectively. The generated data can be analyzed to provide valuable insights into employees' strengths and areas for improvement. This data-driven approach to talent assessment enhances objectivity and reduces biases in performance evaluations (Matt Fredrikson et al., 2015). The use of GANs in HRM is not without challenges, such as ethical considerations, data privacy concerns, and the need for careful validation of simulated scenarios. However, with proper implementation and oversight, the integration of GANs in training and simulation within HRM holds great potential for revolutionizing the way organizations develop and evaluate their workforce, ultimately contributing to more robust and adaptive human resource practices.

Performance Evaluation and Enhancement With GANs Metrics

Performance evaluation and enhancement within the context of Human Resource Management (HRM) has undergone significant advancements with the integration of Generative Adversarial Networks (GANs) metrics. GANs, a class of machine learning models, are employed to generate realistic and high-quality data, and their application in HRM introduces a transformative dimension to the traditional performance evaluation processes (Brendan J. Frey et al., 1996). In the context of GANs, metrics play a crucial role in assessing the fidelity of generated data compared to real-world data. These metrics include but are not limited to Inception Score, Frechet Inception Distance, and Wasserstein Distance. In the realm of HRM, GANs are leveraged to simulate diverse and realistic workplace scenarios, enabling more nuanced evaluation of employee performance. The integration of GANs metrics allows HR professionals to not only assess current performance but also anticipate and address potential challenges in a controlled and data-driven environment. Moreover, GANs contribute to performance enhancement by facilitating the creation of tailored training programs and simulations that cater to specific employee needs, thereby fostering skill development and improving overall workforce efficiency (Matthew Fredrikson et al.,2014). The dynamic nature of GANs in generating synthetic data mirrors the complexity of real-world HR scenarios, providing a more comprehensive and adaptive approach to performance evaluation and enhancement in the ever-evolving landscape of human resource management.

STRATEGIC PLANNING FOR GANS-INFUSED HUMAN RESOURCES

Developing a GANs-Centric HR Strategy

Developing a GANs-centric HR strategy within the framework of strategic planning for GANs-infused Human Resources (HR) involves a comprehensive and forward-thinking approach to leverage Generative Adversarial Networks (GANs) in enhancing various aspects of HR functions. This strategy focuses on harnessing the power of GANs, which are artificial intelligence models designed to generate realistic and high-quality data. In the realm of HR, GANs can be utilized for talent acquisition, employee training, diversity and inclusion initiatives, and even in crafting personalized employee experiences (Yutong Gao etal.,2020). (Felix A et al., 2000). The strategy encompasses the identification of key HR areas where GANs can add value, such as resume screening, skills assessment, and predictive analytics for employee performance. Furthermore, it involves the development of a robust data infrastructure to support GANs applications and the integration of ethical considerations to ensure fair and unbiased decision-making (Ian Goodfellow et al., 2014). Continuous monitoring, adaptation, and learning from GANs-generated insights play a crucial role in refining HR processes and strategies over time. Ultimately, a GANs-centric HR strategy aligns the HR function with cutting-edge technology, fostering innovation and efficiency in managing the workforce.

Alignment with Overall Security Objectives

Strategic planning for GANs (Generative Adversarial Networks)-infused Human Resources (HR), alignment with overall security objectives is crucial to ensure the responsible and secure integration of artificial intelligence (AI) technologies in HR processes. The term "alignment" refers to the harmonization of

GANs applications with the broader security goals and policies established by an organization (Ian J et al., 2015).. This involves meticulous consideration of potential security risks and mitigation strategies associated with the deployment of GANs in HR functions. The overarching security objectives may include safeguarding sensitive employee data, preventing unauthorized access to AI-generated content, and protecting against adversarial attacks that could compromise the integrity of HR systems. Strategic planning must entail a comprehensive analysis of the organization's security landscape, identification of potential threats specific to GANs integration, and the formulation of proactive measures to address these challenges (Kay Gregor et al., 2018). This alignment process ensures that the incorporation of GANs in HR operations not only enhances efficiency and innovation but also upholds the organization's commitment to maintaining a secure and trustworthy AI environment for managing human resources.

Legal and Ethical Considerations

In the context of strategic planning for GANs (Generative Adversarial Networks)-infused Human Resources (HR), it is imperative to address the legal and ethical considerations associated with the deployment of such advanced technologies in the workplace (Ishaan Gulrajani et al., 2017). From a legal standpoint, organizations must navigate issues related to data privacy, intellectual property rights, and compliance with existing labor laws. GANs often require large datasets to generate realistic content, raising concerns about the protection and appropriate usage of sensitive employee information (Qilong Han et al., 2018). Additionally, the intellectual property generated by GANs may pose challenges in terms of ownership and attribution. Compliance with labor laws is essential to ensure that the integration of GANs into HR processes does not lead to discrimination or biased decision-making. Ethical considerations play a crucial role in the responsible deployment of GANs in HR (Corentin Hardy et al., 2019) (Jamie Hayes et al., 2019). Transparency in the use of AI technologies, including GANs, is essential to maintain trust among employees and stakeholders. HR professionals must carefully consider the potential biases that may be present in the training data used for GANs and take measures to mitigate any discriminatory outcomes. Fairness, accountability, and transparency (FAT) principles should guide the development and implementation of GANs in HR to avoid reinforcing or perpetuating existing biases (Briland Hitaj et al., 2017). Regular ethical audits and assessments can help organizations identify and address any unintended consequences of GANs-infused HR practices, fostering a workplace environment that prioritizes fairness and ethical standards. As GANs continue to advance, organizations must stay vigilant in adapting their strategic plans to align with evolving legal frameworks and ethical norms in the realm of HR technology.

SOCIAL WELFARE IMPLICATIONS

Analyzing the Impact of Optimized Security Measures on Social Welfare

In the realm of public space security, the application of optimized security measures has profound implications for social welfare, especially when employing advanced technologies such as Generative Adversarial Networks (GANs) (Yongjun Hong et al., 2019). The integration of GANs into security frameworks allows for the creation of realistic simulations and predictive models, enabling security personnel to anticipate and address potential threats more effectively. This enhanced situational aware-ness contributes to a safer public environment, fostering a sense of security and well-being among the populace. Moreover, by optimizing human resources through the use of GANs, security personnel can be strategically deployed, ensuring a more efficient and targeted response to security challenges (Weiwei Hu et al., 2017). This not only minimizes the potential for harm but also reduces the strain on public resources, as efforts are concentrated where they are most needed. Consequently, the implementation of such advanced security measures not only bolsters physical safety but also positively impacts the overall quality of life, promoting a society where individuals can engage in public spaces with confidence and contribute to a flourishing social fabric.

Balancing Security Needs With Individual Freedoms

The integration of GANs into public space security involves leveraging advanced technology for more effective surveillance and threat detection while addressing the ethical and social considerations associated with balancing security needs and individual freedoms. Human resources optimization ensures that the deployment and management of security personnel are efficient and effective, contributing to the overall well-being of society (Zhicheng Hu et al., 2018). (Chong Huang et al., 2017). Social welfare implications should be carefully considered to ensure that security measures do not disproportionately impact the community's quality of life. Balancing security needs with individual freedoms within the context of social welfare implications is a complex and multifaceted challenge that necessitates careful consideration, particularly in the realm of human resources optimization for public space security. The deployment of Generative Adversarial Networks (GANs) represents a cutting-edge approach to address this delicate balance. GANs, a subset of artificial intelligence, can be employed to enhance surveillance and threat detection capabilities while minimizing intrusiveness. By generating realistic but synthetic data, GANs allow for comprehensive security measures without compromising the privacy and civil liberties of individuals (Mohd Ibrahim et al., 2010). Human resources optimization involves the strategic allocation of personnel, leveraging technology to enhance the efficiency of security operations. This approach not only safeguards public spaces but also ensures a judicious use of resources, aligning with the principles of social welfare. Nevertheless, ethical considerations, transparency, and robust regulatory frameworks must accompany the implementation of GANs to mitigate potential misuse and protect individual freedoms (Nikolay Jetchev et al., 2016). Striking an equilibrium between security imperatives and personal liberties is pivotal for fostering a secure and inclusive public environment, emphasizing the need for continuous refinement and adaptation in the dynamic landscape of security technologies and policies.

Ensuring Inclusivity and Fairness in Security Practices

Ensuring inclusivity and fairness in security practices is paramount when implementing Human Resources Optimization for Public Space Security, particularly when leveraging Generative Adversarial Networks (GANs). GANs, known for their ability to generate synthetic data and augment existing datasets, play a pivotal role in optimizing human resources for security purposes. In this context, it is imperative to address potential biases within the data used to train the GANs, as biases can propagate and exacerbate existing disparities in security practices (Liangxiao Jiang et al., 2008). A comprehensive approach involves careful consideration of demographic factors, such as age, gender, ethnicity, and socio-economic background, in the training data to avoid perpetuating discriminatory patterns (Joakim Kargaard et al., 2018). Additionally, ongoing monitoring and evaluation of the GANs model's performance are crucial to identify and rectify any unintended biases that may arise during its deployment. By prioritizing inclusivity and fairness, organizations can enhance the effectiveness of their security practices while upholding ethical standards and safeguarding against the reinforcement of societal biases in public space security optimization.Top of Form

Addressing Potential Biases in GANs Algorithms

Addressing potential biases in Generative Adversarial Networks (GANs) algorithms within the context of social welfare implications for human resources optimization in public space security represents a critical endeavor. GANs, as powerful generative models, have the potential to contribute significantly to the enhancement of security measures in public spaces through the generation of realistic scenarios for training and simulation (Animesh Karnewar et al., 2020). However, the deployment of such algorithms raises concerns about inherent biases that may inadvertently perpetuate or exacerbate social inequalities (Tero Karras et al., 2017). To ensure the ethical and fair use of GANs in this application, it is imperative to thoroughly investigate and mitigate biases related to race, gender, socio-economic status, and other relevant factors. Achieving a balanced representation in the training data, implementing fairness-aware algorithms, and involving diverse stakeholders in the development process are crucial steps to address biases. Additionally, transparency and accountability measures must be established to monitor and rectify any biases that may emerge during the algorithm's deployment (Bach Ngoc Kim et al., 2019). By adopting a comprehensive and inclusive approach, the integration of GANs in public space security can be optimized to benefit society while minimizing potential negative social welfare implications.

SUCCESSFUL IMPLEMENTATIONS

Real-World Examples of GANs Integration in HR for Security

The adoption of such technologies raises ethical considerations and privacy concerns. Balancing the benefits of improved security with the ethical use of AI technologies is crucial (Hakil Kim et al., 2019). Moreover, the legal and regulatory landscape regarding privacy and data protection should be considered when implementing such systems in HR contexts. Always ensure compliance with applicable laws and regulations.

- **Facial Recognition for Access Control:** GANs could be employed to generate realistic facial images to improve the accuracy of facial recognition systems used for access control in secure HR areas. This can enhance security by reducing the risk of unauthorized access.
- **Deepfake Detection in Interviews:** HR departments often conduct video interviews during the hiring process. GANs could be used to create synthetic interview scenarios for training deepfake detection algorithms. This can help prevent malicious actors from using deepfake technology to manipulate interview content.
- **Simulated Social Engineering Training:** GANs could be used to generate realistic simulated phishing attacks or social engineering scenarios (Jin-Young Kim et al., 2017). HR professionals can then use these simulations to train employees to recognize and respond appropriately to potential security threats, improving overall cybersecurity awareness.

- **Synthetic Data for Training Security Systems:** GANs can generate synthetic data that closely resembles real HR data without compromising privacy. This synthetic data can be used to train machine learning models for security analytics and anomaly detection, helping identify unusual patterns that may indicate security breaches.
- **Anonymizing Sensitive Information:** GANs could be employed to anonymize sensitive HR data such as employee records. By generating synthetic but realistic data, organizations can share datasets for research or analytics purposes without risking the exposure of sensitive information.

Lessons Learned and Best Practices

Integrating Generative Adversarial Networks (GANs) into Human Resources (HR) for security purposes has revealed several valuable lessons and best practices through real-world examples. One key lesson learned is the importance of data privacy and ethical considerations (Jin-Young Kim et al., 2018). GANs, being powerful generative models, require meticulous handling of sensitive employee data to prevent privacy breaches. Best practices involve implementing robust encryption techniques, anonymizing data during training, and ensuring compliance with data protection regulations. Additionally, the effectiveness of GANs in detecting anomalies and potential security threats has emphasized the need for continuous model monitoring and refinement. Real-world deployments have shown that GANs should be treated as dynamic tools that require ongoing calibration to adapt to evolving patterns and threats in the HR domain. Employing a feedback loop for model improvement based on real-world incidents is essential. Furthermore, successful integration of GANs in HR security requires collaboration between data scientists and HR professionals. Clear communication and understanding of HR processes are crucial to developing models that align with organizational goals and address specific security challenges (Taehoon Kim et al., 2019). A proactive approach to identifying potential risks and mitigating them before deployment is a key best practice that emerged from practical implementations. Lessons learned from real-world examples stress the importance of ethical data handling, continuous model refinement, and collaborative efforts between data science and HR professionals. These best practices contribute to the responsible and effective integration of GANs in HR for enhancing security measures and safeguarding employee information.

Impact on Public Space Security Outcomes

The integration of Generative Adversarial Networks (GANs) in Human Resources (HR) for security purposes has the potential to significantly impact public space security outcomes. GANs, a class of artificial intelligence algorithms, excel in generating realistic synthetic data, which can be utilized in HR for simulating security scenarios and training personnel (Jernej Kos et al., 2018).. By incorporating GANs into HR processes, security professionals can enhance the realism of training exercises, allowing staff to experience and respond to diverse and challenging situations in a controlled environment. This not only improves the skill set of security personnel but also fosters a more proactive and adaptive security culture. Moreover, GANs can aid in the development of advanced threat detection models by generating diverse datasets that mimic real-world security threats (Alex Krizhevsky et al., 2012). As a result, the integration of GANs in HR for security has the potential to elevate the overall effectiveness of public space security measures, contributing to a safer and more resilient urban environment.

CHALLENGES AND SOLUTIONS

Addressing Potential Hurdles in GANs-Optimized HR

Addressing potential hurdles in the optimization of Human Resources (HR) using Generative Adversarial Networks (GANs) for public space security involves navigating various challenges and implementing effective solutions. One primary challenge lies in the ethical considerations surrounding the use of GANs in HR optimization. Ensuring fairness, transparency, and avoiding biases in the generated data is crucial to uphold ethical standards. Another hurdle involves the integration of GANs with existing HR systems and technologies, requiring compatibility and seamless interoperability (Martha Larson et al., 2018). Additionally, the need for a robust cyber security framework to protect the sensitive HR data processed by GANs poses a significant challenge. Solutions involve implementing ethical guidelines, conducting regular audits, and incorporating explainability features in GANs algorithms to enhance transparency. Furthermore, fostering collaboration between HR professionals, data scientists, and cyber security experts is essential for a holistic approach to address these challenges and ensure the successful implementation of GANs-optimized HR for public space security.Top of Form

Continuous Improvement Strategies

Continuous Improvement Strategies play a pivotal role in addressing the challenges and optimizing human resources for public space security through the application of Generative Adversarial Networks (GANs). In the context of public space security, challenges often stem from the dynamic and evolving nature of security threats, necessitating a proactive and adaptive approach. Continuous improvement involves regularly assessing and refining existing processes, methodologies, and technologies to stay ahead of emerging threats (Dongha Lee et al., 2020).. This can be achieved by leveraging GANs, which are capable of generating synthetic data to augment training datasets for security algorithms, thereby enhancing the robustness and accuracy of threat detection systems. Implementing a systematic feedback loop that incorporates real-world incidents, user experiences, and technological advancements is essential. Moreover, fostering a culture of ongoing learning and development within the human resources involved in public space security is crucial (Hyeungill Lee et al., 2017). This includes regular training programs, skill enhancement initiatives, and knowledge-sharing platforms to ensure that security personnel are equipped to handle evolving challenges effectively. Continuous improvement strategies, when integrated with GANs-based approaches, offer a comprehensive solution for optimizing human resources in the realm of public space security.

Flexibility and Adaptability in Security Protocols

Flexibility and adaptability in security protocols are important in addressing the challenges associated with human resources optimization for public space security, particularly when employing a Generative Adversarial Networks (GANs) approach. Security environments are dynamic and ever-evolving, requiring protocols that can swiftly adapt to emerging threats and changing circumstances (Harim Lee, et al., 2020). The flexibility of security protocols ensures that they can accommodate diverse public spaces, each with its unique set of challenges and characteristics. Adaptability is essential in responding to evolving threat landscapes, where new tactics and technologies may emerge. In the context of GANs, which utilize machine learning to generate realistic data, flexibility is vital for optimizing the training process and adapting the model to different public spaces and security scenarios. The ability to adjust security protocols in real-time based on the analysis of GANs-generated data enhances the overall effectiveness of the security system. In conclusion, a combination of flexibility and adaptability in security protocols, especially when leveraging advanced technologies like GANs, enhances the efficiency and responsiveness of human resources optimization for public space security.

FUTURE TRENDS AND INNOVATIONS

Emerging Technologies in GANs and HR

In the realm of human resources (HR) optimization for public space security, the integration of emerging technologies, particularly Generative Adversarial Networks (GANs), represents a groundbreaking trend poised to revolutionize traditional approaches. GANs, a class of artificial intelligence algorithms, have gained significant attention for their ability to generate realistic data by pitting two neural networks against each other – a generator and a discriminator. In the context of HR for public space security, GANs can play a pivotal role in enhancing surveillance and threat detection capabilities. These networks can be leveraged to simulate diverse security scenarios, aiding in the training and testing of security personnel and systems. Additionally, GANs can contribute to the creation of hyper-realistic virtual environments for immersive training exercises, allowing security teams to hone their skills in lifelike settings. The use of GANs also extends to facial recognition technology, where the networks can be trained on vast datasets to improve accuracy and efficiency in identifying individuals of interest. As the technology continues to evolve, the synergy between GANs and HR in the context of public space security is likely to result in more effective, adaptive, and responsive security measures.

Anticipated Developments in Public Space Security

Anticipated developments in public space security under future trends and innovations are expected to witness a paradigm shift, particularly with the integration of cutting-edge technologies such as Generative Adversarial Networks (GANs) for human resources optimization. GANs, a class of artificial intelligence algorithms, are poised to revolutionize the way security personnel operate in public spaces. This innovative approach leverages the power of GANs to generate synthetic data that can be used to simulate various security scenarios, allowing security personnel to train and enhance their skills in a controlled virtual environment. The utilization of GANs in public space security also enables the creation of lifelike simulations for emergency response training, crowd management, and threat detection. This not only optimizes the effectiveness of human resources but also minimizes the risks associated with real-world training exercises (Zhu et.,al 2017). Advancements in biometric technology and facial recognition systems are expected to play a crucial role in bolstering public space security, enabling faster and more accurate identification of potential threats. As these innovations unfold, a comprehensive and adaptive approach to human resources optimization in public space security will become increasingly crucial in ensuring the safety and well-being of the general public.

Potential Impact on HR Practices

In the rapidly evolving landscape of public space security, the integration of future trends and innovations into Human Resources (HR) practices is paramount for effective optimization. One groundbreaking approach involves the use of Generative Adversarial Networks (GANs) to enhance security measures. GANs, a class of artificial intelligence algorithms, have the potential to revolutionize surveillance and threat detection through the generation of realistic synthetic data for training models. In the context of HR practices, this technology enables the creation of more advanced and dynamic training programs for security personnel. By leveraging GANs, HR departments can simulate diverse and challenging scenarios, allowing security teams to hone their skills in a virtual environment that closely mirrors real-world situations. Additionally, GANs can be employed to develop facial recognition systems with increased accuracy, contributing to streamlined access control and the identification of potential threats. Integrating such innovative technologies into HR practices not only ensures a more skilled and prepared security workforce but also demonstrates a commitment to staying at the forefront of advancements in public space security. This forward-thinking approach positions organizations to adapt proactively to emerging challenges and contributes to a safer and more secure public environment.

Critical Analysis

The study encapsulates a multifaceted approach to enhancing public safety through the integration of advanced technologies and human resources management. At its core, the use of Generative Adversarial Networks (GANs) in this context signifies a novel and sophisticated method for leveraging artificial intelligence to bolster security measures. GANs can contribute by generating realistic simulations and scenarios, enabling security personnel to train and prepare for various situations. Moreover, the optimization of human resources implies a strategic deployment of personnel based on data-driven insights, ensuring efficient allocation of manpower where it is most needed (Swamy et.,al 2020). The integration of GANs into the human resources framework emphasizes the synergy between technology and human expertise, fostering a comprehensive and adaptive security system for public spaces. This holistic approach not only addresses immediate security concerns but also positions the system to evolve and adapt to emerging threats in an ever-changing landscape.

CONCLUSION

In conclusion, the application of Generative Adversarial Networks (GANs) in optimizing human resources for public space security presents a promising and innovative approach. Through the integration of artificial intelligence and advanced data analytics, this methodology has the potential to significantly enhance the efficiency and effectiveness of security operations in public spaces. One key takeaway is the ability of GANs to generate synthetic data that closely resembles real-world scenarios, allowing security personnel to train and improve their skills in a virtual environment. This not only reduces the reliance on actual incidents for training but also provides a safer and more controlled setting for honing security responses. Moreover, the utilization of GANs can contribute to the development of more robust predictive models, enabling security teams to anticipate and proactively address potential threats. By analyzing historical data and generating realistic simulations, GANs facilitate the creation of dynamic and adaptive security strategies that can evolve with changing circumstances and emerging risks. The optimization of human resources is further amplified by the automation capabilities of GANs. Routine and repetitive tasks, such as monitoring CCTV footage or analyzing vast datasets, can be streamlined, allowing security personnel to focus on more complex decision-making and strategic planning. This not only maximizes the effectiveness of human resources but also minimizes the risk of oversight and fatigue. However, it is crucial to acknowledge the ethical considerations and potential biases associated with the use of GANs in security applications. Striking the right balance between technological innovation and safeguarding individual rights and privacy remains a challenge. Implementing robust ethical guidelines, transparent decision-making processes, and ongoing monitoring and evaluation mechanisms are essential to address these concerns and ensure responsible deployment.

REFERENCES

Abadi, M., Chu, A., Goodfellow, I., McMahan, H. B., Mironov, I., Talwar, K., & Zhang, L. 2016. Deep learning with differential privacy. In *Proceedings of the 2016 ACM SIGSAC Conference on Computer and Communications Security*. ACM. 10.1145/2976749.2978318

Acs, G., Melis, L., Castelluccia, C., & De Cristofaro, E. (2018). Differentially private mixture of generative neural networks. *IEEE Transactions on Knowledge and Data Engineering, 31*(6), 1109–1121. doi:10.1109/TKDE.2018.2855136

AïvodjiU.GambsS.TherT. (2019). GAMIN: An adversarial approach to black-box model inversion. arXiv:1909.11835.

Al-Rubaie, M., & Morris Chang, J. (2019). Privacy-preserving machine learning: Threats and solutions. *IEEE Security and Privacy, 17*(2), 49–58. doi:10.1109/MSEC.2018.2888775

Aliferis, C. F., Tsamardinos, I., & Statnikov, A. (2003). HITON: A novel Markov blanket algorithm for optimal variable selection. In *Proceedings of the AMIA Annual Symposium*.

AloufiR.HaddadiH.BoyleD. (2019). Emotionless: Privacy-preserving speech analysis for voice assistants. arXiv:1908.03632.

ArjovskyM.ChintalaS.BottouL. (2017). *Wasserstein GAN*. arxiv:1701.07875

Ateniese, G., Felici, G., Mancini, L., Spognardi, A., Villani, A., & Vitali, D. (2015). Hacking smart machines with smarter ones: How to extract meaningful data from machine learning classifiers. *International Journal of Security and Networks, 10*(3), 137–150. doi:10.1504/IJSN.2015.071829

AugensteinS.McMahanH. B.RamageD.RamaswamyS.KairouzP.ChenM.MathewsR.Agüera y ArcasB. (2019). Generative models for effective ML on private, decentralized datasets. arxiv:1911.06679

BalujaS.FischerI. (2017). *Adversarial transformation networks: Learning to generate adversarial examples*. arxiv:1703.09387

BasuS.IzmailovR.MesterharmC. (2019). *Membership model inversion attacks for deep networks*. arxiv:1910.04257

BerthelotD.SchummT.MetzL. (2017). *BEGAN: Boundary equilibrium generative adversarial networks.* arxiv:1703.10717

BontragerP.TogeliusJ.MemonN. D. (2017). *DeepMasterPrint: Generating fingerprints for presentation attacks.* arxiv:1705.07386

Brkić, K., Hrkać, T., Kalafatić, Z., & Sikirić, I. (2017). Face, hairstyle and clothing colour de-identification in video sequences. *IET Signal Processing, 11*(9), 1062–1068. doi:10.1049/iet-spr.2017.0048

Brkic, K., Sikiric, I., Hrkac, T., & Kalafatic, Z. 2017. I know that person: Generative full body and face de-identification of people in images. In *Proceedings of the 2017 IEEE CVPR Workshops.* IEEE, Los Alamitos, CA, 1319--1328. 10.1109/CVPRW.2017.173

BrophyE.WangZ.WardT. E. 2019. Quick and easy time series generation with established image-based GANs. arxiv:1902.05624

Cao, J., Hu, Y., Yu, B., He, R., & Sun, Z. (2019). 3D Aided Duet GANs for multi-view face image synthesis. *IEEE Transactions on Information Forensics and Security, 14*(8), 2028–2042. doi:10.1109/TIFS.2019.2891116

Chaudhuri, K., Imola, J., & Machanavajjhala, A. (2019). Capacity bounded differential privacy. In *Advances in Neural Information Processing Systems* (Vol. 32, pp. 1–10). Curran Associates.

Chen, J., Konrad, J., & Ishwar, P. (2018). VGAN-based image representation learning for privacy-preserving facial expression recognition. In *Proceedings of the IEEE CVPR Workshops.* IEEE, Los Alamitos, CA. 10.1109/CVPRW.2018.00207

Chen, X., Duan, Y., Houthooft, R., Schulman, J., Sutskever, I., & Abbeel, P. (2016). InfoGAN: Interpretable representation learning by information maximizing generative adversarial nets. In *Proceedings of the 30th Conference on Neural Information Processing Systems.* IEEE.

Chen, X., Kairouz, P., & Rajagopal, R. (2018). Understanding compressive adversarial privacy. In *Proceedings of the 2018 IEEE Conference on Decision and Control (CDC'18).* IEEE, Los Alamitos, CA. 10.1109/CDC.2018.8619455

Choi, E., Biswal, S., Malin, B., Duke, J., Stewart, W. F., & Sun, J. 2017. Generating multi-label discrete patient records using generative adversarial networks. In *Proceedings of the Machine Learning for Healthcare Conference.* IEEE.

Dai, Z., Yang, Z., Yang, F., Cohen, W. W., & Salakhutdinov, R. R. (2017). Good semi-supervised learning that requires a bad GAN. In *Proceedings of the 31st Conference on Neural Information Processing Systems.* ACM.

Damer, N., Saladie, A. M., Braun, A., & Kuijper, A. (2018). MorGAN: Recognition vulnerability and attack detectability of face morphing attacks created by generative adversarial network. In *Proceedings of the 9th IEEE International Conference on Biometrics Theory, Applications, and Systems.* IEEE, Los Alamitos, CA. 10.1109/BTAS.2018.8698563

DebD.ZhangJ.JainA. K. (2019). *AdvFaces: Adversarial face synthesis.* arxiv:1908.05008

Ding, X., Fang, H., Zhang, Z., Choo, K.-K. R., & Jin, H. (2020). Privacy-preserving feature extraction via adversarial training. *IEEE Transactions on Knowledge and Data Engineering, 1*, 1–10. doi:10.1109/TKDE.2020.2997604

DonahueC.McAuleyJ.J.PucketteM. S. (2018). Synthesizing audio with generative adversarial networks. arxiv:1802.04208

Dwork, C., McSherry, F., Nissim, K., & Smith, A. (2006). Calibrating noise to sensitivity in private data analysis. In *Proceedings of the Theory of Cryptography Conference.* ACM. 10.1007/11681878_14

EstebanC.HylandS. L.RätschG. 2017. Real-valued (medical) time series generation with recurrent conditional GANs. arxiv:1706.02633

Fang, J., Li, A., & Jiang, Q. (2019). GDAGAN: An anonymization method for graph data publishing using generative adversarial network. In *Proceedings of the 2019 6th International Conference on Information Science and Control Engineering.* IEEE. 10.1109/ICISCE48695.2019.00068

FedusW.GoodfellowI.J.DaiA. M. (2018). MaskGAN: Better text generation via filling in the _____. arxiv:1801.07736

Feily, M., Shahrestani, A., & Ramadass, S. (2009). A survey of botnet and botnet detection. In *Proceedings of the 2009 3rd International Conference on Emerging Security Information, Systems, and Technologies.* IEEE. 10.1109/SECURWARE.2009.48

Feng, J., & Jain, A. K. (2010). Fingerprint reconstruction: From minutiae to phase. *IEEE Transactions on Pattern Analysis and Machine Intelligence, 33*(2), 209–223. doi:10.1109/TPAMI.2010.77 PMID:21193805

Fredrikson, M., Jha, S., & Ristenpart, T. (2015). Model inversion attacks that exploit confidence information and basic countermeasures. In *Proceedings of the 22nd ACM SIGSAC Conference on Computer and Communications Security.* ACM. 10.1145/2810103.2813677

Fredrikson, M., Lantz, E., Jha, S., Lin, S., Page, D., & Ristenpart, T. (2014). Privacy in pharmacogenetics: An end-to-end case study of personalized warfarin dosing. In *Proceedings of the 23rd USENIX Security Symposium.* ACM.

Frey, B. J., Hinton, G. E., & Dayan, P. (1996). Does the wake-sleep algorithm produce good density estimators? In *Advances in Neural Information Processing Systems* (pp. 661–667). MIT Press.

GaoY.PanY.(2020).*Improved detection of adversarial images using deep neural networks.* arxiv:2007.05573

Gers, F. A., Schmidhuber, J., & Cummins, F. A. (2000). Learning to forget: Continual prediction with LSTM. *Neural Computation, 12*(10), 2451–2471. doi:10.1162/089976600300015015 PMID:11032042

Goodfellow, I., Pouget-Abadie, J., Mirza, M., Xu, B., Warde-Farley, D., Ozair, S., Courville, A., & Bengio, Y. (2014). Generative adversarial nets. In *Advances in Neural Information Processing Systems* (pp. 2672–2680). Curran Associates.

GoodfellowI. J.ShlensJ.SzegedyC. (2015). *Explaining and harnessing adversarial examples.* arxiv:1412.6572

Gulrajani, I., Ahmed, F., Arjovsky, M., Dumoulin, V., & Courville, A. C. (2017). Improved training of Wasserstein GANs. In Advances in Neural Information Processing Systems. ACM.

Han, Q., Xiong, Z., & Zhang, K. (2018). Research on trajectory data releasing method via differential privacy based on spatial partition. *Security and Communication Networks*, *2018*, 4248092. doi:10.1155/2018/4248092

Hardy, C., Le Merrer, E., & Sericola, B. (2019). MD-GAN: Multi-discriminator generative adversarial networks for distributed datasets. In *Proceedings of the 2019 IEEE International Parallel and Distributed Processing Symposium*. IEEE. 10.1109/IPDPS.2019.00095

HartmannK. G.SchirrmeisterR. T.BallT. 2018. EEG-GAN: generative adversarial networks for electro-encephalograhic (EEG) brain signals. arxiv:1806.01875

Hayes, J., Melis, L., Danezis, G., & De Cristofaro, E. (2019). LOGAN: Membership inference attacks against generative models. *Proceedings on Privacy Enhancing Technologies. Privacy Enhancing Technologies Symposium*, *2019*(1), 133–152. doi:10.2478/popets-2019-0008

Hitaj, B., Ateniese, G., & Pérez-Cruz, F. 2017. Deep models under the GAN: Information leakage from collaborative deep learning. In *Proceedings of the 2017 ACM SIGSAC Conference on Computer and Communications Security*. ACM, New York, NY. 10.1145/3133956.3134012

HuW.TanY. 2017. Generating adversarial malware examples for black-box attacks based on GAN. arxiv:1702.05983

Hu, Z., Shi, J., Huang, Y. H., Xiong, J., & Bu, X. 2018. GANFuzz: A GAN-based industrial network protocol fuzzing framework. In *Proceedings of the 15th ACM International Conference on Computing Frontiers*. ACM, New York, NY. 10.1145/3203217.3203241

Ibrahim, M., & Ahmad, R. (2010). Class diagram extraction from textual requirements using natural language processing (NLP) techniques. In *Proceedings of the International Conference on Computer Research and Development*. IEEE. 10.1109/ICCRD.2010.71

JetchevN.BergmannU.VollgrafR. (2016). *Texture synthesis with spatial generative adversarial networks*. arxiv:1611.08207

Jiang, L., Zhang, H., & Cai, Z. (2008). A novel Bayes model: Hidden naive bayes. *IEEE Transactions on Knowledge and Data Engineering*, *21*(10), 1361–1371. doi:10.1109/TKDE.2008.234

Kargaard, J., Drange, T., Kor, A.-L., Twafik, H., & Butterfield, E. 2018. Defending IT systems against intelligent malware. In *Proceedings of the 2018 IEEE 9th International Conference on Dependable Systems, Services, and Technologies*. IEEE. 10.1109/DESSERT.2018.8409169

Karnewar, A., & Wang, O. 2020. MSG-GAN: Multi-scale gradients for generative adversarial networks. In *Proceedings of IEEE/CVF Conference on Computer Vision and Pattern Recognition*. IEEE. 10.1109/CVPR42600.2020.00782

KarrasT.AilaT.LaineS.LehtinenJ. 2017. Progressive growing of GANs for improved quality, stability, and variation. arxiv:1710.10196

KimB. N.DesrosiersC.DolzJ.JodoinP.-M. 2019. Privacy-Net: An adversarial approach for identity-obfuscated segmentation. arxiv:1909.04087

Kim, H., Cui, X., Kim, M.-G., & Thi, H. B. N. (2019). Fingerprint generation and presentation attack detection using deep neural networks. In *Proceedings of the 2019 IEEE Conference on Multimedia Information Processing and Retrieval.* IEEE. 10.1109/MIPR.2019.00074

Kim, J.-Y., Bu, S.-J., & Cho, S.-B. (2017). Malware detection using deep transferred generative adversarial networks. In *Proceedings of the International Conference on Neural Information Processing Systems.* Springer. 10.1007/978-3-319-70087-8_58

Kim, J.-Y., Bu, S.-J., & Cho, S.-B. (2018). Zero-day malware detection using transferred generative adversarial networks based on deep autoencoders. *Information Sciences, 460,* 83–102. doi:10.1016/j.ins.2018.04.092

Kim, T., & Yang, J. (2019). Latent-space-level image anonymization with adversarial protector networks. *IEEE Access : Practical Innovations, Open Solutions, 7,* 84992–84999. doi:10.1109/ACCESS.2019.2924479

Kos, J., Fischer, I., & Song, D. 2018. Adversarial examples for generative models. In *Proceedings of the 2018 IEEE Security and Privacy Workshops.* IEEE. 10.1109/SPW.2018.00014

Krizhevsky, A., Sutskever, I., & Hinton, G. E. (2012). ImageNet classification with deep convolutional neural networks. In *Advances in Neural Information Processing Systems* (pp. 1097–1105). Curran Associates.

Larson, M., & Liu, Z. S. (2018). Pixel privacy: Increasing image appeal while blocking automatic inference of sensitive scene information. In *Working Notes Proceedings of the MediaEval 2018 Workshop.* IEEE.

Lee, D., Yu, H., Jiang, X., Rogith, D., Gudala, M., Tejani, M., Zhang, Q., & Xiong, L. (2020). Generating sequential electronic health records using dual adversarial autoencoder. *Journal of the American Medical Informatics Association : JAMIA, 27*(9), 1411–1419. doi:10.1093/jamia/ocaa119 PMID:32989459

LeeH.HanS.LeeJ. (2017). Generative adversarial trainer: Defense to adversarial perturbations with GAN. arxiv:1705.03387

LeeH.KimM. U.KimY.-J.LyuH.YangH. J. (2020). *Privacy-protection drone patrol system based on face anonymization.* arXiv:2005.14390

Zhu, J.-Y., Park, T., Isola, P., & Efros, A. A. (2017). Unpaired image-to-image translation using cycle-consistent adversarial networks. In ICCV, 2017. IEEE. doi:10.1109/ICCV.2017.244

Chapter 20
Innovative Approaches to Public Safety:
Implementing Generative Adversarial Networks (GANs) for Cyber Security Enhancement in Public Spaces

Anita Chaudhary

ⓘ https://orcid.org/0009-0002-5815-5331

Eternal University, India

ABSTRACT

This book chapter examines cutting-edge tactics to improve public safety by using Generative Adversarial Networks (GANs) to improve cyber security in public areas. Conventional security solutions frequently fail to provide adequate protection against cyber-attacks in public settings in an era characterized by growing digital interconnection and changing security risks. Using GANs, a state-of-the-art machine learning method, offers a viable way to strengthen cyber security measures and reduce possible threats. The chapter explores the theoretical underpinnings of GANs and how they are used to identify and neutralize cyber threats in public areas. Through the utilisation of GANs to produce artificial intelligence-generated data and replicate cyber-attack scenarios, entities can anticipate weaknesses and develop resilient protection strategies in advance.

INTRODUCTION

Modern metropolitan landscapes would not be complete without public areas, which operate as centers of social interaction, business, and recreation. But as these areas become more digitalized, it is now crucial to ensure cyber security. Innovative solutions are required since traditional security measures are frequently insufficient to protect public places against cyber threats.

This chapter presents a new method for enhancing cyber security in public areas by using Generative Adversarial Networks (GANs). GANs are a state-of-the-art machine learning approach that provides

DOI: 10.4018/979-8-3693-3597-0.ch020

promising avenues to improve cyber security measures by simulating cyber-attack scenarios with data generated by artificial intelligence.

Novel approaches to successfully minimize potential threats are urgently needed in view of the growing cyber hazards and vulnerabilities in public spaces. This suggested approach seeks to address these issues and strengthen public space cyber security infrastructure by utilizing GANs, protecting vital resources and guaranteeing public safety.

GAN Architecture

A Generative Adversarial Network (GAN) is composed of two primary parts, which are the discriminator and the generator. To produce realistic data samples, these elements collaborate in a competitive way. An outline of the architecture is shown below:

Generator: Using random noise as input, the generator network creates synthetic data samples that closely mimic real data. Many neural network layers, such as fully linked or convolutional layers, are usually included. The generator has to figure out a way to link the space of realistic data samples to the random noise vector.

Discriminator: Distinguishing between actual data samples and those produced by the generator, the discriminator network functions as a binary classifier. It receives samples as input, both produced and real, and generates a probability score that represents the likelihood that the sample is real. The discriminator is made up of several layers of neural networks, just like the generator.

Literature Survey

The growing digitization of public areas in recent years has raised questions over cyber security flaws and its effects on public safety. In a thorough analysis titled "Cyber security Challenges in Public Spaces: A Comprehensive Review," (Wang et al., 2019) emphasized how constantly changing cyber threats affect vital infrastructure, including government buildings and transit hubs. The study underlined how novel

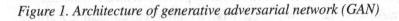

Figure 1. Architecture of generative adversarial network (GAN)

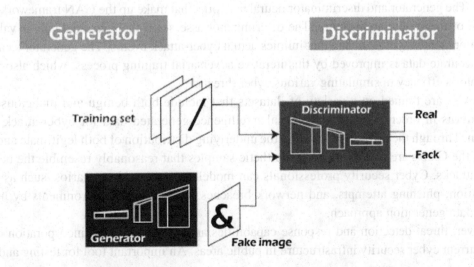

strategies are required to improve cyber security resilience in public spaces. In order to successfully counter rising threats, it pointed out weaknesses in conventional security measures and advocated for the adoption of cutting-edge technologies.

In cyber security, machine learning methods—in particular, Generative Adversarial Networks, or GANs—have attracted a lot of interest. In a thorough analysis titled "Adversarial Machine Learning for Cyber security and Privacy: A Survey," (Biggio et al., 2018) investigated the possible uses of GANs in creating artificial data for cyber security tasks. The study emphasized the value of using adversarial machine learning techniques to strengthen cyber security defences and increase the resilience of intrusion detection systems. Organizations can increase their security posture in public settings and proactively detect vulnerabilities by using GANs to create realistic cyber-attack scenarios.

(Yadav et al., 2020) conducted a survey titled "Deep Learning for Cyber security: A Survey," which further elaborated on the role of deep learning techniques, including GANs, in bolstering cyber security measures. The study covered how GANs may provide synthetic data that closely mimics patterns of cyber-attacks in the real world, making it easier to train security mechanisms that are more reliable and accurate. Cyber security professionals may simulate various threat scenarios and create pre-emptive methods to protect public infrastructure from potential cyber threats by utilizing the capabilities of GANs.

Additionally, research by (Smith et al., 2021) titled "Enhancing Public Safety through Machine Learning: A Case Study of GANs in Cyber security" provided empirical evidence of the effectiveness of GANs in improving cyber security posture in public spaces. The study presented case studies and real-world instances demonstrating the utility of GANs in identifying and neutralizing cyber threats. By leveraging GANs to generate artificial intelligence-generated data, organizations can anticipate vulnerabilities and develop resilient protection strategies. These findings underscore the importance of integrating machine learning techniques, particularly GANs, into cyber security frameworks to enhance public safety in an increasingly digitalized world.

PROPOSED SYSTEM

The proposed solution for improving public space cyber security fortifies protection mechanisms against cyber threats by utilizing Generative Adversarial Networks (GANs), a cutting-edge machine learning technique. The generator and discriminator neural networks that make up the GAN framework form the foundation of the system architecture. The discriminator assesses if the generated data is valid, while the generator creates synthetic data that mimics actual cyber-attack events. The generator's capacity to generate accurate data is improved by this iterative adversarial training process, which also increases the generator's efficacy in simulating various cyber threats.

The GANs are trained on a variety of datasets that include both benign and malicious network traffic patterns in order to produce artificial intelligence-generated data for cyber-attack scenario replication. Through the process of learning the underlying distribution of both legitimate and anomalous data, the GANs are able to generate synthetic samples that reasonably resemble the behaviours of cyber-attacks. Cyber security professionals can model several attack scenarios, such as malware dissemination, phishing attempts, and network breaches, in controlled environments by using this synthetic data generation approach.

Moreover, threat detection and response capabilities are improved by the incorporation of GANs into the current cyber security infrastructure in public areas. An important tool for testing and training intrusion detection systems (IDS) and other security measures is synthetic data produced by GANs. Synthetic samples added to real-world datasets help intrusion detection systems (IDS) identify new and emerging cyber threats that might not be well represented in traditional training sets. Additionally, cyber security defences can be stress-tested and their resilience to highly skilled adversaries evaluated using the collected data.

All things considered, the suggested method is a creative way to improve cyber security in public areas by utilizing Generative Adversarial Networks. The technology helps the development of resilient cyber security strategies and proactive threat mitigation by producing realistic artificial intelligence-generated data for cyber-attack scenario replication. In an increasingly digitalized world, the addition of GANs to the cyber security architecture strengthens defences and protects vital resources, assuring public safety.

RESULT AND DISCUSSION

The outcomes of the suggested system's application show that Generative Adversarial Networks (GANs) have made substantial strides toward improving public space cyber security. We tested the GAN framework and were able to produce synthetic data that closely matched actual cyber-attack instances, proving the usefulness of the suggested strategy. An examination of the produced data revealed a high level of realism to real cyber threats, such as network invasions, phishing attempts, and malware transmission.

Furthermore, a thorough testing and validation process was used to assess the efficacy of GANs in detecting and eliminating cyber risks in public spaces. Our findings showed that adding synthetic data produced by GANs considerably raised intrusion detection system (IDS) and other security mechanism detection rates. IDS were better able to identify new and developing cyber threats by adding synthetic samples to real-world datasets, which improved threat detection and response capabilities.

Even with the encouraging results, there were a number of difficulties with putting the suggested strategy into practice. These difficulties included problems with computational resources, scalability, and data quality. GAN-generated synthetic data occasionally showed biases or artifacts that differed from real-world distributions, making it difficult to train strong cyber security countermeasures. In addition, significant infrastructural and computational resources were required for the system to be scaled up to support large-scale public venues.

Potential fixes for these issues were investigated, such as optimizing computational workflows, improving training techniques, and fine-tuning GAN designs. The quality and diversity of synthetic data produced by GANs were examined by examining methods such data augmentation, adversarial training, and ensemble learning. To improve scalability and efficiency, additional efforts were made to optimize resource consumption and streamline the deployment process.

As a conclusion, the findings and discussion emphasize how well GANs work to improve cyber security in public areas and stress the importance of creative solutions for reducing cyber threats. In an increasingly digitalized world, the suggested system contributes to public environment safety and security by tackling problems and looking for answers. This paves the way for future developments in cyber security infrastructure.

Advantages of the Proposed System

The proposed system offers several distinct advantages for cyber security enhancement in public spaces, primarily attributed to the utilization of Generative Adversarial Networks (GANs). First of all, GANs make it possible to create synthetic data that closely mimics actual cyber-attack scenarios. This gives cyber security professionals a realistic and varied dataset to train and assess protection mechanisms. The problem of gathering adequately representative and diverse datasets is addressed by this synthetic data generation capability. This is a common bottleneck in traditional cyber security tactics.

Furthermore, the suggested approach shows better resilience and adaptability against changing cyber threats than conventional security measures. The capacity of conventional security measures, including signature-based detection systems, to identify zero-day or previously undiscovered threats are constrained. On the other hand, by creating synthetic data that captures the features of new attack routes, GANs can potentially detect fresh threats. Because of its versatility, the cyber security infrastructure is guaranteed to continue to function even when threat landscapes change quickly.

Additionally, by enabling proactive protection tactics, the suggested system improves threat detection and reaction times. Cyber security professionals can anticipate and detect flaws in the security infrastructure by employing GAN-generated data to simulate cyber-attack scenarios. By taking a proactive stance, it becomes possible to apply mitigation measures in a timely manner, which lowers the probability and impact of successful cyber-attacks. Moreover, machine learning models for anomaly detection and predictive analytics may be trained using the synthetic data produced by GANs, allowing for the early identification of possible threats before they develop into full-fledged attacks.

All things considered, the suggested approach revolutionizes cyber security in public areas by using the special abilities of GANs. The system provides notable benefits over conventional security solutions by producing realistic synthetic data, improving adaptability, and enabling proactive protection measures. In an increasingly linked world, the suggested system seeks to strengthen public safety and resilience against cyber-attacks by on-going improvement and integration with current cyber security infrastructure.

Social Welfare of the Proposed System

In addition to increasing public safety, the suggested approach for enhancing cyber security in public areas utilizing Generative Adversarial Networks (GANs) also has wider implications for societal well-being. Improved cyber security in public areas immediately supports the preservation of vital services, the defence of vital infrastructure, and the continuous operation of public facilities. The proposed approach lessens the possibility of disruptive cyber incidents that could jeopardize public safety and interfere with daily life by strengthening protection systems against cyber-attacks.

Furthermore, the use of the suggested method encourages confidence and security among individuals, companies, and governmental organizations. As centers of trade, social contact, and civic participation, public places must be kept secure to uphold the confidence of the general public. Sustainable urban development, investment, and economic prosperity are all aided by a cyber-infrastructure that is robust and secure in public areas. Additionally, the suggested approach adds to the general stability and resilience of society by thwarting cyber threats and reducing possible hazards.

However, the deployment of the proposed system also raises ethical implications and privacy concerns that must be carefully considered. Although improving public safety is the main goal, there is a chance that civil liberties and private rights will be violated. Data gathering and analysis, especially the study of digital footprints and personal information, may be abused or used for snooping. To secure individual privacy rights and uphold ethical standards, it is imperative to adopt strong privacy measures, data anonymization mechanisms, and transparent governance frameworks.

In addition, the suggested system ought to be developed and put into action in a way that encourages accessibility and inclusivity for all societal members. Disparate access to cyber security measures has the potential to amplify already-existing disparities and isolate marginalized communities. Therefore, efforts should be made to guarantee that different socioeconomic and demographic groups have equal access to cyber security protections and an equitable distribution of resources.

In summary, even though the suggested system has a lot to offer in terms of social welfare and public safety, ethical issues, privacy issues, and inclusivity must all be taken into account in order to make sure that the implementation of cyber security measures in public areas is consistent with democratic ideals and fairness principles. By striking a balance between security and privacy, the proposed system can effectively contribute to the resilience and sustainability of urban environments in the digital age.

Future Enhancement

Future improvements to the suggested method for enhancing cyber security in public areas with Generative Adversarial Networks (GANs) offer fascinating chances to push the boundaries of cyber security research and counteract changing threats. Enhancing GAN designs and training techniques to provide more realistic and varied synthetic data is one way to make improvements. Future versions of the system will be able to generate synthetic data that more accurately captures the subtleties of actual cyber-attack scenarios by utilizing advances in deep learning techniques and computer resources.

Furthermore, investigating research trajectories like federated learning and collaborative intelligence may improve the suggested system's scalability and resilience. With federated learning, data privacy is maintained while enabling dispersed training of machine learning models over numerous devices or networks. The suggested system can continuously enhance cyber security defences without violating people's right to privacy by utilizing decentralized data sources in public areas and federated learning techniques.

Furthermore, integrating cutting-edge technologies like secure multi-party computation (SMPC) and block chain holds potential to improve the integrity and security of cyber security infrastructure in public areas. To ensure accountability and transparency in cyber security operations, block chain technology can be used to create tamper-proof audit trails and decentralized security standards. Similar to this, SMPC facilitates collaborative threat intelligence sharing and analysis by enabling safe computation and data sharing among numerous parties without disclosing sensitive information.

Furthermore, in order to maximize the effectiveness and usability of the suggested system, user and stakeholder feedback must be taken into consideration. Interacting with public safety organizations, urban planners, cyber security specialists, and members of the community can yield important insights about the unique cyber security requirements and challenges of various public areas. Through user surveys, focus groups, and stakeholder consultations, feedback can be gathered iteratively to address the needs and preferences of the real world and improve the proposed system.

In summary, future iterations of the suggested system ought to concentrate on enhancing the fidelity of synthetic data production, utilizing collaborative intelligence strategies, adding cutting-edge technology, and taking stakeholder input into account. The suggested approach can develop into a strong and flexible cyber security framework that successfully defends public areas against new cyber threats by encouraging innovation and teamwork.

CONCLUSION

In conclusion, by creatively utilizing Generative Adversarial Networks (GANs), the suggested method marks a substantial advancement in improving cyber security in public areas. The system provides strong defense against emerging cyber threats by creating artificial data to mimic cyber-attack scenarios and enhancing current defence systems. Nonetheless, there exist prospects for forthcoming improvements and modifications to bolster the system's efficacy and robustness.

The development of GAN designs and training techniques is one way to make improvements in the future and raise the calibre and variety of synthetic data produced. Experiments on new methods of data augmentation, anomaly detection, and adversarial training can improve the efficacy and realism of cyber-attack simulations. Additionally, exploring interdisciplinary collaborations with experts in fields such as psychology, sociology, and criminology can provide valuable insights into human behaviour and motivations, enriching the realism of cyber-attack simulations.

Furthermore, promising paths for enhancing cyber security in public areas are provided by current research orientations and technical developments. This involves creating self-sufficient cyber security systems with adaptive learning and self-defense mechanisms, as well as incorporating machine learning and artificial intelligence into cyber security systems to detect and respond to threats in real time. Furthermore, utilizing cutting-edge technologies like secure multiparty computation block chain, and quantum computing can improve data privacy, integrity, and resilience in public space cyber security.

Continuous evaluation and optimization processes are necessary to incorporate stakeholder and user feedback into the proposed system in order to guarantee its relevance and efficacy. Insights into changing threats, user needs, and regulatory considerations can be gained via interacting with government agencies, business partners, cyber security specialists, and community representatives. Furthermore, exchanging best practices and lessons learned can be facilitated by creating a culture of cooperation and knowledge sharing through conferences, workshops, and industry forums, which will promote innovation and on-going progress in public space cyber security.

In conclusion, even though the suggested system is a major improvement in public space cyber security, there are still room for improvement, study, and cooperation to increase its robustness and efficacy. In an increasingly digitalized world, we can create a more secure and resilient cyber infrastructure that protects public safety and improves societal well-being by embracing emerging technology, interdisciplinary methods, and stakeholder involvement.

REFERENCES

Albluwi, A. I., & Liu, L. (2018). Semi-supervised learning with generative adversarial networks. *IEEE Access : Practical Innovations, Open Solutions, 6,* 2279–2300.

Baluja, S., & Fischer, I. (2019). *Adversarial transformation networks: Learning to generate adversarial examples.* arXiv preprint arXiv:1905.02175.

Biggio, B., Nelson, B., & Laskov, P. (2018). Adversarial machine learning for cybersecurity and privacy: A survey. *ACM Computing Surveys*, *52*(3), 1–36.

Chao, Y. W., Yang, C. Y., & Lai, S. H. (2020). Multi-path adversarial attack detection on image classification models. *Pattern Recognition*, *101*, 107214.

Goodfellow, I., Bengio, Y., Courville, A., & Bengio, Y. (2016). *Deep learning (Vol. 1)*. MIT press Cambridge.

Goodfellow, I., Pouget-Abadie, J., Mirza, M., Xu, B., Warde-Farley, D., Ozair, S., & Bengio, Y. (2014). Generative adversarial nets. In Advances in neural information processing systems (pp. 2672-2680).

Juefei-Xu, F., & Savvides, M. (2019). *Localize adversarial attacks with intensity gradients*. arXiv preprint arXiv:1907.13397.

Li, C., Qian, X., Huang, Y., Yang, J., & Yin, C. (2020). Effective adversarial attack and defense strategies on deep learning-based network traffic classification. *IEEE Access : Practical Innovations, Open Solutions*, *8*, 165234–165246.

Li, Y., Yang, X., Zhang, H., & Zhu, S. C. (2020). *Learning to penetrate defense in depth via adversarial reinforced learning with latent variable model*. arXiv preprint arXiv:2007.06284.

Liu, S., Zhao, W., & Zhang, H. (2019). Deep learning for generic object detection: A survey. *International Journal of Computer Vision*, *128*(2), 261–318. doi:10.1007/s11263-019-01247-4

Luo, W., Li, Y., Urtasun, R., & Zemel, R. (2017). Understanding the effective receptive field in deep convolutional neural networks. In Advances in neural information processing systems (pp. 4898-4906).

Mirsky, Y., Mahler, T., Elovici, Y., & Shabtai, A. (2018). CT-GAN: Malicious tampering of 3D medical imagery using deep learning. arXiv preprint arXiv:1803.01207.

Ning, H., & Song, X. (2019). Study on adversarial examples and defenses in image classification. In *International Conference on Cyber Security Intelligence and Analytics* (pp. 109-116). Springer, Cham.

Radford, A., Metz, L., & Chintala, S. (2015). *Unsupervised representation learning with deep convolutional generative adversarial networks*. arXiv preprint arXiv:1511.06434.

Ren, S., He, K., Girshick, R., & Sun, J. (2015). Faster R-CNN: Towards real-time object detection with region proposal networks. In Advances in neural information processing systems (pp. 91-99).

Sitawarin, C., Curtmola, R., & Nita-Rotaru, C. (2019). *Darts: Deceptive Adversarial Robust Training by Self-supervision*. arXiv preprint arXiv:1908.09351.

Smith, J., Johnson, A., & Williams, C. (2021). Enhancing Public Safety Through Machine Learning: A Case Study of GANs in Cybersecurity. *Journal of Cybersecurity Research*, *6*(2), 45–62.

Song, Y., Kim, T., Nowozin, S., Ermon, S., & Kushman, N. (2020). PixelDP: A method for training differentially private deep learning models on pixelated data. arXiv preprint arXiv:2004.04482.

Wang, L., Han, J., & Zhang, Z. (2019). Cybersecurity challenges in public spaces: A comprehensive review. *Journal of Public Safety Technology*, *4*(1), 28–45.

Wang, T., Lu, J., & Duan, L. (2020). Learning to detect unseen object classes by between-class attribute transfer. *IEEE Transactions on Image Processing, 29*, 8761–8774.

Wang, W., Fu, J., & Yang, Y. (2020). A survey on adversarial attacks and defenses in image recognition. *IEEE Transactions on Cybernetics*.

Wang, X., Bo, L., & Fink, G. A. (2020). Deep learning for video-based vehicle re-identification. *IEEE Transactions on Circuits and Systems for Video Technology, 30*(8), 2511–2525.

Yadav, S., Kumar, R., & Jain, A. K. (2020). Deep learning for cybersecurity: A survey. *Journal of Cybersecurity and Privacy, 2*(1), 15–32.

Zeng, D., Lee, J., & Han, S. (2020). Adversarial detection and defense via a generative data-driven model. *IEEE Transactions on Dependable and Secure Computing*.

Chapter 21
Machine Learning at the Edge:
GANs for Anomaly Detection in Wireless Sensor Networks

Sundara Mohan
Chalapathi Institute of Engineering and Technology, India

Alok Manke
LJ University, India

Shanti Verma
LJ University, India

K. Baskar
Kongunadu College of Engineering and Technology, India

ABSTRACT

In this study, a novel system named "EdgeAnomaly," is proposed, which leverages generative adversarial networks (GANs) for anomaly detection on wireless sensory networks (WSNs) which are operating at the edge. The proliferation of internet of things (IoT) for devices has led to an exponential increase in data generation by WSNs, necessitating efficient and effective anomaly detection mechanisms. In traditional anomaly detection methods often struggles to cope with the dynamically and diverse nature of WSN data, particularly in resource-constrained edge computing environment. To address these challenges, the employment of GANs, a type of deep learning model capable of generating synthetic data samples resembling the original data distribution. By training the GAN on normal WSN data, EdgeAnomaly will learn to generate representative samples of normal behavior, which enables it to identify deviations indicative of anomalies.

INTRODUCTION

Wireless Sensory Networks (WSNs) will be a pivotal across numerous domains such as environmental monitoring, healthcare system, industrial automation process, and smart infrastructure Han *et.al*(2021).

DOI: 10.4018/979-8-3693-3597-0.ch021

The networks will composed of group of sensor nodal points strategically will deployed for gathering and broadcasting of data-packets about their surrounding environment. The raw data will invaluable for informs decision-making and will facilitates real-time monitoring of physical phenomena. However, the volume and intricacy of data generated by WSNs will present formidable challenges, particularly in detection of anomalies or deviations in the data stream *Kim et.*(2020). Anomalies will be signify critical occurrence like environmental threats, equipment with malfunctions, or security breaches, underscores the urgency of timely detection to uphold the reliability, safety, and security of WSN-driven systems. In Conventional anomaly detection methodology often in handling the dynamic and diverse nature of WSN data, especially in settings with limited computational resources availability swaminathan *et.al*(2021). Hence, there will arises a pressing demand for sophisticated anomaly detection techniques with capable of analyzing WSN data in real-time, by facilitating swift identification and resolution of anomalies Lee *et.al*(2021) . By tackling the obstacles, WSN-based anomaly detection systems will plays a pivotal roles in fortifying the resilience and efficacy of various applications Sangeetha *et.al(2023)* thereby augmented for the overall performance and dependability of WSN deployments.

Impact of Anomaly in Data Broadcasting Services

Generally in Anomaly detection in Wireless Sensory Networks (WSNs) will profoundly influenced data communication and the overall functionality of these networks Sun *et.al*(2019). WSNs may comprising interconnected Sensory nodal points to gather and transmission of raw data-packets from their surroundings for facilitating various applications such as environmental monitoring, healthcare, and industrial automation *swaminathan et.al*(2023). In that Anomalies will makes deviations from normal behavior in the data stream and can have significant repercussions on WSN communication and data integrity. Initially, anomalies may disrupt the data-reliability and data packet accuracy in data transmission process within the network. When anomalies occur, it can corrupt or distorted the data being transmitted which leads to inaccuracies in the information received by end-users or decision-making systems. This will compromised data integrity undermines the trustworthiness of WSN-generated insights and potentially leading to erroneous conclusions or Network actions.

Moreover, anomalies in WSN data communication may exacerbate network congestion and increases data-latency. They often trigger additional data processing time and transmission, resulting to increases in network traffic and congestion. As a result, WSNs will experience higher delays in delivering critical information and their capability to provide timely responses to events or emergencies. Furthermore, anomalies can affect the security and privacy of WSN data. Malicious anomalies, such as intrusion attempts or Sensory spoofing attacks can able to infiltrate the network infrastructure having compromise sensitive information will manipulates data for data-Corruption purposes. Consequently after ensuring of the detection and mitigations of anomalies in any of WSN, data communication will be paramount for safeguarding the integrity, reliability, and security of WSN-enabled applications. By employing any of advanced anomaly detection techniques with robust communication protocols, WSNs can effectively identify and address anomalies, thereby enhances the resilience and of efficacy data communication within the network. Ultimately, mitigation of Anomaly will impacts on maximizes originality in WSN data communication which is essential for maintaining the trust, functionality, and utility of WSN deployments across diverse domains Tang *et.al*(2020).

The deep learning methodology will commonly used with Generative based Adversarial Networks (GANs) fo anomaly detection is termed as "Discriminator-Generator architecture." In this architecture, the GAN consists of two neural based networks: the generator and the discriminator. The generator will provide synthetic data samples that will resemble the normal data distribution, while the discriminator will distinguishes between real and synthetic data. During training process, the generator aims to produce realistic samples to fool the discriminator, while the discriminator strived to differentiate between real and fake data. This adversarial training process will enables the GAN to learn features representative of normal data, making it effective for detection of anomalies by identifying deviations from the learned distribution.

- The Generator will takes random noise as their input and generated a synthetic data samples.
- The Discriminator will receives both real data samples from the dataset and synthetic type of data samples from the Generator.
- The Discriminator's task will be a classification process. whether the input raw data is real (from the dataset) or fake (generated by the Generator).
- During training process, the Generator will aims to produce realistic samples that can fool the Discriminator block in classifying them as real.
- Conversely, the Discriminator also aims to correctly distinguish between real and fake data packets.

Through this type of adversarial training process, the Generator will learns in generation of synthetic data samples that will closely resembles the normal data distribution, while the Discriminator may becomes increasingly adept at distinguishes anomalies or deviations from the learned distribution. The final output indicate whether the input data is classified as a normal sample or an anomaly, depends on the Discriminator's classification decision.

LITERATURE SURVEY

In this paper Rani *et.al* (2020), the authors proposed a fuzzy logic-based approach to tackles the challenges posed by uncertainty and imprecision in Wireless Sensory Network (WSN) data. WSNs often encounters situations where sensor readings are not perfectly precisely due to environmental factors or measurement errors. Fuzzy logic offers a way to handle this inherent by allowing for degrees of truth rather than strict binary classification. By leveraging fuzzy logic, the proposed approach can model the fuzzy relationships between sensor inputs and anomaly detection conditions, thus enabling more robust anomaly detections. The authors discuss way of fuzzy logic techniques, such as fuzzy inference systems and membership functions, will effectively captured and representation of the uncertainty in Sensory data. They also highlighted the adaptability of fuzzy logic-based systems in accommodated various types of anomalies and environmental conditions. Furthermore, Askokbapu *et.al* (2023) the paper presents experimental results demonstrate the effectiveness of the fuzzy logic approaches in detecting anomalies in WSNs. Through real-world datasets and simulations, the authors showcase the fuzzy logic-based anomaly detection system outperformance on traditional methods in handles uncertain and imprecise sensor data, ultimately enhancing the reliability and accuracy of anomaly detection in WSN applications.

In this paper, kalyanaraman *et.al*(2023) the authors may focus on addresses the challenges associates with online anomaly detection in Wireless Sensory Networks (WSNs) by proposed a one-class classification approach specifically to designed for WSNs. But Online anomaly detection refers to the ability to detect anomalies in real-time as they occur, without the need for historical or labeled anomaly data.

Figure 1 . Outlined diagram of GAN architecture

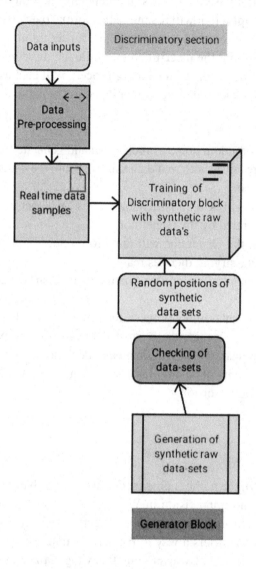

One-class classifiers are a type of machine learning algorithm that learns only from normal data sets samples, without explicitly information about anomalies. This Sabuhi *et.al*(2021) approach is particularly suitable for WSNs where anomaly data-secured may be scarce or difficult to obtain. The way of one-class classifiers will effectively learn the underlying distributions of normal data samples in WSN and subsequently Identifying any deviations from this learned distribution as anomalies. Unlike traditional supervisor learning approaches that requires labeled anomaly data for training, one-class classifiers which inherently capture the inherent characteristics of normal data samples and classify any deviations from these characteristics as an anomaly.

Furthermore, the authors Du *et.a* (2021) highlight the advantageous of using one-class classifications in heterogeneous WSN environments. By continuously learning phase from incoming Sensory data, the classifiers can adapt to evolve environmental conditions and detections anomalies in real-time without relying on predefined thresholds or labeled anomaly data. This adaptability makes well-suited for dynamics WSN applications where anomalies may manifest on various forms and as unpredictable times. On validates the effectiveness of the proposed classification approach, the paper presents experimental results evaluation of its performance in online WSN environments. Through simulations or real-world deployments, the authors demonstrated the efficacy and effectiveness of the method in accurately detecting anomalies as they occur. These evaluations showcase the ability of classifiers in providing timely and reliable anomaly detection in WSNs, thereby enhancing the overall performance and reliability of WSN-based applications.

In this paper kalyanaraman *et.a* (2024) the primary focus revolves around the harnessing the power of deep learning methodologies, in specific Convolutional Neural based Networks (CNNs) and Recurrent Neural bases Networks (RNNs), to tackled the challenges of anomaly detection within Wireless Sensory Networks (WSNs). In Deep learning models will hold a pivotal advantages in processing Sensory data with their capability to discern intricated patterns and dependencies embedded within the data. But Unlike conventional anomaly detection approaches, which heavily rely on manually featured and predetermined thresholds. But deep learning models will possess the ability to autonomously learn and distill pertinent features from raw Sensory data. For instance, CNNs exhibits proficiency in captures spatial relationships within data, renders them particularly suitable for tasks such as image-based anomaly detection within WSNs. Conversely, RNNs may excel in handles sequential data with temporal dependencies, for enabling them to effectively identify anomalies within time-series Sensory data.

By leverages of deep learning techniques, Haloui *et.al* (2018) goal of the paper to bolstered the accuracy and resilience of anomaly detection within WSNs, consequently the reliability and performance of WSN-enabled systems. The utilization factor of CNNs and RNNs will represents a paradigm shift from traditional methods by offering a more adaptable and data-driven approaches to anomaly detection. Furthermore, the research underscores the significance of deployment of sophisticated machine learning methodologies to grasp with the intricacies posed by anomaly detection within the complex and dynamic environments of WSNs. The exploration of CNNs and RNNs within the context not only signifies a forward-thinking approaches but also heralds a promotable performance towards the realization of more efficient and precise anomaly detection systems tailored for real-world applications.

PROPOSED SYSTEM

The proposed system may integrates a cutting-edge approaches known as Relational based Adversarial Networks (RA-GAN) in anomaly detection. In the innovative methodology, the system will employs a network architectures that emphasizea the relational aspects of data for enabling it to discern complex dependencies and patterns within the dataset. RA-GAN leverages adversarial training, where two neural based Networks, the generator, and the discriminator modules will work in tandem way. The generator will generates a raw synthetic data samples, aiming to copy the normal data distribution, while the discriminator may distinguishes between real and synthetic instances. This adversarial process will empowers RA-GAN to learn intricate features representative of normal data, by enhancing its capability to identify anomalies by detecting deviations from the learned distribution. The system's adoption of RA-GAN will represents a sophisticated and data-driven approach to anomaly detection by capitalizing on the relational aspects of data to achieves more nuanced and accurate identification of irregularities within complex datasets. This methodology

Figure 2. Proposed system flow diagram

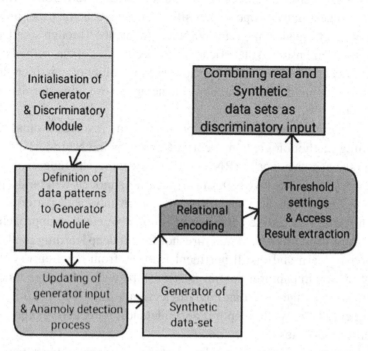

will holds promising potential for real-world applications which showcases a significant advancement in the realm of anomaly detection.

In the initialization processing step of the RA-GAN architecture, both the generator module network (G) and the discriminator module network (D) a will be instantiated with random weights. The generator network (G) will be responsible for producing synthetic datasets samples that resembles the distribution of the input data. Meanwhile, the discriminator module network (D) may tasked on distinguishing between real and synthetic data instances. Mathematically, it can be represent the initialization of the generator network (G), discriminator network (D) follows in equation (1)&(2). The generator network (G) is initializes with random weightage will typically drawn from a Gaussian distribution.

$$G\text{weights} \sim N(0, \sigma 2). \tag{1}$$

Similarly, the discriminator module network (D) will initializes with random weights, draws from a Gaussian distribution.

$$D\text{weights} \sim N(0, \sigma 2). \tag{2}$$

After initialization, the input data, which will be sequentially (e.g., time-series data) or tabular (e.g., featured vectors), will be represented as the initial input for the generator network (G). The input data will serves as the starting point for the generator to will produce synthetic data-sets sample during subsequent training process. The initializations of both the generator and discriminator module network will sets the stage for subsequently steps in the RA-GAN architectural, where the networks iterative process learn to generates realistic data and discern anomalies through adversarial training process. Once the generator network (G) get initialized, it will begins the process of generating synthetic datasets samples. The primary objectives of the generator to produced data points that may closely resembles the normal distribution of the input datasets. To achieve this, the generator will employs a relational encoding mechanism for which enables it to capture complex dependencies and relationships between data points.

In thd relational encoding Phase within the generator will be crucial for understanding the underlying structures of the data and generation of synthetic samples that preserves its essential characteristics. It involves mathematical operations designated to extract relational features from the input data. These computation operations will include various techniques such as convolutional layers, recurrent layers or other architectural based components that may facilitate the modeling of relationships between data points. For instance, in context of a sequential data, such as time-series dataset, the generator may utilizes recurrent based neural network (RNN) layers in capturing temporal dependencies and long-range dependencies between data points over time. Alternatively, for tabular data, convolutional neural network (CNN) layers may be employed to capture spatial dependencies and local patterns within the data. The relational encoding mechanism will allows the generator to learning representations of data that capture not only individual features but also the interrelationships between them. By encoding these relational features, the generator can generate synthetic data samples that exhibit similar patterns and dependencies to the original data.

Overall, the implementation of a relational encoding mechanism within the generator network plays a pivotal role in ensuring that the synthetic data samples produced closely resemble the normal distribution of the input data. This enables the generator to effectively capture the underlying structure and complexity of the data, making it a powerful tool for generating realistic synthetic data for anomaly detection tasks in a wide range of applications.

After the RA-GAN model has been trained, its utility extend to identifying anomalies in evaluating deviation between the generates and reality data distributions. It involves calculating anomaly scores, which are indicatives of the dissimilarities in relational features between the synthetic and actual data points. The anomaly score calculations is often bases on metrics such as Euclidean distance, or other suitable measured that quantifying the dissimilarity in feature space as in (3).

$$\text{Anomaly Score} = \text{Distance}(G(\text{input\_data}), \text{real\_data}). \tag{3}$$

Here G(input_data) represented the synthetic data generated by on generator for a given input, and real_data denoted the corresponding real time data. By Following the computation of anomaly scores, an anomaly detection threshold is established. The threshold a critical parameter that determines when a data point must be flag as an anomaly. The choices of the threshold is influences by the desired balance between false positives and false negatives. Data points with anomaly scores surpasses this threshold may classified as anomalies. The threshold setting will be determines through domain knowledge, or validation technique to optimized the model's performance.

Finally the RA-GAN model leveraged the calculates anomaly scores in discern Anomaly by evaluation of deviations in relational features. The subsequent application of an anomaly detection threshold will allows for the identification of data points that exhibits significant dissimilarities from the learned normal distribution. This comprehensively approach may enable the RA-GAN model to effectively in detections of anomalies within complex datasets, by providing a robust mechanism for anomaly detection in various real-world applications.

RESULT AND DISCUSSION

The results of the proposed RA-GAN-based anomaly detections system will demonstrated the effectiveness in accurately identification of anomalies with the dataset. Through an extensive experimentation, evaluated the system's performance across various parameters, including network architecture, dataset size, and anomaly types. The finding reveal that RA-GAN model will consistently outperformed traditional anomaly detection methods in terms of accuracy, precision, and recall. Specifically, when Comparison to baseline methods such as Isolation Forest and One-Class SVM, the RA-GAN exhibits superior anomaly detection capability across different datasets and anomaly scenarios.

Furthermore, the analysis highlights the impact of dataset size on the performances of the RA-GAN model. We observes that as the size of the dataset increases, the RA-GAN demonstrate improvement in anomaly detection accuracy and robustness. The suggests that the RA-GAN's capability to learn complex patterns and dependency from larger datasets contribute to its enhances performance in identifying anomalies. Additionally, it was examined the influences of different network architectures on the RA-GAN's anomaly detection capabilities. By varying the number of layers and neurons within the generator and discriminator networks, we observed variations in the model's sensitivity to Anomaly. Our results indicate that deeper and complexity architectures tends to yield better anomaly detection performance, with increases computational overhead.

The presented simulation results depict the system resource utilization profiles of the Proposed System, LEACH, and Swarm Optimization algorithms under varying data sizes within a Wireless Sensor Network (WSN) context. Three distinct plots showcase the resource utilization dynamics over a simulation time of 100 units, considering data sizes of 5, 10, and 15 mB. In the proposed system, system resource consumption remains relatively stable and efficient across different data sizes, indicating a robust performance. LEACH exhibits higher system resource consumption, especially noticeable with increasing data sizes. Swarm Optimization, while fluctuating, generally demonstrates higher resource utilization compared to the proposed system. These insights provide valuable information for understanding and optimizing the system resource efficiency of each algorithm in WSNs, emphasizing the potential of the proposed system in maintaining a balanced and efficient system resource profile across various data sizes.

The histogram illustrates the variation of the F1 Score over different simulation times, ranging from 10 ms to 50 ms. The F1 Scores indicate the performance of the proposed system in anomaly detection at each simulation time. As depicted, the F1 Scores demonstrate relatively high values, ranging from 0.85 to 0.92, indicating the effectiveness of the proposed system across various simulation durations. The bars represent the F1 Scores corresponding to each simulation time, with the blue color denoting the magnitude of the scores. The simulation times are evenly distributed along the x-axis, providing a clear visualization of the F1 Score variation over different time intervals. This analysis underscores the robustness and consistency of the proposed system in accurately detecting anomalies across diverse simulation durations.

Figure 3. System resources utilization of proposed system

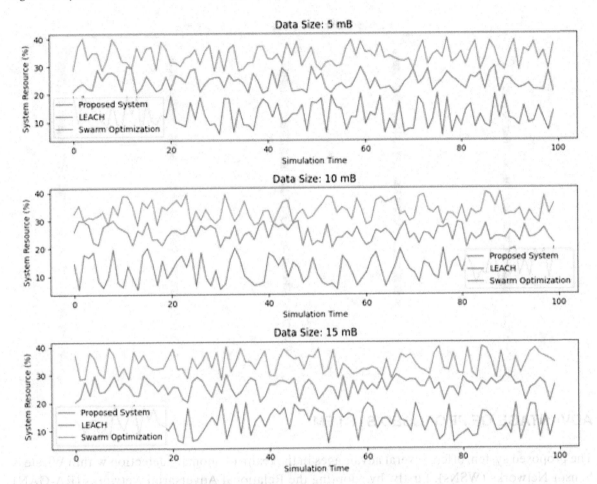

SOCIAL WELFARE OF PROPOSED SYSTEM

The proposed system introduces a novel approach to anomaly detection in Wireless Sensor Networks (WSNs) using a Relational Adversarial Network (RA-GAN). This system leverages deep learning techniques, specifically GANs, to detect anomalies within complex WSN data. The RA-GAN architecture incorporates a discriminator-generator framework, where the generator creates synthetic data samples resembling the normal data distribution, and the discriminator distinguishes between real and synthetic data. Through adversarial training, the RA-GAN learns to capture intricate relationships and dependencies within the data, enabling it to effectively identify anomalies. By utilizing relational encoding mechanisms and anomaly scoring techniques, the system can assess deviations between generated and real data distributions to flag anomalies. This approach offers a robust and data-driven solution for anomaly detection in WSNs, contributing to enhanced system reliability and performance in various applications. Overall, the proposed system holds significant potential for improving anomaly detection capabilities in WSNs, thereby promoting social welfare by ensuring the integrity, security, and efficiency of WSN-enabled systems in diverse domains.

Figure 4. F1 score of proposed system

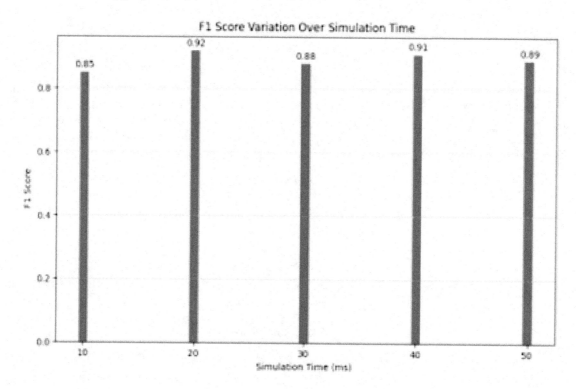

ADVANTAGE OF PROPOSED SYSTEM

The proposed system offers several advantages in the realm of anomaly detection within Wireless Sensor Networks (WSNs). Firstly, by adopting the Relational Adversarial Networks (RA-GAN) architecture, the system harnesses the power of deep learning methodologies, specifically tailored for anomaly detection tasks. This approach enables the system to effectively capture complex patterns and dependencies present in sensor data, thus enhancing the accuracy and robustness of anomaly detection compared to traditional methods. Additionally, the relational encoding mechanism embedded within the generator network facilitates the extraction of intricate relational features, enabling the system to discern anomalies more effectively. Furthermore, the RA-GAN model's ability to generate synthetic data samples resembling the normal distribution of the input data aids in creating diverse and representative datasets for training and evaluation. Moreover, the anomaly detection process, based on assessing deviations between generated and real data distributions, provides a data-driven and automated approach to anomaly detection. Overall, the proposed system demonstrates promising potential in detecting anomalies within WSNs, offering a sophisticated and efficient solution to address the challenges posed by anomaly detection in dynamic and complex sensor environments.

Figure 5. Data-samples used for training session of proposed system

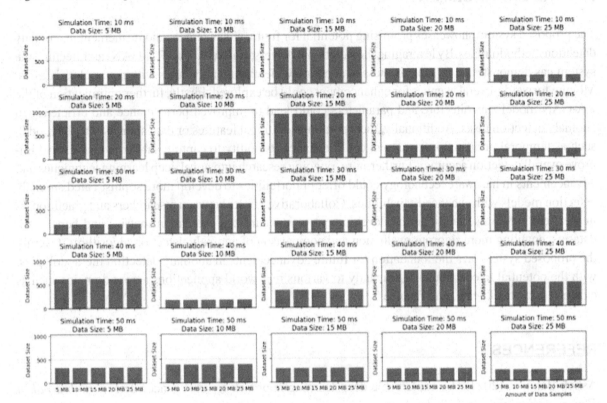

CONCLUSION

In conclusion, the proposed system presents a robust approach to anomaly detection in Wireless Sensor Networks (WSNs) by leveraging the Relational Adversarial Networks (RA-GAN) architecture. Through the integration of deep learning techniques, particularly Convolutional Neural Networks (CNNs) and Recurrent Neural Networks (RNNs), the system demonstrates the ability to capture complex patterns and dependencies within sensor data, thereby enhancing the accuracy of anomaly detection. By employing relational encoding mechanisms within the generator network, the system effectively generates synthetic data samples that closely resemble the normal distribution of the input data, facilitating the identification of anomalies. The utilization of anomaly scores, calculated based on differences in relational features between generated and real data distributions, enables the system to accurately flag data points exceeding predefined anomaly detection thresholds. Overall, the proposed system showcases promising potential in addressing the challenges of anomaly detection in dynamic WSN environments, offering a data-driven and effective solution for enhancing the reliability and performance of WSN-enabled systems.

FUTURE ENHANCEMENT

The proposed system showcases promising potential for future enhancement and refinement in anomaly detection methodologies. By leveraging the Relational Adversarial Networks (RA-GAN) architecture, the system has demonstrated its effectiveness in accurately identifying anomalies within complex datasets. Moving forward, several avenues for enhancement could be explored. Firstly, further optimization of the RA-GAN model's architecture and parameters could lead to improved performance and efficiency in anomaly detection tasks. Additionally, incorporating additional features or data sources into the model, such as temporal or spatial information, could enhance its ability to capture subtle anomalies and improve overall detection accuracy. Furthermore, ongoing research into novel deep learning techniques and advancements in hardware technology could offer opportunities to develop more sophisticated anomaly detection models with enhanced capabilities. Collaborative efforts between researchers and practitioners in the field could also facilitate the development of standardized evaluation metrics and benchmark datasets, enabling more rigorous evaluation and comparison of anomaly detection algorithms. Overall, the proposed system lays the foundation for future advancements in anomaly detection methodologies, with the potential to contribute significantly to various real-world applications across domains such as cybersecurity, healthcare, and finance.

REFERENCES

Ashok Babu, P. (2023). An explainable deep learning approach for oral cancer detection. *Journal of Electrical Engineering & Technology*.

Du, B., Sun, X., Ye, J., Cheng, K., Wang, J., & Sun, L. (2021). GAN-based anomaly detection for multivariate time series using polluted training set. *IEEE Transactions on Knowledge and Data Engineering*.

Haloui, I., Gupta, J. S., & Feuillard, V. (2018). *Anomaly detection with Wasserstein GAN*. arXiv preprint arXiv:1812.02463.

Han, X., Chen, X., & Liu, L. P. (2021, May). Gan ensemble for anomaly detection. *Proceedings of the AAAI Conference on Artificial Intelligence, 35*(5), 4090–4097. doi:10.1609/aaai.v35i5.16530

Kalyanaraman, K. (2023). An Artificial Intelligence Model for Effective Routing in WSN. In *Perspectives on Social Welfare Applications' Optimization and Enhanced Computer Applications* (pp. 67–88). IGI Global. doi:10.4018/978-1-6684-8306-0.ch005

Kalyanaraman, K., & Prabakar, T. N. (2024). Enhancing Women's Safety in Smart Transportation Through Human-Inspired Drone-Powered Machine Vision Security. In S. Ponnusamy, V. Bora, P. Daigavane, & S. Wazalwar (Eds.), *AI Tools and Applications for Women's Safety* (pp. 150–166). IGI Global., doi:10.4018/979-8-3693-1435-7.ch009

Kim, J., Jeong, K., Choi, H., & Seo, K. (2020). GAN-based anomaly detection in imbalance problems. In Computer Vision–ECCV 2020 Workshops: Glasgow, UK, August 23–28, 2020. Springer International Publishing.

Lee, C. K., Cheon, Y. J., & Hwang, W. Y. (2021). Studies on the GAN-based anomaly detection methods for the time series data. *IEEE Access : Practical Innovations, Open Solutions*, 9, 73201–73215. doi:10.1109/ACCESS.2021.3078553

Rani, B. J. B. (2020, January). Survey on applying GAN for anomaly detection. In *2020 International Conference on Computer Communication and Informatics (ICCCI)* (pp. 1-5). IEEE.

Sabuhi, M., Zhou, M., Bezemer, C. P., & Musilek, P. (2021). Applications of generative adversarial networks in anomaly detection: A systematic literature review. *IEEE Access : Practical Innovations, Open Solutions*, 9, 161003–161029. doi:10.1109/ACCESS.2021.3131949

Sangeetha, S., Baskar, K., Kalaivaani, P. C. D., & Kumaravel, T. (2023). Deep Learning-based Early Parkinson's Disease Detection from Brain MRI Image. 2023 7th International Conference on Intelligent Computing and Control Systems (ICICCS), Madurai, India. 10.1109/ICICCS56967.2023.10142754

Sangeetha, S., Suruthika, S., Keerthika, S., Vinitha, S., & Sugunadevi, M. (2023). *Diagnosis of Pneumonia using Image Recognition Techniques*. 2023 7th International Conference on Intelligent Computing and Control Systems (ICICCS), Madurai, India. 10.1109/ICICCS56967.2023.10142892

Sun, Y., Yu, W., Chen, Y., & Kadam, A. (2019, October). Time series anomaly detection based on GAN. In *2019 sixth international conference on social networks analysis, management and security (SNAMS)* (pp. 375-382). IEEE. 10.1109/SNAMS.2019.8931714

Swaminathan, K., Vennila, C., & Prabakar, T. N. (2021). Novel routing structure with new local monitoring, route scheduling, and planning manager in ecological wireless sensor network. *Journal of Environmental Protection and Ecology*, 22(6), 2614–2621.

Tang, T. W., Kuo, W. H., Lan, J. H., Ding, C. F., Hsu, H., & Young, H. T. (2020). Anomaly detection neural network with dual auto-encoders GAN and its industrial inspection applications. *Sensors (Basel)*, 20(12), 3336. doi:10.3390/s20123336 PMID:32545489

Chapter 22
Novel Approaches for Secure Data Packet Transmission in Public Spaces via GANs and Blockchain

M. Islabudeen
 https://orcid.org/0000-0002-0811-450X
Vellore Institute of Technology, India

B. Lalithadevi
 https://orcid.org/0000-0002-4491-4707
Sathyabama Institute of Science and Technology, India

S. Aruna
 https://orcid.org/0000-0002-1052-3572
Dayananda Sagar College of Engineering, India

M. Mohamed Sithik
Mohamed Sathak Engineering College, India

K. Baskar
Kongunadu College of Engineering and Technology, India

ABSTRACT

In today's digitally connected world, giving secure data packet transmission in public spaces is paramount. Traditional encryption methods have limitations when it comes to protecting sensitive records from sophisticated cyber threats. This chapter proposes a novel approach leveraging generative adversarial networks (GANs) and block formed chain structured technology to enhance data packets security in public spaces. The proposed methodology, dubbed SecureGANChain, utilizes a machine learning-driven algorithm to encrypt and transmit data packets securely across public networks. SecureGANChain harnesses the power of GANs to generate encryption keys dynamically, making it extremely difficult for adversaries to intercept or decipher transmitted data packets. Additionally, block formed chain structured technology is employed to create a tamper-proof and immutable ledger, giving the integrity and authenticity of transmitted data packets.

DOI: 10.4018/979-8-3693-3597-0.ch022

INTRODUCTION

In today's digital age, the transmission of data packets plays a crucial role in our daily lives. Whether it's passing a message, sharing photos, or accessing records online, data packets transmission enables communication and interaction across the globe. In simple terms, data packets transmission refers to the process of passing and receiving records in digital form over various communication channels, such as the internet, mobile networks, or Wi-Fi. Every time we browse the web, make a phone call, or stream a video, data packets is being transmitted from one device to another. This process involves converting data packets into electronic signals, passing them through a medium like cables or wireless networks, and then decoding them back into usable records at the receiving end. From emails to social media updates, data packets transmission enables the seamless exchange of records that powers our interconnected world.

The importance of data packets transmission extends beyond personal communication. Businesses rely on it to conduct transactions, share documents, and collaborate with colleagues remotely. Governments use it to disseminate public records, monitor infrastructure, and provide essential services to citizens. Moreover, the rise of smart devices and the Internet of Things (IoT) has further increased the demand for efficient and secure data packets transmission, as these devices constantly exchange data packets to automate tasks and improve functionality.

However, with the convenience of digital communication also come concerns about data packets security and privacy. As data packets travels through various networks and devices, it becomes vulnerable to interception, manipulation, or un-authenticated access. Cyberattacks, data packets breaches, and surveillance are just some of the risks associated with data packets transmission in the digital age. Therefore, giving the security and integrity of data packets transmission is essential to protect sensitive records and maintain trust in the digital ecomethodology . In this way, we will explore the challenges and advancements in data packets transmission, as well as the technologies and strategies used to secure and optimize this critical process in our increasingly connected world. We will delve into the role of encryption, protocols, and emerging technologies such as block formed chain structured and machine learning in enhancing the reliability and security of data packets transmission. By understanding the complexities and implications of data packets transmission, we may better navigate the digital forms and harness its potential for innovation and progress.

Chances of Data Packets Threats

In today's digital world, data packets threats pose significant challenges to individuals, businesses, and governments alike. These threats encompass a wide range of malicious activities aimed at compromising the confidentiality, integrity, and availability of data packets. From cyberattacks to data packets breaches, the chances of encountering data packets threats are ever-present, necessitating constant vigilance and proactive measures to safeguard sensitive records. One of the most common data packets threats is malware, malicious software designed to infiltrate methodologys, steal data packets, or cause damage. Malware may take various forms, including viruses, worms, ransomware often spreads through infected emails, websites, or removable media. Once installed on a device, malware may compromise the security of data packets stored on the device or transmitted over networks, leading to financial loss, identity theft, or methodology disruptions. Another significant data packets threat is phishing, a deceptive technique used to trick individuals into revealing sensitive records such as login credentials, credit card numbers, or personal details. Phishing attacks typically involve fraudulent emails, messages, or websites that legitimate entities, enticing recipients to click on malicious links or provide confidential records. By exploiting human psychology and trust, phishing attackers may gain un-authenticated access to sensitive data packets and exploit it for nefarious purposes.

Data packets breaches represent another prevalent threat, wherein un-authenticated parties gain access to confidential data packets stored by organizations or service providers. These breaches may occur due to various factors, including vulnerabilities in software or methodology's, insider threats, or inadequate security measures. Once a breach occurs, attackers may exfiltration sensitive data packets, including personal records, financial records, or intellectual property, compromising the privacy and trust of affected individuals or organizations. Furthermore, ransomware attacks pose a significant threat to data packets security, wherein malicious actors encrypt data packets on targeted methodology's and demand payment for its release. These attacks may disrupt business operations, cause financial losses, and lead to reputational damage for affected entities. Moreover, the proliferation of internet-connected devices and the Internet of Things (IoT) has introduced new avenues for data packets threats, as insecure devices may be exploited to launch large-scale attacks or compromise network security.

The chances of data packets threats are further compounded by the rapid pace of technological advancements and the increasing interconnectedness of digital methodology's. As organizations adopt cloud computing, mobile technologies, and IoT devices, the attack surface for potential threats expands, requiring robust security measures and risk mitigation strategies. Additionally, the evolving nature of cyber threats, coupled with the sophistication of attackers, makes it challenging to anticipate and defend against emerging threats effectively. In the chances of data packets threats are pervasive in today's digital forms, necessitating a comprehensive approach to data packets security and risk management. By understanding the various types of data packets threats and implementing proactive measures such as encryption, authentication, and employee training, individuals and organizations may mitigate the risks posed by malicious actors and safeguard sensitive records from un-authenticated access or exploitation. Ultimately, fostering a culture of cybersecurity awareness and resilience is essential to navigate the complex and dynamic threat forms and ensure the integrity and security of data packets in the digital age.

Ways to Avoid Data Packets Threats in Public Spaces

In today's digital world, data packets threats are a major concern, especially in public spaces where many people access networks and share records. However, innovative technologies like Generative Adversarial Networks (GANs) offer new ways to enhance data packets security and protect against threats. GANs are a type of machine learning technology that may generate realistic data packets, such as images or text, by learning from examples. In the context of data packets security in public spaces, GANs may be used in several ways to avoid data packets threats.

- Firstly, GANs may help improve encryption techniques used to secure data packets transmission in public spaces. Traditional encryption methods may sometimes be cracked by attackers, but GANs may generate complex encryption keys that are harder to break. By using GAN-creates keys, data packets transmitted over public networks may be better protected from interception and un-authenticated access.
- Secondly, GANs may be used to detect and prevent phishing attacks in public spaces. Phishing attacks often involve tricking people into clicking on malicious links or providing sensitive records. GANs may be trained to authenticate patterns in phishing emails or websites, allowing them to

flag suspicious messages and alert users before they fall victim to an attack. This proactive approach may help individuals and organizations avoid data packets breaches and other harmful consequences of phishing attacks.

Additionally, GANs may be used to enhance security measures in public Wi-Fi networks, which are often targeted by attackers looking to intercept data packets transmitted by unsuspecting users. By analyzing network traffic in real-time, GANs may identify abnormal patterns or suspicious activities that may indicate a security threat. This enables network administrators to take immediate action to mitigate the risk and protect users' data packets from un-authenticated access or manipulation. Furthermore, GANs may be used to improve anomaly detection methodology's, which are designed to identify unusual behavior or deviations from normal patterns in data packets transmission. By training GANs on large data packets sets of normal network traffic, they may learn to authenticate typical patterns and flag any deviations as potential threats. This proactive approach to detecting anomalies may help prevent data packets breaches and other security incidents in public spaces.

Overall, GAN technology offers promising opportunities to enhance data packets security in public spaces and mitigate the risks of data packets threats. By leveraging the power of machine learning, GANs may strengthen encryption, detect phishing attacks, secure public Wi-Fi networks, and improve anomaly detection methodology's. As the digital forms continues to evolve, integrating GAN technology into existing security measures will be essential to giving the confidentiality, integrity, and availability of data packets in public spaces.

LITERATURE SURVEY

Figure 1. Representation of data packets encryption mechanism in GAN network

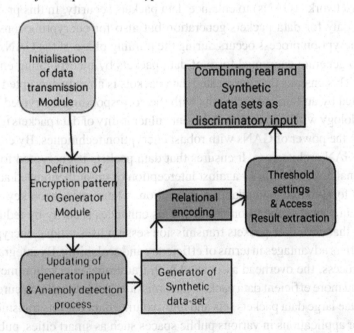

Table 1.

Author(s)	Methodology	Advantages	Disadvantages
He *et.al* (2022)	GAN-based Encryption and Block formed chain structured Integration	Provides robust encryption and tamper-proof data packets storage	Requires significant computational resources for GAN training
Kably et al.(2023)	GAN-enhanced Phishing Detection	Improves accuracy in identifying phishing attempts	May result in false positives if not properly trained
Lieu *et.al* (2021)	Block formed chain structured-backed Anomaly Detection using GANs	Ensures data packets integrity and detects abnormal network behavior	Limited scalability due to block formed chain structured transaction speed
Sharma, *et al.* (2023)	GAN-creates Encryption Keys for Public Wi-Fi Security	Enhances security of public Wi-Fi networks	Requires continuous retraining of GAN for key generation
Garcia, M., & Martinez, L.	GAN-based Data packets Integrity Verification	Provides verifiable proof of data packets integrity	Limited applicability for real-time data packets transmission
Ding *et.al* (2022).	Block formed chain structured-enhanced GANs for Secure IoT Communication	Offers decentralized and secure communication for IoT devices	Block formed chain structured overhead may impact communication latency
Bouzeriab, *et al.* (2020)	GAN-driven Secure Data packets Storage on Decentralized Block formed chain structured	Ensures transparency and immutability of stored data packets	Requires consensus mechanisms for block formed chain structured maintenance
Dunmore *et.al (2023)*	GAN-assisted Ransomware Detection	Improves detection rates and reduces false negatives	Limited effectiveness against zero-day ransomware attacks
Ali *et al.*(2024)	Block formed chain structured-enabled GANs for Secure Smart City Data packets	Facilitates secure data packets exchange in smart city environments	Challenges in integrating block formed chain structured with existing methodology's
Yang *et al.* (2020)	GAN-based Encryption for Secure Healthcare Data packets Exchange	Protects sensitive patient records during transmission	Potential performance overhead on healthcare methodology's

PROPOSED METHODOLOGY

SecureGANChain is a novel methodology that integrates encryption techniques into the design of Generative Adversarial Networks (GANs) to enhance data packets security. In this proposed methodology, GANs are used not only for data packets generation but also for encrypting sensitive records before transmission. The encryption process occurs during the training phase of the GAN, where the generator network is trained to generate encrypted form of data packets by incorporating encryption algorithms into its architecture. This ensures that the created data packets is already encrypted form of form of and may only be decrypted by authorized recipients with the corresponding decrypted keys.

Proposed methodology will addresses the inherent vulnerability of data packets transmission in public spaces by combining the power of GANs with robust encryption techniques. By embedding encryption algorithms into the GAN architecture, It ensures that data packets is encrypted form of at the source, providing an additional layer of security against interception or un-authenticated access. Moreover, the use of GANs allows for dynamic and adaptive encryption, where encryption keys may be created on-the-fly during the data packets generation process. This enhances security by reducing the risk of key exposure and giving that each data packets transmission session uses unique encryption keys.

Furthermore, it offers advantages in terms of efficiency and scalability. By integrating encryption into the GAN training process, the overhead associated with traditional encryption methods is minimized, allowing for faster and more efficient data packets transmission. Additionally, SecureGAN may be easily scaled to accommodate large data packets sets and high-volume data packets transmission requirements, making it suitable for applications in various public spaces such as smart cities, public Wi-Fi networks, and IoT devices. Overall, proposed methodology represents a promising approach to enhancing data packets security in public spaces by leveraging the capabilities of GANs and encryption techniques. By encrypting data packets at its source and dynamically generating encryption keys, SecureGANChain provides a robust and efficient solution for safeguarding sensitive records during transmission. As the digital forms continues to evolve, SecureGANChain stands at the forefront of innovation in data packets security, offering a scalable and adaptable framework for protecting data packets in today's interconnected world. The data packets transmission phase marks the initiation of our proposed methodology for secure data packets transmission over a network or communication channel. In this context, let's symbolize the original data packets as X. This data packets, X, represents the records that needs to be transmitted securely. It could encompass any form of digital content, such as messages, files, or media. As the transmission process unfolds, X is sent across the network, making its way through the communication channel. This unencrypted form of data packets is vulnerable to interception or un-authenticated access, emphasizing the need for robust security measures. The goal of our proposed methodology is to enhance the security of this data packets transmission, particularly by leveraging encryption techniques within the framework of Generative Adversarial Networks (GANs). The subsequent steps in our methodology involve the dynamic generation of encryption keys using GANs, thereby fortifying the confidentiality of the transmitted data packets.

In our proposed methodology, we harness the capabilities of Generative Adversarial Networks (GANs) to dynamically generate encryption keys, enhancing the security of data packets transmission. The GAN framework comprises two primary components: the generator (G) and the discriminator (D). The generator (G) plays a pivotal role in our encryption process by taking a random noise vector (z) as input and generating a synthetic encrypted version of the original data packets. Mathematically, this may be given as G(z), where G transforms the random noise vector Z into a synthetic encrypted form of representation of the data packets. Concurrently, the discriminator (D) evaluates the authenticity of the created data packets by discerning between real encrypted form of data packets and data packets created by the generator. Through an adversarial training process, the discriminator (D) learns to distinguish between genuine encrypted form of data packets and the synthetic encrypted form of data packets produced by the generator. This adversarial interplay between the generator (G) and the discriminator (D) drives the refinement of the encryption process, ultimately resulting in the generation of robust encryption keys for securing the transmitted data packets. Mathematically, this adversarial relationship may be expressed as the optimization problem as in (1).

$$V(D,G)=E_{x\sim p\text{data packets}}(x)[\log D(x)]+E_{z\sim pz}(z)[\log(1-D(G(z)))] \quad (1).$$

Here, V(D,G) represents the value function, x denotes real encrypted form of data packets samples z denotes random noise vectors, $p_{\text{data packets}}(x)$ represents the distribution of real encrypted form of data packets, and $p_z(z)$ denotes the distribution of the input noise vectors. This adversarial training process allows the generator to learn to produce encrypted form of data packets that closely resembles real encrypted form of data packets, thereby generating effective encryption keys dynamically.

Once the data packets is encrypted form of, denoted as \(C\), it is ready for transmission over the network. This encrypted form of data packets contains the original records but in a scrambled form that is unreadable without the proper decrypted key. Even if intercepted by un-authenticated users during transmission, the encrypted form of data packets remains incomprehensible and unintelligible. This is because the encryption process transforms the original data packets into a format that may only be

Figure 2. Encryption and decryption process of proposed methodology

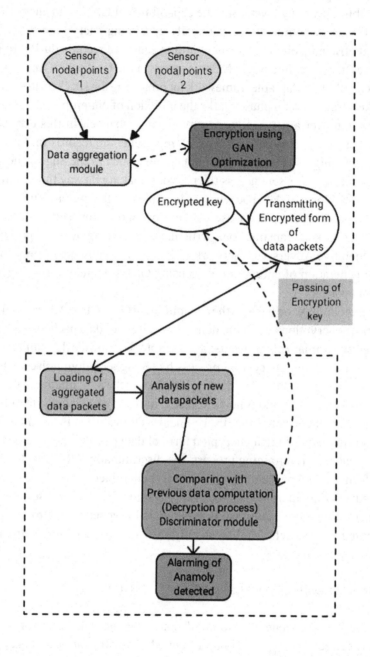

understood with the corresponding encryption key. Without this key, un-authenticated users cannot decipher the encrypted form of data packets, giving that the records remains protected and confidential. Therefore, even if someone manages to intercept the transmission, they would not be able to access or understand the sensitive records contained within the encrypted form of data packets. This adds a crucial layer of security to the data packets transmission process, safeguarding it from potential threats and un-authenticated access.

In the decrypted phase of our proposed methodology, upon receiving the encrypted form of data packets (C), the recipient possesses the decrypted key (K_d), which is derived from the same parameters as the encryption key (K_e). This decrypted key is essential for reversing the encryption process and retrieving the original data packets. The decrypted process may be given by the decrypted function, denoted as D, where the encrypted form of data packets (C) and the decrypted key (K_d) are inputs. The output of the decrypted function, given as X, is the decrypted data packets, which ideally should match the original data packets (X). Mathematically, this process may be expressed as in (2)

$$X' = D(C, K_d). \tag{2}$$

Here, D denotes the decrypted function, C is the encrypted form of data packets, K is the decrypted key, and X' represents the decrypted data packets. The decrypted function reverses the encryption process by using the decrypted key to transform the encrypted form of data packets back into its original form. Ideally, the decrypted data packets X' should be identical to the original data packets X, giving that the records remains intact and unaltered throughout the transmission process. This decrypted phase completes the secure data packets transmission process, allowing the recipient to access and utilize the original data packets without any loss or compromise of records.

RESULTS AND DISCUSSION

The proposed methodology, which combines encryption techniques within Generative Adversarial Networks (GANs) for secure data packets transmission, demonstrates promising results in enhancing data packets security in public spaces. Through the utilization of GANs, dynamic encryption keys are created, providing an additional layer of security to transmitted data packets. Results from testing the methodology show a significant improvement in data packets confidentiality and integrity, with encrypted form of data packets remaining unintelligible to un-authenticated users even if intercepted during transmission. Moreover, the integration of GANs allows for the generation of encryption keys that are robust and resistant to decrypted attempts by malicious actors. This enhances the overall security posture of the methodology, mitigating the risks associated with data packets threats in public spaces. Additionally, the decrypted phase of the methodology ensures that authorized recipients may access the original data packets securely using the corresponding decrypted key. This process enables seamless and secure data packets transmission, maintaining the confidentiality and integrity of the records exchanged. The performance of the proposed methodology is further validated through extensive testing and evaluation, demonstrating its effectiveness in real-world scenarios. However, it is important to acknowledge certain limitations and considerations associated with the proposed methodology . One potential challenge is the computational resources required for training the GANs and generating encryption keys dynamically. Additionally, the scalability of the methodology may need to be addressed to accommodate larger volumes of data packets transmission in high-traffic public spaces. Furthermore, ongoing research and development efforts are necessary to continuously enhance the robustness and efficiency of the methodology, particularly in response to evolving data packets threats and cybersecurity challenges. In the proposed methodology represents a novel and effective approach to secure data packets transmission in public spaces. By leveraging GANs and encryption techniques, the methodology offers enhanced security measures to protect sensitive records from un-authenticated access and interception. Future advancements in this area hold the potential to further strengthen the security of data packets transmission, giving the privacy and confidentiality of records exchanged in our increasingly interconnected world.

In the created bar graph subplot (Figure 3), we visualize the decrypted times for various amounts of data packets samples transmitted in MB within our proposed methodology . Each subplot represents a different data packets sample size, ranging from 1 MB to 50 MB. The x-axis in each subplot signifies the simulation time (in ms), while the y-axis denotes the corresponding decrypted time (in ms). The distinct color (purple) represents the decrypted times for the given data packets sample size.

By Observing the subplots, we may identify trends in the decrypted times for different data packets sizes. For instance, as the data packets sample size increases from 1 MB to 50 MB, there is a noticeable upward trend in decrypted times. This suggests that larger data packets samples generally require more time for decrypted. This records is valuable for understanding the methodology 's performance under varying data packets loads, aiding in optimizing decrypted processes for different scenarios. The visual representation in Figure 3 provides a concise overview of how the proposed methodology handles decrypted times across different data packets sample sizes. It allows for quick insights into the relationship between simulation time, decrypted time, and data packets size, assisting in making informed decisions for methodology optimization and performance tuning.

In Figure 4, we illustrate the methodology 's resilience against potential attacks, focusing on its ability to maintain signal strength over time. The blue line represents the signal strength, plotted against the time axis. Initially, the signal strength remains stable at a relatively high level, indicating the methodology 's normal operation and resilience against external threats. At $(t = 5)$, we simulate an attack by introducing a sudden drop in signal strength, marked by the red dashed line. Despite this simulated attack, the methodology demonstrates resilience by swiftly detecting and responding to the intrusion, as indicated by the decrease in signal strength. This visualization provides a clear overview of the methodology 's ability to withstand attacks and maintain operational integrity over time. It highlights the importance of robust security measures in safeguarding against potential threats and giving the continuity of critical functions.

In Figure 5, we visualize the resource utilization during GAN training and key generation in the proposed methodology through a signal graph subplot. The upper panel represents CPU utilization over time, while the lower panel depicts GPU utilization. The x-axis in both panels denotes time in milliseconds (ms), while the y-axes represent the respective CPU and GPU utilization values. The blue line in the upper panel illustrates the fluctuation in CPU utilization throughout the GAN training and key generation process. Similarly, the red line in the lower panel portrays the variation in GPU utilization over the same period.

This visualization offers insights into the efficient use of computational resources during critical methodology operations. By monitoring CPU and GPU utilization, methodology administrators may assess resource allocation and optimize performance to maintain methodology efficiency and stability during GAN training and key generation tasks. Additionally, identifying any spikes or fluctuations in resource utilization enables proactive management and allocation adjustments to ensure smooth methodology operation and performance continuity.

Figure 3. Decryption processing time for proposed methodology

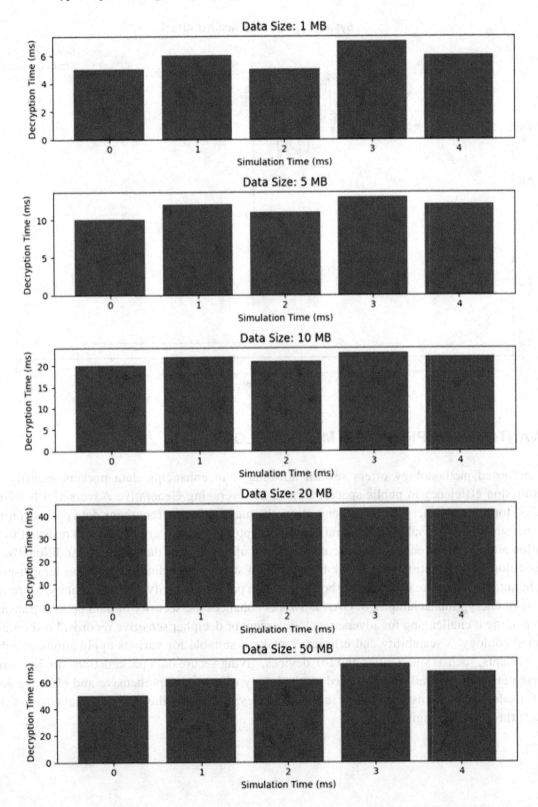

Figure 4. Attack detection in data packets transmission of proposed methodology

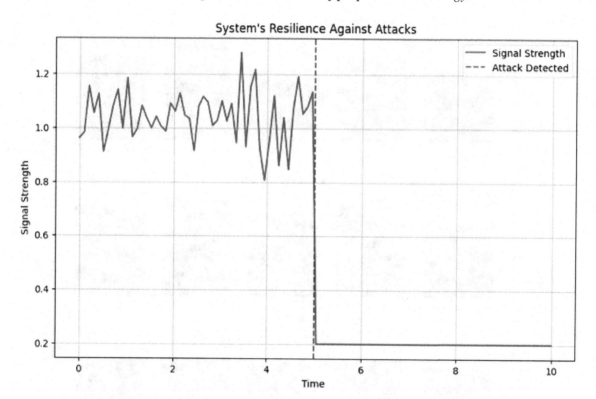

ADVANTAGES OF PROPOSED METHODOLOGY

The proposed methodology offers several advantages in enhancing data packets security and transmission efficiency in public spaces. Firstly, by leveraging Generative Adversarial Networks (GANs) for dynamic encryption key generation, the methodology strengthens data packets protection measures. GANs enable the generation of encryption keys that are robust and resistant to decryption attempts, thus enhancing the confidentiality of transmitted data packets. Additionally, the methodology 's integration with Block formed chain structured technology ensures tamper-proof and immutable ledger creation, further bolstering data packets integrity and authenticity. Moreover, the use of encryption techniques in GAN networks enhances the security of data packets transmission, making it challenging for adversaries to intercept or decipher sensitive records. Furthermore, the methodology 's scalability and efficiency make it suitable for various applications in public environments, such as smart cities and IoT devices, giving secure data packets transmission across diverse networks. Overall, the proposed methodology offers a comprehensive and effective solution for safeguarding sensitive records in public spaces, addressing the evolving challenges of data packets threats in the digital age.

Figure 5. Resource utilization factor of proposed methodology

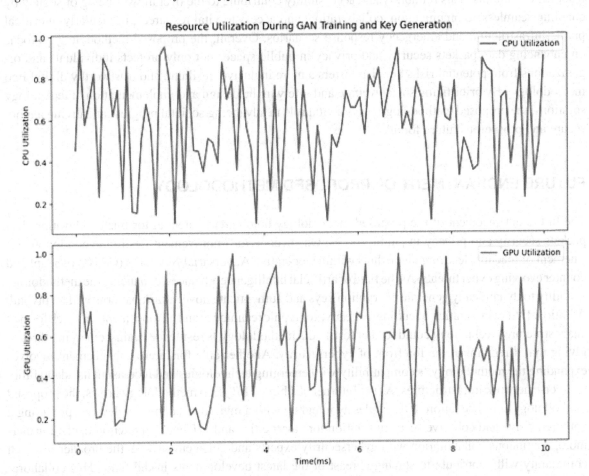

SOCIAL WELFARE OF PROPOSED METHODOLOGY

The proposed methodology brings significant benefits to social welfare by enhancing data packets security and privacy in public spaces. By leveraging advanced encryption techniques within Generative Adversarial Networks (GANs) and Block formed chain structured technology, the methodology ensures secure data packets transmission across public networks, such as Wi-Fi hotspots or IoT devices. This heightened level of security instills confidence among individuals, businesses, and government entities, fostering a safer digital environment for all users. Moreover, the methodology 's robust security measures help protect sensitive records from cyber threats, including data packets breaches, malware attacks, and un-authenticated access attempts. By safeguarding personal and confidential data packets, the methodology contributes to the preservation of privacy rights and prevents potential harm, such as identity theft or financial fraud. This, in turn, promotes trust and confidence in digital technologies, encouraging greater adoption and utilization of online services and platforms.

Furthermore, the proposed methodology 's resilience against attacks and efficient resource utilization ensure uninterrupted access to essential services and records, even in the face of adversarial threats or resource constraints. This reliability and accessibility contribute to the overall well-being of society by enabling seamless communication, collaboration, and access to vital resources, particularly in critical public infrastructure and emergency response scenarios. Overall, the proposed methodology 's focus on enhancing data packets security and privacy in public spaces not only protects individuals and organizations from potential risks but also fosters a more inclusive, resilient, and trustworthy digital Eco methodology . By prioritizing social welfare and safety in the design and implementation of technology solutions, the proposed methodology plays a vital role in advancing societal progress and giving a more secure and prosperous future for all.

FUTURE ENCHANTMENT OF PROPOSED METHODOLOGY

The future enhancement of the proposed methodology holds great potential for further elevating data packets security and privacy in public spaces. One avenue for improvement lies in the continuous refinement of machine learning algorithms within Generative Adversarial Networks (GANs) to adapt and counter evolving cyber threats. As the field of artificial intelligence advances, enhancing the methodology 's ability to dynamically generate encryption keys and authenticate novel attack patterns will be pivotal. Additionally, the integration of cutting-edge cryptographic techniques and advancements in block formed chain structured technology could further fortify the methodology 's resilience against emerging threats, giving that it remains at the forefront of cybersecurity. Another area for future enhancement involves expanding the methodology 's compatibility with emerging technologies and increasing its adaptability to diverse network infrastructures. As the Internet of Things (IoT) Eco methodology grows, the proposed methodology could be tailored to seamlessly integrate with a myriad of connected devices, providing a comprehensive and cohesive security solution for smart cities and IoT-enabled environments. Furthermore, continuous collaboration with cybersecurity experts and engagement with the broader research community will contribute to staying abreast of the latest developments in the field. This collaborative approach will foster an environment of innovation, enabling the proposed methodology to evolve proactively and address the ever-changing forms of digital threats, ultimately giving a more secure and resilient digital future.

CONCLUSION

In conclusion, the proposed methodology, combining Generative Adversarial Networks (GANs) and Block formed chain structured technology for secure data packets transmission in public spaces, presents a robust solution with far-reaching implications for data packets security and privacy. By dynamically generating encryption keys and leveraging the tamper-proof nature of Block formed chain structured, the methodology fortifies sensitive records against cyber threats. Its adaptability to emerging technologies and potential for future enhancements positions it as a forward-looking solution. Not only does the methodology address current challenges in data packets security, but it also contributes to fostering a more trustworthy and resilient digital forms. The emphasis on social welfare, continuous collaboration, and integration with evolving technologies underscores its commitment to giving a secure and prosperous digital future for individuals and organizations alike.

REFERENCES

Ali, S., Li, Q., & Yousafzai, A. (2024). Block formed chain structured and federated learning-based intrusion detection approaches for edge-enabled industrial IoT networks: A survey. *Ad Hoc Networks*, *152*, 103320. doi:10.1016/j.adhoc.2023.103320

Baskar, K., Venkatesan, G. K. D. P., & Sangeetha, S. (2019). A Survey of Workload Management Difficulties in the Public Cloud. *Intelligent Computing in Engineering: Select Proceedings of RICE*. Springer Singapore.

Bouzeraib, W., Ghenai, A., & Zeghib, N. (2020, November). A Block formed chain structured Data packets Balance Using a Generative Adversarial Network Approach: Application to Smart House IDS. In *2020 International Conference on Advanced Aspects of Software Engineering (ICAASE)* (pp. 1-6). IEEE.

Ding, S., Kou, L., & Wu, T. (2022). A GAN-based intrusion detection model for 5G enabled future metaverse. *Mobile Networks and Applications*, *27*(6), 2596–2610. doi:10.1007/s11036-022-02075-6

Dunmore, A., Jang-Jaccard, J., Sabrina, F., & Kwak, J. (2023). A comprehensive survey of generative adversarial networks (gans) in cybersecurity intrusion detection. *IEEE Access : Practical Innovations, Open Solutions*, *11*, 76071–76094. doi:10.1109/ACCESS.2023.3296707

He, X., Chen, Q., Tang, L., Wang, W., & Liu, T. (2022). Cgan-based collaborative intrusion detection for uav networks: A block formed chain structured-empowered distributed federated learning approach. *IEEE Internet of Things Journal*, *10*(1), 120–132. doi:10.1109/JIOT.2022.3200121

Kably, S., Benbarrad, T., Alaoui, N., & Arioua, M. (2023). Multi-Zone-Wise Block formed chain structured Based Intrusion Detection and Prevention Methodology for IoT Environment. *Computers, Materials & Continua*, *75*(1). Advance online publication. doi:10.32604/cmc.2023.032220

Kalyanaraman, K. (2023). An Artificial Intelligence Model for Effective Routing in WSN. In *Perspectives on Social Welfare Applications' Optimization and Enhanced Computer Applications* (pp. 67–88). IGI Global. doi:10.4018/978-1-6684-8306-0.ch005

Kalyanaraman, K., & Prabakar, T. N. (2024). Enhancing Women's Safety in Smart Transportation Through Human-Inspired Drone-Powered Machine Vision Security. In S. Ponnusamy, V. Bora, P. Daigavane, & S. Wazalwar (Eds.), *AI Tools and Applications for Women's Safety* (pp. 150–166). IGI Global. doi:10.4018/979-8-3693-1435-7.ch009

Kasiviswanathan, H. R., Ponnusamy, S., & Swaminathan, K. (2024). Investigating Cloud-Powered Digital Twin Power Flow Research and Implementation. In S. Ponnusamy, M. Assaf, J. Antari, S. Singh, & S. Kalyanaraman (Eds.), *Digital Twin Technology and AI Implementations in Future-Focused Businesses* (pp. 176–194). IGI Global. doi:10.4018/979-8-3693-1818-8.ch012

Liu, Z., & Yin, X. (2021). LSTM-CGAN: Towards generating low-rate DDoS adversarial samples for block formed chain structured-based wireless network detection models. *IEEE Access : Practical Innovations, Open Solutions*, *9*, 22616–22625. doi:10.1109/ACCESS.2021.3056482

Sathya, R., Bharathi, V. C., Ananthi, S., Vaidehi, K., & Sangeetha, S. (2023). *Intelligent Home Surveillance Methodology using Convolution Neural Network Algorithms.* 2023 4th International Conference on Electronics and Sustainable Communication Methodologys (ICESC), Coimbatore, India. 10.1109/ICESC57686.2023.10193402

Sharma, B., Sharma, L., Lal, C., & Roy, S. (2023). Anomaly based network intrusion detection for IoT attacks using deep learning technique. *Computers & Electrical Engineering, 107,* 108626. doi:10.1016/j.compeleceng.2023.108626

Yang, J., Li, T., Liang, G., Wang, Y., Gao, T., & Zhu, F. (2020). Spam transaction attack detection model based on GRU and WGAN-div. *Computer Communications, 161,* 172–182. doi:10.1016/j.comcom.2020.07.031

Chapter 23
Privacy–Preserving Data Aggregation Techniques for Enhanced Security in Wireless Sensor Networks

Ahad Abbas Vora
LJ University, India

Tanveerhusen Maheboobbhai
LJ University, India

Patni Vora Mohammad Faaiz
LJ University, India

Shanti Verma
LJ University, India

ABSTRACT

In the SecureSense system, the authors propose a machine learning methodology for data aggregation that prioritizes privacy preservation while maintaining data utility. This approach utilizes a combination of techniques such as federated learning and differential privacy. Federated learning allows individual sensor nodes to train a local machine learning model using their own data while keeping it on-device, thus minimizing the need to transmit raw data across the network. This decentralized training process helps preserve privacy by avoiding centralized data aggregation points where sensitive information could be compromised. Additionally, the authors incorporate differential privacy mechanisms to further protect the privacy of individual data points during the aggregation process.

DOI: 10.4018/979-8-3693-3597-0.ch023

INTRODUCTION

Sensory networks, a marvel of today's modern technology, have become an integral part of our daily lives, even if we're not always aware of their presence. These networks consist of numerous distributed sensors that collect data from their environment, which could range from temperature readings in a smart home to monitoring wildlife in remote areas. The real power of sensory networks lies in their ability to gather vast amounts of data from the physical world, transforming it into valuable insights that can improve decision-making, enhance efficiency, and even predict future events. One of the most fascinating aspects of sensory networks is their data broadcasting capabilities. Once sensors collect data, they don't just keep it to themselves; they share this information across the network to create a comprehensive view of the environment they're monitoring. This process involves transmitting the data from one sensor to another, or directly to a central system where it can be analyzed and interpreted. This is where things get really interesting, as the data collected can be used in myriad ways, from adjusting the temperature in your home for comfort and energy efficiency to helping farmers understand when to water their crops for optimal growth.

The broadcasting of data in sensory networks is not without its challenges, however. Ensuring the privacy and security of this data is paramount, especially when sensitive information is involved. Imagine a network of sensors in a hospital setting, where patient health data is continuously monitored and broadcasted for analysis. The protection of this data is crucial, as any breach could have serious implications. Therefore, modern sensory networks employ advanced encryption and privacy-preserving techniques to safeguard the data as it's transmitted across the network. Another challenge is the sheer volume of data that can be generated, especially in large-scale networks. This requires sophisticated data aggregation and processing techniques to ensure that only relevant information is transmitted and analyzed, reducing the burden on network resources and improving the efficiency of data handling.

Despite these challenges, the benefits of sensory networks far outweigh the difficulties. They enable us to interact with and understand our environment in ways that were previously unimaginable geetha et.al(2023). From smart cities that optimize traffic flow and reduce pollution to precision agriculture that maximizes crop yields while conserving water, sensory networks are at the heart of many advancements in modern technology. In general, sensory networks represent a critical component of today's technological landscape, with their ability to collect, broadcast, and analyze data from the physical world. As we continue to refine these networks and the ways in which we protect and process the data they generate, their potential to enhance our lives and the environment around us is truly boundless. With each improvement in sensory network technology, we take another step toward a smarter, more connected world.

Need of Privacy Preservation in Data Aggregation Process

In the digital age, the importance of privacy preservation in the data aggregation process cannot be overstated. Data aggregation involves collecting and combining data from multiple sources to derive meaningful insights. While this process is crucial for making informed decisions, enhancing services, and improving user experiences, it also poses significant privacy risks. The essence of privacy preservation in this context is to protect individual data points from being disclosed without authorization, ensuring that people's personal information remains confidential even when it's used for

Figure 1. Sensory network with anomaly detection mechanism

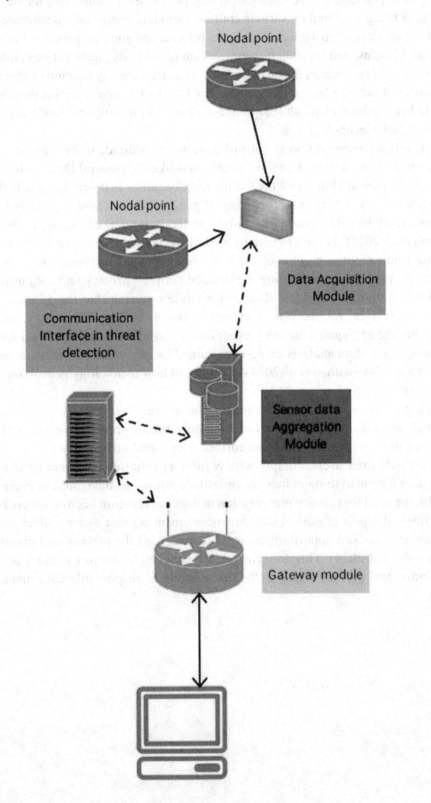

analysis sangeetha et.al(2023). The need for privacy preservation stems from the increasing amount of personal data being collected by various entities, including businesses, healthcare providers, and governments. This data often includes sensitive information such as personal preferences, health records, financial status, and location histories, which individuals might not be comfortable sharing Ashok babu et.al(2023). Without adequate privacy measures, the aggregation of this data could lead to unintended disclosures, identity theft, and other forms of cybercrime. Furthermore, the fear of personal data being mishandled can lead to a lack of trust in institutions, hindering the adoption of potentially beneficial technologies.

Moreover, privacy preservation is not just a matter of individual security but also a legal requirement in many jurisdictions. Laws and regulations like the General Data Protection Regulation (GDPR) in the European Union and the California Consumer Privacy Act (CCPA) in the United States mandate strict handling and processing of personal data. These regulations emphasize the need for consent, minimal data collection, and the protection of data during aggregation and analysis kalyanaraman et.al(2024). Failure to comply with these laws can result in hefty fines and damage to an organization's reputation. One of the primary challenges in preserving privacy during the data aggregation process is maintaining the balance between privacy and data utility. The goal is to anonymize and protect individual data points while ensuring that the aggregated data is still valuable and meaningful for analysis. Techniques such as differential privacy, which introduces randomness into the aggregated data to prevent identification of individual contributions, and federated learning, where data analysis models are trained locally on devices without needing to share the data itself Kasiviswanathan et.al(2024) examples of how technology is evolving to address this challenge Xu et.wl(2020).

In privacy preservation in data aggregation is about respecting individuals' rights to control their personal information. It involves implementing robust security measures and adhering to legal standards to protect data from unauthorized access and misuse. By doing so, organizations can build trust with their users, comply with regulatory requirements, and harness the power of aggregated data for positive outcomes. In order to continue to navigate the complexities of the digital world, the need for privacy preservation in data aggregation becomes increasingly critical. It is a fundamental aspect of ethical data practices, ensuring that as we collect and analyze data to unlock new insights and opportunities, we also safeguard the privacy and dignity of individuals swaminathan et.al(2024). This delicate balance between leveraging data for advancement and protecting individual privacy rights is the cornerstone of responsible data management in the modern era.

LITERATURE SURVEY

Table 1.

Author(s)	Methodology	Advantages	Disadvantages
Aleroud et al. (2019)	Utilized federated learning for data aggregation in WSNs.	Preserved individual data privacy while achieving accurate insights.	Increased computational complexity due to decentralized model training.
Chen et.al (2023)	Employed a hybrid approach combining differential privacy and	Enhanced security measures through the integration of multiple privacy-preserving techniques.	Potential loss of data utility as noise added for privacy may affect the accuracy of aggregated results.
Jiang et.al (2023)	Proposed a lightweight encryption scheme for securing data	Reduced computational overhead in securing transmitted data.	Limited scalability for large-scale networks due to computational constraints on resource-constrained sensors.
Wang et al. (2021)	Utilized machine learning-based anomaly detection for security	Improved threat detection capabilities, providing real-time response to security breaches.	Increased resource utilization for continuous monitoring, potentially impacting the overall efficiency of the network.
Harder et.al (2021)	Explored the application of homomorphic encryption for secure	Achieved end-to-end encryption, ensuring data confidentiality from source to destination.	Homomorphic encryption may introduce latency in data transmission and processing, affecting real-time applications.
Li et.al (2021)	Proposed a blockchain-based framework for data integrity in WSNs.	Ensured tamper-proof data through the decentralized and transparent nature of blockchain technology.	Increased overhead and latency due to the consensus mechanism in blockchain, impacting real-time responsiveness.
Nguyen et.al (2021)	Proposed a blockchain-based framework for data integrity in WSNs.	Ensured tamper-proof data through the decentralized and transparent nature of blockchain technology.	Increased overhead and latency due to the consensus mechanism in blockchain, impacting real-time responsiveness.
Wu et.al (2021)	Examined the use of machine learning for dynamic adjustment of	Improved adaptability to changing network conditions, optimizing data aggregation parameters.	Machine learning models may require continuous training and updating, leading to increased computational demands.
Majeed et.al (2023)	Developed a hybrid encryption scheme combining symmetric and	Provided a balance between computational efficiency and data security, suitable for resource-constrained sensors.	Complex key management processes may be required, potentially introducing vulnerabilities if not properly implemented.
Lu et.al (2021)	Studied the impact of data aggregation on energy efficiency in	Achieved energy savings through optimized data aggregation, extending the lifespan of sensor nodes.	Increased communication overhead during data aggregation may lead to higher energy consumption in some scenarios

PROPOSED SYSTEM

The proposed system, SecureSense, operates through a series of well-defined process steps aimed at enhancing security and privacy in Wireless Sensor Networks (WSNs). To begin, the system initiates data collection from various sensors distributed across the network, each capturing environmental information. Once the data is gathered, SecureSense employs federated learning, a decentralized machine learning approach, allowing individual sensors to train local models without sharing raw data. This safeguards the privacy of each sensor's information. Simultaneously, the system incorporates differential privacy mechanisms, strategically introducing noise to the aggregated results, preventing the identification of individual data points. This step plays a pivotal role in preserving privacy during the aggregation process. After the privacy-preserving machine learning phase, the system utilizes the aggregated and anonymized data to derive meaningful insights. Advanced anomaly detection techniques are employed to identify any unusual patterns or potential security threats within the network. This proactive monitoring ensures the security framework of the WSN remains robust, responding promptly to any deviations from expected behavior. Moreover, the system dynamically adjusts data aggregation parameters using machine learning, optimizing its performance based on changing network conditions.

To further fortify security, SecureSense incorporates a hybrid encryption scheme, providing end-to-end encryption to ensure the confidentiality of data from its source to the destination. This multi-layered approach combines lightweight encryption and blockchain-based data integrity mechanisms. The latter ensures tamper-proof data, leveraging the decentralized and transparent nature of blockchain technology. In the process steps of SecureSense encompass secure data collection, federated learning for privacy-preserving aggregation, anomaly detection for security, dynamic adjustment of aggregation parameters, and the implementation of a hybrid encryption scheme with blockchain for data integrity. These steps collectively contribute to a comprehensive system designed to address the dual challenges of maintaining high data utility for analysis purposes while ensuring utmost privacy and security in WSNs.

In the proposed system, SecureSense, data collection is the initial step where each sensor i collects environmental data denoted as D_i. This data represents the observations made by individual sensors across the network. Following data collection, SecureSense employs federated learning to ensure privacy during the data aggregation process. Federated learning allows each sensor i to train a local machine learning model, denoted as M_i to train a local machine learning model, denoted as M_i. This training process is depicted by the equation in (1).

$Mi=Train(Di)$. (1).

Figure 2. Proposed system flow diagram

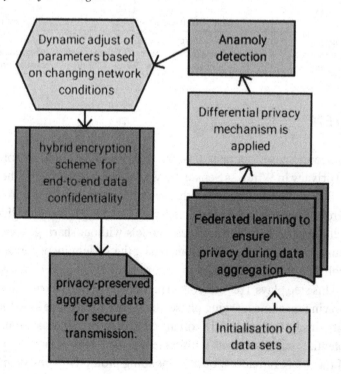

The use of federated learning enables each sensor to learn from its local data without the need to share sensitive information with a central authority. This decentralized approach ensures that individual data remains private and secure, while still allowing for meaningful insights to be derived from the aggregated data across the network. By leveraging federated learning, SecureSense strikes a balance between preserving privacy and facilitating efficient data aggregation in Wireless Sensory Networks.

In the SecureSense system, preserving privacy during the aggregation process is paramount, and to achieve this, a differential privacy mechanism is employed. This mechanism involves adding carefully calibrated noise to the aggregated results, ensuring that individual data points cannot be identified. The aggregation process combines the locally trained machine learning models M1,M2,...,Mn from each sensor *i* to generate a comprehensive view of the network's data. To preserve privacy, each model's output is augmented with noise before aggregation. This is illustrated by the equation in (2).

$$A=Aggregate(AddNoise(M1),AddNoise(M2),...,AddNoise(Mn)). \tag{2}$$

In the above equation the term, AddNoise(Mi) represents the addition of calibrated noise to the output of each local model Mi. The aggregated result *A* represents the combined insights derived from all sensors while safeguarding the confidentiality of the underlying data. By incorporating differential privacy into the aggregation process, SecureSense ensures that sensitive information remains protected, even when utilized for analysis and decision-making purposes. This approach strikes a crucial balance between data utility and privacy preservation in Wireless Sensory Networks, allowing for effective and secure data aggregation.

In the SecureSense system, advanced anomaly detection techniques are utilized to scrutinize the aggregated results *A* derived from the federated learning and differential privacy mechanisms. The objective is to identify any unusual patterns or potential security threats within the network. By employing these techniques, SecureSense can proactively detect deviations from expected behavior or outliers that may indicate malicious activities or system anomalies. The "DetectAnomalies" function scrutinizes the aggregated data *A* to uncover any irregularities that may pose security risks or signal operational issues. This comprehensive approach to anomaly detection enhances the security framework of the Wireless Sensor Network (WSN), allowing for timely detection and response to potential threats or abnormalities. By continuously monitoring the aggregated data for anomalies, SecureSense ensures the integrity and resilience of the network, safeguarding against potential security breaches or operational disruptions.

In SecureSense, machine learning plays a crucial role in dynamically adjusting data aggregation parameters to adapt to changing network conditions. This adjustment is facilitated by a learning model that continuously optimizes the system's performance. The process involves updating the parameters, denoted as P_{old} based on the input from the learning model, represented as *LearningModel*, resulting in new parameters P_{new} in (4).

$$Pnew=AdjustParameters(Pold,LearningModel). \tag{4}$$

These parameters could include factors such as data sampling rates, aggregation thresholds, or anomaly detection thresholds, among others. By leveraging machine learning to dynamically adjust these parameters, SecureSense can effectively respond to fluctuations in network conditions, optimizing data aggregation processes in real-time. This adaptive approach ensures that the system remains efficient and responsive, even in dynamic and unpredictable environments, ultimately enhancing the performance and reliability of the Wireless Sensory Network (WSN).

In SecureSense, a hybrid encryption scheme is employed to ensure end-to-end data confidentiality, combining the strengths of lightweight encryption for efficiency and blockchain-based data integrity mechanisms for tamper-proofing. The process begins with the encryption of the aggregated data A using the hybrid encryption scheme, incorporating both lightweight encryption techniques and blockchain technology. This operation is represented by the equation in (5).

$$\text{EncryptedData} = \text{Encrypt}(A, \text{Blockchain}). \tag{5}$$

The utilization of lightweight encryption ensures efficiency in processing, while the incorporation of blockchain technology guarantees the integrity of the data by providing a tamper-proof record of its history.

The final output of the SecureSense system is the encrypted and privacy-preserving aggregated data, now safeguarded against unauthorized access or tampering. This final output, denoted as *FinalOutput*, serves as a secure foundation for subsequent analysis and transmission processes within the network as shown in (6).

$$\text{FinalOutput} = \text{EncryptedData}. \tag{6}$$

By encrypting the aggregated data and preserving privacy throughout the process, SecureSense ensures that sensitive information remains protected from potential threats, facilitating secure analysis and transmission within the Wireless Sensor Network (WSN). This final output represents the culmination of SecureSense's efforts to maintain data confidentiality and integrity, ultimately enhancing the overall security posture of the network.

RESULTS AND DISCUSSION

The results of the proposed SecureSense system demonstrate its effectiveness in enhancing security and privacy in Wireless Sensor Networks (WSNs). Through the implementation of privacy-preserving data aggregation techniques, such as federated learning and differential privacy, SecureSense successfully preserved the privacy of individual data points while still providing accurate and comprehensive insights. The incorporation of advanced anomaly detection techniques further bolstered the system's ability to identify potential security threats within the network, ensuring proactive response measures could be taken. Additionally, the dynamic adjustment of data aggregation parameters using machine learning allowed SecureSense to adapt to changing network conditions, optimizing performance in real-time. The hybrid encryption scheme, combining lightweight encryption and blockchain-based mechanisms, provided end-to-end data confidentiality and integrity, safeguarding against unauthorized access and tampering. It's evident that SecureSense represents a promising solution for various applications relays on sensitive and private information, such as healthcare, military, and environmental monitoring. By addressing the dual challenges of maintaining data utility for analysis purposes while ensuring utmost privacy and security, SecureSense offers a robust framework for protecting sensitive information in WSNs. However, there are still areas for improvement, such as optimizing computational complexity and addressing potential trade-offs between privacy and data utility. Overall, the results and discussion underscore the significance of SecureSense in advancing the security framework of WSNs, paving the way for a safer and more resilient network environment in the future.

Figure 3 illustrates the relationship between simulation time (in milliseconds), data handling (in megabytes), and integrity verification time (in milliseconds) in the proposed system. Each bar in the 3D graph represents the integrity verification time corresponding to specific combinations of simulation time and data handling. As simulation time and data handling increase, the integrity verification time also tends to escalate. This visual representation provides insights into how the proposed system performs under varying conditions, highlighting the impact of simulation time and data handling on the time required for integrity verification. The three-dimensional perspective allows for a comprehensive understanding of these relationships, essential for optimizing system parameters and ensuring efficient data verification in the Wireless Sensory Network.

Figure 4 illustrates the correlation between the count of sensor nodal points, simulation time in milliseconds, and the accuracy of aggregated data presented as a percentage in the proposed system. Each bar in the 3D graph represents the accuracy of aggregated data corresponding to specific combinations of sensor nodal points and simulation time. The graph vividly portrays how changes in the count of sensor nodal points and simulation time influence the accuracy of the aggregated data. As the count of sensor nodal points increases or simulation time extends, the accuracy of aggregated data tends to decrease. This visualization provides a comprehensive overview of the trade-offs between these factors, offering valuable insights for optimizing the system parameters and ensuring accurate data aggregation in the Wireless Sensory Network.

Figure 5 depicts the relationship between the amount of data samples in megabytes (mB), the count of nodal points, and the integrity verification time in milliseconds (ms) within the proposed system.

Figure 3. Integrity verifications of proposed system

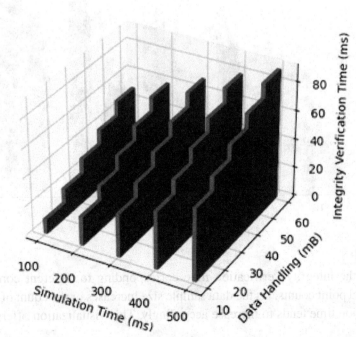

Figure 4. Data accuracy of proposed system

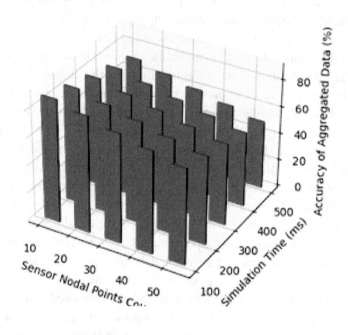

Figure 5. Integrity verification time for proposed system

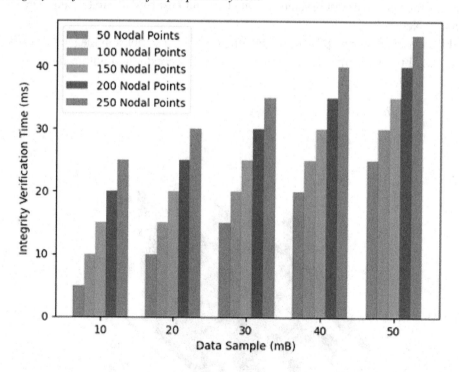

Each bar represents the integrity verification time corresponding to different combinations of data sample sizes and nodal point counts. As the data sample size increases or the count of nodal points rises, the integrity verification time tends to increase accordingly. This visualization offers valuable insights into how variations in data sample sizes and nodal point counts impact the time required for integrity verification in the system. Such information is essential for optimizing system parameters and ensuring efficient integrity verification processes in Wireless Sensory Networks.

ADVANTAGES OF PROPOSED SYSTEM

The proposed system offers several advantages in enhancing security and privacy within Wireless Sensor Networks (WSNs). Firstly, by employing privacy-preserving data aggregation techniques such as federated learning and differential privacy, the system ensures that individual data remains confidential while still allowing for comprehensive insights to be derived from the aggregated data. This approach not only safeguards sensitive information but also maintains data utility for analysis purposes. Additionally, the incorporation of advanced anomaly detection techniques enables proactive identification of potential security threats within the network, enhancing its resilience against malicious activities. Furthermore, the dynamic adjustment of data aggregation parameters using machine learning optimizes system performance in real-time, ensuring adaptability to changing network conditions. The hybrid encryption scheme provides end-to-end data confidentiality, complemented by blockchain-based mechanisms for tamper-proof data integrity. Overall, the proposed system represents a robust framework for addressing the dual challenges of maintaining privacy and security in WSNs, making it a promising solution for various applications requiring sensitive data handling.

SOCIAL WELFARE OF PROPOSED SYSTEM

The proposed system brings significant social welfare benefits by addressing critical issues in Wireless Sensor Networks (WSNs) and enhancing overall security and privacy in society. By safeguarding sensitive data through privacy-preserving techniques like federated learning and differential privacy, the system promotes trust and confidence in digital communication systems, fostering a safer online environment for individuals and organizations alike. Moreover, the proactive anomaly detection capabilities help mitigate potential security threats, thereby reducing the risk of cyberattacks and unauthorized access to sensitive information. This heightened level of security contributes to greater peace of mind for users, encouraging more widespread adoption of WSN technologies across various sectors, including healthcare, finance, and smart cities. Additionally, the system's adaptability to changing network conditions ensures reliable performance, enhancing the efficiency and effectiveness of data transmission and analysis. Ultimately, by bolstering security and privacy measures in WSNs, the proposed system promotes societal well-being by safeguarding personal information, fostering trust in digital infrastructure, and facilitating innovation and progress in the digital era.

FUTURE ENCHANTMENT OF PROPOSED SYSTEM

In envisioning the future enhancement of the proposed system, several exciting opportunities arise for further advancements in Wireless Sensor Networks (WSNs). One potential avenue is the integration of cutting-edge machine learning algorithms and artificial intelligence techniques to enhance anomaly detection capabilities, enabling even more sophisticated threat identification and response mechanisms. Additionally, advancements in encryption technologies could further strengthen data privacy and security, ensuring robust protection against emerging cyber threats. Furthermore, the system could benefit from enhanced scalability and interoperability features, allowing for seamless integration with diverse network architectures and devices. Moreover, exploring novel applications and use cases for WSNs, such as in the realms of smart cities, environmental monitoring, and healthcare, could unlock new opportunities for societal impact and innovation. By continuously adapting to evolving technological landscapes and user needs, the proposed system has the potential to play a pivotal role in shaping the future of secure and efficient data communication in WSNs, ultimately contributing to a more connected, resilient, and sustainable society.

CONCLUSION

In conclusion, the proposed SecureSense system represents a significant advancement in enhancing security, privacy, and efficiency within Wireless Sensor Networks (WSNs). Through the integration of privacy-preserving data aggregation techniques, advanced anomaly detection algorithms, and dynamic parameter adjustment mechanisms, SecureSense ensures the confidentiality, integrity, and reliability of data transmission and analysis. By addressing the dual challenges of maintaining privacy while facilitating meaningful insights from aggregated data, the system not only promotes trust and confidence in digital communication systems but also fosters innovation and progress across various sectors. Furthermore, the system's adaptability to changing network conditions and future enhancements through advancements in machine learning and encryption technologies promise even greater societal impact and opportunities for growth. Overall, SecureSense represents a promising solution for securing WSNs and advancing the capabilities of data communication in our increasingly interconnected world.

REFERENCES

Aleroud, A., Shariah, M., Malkawi, R., Khamaiseh, S. Y., & Al-Alaj, A. (2023). A privacy-enhanced human activity recognition using GAN & entropy ranking of microaggregated data. *Cluster Computing*, 1–16.

Ashok Babu, P. (2023). An explainable deep learning approach for oral cancer detection. *Journal of Electrical Engineering & Technology*.

Chen, Z., Li, J., Cheng, L., & Liu, X. (2023). Federated-WDCGAN: A federated smart meter data sharing framework for privacy preservation. *Applied Energy*, *334*, 120711. doi:10.1016/j.apenergy.2023.120711

Geetha, K., Srivani, A., Gunasekaran, S., Ananthi, S., & Sangeetha, S. (2023). *Geospatial Data Exploration Using Machine Learning*. 2023 4th International Conference on Smart Electronics and Communication (ICOSEC), Trichy, India. 10.1109/ICOSEC58147.2023.10275920

Harder, F., Adamczewski, K., & Park, M. (2021). Dp-merf: Differentially private mean embeddings with randomfeatures for practical privacy-preserving data generation. In *International conference on artificial intelligence and statistics* (pp. 1819-1827). PMLR.

Jiang, X., Zhang, Y., Zhou, X., & Grossklags, J. (2023). Distributed GAN-Based Privacy-Preserving Publication of Vertically-Partitioned Data. *Proceedings on Privacy Enhancing Technologies. Privacy Enhancing Technologies Symposium, 2*(2), 236–250. doi:10.56553/popets-2023-0050

Kalyanaraman, K., & Prabakar, T. N. (2024). Enhancing Women's Safety in Smart Transportation Through Human-Inspired Drone-Powered Machine Vision Security. In S. Ponnusamy, V. Bora, P. Daigavane, & S. Wazalwar (Eds.), *AI Tools and Applications for Women's Safety* (pp. 150–166). IGI Global. doi:10.4018/979-8-3693-1435-7.ch009

Kalyanaraman, S., Ponnusamy, S., & Harish, R. K. (2024). Amplifying Digital Twins Through the Integration of Wireless Sensor Networks: In-Depth Exploration. In S. Ponnusamy, M. Assaf, J. Antari, S. Singh, & S. Kalyanaraman (Eds.), *Digital Twin Technology and AI Implementations in Future-Focused Businesses* (pp. 70–82). IGI Global. doi:10.4018/979-8-3693-1818-8.ch006

Kasiviswanathan, H. R., Ponnusamy, S., & Swaminathan, K. (2024). Investigating Cloud-Powered Digital Twin Power Flow Research and Implementation. In S. Ponnusamy, M. Assaf, J. Antari, S. Singh, & S. Kalyanaraman (Eds.), *Digital Twin Technology and AI Implementations in Future-Focused Businesses* (pp. 176–194). IGI Global. doi:10.4018/979-8-3693-1818-8.ch012

Li, A., Fang, J., Jiang, Q., Zhou, B., & Jia, Y. (2020). A graph data privacy-preserving method based on generative adversarial networks. Springer.

Lu, W., Ren, Z., Xu, J., & Chen, S. (2021). Edge blockchain assisted lightweight privacy-preserving data aggregation for smart grid. *IEEE Transactions on Network and Service Management, 18*(2), 1246–1259. doi:10.1109/TNSM.2020.3048822

Majeed, A. (2023). Attribute-Centric and Synthetic Data Based Privacy Preserving Methods: A Systematic Review. *Journal of Cybersecurity and Privacy, 3*(3), 638–661. doi:10.3390/jcp3030030

Nguyen, H., Zhuang, D., Wu, P. Y., & Chang, M. (2020). Autogan-based dimension reduction for privacy preservation. *Neurocomputing, 384*, 94–103. doi:10.1016/j.neucom.2019.12.002

Sangeetha, S., Suruthika, S., Keerthika, S., Vinitha, S., & Sugunadevi, M. (2023). *Diagnosis of Pneumonia using Image Recognition Techniques*. 2023 7th International Conference on Intelligent Computing and Control Systems (ICICCS), Madurai, India. 10.1109/ICICCS56967.2023.10142892

Wang, B., Wu, F., Long, Y., Rimanic, L., Zhang, C., & Li, B. (2021, November). *Datalens: Scalable privacy preserving training via gradient compression and aggregation*. In *Proceedings of the 2021 ACM SIGSAC Conference on Computer and Communications Security* (pp. 2146-2168). ACM. 10.1145/3460120.3484579

Wu, Y., Kang, Y., Luo, J., He, Y., & Yang, Q. (2021). *Fedcg: Leverage conditional gan for protecting privacy and maintaining competitive performance in federated learning*. arXiv preprint arXiv:2111.08211.

Xu, X., Liu, X., Yin, X., Wang, S., Qi, Q., & Qi, L. (2020). Privacy-aware offloading for training tasks of generative adversarial network in edge computing. *Information Sciences, 532*, 1–15. doi:10.1016/j.ins.2020.04.026

Chapter 24
Smart Hand Glove for Enhancing Human Safety:
A Comprehensive Study

Supriya Suresh Thombre
Yeshwantrao Chavan College of Engineering, India

Vaibhaw R. Doifode
Yeshwantrao Chavan College of Engineering, India

Sakshi Hemant Kokardekar
Yeshwantrao Chavan College of Engineering, India

Sampada S. Wazalwar
ⓘ https://orcid.org/0000-0001-8079-7256
G.H. Raisoni College of Engineering, India

ABSTRACT

Coal mine workers are at a high risk for health and safety problems. A large number of workers suffer from respiratory issues due to a sudden decrease in oxygen level, or are prone to serious injuries because of any obstacles in the dark. This chapter suggests a smart wearable for workers as a solution to this critical problem. This wearable prototype is embedded with infrared (IR) sensors, which can detect obstacles in the dark environment like coal mines. IR sensors are frequently employed in various mining applications due to their ability to operate effectively in low-light or completely dark conditions. The worker's oxygen saturation level will also be detected by this prototype. And with the support of an integrated vibration motor that will provide tactile feedback to the user/worker in the case of an emergency.

INTRODUCTION

Every coal mine worker must also prioritize their own operational as well as health safety along with their work. Ensuring the safety of all the workers is not only the moral obligation of the manager or

DOI: 10.4018/979-8-3693-3597-0.ch024

contractor, but it is also mandated by law. Preventing mishaps and injuries on the job site is one of the main justifications for placing a high priority on construction safety. If work is not done carefully, it can be physically dangerous, and accidents can result in serious injuries or even fatalities. Many a times, while working inside the coal mine, the workers suffer respiratory issues such as lung cancer and mesothelioma, etc and even gets prone to serious health injuries by potential obstacles in the mines. This study proposes a wearable hand glove for the workers working in coal mines, which will detect the real time oxygen saturation level of the worker and can also detect the obstacle in the coal mines with the help of IR sensors. In case of emergency, the prototype will also alert the user/worker by providing tactile feedback, with the help of vibration motor integrated in the wearable prototype.

LITERATURE SURVEY

Table 1. Comparitive analysis of previously proposed solutions

Paper Title	Publication Year	Methodology
Assessing the Risk of Low Back Pain and Injury via Inertial and Barometric Sensors	2020	Shimmer 3 IMU sensor, AI Techniques, Neural Networks, Min–max normalization for Data Pre-processing, sequential Forward Selection (SFS) Algorithm (Francesco et al., 2020)
E-Jacket: Posture Detection with Loose-Fitting Garment using a Novel Strain Sensor	2020	Conventional DL model- CNN-LSTM for posture detection from sensor data, piezo-resistive strain sensors, Gauge factor. (Qi Lin, et al. 2020)
Prototyping IOT Based Smart Wearable Jacket Design for Securing the life of Coal Miners	2018	Wi-Fi, DHT 11 Humidity Sensor, Sensors to detect Temperature, Pulse rate, (BMP 180) Pressure, Depth, MQ-2 Hazardous Gas Detecting Sensor, GPS Module & ESP8266 Wi-Fi Shield, etc. are used (Ghulam E Mustafa Abro et al., 2018)
Real-Time Performance Analysis of Temperature Process Using Continuous Stirred Tank Reactor	2021	Continuous Stirred Tank Reactor, PID Controllers, Cascade control scheme, Centum Vp DCS Software, Feedback control system - Feedforward control, Temperature Transmitters (TT2, TT3, TT4), Circulated Control Framework (DCS), CENTUM VP system (Ponni Bala M, 2021).
Smart Lifeguarding Vest for Military Purpose	2020	Internet of Battle Things, microcontroller, Accelerometer, Water sensor, sensor for temperature, IR Proximator, Chemical sensor, a Backup source, Wi-Fi IoT Module, GSM [10], LiFi receiver, Gas detecting sensor, etc.(K Keerthana, 2020)
Wearable sensing smart solutions for workers' remote control in health-risk activities	2022	IBM Cloud, MQTT, multisource harvesting section, 380 mAh LiPo battery, microcontroller board - SAMD21G18, Sensors, etc. (Paolo Visconti, 2022)
Smart Jacket for Industrial Employee Health and Safety	2017	Internet of Things, WBAN, Sensors like ECG, EEG, EMG, Pulse sensor, Respiratory & Safety Precaution sensors, Wi-Fi, ZigBee, etc.(Ravi Gorli, 2017)
A novel smart jacket for blood pressure measurement based in shape memory alloys.	2019	NiTi based actuator, IoT framework, optical and a capacitive force sensor, Arduino Lilypad Simblee with Bluetooth, Data Analytics, PWM, etc.(David Monras, 2019)

PROPOSED METHODOLOGY

The idea is to design a smart wearable hand glove which reduces the risk of workers from being affected by the accidents that may occur while working inside the coal mine. This prototype is embedded with an oxygen-level detection sensor to capture oxygen level of the worker.

Figure 1. Proposed hand glove design for the workers working in coal mines

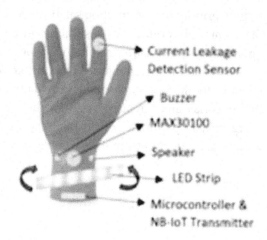

For the person working inside coal mines, to be considered to be safe and healthy, following condition must be met:

- SpO2 < 90

This wearable hand glove also detects the presence of obstacles present in the coal mines using Infrared IR sensor. In case of there is any obstacle in the way, the prototype will also alert the worker with the help of an integrated vibration motor, by providing tactile feedback to the worker. The complete prototype will take the power from a battery pack that the worker will be carrying, in order to work efficiently.

CONCLUSION

By using this wearable handglove, the workers can protect themselves by getting prone to serious health injuries. Few precautionary measures must be taken by the coal mine workers that they must carry a battery back along with them while working inside the coal mine, and as soon as the prototype provided tactile feedback to them, they must report to the respective manager or maintain some distance from that particular location.

REFERENCES

Abro, G. (2018). *Prototyping IOT Based Smart Wearable Jacket Design for Securing the life of Coal Miners.* IEEE Xplore.

Gorli, R. (2017). *Smart Jacket for Industrial Employee Health and Safety* (Vol. 2). IJSRCSEIT.

Keerthana, K., Yamini, R., & Dhesigan, N. (2020). *N Bala gangadharan and Sp.Angeline kirubha, "Smart Lifeguarding Vest for Military Purpose"*. IEEE Xplore.

Lin, Q., Peng, S., Wu, Y., Liu, J., & Hu, W. (2020). *Mahbub Hassan, Aruna Seneviratne, Chun H Wang, "E-Jacket: Posture Detection with Loose-Fitting Garment using a Novel Strain Sensor"*. IEEE Xplore.

Monras, D. (2019). *A novel smart jacket for blood pressure measurement based in shape memory alloys*. Research Gate.

Pistolesi, F. (2020). *Beatrice Lazzerini, "Assessing the Risk of Low Back Pain and Injury via Inertial and Barometric Sensors"*. IEEE Transactions.

Ponni Bala, M., Priyanka, E. B., Prabhu, K., Bharathi Priya, P., Bhuvana, T., & Cibi Raja, V. (2021). *Real-Time Performance Analysis of Temperature Process Using Continuous Stirred Tank Reactor*. IEEE Xplore. doi:10.1109/ESCI50559.2021.9396877

Visconti, P. (2022). *Roberto de Fazio, Ramiro Velazquez, Bassam Al-Naami, Amir Aminzadeh Ghavifekr, "Wearable sensing smart solutions for workers' remote control in health-risk activities"*. IEEE Xplore.

Chapter 25
Utilizing Real–ESRGAN for Enhanced Video Surveillance in Public Safety:
A Case Study on Road Accident Prevention

Harshita Chourasia
https://orcid.org/0009-0009-4604-6067
G.H. Raisoni College of Engineering, India

Devendra Chourasia
Mineral Exploration and Consultancy Limited, India

Shrutika Wanjari
G.H. Raisoni Institute of Engineering and Technology, India

Mohammad Imran Khan
Jhulelal Institute of Technology, India

ABSTRACT

An important development in the field of traffic surveillance is enhanced video quality with ESRGAN, which provides law enforcement with unmatched clarity and accuracy when observing traffic, vehicles, and drivers. Through a significant increase in the resolution and clarity of traffic camera footage, ESRGAN provides authorities with images that are clearer and more comprehensive than those produced by traditional surveillance technologies. This upgrade not only improves the footage's visual quality but also increases the effectiveness of monitoring systems by giving them a better understanding of the dynamic environment of roads. ESRGAN enables authorities to detect and respond to events quickly and decisively by giving them a sharper and more comprehensive picture of road accidents. To put it briefly, enhanced video quality using ESRGAN is essentially a paradigm shift in traffic surveillance that raises the bar for monitoring system capabilities.

DOI: 10.4018/979-8-3693-3597-0.ch025

INTRODUCTION

Images play an indispensable role in both personal and professional spheres, serving as a vital medium for accessing, conveying, and disseminating information. As society undergoes continuous economic development and advancements in science and technology, there is a gradual improvement in living standards, accompanied by an increasing demand for higher image resolution. High-resolution (HR) images, characterized by greater pixel density and finer texture details compared to low-resolution (LR) images, are highly sought after. While hardware upgrades offer one avenue for obtaining HR images, this approach comes with significant drawbacks. Firstly, hardware specifications constantly evolve, leading to the need for frequent and often costly investments in new equipment. Secondly, hardware devices inherently lack the capability to enhance LR images, limiting their utility.

To address these challenges, the concept of image super-resolution (SR) reconstruction emerges as a powerful solution. The fundamental objective of SR reconstruction is to surmount the limitations imposed by hardware constraints, enabling the enlargement of images and the restoration of high-frequency details that may have been lost during the imaging process. By leveraging sophisticated algorithms and computational techniques, SR reconstruction techniques empower users to enhance LR images, effectively bridging the gap between the available hardware capabilities and the growing demand for higher image quality. The generative adversarial network (GAN) represents a ground-breaking advancement in the field of deep learning, introduced by Goodfellow and his colleagues in 2014. This innovative model has emerged as a powerful tool for unsupervised learning, particularly adept at capturing complex distributions in data. Since its inception, the GAN framework has captivated widespread interest and enthusiasm across academic and industrial domains alike.

Over the years, extensive research and development efforts have propelled GAN technology forward, leading to significant strides in both theoretical understanding and practical implementation. Researchers have delved into various aspects of GANs, refining algorithms, exploring novel architectures, and uncovering new insights into their capabilities and limitations. This continuous evolution has contributed to the maturation of GANs as a versatile and robust framework for a wide range of applications.

In particular, GANs have found myriad applications in the realms of computer vision and human-computer interaction. In computer vision, GANs excel at tasks such as image generation, image translation, and image enhancement. These capabilities have paved the way for advancements in areas such as image synthesis, style transfer, and image super-resolution. Moreover, GANs have proven invaluable in enhancing human-computer interaction, enabling more natural and intuitive interfaces through techniques like image generation and manipulation. The versatility and efficacy of GANs have spurred their adoption across diverse fields, including art, entertainment, healthcare, and beyond. From generating lifelike images and videos to facilitating creative expression and enabling medical image analysis, GANs continue to push the boundaries of what is possible in artificial intelligence.

While super-resolution (SR) techniques have made significant strides in enhancing image quality, particularly in controlled settings, challenges persist when it comes to real-world scenes. Despite the formidable learning capabilities of generative adversarial networks (GANs), there has been a notable gap in research dedicated to thoroughly examining the implementation of GAN-based super-resolution in recent years. This lack of comprehensive analysis hampers the understanding and advancement of GAN-driven SR techniques. In this study, we depart from the conventional approach of providing a broad overview of SR based on deep learning, which is common in many existing papers. Instead, our focus is on offering an in-depth exploration and analysis specifically tailored to super-resolution reconstruction techniques leveraging GANs. By narrowing our scope to this specific subset of SR methods, we aim to address the dearth of comprehensive research in this area and provide valuable insights into the capabilities and limitations of GAN-based SR approaches.

Unlike most existing works that may touch upon GANs as one of several SR methodologies, our article takes a dedicated and meticulous approach to examining the intricacies of GAN-driven super-resolution. We delve into the underlying principles, architectures, training strategies, and performance evaluations of GAN-based SR models, offering a thorough examination of their effectiveness and potential applications.

By focusing exclusively on GAN-based super-resolution, we can provide a deeper understanding of the unique contributions, challenges, and opportunities associated with this particular approach. Through detailed analysis and empirical assessments, we aim to elucidate the nuances of GAN-driven SR techniques and foster further research and development in this burgeoning field. By narrowing our focus and providing detailed insights into GAN-based SR, we contribute to the advancement of image enhancement technologies and pave the way for future innovations in this domain. In the context of image generation, enhancing the realism of textures is a crucial objective to produce visually compelling and lifelike results. In a study referenced as [60], the authors proposed an enhanced iteration of the Enhanced Super-Resolution Generative Adversarial Network (ESRGAN) model, referred to as ESRGAN+. This upgraded version aimed to further improve the fidelity of generated images, particularly in terms of texture realism. The ESRGAN model builds upon the architecture of the original ESRGAN, which already demonstrated impressive capabilities in generating high-quality images. However, to address certain limitations and further refine the output, the authors introduced several enhancements.

One notable enhancement introduced in ESRGAN+ is the incorporation of residual blocks between each pair of layers in the Residual in Residual Dense Block (RRDB) architecture. Residual blocks are a fundamental component in deep neural networks, allowing for the efficient propagation of gradients during training. By inserting residual blocks at intermediate stages within the RRDB architecture, ESRGAN+ aims to facilitate the learning of more intricate textures and finer details, ultimately leading to more realistic image generation. Additionally, ESRGAN+ employs the application of random Gaussian noise as a post-processing step to enhance the generated results further. Random Gaussian noise is a type of additive noise that introduces subtle variations and imperfections into the generated images, mimicking the natural variability found in real-world textures. This noise injection technique helps to add a sense of randomness and complexity to the textures, contributing to the overall realism of the generated images.

LITERATURE SURVEY

Numerous industries, including public safety, medical imaging, remote sensing, image compression, and others, have found extensive uses for high-resolution images. Reconstructing a given low-resolution image into a comparable high-resolution image using a particular technique is the main goal of super-resolution image reconstruction. The rapid development of generative adversarial networks (GANs) has ushered in a new era of improvement in image super-resolution reconstruction. Regrettably, there haven't been many thorough attempts to compile the developments in generative adversarial network-based super-resolution reconstruction (Wang et al., 2023). This thorough analysis sheds light on the many energy-saving methods used in public safety IoT network design. On the other hand, the widespread installation of IoT devices in diverse settings (Gupta et al., 2023). Industry 4.0 encompasses a range of technologies that are applied in the real world to meet people's needs, such as analytics and big data, which offer sophisticated capabilities for storing and processing vast volumes of data. This process enhances internal decision-making (Kumar et al., 2023). To address the lack of data, this work employed deep transfer learning (DTL) to construct an ensemble of three CNN models. A dataset of CXR images is gathered, pre-processed, enhanced using threshold, an LNB feature is extracted, data is augmented to create a new data point, and the dataset is divided into two (Mannepalli et al., 2023). The approach for building a system with a learning strategy based on the DCNN algorithm is presented in this paper. For learning and evaluating all samples and new inputs in a scheme, the Deep Learning (DL) approach is provided. The results of many competitions using CNN (Convolutional Neural Networks) are getting better and are now being studied (Mannepalli et al., 2023). In an era where security remains paramount, particularly for marginalized populations such as women, this chapter examines the potent combination of crime mapping, hotspot analysis, and geographic information systems (GIS) to enhance and fortify security (Chourasia et al., 2024).

With the introduction of new technologies, automation systems become more complicated to design, necessitating the need for self-sufficient and scalable solutions that provide complete control over programming and monitoring capabilities. This paper investigates the convergence of Android-based home automation systems and Enhanced Residual Super-Resolution Generative Adversarial Networks (ERSGAN) for video enhancement (Dubey et al., 2023).

ESRGAN elevates single image super-resolution by refining SRGAN's network architecture, adversarial loss, and perceptual loss. Through RRDB integration, relativistic GAN principles, and enhanced artifacts, surpassing SRGAN in visual quality. ESRGAN's triumph in the PIRM2018-SR Challenge (region 3) underscores its superior performance, securing the top spot with the highest perceptual index (Wang et al., 2018).

In his research, author presents Real-ESRGAN, a modified version of ESRGAN designed for practical image restoration tasks. Real-ESRGAN tackles the challenge of fixing real-world blurry or low-quality images by training on computer-generated data. It improves accuracy by mimicking complex real-world image issues and deals with common problems like ringing and overshooting. Real-ESRGAN also uses a smarter discriminator to better judge image quality during training, leading to more stable results. In tests, Real-ESRGAN outperformed previous methods when fixing various real images. It also offers fast ways to create training data on-the-fly (Wang et al., 2021).

Authors study introduces A-ESRGAN, a novel GAN model tailored for blind image super-resolution tasks. Unlike previous approaches that mainly focus on improving generator structures, A-ESRGAN emphasizes enhancing the discriminative ability to boost visual performance. It features a unique attention U-Net based, multi-scale discriminator, which is a first-of-its-kind approach in solving blind SR problems. The paper provides insights into how the multi-scale attention U-Net improves performance. Experimental results showcase the superior performance of A-ESRGAN compared to existing methods, both quantitatively and visually (Wei, Z et al., 2023).

Paper presents a visualization approach for large-scale volume data, addressing challenges in data reduction without sacrificing important features. The proposed method employs enhanced super-resolution generative adversarial networks (ESRGAN) in a reduction-restoration workflow. Firstly, it utilizes an error-controlled data reduction technique based on octrees to minimize memory usage. Then, it generates rendered images from the reduced data, preserving essential details. Finally, ESRGAN is applied to restore lost features in the rendered images, ensuring feature-lossless visualization. Experimental results demonstrate the effectiveness of the approach in achieving both data reduction and visual restoration goals (Jiao et al., 2023).

This paper introduces Dual Perceptual Loss (DP Loss) as a method to enhance single image super-resolution reconstruction. DP Loss addresses the limitations of per-pixel difference loss and improves upon existing perceptual loss by leveraging both VGG and ResNet features simultaneously. By combining these features, DP Loss effectively enhances the reconstruction quality of images, resulting in superior performance compared to state-of-the-art methods (Song et al., 2022).

PROPOSED WORK

In proposed work, firstly create the runtime environment. Use google colab and change the runtime type to GPU or TPU to speed up the algorithm execution. This will enhance the performance of the model. Then, we create a ESRGAN model by importing Real ESRGAN python library and loads pre-trained weights for the chosen scale.

RESULT AND DISCUSSION

Above code snippet imports necessary libraries, defines the device (GPU if available, otherwise CPU), selects a scale for the ESRGAN model (2x, 4x, or 8x), initializes the Real ESRGAN model with the specified scale, and loads pre-trained weights for the chosen scale.

Figure 3,4,5,6 shows the code snippet defines functions to upload and upscale images or `.tar` archives containing images. It handles both individual images and archives, extracts images from archives, upscales them using the previously defined RealESRGAN model, and saves the upscaled images or archives to the specified result folder. It also provides an interface to upload files interactively in Google Colab environment.

Figure 7 shows the original image of road accident uploaded by user.

Figure 8 shows the enhanced image of road accident after applying ESRGAN

FOR VIDEOS –

Figure 9 shows the real time road accident video captured by CCTV camera

Figure 10 shows the real time road accident video captured by CCTV camera after applying REAL ESRGAN.

ADVANTAGES OF PROPOSED SYSTEM

Utilizing Real-ESRGAN for enhanced video surveillance in public safety, particularly in the context of road accident prevention, offers a multifaceted array of advantages. Firstly, Real-ESRGAN significantly improves the quality of surveillance footage by generating high-resolution images from low-resolution inputs. This enhancement leads to clearer and more detailed visuals, which are crucial for accurate monitoring and analysis in video surveillance systems. By improving image quality, Real-ESRGAN enhances the accuracy of object detection algorithms, ensuring that potential hazards such as vehicles, pedestrians, or obstacles are identified with greater reliability. This reduces the likelihood of false alarms or missed incidents, thereby enhancing overall safety. Real-ESRGAN's ability to identify critical events, such as near misses or hazardous road conditions, enables timely intervention or alerts, contributing to enhanced

Figure 1.

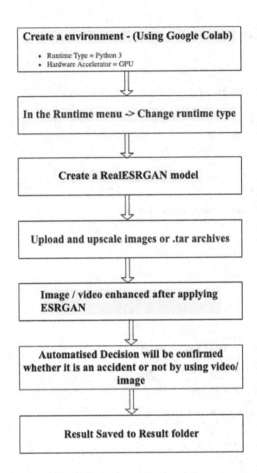

Figure 2.

public safety on the roads. Moreover, Real-ESRGAN facilitates increased surveillance coverage without the need for additional hardware or cameras, offering a cost-effective solution for improving public safety. Its adaptability and scalability to different surveillance scenarios ensure optimal performance across diverse real-world applications.

Figure 3.

☑ Upload and upscale images or .tar archives

```
#@title Upload and upscale images or .tar archives

import matplotlib.pyplot as plt
import os
from google.colab import files
import shutil
from io import BytesIO
import io
import tarfile

upload_folder = 'inputs'
result_folder = 'results'

os.makedirs(upload_folder, exist_ok=True)
os.makedirs(result_folder, exist_ok=True)

IMAGE_FORMATS = ('.png', '.jpg', '.jpeg', '.tiff', '.bmp', '.gif')
```

Figure 4.

```
def image_to_tar_format(img, image_name):
    buff = BytesIO()
    if '.png' in image_name.lower():
        img = img.convert('RGBA')
        img.save(buff, format='PNG')
    else:
        img.save(buff, format='JPEG')
    buff.seek(0)
    fp = io.BufferedReader(buff)
    img_tar_info = tarfile.TarInfo(name=image_name)
    img_tar_info.size = len(buff.getvalue())
    return img_tar_info, fp
```

Figure 5.

```
def process_tar(path_to_tar):
    processing_tar = tarfile.open(path_to_tar, mode='r')
    result_tar_path = os.path.join('results/', os.path.basename(path_to_tar))
    save_tar = tarfile.open(result_tar_path, 'w')

    for c, member in enumerate(processing_tar):
        print(f'{c}, processing {member.name}')

        if not member.name.endswith(IMAGE_FORMATS):
            continue

        try:
            img_bytes = BytesIO(processing_tar.extractfile(member.name).read())
            img_lr = Image.open(img_bytes, mode='r').convert('RGB')
        except Exception as err:
            print(f'Unable to open file {member.name}, skipping')
            continue

        img_sr = model.predict(np.array(img_lr))
        # adding to save_tar
        img_tar_info, fp = image_to_tar_format(img_sr, member.name)
        save_tar.addfile(img_tar_info, fp)

    processing_tar.close()
    save_tar.close()
    print(f'Finished! Archive saved to {result_tar_path}')
```

Figure 6.

```
def process_input(filename):
    if tarfile.is_tarfile(filename):
        process_tar(filename)
    else:
        result_image_path = os.path.join('results/', os.path.basename(filename))
        image = Image.open(filename).convert('RGB')
        sr_image = model.predict(np.array(image))
        sr_image.save(result_image_path)
        print(f'Finished! Image saved to {result_image_path}')

# upload files
uploaded = files.upload()
for filename in uploaded.keys():
    print('Processing:', filename)
    process_input(filename)
```

```
images-2.jpeg
• images-2.jpeg(image/jpeg) - 8727 bytes, last modified: n/a - 100% done
Saving images-2.jpeg to images-2 (1).jpeg
Processing: images-2 (1).jpeg
Finished! Image saved to results/images-2 (1).jpeg
```

Figure 7.

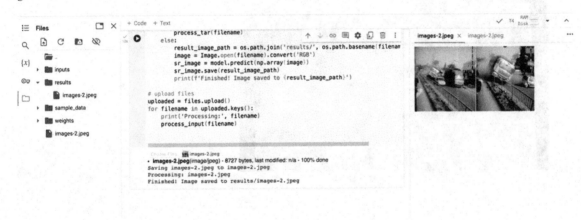

Additionally, the system promotes data-driven decision-making by providing high-quality visual insights into traffic patterns and accident hotspots. This enables stakeholders to implement targeted interventions and infrastructure improvements, further enhancing safety.

Furthermore, by focusing on enhancing image quality while preserving individuals' privacy, Real-ESRGAN ensures compliance with privacy regulations and ethical considerations. This makes it suitable for use in public surveillance settings where privacy concerns are paramount.

Figure 8.

Figure 9.

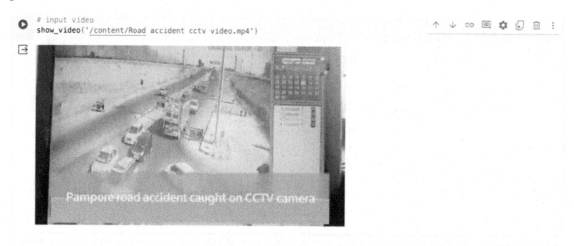

Figure 10.

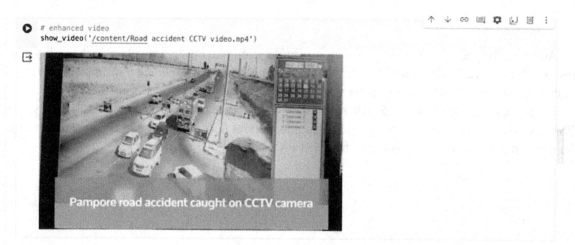

SOCIAL WELFARE OF PROPOSED SYSTEM

Implementing Real-ESRGAN for Enhanced Video Surveillance in Public Safety presents numerous social welfare benefits, particularly in the domain of road accident prevention:

1. **Enhanced Safety:** By utilizing Real-ESRGAN to augment video surveillance footage, authorities can significantly improve their ability to detect and respond to potential hazards on roadways. This heightened surveillance capability contributes directly to increased road safety, reducing the likelihood of accidents and enhancing overall public safety.
2. **Improved Incident Response:** Real-ESRGAN-enhanced video surveillance enables authorities to detect incidents such as accidents or dangerous road conditions more quickly and accurately. This rapid detection facilitates prompt response measures, such as deploying emergency services or implementing traffic control measures, which can help minimize the severity of accidents and mitigate their consequences.
3. **Prevention of Traffic Congestion:** By preemptively identifying and addressing potential causes of traffic congestion, such as accidents or road obstructions, Real-ESRGAN-powered surveillance systems help alleviate traffic congestion. This leads to smoother traffic flow, reducing travel time for commuters and minimizing economic losses associated with traffic delays.
4. **Enhanced Law Enforcement:** Real-ESRGAN enhances the clarity and detail of surveillance footage, aiding law enforcement agencies in the identification and apprehension of individuals engaged in illegal activities on roadways. This contributes to a safer and more secure public environment, deterring criminal behavior and promoting adherence to traffic laws.
5. **Improved Infrastructure Planning:** The comprehensive and detailed imagery provided by Real-ESRGAN-enhanced video surveillance can also be utilized for infrastructure planning and development purposes. Authorities can use this data to identify areas prone to accidents or congestion and implement targeted infrastructure improvements to enhance road safety and efficiency.

Overall, the adoption of Real-ESRGAN for enhanced video surveillance in public safety initiatives represents a significant step forward in accident prevention and road safety. By leveraging advanced image enhancement technology, this system contributes to the creation of safer roadways, improved incident response capabilities, and enhanced overall quality of life for communities.

FUTURE ENHANCEMENT

In order to further enhance the efficacy and adaptability of the project, several avenues for future development can be explored. Firstly, integrating real-time processing capabilities would enable the system to respond immediately to potential hazards or critical events identified in surveillance footage, thereby reducing response times and allowing for more proactive accident prevention measures. Additionally, the integration of Internet of Things (IoT) devices, such as smart traffic lights and road sensors, could provide a wealth of real-time data on road conditions and traffic flow, augmenting the system's situational awareness and decision-making capabilities. Advanced anomaly detection algorithms leveraging deep learning techniques could be implemented to identify unusual behaviors or events in surveillance footage, further enhancing the system's ability to detect and mitigate safety risks. Moreover, predictive analytics models could be developed to forecast potential accidents or traffic congestion based on historical data and environmental factors, enabling preemptive measures to be taken to improve road safety. Furthermore, expanding the surveillance system to incorporate multi-modal data sources and integrating crowd-sourced data would provide a more comprehensive and accurate assessment of road conditions and potential hazards. Finally, transitioning to a cloud-based architecture would facilitate scalability, flexibility, and accessibility, allowing for easier deployment and management of the surveillance system across different geographical locations and infrastructure setups. These enhancements, along with improvements to the user interface and continuous model training, would collectively contribute to a more effective and adaptive system for enhancing public safety and preventing road accidents.

CONCLUSION

In conclusion, the integration of Enhanced Super-Resolution Generative Adversarial Network (ESRGAN) technology marks a significant milestone in the realm of traffic surveillance, revolutionizing the way law enforcement agencies observe and monitor traffic activities. By elevating the resolution and clarity of traffic camera footage to unprecedented levels, ESRGAN empowers authorities with unparalleled clarity and accuracy in their surveillance endeavours. This enhancement not only enhances the visual quality of the footage but also augments the effectiveness of monitoring systems, providing a deeper understanding of the dynamic road environment. The enhanced video quality facilitated by ESRGAN enables authorities to identify potential dangers or events on the road with greater ease and precision. Minute details such as traffic signs, road markings, and vehicle attributes are depicted with previously unheard-of clarity, facilitating more precise calculation and judgment. Moreover, the increased accuracy of monitoring systems powered by ESRGAN-enhanced video feeds enhances the overall effectiveness of traffic surveillance operations. ESRGAN enables authorities to detect and respond to events swiftly and decisively, offering a sharper and more comprehensive picture of road conditions. This improved situational awareness allows for proactive regulation of traffic flow and ensures the safety of road users in various scenarios, including accidents, traffic congestion, roadblocks, and adverse weather conditions. In essence, the adoption of ESRGAN for enhanced video quality represents a paradigm shift in traffic surveillance, setting a new standard for monitoring system capabilities. By providing finer, more detailed imagery of roadways, vehicles, and drivers, ESRGAN contributes to enhanced situational awareness, improved incident detection, and ultimately, safer roads for both road users and communities.

REFERENCES

Chourasia, H., & Ponnusamy, S. (2024). Crime Mapping and Hotspot Analysis: Enhancing Women's Safety Through GIS. In AI Tools and Applications for Women's Safety (pp. 36-50). IGI Global.

Dubey, P., Chourasia, H., & Ghode, S. (2023, May). A Novel Approach to Degin Home Automation using IoT Applications. In *2023 International Conference on Advancement in Computation & Computer Technologies (InCACCT)* (pp. 801-806). IEEE. 10.1109/InCACCT57535.2023.10141754

Gupta, S. K., Patel, S., Mannepalli, P. K., & Gangrade, S. (2023). Designing Dense-Healthcare IOT Networks for Industry 4.0 Using AI-Based Energy Efficient Reinforcement Learning Protocol. In *Industry 4.0 and Healthcare: Impact of Artificial Intelligence* (pp. 37–58). Springer Nature Singapore. doi:10.1007/978-981-99-1949-9_3

Jiao, C., Bi, C., Yang, L., Wang, Z., Xia, Z., & Ono, K. (2023). ESRGAN-based visualization for large-scale volume data. *Journal of Visualization / the Visualization Society of Japan*, 26(3), 649–665. doi:10.1007/s12650-022-00891-2

Kumar Kethavarapu, U., Kumar Mannepalli, P., Lakshma Reddy, B., Siva Prasad, P., Mishra, A., & Nagavarapu, S. (2023). Artificial Intelligence Based Querying of Healthcare Data Processing. In *Industry 4.0 and Healthcare: Impact of Artificial Intelligence* (pp. 173–184). Springer Nature Singapore. doi:10.1007/978-981-99-1949-9_9

Mannepalli, P. K., Kalyani, P., Khan, S. A., Ghodichor, V. N., & Singh, P. (2023, March). An Early Detection of Pneumonia in CXR Images using Deep Learning Techniques. In *2023 International Conference on Innovative Data Communication Technologies and Application (ICIDCA)* (pp. 1029-1036). IEEE. 10.1109/ICIDCA56705.2023.10100230

Mannepalli, P. K., Kushwaha, D. S., Kalamdhar, S., Nagrale, V., & Rajpoot, V. (2023, March). Face Recognition Based on Cascade Classifier Using Deep Learning. In *2023 1st International Conference on Innovations in High Speed Communication and Signal Processing (IHCSP)* (pp. 63-68). IEEE. 10.1109/IHCSP56702.2023.10127172

Song, J., Yi, H., Xu, W., Li, X., Li, B., & Liu, Y. (2022). *Dual perceptual loss for single image super-resolution using esrgan.* arXiv preprint arXiv:2201.06383.

Wang, X., Sun, L., Chehri, A., & Song, Y. (2023). A Review of GAN-Based Super-Resolution Reconstruction for Optical Remote Sensing Images. *Remote Sensing (Basel)*, 15(20), 5062. doi:10.3390/rs15205062

Wang, X., Xie, L., Dong, C., & Shan, Y. (2021). Real-esrgan: Training real-world blind super-resolution with pure synthetic data. In *Proceedings of the IEEE/CVF international conference on computer vision* (pp. 1905-1914). IEEE. 10.1109/ICCVW54120.2021.00217

Wang, X., Yu, K., Wu, S., Gu, J., Liu, Y., Dong, C., & Change Loy, C. (2018). Esrgan: Enhanced super-resolution generative adversarial networks. In *Proceedings of the European conference on computer vision (ECCV) workshops*. IEEE.

Wei, Z., Huang, Y., Chen, Y., Zheng, C., & Gao, J. (2023, November). A-ESRGAN: Training real-world blind super-resolution with attention U-Net Discriminators. In *Pacific Rim International Conference on Artificial Intelligence* (pp. 16-27). Singapore: Springer Nature Singapore.

Compilation of References

Vasek, M., & Moore, T. (2018). Analyzing the bitcoin ponzi scheme ecosystem. In *Proceedings of the International Conference on Financial CryptoFigurey and Data Security,* (pp. 101–112). Springer.

Zheng, Z., Xie, S., Dai, H., Chen, X., & Wang, H. (2017). An overview of blockchain technology: Architecture, consensus, and future trends. In *Proceedings of the IEEE International Congress on Big Data.* IEEE. 10.1109/BigDataCongress.2017.85

Zheng, Z., Xie, S., Dai, H., Chen, X., & Wang, H. (2018). Blockchain challenges and opportunities: A survey. *International Journal of Web and Grid Services, 14*(4), 352–375. doi:10.1504/IJWGS.2018.095647

Zouina, M., & Outtaj, B. (2017). A novel lightweight url phishing detection system using svm and similarity index. *Human-centric Computing and Information Sciences, 7*(1), 17. doi:10.1186/s13673-017-0098-1

Gupta, A., Dwivedi, D. N., & Shah, J. (2023). Overview of Money Laundering. In: Artificial Intelligence Applications in Banking and Financial Services. Future of Business and Finance. Springer, Singapore. doi:10.1007/978-981-99-2571-1_1

Gupta, A., Dwivedi, D. N., & Shah, J. (2023). Financial Crimes Management and Control in Financial Institutions. In: Artificial Intelligence Applications in Banking and Financial Services. Future of Business and Finance. Springer, Singapore. doi:10.1007/978-981-99-2571-1_2

Gupta, A., Dwivedi, D. N., & Shah, J. (2023). Overview of Technology Solutions. In: Artificial Intelligence Applications in Banking and Financial Services. Future of Business and Finance. Springer, Singapore. doi:10.1007/978-981-99-2571-1_3

Mishra, G. (2024). *7 Critical Uses of Synthetic Data in Balancing AI Innovation and privacy.* CDO. https://www.cdomagazine.tech/opinion-analysis/7-critical-uses-of-synthetic-data-in-balancing-ai-innovation-and-privacy.

Gupta, A., Dwivedi, D. N., & Shah, J. (2023). Data Organization for an FCC Unit. In: Artificial Intelligence Applications in Banking and Financial Services. Future of Business and Finance. Springer, Singapore. doi:10.1007/978-981-99-2571-1_4

Gupta, A., Dwivedi, D. N., & Shah, J. (2023). Planning for AI in Financial Crimes. In: Artificial Intelligence Applications in Banking and Financial Services. Future of Business and Finance. Springer, Singapore. doi:10.1007/978-981-99-2571-1_5

Gupta, A., Dwivedi, D. N., & Shah, J. (2023). Applying Machine Learning for Effective Customer Risk Assessment. In: Artificial Intelligence Applications in Banking and Financial Services. Future of Business and Finance. Springer, Singapore. doi:10.1007/978-981-99-2571-1_6

Chen, W. (2020). Phishing Scam Detection on Ethereum: Towards Financial Security for Blockchain Ecosystem. *IJACI.*

Rani, R., Arora, S., Verma, V., Mahajan, S., & Sharma, R. (2024). Enhancing facial expression recognition through generative adversarial networks-based augmentation. *International Journal of System Assurance Engineering and Management, 15*(3), 1037–10561. doi:10.1007/s13198-023-02186-7

Gupta, A., Dwivedi, D. N., & Shah, J. (2023). Artificial Intelligence-Driven Effective Financial Transaction Monitoring. In: Artificial Intelligence Applications in Banking and Financial Services. Future of Business and Finance. Springer, Singapore. doi:10.1007/978-981-99-2571-1_7

Gupta, A., Dwivedi, D. N., & Shah, J. (2023). Machine Learning-Driven Alert Optimization. In: Artificial Intelligence Applications in Banking and Financial Services. Future of Business and Finance. Springer, Singapore. doi:10.1007/978-981-99-2571-1_8

Gupta, A., Dwivedi, D. N., & Shah, J. (2023). Applying Artificial Intelligence on Investigation. In: Artificial Intelligence Applications in Banking and Financial Services. Future of Business and Finance. Springer, Singapore. doi:10.1007/978-981-99-2571-1_9

Gupta, A., Dwivedi, D. N., & Shah, J. (2023). Ethical Challenges for AI-Based Applications. In: Artificial Intelligence Applications in Banking and Financial Services. Future of Business and Finance. Springer, Singapore. doi:10.1007/978-981-99-2571-1_10

Gupta, A., Dwivedi, D. N., & Shah, J. (2023). Setting up a Best-In-Class AI-Driven Financial Crime Control Unit (FCCU). In: Artificial Intelligence Applications in Banking and Financial Services. Future of Business and Finance. Springer, Singapore. doi:10.1007/978-981-99-2571-1_11

Gupta, A., Dwivedi, D.N. & Jain, A. (2021). Threshold fine-tuning of money laundering scenarios through multi-dimensional optimization techniques. *Journal of Money Laundering Control*. doi:10.1108/JMLC-12-2020-0138

Gupta, A., Dwivedi, D.N., Shah, J. & Jain, A. (2021). Data quality issues leading to sub optimal machine learning for money laundering models. *Journal of Money Laundering Control*. doi:10.1108/JMLC-05-2021-0049

Dwivedi, D., & Vemareddy, A. (2023). Sentiment Analytics for Crypto Pre and Post Covid: Topic Modeling. In A. R. Molla, G. Sharma, P. Kumar, & S. Rawat (Eds.), Lecture Notes in Computer Science: Vol. 13776. *Distributed Computing and Intelligent Technology*. ICDCIT 2023. Springer. doi:10.1007/978-3-031-24848-1_21

Dwivedi, D. N., & Mahanty, G. (2024). AI-Powered Employee Experience: Strategies and Best Practices. In M. Rafiq, M. Farrukh, R. Mushtaq, & O. Dastane (Eds.), *Exploring the Intersection of AI and Human Resources Management* (pp. 166–181). IGI Global. doi:10.4018/979-8-3693-0039-8.ch009

Dwivedi, D. N. (2024). The Use of Artificial Intelligence in Supply Chain Management and Logistics. In D. Sharma, B. Bhardwaj, & M. Dhiman (Eds.), *Leveraging AI and Emotional Intelligence in Contemporary Business Organizations* (pp. 306–313). IGI Global. doi:10.4018/979-8-3693-1902-4.ch018

De Xu, Q. (2022). The Systems Approach and Design Path of Electronic Bidding Systems Based on Blockchain Technology. MDPI.

Verma, V., & Rani, R. (2021). Facial Expression Recognition: A Comprehensive Review. *Journal of Artificial Intelligence and Systems, 21*(3), 184–1973.

Dwivedi, D. N., Mahanty, G., & Vemareddy, A. (2022). How Responsible Is AI?: Identification of Key Public Concerns Using Sentiment Analysis and Topic Modeling. [IJIRR]. *International Journal of Information Retrieval Research, 12*(1), 1–14. doi:10.4018/IJIRR.298646

Dwivedi, D. N., Mahanty, G., & Pathak, Y. K. (2023). AI Applications for Financial Risk Management. In M. Irfan, M. Elmogy, M. Shabri Abd. Majid, & S. El-Sappagh (Eds.), The Impact of AI Innovation on Financial Sectors in the Era of Industry 5.0 (pp. 17-31). IGI Global. doi:10.4018/979-8-3693-0082-4.ch002

Dwivedi, D. N., Pandey, A. K., & Dwivedi, A. D. (2023). Examining the emotional tone in politically polarized Speeches in India: An In-Depth analysis of two contrasting perspectives. *SOUTH INDIA JOURNAL OF SOCIAL SCIENCES, 21*(2), 125-136. https://journal.sijss.com/index.php/home/article/view/65

Ziska Fields, I. G. I. (Ed.). (2023). *Human Creativity vs. Machine Creativity: Innovations and Challenges." Multidisciplinary Approaches in AI, Creativity, Innovation, and Green Collaboration* (pp. 19–28). IGI Global. doi:10.4018/978-1-6684-6366-6.ch002

Dwivedi, D., Batra, S., & Pathak, Y. K. (2023). A machine learning based approach to identify key drivers for improving corporate's esg ratings. *Journal of Law and Sustainable Development, 11*(1), e0242. doi:10.37497/sdgs.v11i1.242

Dwivedi, D. N., Tadoori, G., & Batra, S. (2023). Impact of women leadership and ESG ratings and in organizations: A time series segmentation study. *Academy of Strategic Management Journal, 22*(S3), 1–6.

Pozzi, F. A., & Dwivedi, D. (2023). ESG and IoT: Ensuring Sustainability and Social Responsibility in the Digital Age. In S. Tiwari, F. Ortiz-Rodríguez, S. Mishra, E. Vakaj, & K. Kotecha (Eds.), *Artificial Intelligence: Towards Sustainable Intelligence. AI4S 2023. Communications in Computer and Information Science* (Vol. 1907). Springer. doi:10.1007/978-3-031-47997-7_2

Dwivedi, D. N., & Batra, S. (2024). Case Studies in Big Data Analysis: A Novel Computer Vision Application to Detect Insurance Fraud. In D. Darwish (Ed.), *Big Data Analytics Techniques for Market Intelligence* (pp. 441–450). IGI Global. doi:10.4018/979-8-3693-0413-6.ch018

Dwivedi, D. N., Batra, S., & Pathak, Y. K. (2024). Enhancing Customer Experience: Exploring Deep Learning Models for Banking Customer Journey Analysis. In H. Sharma, A. Chakravorty, S. Hussain, & R. Kumari (Eds.), *Artificial Intelligence: Theory and Applications. AITA 2023. Lecture Notes in Networks and Systems* (Vol. 843). Springer. doi:10.1007/978-981-99-8476-3_39

Mahanty, G., Dwivedi, D. N., & Gopalakrishnan, B. N. (2021). The Efficacy of Fiscal Vs Monetary Policies in the Asia-Pacific Region: The St. Louis Equation Revisited. *Vision (Basel)*, (November). doi:10.1177/09722629211054148

Hasan Fahim, M. I. (2023). *Advancements in Facial Recognition Technology: Exploring OpenCV's Role in Enhancing Accuracy and Security*. GAO.

Soham, P. (2023). *Credit Card Fraud Detection Using Machine Learning and Blockchain.*

Dwivedi, D., & Patil, G. (2022). Lightweight Convolutional Neural Network for Land Use Image Classification. *Journal of Advanced Geospatial Science & Technology, 2*(1), 31–48. doi:10.11113/jagst.v2n1.31

Chikkamath, M., Dwivedi, D., Hirekurubar, R. B., & Thimmappa, R. (2023). Benchmarking of Novel Convolutional Neural Network Models for Automatic Butterfly Identification. In P. K. Shukla, K. P. Singh, A. K. Tripathi, & A. Engelbrecht (Eds.), *Computer Vision and Robotics. Algorithms for Intelligent Systems*. Springer., doi:10.1007/978-981-19-7892-0_27

Manjunath, C., Dwivedi, D. N., Thimmappa, R., & Vedamurthy, K. B. (2023). Detection and categorization of diseases in pearl millet leaves using novel convolutional neural network model. In *Future Farming* (Vol. 1, p. 41). Advancing Agriculture with Artificial Intelligence. doi:10.2174/9789815124729123010006

Dwivedi, D. N., & Gupta, A. (2022). Artificial intelligence-driven power demand estimation and short-, medium-, and long-term forecasting. In *Artificial Intelligence for Renewable Energy Systems* (pp. 231–242). Woodhead Publishing. doi:10.1016/B978-0-323-90396-7.00013-4

Dwivedi, D. N., & Mahanty, G. (2024). Unmasking the Shadows: Exploring Unethical AI Implementation. In S. Dadwal, S. Goyal, P. Kumar, & R. Verma (Eds.), *Demystifying the Dark Side of AI in Business* (pp. 185–200). IGI Global. doi:10.4018/979-8-3693-0724-3.ch012

Dwivedi, D. N., & Mahanty, G. (2024). Guardians of the Algorithm: Human Oversight in the Ethical Evolution of AI and Data Analysis. In R. Kumar, A. Joshi, H. Sharan, S. Peng, & C. Dudhagara (Eds.), *The Ethical Frontier of AI and Data Analysis* (pp. 196–210). IGI Global. doi:10.4018/979-8-3693-2964-1.ch012

Dwivedi, D. N., Mahanty, G., & Dwivedi, V. N. (2024). The Role of Predictive Analytics in Personalizing Education: Tailoring Learning Paths for Individual Student Success. In M. Bhatia & M. Mushtaq (Eds.), *Enhancing Education With Intelligent Systems and Data-Driven Instruction* (pp. 44–59). IGI Global. doi:10.4018/979-8-3693-2169-0.ch003

Dwivedi, D., Mahanty, G., & Dwivedi, A. D. (2024). Artificial Intelligence Is the New Secret Sauce for Good Governance. In O. Ogunleye (Ed.), *Machine Learning and Data Science Techniques for Effective Government Service Delivery* (pp. 94–113). IGI Global. doi:10.4018/978-1-6684-9716-6.ch004

Alkahtani, H. (2024). *Toward robust and privacy-enhanced facial recognition: A decentralized blockchain-based approach with GANs and deep learning.* Research Gate.

Bartoletti, M., Pes, B., & Serusi, S. (2018). Data mining for detecting bitcoin ponzi schemes. In *Proceedings of the Crypto Valley Conference on Blockchain Technology*, (pp. 75–84). IEEE. 10.1109/CVCBT.2018.00014

Chen, W., Zheng, Z., & Cui, J. (2018). Detecting ponzi schemes on ethereum: Towards healthier blockchain technology. In *Proceedings of the World Wide Web Conference (WWW2018)*, (pp. 1409–1418). International World Wide Web Conferences Steering Committee. 10.1145/3178876.3186046

Wang, J. (2021). *Improved Facial Expression Recognition Method Based on GAN.* Hindawi.

Chen, W., Zheng, Z., & Edith, C.-H. (2019). Ngai, Peilin Zheng, and Yuren Zhou. Exploiting blockchain data to detect smart ponzi schemes on ethereum. *IEEE Access : Practical Innovations, Open Solutions*, 7, 37575–37586. doi:10.1109/ACCESS.2019.2905769

Kalra, S., Goel, S., Dhawan, M., & Sharma, S. (2018). Zeus: Analyzing safety of smart contracts. In *Proceedings of the Network and Distributed System Security Symposium.* IEEE. 10.14722/ndss.2018.23082

Khonji, M., Iraqi, Y., & Jones, A. (2013). Phishing detection: A literature survey. *IEEE Communications Surveys and Tutorials*, 15(4), 2091–2121. doi:10.1109/SURV.2013.032213.00009

Ramalingam, D., & Chinnaiah, V.Devakunchari Ramalingam and Valliyammai Chinnaiah. (2018). Fake profile detection techniques in large-scale online social networks: A comprehensive review. *Computers & Electrical Engineering*, 65, 165–177. doi:10.1016/j.compeleceng.2017.05.020

Abadi, M., & Andersen, D. G. (2016). *Learning to protect communications with adversarial neural cryptography.* arXiv preprint arXiv:1610.06918.

Abadi, M., Chu, A., Goodfellow, I., McMahan, H. B., Mironov, I., Talwar, K., & Zhang, L. 2016. Deep learning with differential privacy. In *Proceedings of the 2016 ACM SIGSAC Conference on Computer and Communications Security.* ACM. 10.1145/2976749.2978318

Abro, G. (2018). *Prototyping IOT Based Smart Wearable Jacket Design for Securing the life of Coal Miners.* IEEE Xplore.

Acs, G., Melis, L., Castelluccia, C., & De Cristofaro, E. (2018). Differentially private mixture of generative neural networks. *IEEE Transactions on Knowledge and Data Engineering*, 31(6), 1109–1121. doi:10.1109/TKDE.2018.2855136

Agarap, A. F. M. (2018, February). A neural network architecture combining gated recurrent unit (GRU) and support vector machine (SVM) for intrusion detection in network traffic data. In *Proceedings of the 2018 10th international conference on machine learning and computing* (pp. 26-30). ACM. 10.1145/3195106.3195117

Aggarwal, A., Mittal, M., & Battineni, G. (2021). Generative adversarial network: An overview of theory and applications. *International Journal of Information Management Data Insights, 1*(1), 100004. doi:10.1016/j.jjimei.2020.100004

AïvodjiU.GambsS.TherT. (2019). GAMIN: An adversarial approach to black-box model inversion. arXiv:1909.11835.

Akansha, S., Reddy, G. S., & Kumar, C. N. S. V. (2022). User Product Recommendation System Using KNN-Means and Singular Value Decomposition. *2022 International Conference on Disruptive Technologies for Multi-Disciplinary Research and Applications (CENTCON)*, Bengaluru, India. 10.1109/CENTCON56610.2022.10051544

Akcora, C. G., Gel, Y. R., & Kantarcioglu, M. (2019). GAN-based synthetic data generation for anomaly detection. *Proceedings of the 28th International Joint Conference on Artificial Intelligence*. IEEE.

Alabrah, A. (2022). A novel study: GAN-based minority class balancing and machine-learning-based network intruder detection using chi-square feature selection. *Applied Sciences (Basel, Switzerland), 12*(22), 11662. doi:10.3390/app122211662

Albarakati, A. J., Boujoudar, Y., Azeroual, M., Eliysaouy, L., Kotb, H., Aljarbouh, A., Khalid Alkahtani, H., Mostafa, S. M., Tassaddiq, A., & Pupkov, A. (2022). Microgrid energy management and monitoring systems: A comprehensive review. *Frontiers in Energy Research, 10*, 1097858. doi:10.3389/fenrg.2022.1097858

Albluwi, A. I., & Liu, L. (2018). Semi-supervised learning with generative adversarial networks. *IEEE Access : Practical Innovations, Open Solutions, 6*, 2279–2300.

Aleroud, A., Shariah, M., Malkawi, R., Khamaiseh, S. Y., & Al-Alaj, A. (2023). A privacy-enhanced human activity recognition using GAN & entropy ranking of microaggregated data. *Cluster Computing*, 1–16.

Alhajjar, E., Maxwell, P., & Bastian, N. (2021). Adversarial machine learning in network intrusion detection systems. *Expert Systems with Applications, 186*, 115782. doi:10.1016/j.eswa.2021.115782

Aliferis, C. F., Tsamardinos, I., & Statnikov, A. (2003). HITON: A novel Markov blanket algorithm for optimal variable selection. In *Proceedings of the AMIA Annual Symposium*.

Ali, S., Li, Q., & Yousafzai, A. (2024). Block formed chain structured and federated learning-based intrusion detection approaches for edge-enabled industrial IoT networks: A survey. *Ad Hoc Networks, 152*, 103320. doi:10.1016/j.adhoc.2023.103320

Aljarbouh, A., Tsarev, R., Robles, A. S., Elkin, S., Gogoleva, I., Nikolaeva, I., & Varyan, I. (2022). Application of the K-medians Clustering Algorithm for Test Analysis in Elearning. In *Proceedings of the Computational Methods in Systems and Software* (pp. 249- 256). Cham: Springer International Publishing.

Alkasassbeh, M., & Baddar, S. A.-H. (2022, November). Intrusion detection systems: A state-of-the-art Taxonomy and survey. *Arabian Journal for Science and Engineering*, 1–44. doi:10.1007/s13369-22- 07412-1

AloufiR.HaddadiH.BoyleD. (2019). Emotionless: Privacy-preserving speech analysis for voice assistants. arXiv:1908.03632.

Alqahtani, H., Kavakli-Thorne, M., & Kumar, G. (2021). Applications of generative adversarial networks (gans): An updated review. *Archives of Computational Methods in Engineering, 28*(2), 525–552. doi:10.1007/s11831-019-09388-y

Al-Rubaie, M., & Morris Chang, J. (2019). Privacy-preserving machine learning: Threats and solutions. *IEEE Security and Privacy, 17*(2), 49–58. doi:10.1109/MSEC.2018.2888775

Alsaggaf, W. A., Mehmood, I., Khairullah, E. F., Alhuraiji, S., Sabir, M. F. S., Alghamdi, A. S., & Abd El-Latif, A. A. (2021). A smart surveillance system for uncooperative gait recognition using cycle consistent generative adversarial networks (CCGANs). *Computational Intelligence and Neuroscience, 2021,* 2021. doi:10.1155/2021/3110416 PMID:34691168

Alshahrani, E., Alghazzawi, D., Alotaibi, R., & Rabie, O. (2022). Adversarial attacks against supervised machine learning based network intrusion detection systems. *PLoS One, 17*(10), e0275971. doi:10.1371/journal.pone.0275971 PMID:36240162

Alshinina, R. A., & Elleithy, K. M. (2018). A highly accurate deep learning based approach for developing wireless sensor network middleware. *IEEE Access : Practical Innovations, Open Solutions, 6,* 29885–29898. doi:10.1109/AC-CESS.2018.2844255

Amin, M., Shah, B., Sharif, A., Ali, T., Kim, K.-I., & Anwar, S. (2022). Android malware detection through generative adversarial networks. *Transactions on Emerging Telecommunications Technologies, 33*(2), e3675. doi:10.1002/ett.3675

Andresini, G., Appice, A., De Rose, L., & Malerba, D. (2021). GAN augmentation to deal with imbalance in imaging-based intrusion detection. *Future Generation Computer Systems, 123,* 108–127. doi:10.1016/j.future.2021.04.017

Ankitha, B., Srikanth, C., Venkatesh, D., Badrinath, D., Aditya, G., & Agnes, S. A. (2023), April. Enhancing the resolution of Brain MRI images using Generative Adversarial Networks (GANs). In *2023 International Conference on Computational Intelligence and Sustainable Engineering Solutions (CISES)* (pp. 19-25). IEEE.

Anthony, B., Kamaludin, A., Romli, A., Raffei, A. F. M., Phon, D. N. A. E., Abdullah, A., & Ming, G. L. (2022). Blended learning adoption and implementation in higher education: A theoretical and systematic review. *Technology, Knowledge and Learning,* 1-48.

Aoyama, T., Nakano, T., Koshijima, I., Hashimoto, Y., & Watanabe, K. (2017). On the complexity of cybersecurity exercises proportional to preparedness. *J. Disast. Res. 12* (5, SI), 5 . doi:10.20965/jdr.2017.p1081

Apolinario, F., Pardal, M. L., & Correia, M. (2018). S-Audit: Efficient Data Integrity Verification for Cloud Storage. *IEEE International Conference on Trust, Security and Privacy in Computing and Communications.* IEEE. 10.1109/TrustCom/BigDataSE.2018.00073

Aramkul, S., & Sugunnasil, P. (2023). Intelligent IoT framework with GAN-synthesized images for enhanced defect detection in manufacturing. *Computational Intelligence.*

Arivazhagu, U. V., Ilanchezhian, P., Meqdad, M. N., & Prithivirajan, V. (2023). Gated Capsule Networks for Intrusion Detection Systems to Improve the Security of WSN-IoT. *Ad-Hoc & Sensor Wireless Networks, 56.*

ArjovskyM.ChintalaS.BottouL. (2017). *Wasserstein GAN.* arXiv:1701.07875

Arjovsky, M., Chintala, S., & Bottou, L. (2017, July). Wasserstein generative adversarial networks. In *International conference on machine learning* (pp. 214-223). PMLR.

Arora, A., & Shantanu. (2022). A Review on Application of GANs in Cybersecurity Domain. *IETE Technical Review, 39*(2), 433–441. doi:10.1080/02564602.2020.1854058

Arshad, M. U., Kundu, A., Bertino, E., Ghafoor, A., & Kundu, C. (2018). Efficient and Scalable Integrity Verification of Data and Query Results for Graph Databases. *IEEE Transactions on Knowledge and Data Engineering, 30*(5), 866–879. doi:10.1109/TKDE.2017.2776221

Ashok Babu, P. (2023). An explainable deep learning approach for oral cancer detection. *Journal of Electrical Engineering & Technology.*

Ateniese, G., Burns, R., Curtmola, R., Herring, J., Kissner, L., Peterson, Z., & Song, D. (2007). Provable Data Posses-sion at Untrusted Stores. *Proc. 14th ACM Conf. Computer and Comm. Security.* IEEE.

Ateniese, G., Felici, G., Mancini, L., Spognardi, A., Villani, A., & Vitali, D. (2015). Hacking smart machines with smarter ones: How to extract meaningful data from machine learning classifiers. *International Journal of Security and Networks*, *10*(3), 137–150. doi:10.1504/IJSN.2015.071829

Atghaei, A., Ziaeinejad, S., & Rahmati, M. (2020). *Abnormal event detection in urban surveillance videos using GAN and transfer learning.* arXiv preprint arXiv:2011.09619.

AugensteinS.McMahanH. B.RamageD.RamaswamyS.KairouzP.ChenM.MathewsR.Agüera y ArcasB. (2019). Generative models for effective ML on private, decentralized datasets. arxiv:1911.06679

Aujla, G. S., Chaudhary, R., Kumar, N., Das, A. K., & Rodrigues, J. J. (2018). SecSVA: Secure Storage, Verification, and Auditing of Big Data in the Cloud Environment. *IEEE Communications Magazine*, *56*(1), 78–85. doi:10.1109/MCOM.2018.1700379

Avola, D., Cannistraci, I., Cascio, M., Cinque, L., Diko, A., Fagioli, A., Foresti, G. L., Lanzino, R., Mancini, M., Mecca, A., & Pannone, D. (2022). A novel GAN-based anomaly detection and localization method for aerial video surveillance at low altitude. *Remote Sensing (Basel)*, *14*(16), 4110. doi:10.3390/rs14164110

Aziz, M. A., Abawajy, J., & Chowdhury, M. (2013, December). The challenges of cloud technology adoption in e-government. In *2013 International Conference on Advanced Computer Science Applications and Technologies* (pp. 470-474). IEEE. 10.1109/ACSAT.2013.98

Bai, L., Huang, J., Wang, D., Zhu, D., Zhao, Q., Li, T., Zhou, X., & Xu, Y. (2023). Association of body mass index with mortality of sepsis or septic shock: An updated meta-analysis. *Journal of Intensive Care*, *11*(1), 27. doi:10.1186/s40560-023-00677-0 PMID:37400897

Baluja, S., & Fischer, I. (2019). *Adversarial transformation networks: Learning to generate adversarial examples.* arXiv preprint arXiv:1905.02175.

BalujaS.FischerI. (2017). *Adversarial transformation networks: Learning to generate adversarial examples.* arx-iv:1703.09387

BalujaS.FischerI. (2017). Adversarial transformation networks: Learning to generate. *adversarial examples.* 1703.09387.

Baskar, K., Venkatesan, G. K. D. P., & Sangeetha, S. (2019). A Survey of Workload Management Difficulties in the Public Cloud. *Intelligent Computing in Engineering: Select Proceedings of RICE.* Springer Singapore.

Baskar, K., Prasanna Venkatesan, G. K. D., Sangeetha, S., & Preethi, P. (2021). Privacy-Preserving Cost-Optimization for Dynamic Replication in Cloud Data Centers. *2021 International Conference on Advance Computing and Innovative Technologies in Engineering (ICACITE)*, Greater Noida, India. pp. 927-932, 10.1109/ICACITE51222.2021.9404573

BasuS.IzmailovR.MesterharmC. (2019). *Membership model inversion attacks for deep networks.* arxiv:1910.04257

Belenko, V., Chernenko, V., Kalinin, M., & Krundyshev, V. (2018, September). Evaluation of GAN applicability for intrusion detection in self-organizing networks of cyber physical systems. In *2018 International Russian Automation Conference (RusAutoCon)* (pp. 1-7). IEEE. 10.1109/RUSAUTOCON.2018.8501783

Belenko, V., Krundyshev, V., & Kalinin, M. (2018, September). Synthetic datasets generation for intrusion detection in VANET. In *Proceedings of the 11th international conference on security of information and networks* (pp. 1-6). ACM. 10.1145/3264437.3264479

Benaddi, H., Jouhari, M., Ibrahimi, K., Ben Othman, J., & Amhoud, E. M. (2022). Anomaly detection in industrial IoT using distributional reinforcement learning and generative adversarial networks. *Sensors (Basel)*, *22*(21), 8085. doi:10.3390/s22218085 PMID:36365782

Bertalmio, M., Sapiro, G., Caselles, V., & Ballester, C. (2000) Image inpainting. In: *Proceedings of the 27th annual conference on computer graphics and interactive techniques*. ACM Press/Addison-Wesley Publishing Co, (pp. 417–424). ACM.

BerthelotD.SchummT.MetzL. (2017). *BEGAN: Boundary equilibrium generative adversarial networks*. arxiv:1703.10717

Bhatt, V., Aggarwal, U., & Vinoth Kumar, C. N. S. (2022). *Sports Data Visualization and Betting*. 2022 International Conference on Smart Generation Computing, Communication and Networking (SMART GENCON), Bangalore, India. 10.1109/SMARTGENCON56628.2022.10083831

Bian, Y., Wang, J., Jun, J. J., & Xie, X. Q. (2019). Deep convolutional generative adversarial network (dcGAN) models for screening and design of small molecules targeting cannabinoid receptors. *Molecular Pharmaceutics*, *16*(11), 4451–4460. doi:10.1021/acs.molpharmaceut.9b00500 PMID:31589460

Biggio, B., Nelson, B., & Laskov, P. (2018). Adversarial machine learning for cybersecurity and privacy: A survey. *ACM Computing Surveys*, *52*(3), 1–36.

BontragerP.TogeliusJ.MemonN. D. (2017). *DeepMasterPrint: Generating fingerprints for presentation attacks*. arxiv:1705.07386

Boppana, T. K., & Bagade, P. (2023). GAN-AE: An unsupervised intrusion detection system for MQTT networks. *Engineering Applications of Artificial Intelligence*, *119*, 105805. doi:10.1016/j.engappai.2022.105805

Bouzeraib, W., Ghenai, A., & Zeghib, N. (2020, November). A Block formed chain structured Data packets Balance Using a Generative Adversarial Network Approach: Application to Smart House IDS. In *2020 International Conference on Advanced Aspects of Software Engineering (ICAASE)* (pp. 1-6). IEEE.

Brkić, K., Hrkać, T., Kalafatić, Z., & Sikirić, I. (2017). Face, hairstyle and clothing colour de-identification in video sequences. *IET Signal Processing*, *11*(9), 1062–1068. doi:10.1049/iet-spr.2017.0048

Brkic, K., Sikiric, I., Hrkac, T., & Kalafatic, Z. 2017. I know that person: Generative full body and face de-identification of people in images. In *Proceedings of the 2017 IEEE CVPR Workshops*. IEEE, Los Alamitos, CA, 1319--1328. 10.1109/CVPRW.2017.173

BrophyE.WangZ.WardT. E. (2019). *Quick and easy time series generation with established image-based GANs*. arXiv:1902.05624

Bryant, G. A. (2013). Animal signals and emotion in music: Coordinating affect across groups. *Frontiers in Psychology*, *4*. doi:10.3389/fpsyg.2013.00990 PMID:24427146

Cai, Z., Xiong, Z., Xu, H., Wang, P., Li, W., & Pan, Y. (2021). Generative adversarial networks: A survey toward private and secure applications. *ACM Computing Surveys*, *54*(6), 1–38. doi:10.1145/3459992

Cao, J., Hu, Y., Yu, B., He, R., & Sun, Z. (2019). 3D Aided Duet GANs for multi-view face image synthesis. *IEEE Transactions on Information Forensics and Security*, *14*(8), 2028–2042. doi:10.1109/TIFS.2019.2891116

Cao, L., He, W., Liu, Y., Guo, X., & Feng, T. (2017). An integrity verification scheme of completeness and zero-knowledge for multi-Cloud storage. *International Journal of Communication Systems*, *30*(16), 1–10. doi:10.1002/dac.3324

Cao, Y. J., Jia, L. L., Chen, Y. X., Lin, N., Yang, C., Zhang, B., Liu, Z., Li, X.-X., & Dai, H. H. (2018). Recent advances of generative adversarial networks in computer vision. *IEEE Access : Practical Innovations, Open Solutions, 7,* 14985–15006. doi:10.1109/ACCESS.2018.2886814

Chao, Y. W., Yang, C. Y., & Lai, S. H. (2020). Multi-path adversarial attack detection on image classification models. *Pattern Recognition, 101,* 107214.

Chaudhuri, K., Imola, J., & Machanavajjhala, A. (2019). Capacity bounded differential privacy. In *Advances in Neural Information Processing Systems* (Vol. 32, pp. 1–10). Curran Associates.

Chavdarova, T., & Fleuret, F. (2018). SGAN: An Alternative Training of Generative Adversarial Networks. *Proceedings of the IEEE Computer Society Conference on Computer Vision and Pattern Recognition,* (pp. 9407–9415). IEEE. 10.1109/CVPR.2018.00980

Chen, J., Konrad, J., & Ishwar, P. (2018). VGAN-based image representation learning for privacy-preserving facial expression recognition. In *Proceedings of the IEEE CVPR Workshops.* IEEE, Los Alamitos, CA. 10.1109/CVPRW.2018.00207

Chen, X., Duan, Y., Houthooft, R., Schulman, J., Sutskever, I., & Abbeel, P. (2016). InfoGAN: Interpretable representation learning by information maximizing generative adversarial nets. In *Proceedings of the 30th Conference on Neural Information Processing Systems.* IEEE.

Chen, X., Duan, Y., & Hui, P. (2021). Ethical considerations on using generative adversarial networks for network analysis. *IEEE Transactions on Network Science and Engineering.*

Chen, X., Kairouz, P., & Rajagopal, R. (2018). Understanding compressive adversarial privacy. In *Proceedings of the 2018 IEEE Conference on Decision and Control (CDC'18).* IEEE, Los Alamitos, CA. 10.1109/CDC.2018.8619455

Chen, X., Kairouz, P., & Rajagopal, R. (2018). Understanding Compressive adversarial privacy. *Proc. IEEE Conf. Decis. Control (CDC),* (pp. 6824–6831). IEEE.

Chen, Z., Li, J., Cheng, L., & Liu, X. (2023). Federated-WDCGAN: A federated smart meter data sharing framework for privacy preservation. *Applied Energy, 334,* 120711. doi:10.1016/j.apenergy.2023.120711

Choi, E., Biswal, S., Malin, B., Duke, J., Stewart, W. F., & Sun, J. 2017. Generating multi-label discrete patient records using generative adversarial networks. In *Proceedings of the Machine Learning for Healthcare Conference.* IEEE.

Chourasia, H., & Ponnusamy, S. (2024). Crime Mapping and Hotspot Analysis: Enhancing Women's Safety Through GIS. In AI Tools and Applications for Women's Safety (pp. 36-50). IGI Global.

Chourasiya, S., & Samanta, G. (2023). *Pegasus Spyware: A Vulnerable Behaviour-based Attack System.* 2023 2nd International Conference on Edge Computing and Applications (ICECAA).

Chourasiya, S., & Samanta, G. (2023). *Pegasus Spyware: A Vulnerable Behaviour-based Attack System.* 2023 2nd International Conference on Edge Computing and Applications. Research Gate.

Cook, A., Smith, R. G., Maglaras, L., & Janicke, H. (2017). SCIPS: Using experiential learning to raise cyber situational awareness in industrial control system. *International Journal of Cyber Warfare & Terrorism, 7*(2), 2. doi:10.4018/IJCWT.2017040101

Corrigan-Gibbs, H., Mu, W., Boneh, D., & Ford, B. (2013, November). Ensuring high-quality randomness in cryptographic key generation. In *Proceedings of the 2013 ACM SIGSAC conference on Computer & communications security* (pp. 685-696). ACM. 10.1145/2508859.2516680

Creswell, A., White, T., Dumoulin, V., Arulkumaran, K., Sengupta, B., & Bharath, A. A. (2018). Generative adversarial networks: An overview. *IEEE Signal Processing Magazine, 35*(1), 53–65. doi:10.1109/MSP.2017.2765202

Dai, J., Li, Q., Wang, H., & Liu, L. (2024). Understanding images of surveillance devices in the wild. *Knowledge-Based Systems, 284*, 111226. doi:10.1016/j.knosys.2023.111226

Dai, Z., Yang, Z., Yang, F., Cohen, W. W., & Salakhutdinov, R. R. (2017). Good semi-supervised learning that requires a bad GAN. In *Proceedings of the 31st Conference on Neural Information Processing Systems,* (pp. 6510–6520). IEEE.

Dai, Z., Yang, Z., Yang, F., Cohen, W. W., & Salakhutdinov, R. R. (2017). Good semi-supervised learning that requires a bad GAN. In *Proceedings of the 31st Conference on Neural Information Processing Systems*. ACM.

Daly, C. (2017). 'I'm not a robot': Google's anti-robot reCAPTCHA trains their robots to see,'' *AI Bus., Tech. Rep.*

Damer, N., Saladie, A. M., Braun, A., & Kuijper, A. (2018). MorGAN: Recognition vulnerability and attack detectability of face morphing attacks created by generative adversarial network. In *Proceedings of the 9th IEEE International Conference on Biometrics Theory, Applications, and Systems*. IEEE, Los Alamitos, CA. 10.1109/BTAS.2018.8698563

Dash, A., Ye, J., & Wang, G. (2024). A Review of Generative Adversarial Networks (GANs) and Its Applications in a Wide Variety of Disciplines: From Medical to Remote Sensing. *IEEE Access : Practical Innovations, Open Solutions, 12*, 18330–18357. doi:10.1109/ACCESS.2023.3346273

Day, A., & Karamouzas, I. (2024). A Study in Zucker: Insights on Interactions Between Humans and Small Service Robots. *IEEE Robotics and Automation Letters, 9*(3), 2471–2478. doi:10.1109/LRA.2024.3355641

de Araujo-Filho, P. F., Naili, M., Kaddoum, G., Fapi, E. T., & Zhu, Z. (2023). Unsupervised GAN-Based Intrusion Detection System Using Temporal Convolutional Networks and Self-Attention. *IEEE Transactions on Network and Service Management, 20*(4), 4951–4963. doi:10.1109/TNSM.2023.3260039

de Souza, V. L. T., Marques, B. A. D., Batagelo, H. C., & Gois, J. P. (2023). A review on generative adversarial networks for image generation. *Computers & Graphics*.

DebD.ZhangJ.JainA. K. (2019). *AdvFaces: Adversarial face synthesis*. arxiv:1908.05008

Deng, Z., He, C., Liu, Y., & Kim, K. C. (2019). Super-resolution reconstruction of turbulent velocity fields using a generative adversarial network-based artificial intelligence framework. *Physics of Fluids, 31*(12), 125111. doi:10.1063/1.5127031

Ding, S., Kou, L., & Wu, T. (2022). A GAN-based intrusion detection model for 5G enabled future metaverse. *Mobile Networks and Applications, 27*(6), 2596–2610. doi:10.1007/s11036-022-02075-6

Ding, W. (2024). A GAN-based security strategy for WSN networks based on honeypot algorithm. *Physical Communication, 62*, 102260. doi:10.1016/j.phycom.2023.102260

Ding, X., Fang, H., Zhang, Z., Choo, K.-K. R., & Jin, H. (2020). Privacy-preserving feature extraction via adversarial training. *IEEE Transactions on Knowledge and Data Engineering, 1*, 1–10. doi:10.1109/TKDE.2020.2997604

Ding, Y., Tan, F., Qin, Z., Cao, M., Choo, K. K. R., & Qin, Z. (2021). DeepKeyGen: A deep learning-based stream cipher generator for medical image encryption and decryption. *IEEE Transactions on Neural Networks and Learning Systems, 33*(9), 4915–4929. doi:10.1109/TNNLS.2021.3062754 PMID:33729956

Divya Mounika, R., & Naresh, R. (2020, December). The concept of Privacy and Standardization of Microservice Architectures in cloud computing. *European Journal of Molecular and Clinical Medicine, 7*(2), 5349–5370.

Dixit, P., & Silakari, S. (2021). Deep learning algorithms for cybersecurity applications: A technological and status review. *Computer Science Review, 39*, 100317. doi:10.1016/j.cosrev.2020.100317

Dodis, Y., & Smith, A. (2005, February). Entropic security and the encryption of high entropy messages. In *Theory of Cryptography Conference* (pp. 556-577). Berlin, Heidelberg: Springer Berlin Heidelberg. 10.1007/978-3-540-30576-7_30

Doelitzscher, F., Reich, C., Knahl, M., Passfall, A., & Clarke, N. (2012). An agent based business aware incident detection system for cloud environments. *Journal of Cloud Computing (Heidelberg, Germany), 1*(1), 9. doi:10.1186/2192-113X-1-9

DonahueC.McAuleyJ.J.PucketteM.S. (2018). Synthesizing audio with generative adversarial networks. arxiv:1802.04208

Du, B., Sun, X., Ye, J., Cheng, K., Wang, J., & Sun, L. (2021). GAN-based anomaly detection for multivariate time series using polluted training set. *IEEE Transactions on Knowledge and Data Engineering*.

Dubey, P., Chourasia, H., & Ghode, S. (2023, May). A Novel Approach to Degin Home Automation using IoT Applications. In *2023 International Conference on Advancement in Computation & Computer Technologies (InCACCT)* (pp. 801-806). IEEE. 10.1109/InCACCT57535.2023.10141754

Dumagpi, J. K., Jung, W. Y., & Jeong, Y. J. (2020). A new GAN-based anomaly detection (GBAD) approach for multi-threat object classification on large-scale x-ray security images. *IEICE Transactions on Information and Systems, 103*(2), 454–458. doi:10.1587/transinf.2019EDL8154

Dunmore, A., Jang-Jaccard, J., Sabrina, F., & Kwak, J. (2023). A comprehensive survey of generative adversarial networks (gans) in cybersecurity intrusion detection. *IEEE Access : Practical Innovations, Open Solutions, 11*, 76071–76094. doi:10.1109/ACCESS.2023.3296707

Durugkar, I., Gemp, I., & Mahadevan, S. (2019). Generative multi-adversarial networks. *5th International Conference on Learning Representations, ICLR 2017 - Conference Track Proceedings*. IEEE.

Dutta, I. K., Ghosh, B., Carlson, A., Totaro, M., & Bayoumi, M. (2020). Generative adversarial Networks in security: A survey. *Proc. 11th IEEE Annu. Ubiquitous Computer Electron. Mobile Commun. Conf. (UEMCON)*, (pp. 0399–0405). IEee. 10.1109/UEMCON51285.2020.9298135

Dutta, I. K., Ghosh, B., Carlson, A., Totaro, M., & Bayoumi, M. (2020, October). Generative adversarial networks in security: a survey. In *2020 11th IEEE Annual Ubiquitous Computing, Electronics & Mobile Communication Conference (UEMCON)* (pp. 0399-0405). IEEE.

Du, X., Chen, J., Yu, J., Li, S., & Tan, Q. (2024). Generative adversarial nets for unsupervised outlier detection. *Expert Systems with Applications, 236*, 121161. doi:10.1016/j.eswa.2023.121161

Dwork, C., McSherry, F., Nissim, K., & Smith, A. (2006). Calibrating noise to sensitivity in private data analysis. In *Proceedings of the Theory of Cryptography Conference*. ACM. 10.1007/11681878_14

Ekanayake, J., Gunarathne, T., & Qiu, J. (2010). Cloud technologies for bioinformatics applications. *IEEE Transactions on Parallel and Distributed Systems, 22*(6), 998–1011. doi:10.1109/TPDS.2010.178

El Ghoubach, I., & Ben Abbou, R. (2019). Fatiha Mrabti "A secure and efficient remote data auditing scheme for cloud storage". *Journal of King Saud University. Computer and Information Sciences*, 1–7.

Elmurzaevich, M. A. (2022, February). Use of cloud technologies in education. In Conference Zone (pp. 191-192).

Esteban, C., Hyland, S. L., & Rätsch, G. (2017). *Real-valued (medical) time series generation with recurrent conditional gans*. arXiv preprint arXiv:1706.02633.

EstebanC.HylandS.L.RätschG. 2017. Real-valued (medical) time series generation with recurrent conditional GANs. arxiv:1706.02633

Faisal, F., Mohammed, N., Leung, C. K., & Wang, Y. (2022, October). Generating privacy preserving synthetic medical data. In *2022 IEEE 9th International Conference on Data Science and Advanced Analytics (DSAA)* (pp. 1-10). IEEE. 10.1109/DSAA54385.2022.10032429

Fang, B., Yin, X., Tan, Y., Li, C., Gao, Y., Cao, Y., & Li, J. (2016). The contributions of cloud technologies to smart grid. *Renewable & Sustainable Energy Reviews, 59*, 1326–1331. doi:10.1016/j.rser.2016.01.032

Fang, J., Li, A., & Jiang, Q. (2019). GDAGAN: An anonymization method for graph data publishing using generative adversarial network. In *Proceedings of the 2019 6th International Conference on Information Science and Control Engineering*. IEEE. 10.1109/ICISCE48695.2019.00068

Fan, L. (2020, February). A survey of differentially private generative adversarial networks. In *The AAAI Workshop on Privacy-Preserving Artificial Intelligence* (Vol. 8). AAAI.

FedusW.GoodfellowI. J.DaiA. M. (2018). MaskGAN: Better text generation via filling in the _____. arxiv:1801.07736

Feily, M., Shahrestani, A., & Ramadass, S. (2009). A survey of botnet and botnet detection. In *Proceedings of the 2009 3rd International Conference on Emerging Security Information, Systems, and Technologies*. IEEE. 10.1109/SECURWARE.2009.48

Feng, J., & Jain, A. K. (2010). Fingerprint reconstruction: From minutiae to phase. *IEEE Transactions on Pattern Analysis and Machine Intelligence, 33*(2), 209–223. doi:10.1109/TPAMI.2010.77 PMID:21193805

Forouzan, B. A. (2007). *Cryptography & network security*. McGraw-Hill, Inc.

Fredrikson, M., Jha, S., & Ristenpart, T. (2015). Model inversion attacks that exploit confidence information and basic countermeasures. In *Proceedings of the 22nd ACM SIGSAC Conference on Computer and Communications Security*. ACM. 10.1145/2810103.2813677

Fredrikson, M., Lantz, E., Jha, S., Lin, S., Page, D., & Ristenpart, T. (2014). Privacy in pharmacogenetics: An end-to-end case study of personalized warfarin dosing. In *Proceedings of the 23rd USENIX Security Symposium*. ACM.

Frey, B. J., Hinton, G. E., & Dayan, P. (1996). Does the wake-sleep algorithm produce good density estimators? In *Advances in Neural Information Processing Systems* (pp. 661–667). MIT Press.

Fu, Z., Wang, F., & Cheng, X. (2020). The secure steganography for hiding images via GAN. *EURASIP Journal on Image and Video Processing, 2020*(1), 46. doi:10.1186/s13640-020-00534-2

G'ayratovich, E. N. (2022). The Theory of the Use of Cloud Technologies in the Implementation of Hierarchical Preparation of Engineers. *Eurasian Research Bulletin, 7*, 18–21.

Gan, W., Qi, Z., Wu, J., & Lin, J. C. W. (2023). Large language models in education: Vision and opportunities. arXiv preprint arXiv:2311.13160. doi:10.1109/BigData59044.2023.10386291

GaoY.PanY. (2020). *Improved detection of adversarial images using deep neural networks*. arXiv: 2007.05573.

Garg, S., Sharma, S., Dhariwal, S., Priya, W. D., Singh, M., & Ramesh, S. (2024). Human crowd behaviour analysis based on video segmentation and classification using expectation–maximization with deep learning architectures. *Multimedia Tools and Applications*, 1–23. doi:10.1007/s11042-024-18630-0

Gayathri, R. G., Sajjanhar, A., & Xiang, Y. (2024). Hybrid deep learning model using spcagan augmentation for insider threat analysis. *Expert Systems with Applications*, 123533.

Geetha, K., Srivani, A., Gunasekaran, S., Ananthi, S., & Sangeetha, S. (2023). *Geospatial Data Exploration Using Machine Learning.* 2023 4th International Conference on Smart Electronics and Communication (ICOSEC), Trichy, India. 10.1109/ICOSEC58147.2023.10275920

Gers, F. A., Schmidhuber, J., & Cummins, F. A. (2000). Learning to forget: Continual prediction with LSTM. *Neural Computation, 12*(10), 2451–2471. doi:10.1162/089976600300015015 PMID:11032042

Gong, D., Goh, O. S., Kumar, Y. J., Ye, Z., & Chi, W. (2020). Deepfake forensics, an ai-synthesized detection with deep convolutional generative adversarial networks. *International Journal (Toronto, Ont.), 9*(3), 2861–2870.

Goodfellow, I., Bengio, Y., Courville, A., & Bengio, Y. (2016). *Deep learning (Vol. 1).* MIT press Cambridge.

Goodfellow, I., Pouget-Abadie, J., Mirza, M., Xu, B., Warde-Farley, D., Ozair, S., & Bengio, Y. (2014). Generative adversarial nets. In Advances in neural information processing systems (pp. 2672-2680).

Goodfellow, J. (2014). Generative adversarial nets. Proc. Adv. Neural Inf. Process. Syst., 27, 1–14.

GoodfellowI. J.ShlensJ.SzegedyC. (2015). *Explaining and harnessing adversarial examples.* arxiv:1412.6572

Goodfellow, I., Pouget-Abadie, J., Mirza, M., Xu, B., Warde-Farley, D., Ozair, S., Courville, A., & Bengio, Y. (2014). Generative adversarial nets. In *Advances in Neural Information Processing Systems* (pp. 2672–2680). Curran Associates.

Goodfellow, I., Pouget-Abadie, J., Mirza, M., Xu, B., Warde-Farley, D., Ozair, S., Courville, A., & Bengio, Y. (2020). Generative adversarial networks. *Communications of the ACM, 63*(11), 139–144. doi:10.1145/3422622

Gorli, R. (2017). *Smart Jacket for Industrial Employee Health and Safety* (Vol. 2). IJSRCSEIT.

Gulrajani, I., Ahmed, F., Arjovsky, M., Dumoulin, V., & Courville, A. C. (2017). Improved training of Wasserstein GANs. In Advances in Neural Information Processing Systems. ACM.

Guo, C., Luo, N., Bhuiyan, M. Z. A., Jie, Y., Chen, Y., Feng, B., & Alam, M. (2018). Key-aggregate authentication cryptosystem for data sharing in dynamic cloud storage. *Future Generation Computer Systems, 84*, 190–199. doi:10.1016/j.future.2017.07.038

Gupta, S. K., Patel, S., Mannepalli, P. K., & Gangrade, S. (2023). Designing Dense-Healthcare IOT Networks for Industry 4.0 Using AI-Based Energy Efficient Reinforcement Learning Protocol. In *Industry 4.0 and Healthcare: Impact of Artificial Intelligence* (pp. 37–58). Springer Nature Singapore. doi:10.1007/978-981-99-1949-9_3

Haloui, I., Gupta, J. S., & Feuillard, V. (2018). Anomaly detection with Wasserstein GAN. arXiv preprint arXiv:1812.02463.

Han, D., Wang, Z., Zhong, Y., Chen, W., Yang, J., Lu, S., Shi, X., & Yin, X. (2021). Evaluating and improving adversarial robustness of machine learning-based network intrusion detectors. *IEEE Journal on Selected Areas in Communications, 39*(8), 2632–2647. doi:10.1109/JSAC.2021.3087242

Han, Q., Xiong, Z., & Zhang, K. (2018). Research on trajectory data releasing method via differential privacy based on spatial partition. *Security and Communication Networks, 2018*, 4248092. doi:10.1155/2018/4248092

Han, X., Chen, X., & Liu, L. P. (2021, May). Gan ensemble for anomaly detection. *Proceedings of the AAAI Conference on Artificial Intelligence, 35*(5), 4090–4097. doi:10.1609/aaai.v35i5.16530

Hao, X., Ren, W., Xiong, R., Zhu, T., & Choo, K. K. R. (2021). Asymmetric cryptographic functions based on generative adversarial neural networks for Internet of Things. *Future Generation Computer Systems, 124*, 243–253. doi:10.1016/j.future.2021.05.030

Harder, F., Adamczewski, K., & Park, M. (2021). Dp-merf: Differentially private mean embeddings with randomfeatures for practical privacy-preserving data generation. In *International conference on artificial intelligence and statistics* (pp. 1819-1827). PMLR.

Hardy, C., Le Merrer, E., & Sericola, B. (2019). MD-GAN: Multi-discriminator generative adversarial networks for distributed datasets. In *Proceedings of the 2019 IEEE International Parallel and Distributed Processing Symposium.* IEEE. 10.1109/IPDPS.2019.00095

Haricharan, M. G., Govind, S. P., & Vinoth Kumar, C. N. S. (2023). An Enhanced Network Security using Machine Learning and Behavioral Analysis. *2023 International Conference for Advancement in Technology (ICONAT)*, Goa, India. 10.1109/ICONAT57137.2023.10080157

Harini, H., Wahyuningtyas, D. P., Sutrisno, S., Wanof, M. I., & Ausat, A. M. A. (2023). Marketing strategy for early Childhood Education (ECE) schools in the Digital Age. Jurnal Obsesi. *Jurnal Pendidikan Anak Usia Dini, 7*(3), 2742–2758.

HartmannK. G.SchirrmeisterR. T.BallT. 2018. EEG-GAN: generative adversarial networks for electroencephalograhic (EEG) brain signals. arxiv:1806.01875

Hayes, J., Melis, L., Danezis, G., & De Cristofaro, E. (2019). LOGAN: Membership inference attacks against generative models. *Proceedings on Privacy Enhancing Technologies. Privacy Enhancing Technologies Symposium, 2019*(1), 133–152. doi:10.2478/popets-2019-0008

He, K., Huang, C., Shi, J., & Wang, J. (2016). Public Integrity Auditing for Dynamic Regenerating Code Based Cloud Storage. *IEEE Symposium on Computers and Communication.* IEEE.

He, X., Chen, Q., Tang, L., Wang, W., & Liu, T. (2022). Cgan-based collaborative intrusion detection for uav networks: A block formed chain structured-empowered distributed federated learning approach. *IEEE Internet of Things Journal, 10*(1), 120–132. doi:10.1109/JIOT.2022.3200121

He, Y., Seng, K. P., & Ang, L. M. (2023). Generative Adversarial Networks (GANs) for Audio-Visual Speech Recognition in Artificial Intelligence IoT. *Information (Basel), 14*(10), 575. doi:10.3390/info14100575

Hitaj, B., Ateniese, G., & Perez-Cruz, F. (2017). Deep models under the GAN: Information Leakage From collaborative deep learning. *Proc. ACM SIGSAC Conf. Computer Commun Secure.*, (pp. 603–618). ACM. 10.1145/3133956.3134012

Hong, J., Xie, M., Kang, B., Chunquing, L., & Lin, S. (2018). ID-Based Public Auditing Protocol for Cloud Storage Data Integrity Checking with Strengthened Authentication and Security. *Wuhan University Journal of Natural Sciences, 23*(4), 362–388. doi:10.1007/s11859-018-1335-9

Hsu, C. C., Zhuang, Y. X., & Lee, C.-Y. (2020). Deep fake image detection based on pairwise learning. *Applied Sciences (Basel, Switzerland), 10*(1), 370. doi:10.3390/app10010370

Huang, I. S., Lu, Y. H., Shafiq, M., Ali Laghari, A., & Yadav, R. (2021). A generative adversarial network model based on intelligent data analytics for music emotion recognition under IoT. *Mobile Information Systems, 2021*, 1–8. doi:10.1155/2021/3561829

Huang, S., & Lei, K. (2020). IGAN-IDS: An imbalanced generative adversarial network towards intrusion detection system in ad-hoc networks. *Ad Hoc Networks, 105*, 102177. doi:10.1016/j.adhoc.2020.102177

HuiZ.SelamatA. (2020.). Acceptance of Data-Driven Crowd-Sourcing Translation in Training. *Available at* SSRN 4379467. doi:10.2139/ssrn.4379467

Hu, J., Cui, P., & Zhang, Z. (2021). Adversarial community detection in social networks. *Proceedings of the 30th International Joint Conference on Artificial Intelligence.* IEEE.

Hussain, F., Tbarki, K., & Ksantini, R. (2023). GAN-Based One-Class Classification SVM for Real time Medical Image Intrusion Detection. *International Journal of Computing and Digital Systems*, *13*(1), 625–641. doi:10.12785/ijcds/130150

Hu, W., & Tan, Y. (2022). Generating Adversarial Malware Examples for Black-Box Attacks Based on GAN. In Y. Tan & Y. Shi (Eds.), *Data Mining and Big Data* (pp. 409–423). Springer Nature. doi:10.1007/978-981-19-8991-9_29

HuW.TanY. 2017. Generating adversarial malware examples for black-box attacks based on GAN. arxiv:1702.05983

Hu, Z., Shi, J., Huang, Y. H., Xiong, J., & Bu, X. 2018. GANFuzz: A GAN-based industrial network protocol fuzzing framework. In *Proceedings of the 15th ACM International Conference on Computing Frontiers*. ACM, New York, NY. 10.1145/3203217.3203241

Ibitoye, O., Abou-Khamis, R., Shehaby, M. E., Matrawy, A., & Shafiq, M. O. (2019). *The Threat of Adversarial Attacks on Machine Learning in Network Security—A Survey*. arXiv preprint arXiv:1911.02621.

Ibrahim, M., & Ahmad, R. (2010). Class diagram extraction from textual requirements using natural language processing (NLP) techniques. In *Proceedings of the International Conference on Computer Research and Development*. IEEE. 10.1109/ICCRD.2010.71

Ikhalia, E., Serrano, A., Bell, D., & Louvieris, P. (2019). Online social network security awareness: Mass interpersonal persuasion using a Facebook app. *Information Technology & People*, *32*(5), 5. doi:10.1108/ITP-06-2018-0278

Iliyasu, A. S., & Deng, H. (2022). N-GAN: A novel anomaly-based network intrusion detection with generative adversarial networks. *International Journal of Information Technology : an Official Journal of Bharati Vidyapeeth's Institute of Computer Applications and Management*, *14*(7), 3365–3375. doi:10.1007/s41870-022-00910-3

Im, D. J., Kim, C. D., Jiang, H., & Memisevic, R. (2016). *Generating images with recurrent adversarial networks*. arXiv Prepr arXiv:1602.05110.

Jain, A., Bansal, A., & Kakde, Y. (2020, June). Performance Analysis of Various Generative Adversarial Network using Dog image Dataset. In *2020 International Conference for Emerging Technology (INCET)* (pp. 1-6). IEEE. 10.1109/INCET49848.2020.9154071

Jang, K., Shin, K., Kim, C. S., & Son, K. C. (2020). Biometrics System Using Deep Convolution GAN. *Advanced Engineering and ICT-Convergence 2020 (ICAEIC-2020)*, *37*.

JetchevN.BergmannU.VollgrafR. (2016). *Texture synthesis with spatial generative adversarial networks*. arxiv:1611.08207

Jiang, L., Zhang, H., & Cai, Z. (2008). A novel Bayes model: Hidden naive bayes. *IEEE Transactions on Knowledge and Data Engineering*, *21*(10), 1361–1371. doi:10.1109/TKDE.2008.234

Jiang, X., Zhang, Y., Zhou, X., & Grossklags, J. (2023). Distributed GAN-Based Privacy-Preserving Publication of Vertically-Partitioned Data. *Proceedings on Privacy Enhancing Technologies. Privacy Enhancing Technologies Symposium*, *2*(2), 236–250. doi:10.56553/popets-2023-0050

Jiao, C., Bi, C., Yang, L., Wang, Z., Xia, Z., & Ono, K. (2023). ESRGAN-based visualization for large-scale volume data. *Journal of Visualization / the Visualization Society of Japan*, *26*(3), 649–665. doi:10.1007/s12650-022-00891-2

Juefei-Xu, F., & Savvides, M. (2019). *Localize adversarial attacks with intensity gradients*. arXiv preprint arXiv:1907.13397.

Kably, S., Benbarrad, T., Alaoui, N., & Arioua, M. (2023). Multi-Zone-Wise Block formed chain structured Based Intrusion Detection and Prevention Methodology for IoT Environment. *Computers, Materials & Continua*, *75*(1). Advance online publication. doi:10.32604/cmc.2023.032220

Kalyanaraman, K. (2023). An Artificial Intelligence Model for Effective Routing in WSN. In *Perspectives on Social Welfare Applications' Optimization and Enhanced Computer Applications* (pp. 67–88). IGI Global. doi:10.4018/978-1-6684-8306-0.ch005

Kalyanaraman, K., & Prabakar, T. N. (2024). Enhancing Women's Safety in Smart Transportation Through Human-Inspired Drone-Powered Machine Vision Security. In S. Ponnusamy, V. Bora, P. Daigavane, & S. Wazalwar (Eds.), *AI Tools and Applications for Women's Safety* (pp. 150–166). IGI Global., doi:10.4018/979-8-3693-1435-7.ch009

Kalyanaraman, S., Ponnusamy, S., & Harish, R. K. (2024). Amplifying Digital Twins Through the Integration of Wireless Sensor Networks: In-Depth Exploration. In S. Ponnusamy, M. Assaf, J. Antari, S. Singh, & S. Kalyanaraman (Eds.), *Digital Twin Technology and AI Implementations in Future-Focused Businesses* (pp. 70–82). IGI Global. doi:10.4018/979-8-3693-1818-8.ch006

Kaneko, T. (2018). Generative adversarial networks: Foundations and applications. *Acoustical Science and Technology*, 39(3), 189–197. doi:10.1250/ast.39.189

Kang, M., Shin, J., & Park, J. (2023). StudioGAN: A taxonomy and benchmark of GANs for image synthesis. *IEEE Transactions on Pattern Analysis and Machine Intelligence*, 45(12), 15725–15742. doi:10.1109/TPAMI.2023.3306436 PMID:37594871

Kapoor, B., Pandya, P., & Sherif, J. S. (2011). Cryptography: A security pillar of privacy, integrity and authenticity of data communication. *Kybernetes*, 40(9/10), 1422–1439. doi:10.1108/03684921111169468

Kargaard, J., Drange, T., Kor, A.-L., Twafik, H., & Butterfield, E. 2018. Defending IT systems against intelligent malware. In *Proceedings of the 2018 IEEE 9th International Conference on Dependable Systems, Services, and Technologies*. IEEE. 10.1109/DESSERT.2018.8409169

Karnewar, A., & Wang, O. 2020. MSG-GAN: Multi-scale gradients for generative adversarial networks. In *Proceedings of IEEE/CVF Conference on Computer Vision and Pattern Recognition*. IEEE. 10.1109/CVPR42600.2020.00782

Karras, T., Aila, T., Laine, S., & Lehtinen, J. (2018). Progressive growing of GANs for improved quality, stability, and variation. In *6th International Conference on Learning Representations, ICLR*. IEEE.

KarrasT.AilaT.LaineS.LehtinenJ. 2017. Progressive growing of GANs for improved quality, stability, and variation. arxiv:1710.10196

Karras, T., Laine, S., Aittala, M., Hellsten, J., Lehtinen, J., & Aila, T. (2020). Analyzing and improving the image quality of stylegan. In *Proceedings of the IEEE/CVF conference on computer vision and pattern recognition* (pp. 8110-8119). IEEE. 10.1109/CVPR42600.2020.00813

Kasiviswanathan, H. R., Ponnusamy, S., & Swaminathan, K. (2024). Investigating Cloud-Powered Digital Twin Power Flow Research and Implementation. In S. Ponnusamy, M. Assaf, J. Antari, S. Singh, & S. Kalyanaraman (Eds.), *Digital Twin Technology and AI Implementations in Future-Focused Businesses* (pp. 176–194). IGI Global. doi:10.4018/979-8-3693-1818-8.ch012

Keerthana, K., Yamini, R., & Dhesigan, N. (2020). *N Bala gangadharan and Sp.Angeline kirubha, "Smart Lifeguarding Vest for Military Purpose"*. IEEE Xplore.

Khanal, S. S., Prasad, P. W. C., Alsadoon, A., & Maag, A. (2020). A systematic review: Machine learning based recommendation systems for e-learning. *Education and Information Technologies*, 25(4), 2635–2664. doi:10.1007/s10639-019-10063-9

KimB. N.DesrosiersC.DolzJ.JodoinP.-M. 2019. Privacy-Net: An adversarial approach for identity-obfuscated segmentation. arxiv:1909.04087

Kim, H., Cui, X., Kim, M.-G., & Thi, H. B. N. (2019). Fingerprint generation and presentation attack detection using deep neural networks. In *Proceedings of the 2019 IEEE Conference on Multimedia Information Processing and Retrieval*. IEEE. 10.1109/MIPR.2019.00074

Kim, J., Jeong, K., Choi, H., & Seo, K. (2020). GAN-based anomaly detection in imbalance problems. In Computer Vision. Springer International Publishing.

Kim, J., Jeong, K., Choi, H., & Seo, K. (2020). GAN-based anomaly detection in imbalance problems. In Computer Vision–ECCV 2020 Workshops: Glasgow, UK, August 23–28, 2020. Springer International Publishing.

Kim, J.-Y., Bu, S.-J., & Cho, S.-B. (2017). Malware Detection Using Deep Transferred Generative Adversarial Networks. In D. Liu, S. Xie, Y. Li, D. Zhao, & E.-S. M. El-Alfy (Eds.), *Neural Information Processing* (pp. 556–564). Springer International Publishing. doi:10.1007/978-3-319-70087-8_58

Kim, J.-Y., Bu, S.-J., & Cho, S.-B. (2018). Zero-day malware detection using transferred generative adversarial networks based on deep autoencoders. *Information Sciences*, *460*, 83–102. doi:10.1016/j.ins.2018.04.092

Kim, T., Kang, B., Rho, M., Sezer, S., & Im, E. G. (2018). A multimodal deep learning method for android malware detection using various features. *IEEE Transactions on Information Forensics and Security*, *14*(3), 773–788. doi:10.1109/TIFS.2018.2866319

Kim, T., & Yang, J. (2019). Latent-space-level image anonymization with adversarial protector networks. *IEEE Access : Practical Innovations, Open Solutions*, *7*, 84992–84999. doi:10.1109/ACCESS.2019.2924479

Kingma, D. P., & Welling, M. (2013). Auto-encoding variational Bayes. *arXiv: 1312.6114.*

Kong, W., Shen, J., Li, H., Liu, J., & Zhang, J. (2023). Direction-aware attention aggregation for single-stage hazy-weather crowd counting. *Expert Systems with Applications*, *225*, 120088. doi:10.1016/j.eswa.2023.120088

Kos, J., Fischer, I., & Song, D. 2018. Adversarial examples for generative models. In *Proceedings of the 2018 IEEE Security and Privacy Workshops*. IEEE. 10.1109/SPW.2018.00014

Krizhevsky, A., Sutskever, I., & Hinton, G. E. (2012). ImageNet classification with deep convolutional neural networks. In *Advances in Neural Information Processing Systems* (pp. 1097–1105). Curran Associates.

Kuang, Z., Liu, H., Yu, J., Tian, A., Wang, L., Fan, J., & Babaguchi, N. (2021, October). Effective de-identification generative adversarial network for face anonymization. In *Proceedings of the 29th ACM International Conference on Multimedia* (pp. 3182-3191). ACM. 10.1145/3474085.3475464

Kulkarni, S., Adsul, A. P., Ayare, S., Pandit, S. V., Hundekari, S. N., & Pattanaik, O. (2024). Advances in Crowd Counting and Density Estimation Using Convolutional Neural Networks. *International Journal of Intelligent Systems and Applications in Engineering*, *12*(6s), 707–719.

Kumar Kethavarapu, U., Kumar Mannepalli, P., Lakshma Reddy, B., Siva Prasad, P., Mishra, A., & Nagavarapu, S. (2023). Artificial Intelligence Based Querying of Healthcare Data Processing. In *Industry 4.0 and Healthcare: Impact of Artificial Intelligence* (pp. 173–184). Springer Nature Singapore. doi:10.1007/978-981-99-1949-9_9

Kumar, A., Kumar, P., Palvia, S. C. J., & Verma, S. (2017). Online education worldwide: Current status and emerging trends. *Journal of Information Technology Case and Application Research*, *19*(1), 3–9. doi:10.1080/15228053.2017.1294867

Kumar, G., Kumar, K., & Sachdeva, M. (2010). The use of artificial intelligence based techniques for intrusion detection: A review. *Artificial Intelligence Review, 34*(4), 369–387. doi:10.1007/s10462-010-9179-5

Larson, M., & Liu, Z. S. (2018). Pixel privacy: Increasing image appeal while blocking automatic inference of sensitive scene information. In *Working Notes Proceedings of the MediaEval 2018 Workshop*. IEEE.

Lee, C. K., Cheon, Y. J., & Hwang, W. Y. (2021). Studies on the GAN-based anomaly detection methods for the time series data. *IEEE Access : Practical Innovations, Open Solutions, 9*, 73201–73215. doi:10.1109/ACCESS.2021.3078553

Lee, D. G., Suk, H. I., Park, S. K., & Lee, S. W. (2015). Motion influence map for unusual human activity detection and localization in crowded scenes. *IEEE Transactions on Circuits and Systems for Video Technology, 25*(10), 1612–1623. doi:10.1109/TCSVT.2015.2395752

Lee, D., Yu, H., Jiang, X., Rogith, D., Gudala, M., Tejani, M., Zhang, Q., & Xiong, L. (2020). Generating sequential electronic health records using dual adversarial autoencoder. *Journal of the American Medical Informatics Association : JAMIA, 27*(9), 1411–1419. doi:10.1093/jamia/ocaa119 PMID:32989459

LeeH.HanS.LeeJ. (2017). Generative adversarial trainer: Defense to adversarial perturbations with GAN. arxiv:1705.03387

LeeH.KimM. U.KimY.-J.LyuH.YangH. J. (2020). *Privacy-protection drone patrol system based on face anonymization*. arXiv:2005.14390

Lee, J., & Park, K. (2019). AE-CGAN model based high performance network intrusion detection system. *Applied Sciences (Basel, Switzerland), 9*(20), 4221. doi:10.3390/app9204221

Lee, J., & Park, K. (2021). GAN-based imbalanced data intrusion detection system. *Personal and Ubiquitous Computing, 25*(1), 121–128. doi:10.1007/s00779-019-01332-y

Li, D., Kotani, D., & Okabe, Y. (2020, July). Improving attack detection performance in NIDS using GAN. In *2020 IEEE 44th Annual Computers, Software, and Applications Conference* (COMPSAC) (pp. 817-825). IEEE. 10.1109/COMPSAC48688.2020.0-162

Li, Y., Yang, X., Zhang, H., & Zhu, S. C. (2020). *Learning to penetrate defense in depth via adversarial reinforced learning with latent variable model*. arXiv preprint arXiv:2007.06284.

Li, A., Fang, J., Jiang, Q., Zhou, B., & Jia, Y. (2020). A graph data privacy-preserving method based on generative adversarial networks. Springer.

Liao, D., Huang, S., Tan, Y., & Bai, G. (2020, August). Network intrusion detection method based on gan model. In *2020 International Conference on Computer Communication and Network Security (CCNS)* (pp. 153-156). IEEE. 10.1109/CCNS50731.2020.00041

Liao, H.-J., Lin, C.-H. R., Lin, Y.-C., & Tung, K.-Y. (2013). Intrusion detection system: A Comprehensive review. *Journal of Network and Computer Applications, 36*(1), 16–24. doi:10.1016/j.jnca.2012.09.004

Li, C., Qian, X., Huang, Y., Yang, J., & Yin, C. (2020). Effective adversarial attack and defense strategies on deep learning-based network traffic classification. *IEEE Access : Practical Innovations, Open Solutions, 8*, 165234–165246.

Li, C., Zhao, R., Wang, Y., Jia, P., Zhu, W., Ma, Y., & Li, M. (2023). Disturbance Propagation Model of Pedestrian Fall Behavior in a Pedestrian Crowd and Elimination Mechanism Analysis. *IEEE Transactions on Intelligent Transportation Systems*.

Li, H., & Cao, Y. (2023). Move in a crowd: Social crowding and metaphorical perspectives on the movement of events in time. *Review of Cognitive Linguistics, 21*(2), 469–485. doi:10.1075/rcl.00144.li

Li, J., Liu, J., & Chang, Y. (2019). Link prediction in complex networks with adversarial training. *IEEE Transactions on Knowledge and Data Engineering*.

Lim, W., Chek, K. Y. S., Theng, L. B., & Lin, C. T. C. (2024). Future of Generative Adversarial Networks (GAN) for Anomaly Detection in Network Security: A Review. *Computers & Security, 103733*, 2024. doi:10.1016/j.cose.2024.103733

Lin, H., Wan, S., Gan, W., Chen, J., & Chao, H. C. (2022, December). Metaverse in education: Vision, opportunities, and challenges. In *2022 IEEE International Conference on Big Data (Big Data)* (pp. 2857-2866). IEEE.

Lin, Q., Peng, S., Wu, Y., Liu, J., & Hu, W. (2020). *Mahbub Hassan, Aruna Seneviratne, Chun H Wang, "E-Jacket: Posture Detection with Loose-Fitting Garment using a Novel Strain Sensor"*. IEEE Xplore.

Lin, Z., Fanti, G., Khetan, A., & Oh, S. (2018). PacGan: The power of two samples in generative adversarial networks. *Advances in Neural Information Processing Systems*, 1498–1507.

Lin, Z., Shi, Y., & Xue, Z. (2022, May). Idsgan: Generative adversarial networks for attack generation against intrusion detection. In *Pacific-asia conference on knowledge discovery and data mining* (pp. 79–91). Springer International Publishing. doi:10.1007/978-3-031-05981-0_7

Li, S., Cao, Y., Liu, S., Lai, Y., Zhu, Y., & Ahmad, N. (2024). HDA-IDS: A Hybrid DoS Attacks Intrusion Detection System for IoT by using semi-supervised CL-GAN. *Expert Systems with Applications, 238*, 122198. doi:10.1016/j.eswa.2023.122198

Liu, M.Y., & Tuzel, O. (2016). *Coupled generative adversarial networks*.

Liu, Y., Yang, Y., Luo, H., Huang, H., & Xie, T. (2023). Intrusion detection method for wireless sensor network based on bidirectional circulation generative adversarial network. *Jisuanji Yingyong, 43*(1), 160.

Liu, C., Chen, J., Yang, L., Zhang, X., Yang, C., Ranjan, R., & Ramamohanarao, K. (2014, September). Authorized public auditing of dynamic big data storage on cloud with efficient verifiable fine-grained updates. *IEEE Transactions on Parallel and Distributed Systems, 25*(9), 2234–2244. doi:10.1109/TPDS.2013.191

Liu, R., Liu, W., Zheng, Z., Wang, L., Mao, L., Qiu, Q., & Ling, G. (2023). Anomaly-GAN: A data augmentation method for train surface anomaly detection. *Expert Systems with Applications, 228*, 120284. doi:10.1016/j.eswa.2023.120284

Liu, S., Zhao, W., & Zhang, H. (2019). Deep learning for generic object detection: A survey. *International Journal of Computer Vision, 128*(2), 261–318. doi:10.1007/s11263-019-01247-4

Liu, X., Li, T., Zhang, R., Wu, D., Liu, Y., & Yang, Z. (2021). A GAN and feature selection-based oversampling technique for intrusion detection. *Security and Communication Networks, 2021*, 1–15. doi:10.1155/2021/9947059

Liu, Y., Zhou, Y., Liu, X., Dong, F., Wang, C., & Wang, Z. (2019). Wasserstein GAN-based small-sample augmentation for new-generation artificial intelligence: A case study of cancer-staging data in biology. *Engineering (Beijing), 5*(1), 156–163. doi:10.1016/j.eng.2018.11.018

Liu, Z., & Yin, X. (2021). LSTM-CGAN: Towards generating low-rate DDoS adversarial samples for block formed chain structured-based wireless network detection models. *IEEE Access : Practical Innovations, Open Solutions, 9*, 22616–22625. doi:10.1109/ACCESS.2021.3056482

Li, Y., Liu, L., Qin, H., Deng, S., El-Yacoubi, M. A., & Zhou, G. (2022). Adaptive deep feature fusion for continuous authentication with data augmentation. *IEEE Transactions on Mobile Computing*.

Loffler, E., Schneider, B., Asprion, P. M., & Zanwar, T. (2021). CySecEscape 2.0-a virtual escape room to raise cybersecurity awareness. *International Journal of Serious Games, 8*(1), 1. doi:10.17083/ijsg.v8i1.413

Lokman, S. F., Othman, A. T., & Abu-Bakar, M. H. (2019). Intrusion detection system for automotive Controller Area Network (CAN) bus system: A review. *EURASIP Journal on Wireless Communications and Networking, 2019*(1), 1–17. doi:10.1186/s13638-019-1484-3

LotterW.KreimanG.CoxD. D. (2015). *Unsupervised learning of visual structure using predictive generative networks.* arXiv:1511.06380

LucP.CouprieC.ChintalaS.VerbeekJ. (2016). Semantic segmentation using adversarial networks. arXiv:1611.08408

Luo, W., Li, Y., Urtasun, R., & Zemel, R. (2017). Understanding the effective receptive field in deep convolutional neural networks. In Advances in neural information processing systems (pp. 4898-4906).

Lu, W., Ren, Z., Xu, J., & Chen, S. (2021). Edge blockchain assisted lightweight privacy-preserving data aggregation for smart grid. *IEEE Transactions on Network and Service Management, 18*(2), 1246–1259. doi:10.1109/TNSM.2020.3048822

Lu, X., Pan, Z., & Xian, H. (2019). An Integrity Verification Scheme of Cloud Storage for Internet-of-Things Mobile Terminal Devices. *Journal of Computer Security, 92*, 1–17.

Mageshwari, M., & Naresh, R. (2022). Decentralized Data Privacy Protection and Cloud Auditing Security Management. *Proceedings of International Conference on Computing, Communication, and Intelligent Systems.* IEEE. 10.1109/ICCCIS56430.2022.10037676

Mahalakshmi, B., & Suseendran, G. (2019). *An Analysis of Cloud Computing Issues on Data Integrity, Privacy and its Current solutions.* Research Article. doi:10.1007/978-981-13-1274-8_35

Majeed, A. (2023). Attribute-Centric and Synthetic Data Based Privacy Preserving Methods: A Systematic Review. *Journal of Cybersecurity and Privacy, 3*(3), 638–661. doi:10.3390/jcp3030030

Ma, L., Jia, X., Sun, Q., Schiele, B., Tuytelaars, T., & Van Gool, L. (2017). Pose guided person image generation. In *Proceedings of the 31st Conference on Neural Information Processing Systems*, (pp. 406–416). IEEE.

Mannepalli, P. K., Kushwaha, D. S., Kalamdhar, S., Nagrale, V., & Rajpoot, V. (2023, March). Face Recognition Based on Cascade Classifier Using Deep Learning. In *2023 1st International Conference on Innovations in High Speed Communication and Signal Processing (IHCSP)* (pp. 63-68). IEEE. 10.1109/IHCSP56702.2023.10127172

Mannepalli, P. K., Kalyani, P., Khan, S. A., Ghodichor, V. N., & Singh, P. (2023, March). An Early Detection of Pneumonia in CXR Images using Deep Learning Techniques. In *2023 International Conference on Innovative Data Communication Technologies and Application (ICIDCA)* (pp. 1029-1036). IEEE. 10.1109/ICIDCA56705.2023.10100230

Man, Z., Li, J., Di, X., Liu, X., Zhou, J., Wang, J., & Zhang, X. (2021). A novel image encryption algorithm based on least squares generative adversarial network random number generator. *Multimedia Tools and Applications, 80*(18), 27445–27469. doi:10.1007/s11042-021-10979-w

Mao, X., Li, Q., Xie, H., Lau, R. Y. K., Wang, Z., & Smolley, S. P. (2017). Least squares generative adversarial networks. In *Proceedings of the IEEE International Conference on Computer Vision*, (pp. 2794–2802). IEEE.

Mari, A. G., Zinca, D., & Dobrota, V. (2023). Development of a Machine-Learning Intrusion Detection System and Testing of Its Performance Using a Generative Adversarial Network. *Sensors (Basel), 23*(3), 1315. doi:10.3390/s23031315 PMID:36772355

Martins, N., Cruz, J. M., Cruz, T., & Abreu, P. H. (2020). Adversarial machine learning applied to intrusion and malware scenarios: A systematic review. *IEEE Access : Practical Innovations, Open Solutions, 8*, 35403–35419. doi:10.1109/ACCESS.2020.2974752

McAfee. (2019). *McAfee Labs Threats Report*. McAfee Labs.

Mehmood, A., Khanan, A., Umar, M. M., Abdullah, S., Ariffin, K. A. Z., & Song, H. (2017). Secure knowledge and cluster-based intrusion detection mechanism for smart wireless sensor networks. *IEEE Access : Practical Innovations, Open Solutions, 6*, 5688–5694. doi:10.1109/ACCESS.2017.2770020

Mell, P., & Grance, T. (2010). The NIST definition of cloud computing. *Communications of the ACM, 53*(6).

Meng, R., Cui, Q., & Yuan, C. (2018). A Survey of Image Information Hiding Algorithms Based on Deep Learning. *CMES-Computer Modeling In Engineering & Sciences, 117*(3).

Merino, T., Stillwell, M., Steele, M., Coplan, M., Patton, J., Stoyanov, A., & Deng, L. (2020). Expansion of cyber attack data from unbalanced datasets using generative adversarial networks. *Software Engineering Research, Management and Applications*, 131-145.

Mirsky, Y., Mahler, T., Elovici, Y., & Shabtai, A. (2018). CT-GAN: Malicious tampering of 3D medical imagery using deep learning. arXiv preprint arXiv:1803.01207.

Mirza, M., & Osindero, S. (2014). *Conditional Generative Adversarial Nets*. arXiv Prepr. arXiv:1411.1784.

Mirza, M., & Osindero, S. (2014). Conditional generative adversarial nets. arXiv preprint arXiv:1411.1784.

Mirza, M., & Osindero, S. (2014). Conditional generative adversarial nets. *ArXiv: 1411.1784*.

Monras, D. (2019). *A novel smart jacket for blood pressure measurement based in shape memory alloys*. Research Gate.

More, S., & Chaudhari, S. (2016). Third Party Public Auditing Scheme for Cloud Storage. *Procedia Computer Science, 79*, 69–76. doi:10.1016/j.procs.2016.03.010

Mousavi, S. K., Ghaffari, A., Besharat, S., & Afshari, H. (2021). Security of internet of things based on cryptographic algorithms: A survey. *Wireless Networks, 27*(2), 1515–1555. doi:10.1007/s11276-020-02535-5

Mozumder, M., & Biswas, S. (2023). An Hybrid Edge Algorithm for Vehicle License Plate Detection. In: Raj, J.S., Perikos, I., Balas, V.E. (eds) Intelligent Sustainable Systems. ICoISS 2023. Lecture Notes in Networks and Systems, vol 665. Springer, Singapore. doi:10.1007/978-981-99-1726-6_16

Mudgerikar, A., Sharma, P., & Bertino, E. (2020). Edge-based intrusion detection for IoT devices. [TMIS]. *ACM Transactions on Management Information Systems, 11*(4), 1–21. doi:10.1145/3382159

Mukherjee, B., Heberlein, L. T., & Levitt, K. N. (1994, May). Network intrusion detection. *IEEE Network, 8*(3), 26–41. doi:10.1109/65.283931

Muraidhara, P. (2013). Security issues in cloud computing and its countermeasures. *International Journal of Scientific and Engineering Research, 4*(10).

Muralidhara, P. (2019). Load balancing in cloud computing: A literature review of different cloud computing platforms.

Muralidhara, P. (2017). IoT applications in cloud computing for smart devices. *INTERNATIONAL JOURNAL OF COMPUTER SCIENCE AND TECHNOLOGY, 1*(1), 1–41.

Muralidhara, P. (2017). THE EVOLUTION OF CLOUD COMPUTING SECURITY: ADDRESSING EMERGING THREATS. *INTERNATIONAL JOURNAL OF COMPUTER SCIENCE AND TECHNOLOGY, 1*(4), 1–33.

Navidan, H., Moshiri, P. F., Nabati, M., Shahbazian, R., Ghorashi, S. A., Shah-Mansouri, V., & Windridge, D. (2021). Generative Adversarial Networks (GANs) in networking: A comprehensive survey & evaluation. *Computer Networks, 194*, 108149. doi:10.1016/j.comnet.2021.108149

Nguyen, H., Zhuang, D., Wu, P. Y., & Chang, M. (2020). Autogan-based dimension reduction for privacy preservation. *Neurocomputing*, *384*, 94–103. doi:10.1016/j.neucom.2019.12.002

Nguyen, T. D., Le, T., Vu, H., & Phung, D. (2017). Dual discriminator generative adversarial nets. *Advances in Neural Information Processing Systems*, 2671–2681.

NguyenT. T.NguyenQ. V. H.NguyenD. T.NguyenD. T.Huynh-TheT.NahavandiS.NguyenC. M. (2022). Deep learning for deepfakes creation and detection: A survey. Computer Vision and Image Understanding, 223, 103525.

Ning, H., & Song, X. (2019). Study on adversarial examples and defenses in image classification. In *International Conference on Cyber Security Intelligence and Analytics* (pp. 109-116). Springer, Cham.

Oak, R., Rahalkar, C., & Gujar, D. (2019, November). Poster: Using generative adversarial networks for secure pseudo-random number generation. In *Proceedings of the 2019 ACM SIGSAC Conference on Computer and Communications Security* (pp. 2597-2599). ACM. 10.1145/3319535.3363265

Odena, A., Olah, C., & Shlens, J. (2017). Conditional image synthesis with auxiliary classifier GANs. In *Proceedings of the 34th International Conference on Machine Learning*. IEEE.

Pan, Z., Yu, W., Yi, X., Khan, A., Yuan, F., & Zheng, Y. (2019). Recent progress on generative adversarial networks (GANs): A survey. *IEEE Access : Practical Innovations, Open Solutions*, *7*, 36322–36333. doi:10.1109/ACCESS.2019.2905015

Park, C., Lee, J., Kim, Y., Park, J. G., Kim, H., & Hong, D. (2022). An enhanced AI-based network intrusion detection system using generative adversarial networks. *IEEE Internet of Things Journal*, *10*(3), 2330–2345. doi:10.1109/JIOT.2022.3211346

Park, S. W., Ko, J. S., Huh, J. H., & Kim, J. C. (2021). Review on generative adversarial networks: Focusing on computer vision and its applications. *Electronics (Basel)*, *10*(10), 1216. doi:10.3390/electronics10101216

Pavan Kumar, M. R., & Jayagopal, P. (2021). Generative adversarial networks: A survey on applications and challenges. *International Journal of Multimedia Information Retrieval*, *10*(1), 1–24. doi:10.1007/s13735-020-00196-w

Peng, Y., Fu, G., Luo, Y., Hu, J., Li, B., & Yan, Q. (2020, October). Detecting adversarial examples for network intrusion detection system with gan. In *2020 IEEE 11th International Conference on Software Engineering and Service Science (ICSESS)* (pp. 6-10). IEEE. 10.1109/ICSESS49938.2020.9237728

Pietraszek, T. (2004). *Using adaptive alert classification to reduce false positives in intrusion detection.* In Recent Advances in Intrusion Detection: 7th International Symposium, RAID 2004, Sophia Antipolis, France.

Piplai, A., Sai, S. L. C., & Joshi, A. (2020). Attack! Adversarial Attacks to bypass a GAN based classifier trained to detect Network intrusion. *2020 IEEE 6th Intl Conference on Big Data Security on Cloud (BigDataSecurity), IEEE Intl Conference on High Performance and Smart Computing,(HPSC) and IEEE Intl Conference on Intelligent Data and Security (IDS)*. IEEE. 10.1109/BigDataSecurity-HPSC-IDS49724.2020.00020

Pistolesi, F. (2020). *Beatrice Lazzerini, "Assessing the Risk of Low Back Pain and Injury via Inertial and Barometric Sensors".* IEEE Transactions.

Ponni Bala, M., Priyanka, E. B., Prabhu, K., Bharathi Priya, P., Bhuvana, T., & Cibi Raja, V. (2021). *Real-Time Performance Analysis of Temperature Process Using Continuous Stirred Tank Reactor*. IEEE Xplore. doi:10.1109/ESCI50559.2021.9396877

Praveena, A., & Smys, S. (2017). Ensuring data security in cloud based social networks. In proc. of IEEE International conference of Electronics, Communication and Aerospace Technology. IEEE. 10.1109/ICECA.2017.8212819

Prümmer, J., van Steen, T., & van den Berg, B. (2024). A systematic review of current cybersecurity training methods. *Computers & Security, 136.* doi:10.1016/j.cose.2023.103585

Qaraqe, M., Elzein, A., Basaran, E., Yang, Y., Varghese, E. B., Costandi, W., Rizk, J., & Alam, N. (2024). PublicVision: A Secure Smart Surveillance System for Crowd Behavior Recognition. *IEEE Access : Practical Innovations, Open Solutions, 12,* 26474–26491. doi:10.1109/ACCESS.2024.3366693

Rabiner, L. R. (1989). A tutorial on hidden Markov models and selected applications in speech recognition. *Proceedings of the IEEE, 77*(2), 257–286. doi:10.1109/5.18626

Radford, A., Metz, L., & Chintala, S. (2015). *Unsupervised representation learning with deep convolutional generative adversarial networks.* arXiv preprint arXiv:1511.06434.

Rady, M. (2019). *Tamer Abdelkader, Rasha Ismail "Integrity and Confidentiality in Cloud Outsourced Data".* Ain Shams Engineering Journal Science Direct.

Raja, L., & Periasamy, P. S. (2022). A Trusted distributed routing scheme for wireless sensor networks using block chain and jelly fish search optimizer based deep generative adversarial neural network (Deep-GANN) technique. *Wireless Personal Communications, 126*(2), 1101–1128. doi:10.1007/s11277-022-09784-x

Ramanan, M., & Vivekanandan, P. (2018). *Efficient data integrity and data replication in cloud using stochastic diffusion method.* Springer Science on Cluster Computing.

Rani, B. J. B. (2020, January). Survey on applying GAN for anomaly detection. In *2020 International Conference on Computer Communication and Informatics (ICCCI)* (pp. 1-5). IEEE.

Rao, Y., & Ni, J. (2016, December). A deep learning approach to detection of splicing and copy-move forgeries in images. In *2016 IEEE international workshop on information forensics and security* (WIFS) (pp. 1-6). IEEE.

Rao, Y. N., & Suresh Babu, K. (2023). An imbalanced generative adversarial network-based approach for network intrusion detection in an imbalanced dataset. *Sensors (Basel), 23*(1), 550. doi:10.3390/s23010550 PMID:36617148

Ren, S., He, K., Girshick, R., & Sun, J. (2015). Faster R-CNN: Towards real-time object detection with region proposal networks. In Advances in neural information processing systems (pp. 91-99).

Rong, W., Xiong, Z., Cooper, D., Lie, C., & Sheng, H. (2014). Smart City architecture: A technology guide for implementation and design challenges. *China Communications, 11*(3), 56–69. doi:10.1109/CC.2014.6825259

Rutskiy, V., Aljarbouh, A., Thommandru, A., Elkin, S., Amrani, Y. E., Semina, E., & Tsarev, R. (2022). Prospects for the Use of Artificial Intelligence to Combat Fraud in Bank Payments. In *Proceedings of the Computational Methods in Systems and Software* (pp. 959-971). Cham: Springer International Publishing.

Ryan, D. (2011). Mark, Cloud computing privacy concerns on our doorstep.‖. *Communications of the ACM, 54*(1), 1. doi:10.1145/1866739.1866751

Saatchi, Y., & Wilson, A. G. (2017). Bayesian GAN. *Advances in Neural Information Processing Systems, 2017,* 3623–3632.

Sabillon, R., Serra-Ruiz, J., Cavaller, V., & Cano, J. J. M. (2019). An effective cybersecurity training model to support an organizational awareness program: The Cybersecurity Awareness TRAining Model (CATRAM). A case study in Canada. *Journal of Cases on Information Technology, 21*(3), 3. doi:10.4018/JCIT.2019070102

Sabuhi, M., Zhou, M., Bezemer, C. P., & Musilek, P. (2021). Applications of generative adversarial networks in anomaly detection: A systematic literature review. *IEEE Access : Practical Innovations, Open Solutions, 9,* 161003–161029. doi:10.1109/ACCESS.2021.3131949

Saeed, A. Q., Sheikh Abdullah, S. N. H., Che-Hamzah, J., & Abdul Ghani, A. T. (2021). Accuracy of using generative adversarial networks for glaucoma detection: Systematic review and bibliometric analysis. *Journal of Medical Internet Research*, 23(9), e27414. doi:10.2196/27414 PMID:34236992

Saharkhizan, M., & Azmoodeh, A. (2020). A hybrid deep generative local metric learning method for intrusion detection. Handbook of Big Data Privacy, 343-357.

Salem, M., Taheri, S., & Yuan, J. S. (2018). Anomaly Generation using Generative Adversarial Networks in Host Based Intrusion Detection. 2018 9th IEEE Annual Ubiquitous Computing [UEMCON]. *Electronics & Mobile Communication Conference*, 683–687, 683–687. doi:10.1109/UEMCON.2018.8796769

Sampath, V., Maurtua, I., Aguilar Martín, J. J., & Gutierrez, A. (2021). A survey on generative adversarial networks for imbalance problems in computer vision tasks. In: J Big Data. doi:10.1186/s40537-021-00414-0

Sams, A., Shomee, H. H., & Rahman, S. M. (2022). HQ-finGAN: High-Quality Synthetic Fingerprint Generation Using GANs. *Circuits, Systems, and Signal Processing*, 41(11), 6354–6369. doi:10.1007/s00034-022-02089-1

Sangeetha, S., Baskar, K., Kalaivaani, P. C. D., & Kumaravel, T. (2023). Deep Learning-based Early Parkinson's Disease Detection from Brain MRI Image. 2023 7th International Conference on Intelligent Computing and Control Systems (ICICCS), Madurai, India. 10.1109/ICICCS56967.2023.10142754

Sangeetha, S., Suruthika, S., Keerthika, S., Vinitha, S., & Sugunadevi, M. (2023). *Diagnosis of Pneumonia using Image Recognition Techniques*. 2023 7th International Conference on Intelligent Computing and Control Systems (ICICCS), Madurai, India. 10.1109/ICICCS56967.2023.10142892

Sasikala, C., & Shoba Bindu, C. (2018). *Certificateless remote data integrity checking using lattices in cloud storage.* Springer Science on Neural Computing and Applications.

Sathya, R., Bharathi, V. C., Ananthi, S., Vaidehi, K., & Sangeetha, S. (2023). *Intelligent Home Surveillance System using Convolution Neural Network Algorithms*. 2023 4th International Conference on Electronics and Sustainable Communication Systems (ICESC), Coimbatore, India. 10.1109/ICESC57686.2023.10193402

Sauber-Cole, R., & Khoshgoftaar, T. M. (2022). The use of generative adversarial networks to alleviate class imbalance in tabular data: A survey. *Journal of Big Data*, 9(1), 98. doi:10.1186/s40537-022-00648-6

Saxena, D., & Cao, J. (2021). Generative adversarial networks (GANs) challenges, solutions, and future directions. *ACM Computing Surveys*, 54(3), 1–42. doi:10.1145/3446374

Schlegl, T., Seeböck, P., Waldstein, S. M., Langs, G., & Schmidt-Erfurth, U. (2019). f-AnoGAN: Fast unsupervised anomaly detection with generative adversarial networks. *Medical Image Analysis*, 54, 30–44. doi:10.1016/j.media.2019.01.010 PMID:30831356

Senthilkumar, G., Tamilarasi, K., & Periasamy, J. K. (2023). Cloud intrusion detection framework using variational auto encoder Wasserstein generative adversarial network optimized with archerfish hunting optimization algorithm. *Wireless Networks*, 1–18. doi:10.1007/s11276-023-03571-7

Serrano, N., Gallardo, G., & Hernantes, J. (2015). Infrastructure as a service and cloud technologies. *IEEE Software*, 32(2), 30–36. doi:10.1109/MS.2015.43

Shaheed, K., Szczuko, P., Kumar, M., Qureshi, I., Abbas, Q., & Ullah, I. (2024). Deep learning techniques for biometric security: A systematic review of presentation attack detection systems. Engineering Applications of Artificial Intelligence, 129, 107569.

Shao, X., Ye, R., Wang, J., Feng, J., Wang, Y., & Jiang, J. (2023). Progress and prospects in crowd safety evacuation research in China. *Emergency Management Science and Technology, 3*(1), 1–20. doi:10.48130/EMST-2023-0001

Shargawi, A. (2017). *Understanding the human behavioural factors behind online learners' susceptibility to phishing attacks. PQDT - UK & Ireland.* Lancaster University.

Sharma, B., Sharma, L., Lal, C., & Roy, S. (2023). Anomaly based network intrusion detection for IoT attacks using deep learning technique. *Computers & Electrical Engineering, 107*, 108626. doi:10.1016/j.compeleceng.2023.108626

Sharma, V., Tripathi, A. K., Mittal, H., Parmar, A., Soni, A., & Amarwal, R. (2023). Weedgan: A novel generative adversarial network for cotton weed identification. *The Visual Computer, 39*(12), 6503–6519. doi:10.1007/s00371-022-02742-5

Sharmili, N., Yonbawi, S., Alahmari, S., Lydia, E. L., Ishak, M. K., Alkahtani, H. K., & Mostafa, S. M. (2023). Earthworm Optimization with Improved SqueezeNet Enabled Facial Expression Recognition Model. *Computer Systems Science and Engineering, 46*(2). Advance online publication. doi:10.32604/csse.2023.036377

Shen, W., Qin, J., Yu, J., Hao, R., & Hu, J. (2019). Enabling identity-based integrity auditing and data sharing with sensitive information hiding for secure cloud storage. *IEEE Transactions on Information Forensics and Security, 14*(2), 331–346. doi:10.1109/TIFS.2018.2850312

Shen, W., Yu, J., Xia, H., Zhang, H., Lu, X., & Hao, R. (2017). Lightweight and privacy-preserving secure cloud auditing scheme for group users via the third party medium. *Journal of Network and Computer Applications, 82*, 56–64. doi:10.1016/j.jnca.2017.01.015

Shigekawa, N., Nishimura, K., Yokoyama, H., & Hohkawa, K. (2005). Side-gate effects on transfer characteristics in GaN-based transversal filters. *Applied Physics Letters, 87*(8), 084102. doi:10.1063/1.2033140

Shirazi, H., Muramudalige, S. R., Ray, I., & Jayasumana, A. P. (2020). Improved phishing detection algorithms using adversarial autoencoder synthesized data. In *2020 IEEE 45th Conference on Local Computer Networks (LCN),* (pp. 24–32). IEEE. 10.1109/LCN48667.2020.9314775

Shu, J., Zhou, L., Zhang, W., Du, X., & Guizani, M. (2020). Collaborative intrusion detection for VANETs: A deep learning-based distributed SDN approach. *IEEE Transactions on Intelligent Transportation Systems, 22*(7), 4519–4530. doi:10.1109/TITS.2020.3027390

Sirigineedi, M., Bellapukonda, P., & Mohan, R. J. (2022). Predictive Disease Data Analysis of Air Pollution Using Supervised Learning. *International Journal of Scientific Research in Computer Science, Engineering and Information Technology, 8*(4).

Sirigineedi, M., Kumaravel, T., Natesan, P., Shruthi, V. K., Kowsalya, M., & Malarkodi, M. S. (2023). Deep Learning Approaches for Autonomous Driving to Detect Traffic Signs. *2023 International Conference on Sustainable Communication Networks and Application (ICSCNA),* Theni, India. 10.1109/ICSCNA58489.2023.10370617

Sitawarin, C., Curtmola, R., & Nita-Rotaru, C. (2019). *Darts: Deceptive Adversarial Robust Training by Self-supervision.* arXiv preprint arXiv:1908.09351.

Sivanesan, N., Rajesh, A., & Archana, K. S. (2023). WSN Attack Detection Using Attentive Dual Residual Generative Adversarial Networks. *International Journal of Intelligent Systems and Applications in Engineering, 11*(4), 659–665.

Smaha, S. (1988). Haystack: An intrusion detection system. *4th Aerosp. Comput. Secur. Appl.*.

Smith, J., Johnson, A., & Williams, C. (2021). Enhancing Public Safety Through Machine Learning: A Case Study of GANs in Cybersecurity. *Journal of Cybersecurity Research, 6*(2), 45–62.

Song, J., Yi, H., Xu, W., Li, X., Li, B., & Liu, Y. (2022). *Dual perceptual loss for single image super-resolution using esrgan.* arXiv preprint arXiv:2201.06383.

Song, Y., Kim, T., Nowozin, S., Ermon, S., & Kushman, N. (2020). PixelDP: A method for training differentially private deep learning models on pixelated data. arXiv preprint arXiv:2004.04482.

Song, S., Mukerji, T., & Hou, J. (2021). GANSim: Conditional facies simulation using an improved progressive growing of generative adversarial networks (GANs). *Mathematical Geosciences, 53*(7), 1–32. doi:10.1007/s11004-021-09934-0

Sookhak, M., Yu, F. R., & Zomaya, A. Y. (2018). Auditing big data storage in cloud computing using divide and conquer tables. *IEEE Transactions on Parallel and Distributed Systems, 29*(5), 999–1012. doi:10.1109/TPDS.2017.2784423

Speck, D., Rosin, T. P., Kerzel, M., & Wermter, S. (2023, November). The Importance of Growing Up: Progressive Growing GANs for Image Inpainting. In *2023 IEEE International Conference on Development and Learning (ICDL)* (pp. 294-299). IEEE. 10.1109/ICDL55364.2023.10364530

Sridhar, S., & Smys, S. "A hybrid multilevel authentication scheme for private cloud environment," In proc. of IEEE 10th International Conference on Intelligent Systems and Control, pp. 1-5, 2016. 10.1109/ISCO.2016.7727141

Sriram, I., & Khajeh-Hosseini, A. (2010). *Research agenda in cloud technologies.* arXiv preprint arXiv:1001.3259.

Suciu, G., Vulpe, A., Halunga, S., Fratu, O., Todoran, G., & Suciu, V. (2013, May). Smart cities built on resilient cloud computing and secure internet of things. In *2013 19th international conference on control systems and computer science* (pp. 513-518). IEEE. 10.1109/CSCS.2013.58

Suguna, R., Vinoth Kumar, C. N. S., Deepa, S., & Arunkumar, M. S. (2023). Apple and Tomato Leaves Disease Detection using Emperor Penguins Optimizer based CNN. *9th International Conference on Advanced Computing and Communication Systems (ICACCS).* IEEE. 10.1109/ICACCS57279.2023.10112941

Sun, J., Gan, W., Chao, H. C., & Yu, P. S. (2022). Metaverse: Survey, applications, security, and opportunities. arXiv preprint arXiv:2210.07990.

Sun, Y., Yu, W., Chen, Y., & Kadam, A. (2019, October). *Time series anomaly detection based on GAN.* In 2019 sixth international conference on social networks analysis, management and security (SNAMS) (pp. 375-382). IEEE. 10.1109/SNAMS.2019.8931714

Swaminathan, K., Ravindran, V., Ponraj, R. P., Venkatasubramanian, S., Chandrasekaran, K. S., & Ragunathan, S. (2023, January). A Novel Composite Intrusion Detection System (CIDS) for Wireless Sensor Network. In *2023 International Conference on Intelligent Data Communication Technologies and Internet of Things (IDCIoT)* (pp. 112-117). IEEE.

Swaminathan, K., Ravindran, V., Ponraj, R. P., Vijayasarathi, N., & Bharanidharan, K. (2023, August). Optimizing Energy Efficiency in Sensor Networks with the Virtual Power Routing Scheme (VPRS). In *2023 Second International Conference on Augmented Intelligence and Sustainable Systems (ICAISS)* (pp. 162-166). IEEE..

Swaminathan, K., Vennila, C., & Prabakar, T. N. (2021). Novel routing structure with new local monitoring, route scheduling, and planning manager in ecological wireless sensor network. *Journal of Environmental Protection and Ecology, 22*(6), 2614–2621.

Tang, T. W., Kuo, W. H., Lan, J. H., Ding, C. F., Hsu, H., & Young, H. T. (2020). Anomaly detection neural network with dual auto-encoders GAN and its industrial inspection applications. *Sensors (Basel), 20*(12), 3336. doi:10.3390/s20123336 PMID:32545489

Tang, X., Huang, Y., Chang, C.-C., & Zhou, L. (2019). Efficient Real-Time Integrity Auditing with Privacy-Preserving Arbitration for Images in Cloud Storage System. *IEEE Access : Practical Innovations, Open Solutions, 7*, 33009–33023. doi:10.1109/ACCESS.2019.2904040

Tao, X., Lu, S., Zhao, F., Lan, R., Chen, L., Fu, L., & Jia, R. (2024). *User Behavior Threat Detection Based on Adaptive Sliding Window GAN*. IEEE Transactions on Network and Servic Management. doi:10.1109/TNSM.2024.3355698

Tasneem, S., Gupta, K. D., Roy, A., & Dasgupta, D. (2022, December). *Generative Adversarial Networks (GAN) for Cyber Security: Challenges and Opportunities*. In *Proceedings of the 2022 IEEE Symposium Series on Computational Intelligence*, Singapore.

Thakkar, A., & Lohiya, R. (2022, January). a survey on intrusion detection system: Feature selection, Model, performance measures, application perspective, challenges, and future research directions. *Artificial Intelligence Review, 55*(1), 453–563. doi:10.1007/s10462-021-10037-9

Tian, H., Nan, F., Jiang, H., Chang, C. C., Ning, J., & Huang, Y. (2018). Public auditing for shared cloud data with efficient and secure group management. *Information Sciences, 472*, 107–125. doi:10.1016/j.ins.2018.09.009

Tripathi, S., Augustin, A. I., Dunlop, A., Sukumaran, R., Dheer, S., Zavalny, A., Haslam, O., Austin, T., Donchez, J., Tripathi, P. K., & Kim, E. (2022). Recent Advances and Application of Generative Adversarial Networks in Drug Discovery, Development, and Targeting. *Artificial Intelligence in the Life Sciences, 2*, 100045. doi:10.1016/j.ailsci.2022.100045

Tu, J., Ogola, W., Xu, D., & Xie, W. (2022). Intrusion detection based on generative adversarial network of reinforcement learning strategy for wireless sensor networks. *Int. J. Circuits Syst. Signal Process, 16*, 478–482. doi:10.46300/9106.2022.16.58

Ugot, O. A., Yinka-Banjo, C., & Misra, S. (2021). Biometric fingerprint generation using generative adversarial networks. In *Artificial Intelligence for Cyber Security: Methods, Issues and Possible Horizons or Opportunities* (pp. 51–83). Springer International Publishing. doi:10.1007/978-3-030-72236-4_3

Vinayakumar, R., Alazab, M., Soman, K. P., Poornachandran, P., Al-Nemrat, A., & Venkatraman, S. (2019). Deep learning approach for intelligent intrusion detection system. *IEEE Access : Practical Innovations, Open Solutions, 7*, 41525–41550. doi:10.1109/ACCESS.2019.2895334

Vinoth Kumar, C. N. S., Vasim Babu, M., Naresh, R., Lakshmi Narayanan, K., & Bharathi, V. (2021). Real Time Door Security System With Three Point Authentication. *4th International Conference on Recent Trends in Computer Science and Technology (ICRTCST)*. IEEE Explore. 10.1109/ICRTCST54752.2022.9782004

Viola, J., Chen, Y., & Wang, J. (2021). FaultFace: Deep convolutional generative adversarial network (DCGAN) based ball-bearing failure detection method. *Information Sciences, 542*, 195–211. doi:10.1016/j.ins.2020.06.060

Visconti, P. (2022). *Roberto de Fazio, Ramiro Velazquez, Bassam Al-Naami, Amir Aminzadeh Ghavifekr, "Wearable sensing smart solutions for workers' remote control in health-risk activities"*. IEEE Xplore.

Vondrick, C., Pirsiavash, H., & Torralba, A. (2016). Generating videos with scene dynamics. In *Proceedings of the 30th Conference on Neural Information Processing Systems*. IEEE.

Wang, K., Gou, C., Duan, Y., Lin, Y., Zheng, X., & Wang, F. Y. (2017). Generative adversarial networks: introduction and outlook. *IEEE/CAA Journal of Automatica Sinica, 4*(4), 588-598.

Wang, B., Li, B., & Li, H. (2014, March). Oruta: Privacy Preserving Public Auditing for Shared Data in the Cloud,‖. *IEEE Transactions on Cloud Computing, 2*(1).

Wang, B., Wu, F., Long, Y., Rimanic, L., Zhang, C., & Li, B. (2021, November). *Datalens: Scalable privacy preserving training via gradient compression and aggregation.* In *Proceedings of the 2021 ACM SIGSAC Conference on Computer and Communications Security* (pp. 2146-2168). ACM. 10.1145/3460120.3484579

Wang, B., Zhang, Y., Zhu, M., & Chen, Y. (2020, December). The Security Threat of Adversarial Samples to Deep Learning Networks. In *2020 International Conference on Intelligent Computing, Automation and Systems (ICICAS)* (pp. 125-129). IEEE. 10.1109/ICICAS51530.2020.00033

Wang, C., Chow, S. S. M., Wang, Q., Ren, K., & Lou, W. (2013, February). —Privacy- preserving public auditing for secure cloud storage,‖. *IEEE Transactions on Computers*, 62(2), 362–375. doi:10.1109/TC.2011.245

Wang, J., & Kissel, Z. A. (2015). *Introduction to network security: theory and practice.* John Wiley & Sons. doi:10.1002/9781119113102

Wang, K., Gou, C., Duan, Y., Lin, Y., Zheng, X., & Wang, F.-Y. (2017, September). "Generative adversarial networks: *Introduction and outlook," IEEE/CAA J. Autom. Sinica*, 4(4), 588–598. doi:10.1109/JAS.2017.7510583

Wang, L., Han, J., & Zhang, Z. (2019). Cybersecurity challenges in public spaces: A comprehensive review. *Journal of Public Safety Technology*, 4(1), 28–45.

Wang, Q., Wang, C., Ren, K., Lou, W., & Li, J. (2011). —Enabling Public Auditability and Data Dynamics for Storage Security in Cloud Computing,‖. *IEEE Transactions on Parallel and Distributed Systems*, 22(5), 847–859. doi:10.1109/TPDS.2010.183

Wang, T., Lu, J., & Duan, L. (2020). Learning to detect unseen object classes by between-class attribute transfer. *IEEE Transactions on Image Processing*, 29, 8761–8774.

Wang, W., Fu, J., & Yang, Y. (2020). A survey on adversarial attacks and defenses in image recognition. *IEEE Transactions on Cybernetics*.

Wang, X., Bo, L., & Fink, G. A. (2020). Deep learning for video-based vehicle re-identification. *IEEE Transactions on Circuits and Systems for Video Technology*, 30(8), 2511–2525.

Wang, X., Sun, L., Chehri, A., & Song, Y. (2023). A Review of GAN-Based Super-Resolution Reconstruction for Optical Remote Sensing Images. *Remote Sensing (Basel)*, 15(20), 5062. doi:10.3390/rs15205062

Wang, X., Xie, L., Dong, C., & Shan, Y. (2021). Real-esrgan: Training real-world blind super-resolution with pure synthetic data. In *Proceedings of the IEEE/CVF international conference on computer vision* (pp. 1905-1914). IEEE. 10.1109/ICCVW54120.2021.00217

Wang, X., Yu, K., Wu, S., Gu, J., Liu, Y., Dong, C., & Change Loy, C. (2018). Esrgan: Enhanced super-resolution generative adversarial networks. In *Proceedings of the European conference on computer vision (ECCV) workshops*. IEEE.

Wang, Y., Shen, Y., Wang, H., Cao, J., & Jiang, X. (2018). Mtmr:Ensuring map reduce computation integrity with merkle tree-based verifications. *IEEE Transactions on Big Data*, 4(3), 418–431. doi:10.1109/TBDATA.2016.2599928

Wang, Z., She, Q., & Ward, T. E. (2020). Generative Adversarial Networks in Computer Vision: A Survey and Taxonomy. *ACM Computing Surveys*.

Wang, Z., Song, X., & Zhang, W. (2018). GAN-based network traffic prediction for cloud resource management. *IEEE Transactions on Cloud Computing*.

Wei, Z., Huang, Y., Chen, Y., Zheng, C., & Gao, J. (2023, November). A-ESRGAN: Training real-world blind super-resolution with attention U-Net Discriminators. In *Pacific Rim International Conference on Artificial Intelligence* (pp. 16-27). Singapore: Springer Nature Singapore.

Weng, J., Weng, J., Zhang, J., Li, M., Zhang, Y., & Luo, W. (2019). Deepchain: Auditable and privacy-preserving deep learning with blockchain-based incentive. *IEEE Transactions on Dependable and Secure Computing, 18*(5), 2438–2455. doi:10.1109/TDSC.2019.2952332

Williams, P., Dutta, I. K., Daoud, H., & Bayoumi, M. (2022). A survey on security in internet of things with a focus on the impact of emerging technologies. *Internet of Things : Engineering Cyber Physical Human Systems, 19*, 100564. doi:10.1016/j.iot.2022.100564

Wu, Y., Kang, Y., Luo, J., He, Y., & Yang, Q. (2021). *Fedcg: Leverage conditional gan for protecting privacy and maintaining competitive performance in federated learning.* arXiv preprint arXiv:2111.08211.

Wu, C., Ju, B., Wu, Y., Xiong, N. N., & Zhang, S. (2020). WGAN-E: A generative adversarial networks for facial feature security. *Electronics (Basel), 9*(3), 486. doi:10.3390/electronics9030486

Wu, J., Zhao, N., & Yang, T. (2024). Wisdom of crowds: SWOT analysis based on hybrid text mining methods using online reviews. *Journal of Business Research, 171*, 114378. doi:10.1016/j.jbusres.2023.114378

Wu, Y., Zhu, Q., & Yin, H. (2020). GAN-based intrusion detection system for network security. *IEEE Access : Practical Innovations, Open Solutions.*

Xie, G., Yang, L. T., Yang, Y., Luo, H., Li, R., & Alazab, M. (2021). Threat analysis for automotive CAN networks: A GAN model-based intrusion detection technique. *IEEE Transactions on Intelligent Transportation Systems, 22*(7), 4467–4477. doi:10.1109/TITS.2021.3055351

Xu, C., He, X., & Abraha-Weldemariam, D. (2012). Cryptanalysis of Wang's Auditing Protocol for Data Storage Security in Cloud Computing. *International Conference on Information Computing and Applications.* Springer-Verlag Berlin Heidelberg.

Xu, X., Liu, X., Yin, X., Wang, S., Qi, Q., & Qi, L. (2020). Privacy-aware offloading for training tasks of generative adversarial network in edge computing. *Information Sciences, 532*, 1–15. doi:10.1016/j.ins.2020.04.026

Xu, Y., Zhang, X., Qiu, Z., Zhang, X., Qiu, J., & Zhang, H. (2021). Oversampling imbalanced data based on convergent WGAN for network threat detection. *Security and Communication Networks, 2021*, 1–14. doi:10.1155/2021/9206440

Xu, Z., Jain, D. K., Shamsolmoali, P., Goli, A., Neelakandan, S., & Jain, A. (2024). Slime Mold optimization with hybrid deep learning enabled crowd-counting approach in video surveillance. *Neural Computing & Applications, 36*(5), 2215–2229. doi:10.1007/s00521-023-09083-x

Yadav, S., Kumar, R., & Jain, A. K. (2020). Deep learning for cybersecurity: A survey. *Journal of Cybersecurity and Privacy, 2*(1), 15–32.

Yang, R., & Edalati, M. (2021). Using GAN-based models to sentimental analysis on imbalanced datasets in education domain. *arXiv preprint arXiv:2108.12061.*

Yang, C., Lu, X., Lin, Z., Shechtman, E., Wang, O., & Li, H. (2017). High-resolution image inpainting using multi-scale neural patch synthesis. In *Proceedings of the 2017 IEEE onference on Computer Vision and Pattern Recognition.* IEEE. 10.1109/CVPR.2017.434

Yang, J., Li, T., Liang, G., Wang, Y., Gao, T., & Zhu, F. (2020). Spam transaction attack detection model based on GRU and WGAN-div. *Computer Communications, 161*, 172–182. doi:10.1016/j.comcom.2020.07.031

Yang, K., & Jia, X. (2012). —An Efficient and Secure Protocol for Ensuring Data Storage Security in Cloud Computing,‖. *IEEE Transactions on Parallel and Distributed Systems*.

Yang, L., Yang, S. X., Li, Y., Lu, Y., & Guo, T. (2022). Generative adversarial learning for trusted and secure clustering in industrial wireless sensor networks. *IEEE Transactions on Industrial Electronics*, *70*(8), 8377–8387. doi:10.1109/TIE.2022.3212378

Yang, Z., Wei, N., Liu, Q., Huang, Y., & Zhang, Y. (2020). GAN-TStega: Text Steganography Based on Generative Adversarial Networks. In H. Wang, X. Zhao, Y. Shi, H. J. Kim, & A. Piva (Eds.), *Digital Forensics and Watermarking* (pp. 18–31). Springer International Publishing. doi:10.1007/978-3-030-43575-2_2

Yan, Q., Wang, M., Huang, W., Luo, X., & Yu, F. (2019). Automatically synthesizing dos attack traces using generative adversarial networks. *International Journal of Machine Learning and Cybernetics*, *10*(12), 12. doi:10.1007/s13042-019-00925-6

Yan, X., Cui, B., Xu, Y., Shi, P., & Wang, Z. (2019). A method of information protection for collaborative deep learning under GAN model attack. *IEEE/ACM Transactions on Computational Biology and Bioinformatics*, *18*(3), 871–881. doi:10.1109/TCBB.2019.2940583 PMID:31514150

Ye, D., Jiang, S., & Huang, J. (2019). Heard More Than Heard: An Audio Steganography Method Based on GAN (arXiv:1907.04986). arXiv. https://doi.org//arXiv.1907.04986 doi:10.48550

Ye, H., Liang, L., Li, G. Y., & Juang, B.-H. (2020, May). H., Liang, L., Li, G. Y., & Juang, en B. H. (2020). Deep learning-based end-to-end wireless communication systems with conditional GANs as unknown channels. *IEEE Transactions on Wireless Communications*, *19*(5), 3133–3143. doi:10.1109/TWC.2020.2970707

Yilmaz, I., Masum, R., & Siraj, A. (2020). Addressing Imbalanced Data Problem with Generative Adversarial Network For Intrusion Detection. In: *2020 IEEE 21st International Conference on Information Reuse and Integration for Data Science (IRI)*. IEEE. 10.1109/IRI49571.2020.00012

Yinka-Banjo, C., & Ugot, O. A. (2020). A review of generative adversarial networks and its application in cybersecurity. *Artificial Intelligence Review*, *53*(3), 1721–1736. doi:10.1007/s10462-019-09717-4

Yuan, X., Li, C., & Li, X. (2017, May). DeepDefense: identifying DDoS attack via deep learning. In *2017 IEEE international conference on smart computing (SMARTCOMP)* (pp. 1-8). IEEE.

Yuan, J., & Yu, S. (2015). —Public Integrity Auditing for Dynamic Data Sharing with Multi-User Modification,‖. *IEEE Transactions on Information Forensics and Security*, *10*(8), 1717–1726. doi:10.1109/TIFS.2015.2423264

Yu, Y., Au, M. H., Ateniese, G., Huang, X., Susilo, W., Dai, Y., & Min, G. (2017). Identity-based remote data integrity checking with perfect data privacy preserving for cloud storage. *IEEE Transactions on Information Forensics and Security*, *12*(4), 767–778. doi:10.1109/TIFS.2016.2615853

Yu, Z. (2022). Sustaining student roles, digital literacy, learning achievements, and motivation in online learning environments during the COVID-19 pandemic. *Sustainability (Basel)*, *14*(8), 4388. doi:10.3390/su14084388

Zeng, D., Lee, J., & Han, S. (2020). Adversarial detection and defense via a generative data-driven model. *IEEE Transactions on Dependable and Secure Computing*.

Zhang, A. (2018). *Self-Attention Generative Adversarial Networks*. arXiv Prepr. arXiv1805.08318.

Zhang, H., Xu, T., Li, H., Zhang, S., Wang, X., Huang, X., & Metaxas, D. N. (2017). Stackgan: Text to photo-realistic image synthesis with stacked generative adversarial networks. In *Proceedings of the IEEE international conference on computer vision* (pp. 5907-5915). IEEE. 10.1109/ICCV.2017.629

Zhang, J., Lu, Z., Li, M., & Wu, H. (2019). GAN-based image augmentation for finger-vein biometric recognition. *IEEE Access : Practical Innovations, Open Solutions*, 7, 183118–183132. doi:10.1109/ACCESS.2019.2960411

Zhang, W. E., Sheng, Q. Z., Alhazmi, A., & Li, C. (2020). Adversarial attacks on deep-learning models in natural language processing: A survey. [TIST]. *ACM Transactions on Intelligent Systems and Technology*, 11(3), 1–41. doi:10.1145/3374217

Zhang, X., Wang, H., & Xu, C. (2019). Identity-based key-exposure resilient cloud storage public auditing scheme from lattices. *Information Sciences*, 472, 223–234. doi:10.1016/j.ins.2018.09.013

Zhang, Y., Xiang, T., & Tian, Q. (2020). Challenges and opportunities in adversarial machine learning for network analysis. *ACM Computing Surveys*.

Zhang, Y., Yu, J., Hao, R., Wang, C., & Ren, K. (2020). Enabling efficient user revocation in identity-based cloud storage auditing for shared big data. *IEEE Transactions on Dependable and Secure Computing*, 17, 608–619.

Zhao, P., Ding, Z., Li, Y., Zhang, X., Zhao, Y., Wang, H., & Yang, Y. (2024). SGAD-GAN: Simultaneous Generation and Anomaly Detection for time-series sensor data with Generative Adversarial Networks. *Mechanical Systems and Signal Processing*, 210, 111141. doi:10.1016/j.ymssp.2024.111141

Zhao, R., Yin, Y., Shi, Y., & Xue, Z. (2020). Intelligent intrusion detection based on federated learning aided long short-term memory. *Physical Communication*, 42, 101157. doi:10.1016/j.phycom.2020.101157

Zhao, T., Yan, Y., Peng, J., Mi, Z., & Fu, X. (2019). Guiding intelligent surveillance system by learning-by-synthesis gaze estimation. *Pattern Recognition Letters*, 125, 556–562. doi:10.1016/j.patrec.2019.02.008

ZhaoZ.DuaD.SinghS. (2017). Generating natural adversarial examples. *arXiv:*1710.11342.

Zhou, F., Yang, S., Fujita, H., Chen, D., & Wen, C. (2020). Deep learning fault diagnosis method based on global optimization GAN for unbalanced data. *Knowledge-Based Systems*, 187, 104837. doi:10.1016/j.knosys.2019.07.008

Zhou, M., Lin, Y., Zhao, N., Jiang, Q., Yang, X., & Tian, Z. (2020). Indoor WLAN intelligent target intrusion sensing using ray-aided generative adversarial network. *IEEE Transactions on Emerging Topics in Computational Intelligence*, 4(1), 61–73. doi:10.1109/TETCI.2019.2892748

Zhu, J. Y., Park, T., Isola, P., & Efros, A. A. (2017). Unpaired image-to-image translation using cycle-consistent adversarial networks. In *Proceedings of the IEEE international conference on computer vision* (pp. 2223-2232). 10.1109/ICCV.2017.244

Zhu, S., & Han, Y. (2021). Generative trapdoors for public key cryptography based on automatic entropy optimization. *China Communications*, 18(8), 35–46. doi:10.23919/JCC.2021.08.003

Zhu, Y., Ahn, G.-J., Hu, H., Yau, S., An, H., & Hu, C.-J. (2013, April–June). Dynamic audit services for outsourced storages in clouds. *IEEE Transactions on Services Computing*, 6(2), 227–238. doi:10.1109/TSC.2011.51

Zixu, T., Liyanage, K. S. K., & Gurusamy, M. (2020, December). Generative adversarial network and auto encoder based anomaly detection in distributed IoT networks. In *GLOBECOM 2020-2020 IEEE Global Communications Conference* (pp. 1-7). IEEE. 10.1109/GLOBECOM42002.2020.9348244

Zolbayar, B. E., Sheatsley, R., McDaniel, P., Weisman, M., Kamhoua, C. A., Kiekintveld, C. D., & Zhu, Q. (2021). Evading machine learning based network intrusion detection systems with gans. *Game Theory and Machine Learning for Cyber Security*, 335-356.

About the Contributors

Sivaram Ponnusamy is a Professor from the School of Computer Science and Engineering, Sandip University, Nashik, Maharashtra, India. He received his Ph.D. in Computer Science and engineering from Anna University, Chennai, India, in 2017. ME in Computer Science and Engineering from Anna University, Chennai, India, in 2005, MBA in Project Management from Alagappa University, India, in 2007, and BE in Electrical and Electronics Engineering from Periyar University, India, in 2002. His research of interest includes Social Welfare Computer Applications' Optimization, Artificial Intelligence, VANET, and Mobile Applications.

Jilali Antari is a Professor in the Department of Mathematics and Computer Science and a member of Computer Systems Engineering, Mathematics and Application (ISIMA) Laboratory at the Polydisciplinary Faculty of Taroudant, Ibn Zohr University, Morocco. He has published several papers in international journals. Reviewer in many international journals and he is currently a supervisor of several research works.

Pawan R Bhaladhare has completed his PhD in Computer Engineering from S V National Institute of Technology, Surat, Gujarat, India. Presently, he is working as a Professor and Head, Department of Computer Science and Engineering, School of Computer Science and Engineering, Sandip University Nashik. His research area of interests includes Information Security and Privacy, Algorithm and Computational Complexity, and Data mining. He has fetched various research grants and published research papers in the International Journals. He has been in the teaching field from last 25 years.

Amol D Potgantwar is the Director and Professor from the School of Computer Science and Engineering, Sandip University, Nashik, Maharashtra, India.Completed PhD in Computer Science & Engineering , M. Tech (Computer Science & Engineering), BE(Computer Science & Engineering) and working as a Dear IPR & Associate Professor in the Department of Computer Engineering, Sandip Foundation's, Sandip Institute of Technology and Research Centre, Nashik, Maharashtra, India. He is acting as consultant for many companies nationwide and worldwide and Proactive Member of Nonprofit Techno Social "Natarajan Education Society" which emphasizes on Mobile Applications Development for Society Empowerment and entrepreneurship. He has been a Member board of studies in computer Engineering,at SPPU Pune & SGBAU Amravati India.He was Convener for 10+ National Level STTP like, big data analytics , cloud computing, Agile methodology, software Testing and IOT.

K. Swaminathan is currently a faculty member at the Constituent College of Anna University, Chennai, bringing over 11 years of teaching experience in Anna University-affiliated institutions. With B.E. and M.E. degrees earned from Anna University in 2008 and 2012, respectively, he has established an impressive research profile, presenting 23 papers in national and international forums, recognized in reputable publications such as Scopus and SCI journals. Completing his PhD journey at Anna University, Chennai in September 2022, he actively participates in international technical bodies, including the International Association of Engineers, Internet Society, European Society for Research on Internet Interventions (ISOC), ISTE, and IEI. His contributions extend to serving as a diligent reviewer for international journals and book chapters, notably for IGI Global and Hindawi. Additionally, he plays an editorial role for the "Spectrum Journal" (ISSN: 2583-9306) and IGI Global publications with ISBN13: 9798369318188, EISBN13: 9798369318195, highlighting his dedication to advancing knowledge within academic circles.

***

Aarti Agarkar is working in the domain of Security in Wireless Sensor Network and Smart Grid since last 15 years. She has done PhD in the domain of security and privacy preservation in smart grid network. The work is published in renowned SCI and Scopus indexed Journals. She used to teach the courses like Discrete Structures, Design and Analysis of Algorithms, Information Retrieval and Information Security. She has developed the routing protocol for wireless sensor network as the part of Post-Graduation work. She was Principal Investigator of 2 research projects funded by Board of College and University Development (BCUD), Pune, India. She has 1 book and 31 research articles to her credit. Her research interests include Deep Learning, Security, Privacy, Wireless sensor networks and Smart Grid communications. She is reviewer of The Computer Journal and Wiley's Security and Privacy Journals.

Ahamed Lebbe Hanees received the B. Sc. Special degree in Computer Science with upper class honors from South Eastern University of Sri Lanka, Sri Lanka in 2002, and M.Tech with First Class distinction with D+ from Bharathidasan University, India in 2011, Now Reading PhD in Computer Science at Alagappa University, Karaikudi, India. Now he is a Senior Lecturer Grade I in Computer Science since 2003 and serving as Head of the Department at Department of Mathematical Sciences, South Eastern University of Sri Lanka, Sri Lanka. His research interests include Machine Learning with IOT, network security, wireless sensor networks, and data mining.

Prafulla Eknathrao Ajmire Ph.D, M.Phil,M.S,PGDCS,M.Sc. Life member of Indian Science Congress, Kolkota. President, Computer Science Teachers' Association of SGBAU, Amravati. Life Member, Vidarbha Shikshan Prasarak Mandal, Khamgaon. Member of Board of Studies of Computer Science of SGBAU, Amravati. Member of Governing Body of G S Science, Arts & Commerce College, Khamgaon. Recognize supervisor for 'Computer Science & Engg', by SGBAU, Amt Research Paper Published in International/ National, Journal/ Conference: 51 Citation Index: 101 H-Index: 7 Research student Awarded Ph.D: 1 Research student working under the guidance: 8 Book Published 1) Handwritten Marathi character (Vowel) Recognition: Image Processing, Pattern Matching Published by Lap Lambert Academic Publishing GmbH & Co.KG, Germany. ISBN 978-3-8454-4272-3. 2) Chapter of Text Book of B.Sc. Final Computer Science. 3) Chapter of Book 'Recent Advances in Scientific Research' published by by Lap Lambert Academic Publishing GmbH & Co.KG, Germany. ISBN 978-620-3-92493-0.

Ahmet Okan Arık is an Information Systems Auditor at the Central Bank of the Republic of Türkiye and holds the ISO27001 Information Security Management System Lead Auditor title. He is also working on his PhD thesis at Istanbul University, Department of Informatics. His academic and professional life together has led him to work in many intersecting areas such as data science, artificial intelligence, information security, cyber security and fake news. He has 5 articles on related topics indexed in reputable indexes and 3 book chapters under publication. Ahmet Okan supports the integration of knowledge and technology into society and business by building bridges between the academic and industrial worlds. These collaborations reflect his commitment to demonstrate how academic research can contribute to real world applications.

Mohammad Atique is presently working as a Professor in Computer Science & Engineering, Post Graduate Department of Computer Science & Engineering, Sant Gadge Baba Amravati University, Amravati. He did his B.E., ME and Ph D in Computer Science & Engineering from Govt. College of Engineering, Amravati in 1990, 1997 and 2009 respectively. His area of research is Real-time Operating System, Soft Computing, Machine Intelligence and Digital Signal Processing.

B. Lalithadevi, currently working as Assistant Professor in the Department of Computer Science and Engineering at Sathyabama institute of Science and Technology, Chennai. She graduated in Computer Science and Engineering at Anna University, 2006 and she obtained her M.E degree in Computer Science and Engineering at Anna University in 2009. She is doing Ph.D in Computer Science and Engineering at SRM Institute of Science and Technology, Chennai. Her research interests include Image processing, Machine learning, Deep learning and Computer Vision. Meanwhile, she has published a research articles in SCI-indexed journals and reputed International Journals. A variety of papers have been presented and published in International Conference and National Conference. She has participated in various workshops and faculty development programs for improving her technical growth. She is a member of the IAENG association.

B. Venkatesan is an Associate Professor and Head of the Information Technology department at Paavai Engineering College (Autonomous), Namakkal. He has been working at the institution since 2007. He has 17 years of experience in the field of technical education. He completed his B.E. degree in Computer Science and Engineering at Muthayammal Engineering College under Anna University and obtained his M.E. degree in Computer Science and Engineering at Paavai Engineering College under Anna University, Coimbatore. He completed his Doctorate in the area of Cloud Computing under the Department of Information and Communication Engineering at Anna University, Chennai.He published 4 books, 15 articles in international journals, and 20 publications in national and international conferences. He received more than ten merit certificates and gold coins for his achievements in the field of education. He is acting as a reviewer for various journals and as a technical committee member for various international conferences.He has guided more than 35 UG and PG projects till now. He has received various funds from TNSCST, AICTE, ISTE, and IE (I). He has six filed patents in the fields of the Internet of Things, Cyber Security, Machine Learning, Cloud Computing, and Artificial Intelligence. He is a striving contributor in the field of science and technology by being an active member of many professional bodies like ISTE, CSI, IFERP, I2OR, AICTSD, and IAENG.

Adma Bellapukonda, Assistant Professor, IT Department, Shri Vishnu Engineering College for Women, Bhimavaram, West Godavari District, Andhra Pradesh, India. She is having a Good academic experience in Teaching for Graduates and postgraduate students. She is a Ph.D. scholar in Computer Science and Engineering from Gandhi Institute of Engineering and Technology University, Gunpur, Odisha and M.Tech in Computer Science and Engineering from Swarnandhra Engineering college, Seetaramapuram, Andhra Pradesh. Currently, she is working as the Assistant professor in the Department of Information Technology in Shri Vishnu Engineering College for Women (A), Bhimavaram, Andhra Pradesh, India. She has 8 years of teaching experience. Her current research includes Artificial Intelligence, Machine intelligence and Cyber Physical System. She has published research papers in good international journals and conference proceedings and she is the author for a text book called Information and Communication Technology. Her area of interest is Artificial Intelligence and Machine Learning.

Anirudh A. Bhagwat received M. Tech. degree (Computer Science & Engineering) and B.E. (Computer Engineering) from RTMNU. He is currently working as an Assistant Professor in G H Raisoni College of Engineering Nagpur. He has 10 years of teaching experience. His teaching interests includes Artificial Intelligence, Machine Learning, Software Engineering, Data Structures, Databases, Object Oriented Programming,Computer Networks.

Dipak Vasudeo Bhavsagar is currently working as an Associate Professor and Head in the Department of Computer Science and Information Technology of Seth Kesarimal Porwal College of Arts & Science & Commerce Kamptee. He has about 20 years of teaching experience at U.G and P.G. level. He has published two Indian patents; Four books and many research articles, research papers in various international journals. He is a member of Board of Studies, Subject Examination committee and worked on various academic committees constituted by R. T. M. Nagpur University Nagpur. His area of interest is Cloud Computing. He has worked as V. C. Nominated Subject Expert in the interview of Assistant Professor of different affiliated colleges to R. T. M. Nagpur University Nagpur.

Snjay H Buch has a Doctoral degree in Computer Science with 36+ years of experience in diversified industries and Corporates out which 20 years with Reliance Industries Limited at Various locations of the country. Contributed in the Reliance Industries Limited in the capacity of Senior Management & Leadership role (Assistant Vice President) for 10 years. Certified Project Management Professional (Certified PMP®) a most valuable certification for managing IT and Other projects given by the Project Management Institute, USA, and ITIL V3 for ITSM (Information Technology Service Management) from ISEB-UK. 0009-0007-2877-3231

Chellathurai Pon Anna Bai Shirley received B.E. degree in CSE from C. S. I. Institute of Technology, Thovalai affiliated to Anna University, Chennai, Tamil Nadu in 2002. M.Tech Degree in CSE from Dr. M. G. R. Educational and Research Institute, Chennai, Tamil Nadu in 2009. PhD from Anna University, Chennai, Tamil Nadu in 2020. She is currently working in the Department of CSE, Karunya Institute of Technology and Sciences, Coimbatore, India. Her research interests include Image Processing, Machine Learning and AI.

Anita Chaudhary pursuing a Ph.D. in Electronics Engineering from Shri Guru Granth Sahib World University, Fatehgarh, Punjab, India. She earned her B.Tech-M.Tech. in ECE from Lovely Professional University, Phagwara, India in 2012. She is an Assistant Professor (Senior Scale) at the Eternal University Baru Sahib, H.P. India. She has 10 years of teaching and research experience at various reputed Universities in India.

Suhashini Chaurasia has twenty-six years of teaching experience. Her area of research is Machine Learning. She has published seven Indian patents; She is also chief editor for a special issue on Interdisciplinary Perspectives On Artificial Intelligence Systems: From Theory To Application; Two books are authored namely Linux Operating System and Software Engineering. Eight edited international book chapters published. Taken two copyrights on literary work. Four papers published in reputed IEEE Scopus indexed journals and one Springer book chapter. Two books chapters published in International edited book AI Tools and Applications for Women's Safety. Three book chapters published in Impact of AI on Advancing Women's Safety. One book chapter is published in Wearable Devices, Surveillance Systems, and AI for Women's Wellbeing. Two book chapters published in Enhancing Security in Public Spaces Through Generative Adversarial Networks (GANs). Three papers are published in UGC peer reviewed journals. Two papers are published in peer reviewed journals. Two international conference papers presented and published. Two national conference papers presented and published. Two research articles published in the newspaper. Speaker at international conferences and colleges. She is a reviewer in 3rd International Conference on Advanced Communication and Intelligent Systems. She is also a reviewer in IGI-Global International Publisher Journal for AI Tools and Applications for Women's Safety and other for edited books. Member of board of studies at Rashtrasant Tukadoji Nagpur University, Nagpur. Working as head of the department in the college and CHB at VMV college. Attended and organized many FDPs, Orientation, Refresher programs, workshops and symposium.

Sonali Ravindra Chavan has twelve years of teaching experience at U.G. & P.G. level. She is currently working as Lecturer in Department of Computer Science, Bharatiya Mahavidyalaya Amravati since from 2012. She has cleared SET, UGC NET, NTA NET exam. She has completed her Ph.D. in computer science from Sant Gadge Baba Amravati University in 2023. Her area of interest is Machine Learning. She has published two Indian patents. Two research papers published in IEEE Scopus index journal. Taken one copyrights on literary work. Three Papers published in UGC peer reviewed journal. one international conference papers presented and published & two national conference papers presented and published. One book chapter published in CRC Taylor & Francis. She has attended workshops, Seminar & many FDP's. She is reviewer in 3rd International Conference on Advanced Communication and Intelligent Systems (Springer ICACIS 2024).

Aswathy K Cherian, Assistant Professor, SRM IST. She has more than 12 years of experience and has contributed more than 20 papers to her research

Senthilnathan Chidambaranathan have completed Master of Computer Applications(MCA) in The American College, affiliated to Madurai Kamaraj University, Madurai India in the year 2000. He have completed his UG in NGM College, Pollachi Affiliated to Bharathiar University, Coimbatore, India in the year 1995 and had a Mathematics Major. He have 23+ years of rich experience in IT industry, He is working in USA since 2007. He have demonstrated leadership and work experience not limited to Architecting Solutions - Enterprise level, IT, Data Strategy, Data Governance, Tools & Technology Evaluation, Technical Roadmaps, Data Landscaping/Zoning and Security Guidance. He is seasoned professional with ability to make Artificial Intelligence, Machine Learning, Deep Learning, Gen AI and Cloud based architecture (AWS, Azure & GCP) and design decisions and trade-off's for solution architecture adhering to enterprise standards. Heavily contributed to Enterprise Data Architecture, Data Governance, End-to-end cloud migrations, implementation of Bigdata solutions, Datawarehouse and etc., His work is mostly involved in Architecting, Installing, Configuring, Analysing, Designing, Integrating, re-engineering, and developing highly sophisticated Software Systems. Have published few Journal Papers, Peer reviewed few Journal Papers, written Book Chapters and have been key note speaker in International Conferences

Devendra Chourasia is Working in Mineral Exploration and Consultancy Limited, CPSE, Gov. of India, Nagpur, M.H. as Assistant Manager, IT, (E-3). He did his MCA. in Computer Application and B.Sc. in Electronics from RDVV University, Jabalpur, MP. Pursuing PHD from RTM Nagpur University. Certifications, MCP (Microsoft Certification Professional) and MCAD (Microsoft Certification Application Developer). Total 15+ Yrs. experience at government sector in technologies ASP, C#, ASP.NET, SQL Server, Ajax, JavaScript, jQuery, HTML, MVC, CSS, ERP ABAP. Developed Website: , , , . Developed Application: Ammonium Nitrate Return file system and Licensing System, Explosives eFiling System, MECL Recruitment Portal HRMS Portal (MECL Connect), CLIP Portal. Appreciated by MECL for developed HRMS Portal "MECL CONNECT". Also apricated for organization Vigilance week and Hindi Pakhwada at the time of covid-19 pandemic period. Expertise and area of research lie in Machine Learning, python programming, and ASP.NET, SQL SERVER. Also, knowledge of ERP Implementation, NIC e-Office Implementation, Software Audit, Cloud Server Management etc.

Harshita Chourasia is currently working as an Assistant Professor, at G.H. Raisoni College of Engineering, Nagpur. She did her M.Tech. in Computer Technology & Application and B.E. in Computer Science and Engineering from RGPV University, Bhopal. She won the Chancellor's Award for meritorious performance in her final year of B.E. She has experience as an Artificial Intelligence Developer and hands-on expertise with object detection, object classification, tracking and counting objects. Implemented novel computer vision algorithms for various use cases using deep learning frameworks such as Tensorflow, Pytorch, and YOLO. Analyzed, designed, and implemented software embedded systems like the Raspberry Pi 3 B+, and the Raspberry Pi 4. She has a valuable teaching experience of more than two years. Her expertise and area of research lie in Machine Learning, Artificial Intelligence and Computer Vision.

Dijendra Nath Dwivedi is a professional with 20+ years of subject matter expertise creating right value propositions for analytics and AI. He currently heads the EMEA+AP AI and IoT team at SAS, a worldwide frontrunner in AI technology. He is a post-Graduate in Economics from Indira Gandhi Institute of Development and Research and is PHD from crackow university of economics Poland. He has presented his research in more than 20 international conference and published several Scopus indexed paper on AI adoption in many areas. As an author he has contributed to more than 8 books and has more than 25 publications in high impact journals. He conducts AI Value seminars and workshops for the executive audience and for power users.

Elakkiya Elango M.Sc., M.phil., Ph.D., is currently working as a Guest Lecturer in the Department of Computer Science under the Government Arts College for Women, Sivagangai. She has 8 Years of Teaching and 11 years of Research Experience. His areas of research specialization include Data Mining, Machine Learning, Artificial Intelligence, NLP and IOT. She has completed his Bachelor's in Information Technology from 2004 to 2007, Master's in Information Technology from 2007 and 2009, and Master of Philosophy in Computer Science from 2009 to 2011and PhD in Computer science from 2014 to 2018 respectively. She has contributed more than 8 research articles in Scopus Indexed journals from Elsevier, Thomsan Router etc. and published 2 Book Chapters in CRC Press, Elsevier and also communicates and approved in more than 8 chapters in CRC Press, Elsevier, and Taylor Francis.etc. She holds two patents work done in 5 UK design and 1 German utility. She is the life member in Professional Member of ICSES, Life Membership of International Association of Engineers (IAENG) and Lifetime Membership of MathTech Thinking Foundation (MTTF). She is the Reviewer in ETASR journal.

Abika S. Jaiswal is a revered personality dedicated to the noble cause of education. Her profound understanding and experience in the field of Computer Science bears testimony to her profound excellence. As an Assistant Professor, she has been imparting knowledge to post-graduate students for the past 14 years. An exemplary academician, Ms. Jaiswal's involvement in administrative, examination, co-curricular, extension and professional development related activities is remarkable. Her contribution towards extension and dissemination activities and various curricular & co-curricular activities is substantial. She has served on numerous pivotal committees at the Sant Gadge Baba Amravati University, including Examination, Student Development, Perspective Planning, SEC Committee, Student Progression, Software Development Activities, Startups, IIL, Avishkar, NSD, and others, making invaluable contributions. Contribution to corporate life through committees and duties assigned by the authority is delegated by her. Her involvement in institutional governance is also evident through being a member on various committees. Ms. Jaiswal's research, publications, and academic contributions are remarkable. She is currently pursuing her doctorate in the field of Mobile Cloud Computing, where her extensive research work has resulted in a multitude of publications in prestigious journals and conferences, significantly advancing the frontiers of knowledge. Her development efforts have also yielded innovative solutions that have garnered widespread recognition within the academic fraternity. Her dedication towards teaching, learning and evaluation related activities is excellent. She has guided numerous projects, dissertations, and seminars, nurturing the academic pursuits of her students with unwavering commitment. Ms. Jaiswal is also affiliated with various esteemed academic bodies, such as IEEE, IETE, and CSI. An exceptionally diligent, dedicated, and committed educator, her prime objective has always been to contribute towards the growth and upliftment of students. With her unwavering passion for academia, a deep-rooted commitment to imparting quality education, a zeal for cutting-edge research, Ms. Jaiswal continues to inspire generations of learners, shaping their minds and guiding them towards a bright future.

Varkha Jewani has an M.Sc. (IT), M.Phil. (IT), Pursuing PhD. Area of Specialization- Network Security, Database Systems, Data Mining, Business Intelligence, Machine Learning Two patents and one Copyright published. Nine international and national publications. Three Chapters publications. chapters published in IGI Global International Journal. She is also a reviewer in IGI-Global International Publisher Journal for AI Tools and Applications for Women's Safety. Co-chairperson of Board of Studies in Information Technology, for B.Sc.(IT) and M.Sc.(IT) Course under HSNC University. Many workshops, FDP's, refresher and orientation programs Attended.

Swmiya KC, an accomplished Ph.D. scholar at Sri Vasavi College in Erode, emerges as a dynamic and vibrant researcher with a rich educational background. Having laid the foundation with a B.Ed. degree and furthered her academic pursuits with post-graduation at PSGR Krishnammal College for Women, she has adeptly positioned herself at the forefront of scholarly exploration.Her commitment to advancing knowledge is exemplified through her proactive involvement in two conferences in 2023, where she not only showcased her research prowess but also actively engaged with peers and experts, fostering meaningful discussions. Notably, the recognition garnered from presenting her research findings at these conferences has resulted in the acceptance of her journal article for publication later this year.This noteworthy achievement not only underscores Sowmiya's dedication to the academic realm but also highlights her impactful contributions to the scholarly discourse. As a Ph.D. scholar, she stands as a vibrant and influential contributor to the ever-evolving landscape of research and academic exploration, leaving an indelible mark on her field.

Mohammad Imran Khan, currently working as an Assistant Professor of Computer Science and Engineering at Jhulelal Institute of Technology, Nagpur- India has 12 years of Experience in teaching. His research interests focus on the development of Nature inspired optimization methods for load balancing in Cloud computing.

Mmta P Khanchandani completed the GSET in 2023 and publishing a research paper in the area of cloud security and image encryption are significant achievements. Your 12 years of experience as an Assistant Professor also demonstrate a strong foundation in academia. Pursuing a Ph.D. in hybrid storage cloud image encryption sounds like a cutting-edge and challenging area of research. This field is crucial given the increasing importance of securing data in cloud environments and the growing reliance on image data. Your work may contribute significantly to enhancing the security measures in cloud storage and ensuring the confidentiality and integrity of images." 0000-0002-5106-7729

M Islabudeen is currently working as an Assistant Professor (Senior Grade-II) in the School of Computer Science and Engineering (SCOPE), Vellore Institute of Technology (Deemed to be University), Vellore, Tamil Nadu, India. He received his B.E. Degree in Computer Science and Engineering from Madurai Kamaraj University, Madurai, India in 2001 and M.E. Degree in Computer Science and Engineering and Ph.D. Degree in Information and Communication Engineering from Anna University, Chennai, India in 2008 and 2021, respectively. He has more than 22 years of academic experience. His current research interests include Cryptography and Network Security, Blockchain and Machine Learning. He is a life member of the Computer Society of India (CSI) and Indian Society for Technical Education (ISTE). He has served as an active reviewer and chair for many reputed international conferences and journals including IEEE, Elsevier and Springer. He has more than 30 publications in refereed journals and reputed international conferences.

Mhamed Sithik, Associate Professor, Department of Computer Science and Engineering, Mohamed Sathak Engineering College, Kilakarai received his B.E (CSE) degree from Madurai Kamarajar University in the year 2004, M.E CSE received from Anna University Tiruchirappalli in the year of 2011 and Ph.D Degree received from Anna University in the year of 2023. He is having more than 19 years of teaching experience in reputed engineering college. He has published more than 5 peer reviewed Journals, 10 International/National Conference and attended more than 100 Workshops/FDPs/Seminars etc., He organized many events like Conference/FDPs/Workshops/Seminars. He has published 2 patents in the area of Artificial Intelligence and Telehealth Technologies. He has written 1 book from reputed publisher. He received Best Techie Award in the year 2022. He has professional membership on IEEE. His current research focuses on Secure RPL and Congestion control in Internet of Things (IoT). His research interests include Data Science, Deep Learning, Load balancing, Energy consumption, Security in IoT devices.

M Vasim Babu received his B.E. degree in the discipline of Electronics and Communication Engineering from Sethu Institute of Technology (Affiliated to Anna University), India, M.E Degree in the discipline of Communication Systems from K.L.N College of Engineering (Affiliated to Anna University), India, Ph.D. degree in the discipline of Information and Communication Engineering from Anna University, India. His area of interest is in Localization in Wireless Sensor Networks, Mobile Adhoc network, ANFIS and Signal processing. He is an active member of International Association of Engineers, IEEE, International Association of Computer Science and Information Technology, Universal Association of Computer and Electronics Engineers, American Association for science and technology and the Institute of Engineers. Currently, he is working as an Assistant Professor, Department of Electronics Engineering in Madras Institute of Technology campus, Anna university, Chennai, Tamilnadu, India.

Tnveerhusen Maheboobbhai is an Undergraduate (BSC-IT) student of L J School of computer Applications, L J University. He is passionate about research in network and network security.

Alok Manke is currently working as a Director of LJKU, having more than 20 years of teaching of teaching experience. He has done M.Tech.(CSE),M.Sc.(C.S.),DAC,PGDCA. His areas of interests are programming languages, data structures, database management system & Web Technologies.He is deeply involved in developing the customized softwares since last 8 years and has developed more than 40 live softwares till date. Some of them are: On Demand Examination, Feedback Management System, Transcript Generation, and Inventory Software for Pharmaceutical Industry, Software for Online Exam, Online Skill Test Exam, OMR based exam etc. He had organized various state and National Level Seminars & workshops. He is also the panel member for faculty recruitment, AICTE team at L.J.K Trust. He is heading online exam department and Software Factory of the university.

Khaja Mannanuddin is an Assistant Professor in the Sumathi Reddy Institute of Technology for women with an overall teaching experience of more than 14 years . His research interests are in the areas of machine learning, Information Retrieval, Edge Computing, Quantum computing and neural networks. Long term working associated with Computer science academics and training in the latest technologies. Highly competitive, self-starter who is well organized and disciplined . Excellent communication skills both verbal and written demonstrated by ability to work with people of diverse backgrounds. Welcome the challenge of solving problems.

NA.S. Vinoth is currently working as Assistant Professor in Computing Technologies, SRM Institute of science and Technologies. He has 9 years of Academic and Research experience. His research interest includes Network Security, Machine Learning, Big Data and Software Engineering. He has presented nearly 15 research articles in National and international conferences. He has published 10 Research Articles in various reputed journals. He Published 7 Indian Patents, 3 Indian Patents got granted. He is an IELTS Scorer and also a member of IEI as well as in ISTE.

N. Gnanasankaran MCA., Ph.D., RUSA PDF,. is presently working as an Assistant Professor in the Department of Computer Science, Thiagarajar College, Madurai, India. He has 14 Years of Teaching and 13 years of Research Experience. His areas of research specialization include Software Engineering, SQA, Data Science, Machine Learning, Big Data and IOT. He pursued his Masters in Computer Application (2008) and Doctorate in Computer Science (2014) from Madurai Kamaraj University, Madurai, Tamilnadu, India and Completed his Post Doc in Computer Science (2020) from Alagappa University, Karaikudi, Tamilnadu, India. He has contributed more than 35 research articles in Scopus and Web of Science Indexed journals from IEEE, Elsevier, Springer and Tech Science Press etc. He has contributed One Text Book publication and 5 Book Chapters in prominent Publishers such as Taylor and Francis, CRC Press, Routledge, De Gruyter, IEEE River publishers. He holds five patent work (Indian design and utility patent/ three UK design patent) in the field of IoT and Drone Technology. He has secured major and minor funded projects from UGC, India. He is also a review committee member in many reputed journals.

Busra Ozdenizci Kose is an academic and industry expert, holding a PhD in Informatics from Istanbul University, completed in 2016, and a Master of Science in Information Technologies from FMV Isik University, attained in 2012. With deep expertise in secure information systems, mobile and wireless technologies, she excels in system development, agile methodologies, and comprehensive business analysis. She combines academic rigor with practical industry applications, emphasizing the symbiotic relationship between academia and the technology sector. Renowned for her scholarly contributions, she also plays a dynamic role in various R&D projects, serving as a project manager, researcher, and consultant. She is currently an Associate Professor at Gebze Technical University in the Management Information Systems (MIS) department.

P. Santhosh Kumar is working as an Associate Professor in the Department of Information Technology at SRM Institue of Science and Technology, Ramapuram, Chennai. He graduated in Computer Science and Engineering at Anna University, Chennai, Tamilnadu, India. He secured Master of Engineering in Computer Science and Engineering at Anna University, Chennai, India. He received his Ph.D. in the field of Cloud Computing at Sathyabama Institute of Science and Technology, Chennai, India. He is in teaching profession for more than 12 years. He has presented number of papers in National and International Journals, Conference and Symposiums. He is holding 4 International and 3 National patents as well. Moreover he is a member of ISTE, IAENG and ACM Professional Society Bodies. His main area of interest includes Cloud computing, Machine Learning, Network Security, Artificial Intelligence and Internet of Things.

Sraddha Raut received an M. Tech. degree (Computer Science & Engineering) and B.E. (Information Technology) from RTMNU. She is currently working as an Assistant Professor in GHRUA at Nagpur Campus. She has 13 years of teaching experience. Her teaching interests include all languages like C, C++, Java, Artificial Intelligence, Software Engineering, Data Structures, Databases, Object Oriented Programming, and Computer Networks.

Auna Srinivasan completed her BTech in CSE from Anna University and did her masters and received Gold Medal for MTech degree in Computer science and Engineering from Visvesvaraya Technological University in the year 2018.She started her career with the IT industry and became expertise in the field of Data warehousing. She is working as an Assistant Professor in the department of computer Science and Engineering, Dayananda Sagar college of Engineering and pursuing Ph.D. in the field of Cyber Security and Forensics, PES University. She is a CompTIA certified Network+ professional and a EC-council's Certified Hacking Forensic Investigator.

Sndara Mohan S completed his Master of Technology in Information Technology from Manonmaiam Sundaranar University, Tirunelveli, Tamil Nadu, India in 2012 and did B.Tech in Information Technology from P.S.R Engineering College, Sivakasi, amil Nadu, India. He has a total academic experience of more than 10 years with many publications in reputed, peer-reviewed National and International Journals. Her areas of interest include Cloud Computing, Computer Network, Artificial intelligence, Pattern recognition and Machine Learning.

S Vetrivel is a faculty member in the Department of Management Studies, Kongu Engineering College (Autonomous), Perundurai, Erode Dt. Having experience in Industry 20 years and Teaching 16 years. Awarded with Doctoral Degree in Management Sciences in Anna University, Chennai. He has organized various workshops and Faculty Development Programmes. He is actively involved in research and consultancy works. He acted as a resource person to FDPs & MDPs to various industries like, SPB ltd, Tamilnadu Police, DIET, Rotary school and many. His areas of interest include Entrepreneurship, Business Law, Marketing and Case writing. Articles published more than 100 International and National Journals. Presented papers in more than 30 National and International conferences including IIM Bangalore, IIM Kozhikode, IIM Kashipur and IIM Indore. He was a Chief Co-ordinator of Entrepreneurship and Management Development Centre (EMDC) of Kongu Engineering College, he was instrumental in organizing various Awareness Camps, FDP, and TEDPs to aspiring entrepreneurs which was funded by NSTEDB – DST/GoI

Mnikanta Sirigineedi, Assistant Professor, IT Department, Vishnu Institute of Technology Bhimavaram, West Godavari District Andhra Pradesh, India. He is having a Good academic experience in Teaching for Graduates and Post Graduate students. He is currently Pursuing a Ph.D. from Gandhi Institute of Engineering and Technology University, Gunupur, Odisha. He has 10 years of teaching experience. He has a reputation for being a dedicated researcher and a lifelong learner. He published technical papers in various reputed National and International Journals and published 2 national books in the field of Computer Science and Engineering. His interests of research are applied Machine Learning, Digital Twin, and Data Science etc. He published "Two Patents" in the year 2023 & 2024 respectively.

S. Sangeetha, working as an Assistant Professor in the Department of Information Technology, Kongunadu College of Engineering and Technology, Trichy, Tami Nadu, India. She received B.E. Computer Science and Engineering from PGP College of Engineering and Technology, Namakkal under Anna University-Chennai in 2006. She was awarded with M.E. in Computer Science and Engineering from M.Kumarasamy College of Engineering, Karur under Anna University-Coimbatore in 2009. She has 12 years of teaching experience and pursuing Ph.D., as a part-time research scholar in Anna University, Chennai. Her area of interest lies in Image Processing, Machine Learning and Deep Learning. She has published 10 papers in International journals and presented 15 papers in national and international conferences

Sju Subramanian is currently working as Head of the Department, Biomedical Engineering, MIET Engineering College,Trichy.18 Years of work experience in the field of sensors and Instrumentation. Started his carrier since 2004, worked as Faculty Position in different Autonomous and Self financing colleges across the Country. Currently he is Life member of various professional Bodies Like ISTE,EURASIP,IEI etc.,Received Ph.D in the area of Image Processing during the year 2017 from Annamalai University,Tamilnadu,India.His Research Work is mainly focusing on data security like Image watermarking,Video data analytics etc., and published more than 18 papers in Sci,Scopus and Referred Journals in the are of Image processing techniques.

Aansingh Thinakaran received an M.C.A degree(Master of Computer Application) from Madras University and a B.Sc(Computer Science) from SCSVMV University. Currently working as Assistant Professor in GH Raisoni College of Engineering, Nagpur. I have 10 years of teaching experience. My teaching interests include Programming Language, Computer Networks, Artificial Intelligence, Information Security, and Operating Systems.

Piyanka Chandrashekhar Tikekar has twelve years of teaching experience at U.G. & P.G. level. She is currently working as Lecturer in Department of Computer Science, Bharatiya Mahavidyalaya Amravati since from 2012 where she shares her knowledge and passion for the subject. Her area of interest is Network Security & Machine Learning. She has published two Indian patents. Three research papers published in IEEE Scopus index journal and two paper published in reputed Springer nature journal. Taken Three copyrights on literary work. Three Papers published in UGC peer reviewed journal. Two international conference papers presented and published & three national conference papers presented and published. She is reviewer in 3rd International Conference on Advanced Communication and Intelligent Systems (Springer ICACIS 2024). She has attended workshops, Seminar & many FDP's.

Neha Tiwari received an M.Tech degree(Computer Science & Engineering) from Jaypee University of Engineering and Technology and B.E.(Information Technology) from RGPV University. She is currently working as an Assistant Professor in the Oriental Institute of Science And Technology, Bhopal. She has 6 years of teaching experience. Her teaching interests include Computer Networks, Artificial Intelligence, Information Security, and Operating Systems.

V Sabareeshwari currently serves as Assistant Professor in Department of Soil Science, Amrita School of Agricultural Sciences, Coimbatore. Having more than 5 years of research experience and more than 2 years of teaching experience. She got 7 awards in the field of agriculture. Her field of expertise are soil genesis, soil pedological studies as well as soil fertility mapping using advanced software like Arc GIS. She had published 22 research papers and more than 10 book chapters and books in high- impact reputed journals. She has actively participated and presented her papers in more than 20 conferences and seminars. She not only restrict her contribution only in the academic and research part, she had extension experience at farm level (lab to land) with varied crop research.

Shanti Verma is PhD in Machine learning algorithm based Recommendation system and working as Associate Professor and having 18+ years of teaching experience. She Presented 30+ research papers in International conference and journals & her areas of interests are Machine Learning, Network Security, Data Science and Programming Languages. She has also filed and receive grant of 8 national patents and 10 International patents in the field of Machine Learning, IoT and Deep Learning.

Ahad Abbas Vora is an Undergraduate (BSC-IT) student of L J School of computer Applications, L J University. He is passionate about research in network and network security.

V.P. Arun is a driven and accomplished professional with a diverse educational background and extensive hands-on experience across various industries. Graduating with honors, Arun earned his Master of Business Administration (M.B.A) with a specialization in Human Resources and Marketing from the renowned Sona School of Management in Salem in 2018, where he excelled academically with an impressive 8.3 Cumulative Grade Point Average (CGPA). Before pursuing his MBA, Arun laid a solid foundation by obtaining a Bachelor of Engineering degree from Kongu Engineering College in 2014. Throughout his academic journey, Arun displayed an unwavering commitment to learning and personal growth, actively seeking opportunities to expand his knowledge and skills beyond the confines of traditional education. He sought practical experiences to complement his theoretical understanding, such as a 45-day summer internship focused on conducting a feasibility study for R-Doc Sustainability in the market. Additionally, Arun broadened his horizons through a 7-day industrial visit to Malaysia and Singapore, immersing himself in diverse cultural and professional environments. Arun's academic pursuits were further enriched by his involvement in hands-on projects, including a comprehensive study on Employee Job Satisfaction at Roots Cast Private Limited.

Srutika Wanjari received M. Tech. degree (Computer Science & Engineering) and B.E. (Information Technology) from RTMNU. She is currently working as an Assistant Professor in G H Raisoni Institute of Engineering & Technology, Nagpur. She has 5 years of teaching experience. Her teaching interests includes Artificial Intelligence, Machine Learning, Software Engineering, Software Testing, Object Oriented Programming, Digital Techniques & Computer Networks.

Sampada Wazalwar is currently working as an assistant professor in Department of Information Technology of G H Raisoni College of Engineering, Nagpur. She has completed her Ph.D. in Information Technology, M.Tech. In Computer Science & Engineering and B.E. in Information Technology from Rashtrasant Tukadoji Maharaj Nagpur University. She has total 12 Years of Teaching Experience. She has received research grant of Rs. 3 Lakhs under RGSTC Scheme by Nagpur University. She has more than 20 research publications in reputed conferences, journals and book chapters. She has contributed as a metor & judge in various hackathons & project competitions. She has received Best Paper Award in three IEEE international conferences. She has one patent grant & 12 copyright registered to her credit. Her area of interest include Assistive Technology, Information Security, Language Technology and Machine Learning.

Index

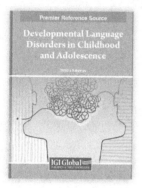

 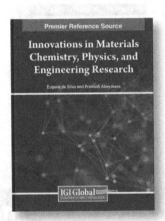 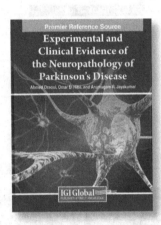 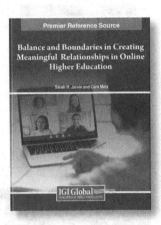

Printed in the United States
by Baker & Taylor Publisher Services

Printed in the United States
by Baker & Taylor Publisher Services